*
*
*

A History of the Kennedy Space Center

UNIVERSITY PRESS OF FLORIDA

Florida A&M University, Tallahassee
Florida Atlantic University, Boca Raton
Florida Gulf Coast University, Ft. Myers
Florida International University, Miami
Florida State University, Tallahassee
New College of Florida, Sarasota
University of Central Florida, Orlando
University of Florida, Gainesville
University of North Florida, Jacksonville
University of South Florida, Tampa
University of West Florida, Pensacola

University Press of Florida
Gainesville
Tallahassee
Tampa
Boca Raton
Pensacola
Orlando
Miami
Jacksonville
Ft. Myers
Sarasota

A History of the Kennedy Space Center

WITHDRAWN

Kenneth Lipartito and Orville R. Butler

To the men and women of the Kennedy Space Center

Copyright 2007 by the National Aeronautics and Space Administration, John
F. Kennedy Space Center
All rights reserved
All photos courtesy of NASA

Printed in the United States of America on acid-free paper

12 11 10 09 08 07   6 5 4 3 2

Library of Congress Cataloging-in-Publication Data
Lipartito, Kenneth, 1957–
A history of the Kennedy Space Center / Kenneth Lipartito
and Orville R. Butler
Includes bibliographical references and index.
ISBN 978-0-8130-3069-2 (alk. paper)
1. John F. Kennedy Space Center—History. 2. Launch complexes
(Astronautics)—Florida. 3. Astronautics—United States—History.
I. Butler, Orville R., 1952– . II. Title.
TL4027.F52L57   2007
387.8—dc22   2007001321

The University Press of Florida is the scholarly publishing agency
for the State University System of Florida, comprising Florida A&M
University, Florida Atlantic University, Florida Gulf Coast University,
Florida International University, Florida State University, New College
of Florida University of Central Florida, University of Florida, University of
North Florida, University of South Florida, and University of West Florida.

University Press of Florida
15 Northwest 15th Street
Gainesville, FL 32611-2079
http://www.upf.com

Contents

Preface

No matter how far away the destination, every spacecraft leaves for its journey from someplace on earth. For most of the history of the United States space program, that place has been Cape Canaveral, at the launch site known as the Kennedy Space Center (KSC). KSC is the most visible part of the American space program. It has the big machinery, the out-scale technology one associates with space ventures. It has the fire and smoke of the rocket's liftoff. Yet the work done there is easily overlooked.

A spaceship has to fly while on the ground before it can fly in space. It is only on the ground that one can control what happens after liftoff, to the extent that it can be controlled. The farther a rocket travels from earth, the farther it flies from terrestrial support and assistance. Most of the hope of mission success rests on what took place before it left, what took place on the ground. Launch operations is the business of getting rockets and their cargo, humans included, ready to fly. Work on the ground assures that the engines will light and the vehicle will lift. This is the least glamorous side of the space program, but unless humans develop some new way to defy gravity, they will depend on such ground work if they ever want space flight to be routine and widely accessible.

The image of flight, since the days of the Montgolfier brothers' hot-air balloons and the Wright brothers' motorized gliders, has been one of lightness and freedom. But the escape from earth is all about heavy lifting. Rockets do not leave earth willingly. They must be persuaded to break the terrestrial speed limit of seven miles a second and slip earth's tenacious grip. They must be coaxed and cajoled, coddled like Thoroughbreds before a big race. From space, humans seem precariously placed on a tiny sphere whirling through the galaxy. On earth, we lie at the bottom of an enormous gravity well, lit by a faint glimmer of starlight from above. Escaping this well is more like climbing a sheer cliff than levitating to the heavens. As writer Norman Mailer aptly put it, rockets leaving earth do not so much burst free as roll up the side of gravity like a marble up the side of a deep bowl.

To fly free of gravity, a rocket must generate thrust equal to and then exceeding its own weight. One iota less and it will crash back to earth, no matter how many millions of gallons of fuel it has spent. These are the laws from the Old Testament of physics. God does not play dice with this universe; he is not even amused. To generate the needed thrust, a rocket must release energy, usually by fire or, more exactly, by a controlled explosion. But it must also lift its own fuel and the oxygen to burn that fuel as it rises from the ground. The more fuel, the more thrust, but also the more weight to carry, creating a need for still more thrust, and on and on. No wonder that the eminent physicist Freeman Dyson, known for his stance against nuclear weapons, once proposed a spacecraft that would leave earth by riding atop the energy pulse of a series of small nuclear explosions.

These earthbound realities are a far cry from the soaring vision of rockets in space or the weightless freedom of zero gravity. They do not capture the imagination the way missions to Mars and space stations do. Rockets have been one of the most highly imagined, symbolically freighted of all technologies. The very term "rocket science," meaning something beyond the ken of ordinary brains, carries with it the implicit promise of an exciting future. Yet, as we shall see, much of space flight is not rocket science at all. Remembering that missions to the outer realm are constructed on the ground helps to reconnect a technology of great fancy with the earthly realities of economics, politics, and society.

Given their science-fiction pedigree, rockets share with other highly imagined technologies a large and at times frustrating gap between the dreams of the builders and the realities of operations. Inventors love to project wonderful futures for their creations. Advertisers proffer us a world filled with shiny new products. But experience wreaks havoc on the bold intentions and fanciful projections of ingenious machine makers. The creator of a new technology soon finds that the child of his mind has a mind of its own. People are not so gullible that they fail to see the gap between promise and reality. They know that their aging autos are really transportation workhorses, mere shadows of the dreams and desires felt at purchase. Even successful technology suffers from a bit of natural deflation once it is in our hands. Computers and related information technology have made startling inroads into our lives, but we rarely experience the frictionless information existence sold in the commercials. If the loss of original promise seems at first disappointing, we should remember that the new avenues of use and possibility opened by real-world experience are themselves a form of innovation.

The tension between invention and use, between design and operation, lies at the heart of this book. Innovation occurring through use and experience is different from innovation by design. The skills needed to translate plans and drawings into functioning systems are distinct yet no less crucial to technology than those of the designers. Sometimes operational skills lie mainly in the hands of nonexperts, the ordinary users who make choices about when to purchase, how to deploy, and even how to adapt technologies to their own needs and purposes. Radio makers were surprised to find that radio customers set up their own amateur communications networks. Only gradually did it dawn on them that the future of their invention lay with something called broadcasting. The Internet grew through the actions and interactions of users and user groups, individuals possessing various levels of technical competence, and widely varying ideas about what the Internet should be.

As a large, centrally controlled technology most often run by the government, rockets have been somewhat less democratic in this respect (though recent efforts to open up the launch market to greater commercial competition may change that). But the work at the Kennedy Space Center exhibits the same pattern of transforming the plans of designers into real-world operations. The skills and approach needed so that a spacecraft can actually fly on its mission are distinct from those needed in design and fabrication. The space operations culture at KSC grew in a different fashion and cultivated different values from the cultures at NASA's design centers. One of the untold stories of NASA has been the successful, if sometimes frustrating, efforts to bring together the culture of the designer and of the operator.

What follows is a history of the Kennedy Space Center from its origins, stretching back to the early years of the American rocket and missile programs of the 1950s through 2000. After this book was under way, the Columbia accident of 2003 occurred. The last chapters will deal with that event and some of its implications. Through this history of launch operations we shall see how the distinctive operator culture of NASA evolved, what it has contributed to the space program, and why perhaps greater heed should be given to the work and learning that take place after the plans are made, but before the ship flies.

Acknowledgments

This book began as a project history sponsored and funded by the Kennedy Space Center. We would like to thank KSC for their financial and institutional and indeed intellectual support. We were especially fortunate to have had the unwavering backing of two Center directors, Roy Bridges and James Kennedy, who both recognize the value of an organization's understanding its own past. NASA's long-standing and successful publication program has underwritten a wide range of research in space history and related areas, always giving scholars complete access and allowing them to write what they find. NASA's encouragement of high-quality independent research is a model for other institutions to follow.

We owe a great debt to JoAnn Morgan, who was head of the Kennedy Space Center's External Affairs Directorate, under which this project was carried out. Unfailingly courteous and helpful in our quest to understand KSC's history, she lent her deep knowledge of the Center and the space program to us in ways that improved this work. Following Morgan's retirement, Lisa Malone took over the project and helped to bring it to a successful conclusion, showing us the same courtesy and giving us the same level of support we had from the beginning. Shannon Roberts at KSC and Roger Launius, former NASA chief historian, helped to design the original project and got us started. Both were valuable history boosters in NASA, and we are thankful for all they did to make sure that KSC now has a published history.

Our first project manager was Dennis Armstrong, who taught us how to penetrate the sometimes opaque KSC organization and made sure that the system worked smoothly for us. When other time demands required Dennis to leave the project, we experienced a seamless transition to Gregg Buckingham. We are especially grateful to Gregg for negotiating between our academic culture and the different world of a government agency. Gregg took a strong intellectual interest in the project, and we benefited from our many discussions with him about KSC's history. Douglas Hendriksen, deputy chief counsel of KSC's legal department and historian of Brevard County in his own right, was also an invaluable ally in our work. He and James Vatne took charge of negotiations with the University Press of Florida to make sure this book came out on time. We are grateful for their support and efforts on behalf of the project.

We could not have completed our research without the day-to-day assistance of Elaine Liston, who heads the KSC Archives. Elaine tracked down documents we never knew existed and introduced us to other members of the Center who had information we needed. Her coworker Barbara Green aided in locating the photographs for the book. At the KSC Library, Susan Byrd took the time to help us get the materials we asked for and made valuable suggestions of her own. They all ensured that our stay at KSC was a pleasant one.

We thank Carey McCleskey and Tracy Young, who served on the committee overseeing the project. We benefited especially from Carey's own research into the life of Kurt H. Debus. We thank as well Marilee Tewksbury for her assistance with records under her control in the Records Management Office and Sharon White, who was the contracting officer for this project.

Several people went beyond the call of duty in helping us with this book. They were willing to subject themselves to several rounds of our often fumbling and ignorant questions on technical matters, provided access to materials or to people we wanted to interview, or served on review panels that checked the manuscript for accuracy. For these and other contributions we thank John Conway, Larry Ellis, Steve Francois, Hugh Harris, Jay Honeycutt, Ray Lugo, Tiffany Nail, John Neilon, Ernie Reyes, Ike Rigell, Stan Starr, Tip Talone, and Michael Woolley.

Although most of our research and contacts at NASA came at the Kennedy Space Center, the book benefited substantially from the assistance of the NASA Headquarters History Office. Jane Odom helped us locate records on the history of KSC held there. Stephen Garber provided our first point of contact in the History Office and along with NASA chief historian Steven Dick shepherded the manuscript through the peer review process. We thank both of them for their input.

At the National Archives and Records Administration in Eastpoint, Georgia, we were fortunate to have the assistance of Charles Reeves, who guided us through their holdings of relevant records, and Andre Wilkerson, who saw that we got what we needed. Kent Carter, archivist at NARA in Dallas, helped us understand NARA holdings relevant to the space program.

Sallie Middleton served as a research assistant for this book and coauthored two of the supplementary monographs that formed part of the larger project. Her work on expendable launch vehicles and on relations between the Kennedy Space Center and its surrounding community contributed to several chapters of this book, and we are extremely grateful for her assistance.

Elisabeth O'Kane worked on the research and writing of several chapters, and her contributions to chapter 7 were especially valuable. We thank her as well for her proofreading and editing of the manuscript.

Three graduate students also worked for us at various times on aspects of KSC's history. Jessica Barrella at Florida International University and Nanci Schwartz at the University of Central Florida conducted research on safety issues and contributed to a monograph on that subject. Tim Palmer from the University of Florida did research on labor issues. Students in Kenneth Lipartito's undergraduate classes on the history of technology indulged his newly discovered enthusiasm for space history and took up his challenge to write seminar papers in this area. Three of them, Kristen Merino, Robert Carmenate, and Philip Slama, made contributions that shaped our writing of this book.

We also express our thanks to colleagues who helped us to better understand space history or who thoughtfully commented on our manuscript at various stages: Andrew Butrica, Glenn Bugos, Virginia Dawson, Dennis Jenkins, Stephen Johnson, Roger Launius, David Mindel, Patrick Moore, Michael Neufeld, and David Sicilia.

Our appreciation as well to John Byram at the University Press of Florida, who enthusiastically supported the publication of this book, and to Ann Marlowe for her excellent copyediting. Our thanks to Gerry Ryan of Ryan Reporting, who handled the interview transcriptions.

Finally, Orville Butler would like to thank his daughter Hsieyun Butler-Yang for her support and sacrifices so that he could devote time to the KSC project, and Kenneth Lipartito thanks his family for putting up with his time away from home playing with rockets at the Cape.

To all these and to the many nameless others who helped, we extend our gratitude. Responsibility for any errors remains, of course, ours alone.

Abbreviations

AW&ST	*Aviation Week & Space Technology*
CAIB	Columbia Accident Investigation Board
DOD	Department of Defense
ELV	Expendable Launch Vehicle
GSE	Ground Support Equipment
GOCO	Government Owned, Contractor Operated
IGY	International Geophysical Year
IPT	Integrated Product Team
ISS	International Space Station
IUS	Inertial Upper Stage (originally, Interim Upper Stage)
JPL	Jet Propulsion Laboratory (CalTech, Pasadena)
JSC	Johnson Space Center (Houston)
KSC	Kennedy Space Center
LC	Launch Complex
LCC	Launch Control Center
LEM	Lunar Excursion Module (later, Lunar Module)
LOC	Launch Operations Center
LOD	Launch Operations Directorate
LPS	Launch Processing System (software)
MCP	Mission Control Program
MEIT	Multi-Element Integrated Testing
MSC	Manned Spacecraft Center (after 1973, JSC)
NACA	National Advisory Committee on Aeronautics
NARA	National Archives and Records Administration
NASA	National Aeronautics and Space Administration
O&C	Operations and Checkout
OPF	Orbiter Processing Facility
PERT	Program Evaluation Review Technique
SCA	Shuttle Carrier Aircraft
SFOC	Space Flight Operations Contract

SPC   Shuttle Processing Contract
SRB   Solid Rocket Booster
SSME   Space Shuttle Main Engine
SSPF   Space Station Processing Facility
STAG   Shuttle Turnaround Analysis Group
STS   Space Transportation System (space shuttle)
TPS   Thermal Protection System (tiles)
VAB   Vehicle Assembly Building

1

*
*
*

Moment of Truth

*The liftoff of an Apollo space vehicle with three
men aboard is an awesome "moment of truth," but
it is also just the top of an engineering iceberg.*

Rocco Petrone

On July 16, 1969, *Apollo 11* sat on its launch pad at Merritt Island, Florida, awaiting its quarter-million-mile journey to the moon. Sometime that morning, the Saturn rocket's mammoth first-stage engines would ignite. In less than three minutes, they would burn through 200,000 gallons of kerosene, generating enough thrust to release the six-and-a-half-million-pound vehicle free from earth's gravity. The blast of those engines would echo one from twenty-four years earlier, one equally resonant and symbolic. On July 16, 1945, at the Trinity test site in Alamogordo, New Mexico, not far from where the American space program began, the first atomic bomb exploded. *Apollo 11* was born in the Cold War that atomic weapons helped to start.

For the previous five months, this beast of a rocket had been carefully tended and prepared and sometimes pounded into shape by engineers at the Kennedy Space Center.[1] They worked in a complex carved out of the Florida scrub only five years before. A few miles to the east of where they worked, other tests were taking place as Minuteman missiles, the backbone of America's strategic nuclear arsenal, underwent their final verification before deployment. Cold War fears and hopes for the future sat side by side in Florida that day.[2]

At 9:32 A.M., the massive 363-foot-high Saturn roared to life. Nearly a million pairs of eyes turned upward, the spectators silent as they watched the column of fire from the five first-stage F-1 engines begin to accelerate the vehicle toward its escape velocity of seven miles a second. As *Apollo 11* rose, a shock wave and blast of sound raced across three and a half miles of flatness, drowning out any possible conversation. With awesome slowness the spaceship cleared the 400-foot launch tower. At that point, leaving the

1-1. Bathed in light, *Apollo 11* awaits its epic journey.

home it had known for five months, it was handed over from the Kennedy Space Center to Mission Control in Houston.

The flight of *Apollo 11* would bring out the poet in all who witnessed it. Its lunar trajectory was a sweeping arc of human destiny, its voyage a rendezvous between the moon and history. To mark the lunar landing, composer Duke Ellington wrote a jazz score.[3] When Neil Armstrong alighted on the moon's surface, President Richard Nixon called the first steps "a moment of transcendent drama." But the launch itself, what was that? "A really good ride," reported the astronauts. "It feels good" was all that Armstrong could say before his voice was lost in the engines' roar.[4] And launch preparations? They were largely forgotten once the bird was in the air. The best compliment may have been an unintended one from astronaut Buzz Aldrin. When asked what he had felt just before liftoff, he replied, "I can't remember feeling much of anything before T-zero. How about the rest of you?"[5]

The Five-Month Journey

Barely a decade after NASA's founding, America was fulfilling President Kennedy's 1961 challenge to send a man to the moon. But the launch of *Apollo 11* had followed the climb of the Kennedy Space Center up a steep learning curve. By the time *Apollo 11* was scheduled for flight, KSC had well-honed methods of getting rockets ready for their journeys. These methods drew on knowledge and experience that stretched back to NASA's beginnings. They reflected lessons learned in flying the smaller Saturn I and IB predecessors to the giant Saturn V, and in sending Gemini and Mercury astronauts on their way atop Redstone, Atlas, and Titan missiles. Experience had been acquired as well in many flights from Cape Canaveral with no humans aboard. Delta, Agena, and Centaur rockets had already completed some eighty-eight missions to study the planets of the solar system, and twenty-five more to observe the earth. The myriad steps of launch procedure now resided in thick books. And yet, as with any complex system of technology, nothing could be done simply by the book. Preparing *Apollo 11* for its historic flight presented its own challenges and unexpected turns of events. The moment of truth began long before liftoff, which was indeed the tip of an iceberg of preparation, testing, retesting, last-minute changes, and constant worrying.

First mention of the vehicle that would take three Americans to the moon appeared in the Daily Status Reports of Kennedy Space Center on February 24, 1969, five months before "T-0" or T-time minus zero launch. But in that same report many other concerns, more pressing, came first. *Apollo 9* was still awaiting its trip. How did things look for this, the first mission to test all of the hardware for the moon descent and landing? During a chill-down test, two of three valves failed and had to be replaced. Workers discovered a fault in a spacecraft battery line, and the "Z" Pipa Bias was out of tolerance. In other words, pretty much the normal daily events of preparing for a launch. The same sort of things would mark *Apollo 11*'s time at KSC.[6]

Preparing an Apollo-Saturn system for flight began when parts arrived at the Cape months before blastoff. Big pieces of equipment were put on ships at aerospace factories in California and traveled to Florida via the Panama Canal. Others arrived by rail and truck. Preparations involved assembling the pieces and subjecting them to rigorous tests. The tests sought out faults in systems, subsystems, and individual components, the baroque architecture of technology that made up rocket and spacecraft. Similar work took place with ground support equipment (GSE), the machinery that would launch the rocket into space. Hydrostatic tests, pressurization tests, leak tests, instrumentation tests, and, according to a preset schedule, a series of construction operations—all these tasks had to be finished before the separate stages of Saturn could be stacked into a three-stage rocket. After similar preparations on the Apollo spacecraft, workers mated the two to form a complete space vehicle.

In the early months at KSC, *Apollo 11*'s life was dictated by the schedule of the missions before it. *Apollo 9* and *Apollo 10* were to fly first, and *Apollo 9* had already slipped its launch date. No one doubted that *Apollo 11* would eventually depart, but when was still not certain. By March 13 the Saturn rocket for *Apollo 11* was three days behind schedule, the command service module (CSM) four days, and the lunar excursion module (LEM) three days. There was no single cause for such delays: a kink here, a glitch there, a leak somewhere else. Personnel shortages were a constant problem with work that required hundreds of experts processing three ships simultaneously. Crews who should have been at work on *Apollo 11* were busy ironing out problems with the preceding craft. Still, there was time to make all this up. Each day, in Firing Room 4 of the Launch Control Center (LCC), Launch Operations Director Paul Donnelly updated the schedules. He and his team wrestled as much with sequence as with hardware. Some steps simply had to be completed before others; some work could take place only at certain times. Before the tanks could be loaded, workers had to test the fuel lines for leaks. Integrated tests had priority over individual system tests. Dangerous work involving live explosives took place on weekends, when fewer people were around.[7]

Donnelly aimed to meet an important date, April 8, when the Saturn booster would join the Apollo spacecraft. But testing only uncovered more problems to solve. It was all the natural result of the system's complexity. Faults could occur in individual components, combinations of components, or larger congregations of parts that formed their own intricate subsystems. Despite best efforts, it was soon clear that the Apollo vehicle would be late for the April 8 rendezvous. The mating was postponed.[8]

Finally, on April 14, workers maneuvered the Apollo spacecraft into the enormous Vehicle Assembly Building (VAB) and began preparations to join Apollo with Saturn. Inside this 525-foot-high steel box, Saturn's three stages had already been stacked. Huge overhead cranes brought stages across the transfer aisle and into the high bay. Crane operators hoisted the cavernous upper stages, then lowered them at the rate of one inch per minute, slower than the eye could follow. In the high bay, engineers and technicians shuffled around the rocket in a workspace with floors that slid up and down and walls that rolled back and forth. Watching this beehive of activity, as powerful cranes placed rocket stages weighing hundreds of thousands of pounds with faultless precision, one saw clearly that KSC was the brawn and muscle of the space program. Missions went forward only after men with big forearms had done their work, and done it well. Test managers supervised this constant buzz of activity from offices lining the high bay. The VAB was simultaneously a shipyard for spaceships, a vertical assembly line, and an office high-rise.

The innovative and sometimes troublesome Apollo spaceship had undergone its own tests at KSC's Manned Spacecraft Operations Building.[9] All the Apollo systems worked individually and with each other, but what would happen when they were joined to the Saturn rocket? The only way to know was with further testing. First, KSC engineers put the combined vehicle through a "space vehicle overall test," or OAT, to verify that the merged vehicles were ready to play together. This was done "with the plugs in," meaning the vehicle received power from the ground. Later, on the pad with the plugs out, *Apollo 11* could prove itself independent of terrestrial support. In the meantime the spacecraft took its first flight, simulated. Before the OAT finished, all moving parts proved that they could function as required. The completed vehicle demonstrated that it could speak with itself, and with ground support equipment and off-site facilities. It showed how it would handle an emergency abort. It had gone through a full launch, including loading of propellants. That was always a tricky moment, when fuel was put on board, but this time it was only simulated. Later there would be an actual preflight test of the loading of the volatile fuels.

At this point *Apollo 11* was like a child in primary school, being carefully walked through the basics. But soon it would have to face real risks. The first of these came when KSC workers installed live ordnance, put out the smoking lamp, and put aboard the explosives that were to propel astronauts free in a launch escape system, should anything go wrong at liftoff.[10]

Apollo 11's time in the VAB was nearing an end. It was getting closer to graduation day, when it would roll down the transfer aisle and out to the pad. On April 25 the vehicle that would fly the second moon mission, *Apollo 12*, entered the daily reports. On May 18, *Apollo 10* was away. Now nothing stood between *Apollo 11* and its date with destiny. It was next to go.[11]

On May 20 the spacecraft took its long, slow promenade to the pad. Rollout is always a big moment. The 45-story-high VAB doors retract, and the rocket moves ponderously into the light, the bright sunshine of Florida glinting off its metal skin for the first time. Cranes loaded *Apollo 11* onto the

1-2. Stacked in the enormous Vehicle Assembly Building, *Apollo 11* starts to move out to the launchpad.

squat and well-named crawler transporter. It is hard to imagine something weighing half a million pounds being lowered onto a platform. Even more remarkable was what it was lowered onto. The crawler held the spacecraft perfectly upright as it crept one-half mile per hour to the launchpad. One more thing happened when *Apollo 11* left the VAB. It got its launch date—July 16. No one knew it at the time, but this date *Apollo 11* would keep.

There was still plenty to do before the launch director could give the "go" signal. Any snag would ripple back through the schedule of upcoming launches and wreak havoc on the nation's plans for putting Americans first on the moon. The Soviet Union had given up, unofficially, any hope of beating the United States at the manned lunar landing game. But rumors were circulating about a possible last-minute effort to steal American thunder by landing a robotic vehicle on the moon, scooping up some soil, and dashing back to earth ahead of the American astronauts. That June, in fact, *Luna 15* left the Soviet Union. It would arrive in lunar orbit two days ahead of the *Apollo 11* crew. The race would not finally be won until July 20, when Neil Armstrong and Buzz Aldrin walked on the moon while the Russian robot crashed into a lunar mountain.

No matter, the steps to prepare *Apollo 11* had to be taken, in order, with little room for deviation. Volunteers dressed in flight suits tested emergency escape procedures, lying "on the white room floor in the supine position," while supervisors read through the escape plan. The volunteers were then lifted into the escape mechanism, a basket on a wire, and slid from the top of the tower down to the ground. Next, the flight readiness test (FRT) verified that the vehicle was in "proper launch configuration." That toneless phrase belied the true nature of this test, which involved not only a simulated countdown and launch but an entire simulated flight to the moon and back, complete with a simulated splashdown, as well.[12]

1-3. Vehicle with launch tower on the pad, mobile service structure to right.

Work done at the pad took place on the mobile service structure (MSS) that embraced the vehicle. Through half a dozen swing arms, workers accessed the inner workings of the rocket from top to bottom. Although *Apollo 11*'s fate was no longer determined by the schedule of preceding launches, on the pad it was subject to the whims of weather. In hot, humid Central Florida, summer thunderstorms are daily events, and Florida has more lightning strikes than anywhere else in the United States. A flash of lightning even five miles from the pad meant work stopped. *Apollo 11* lost ten valuable hours to weather that summer.[13]

Presumably the major problems had been detected and fixed within the controlled confines of the VAB. Presumably, but each vehicle was unique and no set of standard procedures was foolproof. Launching relied on checks, validations, and rechecks. This was not a mass-produced vehicle. Workers fit parts by hand, drilled holes, shaved metal, and spliced wires. Progress was made by hewing to an industrial pace: tasks done on schedule, a certain number each day. A typical day on *Apollo 11* involved a dozen or more major items of work. During one twenty-four hour cycle, workers tested launch control mechanisms, detonators, and igniters. They replaced a malfunctioning digital multiplexer, troubleshot the flight control computer, and repaired damage to the LEM bulkhead. The tasks on the list were discrete, but the hum of activity at the mobile service structure was continual, a flow of preparation work that reflected both the needs of the technology and the years of accumulated experience with testing, preparing, and flying rockets.

Some of this work was purely mechanical, such as testing the steel arms that held rocket to pad, to see that they retracted precisely on time. At launch, a millisecond too long spelled disaster. Other tasks were troubling and puzzling, such as figuring out why the launch vehicle computer kept scrambling. The unglamorous side of going to the moon had no complex calculations of trajectory to charm mathematicians, no neat design problems to absorb engineers. But grinding out work on schedule was nerve-wracking as the big day approached. No one knew if a single mistake might cause a malfunction that triggered a problem that lost the mission. The Apollo command module alone had two million functional parts and fifteen miles of wire. Considering spacecraft, launch vehicle, and ground equipment, work at KSC was "for want of a nail" with a vengeance.

It was also organized work, teamwork, though more the sort found in a factory than in a lab. Getting to the moon required coordination across three major NASA installations, dozens of contractors, and sundry other individuals and institutions. Nowhere was the team nature of the work more apparent than in the processing and preparation for launch, "a team whether you push a broom or the big button."[14] At KSC the launch corps embraced government employees and contract workers from the private sector. The Center operated on five main contracts: launch support, instrumentation, communications, administration, and base operations.[15] NASA employees—civil servants—supervised this work, though not from an office but by getting their fingernails dirty side by side with contract workers. More than later space missions, the moon shot involved government engineers doing hands-on engineering. Still, the coordination and management challenges were enormous.

Personnel from KSC, the Manned Spacecraft Center in Houston, and the Marshall Space Flight Center in Huntsville all worked on the vehicle while it was at Cape Canaveral. They also had to work with the prime contractors responsible for each major system component. Boeing built the Saturn rocket's first stage, North American Aviation the second, and Douglas Aircraft the third. North American's Rocketdyne Division supplied the engines for all three stages. IBM provided the instrument unit, Grumman the lunar module, and Rockwell the service module and the command module. Lockheed was responsible for the crew escape system.[16]

On June 1, *Apollo 11* passed its flight readiness test. It had gone exceedingly well. Now all that needed to be done was to get rid of the ice crystals forming in the liquid hydrogen, add a pneumatic reservoir and check valve, and replace a leaking disk in the liquid hydrogen system. Nothing that the Center could not handle, though the thought of a problem at this point with liquid hydrogen, a difficult and volatile fuel, would seem disconcerting to an amateur. Still, it was not hardware problems alone that might threaten the launch. One item still to be resolved was an inconsistency in the rules for an abort. While one set of rules put the abort ceiling at 1,500 feet, another said that abort could take place only at an altitude that permitted visual monitoring, 500 feet.[17]

Inconsistencies were slowly ironed out in the testing process. Testing in fact was not a linear progression. Power might be turned on for one stage, then turned off again until later. Any test performed usually required subsequent work to verify what was done, or to recalibrate, validate, or sample the system tested. A failure or problem at any one point might stop the entire process. Countdown allowed for holds, and even had them built in, but if problems could not be corrected within a certain time, then it would be impossible to get back on schedule.

So before *Apollo 11* could fly, it was necessary to go through a practice countdown in the same sequence as the actual countdown. The objective was to go all the way to T-0 without a hitch.[18] That meant a run-through with all the built-in holds, practicing all the operations, including moving the mobile service structure to a safe distance, setting up roadblocks, and

1-4. A key moment of flight preparation, the CDDT or countdown demonstration test.

clearing the launch area. It was during this test that a fire aboard *Apollo 1* had killed three astronauts just two years earlier. This was a tense moment.

On June 26, all went quiet around the pad for the countdown demonstration test (CDDT). Now the plugs were out and the vehicle was running on its own power, the only power it would have when it left earth. The first part of the CDDT, the "wet" test, involved loading propellants to be sure there were no leaks. Once the wet test reached the ignition point, conductors called a halt and drained the fuels. Then they commenced the "dry" portion of the test. It was safer, but it also took place with the crew on board, sealed in the command module and breathing air from the life support system.

By this point, workers had learned all the quirks of the vehicle. They had heard its special squeaks and groans, the sounds it made as it swayed on the pad, the noises of valves opening and closing, pipes expanding and contracting, fittings and joints adjusting position. It was speaking to them, and they were listening carefully. They were documenting the steps to be taken for launch. The documentation was thick, some 2,000 steps, many with substeps, to be performed in the last twenty-eight hours of the countdown alone.

* * *

As complex as the test procedures was the public relations plan for *Apollo 11*. NASA had always operated in the open, but it would never have a day as big as this launch. Some 24,000 guests were expected for official ceremonies that began three days before the main event. Five thousand VIPs, including 100 ambassadors and 225 members of Congress, 19 governors, 40 mayors, and an assortment of 275 leaders from commerce and industry were scheduled to fly in for the launch (and fly out as soon as it was over).[19] Every major newspaper, television, and radio station sent correspondents. Twenty-seven hundred members of the press showed up—twice that of any previous launch—representing fifty-six nations, a legion that mandated its own management team from KSC public affairs. Meanwhile, an estimated one million people would witness the launch at surrounding locales.[20] Among those ready to comment after it was over were the voice of the American political right, William F. Buckley Jr., and the voice of the left, Norman Mailer. Failure would have enormous repercussions for NASA's future.

As *Apollo 11* underwent tests and preparations, people began pouring into Brevard County and vicinity. Many simply parked their cars along the beaches, causeways, and bridges in the neighboring towns of Titusville and Cocoa Beach, set up camp, and waited for the rocket's glare. Others slept rumpled in their cars or relaxed on boats, a thousand of which lined the Banana River. Weeks in advance, trailers and campers claimed the best viewing

1-5. People arrive from around the world to witness the historic launch.

sites along the rivers that separated Cape Canaveral from the mainland. The KSC Visitor Center broke attendance records every day.

The launch meant boom times for the famous astronaut hangout of Cocoa Beach just down the road. Area bars stocked up as patrons planted themselves on bar stools equipped with safety belts and downed special cocktails like the Apollo (vodka, lime juice, and Galliano) while bands and jukeboxes played endless versions of "Fly Me to the Moon." It was to be the last big boom for the Space Coast. Anticipating a wind-down of the frenetic pace of work, the Kennedy Space Center had already announced thousands of layoffs. But for now the good times were rolling. Nearly five thousand hotel rooms in Brevard County had been booked solid since January 1. Between July 14 and 17, hotel occupancy hit 100 percent.[21] "We've been paying taxes, we figured we'd like to see what we've been paying for," a retired railroad worker from Harrisburg, Pennsylvania, told reporters. The Cocoa Beach Hilton, in a prime viewing spot along the Atlantic, was so full that it turned away the chain's president, Barron Hilton. Local officials worried about the traffic jams on the bottleneck of causeways and bridges surrounding the Cape as 300,000 cars poured into the area. Placed bumper to bumper, they would make a line 1,000 miles long, exactly the number of miles of highway in Brevard County.[22] A caravan of 150 Volkswagen Beetles was due to arrive from Jacksonville. Italian cyclist Enno Ponte was peddling in from Houston. Australian Bill Emmenton was running the same 1,034 miles, and would arrive the day before launch.[23]

KSC planned a VIP list that included former president Lyndon Johnson and Vice President Spiro Agnew. Distinguished attendees ranged from Prince Claus of the Netherlands to National Gallery of Art director J. Carter Brown to comedians Jack Benny and Johnny Carson. Diplomatic representatives from Afghanistan to Zambia reserved a spot. The guest list posed delicate questions for NASA public affairs. Protocol officials sweated to avoid etiquette nightmares, making sure, for example, that former president Johnson was seated before Vice President Agnew arrived. Though Richard Nixon would not be in attendance—no president had ever attended an Apollo launch—prime spots in the Launch Control Center VIP viewing area were reserved for White House staff. Among those seated just feet away from the launch button were some of the president's most trusted men and women: H. R. Haldeman, John Erlichman, and Rose Mary Woods.[24]

Countdown

With the successful countdown test, 95 percent of the work was done. The last 5 percent, though, provided its own share of headaches. In the last two weeks before launch a string of things had to be replaced—an electrical bracket, a flow meter, an instrument unit. But the launch date set two

1-6. Cocoa Beach offers a free spot for spectators to wait.

months earlier held firm: blastoff on July 16. On July 10, with less than a week to go, engineers were tracking down a helium leak in the first stage and replacing a ruptured disk in the second. Maintenance was patching up a few paint and cork defects on the instrumentation unit. Then, on July 12, the countdown of *Apollo 11* officially began. When it did, the attention of some members of the ground crew turned to *Apollo 12*, which had been progressing steadily.

In a manner of speaking, a countdown is also a test. Since the early years of missiles, launch operations had sequenced the steps to liftoff through the discipline of a clock. The clock assured that the steps were taken at the right moment and in the right order, while moving the vehicle to the point of launch within the desired window of time. As missiles got larger and more complicated, so the number of preparation and verification activities grew, making the countdown longer and more complex. But the basic rule remained: a countdown was a series of acts to verify the vehicle was ready to go. Everything down to liftoff itself was oriented to seeing that *Apollo 11* was performing as it should. Only when it rose higher than the launch tower would the testing be done. Only then, the ship in the hands of Mission Control in Houston, would the men and women of the Kennedy Space Center know their work had been successful.[25]

Countdown began at T-4 days 20 hours 35 minutes. For the first twelve hours or so, little seemed to be happening. At T-4 days 8 hours, KSC engineers indicated that they were ready to proceeded to the "precount," which would last almost three days. At exactly T-3 days 21 hours 0 minutes, with the launch director counting backward from 5, precount operations began. Now things started to happen. Technicians flipped the switches to power up the Saturn launch vehicle and Apollo spacecraft. Guards cleared nonessential personnel from the danger zones and ordered radios silenced as specially trained technicians put live ordnance on board. At T-3 days 8 hours 45 minutes, another hazardous operation took place, hooking up propellant vent lines and pressurizing the tanks.

Suddenly there were lots of things to do: UHF equipment, flight code plugs, and other things most people never knew were part of a spacecraft all had to be activated or tested. One by one the launch team ticked off the several thousand steps to launch. At T-1 day 17 hours, workers started the flow of liquid hydrogen into the tanks of the command service module. This fuel would propel *Apollo 11* from earth orbit to the moon and back.

As July 16 approached, signs at the KSC gates followed the countdown—3 days to launch, 2 days to launch. Now they read: 1 day to launch. Guards at the Launch Control Center began to check badges more closely, so that the men and women at work there had as few distractions as possible. *Apollo 11*, the star of the show, sat bathed in lights during its last evening on earth. All the key preflight tests had been completed. Some procedures were practiced several times. Many systems had gone through three major simulations.[26]

The day before launch, Cape festivities moved to crescendo. Temperatures had been at their midsummer peak for a week, some afternoons reaching 100 degrees. Weather predictions were for cloudy skies on the sixteenth, which would limit the viewing distance, but rain was expected to hold off until late afternoon, when thunderstorms would rake the Cape. Towns in Brevard County had scheduled events starting on July 15. On the mainland, Titusville citizens dedicated their new post office in the afternoon, held a band concert and a square dance that evening, and started launch day with a pancake breakfast at St. Teresa's Parish Hall. For weeks, local stores had been running specials on items like "moon cheese." The Searstown Mall stayed open until 10:00 P.M. for Moonshot Madness sales, with free space masks and helium-filled balloons for children. Rows of bleachers at area high schools were reserved for lower level VIPs who did not have a badge to enter KSC property. The local Jaycees stocked free Florida orange juice to hand out at Welcome Stations, where visitors would find souvenirs ranging from bumper stickers to copies of the Mission Profile.[27]

The entire earth was experiencing its own moonshot madness. A man in Tokyo was going to mark the occasion in a hotel room wearing a space suit and eating "astronaut food" for the duration of the mission. Buddhists worshipped at shrines resembling the Apollo ship. And a few miles south of the launch site at the town of Cocoa, another gathering was taking place.

Five hundred marchers from the Poor People's Campaign led by civil rights activists Hosea Williams and Ralph Abernathy had converged on the Cape.[28] With America spending some $24 billion to send a handful of men to the moon, they asked, how could the nation not afford to tackle poverty at home? Already, in fact, the tide of public opinion was turning away from space exploration, in the increasingly divided culture of the 1960s. Even before *Apollo 11* lifted off, public opinion polls in France showed that a majority thought the moon shot not worth the expense. Americans themselves were closely divided on the question. A Harris Poll conducted the day before launch registered support hovering at 51 percent, a majority but a bare one, and just two points higher than it had been a year earlier when the success of Project Apollo was far less certain.[29] "We have a lot of problems here on earth we have to face up to," stated Montana senior senator Mike Mansfield. Critics suggested it would be more cost-effective to send "computers, not men into space."[30] Edward Kennedy, brother of the president who had started it all, called for putting earth needs such as "poverty, hunger, pollution and housing" ahead of space.[31]

Protestors from the Poor People's Campaign held an all-night vigil as the countdown proceeded.[32] The next day, they marched behind two mule-drawn wagons, a reminder that poverty lingered among many African Americans. Abernathy and forty of his contingent received VIP badges and seats in the viewing stands at KSC. The remaining protestors started a slow trek toward the Center. "We do not oppose the moon shot," declared Hosea Williams. "Our purpose is to protest America's inability to choose human priorities."[33] "We're wishing the astronauts all good luck," Abernathy added. "But we think attention should be given to poor people too."[34]

Along the riverbanks, bay shores, and beaches of the Cape, excitement was now palpable. Exasperated parents struggled to control overexcited children.[35] Babies dozed on the grass alongside bottles of suntan lotion and six-packs. Men in sharkskin suits and women in floral bikinis looked over peace signs stenciled in the sand. It all reminded one reporter of a "mammoth family picnic." Or a carnival, where "everyone [had] their own booth."[36] Reporters interviewed the wives of the astronauts, who expressed a mixture of concern for their husbands' safety and confidence that all had been done to assure a successful mission. Astronaut Mike Collins told everyone that he was going to spend his last day on earth sleeping, lying in the sun, and rereading the flight plan.[37] At KSC there was no time to lie in the sun, but there were similar expressions of confidence. "We have been preparing for this mission for several years. Now we are ready to go," stated one KSC engineer.[38] Ready, yes, but finished, not quite.

A launchpad is never dull when a bird is there. It turns into a controlled frenzy of activity as the final hours of launch approach. "I'm telling you, you go out to the launchpad the night before a launch," engineer Gene Sestile remembered. "I've never seen anything like it. It's awesome."[39] He meant the motion, the focus on getting things done, tasks crossed off lists, open items checked, verified, and closed up. It was work that involved calibrating delicate pieces of equipment one minute—equipment on which human lives depended—and then moving machines of gigantic proportions the next. Space technology simultaneously combined the incredibly delicate and sensitive with the gargantuan. The rocket, sixty feet taller than the Statue of Liberty, was overshadowed by the launch tower, an interlaced bridgework of steel trusses. Despite the tremendous weight of a fully loaded Saturn, the rocket's skin was surprisingly thin, an aluminum shell of one-twenty-fifth of an inch in some places.

At T-20 hours, workers readied the launch equipment. They took out the safety pins on the massive hold-down arms. These kept the vehicle in place for some eight seconds after the engines fired, then quickly swung away to release it. With fifteen hours to go, the Cape's Range Safety Office had completed its checks; the rocket could be destroyed in an emergency. With ten hours left, workers secured, jacked, and moved the mobile service structure to a safe distance. This 400-foot steel tower was no match for the fires of blastoff. Now only the rocket and launch tower stood at the pad. Almost every fifteen minutes brought the start or completion of another task. Inch by inch the curtain on the *Apollo 11* performance was rising.

At T-9 hours, counting stopped for six hours. This built-in hold allowed everyone to catch up on work. It wasn't a time for rest, though. The time out was to prepare for the last big, dangerous step—loading propellants into the Saturn. Only those with special badges, no more than twenty people, were permitted on the pad during tanking. Loading nearly a million gallons of explosive fluid was hair-raising work, both dangerous and difficult. The more tractable RP-1, essentially kerosene, fueled the first-stage rockets. But the upper stages needed fuel that delivered more bang for the buck—hydrogen. In its gaseous state, this lightest element would take up a huge amount of space. Cooled to a liquid, it was compact enough to fit in the rocket's tanks. But fire needs oxygen, and the upper stages would be burning above earth's oxygen-rich atmosphere. So the rocket took along its own oxygen, also cooled to an extreme temperature.

Substances at minus-423 degrees Fahrenheit were not to be fooled with. Even getting cryogenic fuels into the vehicle tanks was difficult. Before starting full propellant flow, technicians prechilled the lines and checked carefully for leaks. Invariably leaks would occur in the quarter-mile journey from the storage tank as the near-frozen fuel rose ever so slightly in temperature. The slight rise was enough to expand the pipes' supercooled joints, letting some of the cryogenic liquid ooze onto the ground. The trick was to keep leaks within a tolerable limit. Every pipe had a redundancy, an alternate route should one path fail. After six hours of painstaking work, tanking was complete. The rocket, loaded with fuel, had grown from half a million pounds to six and a half million.

Now the launch team prepared to receive the crew. They checked the cabin inventory, down to the crew's seventy-two aspirin tablets. At 4:00 A.M., Neil Armstrong, Edwin Aldrin, and Michael Collins awoke and ate the traditional astronaut breakfast of steak and eggs, orange juice, toast, and coffee, their last earth food for eight days. Then they left their KSC home in the Manned Spacecraft Operations Building, and at 6:52 A.M. were ready to board. Exactly an hour later, the hatch was closed.

With forty-five minutes remaining, the pad area was cleared and the launch tower elevator locked. The only humans left near *Apollo 11* were the astronauts and a fourteen-man emergency crew, stationed in a bunker three-quarters of a mile away. Tension in the firing room rose to maximum levels, made worse when the order was given to extinguish all cigarettes. Not even the distraction of smoking was allowed at this point. Every technician focused on his or her screen, watching the redlines, alert for deviations from expected values. Every ten seconds the count came over voice channels. After T-40 seconds, it would come every five seconds until T-11 seconds, when the voice would count each second backwards to zero.

At T-10 minutes, cryogenic fuel circulated through the thrust chambers of the giant rocket engines to cool them, a key measure of protection against the heat of the blast. At T-6 minutes, the spacecraft was go for launch, verified by the mission director in Houston and the director of launch operations at KSC.

In every launch, then as today, comes that moment of truth when each major system reports in. In flat, clipped voices come the words: "S-IC is go"; "S-II is go"; "S-IVB go"; "CSM go, LEM go, SRO go." Each stage, each system—propulsion, computer, guidance, stabilization—signals readiness with a definite affirmative. They come in rapid succession, building tension until the hairs on your neck stand up as if they themselves were craning for a better view.

All the major directors now agreed, *Apollo 11* was ready. Director of Launch Operations Paul Donnelly, Test Conductor Skip Chauvin, and finally Launch Director Rocco Petrone all gave their thumbs-up. At T-3 minutes 20 seconds, the automatic sequencer took over. Now the series of checks and moves needed to reach ignition would be handled by computer. It was still possible to hold and recycle the clock if needed, or scrub entirely, but the window for a decision was rapidly closing. With less than a minute to go, vehicle systems were running fully on internal power. At T-11 seconds, there were no more chances. The computer would decide to fire the engines, or shut them down if the vehicle failed to lift. Human hands would intervene only if automation failed.

At T-8.9 seconds, 500 volts of electricity jolted the first-stage engines to life. A column of flame shot down from the combustion chambers. It was split by the 40-foot-high flame deflector sending twin rivers of fire along the flame trench, where they curled up at the ends. Instantly nozzles released 50,000 gallons of water to cool the pad, sending white steam billowing up around the Saturn.

For six seconds the rocket built up thrust, first equal to its own weight and then over. Once thrust exceeded weight, the craft could rise, but the hold-down arms still kept it anchored. Only at 7.5 million pounds of thrust—which allowed a sufficient margin for error—did they let go. In one-twentieth of a second, at exactly the same instant, all the arms released. At

1-7. The journey begins as *Apollo 11* starts to rise.

T-0 *Apollo 11* was free to start its journey. As it rose, 120 decibels of sound rumbled through the LCC, shaking dust from the ceiling tiles.

Viewed from the ground miles away, the giant rocket appeared to stutter. Saturns do not make a perfectly smooth ascent. One second after liftoff, they automatically turn away from the launch tower. Despite its size and heft, the Saturn is not sturdy enough to resist strong gusts of wind, so it instead bends with them and then quickly readjusts course as, in a fraction of a second, the instrument unit computes a new trajectory. Ten seconds after starting its as-

1-8. Former president Lyndon Johnson and then–vice president Spiro Agnew stare up at the rising rocket.

cent, *Apollo 11* cleared the tower, with a farewell from KSC's Paul Donnelly: "Good luck and Godspeed from the launch crew."

Away and After

Immediately after Houston took control, KSC personnel began safing-and-securing operations. At T+6 minutes, postlaunch inspection plans went into effect. Within twenty minutes a safety team approached the 7,000-foot blast danger line. They purged liquid hydrogen and vented the fuel lines. Two hours later the last of the countdown steps were completed.

Like every launch, *Apollo 11* was a learning opportunity. It began with an immediate evaluation, a "quick look." Engineers noted each variation from the expected, and where performance stayed within norms, that was noted too. How did the second stage do? Fine, but at T-33 seconds, a pressure measurement was 5 psi too low. A leak? No, the pressure was increasing normally. Low pressure must have been due to a miscalibrated regulator. The ground crew would follow up later to correct the setting. They would also perform an analysis on one of the batteries, which had failed. Study later showed that a slight trace of electrolyte had created a path between the battery and its casing, draining the cell. Fortunately, they found no evidence of a crack, which might have indicated a defect in manufacturing requiring follow-up back to the factory.[40] How about the lunar module, which would soon be called on to take Armstrong and Aldrin to the lunar surface? A problem here could scrub the landing or, worse, leave them with no way back. Tests taken throughout the countdown showed a persistent problem of crystals in the water-glycol system. Nothing that should endanger the mission, but this would require more work. On and on the report went, noting each condition, each anomaly, marking areas for further investigation. Why had a service arm taken 64 milliseconds longer than specifications to withdraw? Why hadn't the LH_2 heat exchanger on the S-II stage operated properly? What sort of launch had this been? A nearly flawless one, late by only 724 milliseconds.

All the work leading up to liftoff was forgotten the moment the rocket cleared the tower, forgotten, and largely unknown by the millions around the world who watched the 250,000 mile journey of *Apollo 11* to an alien world. The day-by-day progress of preparing for that journey was not their concern. It was important only the way Buzz Aldrin put it; there was nothing to feel, nothing that was not as it should be, nothing that had not been made as ready as it could be by human hands.

Across the United States, and indeed much of the world, people sat transfixed in front of television screens when *Apollo 11* lifted off. Unknown numbers watched in thirty-three other nations, or heard the broadcast on radio. Most of those at the Cape, viewing from lawn chairs, car roofs, or even atop portable toilets, just looked and stared. There is no more appropriate time to be struck silent than when seeing the dragon tail of fire, hearing the roar, and feeling the pulse of a Saturn V at full throttle. Those on the ground were too stunned to applaud. Many, though, cried. One visitor remarked, "Once they land on the moon, it will represent a quantum jump of mankind similar to the transition of animals from water to land." Some sought the meaning of what they had just seen in archaeology: "It's like mankind has developed fire all over again." Some searched history: "I wonder if Columbus had this kind of send-off?" Still others turned to the sublime: "I sat there and admired all those stars," said one witness, recounting his nighttime vigil with the rocket.[41] No single angle could cover what had just happened, this mixture of science and poetry. Novelist Norman Mailer professed himself awed and baffled by "a sex-stripped mystery of machines which might have a mind, and mysterious men who managed to live like machines." Only contradiction could capture the moment, an "adventure in space so vast that one thought of the infinities of a dream," yet on the ground "conventional, techni-cal, hardworking." Bureaucracy had been set in pursuit of surreal ends.[42] Or was *Apollo 11* a resolution? Perhaps the best last word came from someone who had also asked the most difficult questions. Speaking after the launch, Ralph Abernathy reflected, "Just as the shot was made I forgot for the first time since my youth that our nation is divided into two worlds. I lived in one world for a time."[43]

Operations and Learning

The last entry on *Apollo 11* in the status report dutifully appeared the next day: "Apollo 11 (AS 506) was successfully launch[ed] from LC-39/Pad A, Kennedy Space Center, at 0932 hours on July 16, 1969."[44] After that, it dis-appeared forever. Not even a whisper four days later when the men it had ferried stepped onto the lunar surface. By then KSC workers were busy pre-paring *Apollo 12*. Someone was high up on the launch tower, repainting spots of paint chipped or burned off in the launch of *Apollo 11*. Then on July 28, a week and a day after Neil Armstrong set foot on the moon, *Apollo 13* appeared in the report.

As Norman Mailer perceived, there was much about this event, and the American space program in general, that was industrial and bureaucratic. Where the public saw a flawless arc of ascent, those at KSC experienced the daily grind of working on the assembly line to the stars. Indeed, the bureaucratic nature of the space program is often seen as its greatest flaw, a detraction from the noble goals of exploration, innovation, and scientific investigation.[45] But this claim depends on a particular view of science and technology. Images of the solitary scientist in the laboratory or the cranky inventor tinkering in a garage are at the opposite pole from a large, bu-reaucratic space program. Yet contrary to popular myth, big science and big technology have, throughout the twentieth century, required substan-tial attention to matters of organization and management.[46] This is hardly the heroic side of the story of knowledge, but it is there nonetheless. Even the most exceptional inventor—the Henry Ford or the Bill Gates—needs an organization to bring his vision to fruition.[47] While two Dayton bicycle mechanics might build a prototype airplane, designing and operating a 747 cannot be done in the Wright brothers' bicycle shop.

Moving beyond invention to a full-scale system for putting humans into space on a regular basis, sending robots to study distant planets, or con-structing an orbital station requires close attention to organization, manage-ment and engineering. It also requires, as we have just seen, some old-fashioned "wrench turning." A somewhat more professional word for this sort of work—the work that goes on at Kennedy Space Center—is "operations."

If unromantic, operations work is not simple. Getting the right wrench turned at the right time can be as difficult a task, from a management and operations point of view, as designing a rocket or planning a deep space journey. To prepare, launch, land, and prepare again for the next flight, on schedule, within a budget, is an even more difficult task. And more difficult still is sustaining such work at a high level of performance, while accumulating the necessary skills and knowledge to deal with innovation and change.

Operations have in fact been crucial to the success of NASA and the space program since their earliest days. Only the tendency to separate scientific research and technological innovation from operations keeps us from seeing this.[48] Part of the problem comes from the incorrect assumption that matters such as maintenance and service are ordinary and basic, that they cannot provide fundamental insights into technology. Yet as astute businesses have now begun to recognize, it is often the "maintenance" departments, such as warranty claims and help desks, that reveal the problems that designers and builders missed, or could not have foreseen. The unexpected is discovered only in operations.[49] At least one student of high-risk, high-performance environments has argued that operations should be treated more like scientific experiments than like the routine following of established procedures.[50] At ground level, operational work provides real-world experience that proves plans and designs. It results in knowledge and understanding that can be fed back to the developers for more efficient, and safer, future products and technologies.

For all this to happen, organizations must have several things. First, they must have talented people working for them. Particularly in operations, much knowledge is tacit; it comes by doing, not studying. It is picked up on the job, not read out of books. Good personnel who can learn as they work are thus crucial to operational performance. Fortunately, as we shall see, the ability to attract talented workers, often at wages below those prevailing in the private sector, has never been a major problem at the Kennedy Space Center, and at NASA in general. The prestige of space has attracted many high-quality scientists, engineers, and technicians.

Organizations are more than the sum of their parts, however. After all, if they were *only* the sum, then we could dispense with them. More important even than individual talent is organizational learning. NASA in fact has a long tradition of learning. KSC and other centers have maintained strong ties to universities and secondary schools, and have used these education programs to recruit workers and to bring the fruits of space research to school curriculums. Internal training and connections to outside institutions of scientific and engineering research, to the professions and disciplines of knowledge used in the space business, and to private-sector contractors have been crucial to the success of space programs.[51] But the success of an organization depends on its ability to adapt, change, and "learn" as an organization.[52]

Organizational learning takes place culturally. Old hands teach newcomers. They talk among themselves about the "lessons" they have gathered, making their experiences part of the accepted wisdom of organizational life. Particularly in operations, the tacit nature of knowledge makes these personal connections all the more valuable. In fact, since the keenest insights sometimes come from the lowest levels of operations, learning must flow up from the bottom as well as down from on high.[53]

There is a belief that noncompetitive governmental organizations are less motivated to learn.[54] As we shall see, however, KSC contradicts this assumption. KSC has learned over time. It has made incremental improvements in its procedures and routines. It has learned to launch vehicles more efficiently. It has become more proficient at finding and correcting errors. And it has learned to handle a wide variety of new vehicles, some of which, such as the space shuttle, broke significantly from past designs.

Students of technology have posited that there are two types of innovation: incremental and radical. The first involves improvements in existing systems of technology, existing processes and methods. The second involves a sharper break with the past to embrace strikingly new machines, methods, and procedures. Existing organizations are often good at the first, but newcomers are often the only ones with a clean enough slate to achieve the second.[55] Since government agencies do not face competition and rarely go out of business, critics of the public sector have argued that they are incapable of making radical technological innovations. This belief has provided ammunition for those who would privatize governmental activities, including the space program.

The history of KSC, however, challenges this assumption as well. It argues against a sharp separation between incremental and radical innovation. At the level of operations, incremental improvements and knowledge gained from hands-on work can often have radical implications. Striking breakthroughs can be built on the accumulation of small but continuous improvements of the sort that happen at the operational level.[56]

None of this is to say that the history of KSC, and of NASA more broadly, has been one of undeflected progress. Individuals can be lazy. Alienated employees can underperform. But just as learning is an organizational matter, beyond what individuals do, so too many of the problems of innovation and learning go beyond individual actions.

All organizations, no matter how successful they are at one moment, can suffer from myopia and succumb to breakdowns at the next. Experience can make strong organizations learn "all too well" what to do. These "competency traps" breed complacency about change, complacency only reinforced by past successes. Problem solving becomes narrowly defined, and misses new opportunities. The good becomes the enemy of the better.[57]

More important to the history of the space program, however, has been another issue. In complex organizations, such as those performing big science and engineering projects, tasks are broken down and subdivided into smaller units and specialties. Various groups of people perform various functions—engineers, managers, blue-collar workers, clerical workers. Across these functional categories are differences in outlook and experience, differences in professional standards, practice, and education. Good organizations coordinate these varied forms of knowledge and expertise. But as organizations divide tasks into smaller units, they also construct walls or boundaries. Individuals tend to identify most closely with their own unit. The result is the familiar problem of organizational turf, sandboxes, silos, and other borders that block change and innovation.[58]

The history of the space program, as seen from KSC, has been limited by a fundamental organizational boundary of this sort. It is found in the tension between those who do operations and those who design and build spacecraft and plan missions.[59] Design and development personnel, if they are isolated from real-world operations, tend to dismiss as simply "a problem" any information coming in from the field that does not match their expectations.[60] They ask operating personnel to overcome or work around such problems, but do not consider the deeper implications for design issues that such problems may be providing. In perhaps the most tragic example of this in the American space program, failure to respond to an anomaly in the solid rocket booster joints led to the *Challenger* disaster.

Overcoming the barriers between the operational culture and the design culture of NASA has been a major challenge, and one that KSC has struggled with throughout its history. In what follows, we shall see how this tension between operations and design has manifested itself, where KSC has been able to overcome it, and where it has not.

*   *   *

As Apollo launch director Rocco Petrone once said, the launch of *Apollo 11* had been in preparation ever since President John F. Kennedy first proposed a mission to the moon in 1961. In the next chapters, we trace the origins of that moment back to the early test flights of rockets at the Cape, back even to the work of Wernher von Braun at White Sands, New Mexico, 160 miles from the explosion of the first atomic bomb. And we move forward from the launch of *Apollo 11* to the rest of the Apollo program, to the human and robotic missions of the 1970s, to the flying of the space shuttle, and into the present day of the International Space Station and missions still being defined.

2

*
*
*

Rockets and Alligators

*There are four several ways whereby this flying in the air hath been
or may be attempted. 1. By spirits or angels. 2. By the help of fowls.
3. By wings fastened immediately on the body. 4. By a flying chariot.*

Bishop John Wilkins, *Mathematical Magick* (1648)

Two Cape Dwellers

Before it was land, it was sea. For thousands of years, the land of Florida lay beneath a warm, shallow ocean. In those waters swam creatures of the sea, eating plants, nibbling at coral reefs, filtering microscopic plankton. Land rose on the skeletons of these prehistoric creatures until it formed a coral outcropping poking through the water as the primordial seas receded. Left in the wake of the retreating ocean was a sandy spit of shore only four or five feet above sea level, a point jutting into the Atlantic, a geographical form commonly known as a cape.

Little is known about the history of Cape Canaveral before Spanish explorers alighted five hundred years ago. Prehistoric bones tell of a people who arrived three millennia before the Spanish, nomadic hunters who pursued game with flint-tipped spears. They roamed lands festooned with cabbage palms and pines and, on higher ground, oak and tropical hardwoods. They climbed along wind-blown dunes and tramped through marshes and lowlands covered by salt water at high tide. They found little they could cultivate in these poorly drained soils, but in the Cape's shallow, brackish waters lived an abundance of marine life, supplying native hunters with fish and shellfish. The remains of their meals formed high mounds or "middens." Hundreds of these mounds, and dozens of burial sites of the early hunters, dot the Cape. Several lie only a few hundred yards from the NASA launch facilities. In the middens and burial mounds are a prehistoric technology of tools made of bones and clay vessels close by the wonders of the space age.[1]

By the time the Spanish arrived, two native groups occupied the region, the Ais and the Timucuan.[2] Settled peoples, they lived in wooden dwellings covered with palmetto leaves. Neither welcomed the European interlopers, in part because European slave raiders had already visited the Florida coast in search of human cargo. When Ponce de León made his second Florida landing in 1513 close to the Cape, he was forced to beat a hasty retreat by attacking Ais. Although Spain signed a peace treaty with the native population in 1570, Spanish crews stranded from shipwrecks still risked their lives waiting for rescue.

Exactly when and how the Cape was christened Canaveral is not known. Early Spanish sailors referred to it as the Cape of Currents, a warning about its shallow shoals and treacherous tides that led many ships to founder. So many, in fact, that the Ais and Timucuan, scavenging among Spanish hulks, added European axes and hatchets to their inventory of tools. The name that stuck, Canaveral, means canebrake or "place of cane." It did not refer to sugarcane, although this now grows close by on the mainland of central Florida, but to a variety of native plants and reeds resembling sugarcane.

To the Spanish, the Cape was a place neither of settlement nor of treasure. It was rather a sign, a distinctive promontory that guided ships plying the waters between the Caribbean and Europe. Seen from the air, the east coast of Florida appears as straight as a paper edge. But heading north, one soon notices a distinctive protrusion. Viewed sideways, this outcropping looks like a mountain rising from a low plane. Pointing proudly out to sea, with a small fingertip extending just northward, Cape Canaveral is an unmistakable landmark. In the sixteenth century, ships' captains guided their vessels along the Florida coast, keeping land in sight until they spotted the Cape. Then they turned to the northeast for the journey to Spain. Otherwise, the Cape, like the rest of Florida, was mainly a piece of second-class real estate passed back and forth in the New World struggles of the major European powers. French Huguenots started a colony nearby, but after the Spanish secured their Florida claim by establishing a fort to the north at St. Augustine in 1565, the French were uprooted in a bloody ordeal that left most of them dead. Uprooted too were most of the native peoples, who were killed or enslaved during raids by English and French intruders.

When Great Britain gained possession Florida at the end of the Seven Years' War in 1763, most of the remaining Indians fled with the Spanish to Cuba. Although part of the British Empire from 1763 until 1783, the Cape was now virtually devoid of humans. English settlers came no closer to it than New Smyrna, on the mainland just to the north. Led by Dr. Andrew Turnbull, the English colonists sought a profit-making venture in sugarcane, but gave up at the end of the American Revolution when Florida passed back into Spanish hands. After negotiations by John Quincy Adams, Spain ceded Florida to the United States in 1821.[3]

At this time the United States was starting an aggressive drive for land, with settlers moving westward. Though ripe for settlement, the Cape was largely ignored during the antebellum decades. Just to the west of the Cape proper on Merritt Island, the present-day site of the Kennedy Space Center, entrepreneur Douglas Dummitt planted orange groves, the first substantial commercial activity in the region. By 1828, Dummitt's Indian River Brand citrus was being marketed along the East Coast. But one could reach Cape Canaveral itself only by boat. By the 1840s a few poor Scots-Irish settlers from Georgia and the Carolinas looking for cheap land had taken up residence there. In 1847 the U.S. government built a lighthouse to warn ships of the dangerous Cape currents. On Merritt Island, families had settled permanently by 1868, growing citrus and sugarcane and raising cattle. But the most significant population growth took place to the west, along the mainland. In Brevard County, northern sportsmen frequently stopped at the Titus House, a sprawling hotel built by "Colonel" Henry Titus. A former Confederate blockade-runner, Titus took on the role of first citizen and became the town's namesake in 1867. Brevard County's reputation as a tropical hunting ground was already well established in 1887 when rail service arrived in the area.

The railroad encouraged development of other small towns in Brevard. Nature's bounty and beauty attracted a growing number of tourists, as did the salubrious climate, which became famous for its healing powers for tuberculosis sufferers. Orange groves and cattle ranches rounded out an economy that increasingly depended on seasonal visitors who came to breathe clean air, hunt wild game, and land big fish.

Even as mainland towns grew, the boat remained the only way out to the Cape. The first bridge was not built until 1923. Beach houses, fishing piers, a parlor-sized general store, and something that passed for a hotel were about all the evidence of human habitation one could find on Cape Canaveral before World War II.[4] The hundred or so souls living there were far outnumbered by the most impressive Cape dweller, the ancient Florida alligator.[5]

All this began to change in 1938 as the U.S. military constructed defense facilities along the Florida coast. On October 1, 1940, the navy opened the Banana River Naval Air Station, about fifteen miles south of Cape Canaveral. During World War II, the air station was used to train pilots and send out patrols, looking for German submarines. But it declined in importance with the end of hostilities, and was decommissioned in 1947. A world at peace seemed to promise the Cape a return to its peaceful, sleepy lifestyle. Then came the Cold War and with it permanent changes to Cape Canaveral. What

2-1. Historic Cape Canaveral Lighthouse, a sign from the Cape's seafaring past.

2-2. Cape and Merritt Island region in their pre–space center topography.

generations of Native American, Spanish, English, and American settlers had failed to do, new technology did: make Cape Canaveral a household name to millions of people around the world. The new Cape born of the Cold War was a sign too, a sign for a spacefaring, not a seafaring, era.

On July 24, 1950, the first rocket lit the sky above Cape Canaveral. As Bumper 8 sped into the atmosphere in a perfect launch arc, rockets joined alligators on the coastal lowlands of Central Florida. These technological marvels represented the modern world just as the alligator, unchanged over five million years of evolution, recalled the prehistoric. In the idiom of the 1950s, nothing was more modern and futuristic than rockets and rocket science. Cape Canaveral was soon to become the major landform in the symbolic geography of rocket science.

Flying Chariots

Before a technology achieves material form, it lives in the human imagination. Images of rockets leaving the earth and literature on space have existed nearly as long as humans have understood themselves to be voyagers on a sea-blue globe whisking through a vast dark universe. After Copernicus showed the earth not to be the center of existence but only one planet circling the sun, scientists, theologians, and poets alike felt a need to explore the new realm of space he had opened. By the nineteenth century, this combination of scientific curiosity and imaginative thought had coalesced into modern science fiction. Before it was physically possible to explore space, science fiction writers argued that space was a place needing exploring.

In *De la terre à la lune* (1866; trans. *From the Earth to the Moon*), Jules Verne outlined a plausible scenario for getting to the moon, down to locating the launch point in Florida. He correctly calculated travel time from the earth, the size and weight of the capsule, and even suggested use of lightweight aluminum (then a new metal) in place of steel, though his method of propulsion was a giant cannon. In *The First Men in the Moon* (1901), H. G. Wells was less obsessed with technical issues, dismissing real problems with invented solutions, such as a gravity-defying metal. Wells gave his readers a critique of imperialism and a warning about the clash of civilizations that blindly reaching out to space might bring, but the lesson was lost on those enthralled by the idea of space travel. In 1898 a Russian schoolteacher named Konstantin Tsiolkovskiy proposed that rockets be used to explore space beyond earth's gravity. Like Verne and even like Wells, Tsiolkovskiy's pursuit of rocketry at the theoretical level brought what had been the most remote and obscure of places—outer space—closer to home. These writers staked out the territory for others who would think seriously about the physical, physiological, and social mechanisms needed to make the leap into space.

Tsiolkovskiy's work was especially important in this regard. Though it might seem hard to understand now, rocket power for space flight had not been deemed realistic enough for either Verne or Wells to use in their books. The Russian, however, drew on a long history of rocket technology, a history that was largely disconnected from astronomy or from musings about outer space. Two thousand four hundred years ago in Greece, Archytas had amazed his friends and neighbors with a wooden pigeon that flew across a wire, propelled by escaping steam. Simple as it was, this ancient device illustrated the Third Law of Motion that Sir Isaac Newton would set down in 1686: For every action there is an equal and opposite reaction. Tsiolkovskiy extended well-known scientific principles when he noted that with escaping gases of sufficient velocity, a rocket could accelerate to 27,000 miles per hour and break free of gravity. Modern rockets are giant reaction motors.

Before the twentieth century, rockets found application not in space but in earthly affairs, notably war. The Chinese invented gunpowder in the first century C.E. and were shooting off fireworks by the year 600. At the battle of Kai-Keng in 1232, Chinese warriors launched bamboo tubes packed with gunpowder at their enemies, the Mongols.[6] From China, gunpowder and rocketry spread west. French knights during the Seventh Crusade were met by Arabs firing gunpowder-propelled arrows. By the late fourteenth century, the Italian word *rocchetta* referred to pyrotechnic devices. "Rocket," in various spellings, made it to English by the seventeenth century. Captain John Smith of the Virginia Colony in North America reported scaring the "poore Salvages" of the New World by firing "rackets" at them.[7] But rockets had only a minor military role in the Western world until the next century. In 1792 at the Battle of Seringapatam, Indian soldiers devastated British troops with rocket barrages. The British responded by developing their own rocket weapons at Woolwich Arsenal. It was the "red glare" of these British rockets that illuminated the American flag over Fort McHenry for Francis Scott Key. For the most part, though, rockets were far less important than artillery. The trajectory of long-range guns, not rockets, led to the ballistic tables that predicted where projectiles would land as they were pulled back to earth by gravity during flight. Rockets and rocket science were largely the province of inventors and scientists more interested in the principles of physics and aerodynamics than in matters of transportation or military armament.

Shortly after the Wright brothers achieved powered flight in 1903, American physicist Robert Goddard began launching rockets toward the upper atmosphere from Worcester Polytechnic Institute in central Massachusetts. After experimenting with solid-fueled devices—the technology that went back to medieval China—Goddard took out patents on higher-velocity liquid-fueled engines and designs for multistage rockets. His scientific investigations culminated in 1920 in a report he issued for the Smithsonian, "A Method of Reaching Extreme Altitudes." In it Goddard provided mathematical theories of rocket propulsion and demonstrated some practical uses, such as placing weather-recording devices high into the atmosphere.[8] Still, even in Goddard's day, the rocket remained more toy than tool of civilian or military application. Like Tsiolkovskiy, Goddard had leapt well beyond accepted science by proposing that rockets could reach beyond the atmosphere, perhaps even to the moon. Such propositions brought him ridicule from the press. Goddard continued his work, however, launching the world's first liquid-fueled rocket in 1926 and publishing his prescient findings, including empirical proof that rocket engines could work in a vacuum.[9]

Goddard's work had more immediate influence on another nation. Following publication of Goddard's Smithsonian study, the *Verein für Raumschiffahrt*, or German Space Society, was founded in 1927. In 1937, Wernher von Braun assembled a team of top German scientists and engineers to work on a secret project in a vast installation on the shores of the Baltic at Peenemünde. Using the basic knowledge developed by Goddard and other pioneers, they produced what Joseph Goebbels named the *Vergeltungswaffe* or "vengeance weapon." A ballistic missile, the liquid-fueled V-2 carried high explosives into London and other allied cities during World War II. Traveling fifty miles into the sky, the 46-foot-long V-2 came screaming back to earth at 3,500 miles per hour. It hit its target before the sound of its supersonic descent reached the ears of victims below. With a full ton of explosives, it packed a payload large enough to destroy a city block. Though inaccurate, the V-2 was used more than three thousand times in the war. The Germans had demonstrated the military potential of rockets once and for all.[10]

The V-2 had no effect on the war's outcome, though to the astute it did suggest what a missile attack with nuclear weapons might do. The German project also brought together a group of scientists, engineers, and technicians who would profoundly shape the American space program a decade later. Naively or not, von Braun had run a Nazi rocket program while retaining his belief that the same technology would be used someday for peaceful exploration of outer space. Even while working on the vengeance weapon, von Braun mapped out plans for a multistage booster capable of more than 2 million pounds of thrust, a true spaceship for the stars.[11]

At the end of World War II, five hundred German rocket scientists packed up all they could carry in three hundred railroad cars and headed west—as luck would have it, right into the American zone of occupation. They were carrying with them V-2 parts, papers, technical drawings, and documents.

American intelligence officers, under Project Paperclip, examined the personnel files of these German scientists and engineers, looking for those who possessed useful knowledge. Despite the missiles' terror over London and the use of concentration-camp slave labor to assemble them, some one hundred German scientists were allowed to enter the United States. With relations between the United States and Russia already cooling, the German expatriates were being recruited to work on the next generation of military hardware.

Cold War Competition

The arrival of the German rocket team gave the United States a significant leg up in rocket knowledge and technique. But institutional barriers remained. Trained in strategy and tactics whose roots were thousands of years old, American military planners were adjusting to the realities of a world in which science and technology could decisively shift the balance of power.[12] The lessons of World War II provided a strong argument for change. That conflict, after all, had introduced not only the German ballistic missiles but also atomic bombs, sophisticated electronic devices such as radar and sonar, and long-range bombers. The Soviet Union, the only other superpower on the globe, saw the advantages of new technology too. Several German rocket scientists had gone to the Russian side, and there they found a Soviet missile research program that nearly matched the German effort in knowledge, if not in results.[13]

In a few short years following the war, the American military establishment changed dramatically. By 1947 the United States had a unified Department of Defense under a single cabinet secretary, advised by a more or less cohesive Joint Chiefs of Staff drawn from the army, navy, marine corps, and a newly independent air force. Now separated from the army, the air force in particular was strongly committed to scientific and technological research. It even created its own think tank, the RAND Corporation.

RAND reports over the next few years laid out plans that would become blueprints for military and civilian space programs. Advances in rocket technology, RAND researchers argued, portended rapid conquest of the upper reaches of the atmosphere. Already jet planes had broken the sound barrier, and rocket-powered missiles carrying weapons (or scientific instruments, or people) were likely to arrive soon. Scientist and writer Arthur C. Clarke had just published a speculative but compelling article in *Wireless World* titled "Extra Terrestrial Relays" in which he argued for building a global communications network with geo-stationary satellites. RAND writers saw satellites as especially useful for intelligence purposes. Without sophisticated electronic spying, the closed Soviet society would be difficult for American intelligence to penetrate.[14]

The RAND reports also mentioned, in fewer words, a role for civilian space exploration. Space captured the public imagination, and the nation that demonstrated mastery of space would be in a position to claim serious technological bragging rights. To the extent that the Cold War was also a battle for the hearts and minds of people on earth, space might well become the proving ground for the technological prowess of capitalism against communism. Thus as early as 1950, civilian space had become connected to political and military agendas. In the minds of the military authorities who read the RAND reports, space had both strategic and propaganda value, value perhaps high enough to override the cost of space ventures.

The realities of American politics in the 1950s, however, did not lend themselves to a broad space agenda. Under President Dwight Eisenhower, military options were assessed soberly in light of fiscal realities. Committed to low taxes and limited spending, the former supreme commander of American forces in Europe was not easily bluffed or bamboozled by the military hard sell. He knew that the quest for superiority, particularly technical superiority, could be trotted out to justify any and all weapons systems in a full-scale arms race. Rather than explore every technnological frontier, therefore, Eisenhower was content to parry threats from the communist world with an arsenal of nuclear weapons and a strong American bomber force. Unlimited research budgets and big-ticket prestige items like space exploration were not high on Ike's shopping list.

Devotees of an ever-expanding air frontier in the U.S. military continued to do research on rockets, picking up the lead from Germany. In 1946 the army had ensconced the German rocket team at Fort Bliss in El Paso, Texas, where they carried out further missile research using the White Sands Proving Grounds in nearby New Mexico. Their main task was to develop military weapons, but von Braun hoped that there would be opportunities to do other things as well. "Like a sideshow," work could proceed on rockets that might orbit the earth and escape gravity for the stars.[15]

At White Sands, the German scientists assembled their imported V-2s and practiced launching them. In charge of launches was a von Braun protégé and fellow immigrant, Kurt Debus. Working with American military and scientific personnel, the rocket team ran more a "firing laboratory" than a missile development and deployment operation. The V-2 rockets, rebuilt and reassembled by the American firm General Electric, were prepared and tested in a laborious process before being wheeled to a firing site on a

2-3. Captured V-2s tested at White Sands, New Mexico.

"Meillerwagen," a German-designed trailer. At the launchpad the rocket was raised to vertical for countdown. These were the same basic launch procedures practiced in Germany during the war.

They tested sixty-seven V-2s before the White Sands program ended. On February 24, 1949, one of these, Bumper 5, combined a V-2 with a WAC Corporal second stage and flew high enough to penetrate outer space, a first for the United States. Other missions included studying cosmic and solar radiation. All the tests resulted in data about engine performance, launch operations, flight, guidance, and telemetry, which would hopefully be useful in future generations of more powerful rockets when the United States was ready to build them.[16]

In June 1949 von Braun and his crew left the arid confines of West Texas for the warm humidity of northern Alabama. There the army had reactivated the old Redstone Arsenal in Huntsville as its Ordnance Rocket Center. It was still unclear if rockets would be primarily a form of advanced artillery, under army control, or a type of aircraft suitable for the air force. Parallel development programs went on in both services as well as in the navy, which envisioned missiles launched from ships. In the summer of 1950 von Braun and his Huntsville team started sending their missiles to a recently activated site on the Central Florida coast.

In 1947 military authorities had selected Cape Canaveral as a missile testing range. The air force took over the old Banana River Naval Air Station and on October 1, 1949, rechristened it Long Range Proving Ground Air Force Base. The following August it became Patrick Air Force Base.[17] Just to the north of the airbase lay the sandy shores of Cape Canaveral, which were to serve as a launch site, with missiles flying over the water in what came to be called the Atlantic Missile Range.

When the Huntsville team arrived at Cape Canaveral, they found a topography little changed from its early American and indeed Spanish days—lovely beaches, fair weather, superb fishing, shrimp boats, tall reeds. One could now reach the beach from the mainland by car, though over a rickety bridge that ended in the middle of a sandy clearing. The main structures nearby were the Cape Canaveral lighthouse, a coast guard station, and a few private houses. Down the road, Patrick Air Force Base was still just a collection of temporary buildings and Quonset huts.[18] Alligators, along with deer, rattlesnakes, and wild pigs, patrolled inland lagoons. But the macro fauna paled in comparison to a much smaller creature—the fierce salt marsh mosquito. In countless numbers the insects greeted the new visitors, turning white shirts black with their bodies. Workers donned hats, gloves, and long-sleeved shirts in 90-degree-plus heat. To keep them at bay they used repellent so strong that it dissolved photographs on security badges. Even so, at night the masters of rocket power sat in their lodgings, besieged by the threat of bugs.[19]

The rockets traveled from White Sands by rail to Melbourne, south of the Cape, and then moved in a convoy of cars and army trucks to Patrick Air Force Base. Fifteen miles farther to the north, crews cut away the canebrakes, burned underbrush, and uprooted palmettos with bulldozers until they had cleared enough land to set up a launch stand. Jeeps sank into sand up to their axles, and materials for a gantry had to be secured from the scaf-

2-4. First launch from the Cape, Bumper 8, a V-2 topped with a WAC Corporal rocket.

folding supplies of local painters. An old oil derrick provided a makeshift rocket service structure. But on July 24 the launch team was ready.

Fueling the rocket directly from tanker trucks, they set one designated Bumper 8 on a 30-meter-wide concrete pad. As the countdown started, the launch crew, composed of personnel from the military, General Electric, and California Institute of Technology, took up positions in a disused swimmers' hut surrounded by sandbags, less than a hundred yards from the rocket. A few days before, moisture problems had delayed the launch of a sister rocket, Bumper 7. But on July 24, 1950, Bumper 8 roared to life and lifted off flawlessly, the first stage separating at ten miles into the air and the second punching the missile an additional fifteen miles high. Birds scattered and alligators lifted their heads to a sound they had in their millions of years on earth never heard before.

Images of the launch show a sleek V-2 moving skyward on an exhaust tail billowing outward, while photographers, who seem to be dangerously close, capture the moment. Although the public was still awakening to the dawn of rocket flight, the image is iconic of the optimism of the early space age. Rockets of this era were human scale. They looked like something you could just step aboard and fly—a serious deception, given the number of early failures. Success required careful handling, preparation, and testing, with every attempt an adventure. Still, the launch gave the world a real-life approximation of the vivid images painted in words by Wells and Verne and in pictures in the pulp science fiction magazines.

If Bumper and other early rocket launches from the Cape could be taken as the first glimpses of a brave new world of space adventure, still other missile tests taking place there in the 1950s opened a much darker view on what this new technology might portend. In 1952, American scientists exploded a fusion (hydrogen) bomb, unleashing a destructive force an order of magnitude greater than the plutonium bombs used to annihilate Hiroshima and Nagasaki. Soon they reduced these fearsome devices to weapons size. Jets already carried nuclear weapons, but a missile capable of delivering them at supersonic speeds could reach its target in a mere half hour. The Cold War arms race had turned up one more frightening notch, and fast, accurate missiles against which there was no defense now seemed neither a luxury item nor a remote possibility, but increasingly a key feature of superpower strategy.

In 1955 the Air Force issued a contract to General Dynamics for missile development under Project Atlas.[20] Atlas proved to be one of the most complex weapons systems programs ever undertaken, necessitating a host of technical and organizational innovations that eventually became standards of the space age. Under General Bernard Schriever, the multiple systems of Atlas—engine, frame, guidance, electronics, nose cone—were developed in coordinated fashion using the techniques of program management and systems engineering. Just two years into the project, the first Atlas was trucked 2,600 miles from California to the Cape and flew on June 11, 1957.[21] Using similar managerial techniques, the air force quickly developed another liquid-fueled rocket, the Titan. The Cape hosted nearly a hundred Atlas and Titan tests in the next few years. The army meanwhile was working on its own intermediate-range missile, Jupiter. The navy had started on a submarine-launched Polaris missile, building a complex of pads, blockhouses, and assembly buildings on Cape Canaveral for testing.[22]

Hardware and management techniques from the early intercontinental ballistic missiles (ICMBs) would eventually find their way into America's

2-5. ICBM launchpads line Cape Canaveral. Some will be used in the early space program.

civilian space program. So too would the rockets. Atlas and Titan served as space boosters carrying both people and satellites above the atmosphere. The rush program to develop ICBMs proved an important learning experience for launch operations as well. Increases in the size and thrust of engines meant bigger pads and flame deflectors and the use of new fuels, such as storable hypergolic liquids (chemicals that ignite on contact).

Over 80 percent of the launches conducted at the Cape in the 1950s were for the air force. These included the new ICBMs as well as a host of other weapons, including a series of winged, air-breathing cruise missiles with names like Lark, Snark, Bomarc, and Navaho.[23] For the army, the von Braun team worked on a more powerful rocket named Redstone, derived from the V-2. Von Braun also refashioned his long-held ideas about the future of space with a powerfully stated, engineeringly exact proposal to use the Redstone in a four-stage configuration to launch earth-orbiting satellites.

By the mid-1950s, von Braun had taken over the role of chief space vision-ary. In a series of well-written, beautifully illustrated articles for the popular weekly *Collier's* magazine, he outlined the future of space travel: rockets to carry people, shuttles to a giant orbiting space station, missions to the moon and Mars. The articles discussed propulsion, trajectories, crew selec-tion and training, emergency escapes, lunar landing and exploration. They were more speculative than scientific, though with enough detail to suggest plausibility. Interestingly, though, the articles included almost no discussion of operations on earth or launching procedures, even though von Braun and his team were performing laborious test and verification work on rockets at the time. Trips to space apparently would be launched with a minimum of fuss and largely routine preparation.[24]

Under Eisenhower's go-slow approach, there seemed little likelihood that this bold vision would materialize anytime soon. Even when laid out by sci-entists like von Braun, trips to the moon and space stations still seemed more fiction than science. That did not mean progress came to a standstill, however. Competition with the Soviet Union kept the United States active in space-related research.

In 1952 scientists around the world designated for 1957 an International Geophysical Year (IGY) dedicated to the launching of a satellite into earth orbit. Satellites had the potential to vastly expand knowledge of the earth and its atmosphere, as well as of space.[25] Russia and the United States both accepted this satellite challenge. In 1955 President Eisenhower asked Con-gress to appropriate $13 million for the effort. A committee of scientists and military personnel investigated proposals from the air force, army, and navy. The army intended to use its Redstone rocket modified as a Jupiter multistage vehicle in Project Orbiter to put an Explorer satellite into space. It would be ready by 1957, Wernher von Braun confidently assured the com-mittee. The air force submitted a plan using its Atlas booster but, focused on the weapons race, was content to play only a backup role in case other projects failed. Eventually the committee approved a navy entry, Project Vanguard, which would use its Viking missile. Since it was clear that the con-fiscated V-2s would not last forever, the Naval Research Laboratory started drawing up plans for its own rocket as early as 1946. Under contract, the Glenn L. Martin Company produced the Viking missile in 1949. This small single-stage rocket was only a modest performer compared to the mature V-2–based Redstone, but it incorporated important new features, such as a gimbaled liquid-fueled rocket engine and an aluminum skin. It would be able to reach space with two additional stages.[26]

In 1956 the Vanguard team arranged to use Launch Complex 18 at Cape Canaveral for testing and launch. The Martin Company took charge of launch services and operations for Vanguard. Through 1956 and 1957, the navy team static-fired rocket engines and flew the individual stages, but the date of the American satellite launch slipped by nearly a year. After success with the first two launch attempts, the Vanguard crew worked through the hot summer of 1957 to debug its third test vehicle in time for the IGY challenge.[27] Nearby, the von Braun team watched, apparently out of the running but still testing its Jupiter configuration.

Then, unexpectedly, everything changed. On October 4, 1957, the Russian satellite Sputnik circled the earth at an altitude of 142 miles. The Soviet Union had beaten the United States with the first payload into space. Media and public relations fallout from Sputnik would last for a decade. Americans suddenly woke up to the possibility that Russia was ahead in the space race. Military strategists voiced fear of a "missile gap" that might well give the Soviets missile supremacy. In the wake of Sputnik, Senate majority leader Lyndon Johnson opened a media-savvy investigation into America's space policy. The Democrat from Texas charged Eisenhower with allowing the missile gap to emerge, as Ike and his staff scrambled to minimize the danger. The administration denounced Sputnik as nothing but a "neat trick," and refused to get drawn into a "game of outer space basketball." Sputnik, the president calmly responded, "didn't bother him one iota."[28] But even if it was only an artifact of crafty partisan maneuvering, the sense that America might be losing the space race contributed to gathering dissatisfaction with the calm, deliberate policies of the Eisenhower era. Like it or not, the United States was in danger of losing the battle for scientific prestige. As Senator Johnson concluded, space was big and "second in space means second in everything." Indeed, Wernher von Braun sagely concurred, space was even "bigger than Texas."[29]

The pressure to catch up with Russia soon proved irresistible. Despite disavowals, moreover, the Eisenhower administration had reason to be worried. The first Sputnik weighed in at 184 pounds, far heavier than the 20 pounds or so the United States was planning to boost into orbit with Vanguard. Then, on November 3, 1957, the 1,120-pound Sputnik II went up from the Soviet Union carrying live cargo, the test dog Laika. The Soviets had proved decisively that their first effort was no fluke. Russia possessed powerful boosters and scientists capable of mastering the design and operational problems connected with guiding man-made objects into orbit. In response, the navy hustled its Vanguard program, while the Pentagon quickly authorized the army's Explorer project as a backup. The von Braun team received approval to work on a second satellite launch. It might be too late to beat the Soviets, but there was still time to meet the IGY deadline.

On September 20, 1956, von Braun and his team had lofted a Jupiter-C 680 miles into the sky from Cape Canaveral. Less than a year later, on August 8, 1957, another Jupiter-C went up. Its nose cone was recovered from space, the first time a reentry vehicle came back from beyond the earth. It would not take much more for the Jupiter to achieve orbital velocity. But the navy was not out of the running yet either. On October 23, a third Vanguard rocket went skyward from the Cape in a perfect launch. If the United States would not match the Soviet success immediately, at least it seemed to be making progress toward a quick move into second place.

The best-laid plans, however, soon came to a fiery end. On December 6, 1957, a fourth Vanguard shot went horribly awry. After lifting four feet off the pad, it came crashing back down and was engulfed in a ball of flame. Once the emergency fire control system had doused the rocket, all that was left was a steaming hunk of metal, and a sad beeping from the nose cone. As it continued to bleat, one frustrated member of the launch team grabbed a shotgun from his truck and put it out of its misery.

Even an extensive investigation could not determine the cause of failure. The bad press stung sharply. "A blow to U.S. prestige," pronounced the *New York Times*. "Most humiliating," proclaimed Lyndon Johnson. At the United Nations the USSR's delegate asked if America wanted help from his country's technical assistance program for underdeveloped nations.[30] America's space program, open and public, got its first taste of public relations failure.

Vanguard was shoved to the background in an effort to mitigate embarrassment with a quick, successful launch. The secretary of defense ordered that the army's Jupiter-C be readied for an attempt to place a satellite in orbit. Partnering with the Jet Propulsion Laboratory (JPL), the Huntsville group's rocket took on board the experiment planned for Vanguard. With years of testing behind it, Jupiter seemed ready to go. On the pad, it required only checking of the upper stages mated to the Redstone base. Wary of inflating public expectations, however, General John Medaris, commander of the army's Ballistic Missile Agency, decided to release the launch date just twenty-four hours in advance. Then, with the launch set for January 29, 1958, upper atmospheric weather conditions forced a two-day hold. Another Vanguard effort was scheduled for February 3. With the two programs sharing the missile range, only one would be able to progress at a time. If Explorer did not fire shortly, it would have to give way to Vanguard once again. The final Explorer attempt started to count down at 1:30 P.M. on January 31. With the crew fighting exhaustion from the previous days' efforts and battling a series of glitches to stay on time, Explorer lifted off the pad at 10:48 P.M., its first-stage Redstone firing perfectly. But with no reliable automatic device for setting off the next stage, an engineer in the blockhouse had to push a second firing button with exact timing to start the second stage. Then everyone waited. Finally, an hour and fifty-three minutes later, word came over the wire: "Goldstone has the bird." The California tracking station had picked up Explorer. America was in space.[31]

Explorer weighed in at 31 pounds, a far cry from even the first Sputnik. But it carried the experiment of University of Iowa physicist James Van Allen, and discovered the belt of radiation circling earth now bearing his name. Vanguard finally made it into orbit on March 17, though the 3.5-pound satellite was dismissed by Soviet premier Khrushchev as a "grapefruit." Russia rubbed it in that May by sending up Sputnik III, a 7,000-pound behemoth. Vanguard could at least claim longevity. Sputnik's orbit decayed after a few months, as did Explorer's a year or so later. The satellite launched by Vanguard is in an orbit that will not bring it back to earth for another two hundred years. It remains the oldest man-made object in space.

With the launches of Explorer and Vanguard, America had tied Russia, but it seemed that the United States program was far behind on booster technology. On September 18, 1959, Project Vanguard finished up with a fourth launch that put the 52-pound satellite Vanguard III into orbit. Redstones and Jupiters continued to be tested at the Cape, as the Huntsville team participated in subsequent launches for the extension of the IGY known as International Geophysical Cooperation. Nine more Jupiters with satellites were lofted from the Cape, four successfully. The last put a 91-pound Explorer VII into orbit in October 1959, using a version of the rocket called Juno, a complex and powerful new system. Meanwhile, the army also tested its Redstone military version as an intermediate-range ballistic missile. Redstone/Jupiter served as a tactical weapon in the U.S. arsenal until 1964.

With the end of the IGY competition and completion of Redstone testing, the army moved on to field weapons, such as the Pershing, a solid-fueled intermediate-range missile that could be fired off a mobile platform. Testing began at the Cape in 1960, and fifty-six trials later it was ready for full deployment. But these programs were hardly the bold mission for space that von Braun had predicted. Debate continued within the space community over the need for a more powerful rocket, one capable of a million or more pounds of thrust, a special booster designed to place people in space. This sort of project needed support beyond that offered by existing military and scientific agendas. Doubts about the future of civilian space missions soon receded, however. In 1958 the United States committed itself to civilian space exploration with the creation of a new governmental agency—NASA.

2-6. Explorer, America's answer to Sputnik, awaits launch.

In the growing climate of concern about space, Lyndon Johnson introduced Senate Resolution 256 on February 5, 1958. It established a Special Committee on Space and Astronautics, which was to frame legislation for a space program. Congress had already authorized a new office within the Department of Defense, the Advanced Research Projects Agency (ARPA), which was to handle military missile and satellite work. It was still unclear if all space-related activities would be placed under military control or if there would be a separate civilian component until Eisenhower decided for a civilian space program within the existing National Advisory Committee on Aeronautics (NACA). This venerable government body had since 1915 carried out research on aviation and aeronautics for military and civilian purposes. On April 2, 1958, the president proposed to Congress that a new National Aeronautics and Space Agency (later Administration) be created, absorbing NACA.[32] After working its way through both houses of Congress, a bill was placed on Eisenhower's desk, which he signed on July 29, 1958, giving birth to NASA.

When President Eisenhower signed the Space Act of 1958, he did three things. First, he created a fully fledged civilian space agency, one in theory separate from the military. The legislation made it clear that NASA was to promote a nonmilitary agenda, with "activities in space . . . devoted to peaceful purposes for the benefit of all mankind."[33] One need not take this declaration at face value. It was assumed, given the commonality of technology, that military and civilian programs would cooperate where possible. But important though military missiles were, they alone could not dominate the space agenda. Preliminary ideas such as running all space programs through the Department of Defense were pushed aside.

The new law signaled America's willingness to go head-to-head with Russia in a prestige space race. A few weeks after Eisenhower signed the bill, a National Security Council report argued that the Soviets had "captured the imagination and admiration of the world" with Sputnik. Soviet achievement in space threatened American status around the world.[34]

Finally, the Republican president saw a civilian agency, and a nonmilitary space program, as a way to help with his favored "open skies" doctrine. With the coming of spy satellites in the near future, it would be possible for the United States to gather considerable information about the Soviet Union from the sky. But no one had yet determined the upward boundary of national sovereignty. Routine civilian and scientific missions orbiting the earth would clearly establish the right of spacecraft to patrol the heavens over any nation. But Eisenhower hedged his bets. NASA's remit was broad, as reflected in the legislative title. It provided for not only research into problems of flight within and outside the atmosphere but "other purposes" un-specified as well. The president refrained from articulating a bold mission goal for NASA. He continued to counsel fiscal prudence, though ambitious members of Congress such as Lyndon Johnson had already called for a new generation of powerful boosters to match the Russians and scientists were talking about missions to the planets.

Building Space Capabilities

Whatever the philosophical merits of big versus small government, the plain fact was that a new federal agency with a research mandate could not be built overnight. Questions of organization preoccupied NASA during the early years. Should, for example, the new agency develop strong in-house capacity to carry out all aspects of space missions? This certainly fit the traditions carried over from its predecessor, NACA. Focused on aeronautical testing and research, NACA was noted for its highly competent technical personnel and impeccable research record. But NACA was not an operational organization. It could not design, build, and fire rockets into space. At the other extreme, the air force relied on private-sector contractors for complex technological projects. Its Atlas and other ICBMs were built this way.

Over time, NASA would incorporate both the in-house and the contactor approach. This would have significant implications for Cape launch operations and the formation of a new entity called the Kennedy Space Center. Particularly important was the move of Wernher von Braun and his team to the new civilian agency. For several years the Huntsville group had been at work on a new "super booster" with funding from ARPA. By 1959 it was clear that a rocket engine capable of generating a million pounds of thrust far exceeded military needs. It would, however, be extremely useful for escaping earth's gravity for missions to outer space. In October, Eisenhower transformed von Braun and his team into NASA civil servants. They formed the nucleus of a new organization, the Marshall Space Flight Center in Huntsville. Included among the 5,000 personnel released from the military were Kurt Debus and nearly 300 members of his Missile Firing Laboratory.[35]

With this transfer NASA incorporated the in-house tradition of an army arsenal. Unlike the air force, the army had long designed, tested, and built its own weapons, a practice that predated the Civil War. The von Braun team itself had long believed more in self than in contractor reliance. At Peenemünde the scientists had designed, stacked, tested, and fired their own rockets, "everything under one roof." The innovative nature of von Braun's work required such an arrangement, as there were no private German firms with the skills or knowledge to develop and design rockets.[36] In the United States, Redstones were at first built in-house (though subsequent assembly was turned over to General Electric), as were early versions of other rockets.

The Germans at Huntsville argued strongly that only with in-house work could NASA be assured of quality results and the necessary knowledge and skill.[37] That had been their experience in Germany, where "dirty hands" engineering was needed to gain insight into a system of technology they were just starting to understand. In Germany they brought research, development, and operations close together, both organizationally and geographically, allowing for the testing of multiple designs and configurations.[38] When trying to fathom a new technology, this sort of structure had advantages. But NASA would not only do research on space flight; it would also be expected to carry out missions on a regular basis. That difference argued for a shift in organization.

NASA started life as a hybrid entity, combining the existing NACA facilities with the German rocket tradition and personnel and missions inherited from predecessor agencies.[39] It added to this mix the U.S. Air Force model of contracting and project management. Starting with jet planes and continuing into the ICBM program, the air force had devised an innovative and, to many observers, highly successful managerial structure for developing weapons systems quickly and efficiently. Recognizing that modern weapons were complicated, interconnected systems, the air force employed systems engineering to manage the integration and interface of these separate parts to assure they combined into a well-functioning whole.[40] The air force model seemed a perfect fit for NASA, which would be coordinating a complex technical system. But the air force relied heavily on contractors, sometimes even using outside firms to handle the systems engineering and management of its prime contractors. In this it contrasted sharply with the in-house approach of the German rocket team.

NASA leadership debated the merits of in-house versus contractor expertise. Using contractors would build a base of skills and capabilities for space among private-sector aeronautical firms, or aerospace firms, as they soon would be known. This external network of firms and personnel could be managed and supported by (and support) strong government institutions for space research and operations. But as von Braun had discovered in Germany, private firms did not start out with the necessary expertise to develop new technologies oriented toward new missions. In-house capacity and cooperative work of government engineers alongside contractors would characterize the first decade or so of NASA's history. In particular, the sensitive area of launch, some members of NASA argued, required a strong in-house presence.[41]

Combining in-house expertise with outside contractors satisfied a variety of political interests as well. Organizations are never neutral in political terms, and managerial policies can be shaped as much by political as technical considerations. NASA was no different in this regard. Contractors located in a variety of congressional districts would provide a strong political network for NASA. The United States could not operate like Nazi Germany. As NASA administrator James Webb would later argue, the hallmark of the American space program was cooperation between government and the private sector. This aspect of NASA's history would be especially clear at KSC, where comradeship across business-government lines proved crucial to getting work done.[42]

The origins and structure of NASA raised a final, particularly controversial issue—the relative role of military and civilian authorities. Up through 1958, the bulk of the research, development, and firing of missiles had been done under military auspices. Redstone and Atlas were fundamentally weapons, though both could be used for scientific exploration. Other parts of NASA also had strong military connections. The JPL, for example, was originally created to help advance rocket technology for military authorities. Missile programs for the air force, navy, and army all pushed ahead in the aftermath of Sputnik. No part of NASA's brief was really untouched by military precedents or considerations. The air force had even been pondering its own "manned" space program with the X-series of supersonic planes and its Agena craft, with funding from the Department of Defense's ARPA.[43] Military authorities lost the argument that they alone should handle the space program when Eisenhower and Congress created NASA.[44] But given the technical commonalities, NASA would walk a fine line between civilian goals and military needs.

On October 11, 1958, the first NASA spacecraft, Pioneer I, left the Cape. Soon after, NASA launched its first live cargo into orbit. A squirrel monkey named Gordo rode a Jupiter-C off Cape Canaveral on December 13, 1958, testing the biological effects of space flight in the hope that some day rockets would carry people. Tiros I flew a few days later on December 18, putting the first true meteorological satellite into orbit.

Using hardware from the military, NASA now had access to a whole series of new vehicle configurations. Liquid-fueled Atlas, Titan, and Delta missiles came over to civilian use. New, more powerful upper stages such as Agena and Centaur were under development as well. NASA soon built its own rocket, Scout, cleverly adapting existing hardware from army and navy solid rockets to create a dependable, low-cost light payload launcher for scientific missions.

Most significantly, though, NASA began to explore the long held dream of human space flight.[45] Not everyone agreed that this was the best use of resources. NASA deputy director Hugh Dryden, in a fit of unchecked candor, told the House Space Committee that sending a man into orbit had about the same value as "the circus stunt of shooting a young lady from a cannon." The congressmen were not amused, but Dryden voiced the concerns of many scientists who feared that valuable opportunities for scientific research would be hijacked by what was now being called the "man in space race." Nonetheless, others at NASA, including Wernher von Braun, understood that "stunts" and races for glory might be one way that space could finally get the backing it needed.[46]

Launch Operations at Early NASA

In the first few years following NASA's founding, Cape Canaveral served as the primary launch site simply by default. As it had been for the army, so it continued to be the home for the launch portion of NASA's new Marshall Center. In many ways, the Cape provided an ideal site, with flat, open land to work on, a wide, blue Atlantic to fly over, and only a few residents nearby in case of accidents. As Jules Verne had foreseen, Florida was at the right latitude to take advantage of the earth's rotation in achieving orbital velocity.

The air force had upgraded facilities at the missile range since the days of Bumper and the early Redstone firings. In 1957 it added a control center and a new launch complex, designated Launch Complex 17. By later standards it was still a crude affair, consisting of a concrete hard stand, flame deflector, and blockhouse. With each new generation of missiles, stands would get bigger, blockhouse firing rooms larger, stronger, and further away, service structures and gantries more commodious to access the rocket as it was stacked and readied on the pad before launch. But no one had yet settled on a specific, purpose-built facility for accommodating the range of possible missions space might entail.

To some, the issues surrounding launch were clear, beginning with who should do the work. Kurt Debus had long served as the launch expert on the German rocket team. He argued firmly that Marshall had to expend its own resources, provide its own personnel, and not merely purchase launch services from the air force. The German rocket team had plenty of hands-on experience from almost two decades of flying V-2s and Redstones. One of the lessons learned at Peenemünde was the difficulty of moving from design to test. Rockets that arrived on the test stand frequently required weeks of work ironing out minor but annoying flaws because of lack of communication between the test and design groups, and serious underestimation of what was needed to get a rocket ready to fly.[47]

Such concerns had motivated von Braun to set up at the Redstone Arsenal the Missile Firing Laboratory run by Debus. The laboratory permitted launch operations to function separately from—but in coordination with—research, development, and design. This was particularly important to assure reliability when failure of even one part could doom a missile. Debus and von Braun agreed that careful testing uncovered the causes of failures, which then told designers what to change. This sort of painstaking work implied a substantial commitment to checking and testing operations.[48]

How would launching work be handled in NASA? Some proposals echoed what Debus and von Braun had found. William Pickering, head of the Jet Propulsion Laboratory, noted that the variety of institutions using the Cape created problems. While the military provided logistics and support, "the extent [of work required] is frequently underestimated."[49] Launch operations were becoming a bottleneck as the Cape filled up with civilian and military rockets.[50] Each user of the Cape should perhaps have its own launch team and facilities. But duplication of facilities and multiple points of contact with military authorities would breed inefficiency. Both Debus and Pickering suggested that a single NASA launch authority would solve this problem. Each also wanted this organization to be under his control.

In 1959, NASA administrator T. Keith Glennan established a NASA office at the Cape to provide a high-level interface between the civilian agency and the Cape military commander, General Leighton Davis. Here was one way to supervise the various NASA personnel and projects that needed the launch facility. Placed under NASA's director of space flight development, the Atlantic Missile Range Operations Office (AMROO) would oversee project officers assigned to specific launches and serve as liaison with Davis and his range officers. But this structure did not suffice. The AMROO head had to recognize the "responsibility and authority of heads of divisions and offices" and was more a coordinating body than an operational one.[51]

The smaller, simpler, lighter rockets of the 1950s might well launch successfully following this script. They required little in the way of unique equipment. Wires ran to concrete blockhouses, where data about the rocket before and during liftoff came in and the signal to launch went out. Radar facilities at the Atlantic Missile Range provided telemetry and tracking, and the air force's range safety officer stood by to see that missiles stayed on course, or gave the signal to destruct if they did not. All along the beach at Cape Canaveral, testing and launching facilities had sprouted up in what became known as ICBM Row. Launch centers were constructed as needed, and then abandoned when rendered obsolete by new rocket designs.

The growth in range, power, and capabilities of rockets, however, raised new issues about the launch. Size alone dictated new assembly, stacking, and integration procedures as rockets became taller and heavier, and engines more powerful. The future seemed to indicate that assembly, integration, checkout, and testing would have to become more careful than ever if humans were aboard. Even if they were not, sending robot missiles upward for exploration meant carrying complicated payloads such as satellites and sensors into an exact orbit or on a trajectory into outer space. Mishaps like those during the exploratory launches of the 1950s would grow costly if important payloads were lost before they ever left the earth. The new missions expected of NASA were going to require new approaches to launch. The question was, what sort of equipment, facilities, and organization would best perform these duties?

Early on, Kurt Debus and his launch team simply piled into cars and made their way from Huntsville to the Cape. On July 1, 1960, however, the Cape became home to Marshall's Launch Operations Directorate (LOD). Launch now stood on a par with other key functions of rocket development within the Marshall organization. The LOD was also given responsibility for scheduling, checkout, and countdown of a number of other NASA missions that left from the Cape. It was authorized to develop (in coordination with the Atlantic Missile Range) launch safety concepts and criteria. It was to perform measuring and tracking, logistical and administrative supervision. It would conduct planning on launch facilities for future projects. NASA disbanded AMROO as the Marshall LOD took charge. Still, this broad ambit by no means covered all of NASA launch affairs. The tension between decentralization of responsibility for missions to individual centers and overall coordination at the launch site had yet to be fully worked out.[52]

None of this, however, slowed what was remarkable progress for an American space program that seemed to be limping behind the Soviet Union's just a few years before. The Cape was almost alive with rockets going up between the late 1950s and early 1960s. On August 12, 1960, the global communications satellite Echo-1 rode into orbit on a Delta rocket. Adapted from the earlier Thor rocket of the air force by Douglas Aircraft Company, Delta would soon become the workhorse for sending communications and scientific payloads into orbit. It was placed under the direction of NASA's new Goddard Space Flight Center outside Washington, D.C., with personnel moving over from the defunct Vanguard program. Robert Gray, former head of Vanguard launches, transferred to Goddard, remaining at the Cape to oversee the Delta launches. Later, Gray and his team would also handle civilian launches of the Atlas and Centaur rockets.[53] Military launches had not slowed down either. Dozens of Titan missiles for the air force and Jupiter and Pershing rockets for the army went skyward from Florida. The navy alone launched more than a hundred tests of its submarine-based Polaris missile between 1958 and 1963.[54]

Human Space Flight

With so much going on, it is not surprising that even the amended organizational structure did not meet the evolving needs of launch operations. This became still clearer with the start of the Mercury program for human space flight. Human space flight had special requirements. Pads had to be purpose-built for the vehicle carrying a human into space to assure maximum reliability. It was thus impossible to use a single pad for multiple vehicles. "The very process of modifying one pad from one vehicle to another" meant a reduction in reliability.[55] As launch engineers were beginning to appreciate, "pads like to see the same bird every time."[56] By May 1960, Kurt Debus was trying to maintain a launch schedule of one Mercury test shot every three weeks to keep the United States on pace with an ambitious Soviet manned space program. It was an almost impossible task, given the limited number of pads and the time needed to check out Mercury boosters and capsules.[57] As the pressures mounted, NASA experienced some spectacular failures. Unoccupied Mercury tests went awry as vehicles lost control and gyrated wildly before being destroyed.

Any hopes that there would be time to overcome these early problems at a leisurely pace were quickly dashed. On April 12, 1961, the Soviets scooped the United States once more by sending cosmonaut Yuri Gagarin into orbit. With rockets still barely more than kerosene-filled tubes, the USSR put a man into space and brought him back alive. Now the space race accelerated into an all-out competition for world acclaim. Once more the United States played catch-up. Alan Shepard left Cape Canaveral in a Mercury capsule riding a Redstone rocket on May 5, 1961, for a suborbital flight. This was cold comfort in the face of cartoons depicting Gagarin in his capsule waving like a celebrity to the peoples of the earth on behalf of the Soviet Union.

The thought of even a former test pilot like Shepard sitting atop what was essentially a V-2 rocket for his journey seems almost incredible. The Redstone, painstakingly tested for almost a decade, had earned the reputation of "old reliable."[58] Still, as a piece of military hardware, it and the Atlas (also used in the Mercury program) were not designed for 100 percent reliability. With a weapon, it was easier and cheaper to build extra missiles, in the expectation that some would fail, than to build redundancy into each piece of ordnance to assure it would perform flawlessly. A common bit of sardonic astronaut humor was "Remember, every piece of equipment came from the low bidder on a government contract." During the first flight test of the Mercury-Atlas configuration, for example, the missile tore apart in flight and no one ever found out why.[59] The rocket for Shepard's flight was "man rated," with extra safety features and additional testing to provide at least a margin of assurance that America's first astronaut would come back a living hero.

Shepard's flight was just a stopgap, though. Real changes were in the works, and they became manifest a few weeks later, on May 25, 1961. During a speech before a joint session of Congress, President John F. Kennedy announced that America should commit itself to sending a man to the moon before the decade was out. His words formed only one part of a larger speech, but the context was clear. Economic progress at home and abroad, military defense, opposition to communist influence in the Third World, were all major challenges for America. One way to meet them was through space. It might seem counterintuitive that an expensive civilian space race could serve economic and military ends, but such was the prestige of space that the public accepted Kennedy's argument. "[I]f we are to win the battle that is now going on around the world between freedom and tyranny," the President summed up, "the dramatic achievements in space . . . should have made clear to us all, as did the Sputnik in 1957, the impact of this adventure on the minds of men everywhere, who are attempting to make a determination of which road they should take."[60]

The charge to America's still young space program implied in this mission was daunting, something that perhaps the president himself realized when he backpedaled a bit on the moon later in his speech.[61] Still, the prophetic words stuck, and Kennedy backed them up with specific dollar amounts before Congress—seven to nine billion dollars over five years. The young Democrat had decisively broken from the grandfatherly Eisenhower by fully committing to the battle for prestige through space in the Cold War. Congress and the American people responded, at least enough to assure that a mission to the moon, soon designated Apollo, would get needed financial support. NASA's budget was increased by 60 percent and a powerful new booster designated Saturn was approved. The moon was still a long way off, though. Before any real headway on such a mission could be attempted, NASA had to put its own house in order.

In 1959, on a plot of land outside Washington, D.C., owned by the Department of Agriculture, NASA's Goddard Space Flight Center came into being. Its original role was to bring together NASA capabilities from existing centers and add personnel for operating space missions. But human space flight and a moon program spurred the creation of yet another new NASA

LUNAR LANDING AND BEYOND

M-MS-G 101-17-62 OCT.1, 62

2-7. With the mission to the moon only just approved, fanciful images of the future of space exploration.

center a few years later—the Manned Spacecraft Center (MSC). Situated about 25 miles south of Houston near the Gulf of Mexico, it was eventually renamed the Johnson Space Center. The MSC would take responsibility for mission control, astronaut training, and other flight-related activities for the deep-space human missions and the moon project. Goddard's role was scaled back to scientific investigations through near-earth flights without human crews. The Jet Propulsion Laboratory in California took responsibility for deep-space scientific missions.

At NASA headquarters, debate continued over the best way to configure launch operations, now complicated by the addition of the lunar program to the space agenda. Kurt Debus presented three options.[62] One argued for a decentralized arrangement, with each NASA project doing its own work at the Cape, and headquarters providing coordination. This was seen as a way to promote the various NASA missions, especially the new one for human space flight. A second approach argued for a single office of launch operations at the Cape but confined to supporting the individual launch teams from NASA centers. The Marshall LOD was already playing this role to an extent. A third option would expand the Marshall LOD into a separate, full-scale NASA launch organization.[63]

Kurt Debus argued strongly for a new organization. Based on long experience, he believed that the future of rocket technology depended on a separate launch facility. Indeed, as early as 1952 he had written that "reliability can only result from a systematical and organized approach to the problem."[64] In his view, not widely shared at the time, launch operations involved many steps of preparation, testing, and integration. This work was not simply an extension of the work done in design and fabrication, but an integrating operation that cut across boundaries, bringing together "all the mission elements . . . for the complex launch operation."[65] Crucial to success and reliability, as Debus saw it, was a launch organization that could work independently but in tandem with engineers designing and building hardware.[66] The LOD had already "developed . . . key ground support equipment of missile hardware [as] an *integral part* of the total missile or space vehicle system."[67] Experiences and learning picked up by testing and launching, Debus believed, could be fed into subsequent development work. The launch organization had to collaborate closely with the "originating laboratories or factories." It was necessary to "close the loop" between testing and design.[68]

A separate launch authority would be best positioned to carry out this work, and to coordinate between different NASA installations, the military, and contractors. For this it also needed significant in-house capabilities. Such "workbench" experience would allow NASA "to keep all the various disciplines' 'share' in actual design, manufacturing and operational angles . . . experience which then, in turn, enables the government to effectively and economically direct contractors."[69]

Debus made a strong case for an independent center following the existing German/Arsenal model of work. Here he was at odds with those in NASA who were being influenced by the U.S. Air Force approach, which relied more on private-sector contractors. But at this point the balance of opinion tended to defer to Debus and the Germans, with their long experience in rocketry. The question of how much should be done by contractors and how much by government civil servants would remain an open one for now. The existing format of having each center assume responsibility for its own launches quickly lost ground. It created huge problems of scheduling and coordination with the military. It also undercut learning, since cumulative launches were expected to result in movement up the "learning curve." If launches were conducted by separate organizations, this cumulative experience would be harder to capture. As with any complex system of technology, there were inevitably tradeoffs. A single, independent launch authority promised standardization, efficiency, and cumulative learning. It would, however, somewhat frustrate Debus's desire to have close connections between operations and design. The question was, which structure would optimize these tradeoffs?

Coming out of Marshall and convinced of the importance of in-house capability, Debus saw a certain logic to having the single launch authority connected to the chief rocket design center, Marshall. This would provide for that needed coordination between operations and design, while eliminating duplication at the Cape. But such an arrangement might seem to favor one NASA center over the others. NASA was a many-sided organization with multiple installations and missions. On the other hand, the traditional decentralization of launch operations clearly would not do either. This sort of division of responsibility, General Davis noted, "could very well result in serious support deficiencies, misunderstandings, and [have an] adverse effect on NASA programs."[70] Such an organizational structure could not handle a diverse menu of missions while at the same time gearing up for the lunar program.[71]

On August 24, 1961, NASA administrator James Webb and Deputy Secretary of Defense Roswell Gilpatric signed an agreement on the management and funding of the lunar program's launch needs.[72] That year Kurt Debus and Leighton Davis were asked to prepare a comprehensive study of launch facilities, beginning with the most basic question of location.[73] Despite the new agreement with the military and all the investment and experience at Cape Canaveral, it was still not certain that this would be the place for NASA launch operations. The Cape's relative isolation had advantages, particularly in the early years, when some 5 percent of launches ended in an explosion.[74] Beyond protecting people, the remote, flat Cape offered a clear line of sight between the operations center and launchpads, which had to be kept far apart because of the danger of explosion. The few hundred meters of distance between early blockhouses and pads clearly would not do with engines capable of generating millions of pounds of thrust.

Davis and Debus surveyed other options as well. By July 1961, a number of sites were under consideration. Besides the Cape, there were Mayauana Island in the Bahamas, the old White Sands Missile Range, Christmas Island in the Pacific, South Point on Hawaii, and a site near Brownsville, Texas. There was even talk of launching from an offshore platform in the Atlantic. The Cape remained the front-runner, however, because it already had the people and facilities needed. Local residents were used to the noise of rocket launches and unlikely to raise objections. It would be relatively easy to gear up at Canaveral for more launches, and there was plenty of land for expansion on nearby Merritt Island. The Atlantic Missile Range, some 1,600 downrange miles and tracking stations in the Bahamas, Brazil, and the Dominican Republic, offered a vast field for flying missiles. Eventually it would encompass some 9,000 miles, with stations in the South Atlantic and special instrumentation ships in the Indian Ocean.[75]

Still, the Cape had enough disadvantages to keep the final choice uncertain. Land was relatively expensive. Labor remained a question mark, with few skilled workers in the nonindustrial state of Florida. In short supply as well were basic materials like copper wire, cable, and transformers. And then there were the hurricanes. Cape Canaveral had had close brushes with them in 1885, 1893, 1926, and 1960, though no direct hits. No one knew for certain what a hurricane would do to launch facilities. Finally, bureaucratic politics had a role. The air force had already expressed interest in running launch operations for NASA by itself.[76] To Kurt Debus, this presented a special danger. A NASA launch center might be "swallowed by existing organizations." Maybe leaving the Cape and moving away from the military facility was best after all, at least if NASA's independence and autonomy were a factor.[77]

In the end, the availability of tracking and range facilities and the existing launch complexes pushed the decision in favor of the Cape. NASA announced on August 24, 1961, that it would purchase some 88,000 acres of land adjacent to the Cape Canaveral Air Force Station on Merritt Island at a cost of $72 million. Located between the Indian and Banana Rivers, this site would provide space for a permanent launch operations facility.

With location settled, NASA now returned to the organizational question. The Marshall Launch Operations Directorate had grown significantly over the years. In 1953, Debus had commanded only 19 people in Huntsville. By 1960 he was overseeing 553.[78] The three options drawn up by Debus in June were still on the table. It was becoming clear that simply retaining a Marshall directorate for launches at the Cape was not going to work. The decentralized approach, on the other hand, was still attractive to many. A small central staff could simply coordinate separate launch divisions controlled by Marshall, the JPL, Goddard, and the MSC. Under this proposal Debus would have "worn two hats," as both central coordinator of NASA launches and launch director for Marshall.[79] Many at the Marshall Center liked this option, because it allowed them to retain their own launch organization, as had been the case in Germany. The advantages here, Debus noted, were that it involved the least change from a personnel and organizational standpoint and conserved the experience already gained.[80]

By October, however, debate narrowed down to just two options. There was now no doubt that, whichever won, the launch authority would be separate from any one center, historic ties between the Cape and Marshall notwithstanding.[81] The decentralized, matrixed option remained on the table. This proposal maintained strong in-house capability and the "workbench"

2-8. Early launches were carried out in cramped blockhouses close to the rocket.

proficiency Debus wanted, while allowing launch personnel to accumulate experience and to move launch operations up the learning curve quickly. Still, this approach could be criticized for necessitating duplication of equipment and making coordination difficult. There would have to be some mechanism to feed the accumulation of knowledge from various launches across NASA.[82]

Debus and von Braun now argued for a single, central launch division, even if it could not stay within Marshall.[83] But they had to satisfy those who were focused on what was rapidly becoming NASA's number one priority, the lunar mission. This program was going to consume substantial time, money, and personnel in the upcoming years and obviously warranted special attention. Even a fully independent center would have to be responsive to its "major user." Debates over these issues continued through 1962.[84]

By February everyone agreed that the launch center had to be independent enough to serve its major user—in the short term, the lunar program—"without unreasonably impeding other programs or missions." One way to do this was to maintain, for now, the existing structure for the ongoing Mercury and Atlas programs. This compromise increased support for the central, independent launch authority now favored by Debus and von Braun. It provided the advantages of central planning and execution, maintained

NASA control of NASA decisions, yet was responsive to the requirements and "operational characteristics" of each NASA facility.[85]

This was basically the plan that NASA approved on March 7, 1962. Debus became head of a new NASA Launch Operations Center (LOC). Separate from Marshall, the LOC served all vehicles at the Cape, but with some special arrangements for key projects. Debus reported to Brainerd Holmes, director of manned space flight at NASA headquarters. But for a time he kept his second hat, heading a Launch Vehicle Operations Division at Marshall in Alabama. This interim arrangement assured that Debus stayed closely connected with Marshall's main project, the Saturn booster. The close connection between vehicle work and launches required these sorts of added organizational lines, at least until the LOC acquired enough experience and built its own connections back to the vehicle centers. The separation agreement severing the LOC from Marshall was signed on June 8, 1962. On the first of July, 375 Marshall employees started to work for a new boss.[86]

3

*
*
*

Launch Operations Center

The Boss

Kurt Debus sat in his office at Marshall Space Flight Center. Smoke from a cigarette curled up around him. He had been in America nearly two decades, an American citizen now, far from the Germany where he had started his career in rocketry. But the thick German accent remained, as it would his whole life. So too did the saber scars from his student fencing days. One carved a deep cleft in his chin and continued briefly along his left cheek. It was incongruous in a way, marks of nineteenth-century masculinity defining a man of science working with the latest technology in the mid-twentieth. But the Germany of Debus's youth still practiced those old traditions—tests of manhood among students imitating the aristocracy.

Born in Frankfurt in 1908, Debus was middle class in origin, though he had experienced the economic trials of the German inflation of the 1920s. His father, Heinrich, worked as a bookkeeper for IG Farben, the giant German chemical combine. His mother, Melly, was a seamstress. An only child, Debus received both his undergraduate and advanced degrees in electrical and mechanical engineering at the Technical University in Darmstadt. He grew up reading the science fiction literature of the early twentieth century, filled with predictions that humans would certainly conquer space. In this, his background exactly matched that of the man who recruited him into the German rocket program, Wernher von Braun.[1]

Like the saber scars, Debus's Germanic education and background distinguished him from the American engineers and scientists working for NASA. He shared with them, though, a devotion to mathematical precision and empirical verification of results. He was not given to theorizing for its own sake, and his American colleagues soon came to see him, with admiration, as a "nuts and bolts engineer," a "guy who liked engines." Debus began his career with von Braun at Peenemünde as an "experimental engineer" at the

3-1. Center director Kurt Debus, a "hands-on rocket guy."

V-2 *Prüfstände*, or test stands.[2] He had so much rocket experience that he found he could tell just by seeing how the engine fired whether the launch was good or not. When Explorer I went into space, he had personally supervised the launch, making the final "go" decision in the seconds leading up to T-0. No one ever doubted that Debus was more chief scientist than manager at the Cape.

Intensely private, by American standards he could appear a bit aloof and aristocratic. Though Debus developed a surprising command of American slang and idiom, he was always suspicious of the casual, happy-go-lucky type. He was systematic, keeping a daily journal and firmly believing that a clean desk indicated an orderly mind. Nor did he suffer fools gladly, expecting from those who worked for him the same attention to technical detail that he made time for even as his duties expanded. It was best to visit him with an appointment firmly booked. But these qualities did not make him unimaginative.

Most who worked for him remembered him as warm and caring beneath the formal facade. The "kinder, gentler side" of the German tradition, some thought. His youthful curiosity had never disappeared, and he often called in his engineers to ask for technical briefings on their specialties. It was the kind of meeting that was both a great opportunity and a natural pitfall for a young employee. Not only did the information have to be absolutely correct, but it also had to be presented to Debus in a way that did not even hint at condescension, no matter the subject. You did not lecture this director. One exuberant presenter, trying to explain a difficult scientific concept, reached for an obvious metaphor, one so elementary that it could have been used on a student. The silence that followed was deafening. But Debus took the role of mentor seriously, as he had in the close-knit paternalistic scientific community at Peenemünde.

It was a combination that many Americans would initially find hard to fathom, a stern sort of paternalism that could be genuinely caring but unsparing when administering discipline or correcting errors. Some of those who worked for Debus, especially older engineers trained in the much different American work culture, found it difficult to penetrate the circle of German scientists and engineers who surrounded Debus during these early days at the Cape. But even among those who found his personality unyielding, there was respect. Working in the high-pressure environment of the space program of the 1960s would produce more than a few hard-driving bosses. Now, Kurt Debus was the boss of NASA launches.

Exactly what he commanded, though, was unclear. On paper NASA had a Launch Operations Center (LOC), but this organization had no facilities of its own at the Cape. Debus still split his time between Alabama and Florida, working out of temporary office space at Cape Canaveral rented from the air force. Some of the people launching vehicles, moreover, were still part of other NASA organizations. The Mercury program belonged to the Manned Spacecraft Center located in Houston. Debus had no formal place in this organization. A Goddard team launching vehicles derived from Project Vanguard was still independent of the LOC. The division of responsibility between NASA and the military had yet to be finalized. Meanwhile, new launchpads and equipment had to be designed and built. It was not even clear what Debus's operation should be called. NASA headquarters suggested National Space Port, or perhaps National Space Operations Base, but neither name stuck.[3] Launch Operations Center would have to do for now. The people under Debus's command came from different backgrounds and experiences, and not all of them adjusted quickly to working for a man from one of the most distinctive cultures within the diverse NASA family. It would take a masterful bureaucratic politician to bring these groups together and begin creating a true spaceport at the Cape.

Debus faced these challenges sure of one thing—that a space program required no justification beyond human beings' "desperate need to explore." From his youth as a follower of von Braun, he was firmly convinced that the quest for knowledge stemmed from "basic needs," "given by nature."[4] "Space flight," he wrote more than once, "will logically follow the pattern of historical development which has characterized the transportation industry." The pattern was "vividly demonstrated" by Henry Ford, the automobile pioneer admired in Germany as much as in the United States. Ford's Model T had revolutionized the car and made it an artifact of daily life. In 1962 only a few people had actually ridden rockets out of the atmosphere. Still, Debus believed that he was working in a "new age of transportation," built on the rocket.[5]

Vague expressions of "man's quest to explore" were a far cry from the sort of hardheaded practicality that Americans usually cherished in their inventors, including Ford. Where was the comparable payoff in space exploration? Even after Kennedy's speech, nearly as many Americans questioned the value of a moon mission as supported it.[6] None of this fazed the new director of launch operations. History, Debus was confident, showed that "even a farsighted and visionary inventor often cannot visualize the ultimate utilization of his invention by the public." It was a point well taken. Few of even the most practical inventions in history start life with total public support or respect. Debus noted ruefully that "every vision is a joke until the first man accomplishes it." Just as streets were built when cars were available, so too the supporting infrastructure of technology would arrive to make rockets useful and practical. At the new launch center, Debus would be building some of that infrastructure.[7]

In this task, Debus could turn from visionary predictions to personal experience. Some 600 rockets had taken flight under his supervision, more than 120 from Cape Canaveral. Debus was used to interaction with other team members, the rocket designers and builders, and he expected to create such loops of communication in NASA. "Anticipating future needs," he noted, "requires close liaison with space vehicle designers in order to initiate on a timely basis the studies in supporting advanced technology which will assure that launch operations capability is in phase with vehicle and mission requirements."[8] Appreciation of the systematic interactions among the parts of a complex engineering project was one of the hallmarks of the well-trained twentieth-century engineer, and Debus was nothing if not systematic. But building these connections would require a new type of management and operation.

Organizing a Center

Debus and his senior directors were all members of the German rocket team. Hans Gruene, having served both at Peenemünde and at White Sands, took charge of launch vehicle operations. Albert Zeiler, another V-2 veteran, worked on mechanical, structural, and propulsion issues. Karl Sendler was chief of instrumentation and tracking, as he had been in Germany. Debus remained most comfortable working with a small, tightly knit circle of fellow engineers. He exhibited a proprietary touch when it came to staff, never letting one of "his" employees go if he could help it. He had a similarly strong sense of personal responsibility about his work, even about physical facilities. Years later, coworkers would recall him walking around the grounds outside blockhouses with a wastebasket at slow moments, picking up scraps of refuse.

As much as NASA depended on the German team, it brought Americans into key functions as well. Next to each German engineer was an American counterpart. Gruene's key personnel included Robert Moser, who had worked on the von Braun team at Huntsville, and Andrew Pickett, who later became Gruene's deputy. Robert Gorman worked with Zeiler at the mechanical office, coming from the old NACA facility in Langley, Virginia. Grady Williams was Sendler's deputy. The German and American technical cultures would mix in various ways during the decade at the Cape, sometimes creatively reinforcing each other, other times showing divergent approaches to the business of launching and testing rockets.[9]

Important as were existing cultures and traditions, much of the operation of the LOC would have to be defined through practice. The LOC was responsible for the "planning and supervision of the integration, test, check and launch" of vehicles, as well as "launch concepts," which would be embodied in a master plan that anticipated "future needs." The master plan was pointing toward a flexible "spaceport" akin to the ports from which ships and more recently airplanes started their journeys. Here at last, after more than two decades of launching, Debus would have the money and scope to sit down at the drawing board and bring his knowledge and experience to a green field.[10]

Before any of this could begin, however, the LOC had to establish its place in the organizational pecking order of NASA. Both human and material resources were in short supply. "There are not enough key people to go around," was the conclusion of a meeting between NASA center directors. No one wanted to give up valuable people under these circumstances. Lines of authority were similarly uncertain. Although the LOC did not expect to control the people or budgets of other centers, it insisted on having a voice in decisions involving work and schedules affecting launchers. With a variety of agencies on its turf, it would have to be able to enforce rules, though it was agreed that those rules would be jointly determined by the major players. Working panels, including contractors, would meet to discuss matters such as ground support equipment and facilities, reflecting the interdependence of launch operations and vehicle design.[11] Wernher von Braun placed particular faith in joint panels chaired by representatives of the centers. Joint panels would act as "law making bodies," with the LOC serving as executive to enforce the laws. This sort of cooperation, it was thought, would build consensus, particularly on matters that cut across different functions and did not fall along clean lines of authority.[12]

Then there were relations with the air force to work out. It was natural for the air force to view the NASA facility as an extension of its own missile test site. After all, rockets, many of them military in origin, would share the same range and some of the same tracking facilities. The Atlantic Missile Range was long accustomed to having other tenants on its property, to whom it provided launch services. Indeed, this seemed very much to be the approach envisioned when NASA administrator James Webb and Deputy Secretary of Defense Roswell Gilpatric signed their 1961 agreement.[13] Recognizing that "major new launch facilities" would be required to meet President Kennedy's challenge to land a man on the moon, the agreement stipulated that it was "in the national interest" for NASA and the Department of Defense to cooperate. New launch facilities "peculiar to [the space] program" would be "important items in fixing the rate at which the program can proceed." Thus the launch site would have to be jointly managed, though NASA would spend its own money for new facilities. But the agreement also seemed to give the air force some key management responsibilities, including range flight and safety management and master planning of the new facilities.[14]

As NASA and particularly its ambitious lunar program grew, this relationship no longer seemed quite right. Plans for the LOC included acquiring land and building new structures in the air force's backyard, on the west side of the Banana River at Merritt Island. Though both civilian and military craft would use the range, the proposed facilities on Merritt Island would be wholly in NASA's control and designed with NASA missions in mind. Problems might arise when it came to sharing space and facilities. Debus wanted to be sure that the LOC retained its own separate identity. This required a true "joint" plan, with neither the LOC nor the Atlantic Missile Range making unilateral decisions. With NASA working on designs for an entirely new Saturn rocket as well as its own unmanned craft for a variety of scientific missions, "existing DOD regulations" on range and launch might not suffice.[15]

It had been assumed that a master planning board composed of both NASA and military personnel would resolve these matters. But the commander of the Atlantic Missile Range, General Leighton Davis, had his own ideas. He proposed that the air force and not NASA should own the land and facilities being contemplated for Merritt Island. This was a major change, one that would have ended the life of the LOC before it really began. The air force's position was obvious. It ran the range and was best placed to handle

SATURN BOOSTER
HORIZONTAL CHECKOUT

3-2. Early version of Saturn, in horizontal position. Note minimal equipment assumed necessary for testing and launch preparation.

the new facilities. Smooth integration would come by having a single supreme authority.

On March 27, 1962, General Davis informed Kurt Debus that he wanted to follow the spirit of the prevailing Webb-Gilpatric agreement, which seemed to make the air force the "single manager" of the entire Cape area. The air force, he argued, should hold title to the new land on Merritt Island. It was a tense moment, with Davis prepared to voice his concerns to Congress. Debus objected strongly. Only if NASA had its own land could it retain "joint participation with DOD in planning and use of AMR." Otherwise, "all improvements, including NASA mission facilities," would become in effect property of the air force. NASA had to control its own missions. Here Debus was voicing a vision of the future. The "mission" to the moon was not going to be a one-shot deal, with NASA only a temporary resident of a military facility. Rather, the creation of NASA signaled the start of a new era of civilian space exploration, and for that it needed the freedom to develop and advance its own launch facilities. It was crucial that the civilian and scientific nature of those missions be clear "in the public eye," something more difficult if the military was in charge. NASA, after all, would be a pretty small customer of the larger military launch operation.[16]

Recounting the original motivation behind NASA, Debus's argument prevailed. NASA was a civilian agency to win the hearts and minds of the peoples of earth by demonstrating capitalism's technological superiority over communism. To that end, NASA had to have its own property at the Cape, and the freedom to design and build facilities according to its own, not DOD, specifications. Secretary of Defense Robert McNamara and NASA administrator James Webb agreed that "the Merritt Island Launch Area is considered a NASA installation, separate and distinct from the Atlantic Missile Range." On that key piece of civilian space property, NASA would be "fully responsible" for master planning and development. The LOC became the "single manager" of the new facilities to be built on Merritt Island, while the air force remained manager of the adjacent Atlantic Missile Range. The air force would still provide key launch services, but on NASA property the LOC would have "full power" to determine how launch functions would be performed.[17] Coordination would come through a joint master planning board. There was some grumbling over whether the parties were living up to the terms of the agreement over the next few months. But all in all, the Webb-McNamara Agreement of 1963 provided a workable framework for civilian and military authorities operating at the Cape.[18]

The LOC was now in a position to be NASA's "single launch Agency at Merritt Island and the AMR." Accordingly it took greater responsibility for NASA functions and services there. These included public relations, community relations, visitor services, industrial relations, purchasing, contracting, legal services, and security. Individual NASA centers retained responsibility for their own vehicles and the contractors working on them, but would submit requirements for support through the LOC.[19] The operations center could even forge its own local agreements without approval by NASA headquarters, proceeding "in a manner most advantageous to NASA and the taxpayer."[20] Although NASA headquarters would provide important overall leadership and coordination through project management offices, it would also allow its centers a high degree of independence.

Debus had argued for a separate organization to handle launch operations. He knew from experience that otherwise designers would keep tinkering with the vehicle up to the last minute. But nothing like this degree of separation between design and launch operations had ever been attempted before. To keep these two functions coordinated, special provisions were needed. Working groups channeled information from those building launch vehicles to those designing the launch equipment. NASA development centers were expected to be "responsive to the LOC's requirements in discharging its overall integration, test, checkout and launch responsibilities." "At the earliest possible time" they were to specify to the LOC their ground support and launch needs."[21] Marshall, Goddard, and the Manned Spacecraft Center would provide "functional requirements" to the LOC, which would coordinate them and meet the needs of these "users." Similarly, the LOC would respect the requirements of the centers, which would send their own and contractor personnel to the launch site to work on vehicles. The LOC would stand ready to provide the support to keep the launch moving forward on schedule.[22]

Initial concepts for LOC organization had envisioned a relatively small central staff and two main functional departments, Facilities and Launch Support Equipment. Much of the work, it was once believed, would actually occur in launch divisions of other NASA centers working at the Cape.[23] But with the LOC's growth and independence, the organizational structure grew more elaborate. Most of the work, it now appeared, would be carried out through LOC directorates, such as launch support and facilities engineering, launch operations, and instrumentation. Gone were the support offices for the other NASA centers. Those centers would have personnel at the Cape, but they would work directly with LOC people, and all operations would report to the LOC director.

That was how it was to work on paper. In reality, though, Debus was one part of a sprawling NASA operation at the Cape, with personnel still reporting to other centers. Programs that had originated at the Lewis, Langley, and Goddard Centers continued with launch teams reporting first to their home centers. When the Vanguard program wound up in 1959, workers transferred to the Delta launch vehicle. Delta, derived from the Thor intermediate-range ballistic missile, had originated in design work done at the Lewis Research Center outside Cleveland, but was given to the new Goddard Space Flight Center. The early human flights in the Mercury program continued under the direction of the Space Task Group at the MSC. This decentralized structure would not change until those early programs ended.

Increasingly, though, it was the pressure to get to the moon that shaped launch operations. The relationship between the LOC and Marshall was, Debus admitted, "unique" because of the nature of the Saturn vehicle and the mission it was to carry. The moon program, bold yet still uncertain, required careful coordination between LOC and Marshall personnel. As Debus warned, "any organizational separation of an experimental launch vehicle from the agency responsible for its development could spell disaster, unless it is assured that the two elements operate as an integral team." Here again he was relying on past experience in Germany, where relations between design and operations had been close. Some of this could be "formalized" through organization, as for example having his launch vehicle chief, Hans Gruene, maintain an office at Marshall as well.[24] Much of the problem, though, would not be fully resolved on the organizational chart. Part of the answer lay with the shared background and experiences of Debus and von Braun and the others. Their common traditions and long working relationships permitted a degree of coordination beyond the formal lines of knowledge and authority. At the same time, experience had to be balanced against new learning. The scale, complexity, and time pressures of the lunar program required new types of organization and a new work culture.[25]

Humans Aboard

There was in fact a tremendous amount to learn simply because almost all past experience had been based on unmanned flights. As the first stage of the Mercury program had already shown, things changed substantially when humans were aboard. Human missions meant a new level of safety and reliability. For the Mercury flights, the test philosophy was to make "no assumption regarding the operational readiness of any spacecraft component or system when the spacecraft was delivered . . . from the factory."[26] That meant that each component, system, and subsystem had to be verified, and then verified again as a complete functioning system before launch.

Mercury missions rode on existing launch vehicles, first Redstone, then Atlas. But they added a wholly new device, a "capsule" in which the astronaut sat. Vehicle designers, astronauts, and an engineering group from the Cape started inspecting the Mercury capsule while it was still being assembled at the factories of the McDonnell Aircraft Corporation in St. Louis. This was something of a departure for the contractor. Used to working for the military and private airlines, McDonnell assumed it had total control until the hardware was delivered to the client. Not so with space vehicles. There was too much that could go wrong, too much to learn, to wait until the hardware was manufactured before learning how to use it. Engineers from the Cape were writing procedures for testing, checking, and launching the Mercury capsule even as workers in St. Louis were assembling it.

Launch work on Mercury followed painstaking procedures going back to the earliest days of missiles. As Debus described it in 1952, launch operations required testing devices and subsystems separately, "disconnecting and isolating the component to undergo test as much as possible from all other systems." Then gradually these elements were reintegrated and retested in more and more integrated systems, until "total configuration" was ready for a simulated flight. Only by testing each system separately, Debus argued, could one isolate the source of a failure.[27]

Not everyone believed that this tradition of painstaking testing should continue. Design engineers working on the Mercury capsule tended to see

3-3. The early Mercury-Redstone missile required far less complex servicing equipment.

much of the work done by LOC engineers and Cape "wrench turners" as un-necessary or redundant. Engineers who built the device assumed that they fully understood how it would perform. All that was necessary once it left their hands, they believed, was to set it up on the launchpad and shoot. The shorthand for this philosophy was naturally "ship and shoot," a phrase that would bedevil launch operations for the next fifty years.

Mercury also introduced a second source of tension in space operations, one that would likewise run through the history of the American space program. NASA began to use increasing numbers of contractors, not only to fabricate equipment but in operations as well. This was only natural, as contractors who had built rockets, capsules, or ground equipment would have to be present during launch operations as the experts on their systems. But working with contractors was new for some at the Cape. Those who came from Marshall in particular were used to doing most of the hands-on work themselves. The question of how much work, as opposed to managing, NASA civil servants should do remained unresolved, however. In these early years, the lines between contractor and civil servant were quite fluid, pro-ducing what some later recalled as an ideal "badgeless" world. Whether one wore the insignia of NASA, the military, or a private contractor mattered little during the working day. All hands contributed their skills to opera-tions, testing, and launch. Particularly in the early human missions, it was still possible for everyone to know everyone else.[28] Knowledge and informa-tion flowed easily across organizational lines in this world. To ensure that everyone had a proper orientation to the task, for example, a contractor was given sufficient information to "understand the mission in order that he have a proper sense of urgency about it." The goal was to build a "true team spirit," with all committed to seeing the mission complete and not merely satisfied that they had done their own part for it.[29]

Following Alan Shepard's suborbital flight, there were six more Mercury missions, including the famous orbital voyage of John Glenn in 1962. The unblemished record of success confirmed the testing philosophy. Mercury combined elements of both missile testing and high-speed aircraft testing, and involved redundancies in critical systems. At the Cape, launch opera-tions followed the step-by-step approach that isolated problems and allowed for follow-up on any discrepancies.

Astronaut safety became the foremost concern in these early human mis-sions. Indeed, astronauts were considered an "integral part of the system during tests."[30] No wonder, as they were boarding an ICBM with the nuclear warhead replaced by a capsule. Although the seven original Mercury astro-nauts were recruited from military test pilots, it was not clear how the space program would stand up to an accident that cost a human life. Indeed, the

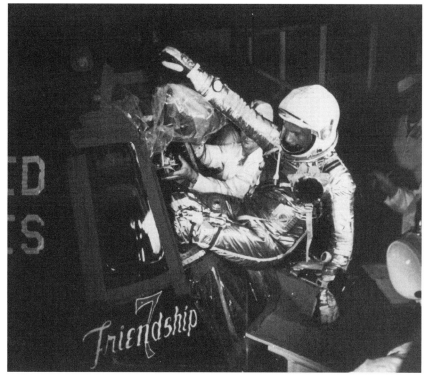

3-4. John Glenn gets ready for his history-making flight, squeezed into a capsule that will ride atop an Atlas ICBM.

quick rise to celebrity status of the Mercury Seven cut two ways. On the one hand, they were seen as bold adventurers who put their lives on the line for America. That might suggest a certain toleration for accidents on the part of the public, in the same way that people accept the death of soldiers in a military campaign. But the celebrity status of these early astronauts also made them something special. Upon his return to earth, John Glenn received a welcome back marked by confetti and ticker-tape parades throughout the world's capitals. The public followed the lives of the Mercury astronauts closely, reading their clean-cut profiles in *Life* magazine and hearing about their unofficial, but perhaps equally admired, lifestyle as young playboys in Corvettes tearing up Cocoa Beach.

Still, for all their celebrity, it was not exactly clear what an astronaut's role would be in flight. "Spam in a can" was the derisive term used by those who feared they would be little more than substitutes for the test primates who had already ridden the rockets. But over time the astronaut role increased. Engineers once feared that a jet jockey itching to get his fingers on the control stick would mess things up. In fact, it turned out to be easier in some respects to have humans perform functions on board than to rely on automated systems that had to be checked and, if critical, made redundant. At the same time, astronaut training and safety procedures became new areas for work at the LOC. Ideas about flight safety that had thus far applied only to aviation crossed over into rocketry.[31] New equipment, such as an escape rocket to blast the capsule free in case of accident, was designed and installed. Preflight preparations included assembling survival kits for the splashdown, with dye markers, distress signals, food and water rations, and shark repellent.

Much of the Mercury program's purpose was to test human performance in space. It did that, and it kept the United States on a par with the Russians in the prestige race. Much as jet test flights to break the sound barrier a decade earlier had shown that humans could survive and perform in extreme flight conditions, so Mercury demonstrated that humans could survive the rigors of takeoff, the searing heat of reentry, and the watery ordeal of an ocean splashdown. Though the Redstone and Atlas boosters were dead ends for human space flight, their launching proved out testing and integration procedures, countdown and launch patterns that would be applied to later rockets. The LOC needed that sort of hands-on, real-time experience. Theoretical work alone could never suffice; actual procedures had to be run, proved, and certified. People had to practice the operational end of space flight.

The Gemini missions that soon followed Mercury were another step in this incremental process of practice and improvement. Testing for Mercury had hewed fairly closely to procedures dating back to the V-2. But Debus and his staff began to recognize that reliability in complex systems might not be possible through the traditional empirical methods. Testing would have to become more efficient if big space projects were going to stay on schedule and meet cost objectives. If new methods of test and checkout were not deployed, the results would be "low returns from our facility investments, exposure to wear-out and corrosion, difficult scheduling and a resultant low probability of meeting astronomical launch windows."[32]

The air force and private industry had been experimenting with statistical techniques to ensure quality for some time. Rather than testing each part, they sampled parts to establish parameters of reliability. By then improving critical parts or building in redundancies, they could reduce the overall odds of failure. These methods would be used in the space program as well. But launches were still relatively rare occurences, so statistical methods alone would not suffice. Each launch had to be treated as a singular event. Each rocket, even each version of the same rocket, had unique characteristics.

Under these conditions, careful prelaunch testing and preparation still had to go on.

Automation and simulation in place of physical testing was one way to improve efficiency. Vehicle designers could also help in reducing launch preparation time by making their hardware easily accessible to technicians—or by designing and incorporating components specifically for testing, so that crucial verification information did not have to be drawn from critical operational parts. Each time a technician laid a hand on a part, he introduced some measure of additional risk. At some point, additional testing added more risk than it subtracted. "We must not permit . . . the emergence . . . of a macrocosmic equivalent to the Heisenberg principle," wrote Debus, referring to the principle from quantum theory that to measure or define an electron is to affect its position.[33] In launching, as in particle physics, there is a price to be paid for gaining knowledge.

These new ideas about launching vehicles came into practice with the two-person Gemini flights that left the Cape from 1963 to 1966. Using the air force's heaviest lifter, the Titan rocket, NASA boosted into space a Gemini craft twice the size of Mercury. This was a major step forward in size and complexity. And Gemini was even more critical to the lunar program than Mercury, for it verified flight and mission procedures that would be used to send astronauts from earth to lunar orbit. Adding to the pressure was the march of time. The end of the decade, which had looked so far away when Kennedy made his speech, was now starting to approach fast. Any mistakes, slippage of schedule, or disasters at this stage would probably make it impossible to complete the moon mission on the president's timetable.

The Gemini mission was designed to prove that it was possible for astronauts to rendezvous in outer space. The plan was for the spacecraft to meet and dock with a target vehicle launched separately. This was a critical point for the trip to the moon. NASA scientists had determined that it would not be possible to make a direct ascent from earth to moon. Such a trip required too much fuel for the return journey, even with the spacecraft blasting off for home in the weak lunar gravity. Fuel for a return trip added weight at takeoff, which meant that the rocket leaving earth would have to be far more powerful than anything on the drawing boards. The only solution was to send a smaller, lighter vehicle to the moon once the main rocket had left earth's gravity. But to do that meant a mission in which two different astronaut teams, operating two vehicles, made a rendezvous in orbit. Gemini would prove out this plan, but it had to stay on schedule, meaning every part of NASA had to do its job, including launch operations.

Fortunately, experience had led to changes that lightened the burden on the launch team. McDonnell, the Gemini contractor, built a modular system, meaning that different parts of the craft could be removed and tested without affecting neighboring parts, something that had not been true of the earlier Mercury craft. This greatly simplified testing and checkout and reduced the possibility of introducing new errors through the testing itself.[34] Gemini's Titan rocket also used hypergolic self-igniting fuel, which was more reliable than the refined kerosene used in the Redstone. Though the toxic hypergolics required careful handling, there was less danger of a fire or explosion on the pad. As a result, one launch procedure was greatly simplified. The Gemini crew did not need a complicated escape rocket to shoot them free in case something went wrong at blastoff; a simpler ejector system sufficed. Finally, in just a few months since Mercury, advances in microelectronics permitted greater use of computers, which provided more real-time data during testing and operations.[35]

Once it had seemed that the Cape would become "a multi-purpose test site," so that rocket manufacturers would not have to build their own facilities for testing at their factories.[36] But Gemini moved the LOC in the opposite direction. To improve reliability, Gemini used more redundancies. As the number of backup systems multiplied, the testing of parts, systems, and their redundancies became enormously time-consuming. Building on the Mercury experience, the launch team undertook substantial work at the points of fabrication. This method allowed the launch team handling the vehicle when it arrived at the Cape to put most of its effort into testing integrated systems. The larger and more complex Gemini vehicle needed integrated testing, so finishing component verification at the factory permitted a considerable gain in time and efficiency.[37]

Still, not everything could be simplified. Advances in microelectronics allowed use of on-board computer systems, but the size, weight, and power consumption limits on these early computers presented challenges in both design and operations. The more "primitive" Mercury craft, by contrast, had relied strictly on ground computers, which could be as big as needed.[38] Two astronauts aboard Gemini meant more work on crew checkout as well. There were two astronauts to train, and a division of labor between them that had to be taught and carefully coordinated. It was one thing to train a single astronaut and go over procedures, but with two people performing different functions, the opportunities for missing a step or for miscommunication multiplied. All of this had to be foolproof before the first mission.

After unmanned testing of Gemini in 1964, the first mission with humans aboard, Gemini 3, went up in March 1965. Twenty months later, the last of ten pairs of astronauts returned safely to earth. Like Mercury, Gemini had finished without a hitch. Despite the obvious dangers of putting people

3-5. Gemini required a much larger scale of rocket and corresponding ground support equipment.

on these early vehicles, the Mercury and Gemini missions had shown that humans could fly in space. Launch Operations had demonstrated that it could meet the challenge of man-rated missions too. But further changes in operational and integration procedures would come swiftly, as the LOC worked to match rapid developments in rocket and spacecraft design. These challenges would arrive at the Cape with the Apollo moon mission. In the meantime, there was still plenty of other excitement.

Several hundred unmanned rockets left the Cape between 1958 and 1967, sometimes as many as two a day. They made the shores around Cape Canaveral a popular spot for rocket buffs. Many were tests of military hardware, such as the navy's submarine-launched Polaris ballistic missile. But NASA launched 130 unmanned or robotic vehicles during this time, for an incredible array of tasks.

These missions were performed under a different organizational and operational structure from the early manned missions. Reflecting the disparate origins of the NASA family, they were handled by personnel from the Lewis Center and the new Goddard Center, many of them moving over from the defunct Vanguard program. Out of Vanguard and from research performed at Lewis came a number of new launch vehicles, including the important liquid-hydrogen-fueled Centaur. This vehicle imposed new requirements on launch operations.

Liquid hydrogen was light and provided tremendous punch, about 40 percent more thrust than the same weight of kerosene. Used in an upper stage, it gave substantial lift to orbit. But it was so dangerous that for a long time Wernher von Braun argued against its use.[39] In the end, though, it became clear that only a hydrogen-fueled engine would do for the moon mission. Mastering the complexities of launching vehicles using this fuel was thus crucial to both early robotic and upcoming human missions. In launch operations, this meant building facilities to store hydrogen at minus-423 degrees Fahrenheit and learning how to manipulate the material in a cryogenic state and then warmed into a gas for use. Given how many of the early rocket launches failed, countdowns with Centaur were "very sensitive, very critical, very stressful. . . . starting at propellant loading, a lot of people were glued to their consoles."[40]

The unmanned program also used an array of other launch vehicles. The Atlas and Titan missiles served to carry nonhuman payloads as well as their more famous human cargo. Still other configurations mated various first-stage boosters with the intermediate-range Thor and Able rockets, a combination launched on the West Coast. But perhaps the most successful vehicle for robotic missions was the Delta. Built by McDonnell, the Delta started out as a military program but ended up as a workhorse of civilian flight. It proved exceptionally reliable. After initial trials, some twenty-two straight successful launches of the Delta took place from the Cape.[41] By 1968 it had been launched sixty-eight times, for missions that gathered geophysical, astronomical, and meteorological data, that placed communication and navigation satellites in orbit, and that sent probes on interplanetary missions.

As with the Mercury and Gemini programs, the unmanned launches required a number of informal but accepted cooperative relationships, especially with the Atlantic Missile Range. Military and NASA people worked side by side on unmanned launches. The basic problems of learning to fly new vehicles were often the same, regardless of whether it was a military mission or a scientific one.[42] There was no doubt, though, that the air force as a military establishment had its own way of doing things. The differences were apparent from the moment one stepped onto the air station. Entering the "Cape side" from the east, just past the port of Cape Canaveral, one passed through a gate little different from that found at any other military installation. The rocket launch complexes along the Cape shore were named in military jargon as SLC (Space Launch Complex) plus a number.

The military test range operated on a far larger scale than did NASA in the early 1960s. It was also part of a far bigger organization with many more facilities and a much more lavish budget. The military way tended to be more bureaucratic as a result, to assure consistency across many programs and bases and to coordinate the vast machinery of modern defense. As we have seen, in the 1960s many members of the air force did not want a separate civilian space agency at all. Yet on a personal level in day-to-day matters, the occasional ruffled feathers aside, cooperation won out. NASA programs emerged from the shadow of the larger military programs at the Cape. With Delta in particular, NASA people felt they had "cut the apron strings" to the air force. Now, on NASA launches, "we sat in the blockhouse running the show and the air force was beside us, consulting as necessary."[43]

Even with a centralized LOC, managing all these mission was difficult, "perhaps impossible to logically implement," in the words of Debus. Part of the problem was the still unresolved issue of organization. Though everyone agreed, at least in principle, that a central authority for launch was logical, other NASA installations were still "accustomed to doing things their own way."[44] The fact was, the space program had multiple goals and competing agendas, even in the early years. Of necessity, there would be "gradual evolution and constant improvisation to meet unforeseen administrative developments."[45] The head of the unmanned section, Robert Gray, kept in daily contact with Debus to assure overall coordination in use of limited facilities and to maintain consistency in dealing with the air force. But in most matters he operated independently with his tight-knit unmanned launch group.

Gray's team, much more modest in size than the evolving manned program being assembled on Merritt Island, was an excellent example of cooperation and teamwork in a small group. Perhaps 120 NASA personnel worked this side of the house.[46] Functional divisions of duties, though obviously necessary, did not result in strict departmental or individual specialization. When the time came for countdown and launch, Gray moved from supervisor of the entire process to launch director "in the blockhouse."[47] It was a process that could never quite be standardized or reduced to a fully documented routine, yet one in which good lines of communication between different functions and lots of sharing of information could result in incremental and continuous improvement. Each launch could not be a *completely* unique event, or there would be no way to pass along insight gained from experience to the next flight. Operations meant not a routine but a research-and-learning process. Flying what were in some ways still experimental vehicles, confronting new payloads and new problems in almost every launch, experiencing both success and failure, sleeping in cots in the blockhouse as work went on round the clock, and sticking together as a group over the years provided the sort of camaraderie and close communications that allowed people to learn lessons and pass on what they learned to others.

Members of the unmanned group believed that this sort of informality and open, communicative approach to work was responsible for the Delta's record of success.[48] It was also necessary in dealing with older technology that remained sensitive and quirky. Atlas missiles flew successfully only when everything was just right. "Tender loving care" was needed for this "people dependent" vehicle, which required a long checkout procedure, one that depended on knowledge won from years of experience. The honeycombed insulation panels on Atlas, for example, could be tested only by having technicians go around the vehicle and tap it with a coin. If it gave back the right sound, it was telling them that the panels were properly glued and would not rip apart at launch.[49] Though the public rarely saw this side of the space age, the fact was that sometimes the most modern of technical systems depended on basic human skills and the primary human faculties of sensation. Design engineers would often see such "workarounds" as deviations from their plans. But the history of space flight would show that intimate knowledge gained from operations could also contribute substantially to mission success.[50]

By the early 1960s, astronomers, meteorologists, and communications companies were demanding so much access to space that NASA's robotic launches ran as high as two a month. In contrast to the human missions, robotic missions came frequently enough to allow the launch team to gain substantial insight into vehicles that could be incorporated into evolving designs. Most of the boosters went through a series of versions and upgrades over the years. Still, with many vehicle configurations and combinations in play, even after dozens of launches with the same rocket it seemed to the launch team that they never really saw the same vehicle twice. Each launch presented new problems, new anomalies to be checked out and solved. One of the most important robotic missions of these early years was the Ranger program, designed to gain greater understanding of the moon through a series of lunar flybys. Four Ranger launches between 1961 and 1962 failed. It was not until 1964 with Ranger 7 that there was a complete mission. Similar problems occurred with the early Mariner missions to the near planets, Mars and Venus.

Feeling that some of the problems with these unmanned missions may have been organizational, NASA headquarters reshuffled responsibilities at the Cape. By 1963, work on the new Merritt Island launch facility was well under way, a major task that required implementation of entirely new launch concepts and the construction of giant new facilities. In the short term, the LOC would focus its energy there. Gray appointed John Gossett to head up a separate Atlas/Centaur organization, which came under the authority of NASA's Lewis Center. The LOC was left to handle only the ground support equipment and the "bricks and mortar needs."[51]

Overall, though, the unmanned group demonstrated remarkable success. Between 1958 and 1964, as the number of NASA launches increased from four to thirty per year, the launch success rate climbed to 90 percent. This was a far cry from the early, stumbling years of the Vanguard program, such as 1958, when zero of four attempts were successful. Some problems remained. Despite the organizational reshuffling, the Atlas booster achieved only a 75–80 percent success rate, and NASA's small-payload launcher called Scout was just a little better at 85 percent. But the Delta and Titan launchers had success rates between 90 and 100 percent.[52] If NASA were asked in the early years what would happen at T-0, the most honest answer would have been "who knows." By the mid-1960s, the honest answer was, it should launch as expected.[53] Clearly, the painstaking work involved in the launch of rockets, going back to White Sands and, for many of the German émigrés, before that to World War II, had produced results.

Defining a Role for Operations

These early years defined the terms of debate about launching that would mark the Apollo years, and indeed to some degree the entire history of the American space program. Size, scale, and speed of operations had resulted in the creation of a separate launch authority. But questions remained on how this organization should best be structured, as the reshuffling of responsibilities for various vehicle programs demonstrated.

Politics as well as technology had argued for the formation of the LOC. But the internal divisions and wranglings of a large organization were more than just politics in the sense of narrow self-interest. Other NASA centers had rightly feared that the "special relationship" between the LOC and Marshall would force them to the back of the line when it came to Cape operations. On the other hand, many at NASA were working from a perspective that treated launching as just the tail end of a more significant development-and-design process. Von Braun and the Marshall engineers who had wanted to retain control of Cape launchings based their position on long experience with rockets, where research, development, design, and operations were carried out "under one roof." Debus himself appreciated the need for an independent launch organization. He was not simply being an empire builder. Unless the operational work of testing and launching had some independence from design and development, it would never be able to provide the insight that came from on-the-ground work and flight experience.

Where exactly the break between design and development lay, and how operational knowledge should feed back into design, however, was still unclear. Mercury and Gemini had shown the advantages of doing testing at the factory. But a pure "ship and shoot" approach quickly fell by the wayside. It was soon apparent that the launch authority needed to have a considerable role in preparing complex vehicles to fly. To stay on any kind of schedule, one could not redesign vehicles after a launch revealed some problem or imperfection; in many cases, those problems simply had to be lived with and overcome by adapting operations to them. But neither was it reasonable to simply pass vehicles on to the launch location and assume that the work of design and development was finished. Designers, developers, and contractors had to be present at the launch site, and considerable information had to flow between launch and design centers.[54]

New ideas about how to organize launches and operate space vehicles had yet to overcome the weight of existing experiences and traditions. "Everyone was trying to get a healthy piece of the action," engineers acknowledged. Section chiefs were certain they knew best how to run their functional areas, and personnel with experience stretching back to the beginnings of their programs had considerable local and intimate knowledge of what they were doing.[55] Some at NASA headquarters were convinced that Kurt Debus could never put aside his loyalty to von Braun and Marshall. For his part, Debus insisted in maintaining certain lines of authority, even over contractors and NASA personnel working for other centers. Could the LOC truly be an independent center serving all of NASA? The question was still in the air, despite the name and the formal organization that said it was.

4
*
*
*

A Bridge to the Moon

The youth gets together his materials to build a bridge to the moon.
Thoreau, *Journal*, July 14, 1852

Rockets were going off daily at Cape Canaveral, sometimes twice daily. Across the Banana River on Merritt Island, workers were busy with far more mundane tasks. Rather than sending rockets into space, they were moving dirt on the ground. Millions of cubic yards of the mosquito-infested marsh NASA purchased on Merritt Island had to be transformed into land suitable for launching vehicles larger and more complex on missions bolder and more complicated than anything yet attempted.

Designs for this new facility existed largely in the head of Kurt Debus and a few of his top-level directors at the LOC. No one really knew what a spaceport for launching men to the moon would look like. Engineers could do the hard calculations, builders could weld steel, but it all had to begin in the mind. A Palos for the space age would reflect the previous twenty years of rocket-launching experience, but it would take inspiration from ideas about space flight discussed by Debus and von Braun as they worked on V-2 rockets. These would be put in service to the Cold War space race with the Soviet Union.

Design Concepts

The imaginative aspects of the new spaceport came out most notably in the ambitious scale of the plans. In these days of seemingly limitless budgets and unlimited space horizons, there was talk of twenty, forty, perhaps one hundred Saturn flights a year. Ideas about orbiting space stations and permanent facilities on the moon were no longer just daydreams. NASA's Future Projects Office was at work investigating these very possibilities, including a mission to Mars. The office also did financial calculations to show how the price per launch would fall as the number of launches went up.[1]

This moment, Debus quickly saw, presented a unique opportunity. It made sense to plan the new launch facilities on Merritt Island on a big scale, anticipating the future. Land was available now, and the budget, if not truly unlimited, was as generous as it was ever likely to get. Under the umbrella of a well-supported Cold War project, Debus sought facilities whose full-scale use would be realized later. It was much the way he and von Braun had seen their work at White Sands or even at Peenemünde, squeezing the future into the practical needs of the moment. Although authorized to build only two new pads for Saturn on Merritt Island, Debus soon proposed launch concepts to reflect a manifest of future missions as yet undefined.

Traditionally, preparing a vehicle for launch, including stacking the stages and all tests and checks, had taken place on the pad itself, in a single, fixed location. But with bigger rockets coming to the Cape, Debus conceived of a "mobile" system for preparation, test, and checkout. Given the size and complexity of the Saturn rocket, it would take months to ready, all the while sitting on the pad exposed to the weather. For six months each year, hurricanes threatened the Florida coast, not to mention lesser storms. So long as the vehicle was on the pad, its delicate machinery risked lightning strikes, wind damage, and salt air corrosion. By assembling and testing the rocket indoors, then wheeling it to the pad only as launch day approached, these dangers would be averted. The mobile launch concept would also permit work to go forward on multiple vehicles at the same time. As one assembled rocket left for the pad, another would take its place. No one vehicle would tie up the center's facilities. This would permit faster launches at a higher rate on a tighter schedule. In launching, as with any other business, Debus noted, "time means money."[2]

Building on the studies of NASA's Future Projects Office, the LOC leadership made a case for economies of scale. If one stuck with the traditional approach, it was true, initial facilities costs were lower. But that cost advantage disappeared as launch rates rose. With fixed launching, a vehicle sat on the pad for as long as two months for repeated checkouts, matings, and rematings. It took still another month to "rehabilitate the pad" after the vehicle was away. At that rate, no more than four vehicles could fly from a single pad each year, "a rather low utilization rate for such an investment in facilities." To launch thirty-six Saturns per year, NASA would need nine traditional fixed structures, at a cost of $900 million.[3] The mobile launch approach would save $150–450 million. Debus, understanding the citizens of his adopted country well, wrote, "The American taxpayer is the stockholder in this vital business of launching space vehicles and, like all stockholders, he wants a return on his investment. This new launch concept can be measured in actual dollar savings and will eventually pay a handsome dividend in national prestige."[4]

· Still, this was long-term thinking. Congress appropriated money on an annual basis, and most members of Congress thought in terms of the next election year. The mobile launch configuration quickly drew critics. "You've got a great big pile of money," one Congress member remarked, "and it is very easy for someone to come along and cut it, really cut it." Maybe America was "trying to do too much in too much of a hurry."[5] Would thirty or more Saturns really be taking flight each year? Here Debus could draw on his experience, which showed that many test flights were needed to "proof" a vehicle. Atlas and Titan each required some fifty test flights. The giant Saturn would probably need still more.

As it turned out, advances in technology and knowledge combined with a shift in test philosophy drastically reduced the number of test flights Saturn would fly. But in the early 1960s no one really knew how many tests were needed to prepare for a trip to the moon. Locking in the LOC with equipment suitable only for the present would stifle future development. During an intense debate on the issue, Wernher von Braun asked whether the space program was "here to stay and will continue to grow" or not.[6] No one could bring themselves to answer "not." Mobile launching and the large-scale plan won the day as a "first class" sendoff the astronauts deserved.[7]

Moving from concept to execution was now the challenge. No one had ever transported a space vehicle weighing perhaps a million pounds perfectly upright, as would be necessary with mobile launching. What if the rocket had to go back for more work? The assembly and transporter facilities would also have to be flexible enough to handle a variety of vehicles, including test versions of Saturn. What would the facilities actually look like, and where would the equipment come from?

Artists' concepts of the proposed facilities show a gleaming industrial landscape dominating the flat marshlands of the Cape with a distant rocket screaming upward, its flame giving the Cape an eerie glow. It was a clean, neat vision of rocket technology, and one that almost completely effaced the basic work of building and construction that made it possible for rockets to soar off the earth. More than anything else, the earthbound facilities set the pace of progress for the space race. Civil engineering, not scientific research or technological breakthroughs, would determine if and when Americans landed on the moon. As NASA administrator James Webb put it, "in a very real sense, the road to the moon is paved with bricks, steel and concrete here on earth."[8]

In an ideal world, designers would specify what was to be built and then

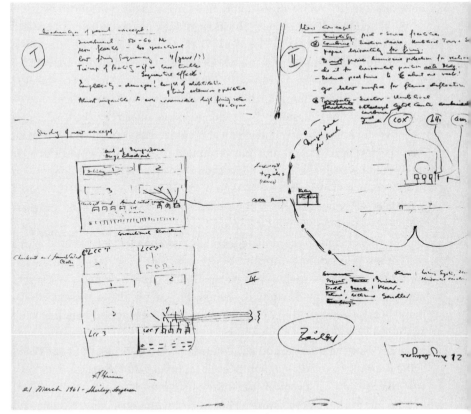

4-1. Kurt Debus's hand drawings of his mobile launch concept.

turn over their specifications to the builders. But the real world of the space program proved much more complicated. Buildings went up even as hardware was still on the drawing board. At a price tag approaching $500 million, the new facilities would take three years to complete. Meanwhile, rocket designers at Marshall kept coming up with bigger boosters, forcing revisions of the launchpad. Changes in midcourse were inevitable. "It was quite a job just pulling the thing together, integrating the whole mess," remembered one participant.[9] The planning team at the Cape worked backward from when the first Saturn V had to be launched to set the schedule for construction.[10]

Simultaneously, NASA advertised more than a dozen major construction projects at the Cape to contractors. Plans called for spending $162 million in 1962–63 alone, for roads and utilities, launchpads, towers, propellant depots, cables, and communications systems. There would be support and operations buildings, canals, barge channels, equipment warehouses, an electric power grid, and other infrastructure. Several items had never been built before: a special assembly building to stack and prepare the giant Saturn vehicle, a transporter mechanism to get it to the pad, and a mobile tower to service the rocket once it was there. Together these items were expected to cost more than 20 percent of the total budget for Merritt Island, a total that was raised to an estimated three-quarters of a billion dollars. In all, some 1,500 engineers would have to prepare 100 tons of specifications and drawings before the launch complex at Merritt Island was ready.[11]

Launching humans on trips to the moon needed a firm footing, literally, on the ground. NASA contracted with the Army Corps of Engineers to handle much of this construction. From office buildings to runways to hangars and launchpads and bunkers, the Corps' work was already visible at Cape Canaveral. Now it had its most ambitious task yet, transforming Merritt Island into a moonport.

The Corps' first task was to secure title to the 88,000 acres of land for the government. In fact, more would soon be needed, an additional 15,000 acres north along the beach going into Volusia County, as revised safety studies called for a circular buffer of at least 20,000 feet around the Saturn. Land acquisition proved a major chore. The Corps had to purchase some fifteen thousand separate tracts, many owned by local farmers who had been there for generations. Acquiring private property for public purposes has never been easy in America, a nation with laws that fiercely protects private property and also give the government broad powers to condemn and take what it needs. Inevitably there were conflicts.

The Corps negotiated directly with owners, which some found a bit unseemly. Should the government be trying to get the land of its citizens at bargain prices? Even using standard appraising procedures, there could be significant variations between adjacent pieces of property. Rumors arose about one family getting a much better price than a neighbor. When negotiations broke down, the Corps initiated condemnation proceedings to force a sale, a sure way to anger locals. In almost every case, landowners lost in court, though some cases dragged on into the late 1960s. Orange growers in particular resented their loss of livelihood. In the end, NASA leased back some twelve square kilometers of citrus trees to growers.[12]

Changes on the once sleepy Cape irked old-time residents who remembered the days before all the dirt and noise, and before bars were permitted to sell liquor on Sundays.[13] The arrival of out-of-state engineers, technicians, and blue-collar workers brought fears of a "second Yankee invasion" in this bucolic part of the South. It did not help when the LOC's publication, *Spaceport News*, ran a headline, "Shiloh Falls to Feds Again," linking a small town on the Brevard-Volusia county line with the eponymous Civil War battle a century earlier.[14]

In its natural state, Merritt Island did not provide suitable footing for pushing rockets into space. Although its lowlands and waterways made transportation of bulky equipment easy, they also made for a swampy launch site. Some of this natural wetland would become a nature preserve surrounding the launch facility. But where launch operations were to take place, land had to be dried out. Civil engineers directed a massive dredging and drainage effort, running surface water off into lakes, ponds, and canals. Where building foundations were to go, they squeezed out excess moisture, by a method called surcharging. Bulldozers made huge sandpiles that pressed down the soggy soil until there was a firm footing.

Much of this work was carried out by a new fraternity of workers who started arriving at Merritt Island in 1962. Driving huge earthmoving machines, they were the members of "E Pilum Dirtum." We don't know who coined the nickname, but it came complete with a hand-drawn crest showing a crossed pick and shovel, palm trees in one corner, mosquitoes in another. So much of the early work on the LOC involved earthmoving that Kurt Debus, eager to get started on launch operations, complained, "Can't you send me anything but dirt pictures?"[15] Debus and his fellow rocketeers would have to wait, however. The work of the civil engineer came first.[16]

Colonel Clarence Bidgood, in charge of the Corps' work at Merritt Island, formed a functional organization with branches of Design Engineering, Construction, Planning, and Real Estate, recruiting his staff from as far away as California. Even if most of the actual labor was to be done by contractor workers, there was more than enough to keep Bidgood fully occupied. When asked what he liked to do in his spare time, he answered, "I sleep."[17] He had little time for anything else. In a few short years, the facilities for the moon launch had to be up and running if the United States wanted to have a chance of meeting President Kennedy's deadline.

While the Corps handled "bricks and mortar" (and dirt), the LOC itself took responsibility for equipment. Theodore Poppel supervised design and construction of the more "esoteric" or specialized technology needed for space flight. A building was a building, and the Corps' civil engineering expertise could handle this work, even down to the concrete launchpads. But anything that touched the skin of a rocket, or any equipment for monitoring, measuring, and controlling operations, was more a matter of development than construction. Even stands, towers, and flame deflectors, long used for military and other rocket programs, did not simply scale up for the lunar program.[18] The LOC employed its own design engineers, men and women who would begin with a blank sheet of paper and come up with something that could serve the special purposes of launch operations.[19] The designs

4-2. Earthmoving equipment scours the Cape to prepare the way for outer-space journeys.

had to be right the first time. There was no time to go back to the drawing board.

Just about everything from moving the completed rocket to the Cape to pushing the launch button was going to be bigger, more complicated, and more risky in the lunar program. The Saturn vehicle dwarfed its predecessors. In final configuration, it stood more than 350 feet tall and used first-stage engines that generated more than 7.5 million pounds of thrust. Even the rocket parts were big. The engines' turbopumps, which sent fuel to the massive combustion chambers, were rated at 40,000 horsepower. They spun fast enough to "drain an Olympic sized swimming pool in ten seconds."[20] Because of Saturn's size and cost, checkout procedures before launch had to be more elaborate, using more automation and gathering more telemetry data than before.

The specialized launch facilities had to match the vehicle. It was crucial to incorporate operational considerations into vehicle designs, and vice versa. The LOC's design engineers worked closely with their counterparts at Marshall. Top design engineer Don Buchanan remained in Huntsville to iron out details of ground equipment as the rocket builders worked on the vehicle. At the Cape, the two chief facility builders, Bidgood and Poppel, reported directly to Debus, as did a third man in charge of Plans, Programs and Resources, Rocco Petrone. In practice Petrone would take more and more responsibility for the construction.[21]

NASA policy was to commission "turnkey" facilities, meaning that the contract covered everything except "people and their tools."[22] The result was a multilevel management structure. On one side were NASA headquarters, the LOC, and the LOC's facilities division. On the other were the Army Corps of Engineers and the contractors who worked for the Corps. Money and directions went from NASA to the LOC to the Corps' district office. Technical information flowed between the LOC's facilities division and the Corps, and from there down to the contractors.[23] Petrone acted as facilitator and coordinator for it all.

Coordinating activity through direct, face-to-face communications was impossible with a project of this size and scope.[24] The working population of Merritt Island mushroomed 400 percent between July 1962 and July 1963. By October 1964, more than 4,000 construction workers and 500 installers were on site. Another 2,000 contract workers provided support services to the Center, and almost 1,000 more were supporting rocket launches. The federal workforce of just under 1,700 was dwarfed by these contract workers. But that was just the start. By 1965, with the construction of the Saturn launch complex at its peak, 15,000 workers would be roaming the island. Nine out of ten were contractors. Many of them were craft and industrial union members.[25]

Labor Conflicts

Thousands of blue-collar workers flocked to the Cape to weld steel, machine metal, fit pipe, and carry out other construction tasks. They arrived to insufficient housing, long daily commutes, shipping delays, and suspicious looks from the local population. Unable to secure accommodations on remote and underdeveloped Cape Canaveral, some had to drive more than a hundred miles each day, from as far away as Daytona and Tampa.[26] Twelve-hour days and seven-day-a-week schedules were not unusual. In extreme cases, such as during the repair of a launchpad following a missile explosion, workers could put in a hundred hours in a single week.[27] As activity on Merritt Island shifted into high gear, many workers would be working at a faster pace than they had during World War II. Conflicts soon arose over hours and conditions.

Labor problems had first emerged in the space program during the early missile tests. Some 327 work stoppages had occurred at federal missile bases by 1960, at a cost of 162,000 lost work days. The majority took place at Cape Canaveral. In May 1961, Senator John McClellan opened an investigation into labor issues at federal missile sites. "Our missile and space program, upon which our very survival in the struggle with world Communism depends," he wrote, was being delayed by those "who have placed greed and profit ahead of their devotion to the safety of our country."[28] McClellan pointed the finger at both workers and contractors, though he left no doubt that he blamed labor more. Taking issue with McClellan, electrical contractor Henry Gable defended his workers: "I doubt if you would find a Communist in the bunch." Nonetheless, he conceded that labor unrest was doing "more harm than any Communists ever could."[29] Though concerned about costs, contractors were under pressure to meet deadlines and saw no choice but to accede to union demands. Workers for their part pointed to contractors who hired nonunion help at lower wages whenever they could get away with it. "The union people all over the country would rather not work on the same job, doing the same type of work, with nonunion people," testified union business agent Bob Palmer.[30] The patriotic thing to do, according to labor representatives, was to use union men every time. This would quell unrest.[31]

The roots of the problem lay in labor laws that stretched back long before there were such things as missiles. In 1931, at the nadir of the Great Depression, Congress had passed the Davis-Bacon Act. Written to protect the jobs of northern union workers from cheap southern (and, frankly, black) labor, it required that all federal construction projects pay union scale wages. At the LOC, workers enjoyed wages comparable to those paid in northern states, at a time when Florida had much lower wage rates. When the act was passed, its sponsors imagined projects such as "highways and schoolhouses," not missile complexes.[32]

In theory, later legislation limited Davis-Bacon's reach. Congress had passed the Taft-Hartley Act in 1947, prohibiting "closed shops," or the requirement that all workers on a site be union members. Many states, starting with Florida, quickly passed their own "right to work" laws that prevented unions from controlling worksites. But high demand for skilled labor forced aerospace contractors to deal almost exclusively with unions, making the Cape, in effect, a closed shop. As one admitted, fighting the union was not usually worth the effort. "If you had a lot of time you could go through the courts and things like that . . . but there were missiles that were supposed to get off the ground."[33]

Committed to his agenda of landing a man on the moon, President Kennedy intervened to keep the industrial peace with Executive Order 10945. It established a Missile Sites Labor Commission, with representatives from

NASA, the Corps, and the major unions.[34] Concerned that they were being portrayed as unpatriotic, the national unions agreed to a no-strike pledge as they had during World War II. In return, the government promised there would be no lockouts during labor disputes. The entire labor arrangement at the Cape was overseen by a Project Stabilization Board, which reviewed agreements and adjudicated conflicts. The board also established a table of compensation to be followed by contractors, which it hoped would reduce uncertainty over labor costs while assuring workers they would be adequately paid.[35]

With high wages guaranteed, workers flocked to the Cape. The Teamsters, the International Brotherhood of Electrical Workers, the United Association of Plumbers and Pipefitters, the International Iron Workers, and other unions sent members to Florida during the early-1960s construction boom. Exhausting hours meant time and a half or double-time wages for overtime. Some workers were earning upwards of $600 per week, more than Wernher von Braun or Kurt Debus.[36] Work at the LOC also had strategic value to unions. It was an opportunity to organize in a right-to-work state.

Between 1961 and 1963, work stoppages and days lost declined significantly at the Cape. But tensions rose quickly with the level and intensity of work. Increased demand for labor and tighter schedules soon put workers in a strong bargaining position. In turn, contractors looked outside the unions for help, or changed job classifications to replace skilled with unskilled workers. The Missile Sites Labor Commission met weekly, but proved unable to stop strikes and walkouts. Even appeals to the National Labor Relations Board or court injunctions were no more than "tourniquets" and resulted in "only a temporary peace."[37]

Behind these labor disputes were deep cultural differences about the nature of work in the space industry. Engineers and managers tended to see what they were doing as a patriotic duty, with American pride on the line. Coming out of Alabama coal mining towns, or growing up chopping cotton on Arkansas farms that still used mules for plowing, they were often the first in their families to go to college, usually at a nearby state school. Their parents had been storekeepers, farmers, mechanics, teachers, nurses, and housewives. These white-collar space workers were not members of the elite; they were strivers. Fresh out of school or the military, gung ho for the space program, they saw sixteen-hour days with no overtime as the road to the future they had read about in *Popular Mechanics* or in science fiction pulps.[38] They worked with a new technology not already claimed by scientists and engineers from the nation's elite institutions of higher learning. When NASA deputy director Albert Siepert suggested that "perhaps the laborers . . . might gain motivation by an orientation on the importance of the work they were doing," he only highlighted a basic difference in outlook.[39] Union workers saw their jobs as an excellent but short-term opportunity to earn high wages. Those in the construction trades would soon be moving on to other projects. It was far more important to them to protect the long-term interests of their trade or craft than to sacrifice all for the short-term goal of a space race with Russia.

These differences came into play with the very technology that enthralled the engineers and gave employment to the workers. Because rockets were new technology, it was uncertain who was responsible for what work or how that work should be done. Jurisdictional disputes became a major source of conflict. Union workers believed that engineers and managers were stepping into their field of craft by demanding control over many activities involved in assembling the launch facilities. Engineers wanted hands-on experience with the hardware that they were developing. In 1960 a committee headed by Solicitor General Harold C. Nystrom recommended that the LOC determine "interface points" where craft workers stopped and engineers took over.[40] As the space program evolved, though, the interface broke down.

Over on the Cape side, the air force allowed union workers to take their work right up to the missile. Union construction workers built the launch sites; union electricians and pipe fitters handled the wiring and conduits. On Merritt Island, NASA balked at this dividing line. The in-house tradition of work followed at Marshall and practiced at the LOC argued for using civil servant technicians for tasks such as wiring and pipe fitting to assure a high standard of result. "We pointed out to them that these were not really simple cables at all, that they were highly technical things built more by technicians than electricians," reflected one civil servant.[41] Kurt Debus argued that while "we have always followed the practice to contract . . . with private enterprise for the construction of the basic launch facility," it was important to retain "for our own employees that part of the ground support equipment which is still undergoing development or is a critical part of the missile system."[42]

Debus saw the LOC as a research facility. Union workers might build the "laboratory," but as soon as the facility was ready, scientists and engineers would step in and conduct the experiment. With technology still in development, the trial-and-error methods inherent in this early phase properly belonged to civil servant engineers. Union technicians, Debus continued, could not "respond to the many developmental changes which take place during the installation and checkout of a facility." The launch site was no mere concrete stand, but in fact "the first stage of the vehicle, dropping off when the flight begins, just as subsequent vehicle stages are separated in flight."[43] The same question of dividing responsibility affected the Center's relationship to the Army Corps of Engineers. The Corps could build buildings, even launchpads, but not research facilities. Throughout the construction phase, the questions came up again and again: What was old, what new? What could be done by army engineers, what by private contractors, what by blue-collar workers, and what had to be done by engineers involved in research?[44]

Following Debus's logic, civil servants and engineers would take over tasks that traditionally belonged to union workers. This spelled trouble, and it was not long before "big rough guys with a growth of beard" started grumbling "they're taking food out of my belly."[45] As workers saw it, they had no choice but to "hold to their guns" and stop a precedent for the future from being set. They were willing to go to extremes, or take symbolic stands to protect jurisdiction. When technicians installed electrical cables, the workers compromised, cutting them in half and then splicing them again. In other cases, union workers "blessed" a piece of equipment, doing nothing to it, but symbolically maintaining it as in their area of work.[46]

Such activities soon brought howls of criticism from the outside. Workers were engaging in an absurd "pagan ritual," one incredulous congressman declaimed. They were riding a "gravy-train at the Cape," dragging their heels for overtime, performing their tasks shoddily, complained others.[47] It was not just union rituals that came in for a drubbing, though. Those who had seen how the air force did things argued that there was no reason why union electricians and plumbers could not install equipment, Debus's fears notwithstanding.[48] In fact, some questioned how different "space technology" really was from anything else. They noted that attempts to limit blue-collar workers' scope hindered productivity, even more perhaps than did union foot-dragging. Rapidly evolving designs often meant that cables and wiring had to be ripped out and replaced as many as four times before a launch. A shortage of supervisors, materials, and tools sometimes left craft workers waiting around, unable to proceed without engineering supervision.[49] The question of jurisdiction was thus another part of the emerging debate over what launch operations and, by extension, the entire space program was to be—a laboratory experiment, of the sort that Debus and von Braun and others had been engaged in during their German and early American years of work, or a program with a definite goal and an emphasis on standard operating procedures?[50]

With so many questions unresolved and lines of jurisdiction open to dispute, industrial relations deteriorated.[51] By 1964, one person-day for every 110 worked disappeared into strikes and job actions.[52] Many of the strikes were not officially sanctioned. The no-strike pledge given by the national unions was not binding on locals, and wildcat walkouts occurred whenever workers felt their interests threatened. The local term for such job actions was "going fishing," which is how workers spread the word not to show up the next day. In other cases, dissatisfaction was expressed by the delivery of mysterious shipments of unwanted lumber, sod, or cinderblocks to contractors suspected of using nonunion help, or through anonymous phone calls in the middle of the night.[53]

The worst moment occurred in 1963–64, in a strike against the Florida East Coast Railway. Though not primarily directed against the Center, pickets appeared outside its gates because an FEC branch line ran through the facility. Picketers from the Order of Railroad Telegraphers virtually shut down construction work as Teamsters refused to cross the line. A second union, the largely black Brotherhood of Maintenance of Way, joined the ORT workers in the walkout in June 1963.[54]

As Center director Kurt Debus noted, besides the direct loss of days worked, the railway strike threatened to disrupt the tightly coupled schedules for completing the facilities and testing the Saturn vehicle. "Each stage in the development of space vehicles is interlocking to every other stage," he warned.[55] Often a single contractor depended on workers from several trades, and the absence of just one prevented the work from proceeding. When construction stopped on launchpads, those lost days would push back the schedule of future test launches. The strike ground on, however, and undelivered loads of steel for construction sat on railroad sidings.

In Florida the FEC had long ago earned a reputation for being a hardnosed antiunion company. Recognizing the threat to the schedule, NASA administrator James Webb prodded FEC executives to settle the strike quickly in the interest of national priorities.[56] The FEC suggested instead that NASA ask for a permanent injunction against the pickets at its gates. Neither Webb nor FEC management was prepared to make the first move in bringing the conflict before the courts, a strategy that might well backfire. "I told [the FEC president] I thought he should make his own decision with respect to this," Webb wrote.[57] Ten days later a federal judge enjoined the pickets at the Center, and also banned other unions from striking in sympathy with the railroad locals.[58] Work could now proceed, though members of the building trades unions made it clear that they would refuse to cross picket lines in the future.[59]

As suspected, the injunction did not end labor difficulties at the launch center. Protest over a single nonunion plumbing contractor led to 1,700 lost days in 1965. This strike too required a court order to end.[60] A 1965 action by the International Association of Mechanics against Boeing, an important Cape contractor, cost still more days—in fact, the most in the decade.

Some of the policies enacted years before to prevent labor disputes now became sources of conflict. The Project Stabilization Board provided tables of "reasonable" wages for contractors to follow, but when demand forced up wages, contractors could not pass on the higher labor costs to the government. This gave them incentive to "work men out of classification" and substitute less skilled workers where they could. Technically such moves were prohibited, though as those on the ground observed, the contractors "could do this when Inspectors were away on another job."[61] Work at the Cape was "not being granted national emergency priority by the labor unions," Senator McClellan lamented. But this time he took note of "profiteering in defense contracts for missile procurement" as well as suspect union activity.[62] It was not the sort of congressional attention NASA relished. Work continued, but labor became as important an issue in the Center's growth as construction and equipment.

Local Development

"Apollo Booms Florida," blared a newspaper headline of the early 1960s. The influx of people, money, and new industry from the lunar program was expected to lead Florida from rural underdevelopment to the industrial and space ages in a single great leap. To support the military and civilian space programs, aerospace manufacturers—Martin-Marietta, North American Aviation, Boeing, General Dynamics, Lockheed and McDonnell-Douglas—located facilities in Central Florida.[63] The Cape and Apollo, wrote financial columnist Sylvia Porter, were "destined to play a drama of dollars as well as dreams."[64]

Brevard County felt the space boom most directly. Brevard's 1950 population of 24,000 ballooned to 111,000 by 1960.[65] It remained one of Florida's fastest-growing counties through the 1960s. Employment rose apace with population, mostly in jobs provided by NASA, the Department of Defense, and their contractors. Many local businesses lost their best employees to the space program, though other sectors of the economy—banking, insurance, retailing, and real estate—were soon thriving thanks to space program paychecks.

Cocoa Beach stood at the epicenter of this boom. The sleepy beach town just down the road from Cape Canaveral had harbored some 750 souls at the end of World War II. Its city hall was a one-room shack. By the time the LOC opened, the town had 12,000 residents, and a new paved sidewalk in front of city hall.[66] For a time, Cocoa Beach had the state's second highest per capita income and its youngest population. Land values shot up, new restaurants, motels, recreational, cultural, and educational institutions appeared.[67] Beachfront land once regarded as practically worthless was selling for $900 an acre. Realtors offered brand-new three-bedroom, two-car-garage homes with modern open-plan designs, casement windows, and large patios for $17,000. Promotional leaflets showed families in convertibles driving by the rocket facilities. Fathers golfed and fished, teenagers water-skied, children frolicked on the beach, looking up to see a Titan or Atlas missile streak over the ocean. For those who missed such moments, the Terra-Luna Gift Shop sold 8mm movies of launches.[68] No one ever accused the Cape region of being a mecca of high culture. During the boom years, reporters christened it Disneyland East, for its neon-decked strip shopping centers and motels. It was a prophetic name, since Disney would soon be building a theme park in nearby Orlando.

At least 60 percent of Cocoa Beach's population was involved in missile work. Transient construction workers jammed into overcrowded trailer parks cheek by jowl with professionals brought in to design and build modern launch facilities. They celebrated at blastoff parties at the Starlight Bar after a successful launch.[69] Astronauts drag-raced their Corvettes down the middle of US A1A. Plumbers and electricians argued sports, space, and politics with them at local watering holes. Motel after motel flashed neon signs featuring rockets, spacesuited astronauts, ringed planets, just about anything connected with space. Establishments ranged from the respectable to the red-light. Local restaurants included the Heidelberg (for the German-born scientists, no doubt) and Mr. Guy's Samoa, with its Island Girl waitresses. Comedians performed endless astronaut routines. Diners relaxed to the sounds of Johnny Boland and his Continental Trio or the Play-Aires.

The frenetic pace left the town's thirty-three-year-old mayor reeling. "I'm getting old fast," he told reporters.[70] Unusual community and work conditions spawned a range of social ills, including a divorce rate nearly double the national average and high rates of alcoholism and illegitimacy.[71] The local police chief had to contend with four suicides in 1962. There had not been a single one in the previous five years. NBC reporter David Brinkley painted Cocoa Beach as a tawdry outpost teeming with shifty inhabitants and sleazy bars. When the mayor objected, Brinkley shrugged and replied that the good side of Cocoa Beach "would not interest viewers."[72]

Still, for all the talk about wild times, the truth was that most of the new residents of Brevard County were a fairly sedate middle-class group. Most came from within the state of Florida or from nearby southern states. Most had been married ten or more years, and most planned to stay permanently. In part because of the intensive nature of the work and long hours put in by male space workers, women played key roles in community affairs through women's clubs and garden clubs. These groups, along with the PTA, pro-

4-3. Time-lapse photograph of *Mariner 6* aboard an Atlas-Centaur rocket flying over the bright lights of Cocoa Beach, 1969.

vided the impetus toward community building.[73] Eventually, as the boom atmosphere abated, the population would take on "more normal character-istics."[74]

In a bid to promote normalcy, NASA personnel worked with local au-thorities to plan growth and development in the region. Center director Debus, Patrick Air Force Base commander Davis, and Florida governor Fer-ris Bryant formed the Joint Community Impact Coordination Committee (JCICC) in 1961. County governments responded with their own planning body, the East Central Florida Regional Planning Council. Together the two groups took on issues such as education, public works, public health, and mosquito control. JCICC secretary John P. Nelson served as liaison between the two, acting as Planning Council secretary-treasurer to coordinate expenditures.[75]

Housing and transportation topped their list of concerns. Accommodations for itinerant construction workers were in short supply and a source of labor friction. At the behest of the local authorities, the Federal Housing Administration lent a hand, providing financing to build more homes.[76] Moving workers closer to work alleviated the long commutes, but lack of adequate infrastructure meant agonizing delays at bridges and causeways leading to Cape Canaveral from the mainland.[77] The Emory L. Bennett Causeway opened in 1962, giving welcome relief to road congestion. In 1964, completion of the Orsino Causeway (later the NASA Causeway) provided direct access from north Brevard to the growing missile complex. These infrastructure projects were generally taken as signs of progress, but not always. One controversial plan called for relieving north-south traffic congestion through a limited-access highway resting on pilings and trestles down the middle of the Banana River. Fisherman, sailors, and longtime settlers stopped the project at a community hearing in 1965.[78]

When NASA took over 88,000 acres of Merritt Island, it faced a potential public relations nightmare. The county's oldest settlement on the Cape as well as residents of northern Merritt Island had to be relocated. In the name of security, the popular Titusville and Playalinda Beaches were closed to public access. Fishing camps and hunting grounds would no longer be available to a region once known as a "sportsman's paradise." Hunting ended on NASA-owned land in 1963. Because of the magnitude of the construction, officials feared that a few of the many workers roaming the area might be accidentally bagged. Citizen complaints about the huge perimeter of land demanded for a missile safety zone put NASA on the defensive. Their voices soon reached the office of Florida senior senator Spessard Holland. NASA responded by working through the Department of the Interior to establish a National Wildlife Refuge on Merritt Island. The cooperative agreement started in August of 1963, with Interior's Bureau of Sport Fisheries and Wildlife placed in charge of 25,000 acres of NASA land.[79] Eventually some 58,000 acres were brought under partial control, leading to the formation of the wildlife refuge at Merritt Island and the national seashore along the Cape. It is the first and only refuge adjacent to a missile range.

These steps protected the natural environment, but the human habitat was feeling strains from construction and from population growth too. Increasing concentrations of people overwhelmed existing sanitary facilities. County medical establishments grew so overcrowded that patients waited in hallways.[80] The high percentage of male workers raised public health concerns about venereal disease. The aggressive salt marsh mosquito plagued newcomers, and not just with minor irritations. Florida suffered its worst outbreak of mosquito-borne St. Louis encephalitis in 1962, with forty-three deaths.[81]

The JCICC supported a number of reforms to improve Space Coast quality of life.[82] It backed a new hospital, which opened in Cape Canaveral in 1962. That same year, the Army Corps of Engineers launched Operation Mosquito. With six airplanes, sixteen aerosol-equipped trucks, two bulldozers, seven draglines, and three operations centers, Brevard County soon boasted the largest and best-equipped mosquito-control facilities in Florida.[83] It took three years, but eventually mosquito breeding areas were rendered "biologically unfit" for the insect's life cycle. The mosquito program perfectly reflected the peculiar rearrangement of landscape for the space program. Missile complexes and suburban houses, their yards now blissfully pest-free, went up in one spot, while in another, longtime residents were moved out of the way to create a new "natural area" complete with alligators, wild pigs, and American eagles.[84]

Cutting-edge aerospace activity now made education a priority for a state traditionally more concerned with tourism and low taxes.[85] In 1962 a consultant working for the JCICC found the public school facilities in the region only "adequate" and higher education programs, especially in engineering and science, "inadequate."[86] The JCICC concluded that Florida's most pressing need was to "provide immediate relief" through the establishment of a graduate center nearby geared to space technology.[87] That recommendation led to the founding of Florida Technological University on June 10, 1963.[88] Later this became the University of Central Florida.[89]

Kennedy Space Center

When NASA personnel first arrived at the Cape, they found the spartan accommodations of a military base. Leftover hangars served as offices, and even these were in short supply. Managers sat behind desks made of overturned orange crates. The LOC headquarters was off base in rented space at Cocoa Beach. Free from the shadow of any one NASA center, the LOC now had to provide its own support services, including offices, transportation, utilities, security, communications, even photography for launches. In the early years, everyone did a bit of everything, from putting out brushfires to fighting mosquitoes and snakes. Only one snakebite was reported in the first seven years, though articles about treating them still appeared in Center publications through the late 1960s.[90]

Gradually at first, then with accelerating speed, the Center rose out of the marsh. Between 1963 and 1965 a three-hundred-member design team over-saw construction of most of the key buildings and equipment for the moon trip. Significantly, the team was led not by an engineer but by an architect, Max Urbahn. Like its surrounding landscape, this center would be a planned entity, a giant machine and a modern city in its own right. If beauty was not the main requirement, the size and audacity of the undertaking would still give the Launch Operations Center a unique presence in the public eye.

The centerpiece of the Merritt Island complex was the Vehicle Assem-bly Building. Taller than a fifty-story skyscraper, one-third again as large as the Great Pyramid at Cheops, the VAB sat completely out of scale with the surrounding countryside. Visible from miles away, it was the tallest structure south of the Washington Monument. This "gigantic hatchery for space vehicles" became perhaps the most striking symbol of the American space program, one for which only superlatives would do. Its doors opened wide enough to admit the United Nations building "without a scratch on the paint." It enclosed more space than the Pentagon and the Chicago Mer-chandise Mart combined, or nearly four Empire State Buildings in volume.[91] On humid Florida summer days it even generated its own weather. High up at its ceiling, cold and warm air collided to send precipitation down onto the heads of workers below. There was nothing subtle or elegant about this "polished box of rather outlandish size."[92]

Size served a purpose, though. Capable of housing four giant Saturn rock-ets at once, it was a spaceship factory, a vertical factory. Rocket stages came in through its massive front doors and were stacked toward its ceiling, as workers made incredibly delicate and precise movements of parts as big as a house. All day long, workers moved up and down, by elevator or stairs, and swarmed around the rocket like bees in a hive.

Constructing the VAB was one of the most impressive feats in the build-ing of the Center. First, draglines and bulldozers scoured the land clean of palmetto and orange trees. Then the giant 4,500-horsepower rotating heads of dredging machines cut through everything in their path, including islands seven feet high. Workers slurried fill dirt to the building site so that by July of 1962 the foundation area had been raised from 1.5 to 7 feet above sea level.[93] Some of the nation's leading construction firms—Morrison-Knudsen, Perini, Hardeman—came to the Cape to erect the superstructure. It was, remarked the construction superintendent, "more like building a bridge straight up" than erecting a traditional high-rise.[94] The simple box design allowed for enclosure of vast amounts of space, but also subjected the structure to tre-mendous stress from high winds—like a giant box-kite, feared the design-ers. The solution was to drive thousands of tubular steel pipes into bedrock 160 feet below the surface. But in the brackish underground water, the steel

4-4. The Vehicle Assembly Building under construction. When completed it would for a time be the world's largest building.

tubes acted like monster wet-cell batteries until welders attached copper wire to ground them on the rebar in the concrete foundation.[95]

Crucial to the mobile launch concept was a means to transport the stacked rocket from the VAB to the pad. Designing a transportation system for a rocket and its launch tower that could traverse four miles without a spill was one of the key engineering challenges of the moon program. Based on its existing earthmoving equipment, the Marion Power Shovel Company came up with a 2,700-metric-ton caterpillar-tread transporter. It was big, though not the biggest machine the company had ever built. Powered by two diesel-electric engines making 2,740 horsepower each, it moved along a tread belt of fifty-seven "shoes," each weighing nearly 2,000 pounds. Capable of speeds up to 3 miles per hour, it was naturally dubbed the crawler. On a platform larger than a baseball diamond, the crawler would hold the Saturn rocket and service tower, and deliver its load within a margin of two inches. For the route, engineers constructed a special road as wide "as the New Jersey Turnpike," a crawlerway made of eight-foot-deep river rock.

The crawler's destination was one of two launchpads four and a half miles from the VAB. These pads were a far cry from the simple stands of a few years earlier. To withstand millions of pounds of rocket thrust required a platform of cellular reinforced concrete and a 40-foot-high flame deflector. It all rested on ground made solid with enough fill dirt for an 80-foot-high pyramid.[96]

Pad, crawler, and VAB formed the main working parts of the mobile launch concept, an industrial process where men moved heavy equipment, turned wrenches, attached hoses, and physically readied and inspected the vehicle. The brain center of the whole affair sat next to the VAB, a sleek new Launch Control Center that would house the computers and consoles to run the countdown. Unlike the VAB, the Launch Control Center was human scale. It was one of the few buildings at the Center designed explicitly with both function and symbolic meaning in mind.

As project architect Martin Stein saw it, if the VAB was the factory, the LCC was the "window to see the world which was to be." Its large windows of tinted glass, two centimeters thick, gave an unimpeded view of the launch-pad. The feeling was of being at the prow of a ship. Covering the outside of the windows were long louvered screens in aluminum frames. They looked

4-5. Key KSC design engineer Don Buchanan rests his hand on one of the outsized caterpillar treads of the crawler.

4-6. The Launch Control Center under construction, next to the Vehicle Assembly Building.

like blast deflectors ready to be lowered in case of an explosion, though in fact they were mere Venetian blinds to filter out glare. Infrared lamps prevented the windows from fogging and blocking the all-important view.[97] A partition between the viewing platform near the windows and the workspace below allowed important visitors to be in the room and partake of the action, while keeping them at a safe distance. Incorporating as much flexibility for the future as possible, the firing rooms were open, with no columns, and had removable floors under which ran cables and wires to the large mainframe computers.

The emerging moonport captivated architects and designers in the 1960s. Despite its outlandish scale and relentless use of concrete (or perhaps because of them), many found the planned technological landscape of the space center a compelling alternative to the unplanned ugliness of the modern urban environment.[98] It was a strange model for architects to take for the future. Little about the launch complex was built with beauty in mind. Little of its specialized equipment and structures served human activity outside of the space program. But the LCC won the 1965 Architectural Award for industrial design nonetheless.

Besides this part of the new Merritt Island facilities—the "shooting end"—there was another called the "industrial area." Here in the Operations and Checkout Building (O&C) the Apollo spacecraft to carry the astronauts was assembled and inspected before moving to the VAB. Since the Apollo vehicle, technically the "payload" of the Saturn rocket, was under the control of the MSC in Houston, the O&C also became the site of MSC's Florida operations. In one wing of the building, astronauts resided while awaiting the start of countdown. Just across the way sat the LOC headquarters. This administrative hub was arguably the grandest building on the property, multiwinged, four stories high, topped with a penthouse containing the offices of upper management. Called simply the Headquarters Building, it stared out at the bizarre complex of pipes, rail lines, extraordinary machines, and immense steel and concrete boxes, providing little more than functional accommodations for NASA and contractor managers. With its pebbled concrete walls and aluminum-framed windows, it resembled an unusually large 1960s-era public high school. Its meaning, and even its charm, lay in the complete lack of pretension. The headquarters cafeteria served the same solid American fare to workers, technicians, engineers, and administrators

4-7. A view on the future: the observation deck inside the Launch Control Center.

4-8. KSC Headquarters Building, designed in appropriately modernist International style.

alike. There were no executive dining rooms. The Headquarters Building's symbolic load, if it could be said to carry any, was the equalitarianism of technical competence.

In a race charged with such heavy freight as freedom-versus-totalitarianism, even the most technical aspects of the space program invariably expressed something. From military origins centuries ago to the skyborne terror of the V-2 and the psychological strain of the nuclear age, rockets had largely been weapons of fear. But in the American civilian space program, rockets were to be linked to peaceful and scientific purposes. Their appearance became less menacing. In 1959, NASA administrator T. Keith Glennan ordered that all NASA vehicles be painted boldly with UNITED STATES in block letters down the side. There would be no mistaking whose vehicle this was, but the lettering also made clear that this was an open program, not a secret one.

Early launches at the Cape had always attracted onlookers, whose cars lined the roads leading to Merritt Island. When those launches were largely military affairs, secrecy took priority over the public's curiosity. Many a time the "official" word was "launch? what launch?" as reporters watched the fire in the sky and heard the roar of the engines.[99] But with the birth of a civilian agency, that began to change. The first of the curious to get a peek at the new NASA facilities in Florida were the families of the Center's workers, who were permitted to drive their cars around the grounds on Sunday afternoons beginning in 1963.[100] That year Congressman Olin Teague persuaded James Webb to give the general public similar access.[101] Self-driven automobile tours were soon permitted between 1 and 4 P.M. every Sunday. The Sunday drivers increased to more than a quarter million in 1964.[102] A single visit often won over even space-race skeptics, demonstrating the symbolic power of the Cape as the "Free World's springboard into space."[103] After his visit, New York congressman Victor Anfuso told colleagues back in Washington that "Cape Canaveral can become the hope (or the graveyard) of the free world."[104]

One prominent visitor affirmed the significance of Cape Canaveral, and gave the launch center the resonant name it would carry down to the present day. John F. Kennedy toured the site three times, in visible demonstration of his commitment to the project he had started. On his first visit, Milt Rosen at NASA headquarters told Center director Debus to place emphasis

4-9. John F. Kennedy, the man who started it all, on one of his visits to what was then called the Launch Operations Center at Cape Canaveral.

on "physical things," not just scientific or conceptual matters. With budget discussions coming up, the president wanted to see "where the money is going."[105] Kennedy continued to follow the program closely, including early tests of the crucial Saturn rocket, which he watched on television. He made another visit on November 16, 1963. After briefings by Debus and Petrone, the president toured Merritt Island by helicopter, observing the pads and the VAB under construction. Still concerned about Russia's head start, he asked what the chances were the United States would pull even with its foe. Then, after viewing the launch of a Polaris missile, Kennedy boarded his plane and returned to Washington. A few days later, he headed to Dallas, Texas.[106]

On November 29, 1963, with the nation still in mourning, President Lyndon Johnson renamed the LOC the John F. Kennedy Space Center and renamed Cape Canaveral Cape Kennedy as well.[107] All NASA property on Merritt Island became known as the John F. Kennedy Space Center. Live television images covering the events and aftermath of the November 22 assassination were beamed around the world. Relay I, a communications satellite that had left Cape Canaveral the previous year, made coverage of Kennedy's funeral the world's first real-time global event.

People of the Cape

On April 14, 1965, workers hoisted a four-ton steel beam covered in autographs 525 feet to the top of the VAB. The steel framework of the great building was complete, and ironworkers celebrated with the traditional "topping out." This ceremony marked a milestone of such significance that the ironworkers were joined by Kurt Debus and other dignitaries in a round of speeches.[108] A few weeks later on May 26, the Kennedy Space Center Headquarters Building formally opened. In mid-September, Operation Big Move brought 7,000 KSC employees and contractors out of the rented space in Cocoa Beach into gleaming new facilities on Merritt Island.

By 1965 the Center had assumed not only the physical but also the organizational form it would have through the Apollo era. That year the Goddard "unmanned" group was transferred to KSC and officially became the Unmanned Launch Directorate, headed by Robert Gray. Transferred intact, the group largely retained its autonomy, but that was a mixed blessing. With the moon race reaching a crucial phase, the "Apollo guys were pretty pushy," Gray remarked. "We kind of got pretty irritated . . . because [when] they wanted to arrange a schedule, they usually got it."[109] Recognizing that "people of both organizations may tend to be reluctant" about the move, Kurt Debus counseled "all personnel of KSC [to] make the GLO [Goddard Launch Operations] group feel welcome."[110]

The origins and years of independence of the Goddard group had given it a strong and distinctive culture. As was true of other groups coming together to form the Kennedy Space Center, culture could be an effective tool for getting the job done. But distinctive subcultures within the organization could also make for mistrust and misunderstandings. Debus and his top people often still spoke German among themselves. No one recalled any animosity about working with German engineers, but occasionally a bit of cultural pique surfaced. A sign mocked trespassers in pidgin German: "Achtung! Alles Lookenspeepers. Das Computenmachine is nicht fur gefingerpoken and mittengraben."[111] More seriously, the different groups that made up Kennedy Space Center had their own ideas about launching, their own experiences with vehicles and missions. These would ferment into differences of opinion about how the work of the Center was best organized and accomplished.

Twenty offices and divisions now reported to Debus.[112] With the exception of NASA's small Scout vehicle, launched from Wallops Island, Virginia, and liftoffs from the Western Test Range in California, KSC had responsibility for checkout and launch of all NASA vehicles. The promise of a single, independent launch center had been fulfilled, but now organization had to become more formal and hierarchical. In the early days, nearly everyone reported directly to Debus, and the director was on the phone often to Gray out at the Cape, Petrone directing the construction of the Apollo facilities, von Braun at Marshall, and NASA headquarters. Debus and his lieutenants maintained a hectic pace of travel, eased slightly by use of a Lockheed Jetstar corporate jet, perhaps the finest of its type available in the 1960s. This centralized system of management reinforced the sense that the director was the "top engineer" or chief scientist of a team of highly trained experts. But it was a management system that could not survive as the Center grew. That was an issue that KSC would soon have to confront.

Through the mid-1960s, though, KSC was still small enough to exhibit certain community-like aspects. This was reinforced by the nature of the work, which was about getting things done on time. The performance of engineer and technician alike bore directly on mission success, even if one was programming a computer and the other was installing a switch. One small mistake by either could lead to failure. Differences and conflicts, such as those with unionized construction and installation workers, generally took place outside this work structure. Those building the facilities were temporary, transient workers. They did not participate in what would become the defining event of the Kennedy Space Center—the launch.

This sort of rough equalitarianism of work did not extend to all aspects of the Center, of course. The space program may have been one of the proudest achievements of modern America, but it was not outside the mainstream of American culture. At KSC as elsewhere, managers and engineers were men, and their secretaries women. Although women had been present from the start, most did not do technical work. They took notes, filed papers, kept the books. A few also worked in space medicine or as computer programmers, more rarely as electrical engineers. Female engineers found themselves hemmed in by rules and traditions that hinted (sometimes subtly, sometimes not) they belonged elsewhere.

Images of life and work at KSC at this time show employees dressed in rather stuffy business attire—dark suits, narrow ties, and white shirts for men; dresses, hose, and heels for women. Yet in an operations center there was simply too much big equipment to move around for the suit to be the defining uniform. Out in the field, even women changed into work pants. They were, however, required to change back into dresses when returning to the office. For some it meant a routine of five or six quick changes a day.[113] Articles about the Center's female staff still resorted to adjectives such as "vivacious," and could not resist highlighting the "only girl" in a group of male workers. Human interest stories told of "Cape Gals" competing in beauty contests. Cartoons joked about supposedly traditional female attributes. "I wish I hadn't been cleared for secret," one showed a secretary lamenting. "It's been driving me crazy not being able to talk."[114]

KSC, and NASA in general, was more welcoming to women and to minority workers than were most private-sector firms or even other government agencies at the time. Perhaps this reflected something of the modern, pioneering, even revolutionary spirit that space exploration carried. In 1963 the Center's publication, *Spaceport News*, reprinted a century-old poem by Kate Field: "They talk about a woman's sphere as though it had a limit. There's not a place in heaven or earth . . . [w]ithout a woman in it." Now, the editorial concluded, the word "space" should be inserted as well.[115] But headlines such as "U.S. Space Program Open to Women" or "Sen. Smith Cites Women's Role in Advancing Space Technology" appeared in the same publications with photos of the "first bikini" of the spring. One article in June 1963 quoted Dr. Nancy Roman saying, "NASA requirements for women scientists are exactly the same as for men. It is strictly a matter of merit and experience—without regard to sex."[116] But others acknowledged reality when they told women to aid the space effort with "efficiency and encouragement," referring mainly to office and secretarial work. The sense of ambivalence about what women were doing at KSC was captured best in another article in the same issue. Although performing mundane chores, it noted, women secretaries and clerks were carrying out duties vital to the success of the

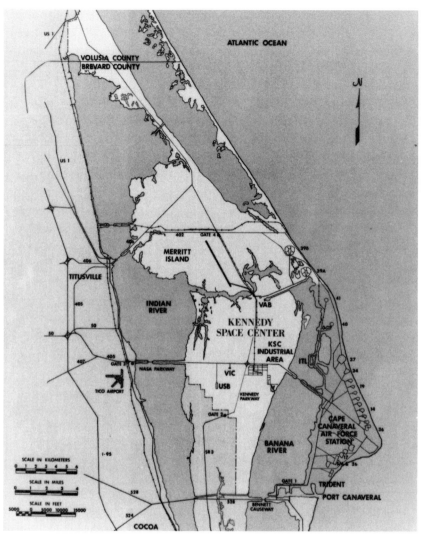

4-10. Map of the Cape and Merritt Island showing the Kennedy Space Center.

program by "relieving her boss so he (or she) may concentrate on more important matters."[117]

With Lyndon Johnson staking much of his Great Society domestic program on civil rights and desegregation, KSC and other NASA facilities became "showcase[s] for equal employment opportunity."[118] If a new federal agency dedicated above all else to science, enlightenment, and the representation of American freedom could not be a beacon of equality, then what part of the government could?

A memo by Kurt Debus noted that "President Johnson has requested that Federal Agencies give special emphasis to improving the employment and advancement opportunities for women." He directed all KSC personnel to "demonstrate full equality of opportunity without regard to sex," and to not permit "personal attitudes to operate aversely against women." Noting that "conventional assumptions of negative employment characteristics of women" had been discredited by a recent study of the Civil Service Commission, he looked for a positive program that would recruit women into the higher levels and pay grades of work at KSC.[119]

Similar progress was expected on race. This proved a greater challenge, as the pool of black applicants was smaller than that of women. Hiring qualified African Americans into KSC's professional ranks suffered because of long-standing segregation practices in Florida and surrounding states, as well as the availability of similar work in California and Massachusetts, states more appealing to well-educated black Americans. Although Florida probably provided a less hostile environment to black recruits than did Alabama, home of the Marshall Center, both installations met only the minimum standards for diversity set by the Kennedy and Johnson administrations.[120]

Roads, bridges, a railroad, steam pipes, water and sewer lines now crisscrossed the land of the Kennedy Space Center. There were service facilities ranging from warehouses and power stations to cafeterias, auditoriums, a barbershop, and a credit union. But the vast launch facilities still needed considerable fine tuning. Like a giant machine just powered up, KSC hummed with anticipation.

5

*
*
*

The World's Greatest Engineering Project

"It was kind of like elephant breeding down there. Nothing happened very fast, and when it happened it was really big."

Donald Scheller

Jules Verne would have liked America's plan for getting to the moon. No magic gravity-defying metal, just the biggest engineering project the world had ever seen. The Apollo program was more audacious than the Panama Canal, more difficult than the Hoover Dam, and more expensive than the Manhattan Project. For all the unknowns about space travel, for all the innovation, in the end, good solid engineering using known techniques and materials made the difference. Nowhere was this more evident than in the blue-collar section of NASA, the Kennedy Space Center. Beyond all the research, mathematics, and fancy hardware, what most stands out during the early years of the moon race was how much back-bending work it required, whether bending over a desk with a pencil or over a 36-inch pipe with a wrench. Workers who had been installing plumbing came to the Cape to build launchpads. Engineers who had been designing sugar mills tested rockets.[1] It was work that brought its own special problems, technical, organizational, and personal.

Moon Widows

"This could be construed as a fan letter," began the wife of one KSC worker, "but as much as I admire and like you, this is a missive about something that bugs me." What was on her mind that prompted this letter to Kurt Debus? Plenty, and the letter revealed an anxious woman afraid for the effect the space program was having on her marriage. "We were brainwashed too many years to ask our husbands any question about what goes on at the Center," and now she did not know what to say to her spouse. Actually, she

5-1. In the pre-Disney era, visitors were content to step into a trailer containing simple displays and artifacts laid out on card tables.

continued, maybe she and her husband had "just lost the knack of talking to each other." It did not require a space program for husbands and wives to lose touch, but perhaps she could reestablish contact if she had a better grasp of what her husband did. "Maybe," she hoped, "we could be better and happier wives if we understood more." A symposium for the layperson, classes to explain in nontechnical terms what was going on at KSC, would help her understand "how one can put a satellite in the heavens and station it there and transpose a picture back to our television sets."[2]

The letter back was gentle. "I have long cherished the hope," Debus replied, "that a way would be possible to make understood the relatively simple principles which underlie space flight." He continued: "I have often wondered how we could get the wives of our space workers and ... the interested public at large" to feel nearer this work. "Your letter," he concluded, "may well hold one of the keys that could help unlock the problem and open the door to a successful solution."[3]

Debus was being honest, for he had become intensely interested in the public face of the space program. In 1965 he would receive authorization to spend $2 million on a full-scale visitor center.[4] By 1967, half a million visitors were flocking to KSC annually, a figure that would double by the end of the decade.[5] But he also understood that better information and adult education would not solve the personal problems contained in this letter. "We need a great many understanding wives here," Debus told an interviewer, and he commissioned studies of how stress affected health and aging.[6] A pediatrician in nearby Titusville, home to many space worker families, even noted a high incidence of ulcers in children. "It is my opinion," the doctor concluded, "that the life generated by the Space Program [is] basically unhealthy for the families of space personnel."[7]

Work and environment bred a special sort of discipline. Young men and women just out of college, lured to the Cape by promises of bold adventure, were ready and able to put in 24-hour workdays. Precisely because they were young, and from rural or small-town worlds far removed from advanced technology, they brought to their tasks a blissful ignorance. "We were too young to know we could fail," many reflected later. The work required intense days that left revved-up workers roaming their houses like caged animals until their next stint. Families and friends were pushed aside, vacation plans rearranged to meet the launch schedule. As the deadline for the moon shot neared, space workers narrowed their lives to that one goal. Looking back years later, a common refrain from those who worked on Apollo was "I missed the 1960s."

Work Culture

The lunar program sparked an intense debate within NASA on how space work should be done. At Peenemünde, von Braun had essentially run a vertically integrated organization. Since people naturally tend to stick with what they know, this earlier work tradition carried over to the American space program.

The German work culture put a premium on individual responsibility and hands-on expertise. There was no elaborate structure of inspectors overseeing the work. Indeed, some who came to NASA from the military were surprised to find that KSC did not originally have a separate quality assurance organization.[8] Those actually doing the work were responsible for quality. It began with give-and-take between the test conductor and assistant engineer.[9] Each engineer had responsibility for his area of work—a particular part, component, or subsystem. At each level, the engineer determined what needed to be done and then supervised technicians who actually did it. Next, the engineer and technician went over the work to see it had been properly completed. If unsure, they were expected to ask someone else to validate it as well.[10] If an engineer determined that a change was necessary, he simply "checked with the boss," the chief engineer, who had "a 90 percent vote."[11] Overall coordination came from the chief engineer, the technical expert on the entire rocket. In the early years, the highest technical authority was Kurt Debus himself. But the fundamental responsibility came much further down the line. Even if he did not fully agree with a move, Debus would back it if one of his trusted engineers was sure, though with a finger in the gut and a "you had better be right" to remind them of what was at stake.[12]

The model this German tradition implied was a scientific laboratory. A team of "rocket scientists" carried out research and development work with the goal of gaining greater knowledge and understanding of engines, guidance systems, flight dynamics, and the like. This extended down to testing and launch operations. Not merely a manager of an organization, Debus was the "chief scientist" of space launch operations.

Those who worked this system remember it as a "tight" but informal one. Since individual responsibility and expert knowledge ranked high, people came to know and understand each other, and know whom they could trust. Knowledge gained from operations was formalized through written books of procedures. But one did not need a massive trail of paper, since the responsible parties for each operation were clear. Particularly in the early years, small scale and close relations made for open lines of communications up and down the hierarchy. People did not stand on ceremony or worry too much about who was assigned what job. "If you needed to install an antenna, you had to get a sack of concrete, you had to dig the ditch to lay the cables for the power to the antenna. I mean you had to do everything." The same informality extended off the job. "Even when folks came from out of town it was still a very small group."[13] Workers would often see Debus and his family on weekends at Cocoa Beach. Von Braun brought his family down for launches as well, even in the rough early days.

Familiarity meant ease of communication and interaction vertically as well as horizontally. Information flowed readily from Debus at the Cape to von Braun at Marshall. Since most of the key technical personnel at the launch center had come from Marshall, they could draw on a wealth of common experience and common knowledge. "We knew them by name," veterans of these years pointed out, and could talk to the design engineers at Marshall about making changes in the field.

The advantage of the German tradition was in finding and correcting errors. "Stressing" rockets "to the breaking point," Debus argued, not only "proved" that the vehicle was ready to fly but actually "achieved" reliability.[14]

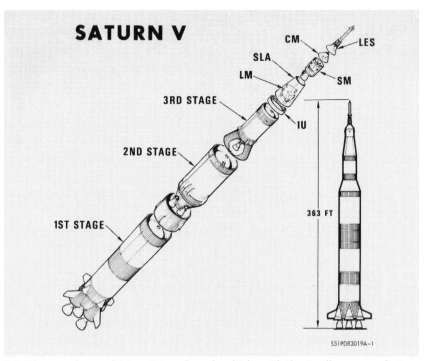

5-2. The complex, multistage Saturn launch vehicle, with the Apollo spacecraft at the top. Many contractors contributed to the different stages.

Step-by-step testing allowed engineers to isolate problems in a scientific manner and incorporate the lessons learned for later designs and operations. This research-oriented approach gave those with hands-on experience plenty of insight about the technology they handled. Americans were amazed when the Germans seemed able to tell by the color of the flame if the rocket was flying right.[15]

This approach worked quite well through the early years at the Center, in part because of the simplicity and small scale of the rockets. Redstone, closely derived from the V-2, was "mom and pop" scale. The new rockets, Saturn in particular, were "a Wal-mart."[16] Size matters, and with the lunar program, technology grew two orders of magnitude in size and scale. The first humans rode Redstone rockets capable of 78,000 pounds of thrust. Titan rockets powered Gemini into orbit with 474,000 pounds of thrust. The Saturn IB that launched early Apollo missions stood three times higher and required six times the fuel to generate ten times the thrust of anything ever launched.[17] That was just the beginning. The Saturn V employed three stages of boosters. The first stage generated 7.5 million pounds, the second more than a million pounds, and the third some 200,000 pounds of thrust.

In the Mercury and even Gemini programs, astronauts sat perched atop the booster in a small capsule with just enough room to carry them as they flew into earth orbit and back. The lunar program, however, required a true spaceship, capable of leaving orbit, traveling to the moon, landing on and blasting off from the lunar surface, and flying back to earth for an ocean splashdown. This much bigger task would be performed by a craft named Apollo. Apollo consisted of two parts, a service and a command module. The service module housed the equipment of space travel, including rockets and fuel for propulsion and maneuvering, oxygen and other life support, and the lunar vehicle that would land on the moon. The crew sat in the much smaller command module, in front of the controls, on takeoff and reentry. Apollo used computers, guidance systems, instrumentation, and environmental technology that far exceeded what had been available for the Mercury capsules.

With the multistage Saturn booster and sophisticated Apollo vehicle, traditional launch methods faced some tough questions. How could informality be maintained as the size of the organization expanded and the number of workers grew? How could one maintain control over all the complex systems and subsystems, and their interfaces, with a multistage, multiengine rocket whose "payload" would be a complicated spacecraft and landing vehicle?

Change in methods and organization at KSC was not driven solely by these technical issues. Like the Germans, the Americans too had traditions they took into the space program. Those included a political tradition averse to big government institutions. From military work with rockets, the private sector in the United States had acquired substantial skill, knowledge, and capacity with aerospace technology. As had been true with the construction of KSC, contractors would play key roles in vehicle design and fabrication, mission control, and launch operation.

From 1963 to 1968, seven-eighths of those working at KSC were contractors.[18] At the height of the lunar program, KSC employed 8,000 contract workers in launch operations, plus another 10,000 providing support functions, all supervised by 800 civil servants.[19] Prominent roles were played by most of the nation's major aerospace firms—McDonnell Douglas, Grumman, North American, Boeing—as well as Chrysler, General Electric, RCA, and IBM. Though these firms received the majority of contracts at KSC, NASA also employed nonprofit institutions, other government agencies, and thousands of small businesses in various capacities, providing research, specialized pieces of hardware, and clerical and cleaning services.[20]

No one had ever done launch operations with this many contractors and on this scale before. The first of the changes came as civil servant technicians doing hands-on work gave way to contractor technicians. In the German model, control ran top to bottom, with the chief engineer supervising those responsible for subsystems, who oversaw the work of those actually touching the rocket. "We had to detach ourselves from doing part of the job and start tracking the efforts of thousands of contractors," noted one veteran of these years.[21] The hands-on work now would be done by contractors from the firms fabricating the part, system, or stage of the rocket. As contractors took over, the old NASA technicians became quality inspectors. It was for many a traumatic experience. These were not college-educated engineers but trade-school-trained technicians who liked "pulling wrenches, hauling cables, hooking up meters." Overnight, they stopped handling the equipment they loved and began looking over the shoulders of others now doing their old jobs.[22] Worse, they had to teach them how to do it. "Teach, but don't do it yourself" was a hard rule to follow, and some simply left, convinced that "the fun went out of the work."[23] Even those who stayed suffered. They thought, incorrectly, that NASA did not trust them anymore.

Supervising contracts involved a "complete job reorientation" for engineers, and KSC held management seminars beginning in 1964 to teach them the new skills required.[24] More formal methods were needed as well for tracking the large number of technical interfaces and coordinating the huge numbers of workers from multiple organizations. Bureaucracy came to NASA. It was not just any bureaucracy, however. Top officials at NASA headquarters looked to the management techniques developed by the air force after World War II for its weapons systems. Going by various names— program management and systems engineering most prominently—they were used in the military ballistic missile development and testing programs running side by side with the NASA programs at the Cape.

The air force techniques differed significantly from the German rocket tradition. They placed emphasis on engineers managing entire systems rather than on being expert in a particular function or discipline. The key technical problem was not how the electrical or mechanical components would function, it was how an entire stage or an entire vehicle, with all its mechanical and electrical systems, its instrumentation and guidance and the like, fared when everything came together. Systems engineers paid special attention to managing the interface points between subsystems, and in this they had authority over the chief engineer of the old German approach. Given that many people were working on a vehicle, it also became crucial to assure quality of work. This was done not by direct lines of authority from chief engineer down, but through increased use of quality inspectors. At KSC, of course, these inspectors were often men who, just a short while before, had been doing the very job they were inspecting, a fortuitous situation that gave them great insight into the work they oversaw.

Perhaps the most crucial actor in the air force model was the program manager, who took charge of the entire project. Now, in addition to the vertical chain of command up and down areas of engineering expertise, there was a crosscutting "horizontal" chain of command in the program office. Certain engineers in fact had two bosses—the head of their engineering unit and a program manager, creating a matrix structure.

The program matrix was ideal for rapidly focusing the attention and skills of diverse technical experts on a specific goal. In this, it contrasted with the traditional functional organizational chart, which was best suited to carrying out routine, repeated actions over the long haul. KSC had functional divisions covering the main engineering disciplines—mechanical, electrical, instrumentation. But this sort of vertical structure bred "silos," or a sort of specialized narrowness. For a project like Apollo, there had to be some way to penetrate those silos and bring the different functions together, for the lunar program needed all these specialties and disciplines.

By cutting across functional lines, program management quickly marshaled the skills of experts on a specific problem, permitting them to learn and adapt as the project developed.[25] Through use of budget and schedule, program managers also revealed the interrelationship between quality, time, and cost. Rather than attending only to their own area or piece of equipment, engineers would hear from the program manager how what they were doing would affect the entire project schedule and budget. Systems engineering bred a similar concern for the project as a whole. In a functional work structure, each line engineer would design or change a piece of equipment to make it perform better. Systems engineers, by contrast, considered the impact of any design change on the overall system, rather than any one part. Program managers approved such a change only after they calculated its effect on cost and schedule. This was rather different from the German tradition, where changes would be made all the time as engineers, through testing and launch, found or learned new things—the "laboratory model." In the air force model, quality improvements were still possible, but now they could be explicitly weighed against financial and time factors, as well as their impact on the entire technical "configuration."

At NASA headquarters George Mueller, who had worked on the air force's ballistic missile program, took charge of the Apollo program in his role as associate administrator. The heads of KSC, Marshall, and MSC reported to him.[26] KSC realigned to meet this new structure, placing Rocco Petrone as head of its own Apollo Program Management Office, which sat on a level just below the director's office in the organizational chart. Petrone, like his program counterparts at the other centers, also reported to NASA headquarters' Program Office, run by General Samuel Phillips. Phillips was a protégé of General Bernard Schriever, the most important figure in the development and use of program management and systems engineering in the air force during the Atlas missile program. Phillips had been brought to NASA precisely to instill these same techniques in the lunar program.

The new approach did not emerge all at once. From the perspective of NASA headquarters, there was resistance in the field, particularly at Marshall, where the German tradition was so dominant. Mueller tried to explain to Wernher von Braun how important it was to embrace systems engineering with the coming increase in rocket size and complexity. He emphasized as well the importance of having control of the interfaces between von Braun's Saturn rocket and the evolving Apollo spacecraft being designed in Houston. All this, Mueller argued, required a program management matrix that put engineering disciplines in communication with each other and also with the aerospace contractors.[27]

Behind these seemingly dry technical matters was in fact an emerging difference in worldview about the space program. Von Braun, coming out of Germany and then the United States Army, still believed that a single organization having complete control over everything would be most efficient. In his view, moreover, each launch was an opportunity to learn something that could contribute to future technological development. As he had written famously in his *Collier's* series, the conquest of the moon was only part of a package that included stations, shuttles, bases, and missions to Mars. From that point of view, time and schedule and budget were less important than learning and improvement and research. This research approach, however, would not meet President Kennedy's deadline. Nor could it work in an American political context. In an ideal world, perhaps von Braun had a point, but in America, management would have to embrace organizational diversity. Mueller, with experience in the air force and big companies such as Bell Labs, foresaw a NASA composed of many geographically separate installations and a large number of contractors, each with its own traditions and organizations. This would require a strong formal system of management to coordinate the work of diverse actors.

Still, neither the use of contractors nor the new management ideas greatly affected life at the Cape, at least not at first. As we shall see, one of the enduring themes in the history of the Center has been its ability to adapt and evolve a variety of work and management cultures. In the early 1960s, the Center remained a "badgeless" world. "We tried to work it as no difference in badges. Badges were a means of identification only," said one engineer.[28] "We never got into, 'Well, I'm the boss cause I'm NASA and you're the contractor, so go do it this way."[29] Contractor technicians supported government engineers, who worked side by side with contractor engineers, preparing tests, evaluating results, solving problems.

This blithe ignoring of lines dividing the public and private sector was all the more surprising given the high percentage of contractors working at KSC. Only 7–9 percent of NASA civil servants worked at Merritt Island in these years, compared to the 20–25 percent working at Marshall. Though small, the civil service workforce at KSC had substantial rocket experience. They "shadowed" the contractors mission by mission.[30] This resulted in some duplication, but those who worked under the structure also believed that it had advantages, a system of checks and balances that assured accuracy and quality.[31] Data would be examined by both NASA and contractor eyes, problems or anomalies discussed between the responsible NASA engineer and his contractor counterpart. Differences of opinion were brought up the next level of the organizational chart. Information flowed up and down this chart, though in accord with the team concept, as division chiefs, systems engineers, and integration engineers pored over problems.

The air force method, by contrast, required an "unbelievable paper trail." Authority was exercised through the system and the program, rather than through the technical expert. Those who had grown up in a world where "accountability and responsibility was vested in the individual" were soon scratching their heads over the myriad signatures they had to get for almost any change. As Wernher von Braun slyly commented, "We can conquer gravity, it is the paperwork that gets us." Aspects of the older, less formal approach could thus still be useful, particularly at the Cape, in operations. Program management, after all, was a tool for governing development and manufacturing, not operations. Theory aside, the hardware still had to work once it got to the Cape, and in this world, one still had to rely heavily on the performance of partners and colleagues. In the "fishbowl" of operations paced by the clock, it was clear when someone messed up. There was no hiding behind the organizational chart. In the end, when it came time to fire the engines, most KSC people wanted to put their trust in a person, "not in a piece of paper that has twenty signatures."[32] Observers often came away puzzled by this strange mixture of "rigid formalism and casual disregard for hierarchies" at KSC.[33]

Debate about organization and management raised once again the question of how operations fit with the design and fabrication of space vehicles. When part of a design center, launch operations had struggled to keep up with almost constant changes in rocket configurations being made by engineers working with a technology still under development. This made it difficult to proceed systematically through testing to discover problems that caused launches to go awry. In Germany, even with everything under one roof and carefully tracking design changes, the tension between development and operations was constant. So by controlling configurations and interfaces, the program management techniques had advantages for KSC. But they came at a cost as well.[34]

When launch operations were attached to Marshall, Debus had been able to "close the loop" between testing and design. The whole philosophy of systems engineering, however, reinforced the sense that operations involved little creative work. Systems engineers, not engineers in the field, made crucial decisions about what to change and what not. Specifications, plans, and integration were all assumed to be done at the design stage.[35] Little new knowledge, it was thought, would come in field operations. Debus continued to argue the contrary. Skillfully designed work-arounds were frequently needed to deal with unexpected problems that arose only at the point of operation. Unique and useful knowledge was being generated by testing. "The preflight and flight operations at the launch site have to be considered as of equal importance to a program as all other design, development and assembly operations," he wrote to Joseph Shea at NASA headquarters. Shea was one of the new breed Mueller had brought in to carry out the new management agenda. Debus's argument followed the logic of the German model, which gave "the flight test engineer the opportunity to introduce his requirements for preflight test into the basic system design."[36] As the Apollo program geared up, however, Debus and others who thought as he did would become voices in the wilderness.

Some believed that needed integration and coordination between design, fabrication, and operations could take place at the top of NASA's chain of command. For a time, headquarters attempted to orchestrate the work of its three main centers for human space flight—Kennedy, Marshall, and MSC. But the independent centers largely resisted that move. In 1962, for example, NASA contracted with General Electric to develop checkout equipment for launch operations, evaluate reliability, and carry out an integration function in Apollo. This followed the air force model, where private contractors not only performed work but also managed and oversaw the work of other contractors. Too much skill, knowledge, and experience, however, resided with the government engineers who had led the early space program. This knowledge allowed them to understand and "penetrate" what their contractors were up to. For all the talk of headquarters supervision, NASA still depended on its strong field centers, where "the real muscle" was.[37] These centers were loath to give up their supervisory function. KSC successfully opposed any move to give GE a management role integrating the Apollo program.[38] Coordination and integration would remain a civil servant task.

Rocco Petrone proved unusually skilled in handling the new manage-rial system, while recognizing its limits and potential problems. Attempts to provide coordination higher up NASA through management councils, Petrone believed, were "largely worthless." Rather, problems of integration had to be resolved at the technical level at each center. At the Cape, Petrone formed panels that brought together different functions, which met regu-larly to make key decisions. These "dotted line" relationships, he noted, cov-ered many things. Decisions made by the panel would then be enacted by the various line organizations.[39]

The type of guy who could "get the job done, whatever it took," Petrone was a natural program manager who handled the Center's external relations with other NASA installations. There was a fundamental conflict built into NASA's structure. Other NASA centers and contractors had every incentive to push work out the door to meet their schedules. When launch opera-tions at "the end of the line" ran behind schedule, the other organizations would complain loudly that KSC was "taking too long." Petrone, ready for this complaint, would then show how the delays were caused by incomplete equipment, changed orders, and other unplanned contingencies dumped into KSC's lap.

While the new ways of working in the Apollo program generated new conflicts and concerns at the management and engineering levels, one old source of tension declined at KSC. Improvements in labor management eliminated or reduced many of the conflicts with blue-collar workers seen in the first half of the 1960s. Center management became more skilled by 1964 in preventing "little walkouts" and slowdowns that reflected unarticulated worker grievances.[40] By monitoring the count of workers passing through the Center gates, KSC management soon was alerted by a sudden reduction in arrivals that something was amiss and quickly moved to investigate. New procedures were issued to contractors on jurisdictional disputes between different craft unions as well. The Program Management Office and the In-dustrial Relations Office established interface points between union respon-sibilities, so it was clear who had control over what work. These efforts paid off, and the Center enjoyed a record run of 250 strike-free days.[41]

The declining volume of construction on Merritt Island naturally tended to ameliorate labor conflict. The number of construction workers on-site fell from a high of 8,000 to fewer than 2,000 by 1966. Construction workers moved from job to job and had only temporary loyalty to any one project. By contrast, the unions that would be working at the Center from now on would be industrial unions, representing employees of various contractors supplying equipment and building vehicles. Industrial workers and their unions enjoyed long-term relationships with employers and hence tended to identify strongly with their industry.[42]

Cultural differences between blue-collar workers and civil servants still caused problems on occasion. A tempest in a teapot brewed up when a handful of workers were found to be "inspecting the wrong kind of heavenly bodies." Ten workers from the Bendix Corporation were caught watching burlesque films in the Bendix shop area near the VAB. The films were dutifully turned over to the Brevard County Sheriff's Department, and the workers were asked to leave. Though this was exactly the wrong sort of publicity for NASA, few at KSC would have been shocked by such behavior in the intensely masculine world of physical labor. A few days later, though, five more employees were fired for playing cards after a ban on gambling had been put into effect. These workers were eventually rehired when it was determined that it was a friendly card game and not on company time, but it was clear that management at the Center was jumpy after the movie incident.[43] Overall, though, the excitement about the moon launch seemed to have quelled the strenuous labor discontent of earlier years. No Apollo launch was cancelled or delayed because of strikes or work disputes.

A New Philosophy

Facilities capable of launching the Apollo-Saturn vehicle were just being completed as the first Saturns arrived at the Cape for testing. The initial Apollo missions, orbiting the earth and using the Saturn IB launcher, would rise from Complexes 34 and 37 on the Cape itself. The Merritt Island facilities, designated Launch Complex 39, could handle the more powerful Saturn V. By 1965 most of the Merritt Island construction work was over, but the launch complex still needed to be rigged and tested. Here the troubles began.

Changes in rockets meant changes in ground equipment and procedures. During the Mercury program, data from tests filled about a page every second. The Apollo-Saturn configuration relayed 300 pages of information each second.[44] The Saturn V required 2,500 connections between ground and launch tower and another 800 between tower and vehicle.[45] Such requirements dictated increases in the amount and sophistication of ground support and launch equipment. All this would have been work enough, but the Saturn vehicle did not evolve in a smooth, predictable way. Even as ground facilities were being completed, the rocket was changing size, adding weight, and growing in complexity. Each vehicle configuration meant a corresponding reconfiguration of ground operations and equipment.

Saturn had evolved into such a big and complex machine that initial assumptions used to design the facilities at KSC soon fell by the wayside. Rather than thirty-plus launches per year, launch rate expectations quickly fell to thirteen, then six, below what Debus had calculated was the minimum to justify his mobile launch approach on financial grounds.[46] The reduction in launch rate was not just a problem for KSC, it was a problem for the entire lunar mission. Launch methodology was evolving incrementally, though fairly rapidly, as the Saturn family matured, but that was not sufficient.

The traditional approach taken by Debus following von Braun of carefully testing each stage and system would require some forty-five flights to qualify the Apollo-Saturn hardware. First there were to be six flights of the uprated Saturn I. Then the components of the Saturn V would be tested step-by-step in six unmanned launches. Testing would proceed until each booster stage had been verified, both separately and in an integrated configuration. At just six launches per year, there was no way America was getting to the moon by decade's end this way.[47] On October 30, 1963, George Mueller at NASA headquarters made the fateful decision. Testing for the Saturn would go "all up." Rather than testing separate stages, the entire rocket would be tested at once.

Mueller based his decision on military experience. Because military hardware always involved a race with one's adversaries, the missile developers at the Department of Defense had abandoned the incremental testing philosophy beginning with the Titan II missile program. All-up testing became de rigeur in the Minuteman program.[48] The air force saved time and, in the end, money by testing all up, Mueller believed. It was the only way to meet the decade deadline.

This was a radical break with the German philosophy of flying each stage separately to isolate problems. Indeed, some saw it as a gauntlet thrown down to the Germans. They had ironed out problems with separate stages or subsystems before conducting integrated tests. This methodical approach, skeptics thought, suited the methodical German personality. But to Debus, it was the way that certainty was produced. Mueller's critics charged that he was forcing them to live with uncertainty. But the real difference was in how knowledge was acquired and what was done with the results.

Both approaches aimed to reduce the risk of failure. Where the Germans did so by acquiring deep insight into how rockets performed in many different environments and configurations, program management emphasized acquiring sufficient knowledge to be sure that the technology would perform as desired under certain circumstances. It was not necessary to know everything about a rocket to know that it would do what it had to for a specific mission. Instead of learning about the rocket empirically through testing, the all-up approach was built on careful control of design and specification during the development and fabrication phases. Along with the new testing philosophy came a greater emphasis on "configuration management," or the fixing and stabilizing of hardware designs so that changes were well understood and fully documented. If a problem should occur, Mueller's approach presumed that it could be traced back through the documentation, rather than isolated by further testing and retesting. Methodical testing procedures, it was true, gave designers opportunities to correct errors. But they introduced their own form of uncertainty. Design changes responding to test results were hard to keep track of. In a small, tight-knit group, operating small-scale vehicles, with close collaboration between designers and testers, that might not matter. In a big, complex project that followed a tight schedule, it would be impossible to maintain the necessary level of communications. The scientist's quest to keep on learning and trying something new and better had to be subordinated to design certainty and performance within a schedule and budget.

Mueller's all-up decision was thus a major departure in test and launch philosophy. But like the new management techniques, it did not unfold exactly as planned. While acknowledging that the traditional approach of testing might not be fast enough, Debus maintained that it would still be necessary to "test to failure." Particularly when trying to isolate problems in "incompatible and immature" parts, some of the traditional methods could be of use. Testing had to be done within the accelerated schedule of the lunar program. Debus intended "to take whatever steps are necessary to keep KSC from becoming the pacing unit" of the program.[49] But where sufficient data could be gathered to establish "statistically significant reliability," some of the older approach would remain.[50] This might be read as resistance to headquarters' preferred policy. But as we shall see, the gap between high-level plans and actual operations at KSC often reflected necessary adaptations to real-world conditions.

Organizing for Apollo

The decision to go all up put pressure on KSC to revamp the way it did business. Complete systems rather than components would arrive at the Cape. The schedule called for flight-testing the Saturn V by 1967, while flights of the Saturn IB with astronauts aboard were to be completed by the end of 1968. Thus two new vehicles would be prepared, tested, and flown at the Cape in overlapping schedules, with a trip to the moon to take place soon after.[51] With the Center moving full tilt toward the lunar mission, further organizational changes were needed.

"You can't fly this thing by the seat of your pants," explained Rocco Petrone. "You have to have a system. There is no human being who can understand it all."[52] The idea that organization might be as important as technology or individual competence in getting to the moon was hard for some to swallow. Those who had started at the Cape working in tiny blockhouses firing human-scale rockets enjoyed a rather democratic environment, one with little need for hierarchy. In this world, "manager" was not a term of respect. Bureaucracy and bureaucratic self-interest were things to oppose. Indeed, many believed that as a fired-up new agency, NASA could overcome the sort of narrow, short-term thinking found in corporate America, and in other branches of the federal government. Charged with a mission of transcendent importance, NASA was supposed to be different.[53]

When KSC gained independence from Marshall in 1962, Debus followed von Braun's practice of having his subordinates write weekly one-page summaries of their activities. These weekly notes would be distributed to top Center management along with Debus's comments, frequently requests for oral reports. While perhaps not so rigidly as his mentor in Huntsville, Debus also scheduled regular meetings of top Center staff. These traditional methods no longer sufficed. Debus had to focus on the big picture. By 1965, reorganization of KSC meant that far fewer people reported directly to him. Instead of hearing from five assistant directors, he now conferred with two deputy directors, one for management and one for operations. These deputies oversaw main Center directorates with such names as Apollo Program, Launch Operations, Technical Support, and Design Engineering.[54] Unmanned Launch Operations director Robert Gray reported to G. Merritt Preston, deputy director for launch operations.[55] In 1966, KSC adjusted its structure to the basic form it would take in the Apollo era. Debus added Albert Siepert as his deputy director for center operations and gave up his role as launch director to Petrone. Under Petrone were the main operational divisions, notably Launch Vehicle and Spacecraft. Petrone now had responsibility for coordinating all the work that prepared craft for their countdown to zero and assured that the many operations moved swiftly and safely to that moment of truth.[56]

Formal organizational change did not, however, forge the space center into a single culture. Healthy tensions, and some unhealthy ones as well, remained among the different groups of workers who made up the space complex. Spacecraft technicians, for example, were under the supervision of Houston, and they let everyone know it by wearing distinctive yellow hard hats labeled MSC (Manned Spacecraft Center) while working at KSC.[57] Facilities engineering and support services, on the other hand, were shaped by the traditions of the Army Corps of Engineers, which had constructed

5-3. In the Operations and Checkout Building adjacent to KSC Headquarters, engineers prepare the Apollo spacecraft, as their counterparts work on the Saturn booster in the VAB.

the Center. Contractors added their own personalities to this frothy cultural mix. Grumman people, from the East Coast, were a boisterous lot, while North American Aviation workers from the West Coast were laid back. "When the Grumman guys would have a problem, there'd be a group of people standing together yelling, arms in the air, waving and things like that," recalled chief engineer Ted Sasseen. "When North American had a problem, there would be a couple of guys hunched over whispering. We had to run after Grumman and we had to push North American."[58] General Electric, contracted by headquarters to impose integration on the various NASA centers, was viewed as headquarters' spy. McDonnell was generally seen as a no-nonsense outfit that quietly got its job done.[59]

In midsummer 1964 Ernie Reyes joined KSC as an operations engineer. Within a month after his arrival two hurricanes, Cleo in late August and Dora in early September, had brushed the Cape, leaving floodwaters and some damage in its wake. The floodwaters bred new generations of small frogs. Reyes and his family had arrived from arid White Sands, and the frogs frightened his wife every time she left the house. When Reyes had a difficult time with a NASA inspector, he blurted out, "You are nothing but a frog. All you do is you eat and you poop. You don't contribute. You ain't helping us." What began as an insult quickly became a badge of honor. Within days NASA quality inspectors were uniformly referred to as "frogs." Other positions had equally colorful nicknames. Technicians, in Reyes's lingo, were mullets, the baitfish in the surrounding waters. Operations engineers were sharks because they ruthlessly ate the baitfish. Contractor inspectors, who sealed their inspections with a reddish substance similar to pelican droppings, became pelicans. These nicknames reflected the informal structure of work at KSC. "Tiger teams," made up of specialists from the Center and key contractors, supervised problem areas. Launch support personnel, who stayed on the launchpad most of the time, were "pad rats."

The mixture of personalities, traditions, and work cultures at KSC subtly undercut the image of bureaucratic super-rationality and technical determinism often expressed in NASA's own public self-image. Publicly, NASA administrator Webb portrayed the space program as a model organization whose methods and structure might be successfully adapted to solve social problems such as urban blight and poverty. "The way in which we have built up our space capabilities and what we have learned in the process," he wrote, ". . . may well constitute as important a contribution to our nation . . . as the space capabilities themselves."[60] As children of the big science, big technology, and military-industrial complex of the Cold War, NASA leaders fervently believed that sophisticated systems of technology required sophisticated systems of management. But the formal structures of management were still populated with real people, who could be imaginative, hardworking, fallible, or stubborn.

Site Activation

Some have compared KSC's Launch Complex 39 to Palos, the port from which Columbus sailed on his fateful voyage.[61] Columbus, however, did not have to build, test, and certify his port before he could use it. Between 1964 and 1968 the pads and other equipment needed for the moon launch were activated or, in essence, "debugged" as a giant computer system might be before delivery to its user. In fact, as with a computer, the debugging took place while the users were using it.

The job was placed in the hands of a new man at Merritt Island, Lieutenant Colonel Donald Scheller. He brought strong qualifications to the task. Scheller had studied mechanical engineering at Johns Hopkins University before joining the Army Air Corps. During World War II he piloted B-17 missions over Europe. After the war Scheller served in a variety of missile research programs, including working on development of the Sidewinder missile. As chief of the Atlas missile program at Vandenberg Air Force Base, Scheller directed twenty-two launches. There he also gained hands-on experience with the air force's program management techniques. Finishing his tour of duty at Vandenberg in 1964, he met his old friend Sam Phillips. Could Phillips, he asked, help him get into the Apollo program? Phillips could not have been more pleased, for he was looking to bring more air force personnel with experience in program management into Apollo. Initially Phillips intended to have Scheller impose program management at Huntsville. But Scheller had a better idea. Why not take advantage of his strong background in launching missiles and send him to KSC?[62]

Knowing that KSC was in danger of falling behind if it did not get its new facilities up and running, Phillips agreed. Time was now crucial. Russia remained a formidable competitor. In October 1964, just as Scheller was settling into his job, Voskhod 1, the first three-person spacecraft, blasted out of Baikonur Cosmodrome in Kazakhstan. The Russians were still very much in the running for lunar glory.

Scheller would need all his skills to keep on top of his job. Forty thousand pieces of equipment had to be brought together from many different contractors, and it all had to fit and work as one system. Just getting it all there required a massive logistics program. Then came months of fitting and testing. Then it all had to be cleaned, as freight cars of cleaning fluid arrived. No wonder everyone thought site activation would be the Achilles' heel of the moon schedule.[63]

Launch Complex 39 differed considerably from those that Scheller had worked on at Vandenberg. The mobile launch concept introduced a host of new technologies, such as the crawler and the mobile launch tower. That plus the constant changes to the configurations of booster and spacecraft made activation like trying to hit a baseball for the first time. A thin stick of wood, a fast-moving sphere, and the unpredictable aerodynamics of flight made batting an art best learned through practice, not by studying the physics in a book. Scheller would have to go beyond what he knew and learn as he went.

Initially Scheller worked with John Potate, setting up "planning and control" in the Apollo Program Office.[64] Potate had graduated from Georgia Tech with a degree in industrial engineering in 1959. Following two years at the Department of Defense he joined KSC in 1961, working site activation for Launch Complexes 34 and 37. His successes there landed him the primary scheduling responsibility for Launch Complex 39 (LC-39).[65]

A lack of configuration management, Scheller recalls, was one of the biggest problems he faced. Phillips's *Apollo Configuration Management Manual* provided the requisite policies for NASA centers, but KSC had had difficulty implementing them during the construction of LC-39.[66] To make matters worse, other centers had been adding equipment and modifying circuits at KSC without proper authority. Scheller quickly argued for a configuration control system to cover all NASA facilities at Merritt Island.[67] But he faced resistance, clashing with the German tradition. Wernher von Braun argued forcefully that the Apollo program required more flexibility than configuration management allowed.[68] The German stage-by-stage approach anticipated leaving room for resolving configuration discrepancies in the testing process. When NASA moved to all-up testing, this was no longer possible. The key part of site activation consisted of an extended march to the 500-F test. This was a dress rehearsal for the first launch of the massive Saturn V rocket. Before that test could take place, eight mission support contractors and five aerospace contractors, in addition to a dozen craft contractors, had to complete their work installing the equipment.[69] Only by carefully controlling and managing changes would it be possible to guarantee that all components would be ready in time.

Rocco Petrone established configuration control boards at the Center, which had to approve major shifts in design. Scheller meanwhile identified some twelve different drawing release systems in use at KSC, none of which guaranteed that designers could maintain configuration. A new part would commonly be given the same number as the old part it replaced. With the ever-changing designs of the Saturn rocket and concomitant design changes of ground support equipment, the result was chaos. Different contractors,

5-4. Verifying KSC as operational required an elaborate site activation process. The chart illustrates the paths of work to complete site activation.

providing various rocket stages and ground support equipment, had no way to be sure that their components would properly fit together when they arrived at Merritt Island. In an attempt to gain control over design changes, Scheller and his assistants adhered to the air force's configuration management manual, often producing regulations by simply replacing "Air Force" with "NASA."[70]

When the U.S. military responded to Sputnik and a feared "missile gap" with its own crash missile program, it needed a way to operate on a tight deadline. One outcome was the Program Evaluation Review Technique (PERT), developed jointly by the U.S. Navy, Lockheed, and the consulting firm Booz Allen Hamilton.[71] PERT began with a listing of all activities necessary for completion of a project and the order in which those activities had to take place. Project managers then made a flow chart of estimated schedules for each activity. Following the flow chart allowed them to pay particular attention to "critical paths," or those activities that would take the longest and therefore determined the completion date of the entire project.

For all its strengths, though, PERT could not be adopted wholesale at KSC. As with other new management techniques, it required significant local adaptation.[72] To schedule activation, John Potate used three interrelated networks and four schedule "flows." In Network A he followed the primary site activation milestones. In Network B he monitored the scheduling of major elements necessary to meet Network A milestones. In Network C he used the traditional PERT diagram to trace the progress of each component required to accomplish the schedules in Network B. Four flow charts tracked the work. One followed facilities and equipment needed for the first launch of the Saturn-Apollo vehicle. Another showed activation work to be completed in time for the second big launch. A third flow tracked the activation of LC-39's Pad B and related facilities that were planned for the launch of the third Saturn V rocket. And Flow 4 handled any remaining facilities not directly needed for the first three launches.[73]

Taking over Firing Room One at the Launch Control Center, Potate installed huge charts displaying the progress of site activation. It became his "war room."[74] Each contractor and each NASA office operating at KSC had a desk in the war room, and there they had to show how they interacted with other contractors or NASA offices. Boeing served as integration contractor, maintaining and running the computer analysis that established the primary, secondary, and tertiary critical paths toward activation. Scheller would use those critical paths to put pressure on the different organizations, identifying those that were falling behind or holding up the work of others.[75] Still, for all its value, PERT had to be applied carefully to be effective. Without modification to accommodate the needs of contractors, it could easily be misused.[76] There were simply not enough hours in the day to look at "every little nook and cranny."

No amount of scheduling refinement could deal with unexpected technical breakdowns or hardware glitches. A number of critical pathways were going to have to be moved along quickly to stay on schedule. The charts soon showed that a problem with the liquid oxygen lines would wreck havoc with the schedule. The lines had not been properly cleaned before installation and as a result were subject to corrosion in the swampy environment of Merritt Island. Dismantling the lines and returning them to the factory for cleaning would push back site activation by a year.[77] Delaying site activation that long would delay the moon landing beyond President Kennedy's goal. Improvisation on the spot was needed to work around this problem. Wyle Labs came to the Cape, set up laboratory trailers, and began cleaning the lines on-site.

As checkout proceeded, more unforeseen problems arose. The mobile launcher that accompanied the Apollo-Saturn vehicle on the crawler came in overweight. The crawler was mighty, but it still could handle only twelve and a half million pounds. There was no time to change the crawler. Instead engineers went back to the drawing board on the service structure. But the new version came in at a mere ten million pounds, seriously underweight. It could not withstand the strain of a speedy mile-and-a-half-per-hour journey, so the crawler speed was cut back to half a mile per hour to keep the tower from swaying.[78]

The crawler's first trip to the pad was scheduled for November 1964, but suddenly another problem emerged. Initially the crawlerway was to consist of a base of sand, covered by selected fill, then a meter of graded lime rock, then an asphalt macadam surface. But when the crawler took to the road, its treads picked up the macadam surface. Loud cracking noises and high hydraulic pressures also disturbed the test crew. KSC engineer Don Buchanan proposed that hydraulic pressures would decrease if the crawlerway were surfaced with a "solid lubricant." A mixture of Alabama river rock and crushed granite eliminated the problem of sticking asphalt. But workers found bearing components strewn along the path. Designers had miscalculated the horizontal coefficient of friction. Redesign would force the moon launch schedule into the next decade. Once again, on-the-spot improvisation was needed. And once again it came from KSC's top design engineer, Don Buchanan. He saved the day by using phosphor bronze bearings in place of the originals. Despite serious skepticism from consultants, the new bearings worked beautifully.[79]

The crawlerway was not finished making a nuisance of itself, however. One morning Scheller noticed a large puddle of water covering both tracks of the path. Soil analysis by the Army Corps of Engineers revealed that one section of the crawlerway rested on an unstable patch of clay. As the heavily laden vehicle crossed that section, pressure pushed the clay through the sand to one side, causing the path to subside. Initially it appeared that the only answer was to dig the clay out and replace it with compacted rock. Once again the schedule was in danger of slipping past the decade goal. The Corps of Engineers provided a timely alternative: drive sheet pilings along the edges of the crawlerway, locking the clay in place. What had appeared to be months of work was reduced to days.

Finally the troublesome crawler was under control, but only just in time for new problems with liquid oxygen lines. These aluminum pipes could carry liquid oxygen to the launch vehicle at a high pressure rate of 10,000 gallons per minute. Before the pumping started, however, technicians would prechill the lines by cracking a valve and letting a small amount of liquid oxygen trickle through. When they tried this on a hot July day, the frigid liquid oxygen ruptured the warm pipes, and 2.7 million liters of liquid oxygen poured on to the ground, temporarily creating the "world's biggest Popsicle." But that was the least of the worry. The inner LOX tank had buckled from the sudden loss of pressure as the liquid oxygen rushed out. Replacement of the LOX tank would have forced serious delays in site activation. Don Buchanan suggested an elegant solution. After draining the remaining liquid oxygen, engineers filled the tank with water until the dent popped back into place. Dye penetration tests showed no cracks in the tank, and within two months LOX was flowing out at Pad A.

It was surprising how often the trip to the moon was made, or saved, by basic engineering, so basic that it went back to ancient times. When tests required a television camera to zoom in on a part of the rocket at launch, the answer was not to design a new camera to withstand the rocket's thrust and flame. Instead, conventional cameras were left unmounted to the structure, attached to bungee cords. When the blast of liftoff blew them back, they fell harmlessly to the ends of their tethers, away from the flame. When it came time to test how much the 360-foot Saturn V rocket would sway in the wind as it sat vertical on the pad, KSC engineers came up with the "tennis shoe test." Half a dozen men lay on their backs on the service structure, wearing tennis shoes to protect the rocket's skin, and pushed with their legs against the nose of the missile. After a few minutes of leg- pumping, they generated enough momentum to start the Saturn moving, enough to measure its oscillation. It was a great example of fancy engineering footwork, and better than building a giant mechanical shaker that might shake the Saturn to pieces.[80]

In mid-November 1965, 72 percent of site activation procedures were behind schedule. Scheller required each contractor to develop its own PERT charts and established biweekly formal reviews.[81] Activities showing "negative slack" became the focus of management attention. Once a delay in the critical paths was identified, Scheller put pressure on the appropriate contractors or NASA offices to bring the schedule into line. By the end of January 1966, events behind schedule had been reduced to 29 percent.[82]

Even as hardware problems were overcome, the schedule confronted problems of logistics. Late deliveries of electrical and pneumatic lines added new "negative slack" to site activation. Some 39 pneumatic lines and 200-odd electrical cables remained uninstalled. The General Electric plant in Daytona Beach appeared to be the source of the problem. While temporary fittings and other work-arounds permitted crucial tests to go ahead on schedule, the failure of GE to deliver equipment became intolerable.[83] But the problem, it turned out, lay with Marshall rather than with GE.

General Phillips called a meeting with Wernher von Braun, Arthur Rudolph, the Saturn V program manager at Marshall, Petrone and Scheller from KSC, and representatives from GE. Scheller outlined the problem of missed schedules. Phillips put up a nine-by-twelve poster showing GE's original proposal and estimated costs, then detailed change after change that the engineers in Huntsville had imposed. General Electric had been unable to complete parts before Huntsville made more modifications to the designs.[84] Phillips insisted that Marshall personnel get together with GE representatives immediately after the meeting and select one set of drawings for GE to use. After that, Scheller recalled, there were no further problems with deliveries.[85]

Program management had, in this case, triumphed over the German tradition of continual development. Petrone sent Willard Holcomb to Huntsville to ensure that the designers there would abide by configuration regulations and keep to the schedules. At KSC, Scheller also froze design changes being made by Launch Facilities Director Theodore Poppel.[86] With design configurations frozen and revised PERT schedules in hand, technicians at KSC still needed to work two shifts a day to complete the support equipment installation in time for the 500-F test. But at least the facilities were nearing readiness. No longer did site activation determine if and when the United States would start on a lunar journey. But plenty else did.

6

＊
＊
＊

Lunar Rendezvous

Rocco Petrone was worried. It was already 1967 and the lunar program was still behind schedule. In 1963 he had confidently predicted, "One day in this decade an American will land on the moon."[1] As a young army ordnance officer, Petrone had helped to launch the first Redstone rocket in 1953. He joined the team at the Cape in 1960. There he had overseen the construction on Merritt Island of a new technological world carved out of scrub and brush. Now he was beginning to wonder, had his prediction in 1963 been overconfident?

Petrone had the right personality for his job, which friends said was "integrating the whole mess."[2] Everything about him suggested a no-nonsense approach to work. A former fullback and captain of the Army football team, his imposing physique, penetrating look, and willingness to master every detail gave him a significance that exceeded any title. He could be brash and demanding, a harsh taskmaster. Even friends noted ruefully that his blunt manner placed him right in step with the Germans in NASA. Petrone didn't schmooze, and he had no qualms about stepping on toes, even the big toes of those higher up. His philosophy seemed to be "management by embarrassment," a common tactic used by aggressive project directors. At his meetings, no one in "the fishbowl" wanted to be the reason why work was being delayed.

Where Debus was the scientist pondering an intellectual problem, Petrone was a hands-on manager, battling crises late into the night when other top officials had gone home. Many thought he might have a photographic memory, catching contradictions in pieces of information relayed

6-1. Perhaps the most important manager at KSC in this era and one of the crucial figures who got America to the moon, Rocco Petrone.

to him months apart. He often knew the real story before the experts. He was so good at cross-examination that someone suggested he had missed his calling as a district attorney. As much as he disliked incompetence, he disliked indecisiveness even more. He cut off meandering subordinates with an order to stop "bugling" (the old army term for it) and give an answer. When it came time to make a decision, Petrone was just the sort of person to make it, knowing that every decision was fraught with some uncertainty.

No one doubted Petrone's competence, nor his ambition. He did not take on the job to be liked, and many believed he met his goal all too well. Those who got on his bad side could seldom be rehabilitated. But others recalled a more complex personality. A "tough, ruthless SOB" when he had to be, he was also "typical Italian . . . Catholic, goes to Mass . . . heart of the world." Those who survived his onslaughts usually thrived, and loved him for his leadership skills and ability to make the tough decision. "It's just like a football team," the former army fullback explained. "I praise and, when I have to, I criticize. Men need to be led, and know that they are being led."[3] The problems he encountered, though, were enormous. The moon mission was a task of Herculean proportions, a race with "calendar, clock, and Russia."[4]

Petrone called together leaders of the Center's main working units. The conference lasted long after 5 P.M. and into the night. As the frustrations with delays and problems grew, he put aside his normally commanding voice and presence for a moment and walked to the window. There was the moon. "Gentlemen," he said softly, "I hope you realize that we are going to be up there in eighteen months."

The Moon in History

Seen on clear nights in the mild Florida winter, the moon is a tempting target. Above Merritt Island it rises so full and sits so low that it almost meets the eye. It looks as a moon should look, perfectly round, dark crater spots visible, bathing the ground in a pale yellow glow. Thin strips of backlit clouds periodically cross its path, as though portending something imminent. It looks so big and full that it seems incredible that anyone ever doubted it could be reached. But the American rocketeers of the 1960s were just the last in a long line of suitors seeking to unveil the lunar mysteries.

Speculation about the moon goes back thousands of years in Western history. Philosophers since Pythagoras have debated the possibility of life on earth's satellite. In the first century, Plutarch wrote *De facie quae in orbe Lunae apparet* (Of the face that appears on the moon), which gave serious thought to lunar geography and climate. Though Plutarch correctly inferred that lack of clouds meant an arid lunar climate, he hoped that the dark spots might be water. We continue to call them *maria*—seas—after his incorrect assumption. In the second century, Lucian of Samosata wrote a story of sailors lifted to the moon by a giant waterspout in the Straits of Gibraltar. It was perhaps the first example of space fiction in Western literature.[5]

Not until the Copernican Revolution of the sixteenth century did speculation about the moon take a scientific as opposed to a philosophical or literary bent. The astronomer Johannes Kepler, though using the literary device of a dream in his story *Somnium*, was also concerned with careful, realistic, scientifically valid astronomical description. In 1638, thirty years after Kepler, the English theologian John Wilkins published *The Discovery of a World in the Moone, or, A Discourse Tending to Prove That 'Tis Probable There May Be Another Habitable World in That Planet*. He sought to reconcile religious truth with the new science. Science and religion, reason and romance, continued to do battle over the moon in the centuries that followed.

The tradition of scientifically informed, but literary and speculative, treatments of the moon and of outer space in general crescendoed in the nineteenth century with the works of Verne and Wells. Wells worried about vexing moral and social questions flowing from the headlong pursuit of technological progress and scientific knowledge. In this the Englishman contrasted with his French counterpart, Jules Verne. The Frenchman applauded American technical know-how and audacity in his fictional account of a trip to the moon. Anticipating correctly the attitude of American space pioneers a century later, he wrote that "their only ambition was now to take possession of that new continent in space and plant the star-spangled banner . . . on its highest peak."[6]

The generation of Americans who would run the space program had grown up seeing the lunar voyage portrayed in cheap pulp magazines such as *Amazing Stories*, and in science fiction films from the early silent *A Trip to the Moon* to the 1950 exercise in Vernean precision *Destination Moon*. The visuals associated with popular stories suggested, against Wells's warnings, that the means of reaching space were advancing smoothly and rapidly. No moral qualms or social issues stood in the way. Sleek metal rocket ships would soon leave earth's tenacious grip and land directly on the lunar surface, ready to blast off again for home at any time. The craft for traveling in space looked like modifications of the streamlined trains, planes, and automobiles of industrial society. Conquering the technical challenges was the main thing; the reason for going needed little further elaboration.

Just at the moment when those means were actually coming together, however, questions about purpose resurfaced. Not everyone had been swept up in the call to arms issued by JFK. In 1963 Philip Abelson, editor of the prestigious journal *Science*, conducted an informal survey of fellow scientists and found that they saw little of value in the moon shot—"two or three television spectaculars and that's that."[7] Around the same time, a Gallup Poll counted 58 percent against versus 33 percent in favor of going to the moon. Indeed, the percentage of people against the moon mission actually rose slightly in the years after Kennedy's pronouncement. When asked in 1965 if America would be better off spending NASA's four billion dollars on space or on antipoverty, Medicare, or national defense, a majority voted for each of these alternatives. Cutting taxes versus spending for NASA was a virtual tie, so this was not a time of fiscal conservatism.[8]

A sense of doubt sometimes reached even to NASA. During the buildup to the Apollo program, articles appeared in the KSC publication *Spaceport News* with titles like "Where's the Pay-Off?" The answer was often found in a quotation from NASA administrator James Webb, who touted the value of exploring the unknown above practical rewards, or even Cold War prestige. "Those who view the lunar program as simply a propaganda effort," Webb wrote, "fail to grasp that not only our prestige, but our capacity for constructive international leadership [and] our economic and military capacity for technological improvement depend on our ability to achieve acknowledged superiority in science and technology." Technological achievement was well enough ingrained in American culture that it could be its own justification. Lyndon Johnson lamented the "fashionable outcry against science itself" when he was asked why go to the moon. Like America's presence in Vietnam, the moon was impossible to abandon once commitment had been made.[9]

In "You and the Moon," Kurt Debus bolstered any wavering confidence of his troops by telling them that the United States had pulled even with the Soviets, who were trying to back out of the race, knowing they could not win. It would be foolish to yield now to "practical" cries of "slow down" and "cut the budget." The moon shot was only a down payment on future missions with bigger payoffs. Space exploration was "here to stay."[10] Imagination and speculation about the unknown still fueled the desire to see the moon close up, as it had 2,500 years earlier in Greece. But now the means were available.

Two Work Cultures

Following Debus's mobile launch concept, KSC had a clear plan for uniting booster and spacecraft. The Saturn was stacked and readied in the VAB. Here it became clear that this, the dominant building on the Cape, really was "not a building but an intricate machine that assembled the vehicle in its final phases." Until they entered the cavernous VAB, the various stages of the rocket had not met. Each stage was fabricated by a different contractor, as were other components. Only late into the processing did all the pieces of technology finally come together. Yet when they met, every wire and every plug had to match, physically, electrically. It was a ponderous task. "When the instrument unit orders 'Go right,' you don't want an engine three stages down to go left," remarked Rocco Petrone.[11]

In theory, the powerful new techniques of management were designed to handle this very issue. They had helped to get site activation on track. They had given rise to a new, innovative approach to testing. Yet reality on the ground at KSC showed that two distinct approaches to work still existed side by side at Merritt Island. Whatever the advantages of the innovative new techniques coming out of NASA headquarters, they were seeded in an environment composed of people who had learned how to launch rockets under a different structure and in a different environment. It was not possible to simply rebuild the Center and its personnel from the ground up. Important actors at the Cape, notably Kurt Debus, Hans Gruene, and others, were German émigrés whose experience and knowledge had been crucial to the early American missile program and early NASA. Though cultural ties of history and language among the German émigrés helped to cement working relationships, this was not an exclusive group. Americans under German mentorship, such as Andy Pickett, who became Debus's protégé, and Ike Rigell, who was likewise close to Hans Gruene, were trained in the same traditions.

The cultural division of work was reflected in the two main technologies of the lunar program. The Saturn launch vehicle, designed at Marshall, was

6-2. Parts arrived at KSC by various means from various manufacturers. They all had to be integrated with other equipment and tested before a launch was possible.

tested and processed by KSC crews who had been trained in the German tradition. The Apollo spacecraft, designed at MSC, was tested and operated by a group under the Houston center. Of course, these divisions of technology and organizational heritage crossed and met at key points. Neither vehicle was wholly the product of one way of working. Still, the divisions were important, and coordinating between the two was crucial.

The spacecraft team, under G. Merritt Preston, operated semiautonomously from the rest of KSC. Through 1965, Preston reported back to Houston, where the design team was led by Max Faget. Debus was a "rocket guy," meaning the booster. Most of the Apollo engineers at Merritt Island had little contact with him. "We didn't have a lot of interface . . . with the launch vehicle," remembered Bob Sieck, though there were "signals passed back and forth between the spacecraft and launch vehicle."[12] His thoughts were echoed by his peers working Saturn. It was a "world divided . . . like we're a totally different program," remembered Tip Talone, who was in the launch vehicle organization.[13]

Spacecraft work was organized around systems. Each system of the craft (eleven in all) had to be tested, and then the entire configuration verified. Similar work had to be performed on the lunar excursion module, the LEM.

These two vehicles also had to work together. This placed responsibility for the working of Apollo largely in the hands of the systems engineers.[14] Much of this work was done in the Operations and Checkout Building next to KSC headquarters, before the spacecraft was moved several miles down the road to the VAB for mating with the booster.[15]

The launch vehicle organization handling Saturn tended to use a more functional, discipline-based engineering structure. Where spacecraft people tried to work end to end on each system, rocket people worked through the technical disciplines of the system. A part, such as a valve, that involved various technical disciplines—mechanical, electrical, instrumentation—would be handled differently in the different work cultures. Spacecraft people would approach it as a single system, with a systems team responsible for the valve. On the launch vehicle, the experts in electrical did the electrical work, mechanical the mechanical, and so forth. The launch vehicle routine reflected the history of how knowledge of rockets had been acquired, by deep penetration of experts in each functional or technical area.[16]

Each vehicle group could point to defects in the other's work culture. Saturn people found the spacecraft organization's approach "a little . . . cumbersome."[17] In the launch vehicle world, work could still be done on the basis of trust and close working relationships, with lots of tacit knowledge and understanding passing back and forth. People, not organizational charts, carried the specific lessons and procedures with them even as they moved into a new environment. Some contractors actually found this sort of relationship too intense, with too much "interference" from the civil servant.[18] It was not an approach designed with contractors in mind. By contrast, the air force methods used on the Apollo spacecraft had grown out of a reliance on contractors, and the need for a system of control and supervision. The spacecraft organization at KSC was therefore better attuned to controlling things, to keeping track of changes, and managing technology as a system.

Naturally, this division of labor led to certain differences of outlook. To Saturn rocket people, the sophisticated Apollo spacecraft was just "the nose cone," a diminutive that went back to the Mercury flights when astronauts literally sat in the nose of the rocket. To spacecraft workers, the mighty Saturn rocket was a mere "booster," something designed to get the astronauts off the earth and then disappear.

Differences in technology also contributed to different patterns of work. "We would go through our schedule, get the work done, and go home at five o'clock," one young Saturn engineer recalled. But spacecraft would continue working straight through with three shifts, exactly the way private aerospace firms operated. A spacecraft technician remembered the same point from a different perspective. "We would joke that the launch vehicle guys had cars without headlights because they always had to go home before dark."[19]

The difference in working hours reflected the different ways the two work processes were organized. Where the spacecraft group operated in teams around each system, the launch vehicle group proceeded step-by-step with supervision from the top engineer in each area. In this latter approach, one could not work round the clock, since it was impossible to have the key supervisor present twenty-four hours a day. Small as they were, such dif-

6-3. Assembling the Saturn instrument unit in the Vehicle Assembly Building.

6-4. Technicians working inside a stage of Saturn.

ferences reflected the sense of belonging to one team versus the other. They also introduced a certain healthy competition. Neither side wanted to be the one that made a crucial error, or slowed down the march to launch day.

As work on the lunar program progressed, it became clear that, rather than conforming to one or the other model, KSC was evolving a mixed work culture that drew on both traditions. Because the two parts of the rocket, Saturn booster and Apollo spacecraft, had to work together, there was a certain amount of cross-fertilization between the two cultures.[20] The Apollo-Saturn program ended up an amalgam of two experiences. Most of those

6-5. Stacking the stages of Saturn inside the VAB.

who worked at the Center in these years eventually came to believe that either approach worked, that each had strengths. By the mid-1960s, "you couldn't tell much difference between the spacecraft organization and the launch vehicle organization."[21]

Like the Apollo vehicle, Saturn involved multiple systems, coordinated by systems engineers and inspected by quality inspectors. The original vertically integrated structure broke down when NASA made the decision to use aerospace contractors to build major Saturn components. These contractors had to do much of the hands-on work during launch operations, making the launch vehicle engineers into contract managers, like their spacecraft counterparts. Likewise, spacecraft people found themselves, de facto, doing far more than just following the grand design of systems engineers. Pieces of the spacecraft arrived at Merritt Island unfinished, with engineering modifications outstanding that had to be closed out. Quality inspections also revealed problems that necessitated redesign, pushing work back to the contractor. When problems occurred, teams of KSC and contractor engineers turned into troubleshooters, tracking down the problem and determining whether the bothersome hardware had to be replaced, refabricated, or redesigned.

Despite the use of contractors on the Apollo spacecraft, KSC spacecraft engineers ended up with a strong sense of "ownership." The word was "you got a problem with your system, be with it."[22] Across contractor and civil servant, a team concept prevailed, much as the team was central to the Saturn vehicle work. Many of the contractor personnel from Grumman, North American, Rockwell, and other aerospace firms remained for long periods at Merritt Island.[23] Like the civil servants, those who got into space work tended to stick with it.

Seen from ground level at KSC, even some of the strongest examples of the new air force–inspired philosophy owed more to the older German tradition than was at first apparent. Mueller's "all up" decision certainly broke with Debus's and von Braun's precedent of painstaking testing to root out faults. Yet all-up testing worked in part because there had already been so much conventional testing. The Saturn vehicle's design derived from the lessons learned about rockets by that same team of German engineers.[24] They had gained a deep penetration of the technology from their hands-on work. Each stage had been fired on test stands. Earlier versions, such as the Saturn I and IB, were thoroughly proofed before moving on to the Saturn V. When the Saturn V flew, it flew with lots of experience behind it.[25]

In 1966 some thought was given to merging spacecraft and launch vehicle operations, at least at certain points. But this was rejected, in part because of the need for "specialized experience and capabilities" to perform what was becoming an elaborate set of tasks. A merger was prevented by "his-

6-6. KSC's chief test conductor, Paul Donnelly *(left)*.

torical differences in the development of the Design Centers" which KSC served. Instead, there would be consultations across specialized areas by senior engineers, and other cross-functional arrangements.[26] As the two vehicles came together, people "integrated across" the two organizations.[27] This became especially strong as the countdown for launch approached. The clock imposed its own special discipline that made differences in approach and outlook simply disappear. "Two weeks before [a launch]," stated Gene Sestile, "you could not believe the cooperation that set in." It was like a switch went off, "brothers and sisters fighting like cats and dogs" and then everyone pulling together "like a family—one of us is under attack, we're all under attack. I've never witnessed anything like it before or since."[28]

In this process, the chief test conductor and launch director were crucial actors. They led the teams that sought out flaws and problems in booster rockets and spacecraft. The test supervisors were headed by Paul Donnelly during the Apollo years. Donnelly was steeped in both traditions, having started in spacecraft operations and then moved to the launch vehicle. The product of an Irish father and a German mother, he felt at ease culturally as well, positioned between the American spacecraft world and the German-influenced launch vehicle world.[29]

Even in the testing process, though, differences remained. Since the Apollo spacecraft would be powered down during its ride through the atmosphere, the role of the spacecraft team was limited until after liftoff. It was the launch vehicle crew that really had to watch the countdown clock and be sure that each step of preparation went off correctly when it was supposed to. Spacecraft engineers were busy checking out the systems on their vehicle, and they had to be done by a certain point, but the flow of work they performed during the hours of countdown did not affect the overall timing of the procedure. They were not disciplined by the clock in the same way.[30]

The master of the clock in this process was the launch director. During the Apollo program, the role of launch director emerged as perhaps the most important of all integrative functions. It was the launch director who brought together Apollo and Saturn engineers, contractors, and civil servants. He also dealt with crucial external actors, such as the air force's range officer and the weather forecasters. The final step of complete integration came when the launch director verified that all systems were go. One hundred people had the power to stop a launch. No one could override the no-go decision of an engineer who saw something wrong. But only the launch director had a "go button" signaling that all was ready. Big issues were at stake in this decision. The danger of launching when not ready was obvious. Less obvious but no less crucial was unnecessary delay, which would rebound back through the entire schedule of tests and launches. If a problem arose on launch day, the launch director had to decide quickly whether or not to pursue a solution. This decision was harder than it might seem, because the launch window was narrow. In space flight, precision of launch and following the clock paid off. The narrower the launch window, the less fuel a rocket needed for course corrections, and the bigger the payload it could carry. Trying to solve intractable problems ahead of the clock was thus an uncertain investment of time and money. It might well be better to cut losses, stop the count early, and wait for another day. Only by thinking ahead to how each step of the launch process affected later steps could this decision be made.

Those who spent time at KSC came to see the strengths of its hybrid work culture. Kurt Debus believed that it was "fortunate" that NASA did not have a "line structured" organization from the beginning. This allowed the centers to do the basic work with minimal interference from above. Project management at headquarters provided just enough coordination, but not so much control as to strangle the strong cultures and expertise at field installations like KSC. Albert Siepert, KSC's deputy director for administration, touted the space program as a "good example of the necessity for gradual evolution and constant improvisation to meet unforeseen administrative developments." Siepert too saw a "wealth of experience in the field," where "local flexibility" produced technological creativity and resourcefulness. The very time-pressured, ad hoc nature of the Apollo program was a source of adaptive strength, as NASA fit its organization and functions to the "needs of the moment."[31]

There was perhaps no better example of "local flexibility" in action during the Apollo years than Rocco Petrone. Though wearing many hats, Petrone basically determined his own areas of responsibility to fit the needs of the moment. Few people at KSC better understood the value of organization to the lunar program than Petrone, but his significance could never be fully measured by a box on the organizational chart.[32] He well understood that individual talent and teamwork required new organizational methods to harness them to the task of getting to the moon. Some people might have argued that a small-scale, organizationally minimal approach, mimicking the work culture of earlier days, was best. But Petrone knew that the size, scale, and schedule of Apollo made such a return impossible. Instead, he activated the organization and breathed life into the empty boxes of the organizational chart. Even in a big organization, knowing people was key. Technique alone was "sterile"; recognizing that every function was performed by a real person, he succeed by being a shrewd judge of character. "Rocco had the uncanny ability to learn quickly who he could trust," those who worked for him recalled. His photographic memory and probing mind were put to use not in doing other people's jobs but in finding those who could do the job right and in pushing aside those who merely filled an office.[33]

In a similar manner, Petrone was able to coordinate work among the many contractors, moving beyond the formal system. Here the heritage of KSC's own technical competence was useful, for contractors were unable to control the situation when civil servants had deep, penetrating knowledge of the technology. The air force used program management to manage contractors, in part because the air force lacked strong in-house capacity, forcing it to depend heavily on contractors. NASA, by contrast, had that in-house expertise, and thus never fully gave up technical control. When conflicts arose, Petrone had a trump card, a government expert who could claim objectivity and independence from the interests of private firms. Petrone did not want "boot licking" from his contractors—he sought out strong management there too—but one reason the program could handle strong contractors was that the depth and capability of the civil servants balanced them out. The result, to use Petrone's own favorite metaphor, was a symphony orchestra playing together in harmony.[34]

Petrone's forceful style combined, like the best project managers, features of the advocate, the entrepreneur, the evangelist, and, one might add, the general, to get work done through people.[35] It was a clear example that even the most modern and complicated of formal organizations is at base a network of social relationships. One of the earliest studies of the space program in fact would note that large, complex projects cannot be managed by purely rational, impersonal methods alone. Programs like Apollo required "not less, but more human ingenuity, improvisation and negotiation than old-style business and government organizations."[36] Later this fundamental insight would be forgotten, even by those who participated in Apollo. Formal organization, more easily represented on a schematic like a chart, was easier to grasp, particularly as the lessons and excitement of the moment faded from memory.

Rough Road to the Stars

Like an orchestra, NASA achieved harmony only through practice, some of it painful. Throughout 1966 NASA administrators worried whether problems with vehicles or site activation would cost the United States the moon. Coordination between KSC and Houston over the Apollo spacecraft proved particularly vexing. The heady innovation needed to build this key part of the lunar system in time to match all the other parts bred a disorderly process. Like Saturn, Apollo was virtually handmade, fit to the needs of mission and crew. North American, prime contractor for the vehicle, worked with dozens of subcontractors and had to make sure that thousands of interface points were compatible. But innovation meant many design changes, a headache for those at KSC responsible for verifying and testing the equipment to get it ready to fly. Despite the more rigorous system of configuration management, many specifications were "TBD" (to be determined), or undergoing change, or simply missing altogether. Personnel from the three or more organizations working on the spacecraft all reported to managers at their own organizations. At times, no one seemed to have overall responsibility.

One checkout, labeled AS-204, had already been delayed because of problems with the Apollo craft to be used in the test. The test vehicle did not make it to the pad until January 21, 1967, nearly six months beyond its original delivery date. Six days later, during a "plugs out" test on Pad 34, the Apollo command module burst into flames, killing astronauts Gus Grissom, Ed White, and Roger Chaffee.

The deaths of the three astronauts rocked the American space program. In the aftermath, some wondered if this was the end of the moon program. Investigations, recriminations, accusations, and finally reform and return to the schedule followed in a matter of months. But the fire also changed things forever, and in ways that were not immediately apparent.

The basic outline of the story of AS-204 (later named *Apollo 1* in memory of the astronauts) is fairly clear. The fire was most likely due to a fault in wiring, though the exact cause was never determined. In the highly pressurized (nearly 17 psi) pure oxygen atmosphere, it would have taken only a small spark to ignite the fire, which quickly spread by consuming flammable plastic materials inside the cabin. As pad personnel scrambled amid smoke and flames to open the module door, toxic smoke inside asphyxiated the three men.

Immediately after the accident, NASA convened the AS-204 Review Board, chaired by Floyd Thompson, director of NASA's Langley Research Center. After several months of investigation, the board identified a number of conditions that had contributed to the accident, beginning with the use of pressurized pure oxygen. Other contributing factors included excess combustible materials in the cabin, vulnerable wiring, and inadequate provisions for crew escape.[37] It took several minutes to open the sealed hatch after the fire was detected, making escape in time all but impossible.

It was, however, investigation into the more remote causes of the fire that proved most disturbing, and that had the long-run impact on NASA. The investigation concluded that no single person, policy, or mistake was responsible. Rather, an accumulated series of decisions had introduced unknown new risks into what was assumed a "nonhazardous" operation. For example, the use of pure oxygen reflected a reasonable testing philosophy of simulating actual flight conditions as closely as possible. But the highly pressurized state of the oxygen at sea level multiplied the risk. Indeed, the possibility of fire in a pure oxygen atmosphere was known from earlier studies commissioned by NASA. One study had concluded that it was likely that "the first casualty in space will occur on the ground."[38] NASA associate administrator George Mueller replied that a fire had been considered "remote" because of "standards of design, manufacture, tests and operations over the last several years."[39]

How had these risks accumulated without anyone noticing them? Understanding that requires going back into the history of the Apollo craft itself, and the problems of scheduling. By the end of 1965 the lunar program was falling behind in its launch schedule. Schedule adjustments resulted in an overlap of the checkout of two of the Apollo-Saturn vehicles, AS-202 and AS-203, which were to undergo unmanned flights. The overlap required the hiring and training of additional personnel to handle the extra work so that the first manned Apollo flight, AS-204, could be brought back on time.[40]

North American Aviation, builder of the Apollo command and service modules, had already been criticized for tardiness. By late 1965 the Apollo program director, General Phillips, had serious doubts about North American's ability to manage its work. After a tough investigation Phillips concluded that the company's quality control was not up to scratch.[41] Quality inspectors were issuing too many discrepancy reports, forcing additional work after a vehicle was delivered to the Cape. There NASA's own quality inspectors found still more discrepancies. When the command module for AS-204 arrived at the Kennedy Space Center in August 1966, for example, it was unfit to fly.[42] The module, complained KSC technicians, had been shipped in "peach baskets." KSC's Apollo program manager, General John G. Shinkle, found at his doorstep a craft with some 164 incomplete engineering change orders. Within a month the change orders exploded to 377. According to Shinkle, 70 percent of the changes should have been identified at North American.[43]

Still, this was not totally abnormal. Contrary to the presumptions of systems engineering, substantial integration work took place at the operations center. To meet schedules, contractors routinely shipped vehicles in an unfinished state, and technicians at Merritt Island completed construction during the mating process. KSC technicians had come to expect this extra work of bringing all the components into a common configuration as part of the launch process.[44] Inevitably, the result was a process of improvisations and work-arounds, lags and catch-up, rather than a smooth progression as on the PERT charts. While Shinkle resolved AS-204's discrepancies, the flight crew of Grissom, White, and Chaffee complained that their Apollo trainer lagged behind spacecraft modifications. Grissom went so far as to hang a lemon by the trainer, expressing his view of its value. Still, he and the others were sure that things would work out, as they always had so far.[45]

Others were not so sure. One inspector at North American, Thomas R. Baron, warned of deep-level problems with quality control. He had earned the nickname DR (Discrepancy Report) because he wrote so many discrepancy reports that his office ran out of the forms. Frustrated by the apparent lack of official response to his warnings, "DR" Baron leaked some criticisms to the press. Soon after, North American fired him.

While many problems with the Apollo spacecraft appeared to be resolved before the fire, others were not. The environmental control system had been replaced once, but continued to malfunction. A balky communication system hindered conversation. Even so, NASA decided to proceed with the next step. The Apollo crew would check out the spacecraft, operating it with "plugs out," or under its own power.

The plugs-out test did not go well from the beginning. Grissom complained of a sour "buttermilk" smell after he hooked up his oxygen line. High oxygen flows sporadically triggered alarms. Environmental control system personnel concluded this was the result of crew movements. Communications failures interrupted Grissom's conversations with the control room. The count stopped for fifty-one minutes while technicians tried to resolve faults in communications lines. During the hold Grissom complained, "How are we going to get to the moon if we can't talk between two or three buildings?"[46]

Seconds after resumption of the count, Chafee announced that he smelled smoke. That was quickly followed by a shout from Ed White—"Fire in the cockpit."[47] At seventeen pounds of pressure per square inch, the oxygen-rich atmosphere could make almost anything burn. NASA had normalized the dangers of the oxygen environment by using it during plugs-out tests throughout the Mercury and Gemini programs. But Apollo introduced new risk elements, including extensive use of Velcro within the command module. Velcro became highly flammable in a pure oxygen environment.

Within seconds, the conflagration consumed the cabin. Firebrands of melting plastic fell on the door, the control panel, the astronauts' suits. Outside the capsule someone saw a hand moving by the hatch window, perhaps one of the astronauts trying to open the door. If so, he stood no chance. The fire caused cabin pressure to spike, putting thousands of pounds of pressure against the inward-opening hatch. Seconds later the capsule ruptured, with tongues of fire shooting out onto the service structure. Pad workers jumped back, and some rushed down to the ground, sure that the fire was going to ignite the escape rocket, or worse. Others ran for extinguishers or scrambled toward the flames. Thick, choking smoke forced them back again. When they finally made it to the spacecraft, they were frustrated by the hatch itself, which had three doors and took a minimum of ninety seconds to open even under ideal conditions. Workers wrestled open the outer door, but the second door, though unsealed, could be lifted and removed only with a special tool. Someone ran back to find the tool as seconds passed. Finally, minutes later, workers opened the inner hatch door to a harrowing scene. Two bodies lay atop each other on the cabin floor, their suits fused together and mixed with melted plastic by the searing heat. The third occupant was still strapped to his seat. But it wasn't flame that had killed them. Long before the hatch was opened, the toxic smoke had ended their lives, probably in less than two minutes from detection of fire.

The men and women of the Kennedy Space Center, and indeed all of NASA, were unprepared for anything like this. Those working the launches had come to know the astronauts well, going back to the Mercury days when the scale of operations was much smaller. Engineers, workers, and astronauts lived close together on Cocoa Beach. They often ate and drank together in the tiny community of early space flight. Many times pad workers had heard the sardonic humor of astronauts counting the number of ways they could die in a space flight. But no one ever thought they would see it happen. Those working during the accident were left stunned. George Page, head of spacecraft operations, recalled sitting in the blockhouse after the fire, just shaking. Others cried openly. Those who had been at home quickly heard of the tragedy, which soon touched all who lived and worked on the Space Coast.

The accident caught NASA management and the public by surprise too. These were the first deaths after sixteen successful human flights and some two dozen Americans in space. It was especially unexpected coming after the early Mercury and Gemini missions, when far less was known about rockets and human space flight. And it was an unexpected ground accident when most of the risks were assumed to be in space or during launches and landings. In the shock, managers did not handle the aftermath well, and NASA was widely criticized in the press for being too closed and secretive. According to one reporter, Debus or Petrone had to personally approve all articles in the *Spaceport News*, the Center newspaper. Other reporters felt excluded from the process. Some complained of outright lies.[48]

Press and public attention now focused not on the space program's achievements but on its inadequacies, even negligence. *Life* magazine produced a special issue on the tragedy, which highlighted the loss of brave young American heroes. Sensationalized accounts such as *Murder on Pad 34* made serious and unsubstantiated accusations against NASA. Members of Congress and the public wondered if space was worth a human life or if the race to the moon had become too intense. Internal KSC publications reflected this sudden sense of doubt. They reaffirmed the Center's commitment to safety, but with the acknowledgement that safety had to have a larger role. Another accident, it was feared, would end the entire human space program.[49]

One significant source of criticism was Thomas Baron, the quality inspector once derided as "DR." Baron had produced a report condemning a variety of practices at the Cape as unsafe or slipshod.[50] His concerns were communicated to Frank Childress in KSC Quality Control and through him to Rocco Petrone and Kurt Debus and finally back to North American Aviation. Baron's report also landed on the desk of the chief of NASA's Regional Inspection Office, John Brooks. But Baron lacked solid evidence and by reporting discrepancies both large and small in the same manner undercut his case.[51] Still, in retrospect, his critique seemed prophetic. It fueled public suspicions that NASA had ignored clear warnings of danger.

These charges were aired in congressional investigations of the fire. There were criticisms of insufficient oversight of private contractors, of communications breakdowns up and down the chain of command, of the rush to the moon, even of the AS-204 Review Board for a lack of independence.[52]

Senator Walter Mondale brought up the Phillips Report of 1965–66, the NASA document highly critical of North American's work and work practices. Baron testified and his earlier report was discussed. When Baron and his family died in a car wreck a week later, conspiracy theorists could only wonder.[53]

After the accident, engineers redesigned the spacecraft hatch for faster access, and test supervisors decreed that pure oxygen could be replaced with a safer mixed-gas environment. Combustible materials were reduced or eliminated, wiring and plumbing checked and redone. People were reassigned. New safety procedures affected all of NASA, including KSC.

KSC had long had a safety office, though in the early days the main safety concern was protecting the public from exploding rockets. But the Review Board urged management to "continually monitor the safety of all test operations and assure the adequacy of emergency procedures."[54] In response, KSC opened a new Flight Safety Office and gave more emphasis to emergency training of pad workers.[55] Following requirements laid down at NASA headquarters, safety programs at the centers now placed more emphasis on identification of hazards, communications about hazardous conditions, and control of known risks. Accidents were to be investigated thoroughly, with prompt follow-up or remedial action. Individual centers were also required to coordinate with each other.

In the wake of the investigations also came recriminations. Many at NASA blamed North American, others the hatch designers, and still others the test supervisors who decided to use pure oxygen.[56] Those at KSC felt that the problem lay largely if not wholly with design rather than test procedures, though the Center, like all NASA, came in for its share of criticism.[57] The Apollo test team, wrote NASA's accident investigators, had "failed to give adequate attention to certain mundane but equally vital questions of crew safety."[58] Much less could be taken for granted now, even in seemingly well understood tests and operations.

The fire and investigation demonstrated in tragic fashion how important management of design really was. The Review Board criticized the "design, workmanship and quality control" of the command module, a charge that required improvements from both contractors and the various NASA centers responsible for their work.[59] The Apollo capsule had been undergoing nearly continual change even while at KSC in a process deemed too uncontrolled and haphazard.[60] With a large number of "open items at the time of shipment of the Command Module" to KSC, engineering change orders were poorly recorded. As a result, "pre-launch test requirements" at KSC were "unresponsive to changing conditions." Better program management and clarification of responsibilities and better communications between NASA centers and contractors were needed.[61]

Now formal procedures grew in importance. NASA headquarters hired Boeing to provide technical integration and evaluation (TIE) oversight for the space program. More than 700 Boeing personnel arrived at the Cape to inspect contractor work.[62] Headquarters also expanded General Electric's role in systems analysis and ground support.[63] There were tougher procedures for making changes in systems, equipment, and craft design. Final authority on such matters rested with George Low, who took over as Apollo spacecraft program manager. Perhaps most important, directors of safety throughout NASA were explicitly given authority to stop actions violating safety procedures or actions deemed too dangerous.[64]

Still, even the fire did not create a top-down management structure running from headquarters to the centers. John Potate, TIE contract manager at KSC, noted: "The TIE contract did not do what a lot of people thought it could do. And I think the reason it did not is . . . it would have had to completely reorganize NASA's way of doing business." Other contractors would not submit to Boeing supervision, since they worked for NASA.[65] Boeing's Clint Wilkinson complained to Potate: "I can't feel the machine, you know. It calls for data . . . and I ain't got the data." Potate sympathetically replied: "I understand your problem, but I can't help you. . . . We're going to give you the data we think that you need . . . to do the job you should be doing. And that is all."[66] In the end, Potate concluded, Boeing saw the lay of the land and adjusted the scope of its work. "They would go to Petrone or Dr. Debus. . . . They never got past that level because they knew they didn't have a leg to stand on." In the end, the Boeing contract may have been more a public relations ploy to quell criticism after the *Apollo 1* fire than anything else.[67] But the issue went beyond tradition and turf defending. Given the technical complexity of the task, many of the most pressing technical problems had to be solved on the ground, at the centers.[68]

More significant than any increasing managerial role for contractors was the change in KSC's supervisory role. Until the fire, contractors working on launch and testing still reported to managers in the respective parts of NASA with whom they had contracted. North American workers took orders from their corporate headquarters in Downey, California, and Downey went to the MSC in Houston. KSC thus had responsibility for tests without supervisory authority over the main body of workers. This structure frustrated configuration management. If Houston personnel wanted to make a change, then they would tell North American management, who would instruct North American people at the Cape, with no direct input from KSC people. After the fire, all workers, even contractors working for another center, were placed firmly under KSC supervision during test and launch operations.[69]

*   *   *

Two plaques now mark the spot at Launch Complex 34 where the *Apollo 1* accident happened. One was placed there in 1988 by the Air Force Space and Missile Museum, which each year conducts a ceremony honoring their lost comrades of space. No one knows who affixed the second. It reads simply "Ad Astra Per Aspera," Latin for "a rough road leads to the stars."

Return to Flight

Return to flight would commence with AS-501, *Apollo 4*, later in 1967. After the fire, investigators evaluated the condition of the command module for *Apollo 4*. Over the next two weeks NASA and North American quality control inspectors uncovered 1,400 wiring discrepancies. By March 24 the number of wiring discrepancies rose to 1,840, and then a month later to 2,200. By that time, technicians had repaired some 1,950 of them, finally finishing the work in mid-June.[70] But problems at the launchpad and with the second stage of *Apollo 4*'s Saturn booster pushed back the launch date once again.

On November 9, 1967, the unmanned *Apollo 4* left Merritt Island from Launch Complex 39. The launch brought a sigh of relief from General Phillips. "It was a powerful operation," he reported. "You could almost feel the will with which it was being carried out. Apollo is on the way to the moon."[71] The flight of *Apollo 4* confirmed the strengths of the launch procedures. KSC and Marshall had tested problems out of the booster's second stage while inspectors rooted out problems in the command module. Both completed their work successfully, allowing this, the first Apollo–Saturn V configuration, to fly a "perfect" mission. All the pieces for lunar conquest were coming into readiness. With *Apollo 4*, LC-39 was fully activated. Now the Center would be up and running at full steam.

Apollo 5 would test the lunar module (LEM) and *Apollo 7* the command module. Both would be launched on the smaller Saturn 1B rocket. *Apollo 6* was to complete the second flow of site activation. Then with *Apollo 8* would come the first test of an Apollo–Saturn V vehicle with people aboard. After that, no major steps would stand between America and its lunar rendezvous. Those were the plans. Meanwhile, though, KSC engineers continued to wrestle with the unexpected and unplanned as vehicles marched their way through the timetable.

Before the *Apollo 1* fire, Phillips had planned the first LEM test for April

1967. But Grumman's lunar module did not arrive at KSC until June 23 that year. Grumman's delays led to creative testing at the launch site. Engineers constructed a plywood LEM mock-up to check ground and electrical support equipment on the launchpad. Garden hoses purchased at a local hardware store stood in for the cable hookups at the pad, another triumph for engineering ingenuity over complex technology. Since the first lunar module would mainly test the propulsion systems, extensive electrical system checkout was not required. Problems of configuration management continued as test engineers found fuel inlet elbows unable to mate with propellant lines. The elbows had been produced to match an earlier engine design.[72] Grumman provided updated elbows on a quick turnaround, and the real lunar module was finally mated to the launch vehicle on November 19, 1967. *Apollo 5* blasted off from LC-37B on January 22, 1968, just a few days shy of the one-year anniversary of the *Apollo 1* fire.

Apollo 6 showed the extent to which the launch team had to be involved in the construction of vehicles—or, rather, reconstruction as they sat on the pad. During the *Apollo 6* plugs-out test on December 28, a second-stage engine control actuator failed, causing a premature engine cutoff. Engineers from North American replaced it in a three-day operation beginning on January 5, 1968. They also installed the spacecraft's Mission Control Program (MCP) Command Controller that day. It malfunctioned during January 7 checkout tests and had to be replaced.[73] As work was being completed, a cracked weld was discovered in a LOX fill-and-drain purge line, which took another three days to replace.[74] Additional replacements delayed the launch till April 4. By this time, though, KSC was well practiced at reconstruction and replacement of components.

Apollo 6's liftoff went, as Rocco Petrone said, "according to script." But the launch had barely cleared the tower—the end of KSC's responsibility—before the unexpected occurred. The rocket suffered a severe "pogo effect" during the last thirty seconds of its first-stage burn. The aptly named pogo effect was a springlike oscillation of the rocket body. The oscillations could place dangerous g-forces on the spacecraft. An answer was needed fast, because the next Saturn launched would have humans aboard.

Fortunately, the dangerous pogo problem was resolved. It stemmed from thrust fluctuations in the engines. The fluctuations struck the vehicle "like a tuning fork," explained George Mueller, setting up resonant frequencies that caused the oscillations.[75] The solution was to fill certain cavities in the stage with helium, changing the harmonic frequency of the rocket so that the oscillations did not rise to a dangerous level.

Now *Apollo 7* could test the full Apollo-Saturn configuration with astronauts on board. The mission reflected the engineering transformation

6-7. In an emergency, astronauts were expected to climb into this escape basket, which would slide down a wire to the ground. Here volunteers test the device at KSC.

that followed the fire. More than 1,800 changes had been made in the new block II command module, where the crew sat, since the fire. Astronaut Frank Borman had gone out to North American's plant in Downey to help with the redesign. Von Braun loaned his assistant, Eberhard Rees, to North American. North American became a virtual subsidiary of NASA.[76]

In spite of NASA's increased supervisory role at Downey, the module still arrived at KSC some two months late. Additional work at the Center on both the spacecraft and the launch vehicle put off the launch date until October 1968. But the launch on October 11 went off with only a minor unscheduled hold in the countdown. The mission, Apollo program director Sam Phillips asserted, "accomplished 101 percent" of NASA's objectives. The mission commander, Wally Schirra, put it more eloquently during the flight. "She's riding like a dream," he said.[77]

In *Apollo 4* through *Apollo 7*, elements of von Braun's step-by-step testing of components had reappeared. For all the orientation to schedule and getting the mission accomplished, there remained a lot of research in the space program—but the methodical learning from each flight was taking place even as preparations were under way for the voyages that would be made possible by that new knowledge.

The next flight, *Apollo 8*, was to test the command module and lunar module together, using a Saturn V. It was pushed by the moon race. Rumors persisted of a Russian rocket with the potential to circle the moon but probably not land.[78] Decisions on *Apollo 8*'s flight appear to have been made at the last minute and stretched KSC's capabilities. Not until April 27, 1968, did Petrone receive word that *Apollo 8* would be a manned mission. Workers had to demate the S-II stage and barge it to NASA's Mississippi Test Facility for further tests.[79] While technicians there modified the rocket engines, KSC personnel performed similar modifications on the third stage. Modifications of electrical support equipment in the firing room further delayed preparations for launch as the RCA computers crashed. During the three weeks from May 12 to June 2, the Change Board approved 117 hardware and 97 documentation changes, numbers made higher than expected by the sudden decision to go manned with *Apollo 8*.[80]

Unfinished equipment shipped from the factory required some 3,500 hours of work for this mission. KSC's Apollo program manager, Rear Admiral R. O. Middleton, noted that though the amount of work was larger than usual, it presented "no particular problem to KSC."[81] But the number of modifications required on the Saturn launcher for *Apollo 8* combined with the large number of open items on the lunar module made it impossible for KSC to meet General Phillips's schedule. In July Debus complained to George Mueller at NASA headquarters that under the current operating schedule, KSC had to simultaneously process three Saturn V rockets in the face of declining budgets that constrained the contractor labor force. Mueller replied that the Center had no choice. It had to do the work to keep the lunar program on schedule. Marshall and MSC would relieve KSC of some spacecraft and launch vehicle modifications.

By the latter part of August, KSC technicians concluded that the lunar module would not be ready for the scheduled launch in early December.[82] While the scrubbing of the lunar module removed one problem for KSC technicians, it created another. Without the lunar module, *Apollo 8*'s earth-orbiting mission would do little more than replicate *Apollo 7*, only riding a Saturn V instead of a Saturn IB. Quietly, NASA officials decided to do something bold amid rumors of a possible Russian lunar voyage. They would send *Apollo 8* around the moon. KSC quickly reconfigured the service module, rebuilding it in the O&C building nearly down to the last bolt and wire.[83]

Following the criticisms of NASA after *Apollo 1*, the space program had taken an unaccustomed backseat to other news coverage, notably of the Vietnam War. Riots at the Democratic National Convention in Chicago in August had blunted the impact of *Apollo 7*'s manned mission. Now *Apollo 8* brought the country together again, temporarily at least, with astronauts Anders, Lovell, and Borman's reading on Christmas Eve of the story of Genesis. *Apollo 7* had been the "Lovely Apollo Room High Atop Everything," but *Apollo 8* truly left the earth behind. Commander Frank Borman would close the reading of the Creation story with "Merry Christmas and God bless all of you—all of you on the good earth."

Ascent to the Moon

After *Apollo 8* world attention focused on NASA like never before. For the first time since President Kennedy's speech, it now seemed that America just might do it. There was no more visible symbol of that looming success than the Kennedy Space Center itself. For three years, visitors from around the world had flocked to Florida to see the spectacle of rockets blasting off, carrying men closer and closer to their lunar target. The guest list for launches grew first into the dozens and then into the hundreds and surged toward the thousands. Particularly notable on several Apollo flights were invitees from Third World nations, Africa for one launch, Asia for another. But it did not require deliberate propaganda efforts to impress the world. The missions themselves were doing that. Center director Debus received unsolicited letters each week from the far reaches of the globe, many handwritten. A welder from Mozambique asked in broken English for the opportunity to work at "Kape Kennedy." "I do vote for what American people they be the first moon to arrive," he ended. Another handwritten missive arrived from a schoolteacher in Nigeria who just wanted to say "congratulations."[84]

Apollos 9, 10, and *11* brought the lunar program to its climax, but they proceeded at the Kennedy Space Center in a process that was smoother than ever before. Only project management remained contentious. North American's home offices left modification work largely up to its crew at KSC. This raised configuration management issues once again, especially after workers at KSC had to modify instrumentation to support the Saturn second stage's new, more powerful engines. But now when problems arose during processing, KSC crews handled them with dispatch. The only unexpected delay in *Apollo 9* came when the astronauts developed colds. By *Apollo 10,* KSC was practiced at cycling launch vehicles and spacecraft into the VAB, stacking them, and sending them to the pad. Each rocket since *Apollo 8* had been stacked before the preceding vehicle left the building. During these missions only minor modifications were made on the spacecraft. By *Apollo*

6-8. Not quite on the moon, astronauts practice scooping up rock samples at the Cape as an armadillo ignores them.

10 the launch vehicle no longer carried research and development instrumentation. Only the lunar module continued to evolve, with mission-related modifications. *Apollo 10* would be the only Apollo launched from Pad B and the only mission to be launched from Firing Room 3. Neither provided complications to liftoff on May 18.

Despite the moment of unity conferred by *Apollo 8*, the race to the moon was still taking place amid an American society growing more divided. War, race, and culture were pulling apart the consensus that had once seemed to mark the nation in the postwar period, and inevitably the space program became a target for controversy. By 1969 the United States had spent some

1 billion dollars preparing the Kennedy Space Center to launch the first human mission to the moon, and much more than that on the Apollo program as a whole.[85] Public opinion polls showed growing skepticism about these expenditures, which peaked at nearly 3.5 percent of the federal budget in 1967. Once again, though, the drama of the moment trumped controversy. As the hour for the lunar launch now seemed finally at hand, everyone wanted a seat for the big show. For *Apollo 11*, one-third of the Senate and nearly half of Congress showed up at the Cape, as did fourteen governors, the army chief of staff, and Vice President Spiro Agnew. Dignitaries present in the Launch Control Center hardly understood what they were seeing. Like most of the world, they were waiting for the dragon's breath, the smoke and fire that signified ignition. What they could not follow was the complex series of calculations being made in real time in the heads of the engineers at their consoles.

Operating a launch in the Apollo era was its own form of knowledge. Much of the work had yet to be automated.[86] Instead, hundreds of men and women watched data stream in, usually in analog form on strip charts, dials, and meters, and quickly assessed what that information meant. Their read-

6-9. Launch operations for Apollo required hundreds of technicians sitting in front of display panels, and much human decision making. Computers and automation would simplify this greatly for the space shuttle.

ings in turn were fed up the chain of command until they reached the launch director, who would have to decide, sometimes in a matter of minutes, what to do next. It was every bit as tense and dramatic as the work at Mission Control in Houston that would follow after the vehicle left earth.

The art of the launch involved a surprising amount of human judgment. Though the engineers who designed the hardware had tested it and determined how it was to perform, operations work at KSC often led to additional understanding of real-world performance. In the LCC, technicians watched levels of temperature and pressure, amplitude and resistance, and other variables. They fixed their eyes on the "redlines" or danger areas that indicated too high a temperature or too low a pressure. Behind the men at the consoles, engineers evaluated what they saw, trying to picture in their minds what was going on inside the rocket. They drew on their intimate familiarity with their system; they searched for data on adjacent systems that could confirm what they believed, or that might reveal more. Was the rise in temperature indicative of an emerging problem that would stop the count? Or was the temperature rising slowly enough that it would still be in the safe area when the launch took place? Did the red light on the board mean a valve was stuck open? Or was that expensive valve operating perfectly, betrayed by a two-dollar microswitch? A check with an adjacent console showed that pressure in the line was where it belonged, giving proof positive the valve was closed. The launch director had to trust the technician reading the dials and the engineer in charge of the system. There was no time to evaluate every potential problem. In other cases, though, it might be necessary to "go to the woodshed" and hash out what to do next. If a turbopump's rpm reading was higher than it should be, a quick conference call to Marshall could bring back word that engineers had tested the turbopump at even higher rpm and never had a problem. The pump's designer had great confidence in the robustness of his design. All the technical knowledge and experience came together in real time like this in launch operations, in a constant flow of communications between operators, designers, and manufacturers.

On the morning of July 16, at 9:32 A.M., a perfect launch began the mission to the moon. A little over five hours earlier, NASA administrator Thomas Paine had guaranteed the astronauts that if they had to abort, they would be the crew on the next attempt. "Your safety," he asserted, "is paramount." Paine's promise was not needed. Translunar injection during *Apollo 11*'s second orbit of earth was so precise that only a three-second burn was needed for a midcourse correction. After a three-day journey and two spins around the lunar disk, a second burn rounded out the orbit to a little over 66 by 54.5 miles above the moon's surface. The next day the *Eagle* landed. Launching from the Kennedy Space Center, America had beaten the Russians, but the

6-10. *Apollo 11* starts to clear the launch tower.

6-11. Viewers watch *Apollo 11* from the Launch Control Center.

record the astronauts left on the lunar surface gave no indication of that competition. The plaque read "Here Men From Planet Earth First Set Foot Upon the Moon. July 1969 A.D. We Came in Peace for All Mankind."

The footprints left by the *Apollo 11* astronauts in the Sea of Tranquility are more permanent than most solid structures on earth. Barring a chance meteorite impact, they will probably last for millions of years. To Wernher von Braun, the footprints meant nothing less than "immortality—not for the individual but for the species or even for the spark of life itself in our corner of the universe." The images of a man leaving his footprints on the moon were reportedly witnessed by one-fifth of the earth's population.

There was, however, surprisingly little time for reflection, especially back at KSC. Getting to the moon may have met President Kennedy's challenge, but there was no question that Americans were going to return for more visits.

On Merritt Island, the whole *Apollo 11* business looked rather different. Number eleven was the big one everyone had been shooting for. But it was not the end of the story. In fact, the first, largely unknown story was, what did the launch teach for the next vehicle in the queue? One thing it taught was a lesson in configuration management. A single bolt almost canceled the trip to the moon. At 5 A.M. during *Apollo 11*'s countdown, the KSC launch crew called for a halt to deal with a liquid hydrogen leak. Fortunately, the redundant ground systems allowed technicians to block the leak and go around it. Only later was the leak's cause uncovered—one out-of-spec bolt that prevented the valve from shutting completely. Someone somewhere in production had run out of $^5/_{16}$-inch bolts and so used a slightly shorter one to finish the job. That fraction of an inch could have been the difference between getting *Apollo 11* to the moon and not.[87]

When Kurt Debus had justified the expenditure of funds to build LC-39, he and other top NASA officials had in mind dozens of Saturn Vs leaving Florida each year. Those numbers proved optimistic. NASA scheduled nine more missions to the moon. Though few members of the public knew it, already the space agency's budget had been scaled back. Workforce reductions had made themselves felt at KSC as early as 1967. Following the return of *Apollo 11* in August, General Phillips resigned as Apollo program manager. Rocco Petrone moved to Washington to succeed him, and Walt Kapryan replaced Petrone as KSC's launch director. A month later Admiral Middleton left KSC's Apollo Program Office to return to the navy. In December Albert Siepert, Debus's deputy director for center management, announced his retirement. The big haul was over and the reshuffling had begun. Already, in fact, it was clear to insiders that NASA would be taking a new direction, that Apollo would soon end and a serious reconsideration of the future of the American space program was about to start. But there were still six more missions to fly, and five of those would land on the moon.

Had *Apollo 11* failed, KSC had *Apollo 12* waiting in the wings for a September try. Once *Apollo 11* made it to the moon, the pressure relented. With *Apollo 12* already stacked in the VAB, the November launch could proceed to final countdown at what must have seemed an almost leisurely pace. Preparations for this mission had resulted in nominal problems—the almost standard change-out of the fuel cells on the command module and cleaning of the lunar module's water-glycol system. No serious issues arose until forty hours before launch, when a fuel cell tank in the service module lost vacuum. Tom O'Malley's crew from North American Aviation changed out the tank on the pad following procedures created just for that purpose. The replacement tank had to be "robbed" from *Apollo 13*. At seventeen hours before launch, the spacecraft was again ready to go.

Apollo 12 faced the challenge of the Cape's capricious weather patterns. Well into the late autumn months, the climate at Cape Canaveral can be warm and humid, conditions that give rise to strong thunderstorms. On sultry afternoons in Central Florida, just about every shape, form, and variety of lightning can be glimpsed shooting through huge black thunderheads. These were the conditions that Petrone's successor, Walt Kapryan, faced on his first launch. Technically competent, Kapryan was a much different figure from his predecessor. Some found him a welcome relief, for Petrone often got what he wanted by pure intimidation, zeroing in on an adversary's weak spot like a heat-seeking missile. Kapryan lacked that commanding presence and probably the encyclopedic command of detail that Petrone awed subordinates with. He had the unenviable task of coming on stage after a human dynamo, finishing up Apollo after the big excitement had died down.

Rules did not prohibit launch into rain, but they forbade liftoff into thunderclouds. Reports from aircraft flying around the Cape assured Kapryan that no cumulus clouds were nearby. The rocket's trail of ionized gases, however, created an ideal trajectory for electron discharge. Thirty-seven seconds after liftoff on November 14, lightning struck the Saturn V. Fifteen seconds later it struck again. All the onboard systems on *Apollo 12* dropped out of commission, and the rocket came within 40 microseconds of abort. The spacecraft switched to backup power as the astronauts worked to restore primary power and quickly rebooted the spacecraft's computers.

The scene sent shock waves through all present, calling up images of disaster put aside since *Apollo 1*. NASA quickly investigated and concluded that Saturn V hardware, vulnerable to lightning strikes, should not be changed. Instead, more rigorous launch restrictions would be put in place. The near miss also started KSC on a research project to understand the behavior of lightning that continues to this day.

In spite of the stormy sendoff, the mission suffered no problems, and five days later astronauts Conrad and Bean landed within 180 meters of the unmanned *Surveyor 3*, which KSC had launched to the moon some two years earlier. The second moon landing crew successfully returned to earth on November 24, but for Pete Conrad the mission was not over "until we go back and thank the folks at Kennedy Space Center." On December 12 he and his fellow astronauts attended a party in the VAB with 8,000 members of the KSC team. Subsequent successful missions followed the precedent established by *Apollo 12*, as astronauts completed their journeys with a return to the Cape.

Unlucky 13

Speaking immediately after *Apollo 11*, KSC director Kurt Debus told his launch team that "the biggest thing that can hurt us is overconfidence." The string of successful Apollo launches meant little when the moment of truth for the next one came. "Every bird we are going to launch," he pointed out, "has no idea what the previous birds have done."[88] He may have felt justified after the near miss a few months later with *Apollo 12*, but he could not have known how prophetic he was until the mission after that. *Apollo 13* would not be struck by lightning, but it quickly turned from success to seeming disaster, only to be plucked from the jaws of tragedy and end as one of NASA's greatest triumphs. It also revealed how far from routine space flight still was, and how easily mistakes and risks could accumulate in a complex technology.

The mission seemed plagued with misfortune before it left earth, as though its number really did mean bad luck. On March 25, 1970, less than a month before launch, three KSC security cars burst into flames and melted, caught in the escaping oxygen vapor from the giant rocket being fueled 1,000 feet away.[89] It was a freak accident and no one was hurt. But the tricky liquid oxygen was already creating headaches for this mission. The day before, on March 24, while *Apollo 13* sat on Pad A of LC-39, a routine preflight test of the Apollo service module ended with an unexpected problem. The test involved checking the tanks by loading them with liquid oxygen and then removing it. During detanking, one of the two tanks discharged only 8 percent of its load. After a second failed try, engineers from MSC, North American Aviation, and Beech Aircraft Corporation met in a teleconference. They decided the best course was to boil off the remaining oxygen by using the tank's heaters, a process that took more than eight hours. All parties concurred that the anomaly was most likely due to a loose fill tube. They could replace the entire oxygen shelf, delaying the mission and affecting the Apollo space program schedule. Replacement was actually riskier than flying with the loose tube, which would not endanger mission or crew. The logic was faultless but, unbeknownst to anyone, the unorthodox detanking procedure had introduced a dangerous defect in the service module.[90]

On April 14, three days after launch, the crew turned on the cryogenic fans and heaters, the same that had been used to detank the LOX during the preflight test. Ninety seconds later they heard a loud bang, which turned out to be the explosion of oxygen tank 2. The blast damaged other parts of the Apollo vehicle, notably oxygen tank 1, which rapidly lost pressure. Happily, emergency response efforts on the ground and by the astronauts in space saved the craft and crew, which returned safely to earth on April 17.

Subsequent investigation confirmed that the original problem was indeed a loose fill tube, possibly broken when the oxygen shelf was jarred and dropped upon installation. More significant was a design flaw in the heater switches, thermostatic protective devices meant to prevent overheating. Apollo service module builder North American Aviation had in 1965 revised its specifications for heater operation from 28 to 65 volts (DC). The maker of the switches, Beech Aircraft, failed to note the change and did not redesign its original 28-volt switch, an error overlooked by both North American and NASA quality inspectors. Subsequent tests also failed to detect the problem, in part because qualification of the equipment did not require a full cycling of the switch. When the recommendation to boil off the unwilling LOX was made, all parties assumed that the switches could handle the requisite voltage. During normal ground tests no problem had ever been detected, even when using the higher-than-rated voltage, because the tank remained cool, preventing overheating of the wiring. But when the LOX was boiled off over eight hours, temperatures rose and the 28-volt switches failed, the current welding them shut. As a result, the thermostats could not open to reduce temperatures, which rose as high as 538 degrees Centigrade during detanking. This intense heat damaged the wiring of the tank's fan motor, causing the short circuit that caused the explosion that nearly doomed *Apollo 13*. It was the perfect example of how even the smallest, simplest piece of equipment is nonetheless a part of the whole and, under the wrong circumstances, can turn into a critical fault.

An internal review also revealed how problems of safety could occur even when no violation of normal procedures was evident. Although the original problem in the switches, going back to 1965 and the days before configuration management, should have been detected, this oversight was due to failures of documentation and quality control, the same problems addressed in the aftermath of the *Apollo 1* fire. The entire *Apollo 13* accident was a series of steps, no one of which was fatal on its own. KSC did not violate any procedure by the special detanking, and all parties concurred that the procedure was safe. The Apollo 13 Review Board did note that pad personnel might have observed the rising temperatures, indicating a problem.[91] But overall, the report was sympathetic to the inherent difficulty of considering all possible interactions within a system as complex as Apollo.

Before the next launch, the command and service modules were redesigned, incorporating recommendations from the *Apollo 13* investigation.

6-12. After the near disaster with *Apollo 13*, a large, happy crowd comes to the Cape to watch the successful liftoff of *Apollo 14*.

Workers removed oxygen tank fans and sheathed heater wiring in stainless steel. They added a third oxygen tank, located away from the existing ones. *Apollo 14* spent nearly a year at KSC while these and other modifications were made. Once they were finished, *Apollo 14* raced through processing. The rocket was stacked in the VAB and sent to the pad in five days' time. Pad tests and servicing revealed no new constraints for a January 31, 1971, launch.

Kennedy Space Center again provided a show to about one million people crowded on the beaches and causeways to see this return to flight. Near disaster had revived flagging public interest in the moon missions. Adding to the drama was the weather once again. Thirty minutes before scheduled liftoff it began to rain, but now the newly installed lightning detectors did their job. At eight minutes before launch, Walt Kapryan ordered a forty-minute hold. There was still a chance the weather would improve. The countdown resumed once the rainstorm had passed over the Cape into the ocean and the lightning detectors showed no activity.

Liftoff at 4:03 P.M. occurred without incident, but KSC's role in the launch was not over. Minor problems plagued the mission. In four tries, command module pilot Stu Roosa could not get the spacecraft to dock with the lunar module. Finally on the fifth try it latched. No further problems occurred until Alan Shepard and Ed Mitchell powered up the lunar module. Then a defective switch forced an abort command in the lunar module computer. Engineers at KSC quickly found a work-around. Ten minutes before the lunar module was scheduled to begin its descent to the moon, engineers at mission control read up numbers for Mitchell to plug into the computer. The work-around had already been practiced on KSC's lunar module simulator and, of course, it worked.

But this triumph could not clear the gathering clouds of concern at KSC, as the entire American space program was placed under the knife of the budget cutters.

7

✳
✳
✳

Transitions to the Future

Many people are shrinking from the future and from participation in the
movement toward a new, expanded reality. And, like homesick travelers
abroad, they are focusing on their anxieties at home.

Margaret Mead, "Man on the Moon"

"My dear fellow worker," began Kurt Debus in a letter to employees of the
Kennedy Space Center in the fall of 1974. What followed next was a shock.
Debus had come to the "difficult, personal decision to retire at an early date."[1]
As the leader of KSC from the beginning, he had both defined and represented the activities that went on there. The most important basic launch
concepts came from his work. He seemed as much a part of the institutional
and physical landscape as the gigantic VAB or the teeming wildlife on Merritt Island. For those who knew him better, though, Debus's decision was less
surprising. "Our type of work . . . it's misery," he had confessed in a 1970 interview. "You've kept the machine going, you have satisfied this problem and
you have solved one over there . . ."[2] Now he told his fellow space workers,
"For thirty years, the pressures of demanding programs have exacted their
toll." It was time for him to rest.[3] There was plenty to look back upon with
pride. "Together we have built up a magnificent installation which is unique
in the Free World while contributing to the steady progress of the National
Space Program," he continued. Always attentive to his responsibilities, Debus was quick to point out that he had chosen to retire at a time when we
are "well along in the design and construction of facilities and supporting
systems to accommodate the Space Shuttle which will open up a wider frontier in space activities in the near future."[4]

Although Debus was striking a confident chord, the years leading up to
his decision had been especially rocky. His early retirement followed in the
wake of disturbing changes at NASA, changes that reshaped the American
space program and took it away from the future that Debus and others of
his generation had imagined. The business of launching rockets was chang-

ing, radically in some ways. The launch concepts that Debus had helped to pioneer would now have to change too. KSC would have to learn and adapt to new ways of doing business, new missions in what had become a dramatically different environment.

From the Moon to Where?

The steps leading to Debus's decision went back to the years just after *Apollo 11*, if not before. The immediate post-Apollo years were demanding ones for NASA, ironically because past success bred doubt and uncertainty. America had won the Cold War space race, but that race seemed less important in the 1970s. There was mounting pressure on the federal government to address domestic issues and turn scarce resources away from big, symbolic politics of the sort that had supported the Apollo program. In all, Apollo had cost almost $25 billion. No other NASA program would match this level.[5] Unlike the Democratic presidents Kennedy and Johnson, the Republican Richard Nixon had little interest in space. NASA now had to defend itself against those who would kill it. No wonder Debus was tired.

Even before the first lunar landing, the question of "what next" had loomed. In early January 1965, NASA administrator James Webb asked center directors for their comments on a report by the Future Programs Task Group. The report outlined "the opportunities and problems involved in our newly opened frontier of space." A consensus of sorts emerged. First on the list was "exploration of Mars through the use of large unmanned soft-landing spacecraft," which would cost in excess of $1 billion. Second was a more modest plan to use hardware built for the lunar program for other projects. "Saturn boosters and the Apollo-LEM manned space flight system," it was believed, could be fitted for use for "a wide variety of scientific and technical missions in near-earth and synchronous orbits." If everything went as planned, the 1970s and 1980s should see "systematic lunar exploration, large orbiting space stations, and manned exploration of Mars."[6]

These post-Apollo proposals—the mission to Mars in particular—had, perhaps, somewhat unconsciously been adopted from ideas that stretched back to the early days of modern space flight. In his famous series of articles for *Collier's* magazine in the 1950s, Wernher von Braun had mentioned space stations, moon stations, and missions to Mars and beyond. When there was time to step back a bit and think grandly about the future, the basic course von Braun had outlined tended to come to the fore at NASA. At KSC, Debus summed up this position nicely when he declared "the lunar landing phase of Apollo is *only a milestone*, a major one, in the national space program."[7]

For KSC, all of these plans implied a move away from the moonport image and its emphasis on the lunar landing. In its place would be a new focus on the operational and launch support that KSC could provide for an expanded menu of missions. Since 1965 engineers at the launch center had been presenting their ideas on what would follow Apollo. Richard Dutton of the Apollo-Saturn Test and Systems Engineering Office urged, for example, that the Saturn IB be used "to orbit the three-man Apollo spacecraft in extended flight missions." The more impressive Saturn V "with its tremendous thrust capacity" could be used to heft a six-person space station into earth orbit, either for terrestrial observation or to support an extended lunar exploration.[8]

The tenor of the times gave KSC personnel their clue on how to pitch the Center's future role. KSC would be the "operational base" for all NASA projects. The Center's structure and facilities had always operated flexibly and incorporated a "growth potential" that could accommodate future goals. Center personnel worked as a team in the "assembly, checkout, and launching of space vehicles, regardless of their size and complexity, and regardless of where they may be developed by the NASA research and development centers."[9] Learning about space exploration took place in a hands-on way, with experience gained from actually testing, preparing, and launching craft.

One way to gain new knowledge was through what was called the Apollo Applications Program. Rocket technology developed for the lunar mission would be adapted to scientific and exploratory endeavors, such as a space lab or station that could be carried into earth orbit by the powerful Saturn V. In November 1965 George Mueller, NASA's associate administrator for manned space flight, had started organizing centers for this program. Mueller believed that the scale of Apollo applications required each center to develop parallel program organizations to handle the two new areas that had emerged: management of experiments and payload integration. Experiments would be planned through NASA headquarters' program offices. Payload integration, on the other hand, was a major new task, since it involved assuring that the experiments and vehicles were compatible with mission and operations plans.[10] Centers would assume various new responsibilities for Apollo applications. Marshall was to handle payloads for lunar excursion missions. The Manned Spacecraft Center would be responsible for command and service module payloads in Apollo vehicles. KSC's role, noted Mueller, would include "nominal spacecraft modifications . . . experiment installation . . . and capability for installation of late-arriving experiments for Follow-on Missions."[11]

The Apollo Applications Program appeared to support the rhetoric that the moon was but a small step on an endless frontier. But there was a hitch.

With Apollo eating up so much of the available budget, very little was left to reinvest in new directions. NASA found itself in the peculiar position of sustaining momentum for the Apollo lunar missions while also looking beyond them. The dual focus was impossible to avoid. Even as men walked on the moon, NASA officials needed enthusiasm for new programs to assure fiscal support. It was a clever strategy, but all the signs indicated that Congress and the American public were not thinking about outer space.

Uncertainty and Cutbacks

In the late 1960s, public concern about education, health, housing, inner-city problems, civil rights, and Vietnam took precedence over futuristic space exploration. Up through the lunar landing, a bare majority of the public had thought the space race was worth the cost. After 1969, NASA even lost that thin edge of support. By 1972, 58 percent of Americans believed too much was being spent to send men to the moon.[12] Sending humans to Mars had even less appeal. In a 1969 poll, less than 40 percent of Americans favored a mission to the red planet. The next year, 40 percent of Americans said that government funding of space exploration should stay the same, while 40 percent believed that it should decrease. Over time, NASA even lost support for the status quo. Between 1973 and 1977, 50–60 percent of Americans polled stated that the agency's budget should be cut.

The hard realities of looming domestic issues combined to weaken enthusiasm for a long-term space program. "We walk safely among the craters of the moon," lamented space skeptics, "but not in the parks of New York or Chicago or Los Angeles." Though no liberal, even President Richard Nixon agreed on putting social needs first. As he told NASA, "we must recognize that many critical problems here on this planet make high priority demands on our attention and our resources."[13]

Not only had space lost its appeal, but NASA itself also had lost some of the respect it once enjoyed as a unifying force in a divided society. When the astronauts of *Apollo 14* went for their traditional ticker-tape parade in New York, police along Broadway had to restrain picketers. In late 1970, KSC went on alert when someone phoned in a threat to "blow up" the moonport. Starting with *Apollo 14*, the Center put into effect new security measures and prepared contingency plans for terrorism.[14]

The job losses of the 1970s strained labor relations at Merritt Island as well. As the final Apollo mission, *Apollo 17*, prepared to blast off to the moon in December 1972, members of the International Alliance of Theatrical Stage Employees (IATSE) who worked at KSC prepared to strike. It was feared that other unions would follow in sympathy. The strike threat ended with a settlement just two days before launch. But even as one problem was resolved, another emerged. Members of the International Association of Machinists (IAM) walked out against Bendix, a prominent contractor.[15] When the machinists finally accepted a new contract two months later, they had broken the record for longest strike at KSC, with a total of 11,780 worker days lost.[16] But that held only until the end of another IAM strike, this time against Boeing.[17] Their 111-day strike left many blue-collar workers embittered. They sported black caps bearing the number 111.

For all the problems, there was at least some evidence that the space program would continue, if in straitened circumstances. Skeptical about the practical benefits of human space exploration, the public still yielded to a fascination with sending people off the earth in rockets. This was particularly evident at the Kennedy Space Center. KSC had developed an extensive plan for public communications, standardized into a series of preflight, during-flight, and postflight briefings, as well as audio and video facilities and hookups.[18] NASA headquarters handled most of the high-level public affairs, such as astronaut visits, television updates, and major press conferences. But the Kennedy Space Center was the place where the public came to experience history being made. KSC, the most industrial part of the space program, represented the romance of space to citizens. Even after the moon shot, attendance at the KSC Visitor Center continued to grow. By 1977 its tours ranked as the fifth most popular Florida attraction, with more than a million visitors a year. Whatever ambivalence public opinion polls showed, there remained a strong, indeed growing, fascination with the business of space launch.[19]

Still, fascination did not translate into federal dollars. The people who came to gawk at KSC's marvelous facilities and watch spine-tingling blast-offs had little idea what it all cost. At the height of the moon race, NASA's budget peaked at just over $5 billion, or 3.4 percent of annual federal spending. That dropped to 2 percent in 1969, the year of the lunar landing, and would fall again to just over 1 percent in 1970. There it hovered throughout most of the 1970s, undercutting the bold plans laid out in the 1960s.[20] Any doubts on this score were driven home in 1971, when budget cuts forced NASA to cancel Apollo missions 18 through 20. Funding restrictions, reported former NASA administrator James Webb, meant that "the United States is not pursuing, for the time being at least, its goal of pre-eminence in space." He feared that the USSR would soon dominate the field.[21]

Webb's appeal to patriotism highlighted the predicament that NASA now found itself in. Remarkably, a joint conference held in 1968 in La Jolla, California, by NASA's Science and Technology Committee and the Office of Manned Flight reaffirmed the space goals identified in the flush times of the early 1960s: colonizing the moon, exploring Mars and other planets, and constructing an orbiting space station. There was, however, one crucial difference. Now this agenda would have to be fulfilled with a smaller number of launches and a more efficient vehicle. Issues of cost and feasibility came to the fore at the La Jolla meeting. If space travel, space science, and space industry were to become "a normal part of human experience," costs had to be drastically reduced. Building support for space missions meant, as Margaret Mead put it, shrinking back from the future and focusing closer to home, with missions to study the earth. But the heart of the NASA response to budget cuts lay with technology—a vehicle that could be used over and over again, a space shuttle.[22]

In September 1969, the Space Task Group (STG), a body established by President Nixon to outline a national space program, submitted its own plans for NASA's future. It incorporated ideas from the La Jolla conference, including the shuttle. With the tightening fiscal belt, however, the Nixon administration chose not to act on the STG report, leaving NASA to redefine or whittle down its plans in the light of declining federal appropriations. The picture looked less than encouraging. The proposed 1971 NASA budget was only a little more than $3 billion. Nixon's director of the Bureau of the Budget (BoB), Robert Mayo, was seeking steep long-term cuts in NASA. Protests that this "would make it impossible to build on and learn from the success of Apollo and other programs, and harm U.S. prestige around the world," no longer carried as much weight as they had at the height of the moon race with the Russia.[23]

The tight budget put NASA into a classic chicken-and-egg dilemma. Programs were cut because the needed technology was not yet ready, but funding for advanced research to create that technology was cut as well. The BoB proposed limiting Apollo lunar exploration flights to one a year. This was, NASA responded, "operationally not feasible from a safety and management point of view." Stopping production of Saturn V launch vehicles would mean that the hardware for continuing human flight would be gone. Reducing funding for developing advanced projects, such as a reusable space shuttle and orbiting space station, would "destroy the continuity and future direction of the manned flight program." The budget axe threatened to eliminate or vastly reduce the number and scope of scientific experiments, to cut NASA's Sustaining University Program, and to shut down the Electronics Research Center, among other things.

At KSC Kurt Debus found this shortsighted approach especially frustrating. His vision of NASA was built on an experimental model of continuous learning. It was always difficult to know which lines of research to pursue, what technology to develop for a future that could not be predicted. But, Debus argued, "future space scientists and designers . . . [would] draw upon the findings of our experiments just as surely as we have followed the principles of rocketry established by Dr. Robert H. Goddard and Hermann Oberth."[24] Without continuous development, knowledge acquisition would cease. If the budget cuts were coming, then the only thing left was to find a way to "preserve, during a period of prolonged austerity, the . . . capabilities that will be needed for a vigorous future space exploration program."[25]

KSC had been preparing itself for such austerity. As early as 1967 George Mueller warned Debus that President Johnson had "clear intent to reduce expenditures to the lowest possible level." Mueller wanted to know how KSC could "best curtail, eliminate, or adjust its operations," including cuts in personnel and closing of facilities. Debus looked into ways of saving on supplies, propellants, and gases, and he found that overtime pay could be cut through better scheduling.[26] Though not wanting to interfere with launch schedule requirements, he still made a 10 percent reduction in the contractor workforce and prepared to deactivate launch complexes 34 and 37 as "expeditiously as possible."[27] Hans Gruene, director of launch vehicle operations at KSC, congratulated his men and women for the successful *Apollo 12* launch and then reminded them that "our future depends heavily on our ability to become more and more *cost effective*."[28] He admonished his team to make saving money a priority. It was a refrain heard through the duration of Apollo missions of the 1970s. "I urge each of you to commit at least a small portion of your work day to thoughts on ways to reduce cost," Gruene wrote to subordinates in 1972.[29]

Nonetheless, these sorts of efficiencies in operations were not going to be enough. President Nixon announced in 1970 that he wanted to "reduce substantially the cost of space operations."[30] This required major cuts, many of which fell on the men and women of the Kennedy Space Center. KSC's budget declined from $375 million in 1970 to $219 million in 1974. Declining budgets meant layoffs and a decreasing workforce, which fell from 26,000 in 1968 to 10,000 in 1974.[31] The decline occurred mainly among contractors at the Cape. Of the 26,000 working there in the late 1960s, only 3,000 had been government employees. By 1974 there were still 2,408 civil servants, but just 7,600 contractors.[32]

This sudden reduction had significant repercussions on employee morale. Contract workers obviously felt vulnerable, but so did civil servants. On July 16, 1970, Debus announced that in order to offset a proposed $9 million shortfall in the NASA budget, eighty-five civil servants would have to go as part of KSC's share of the burden. The timing could not have been worse. Just a few days earlier, *Apollo 14* commander Alan Shepard had said he was concerned that layoffs in the space program might lead to poor workmanship at KSC. "I think we would be naïve if we didn't assume that people are unhappy," Shepard stated bluntly.[33]

Officially denying that morale was a problem, KSC assistant director Miles Ross immediately went to talk with key contractor managers to find out what workers were thinking. Although Ross quickly saw that "lay offs and schedule slow-down" had lowered employee morale, it had not fallen to the point that "mission success is jeopardized," because the "personnel who are in the process of being laid off are not maintained on critical test teams."[34] Still, Shepard's words had such resonance that KSC management feared he had made the workforce anxious. "The reported allegations regarding quality of work and honesty of reporting errors in work, has hurt our contractors and civil servants," Debus remarked. "They feel they have been unjustly accused of a lack of concern for mission success and the well-being of our astronauts."[35]

As KSC management correctly perceived, the low spirits were linked to the cutbacks in personnel as well as scaled-back program aspirations. "The most effective boost to employee morale would be the announcement of a firm operations schedule and a firm manpower level," Debus explained to Dale Myers at NASA's Office of Manned Space Flight in 1970. "This would remove the continuing apprehension that further layoffs are just around the corner." In the meantime, they would try to boost spirits by "keeping . . . people busy."[36] "There must be sufficient challenging work during the impending slow periods," KSC managers understood, "to interest [personnel] . . . as well as to maintain their skill levels and prevent 'stagnation.'"[37] It was proving to be an uphill fight, though. One indication of the anxiety was an uptick in requests by employees for permission to engage in outside employment. For clerical and technical personnel this perhaps reflected a need to supplement income after years of reliable overtime pay. Requests came in from secretaries wanting to take waitressing jobs and from electricians to do housepainting on the side. But higher-level personnel also submitted requests, to start small businesses, sell real estate, or work in clothing stores.[38]

Maintaining skills acquired during the lunar era became the prime focus of personnel management by the early 1970s. Matters that went beyond operational necessity, the optional activities that could help to build, retain, and enhance the workforce, including training and education for employees, were reduced or eliminated.[39] If taking on outside work allowed people to stay at Merritt Island, then it furthered the goal of retaining skilled workers. KSC retention policies encompassed not just upper-level management but all "individuals who play a vital role and who don't have adequate back-up" even those "at the technical level." This was one reason for retaining civil service workers first, even if it meant letting contract workers go, for the civil service workforce was seen as a crucial repository of skill and experience.[40] But skills were also embedded in the contractor workforce. "NASA cannot force contractors to commit individuals for indefinite periods of time," it was understood. But there might be ways to retain contractor personnel, such as offering them guarantees of further employment.[41] However retention was handled, it had to be handled confidentially and with great care, or "a considerable morale problem and possible personnel losses of those not se-lected [for special retention efforts] could result."[42] There was simply no easy way around the challenges that cutbacks in programs imposed on the skills and knowledge built up over the previous decade of work. Nor could new personnel with similar skills be hired and easily trained in this atmosphere. By 1977, NASA administrator James Fletcher noted that "we still have a large number of competent people," but he feared "we are not bringing in new blood."[43]

Cutbacks also seemed to threaten KSC efforts to diversify its workforce. Since the mid-1960s, the Center had recruited qualified minorities, but those efforts had yielded only modest results by the time the cuts came. In 1971, only thirty-four KSC employees were black and another twenty His-panic, Asian, or American Indian, a mere 2 percent of the workforce. This was lower than NASA as a whole, where 4.7 percent of employees were mi-norities. The difference may have reflected the large number of technical and engineering positions at KSC, compared to the higher number of admin-istrative positions in other NASA centers, such as NASA headquarters.[44] Recruitment of minorities into technical and engineering positions tended to lag, both at NASA and in other parts of American business and higher education. Then too, KSC's low number of minorities reflected its southern location.[45] Seventeen percent of KSC employees were women, which was actually slightly better than for NASA as a whole.[46] But the average pay level for KSC women was lower than that of men, even of male minority work-ers. The lower pay for women reflected their concentration in the clerical staff. Only fourteen women worked engineering or scientific positions. No women or minorities were at the top pay grade.[47]

Surprisingly, the number and position of minority workers at KSC actu-ally improved during the 1970s. Reductions in force were generally based on seniority. Since most of the first hired were white males, one might have guessed that force reductions would hit the ranks of blacks, Hispanics, and women hardest. Despite the adverse conditions of the 1970s, though, the Center made significant progress in diversity during this time. Minority em-ployees grew from 2 percent to 6 percent of the labor force, a rate faster than the agency as a whole.[48] No NASA installation did better.

Harder to maintain was the local infrastructure and communities that had grown up around the Kennedy Space Center. NASA and Department of Defense employment in the region reached its apex in the first half of 1968 with just over 43,000 workers. The earnings of federal employees and contractors constituted more than half of all the wages paid in Brevard County.[49] Florida companies had picked up a significant percentage of contracts let by KSC over the Apollo years.[50] Then suddenly 14,500 jobs in Brevard County disappeared between 1969 and 1971. The once booming Space Coast saw only modest increases in population during the 1970s.[51] In July 1970 a local newspaper ran a special report titled "Our Horizons Reach Beyond the Moon," but it might have been more realistically titled "Summer of Discontent." Boldfaced legends showed declines in bank deposits, electric meter connections, and auto sales. The bust of the moon boom turned a housing shortage into a housing glut. Once exhausted by the frenetic pace of work, now Space Coast workers were given "a whole week of Fridays."[52]

Skylab

By the mid-1970s KSC had secured a prominent role in at least one new space program—Skylab. Skylab was the first definite project to emerge out of the Apollo Applications Program. In comparison with Apollo, or the bolder plans for space stations and reusable space planes, Skylab was a modest, relatively low-cost effort, the sort of thing that could be undertaken in a time of reduced budgets. Existing equipment would do for this venture, a sort of cut-rate space station adapting Apollo-era hardware.[53]

The idea of a space station went back to the early 1920s. It matured in the vision of space outlined by von Braun in his magazine articles and by such popular authors as Arthur C. Clarke. In science fiction literature people read descriptions and saw detailed, graphic illustrations of an orbiting habitat where a crew lived and worked, carrying out experiments in life sciences, meteorology, and astronomy, all serviced through "cargo rockets" carrying equipment and supplies launched from the earth. Back in February 1959, NASA deputy administrator Hugh Dryden had made an orbiting laboratory one of the agency's goals. A few months later, NASA held its first conference on the project. By 1962, personnel from NASA headquarters and various centers agreed that work should proceed on the space station project. Development continued over the next several years, with support from the military.[54] In 1969 the space station idea received an unexpected boost from Stanley Kubrick's film *2001, A Space Odyssey.* The movie took its model of a future space habitat almost directly from the illustrations that had accompanied von Braun's magazine pieces—a giant two-rimmed wheel spinning above the clouds. Although the station idea had taken a backseat to the lunar landing, throughout the 1960s George Mueller at NASA headquarters had strongly promoted the concept, as did NASA administrator James Webb and his successor Thomas Paine.

In light of the budget constraints, however, a full station was impossible. Instead, NASA focused on a creative adaptation of the Saturn IB. The rocket's second stage contained a liquid-hydrogen propellant tank of nearly 10,000 cubic feet. It could be used as an orbiting workshop. The initial mission required two launches: one of an Apollo spacecraft carrying a crew of three, and the second putting the rigged-up workshop into orbit. The two would rendezvous and dock in space. Subsequent launches would take place at a fast pace as an ambitious schedule proposed putting several crews in space for months at a time in a number of other orbiting workshops. By the late 1960s, however, the realities of the federal budget had taken their toll and the Skylab program was severely scaled down. There would be a single orbiting station and three crews of three astronauts each.[55]

This shift in mission required several changes in KSC's organizational structure. In 1965, NASA headquarters had assigned the Center responsibility for prelaunch and checkout operations of the Apollo Applications Program, including the space station. In April 1970, in the interests of streamlining, Apollo and Skylab were combined into the Apollo-Skylab Program under one manager. A Sciences and Applications Projects Office dealt with scientific missions and other nonhuman space flights. This office would draw on "previous checkout and launch experience" but would bring together major elements of each mission at an early stage, to develop appropriate ground support equipment and procedures for handling flight hardware as it arrived at the Cape. The lessons of the past would be preserved, but incorporated in the now favored program structure used in Apollo. The hope was that, through these arrangements, KSC operations would maintain communications with specialists in development centers as new projects were prepared. KSC retained its traditional divisions, with a director of launch operations overseeing spacecraft, launch vehicle, and unmanned launches, but now added program and projects elements to deal with future and emerging missions.[56]

For Skylab, KSC took responsibility for launch vehicle checkout and preparation; for spacecraft and payload checkout and preparation; for launch facility design, construction, maintenance, operations, and advanced planning; for operation and coordination of supporting facilities; and for the technical and administrative support services for all NASA elements located in the area.[57] All of this presented a number of new challenges, in particular extensive work to prepare the laboratories and experiments and to ready the crew compartment with supplies for a much longer duration than any previous mission. Payload processing also required new facilities, notably "clean rooms" free of particles that, in zero gravity, might interfere with delicate wiring and instrumentation.[58] Most challenging, Skylab required placing two vehicles on the pad at the same time, one to launch the lab, the other to send up the crew.

In preparation, KSC engineers modified several Apollo facilities. On the mobile launcher built for Saturn V, they constructed a 127-foot pedestal affectionately known as the "milk stool" to serve as a platform for the smaller Saturn IB rocket that would launch astronauts to the Skylab. New clean rooms were installed to handle the lab, which had to be even freer of debris than the Apollo space capsule. The clean rooms included air locks, air showers, sticky mats, and shoe cleaners to remove as much debris as possible from workers. In keeping with the times, every effort was made to adapt existing equipment. Both the work itself and the tools to do the work drew heavily on the Center's prior experience.[59]

In subtle ways, however, the work being done at KSC changed. There was less margin for error, less chance to learn as one went, more need for planning, and more emphasis on designs that could head off problems and increase efficiency. Skylab began with an emphasis on training personnel for jobs before work started, rather than the on-the-job training that had been typical of Apollo. For greater efficiency, there was also a longer lead time for redesign of components, breaking the pattern of adding new components as stopgap measures to solve problems as they arose. But as good as all these new steps sounded, they may have been limited by budget constraints and uncertainty. Peak manpower requirements were not set until late into the Skylab program, making it impossible to train contractor personnel in time. Under tight budgets and some uncertainty as to the final mission, it was difficult to plan ahead, to determine what sort of training might be required, and to be assured that sufficient parts were on hand when needed.[60]

In fact, contrary to the hope that operations and design would be well integrated, budgets and schedules left the two separated. NASA's Aerospace Safety Advisory Panel noted that the launch center had not been included in teams that reviewed Skylab systems and operations. The absence of KSC personnel here "added to the difficulty of examining the compatibility between Skylab Orbital Assembly design and requirements from the point of view of KSC responsibility."[61] Once again, it had proved difficult in real-world conditions to "close the loop" between development and operations.

In May 1973 a two-stage version Saturn V rocket launched the 100-ton Skylab into earth orbit. It did not go off flawlessly, however. During the launch, Skylab's sunshade tore loose, leaving the lab baking in space and exposed to fast-moving meteoroids. To make matters worse, the shield took

7-1. Adapting Apollo-era technology for the Skylab program, KSC design engineers built the "milk stool" to allow the Saturn IB to use a pad and tower built for the much larger Saturn V.

with it one of Skylab's electricity-supplying solar panels and entangled the second so it could not fully deploy. After some fast thinking, a solution was found. The astronauts would rig a substitute shield and free the trapped panel. Eleven days later a manned Apollo command and service module combination was launched into orbit by a Saturn IB rocket and docked with the workshop. The repairs went well enough to make the station functional. The first crew members, Pete Conrad, Joseph Kerwin, and Paul Weitz, spent

28 days aloft, conducting experiments and proving that humans could live and work in space. A second crew stayed for 59 days, and a third for 84 days. They were the final occupants, however, for by this point all attention was focusing on a new program, the recently approved space shuttle. NASA decided that it had invested enough in Skylab, which was abandoned in orbit. The laboratory burned up in the earth's atmosphere in July 1979.[62]

Skylab had served several important purposes for NASA. First, it pushed forward the deep-seated agency agenda of preparing for a permanent human presence in space. In this it foreshadowed the development of a space station in the 1990s. Second, it gave NASA and its centers a major mission to work on at a time of austerity and uncertainty. This mission clearly reflected the temper of a time more interested in scientific research and terrestrial activities, such as earth observation from a laboratory in space. Third, for KSC it provided a new opportunity to extend its mastery of launch procedures and concepts. Out of the Skylab experience came an extensive study of what would be required for a long-term space station project. Included in this plan were proposals for new support buildings, adaptation of the VAB for testing and assembly of the space station itself, and use of the existing barges and canals that had ferried the Saturn elements to the Center. Perhaps most original, the plan included a new approach to management, with greater "coordination with user agencies, development of new program elements," and development of capabilities to "conduct and support the active program." It was a bold departure from the traditional NASA division of responsibility for projects and missions between centers, with mission management functions reserved for the Johnson Space Center in Houston. But it reflected an emerging sense that the complexity of missions and vehicles required greater coordination and planning than had been common in the Apollo era.[63]

Such possibilities still remained in the future. In the meantime, post-Skylab, KSC was prey to growing disquiet and restlessness, like a plane in a holding pattern. It would still be years before the space shuttle arrived at the Cape. The feeling of anxiety was revealed in a February 1973 random survey of employees. In most areas KSC came off badly, particularly concerning "job security." Participants responded that they never knew what was going to happen to their position from one week to the next. Management needed to do a better job of disseminating information. Of those surveyed, 55 percent saw "inconsistency in management's action in granting promotions." The one black member of the survey group felt that "most Blacks are held at GS 12 level, and . . . have very little chance of obtaining higher GS grades and supervisory status." Rather than receiving promotions, African Americans tended to receive incentive awards. This most likely reflected the lack of opportunities for advancement during the slowdown of the 1970s, a problem recognized by KSC directors. "We shall make a concerted effort," wrote the head of Launch Vehicle Operations, Hans Gruene, "to appoint minority individuals to future projects planning and to new programs such as the Space Shuttle." But real advancement might have to wait until "such time as the existing employment and promotion freeze is lifted."[64] Overall, participants in the survey wanted "interesting work, creative projects, opportunity to obtain advanced degrees, and additional training information made available to them." For that to happen, NASA top management should publicly "stand up and fight for our space programs and budgets," and improve public relations by getting the message out.[65]

Only one other human mission took place in the 1970s. In December 1973, KSC awarded a $14.6 million extension to a contract with Rockwell International for support in processing the command and service modules, spacecraft lunar adapter, launch escape system, and docking module for a rendezvous between an Apollo spacecraft and a Soviet Soyuz capsule. In the same month, KSC announced a $10.5 million contract extension to McDonnell Douglas Astronautics to process the Saturn IB second stage for launching and docking the Apollo spacecraft. At a cost of $250 million, the Cold War superpowers would shake hands in space, exchange crews, and conduct joint experiments in the Apollo-Soyuz Test Project.

On July 15, 1975, American astronauts blasted off from the Cape and two days later met with an orbiting Soyuz vehicle. It was an important cultural and political event, and perhaps foreshadowed the sort of international cooperation in space that would become a feature of the post–Cold War 1990s. But beyond testing a universal docking module and honing skills at space rendezvous, it was little more than a public relations mission, marking the final phase of the Apollo era. It was also the last launch scheduled until the shuttle, due in another four years, arrived. Whatever boost the Apollo-Soyuz project provided, a renewed sense of apprehension quickly followed, and the blank future loomed ahead.[66]

Flying without Astronauts

Skepticism about space exploration had robbed NASA of some of its stature, but in one area even skeptics could not deny the agency's accomplishments. Overshadowed by Apollo, scientific missions blossomed in the 1970s. Indeed, some programs seemed to benefit from the very trends that were otherwise troubling NASA's human space flight agenda. For example, Nixon's Space Task Group had emphasized application of space technology to problems on earth. It mentioned communications, natural resource conservation, navi-

7-2. Though fewer humans flew in space in the 1970s, plenty of unmanned missions went up, using vehicles like the reliable Delta.

gation, and national security. These were all things that could benefit from scientific missions sending satellites and experiments into space.[67]

Whereas rockets for human space flight had developed rapidly in the 1960s, robotic mission vehicles took a slower, more evolutionary path. In this they benefited from continuous learning and incremental improvements.[68] Every launch vehicle used for robotic missions in the 1970s had been developed in the 1950s or 1960s. Some, including Atlas and Titan, came from military programs.[69] The workhorse of the fleet, however, was the Delta, used for medium-weight payloads. It provided the thrust for 55 percent of nonhuman missions leaving the Cape between 1958 and 1977.[70] In August 1960, a Thor-Delta launched Echo 1, the world's first communications satellite. Later dropping Thor from its name, Delta played an especially prominent role in the communications revolution. It was the vehicle of choice not only for NASA but for other government agencies and foreign countries as well. Delta and its companion boosters were upgraded several times. These changes were integrated into test and launch procedures, so that the success rate continued to increase. In the 1950s and early 1960s, KSC achieved a launch success rate of 65 percent. Between 1969 and 1979, however, the rate improved to an average of 92 percent.[71]

Launching robotic missions differed in certain ways from launching human missions. With few exceptions, robotic missions took off from Cape Canaveral Air Force Station (CCAFS), adjacent to the Merritt Island facilities. The CCAFS area housed numerous launch assets—launch complexes and pads—overseen by an air force wing commander at Patrick Air Force Base. Responsibility for both the launch facilities and range and flight safety remained with the air force, while responsibility for management of launches fell to the Kennedy Space Center. There was no central "mission control" for the unmanned flights. Each had a different launch team, working out of blockhouses near the pad.[72]

Much as with human space flight, though, KSC oversaw the final assembly and testing of rockets for robotic flights as they arrived at the Cape. KSC personnel determined the facilities needed for processing the mission payload, as well as which launch vehicle to use—an Atlas, Delta, or Titan. Assembled at the Vertical Integration Building (VIB)—the counterpart of the manned program's VAB—the rocket was loaded on a truck or rail car for transport to the launchpad. Testing and checkout continued on the pad, as with human missions, with a series of steps designed to simulate the conditions of launch, including tanking the rocket with volatile fuels and assuring that all vehicle systems operated as designed under their own power.[73] Here one crucial difference emerged. The last step was not installation of astronauts but of the mission payload.

Payloads were developed by a number of NASA centers or, in the case of many commercial satellites, by private firms.[74] Whether a communications satellite or a scientific package for exploring near or far space, the payload comprised a number of sensitive and expensive pieces of hardware. These were loaded in the rocket's nose fairing and checked out before launch. Since each payload had special needs, checkout at the Cape was the responsibility of the builder. But to eliminate any uncertainty at launch time, KSC acted as "payload coordinator." KSC personnel engaged with the payload developer in a long series of coordination meetings, which also included the Cape's range officers. At these meetings the parties determined mission needs and assessed the readiness of the spacecraft for launch. Sometimes the meetings revealed hazardous materials in the mission payload or excessive weight that

7-3. Robert Gray *(left)* headed Unmanned Launch Operations at KSC. He was succeeded by John Neilon *(right)*.

could not be lifted by the launch vehicle.[75] In this "host mode," KSC accommodated the launch needs of government, private industry, and foreign countries. Businesses and foreign countries reimbursed KSC for the launch services it provided.[76]

As with all space flight, robotic missions experienced a trade-off between cost, reliability, and schedule. Greater reliability could be achieved with longer times for preparation and checkout. A shorter schedule with faster turnaround implied less time for testing, and thus higher risks. While not the same as losing a human life, the loss of a robotic spacecraft was expensive. High failure rates or problems with launching could drive up costs and move customers to other launch facilities, such as those being developed in France and Japan.

Different missions involved different judgments about these trade-offs. Commercial users, often facing competition, were especially keen on cost and speed. With scientific missions, however, timing could be the crucial factor. Flights into deep space had to fit in specific launch windows, taking advantage of an alignment of planets that might not occur again for months or years. On the other hand, some scientific payloads were extremely fragile and could not be replicated if the mission failed, so careful preparation was needed to guarantee a successful launch. Adding to these constraints were limits on payload configurations. The principal investigators of scientific missions sought to pack as many experiments into one launch vehicle as possible, to spread the fixed costs. But such packing meant extremely tight space and weight requirements. It was sometimes difficult to predict in advance exactly how the final configuration of payloads would look, with spacecraft and experiments from different teams of investigators evolving simultaneously. Scientists often resented the requirement to mold their experiments to vehicle space and payload configurations. KSC engineers, on the other hand, disliked late changes in payload design.[77]

KSC's involvement in robotic launches had begun with an "unmanned" group operating alongside the more famous human space flight team. Robert Gray joined NASA in 1958 with a proven track record as a launch director for the Vanguard program. Before he left KSC in 1970, he would supervise 145 launches of unmanned spacecraft.[78] Gray's original position was as Goddard launch operations director at the Eastern Test Range (ETR), Cape Canaveral Air Force Station, and the Western Test Range(WTR) at Vandenberg AFB, California. This complicated title reflected the still unformed nature of the early launch site, when it was not clear if separate NASA centers would do their own launching or if there would be a single NASA launch directorate. When KSC became launch center for all of NASA in 1965, Gray became KSC's unmanned launch operations director.[79] In 1970 another veteran of Vanguard, John Neilon, took over from Gray. In the 1960s in particular, when NASA was focused on the lunar program, little of the operational detail of robotic missions made its way up to Center director Debus's office, giving Gray and Neilon substantial latitude in organizing their work.

Early unmanned missions were designed to prepare the way for human flights. The "bioflights" of 1958 and 1959 took primates into space to learn how humans might react. Ranger moon missions from 1959 to 1966 sought to give scientists greater knowledge about the place where the astronauts would land.[80] The Surveyor and Lunar Orbiter programs explored the surface of the moon in greater detail. In addition to sending photographs and television transmissions back to earth, Surveyor touched down on the lunar surface, demonstrating that a soft landing was possible. It also left equipment behind, collecting vital geological information and broadcasting telemetry data back to earth.[81]

The Kennedy Space Center's role in the launch of *Surveyor 1* provides a window onto the crucial position it held in these early missions. Hardware came by truck, plane, or ship and included the launch vehicle (in this case the Atlas-Centaur) and the Surveyor spacecraft, which weighed just over a ton. KSC engineers erected the first stage at Launch Complex 36 on March 21, 1966, followed ten days later by the second stage. After encapsulating the spacecraft inside a protective fairing on April 15, they mated it with the Atlas-Centaur booster. Next came a tanking test to check for leaks and ensure system integrity. In the case of *Surveyor 1*, a Flight Acceptance Composite Test (FACT) revealed problems that required de-encapsulation. After correcting numerous problems, test engineers performed another FACT on May 18, with remating and encapsulating a week later. Launch day came on May 30. These standard operating procedures were used again and again by the unmanned launch group at KSC.[82]

Robots of Science

The early nonhuman missions received less acclaim than the human missions of the 1960s they supported. Robotic missions that did not support the lunar program fared even worse. Before the scaling back of human space flight at the end of the 1960s, they competed for funds at a severe disadvantage. In 1967 a requested $2 billion Mars lander was canceled and replaced with the more modest Viking project (discussed later).[83] Still, during the 1960s, NASA undertook a number of planetary missions that paved the way for an ambitious agenda of robotic space exploration in the 1970s.

Efforts to send robotic vehicles to other planets suffered a high failure rate in the early years. One of two attempts to fly by Venus in the Mariner program failed, as did four straight missions of the Pioneer program, which between 1958 and 1960 sought to study cosmic radiation.[84] Success finally came with the fifth flight, as *Pioneer 5* flew aboard a Thor-Able on March 1, 1960, sending back the first interplanetary radio signal the following June and establishing solar orbit. In all, there were eleven failures of planetary missions in the early 1960s before the Lunar Orbiter project and the soft landings of Surveyors on the moon in the second half of the decade. A second major period of deep space missions in the mid-1970s brought even more impressive results. Between 1971 and 1978, twelve successful launches in a row sent spacecraft to explore the solar system.[85]

Space science increased substantially within NASA's budget to a high of 17 percent during these years. One mission, which had been put on the back burner by the moon shot, now had a second chance. A year before men landed on the moon's surface, NASA approved plans for an unmanned mission to Mars.[86] A new Viking spacecraft carrying two high-resolution cameras would make a soft landing and provide a 354-degree view of the red planet. Viking also carried a mechanical arm, a "soil sampler" capable of scooping up Martian dirt and analyzing its mineral and chemical contents.[87]

The Viking lander arrived at KSC in January 1975, followed a month later by the orbiter portion of the hardware. The next month, the two were mated and a team of engineers from KSC, JPL, and hardware builder Martin Marietta finished checking all systems. Technicians at KSC also sterilized the lander, to be sure that any evidence of life it picked up in the soil samples had not come from planet Earth. This process involved high heat, so the spacecraft's sensitive scientific instruments had to be designed to withstand extremes of temperatures. Finally, on August 11, *Viking 1* was brought to the pad at Launch Complex 41, ready to be launched aboard a Titan heavy-lift rocket.[88]

Viking challenged KSC's Unmanned Launch Operations directorate. Two Viking missions were due to fly within a month of each other. Both had to use the same pad, LC-41, the only one capable of handling the Titan-Centaur booster. As John Neilon explained, "we took the Titan scheduled to fly second to the pad ahead of time and did as much checkout as we could. . . . Then we brought it back and prepared the first Titan for *Viking I*."[89] Countdown to launch was halted after discovery of a faulty control valve and low batteries on the orbiter. Problems with the first Titan delayed the launch for nine days. It finally flew on August 20, 1975. Similarly, *Viking 2* nearly missed its launch window because of problems with the orbiter radio. It launched on September 9. KSC routinely dealt with the kinds of prelaunch problems encountered by the Vikings, although not usually on the same mission.

One of the most ambitious of the deep space missions of the 1970s was Voyager. Voyager's initial planning began in 1967 as a mission to Mars using a Saturn V as the launch vehicle and employing the "capsule bus system" planned to soft-land on Mars in 1973.[90] But this Voyager mission never took off because of budget constraints and NASA's acceptance of Viking as a cost-effective alternative in 1968. Eventually Voyager reemerged as a grand tour of the solar system, taking advantage of a once-in-176-years alignment of the earth with the outer planets.

Voyager 2 flew on August 20, 1977, aboard the Titan-Centaur vehicle. *Voyager 1* followed on September 5. Because of its more efficient flight path, *Voyager 1* arrived at Jupiter first. The craft continued on to photograph Saturn, Uranus, and Neptune. Voyager photos revealed five previously unknown moons around Saturn and detailed the planet's intricate ring system. *Voyager 2* discovered the stormy atmosphere of Neptune, which demonstrated hurricane-like patterns, as well as six unknown moons as it flew a mere 3,100 miles from the surface.[91] Both Voyagers left the solar system, but will send back telemetry until the year 2020.

During this same period, near-earth missions for terrestrial purposes also picked up. Use of space beyond the ionosphere for communications had been explored as far back as the 1950s through experiments conducted by the Naval Research Laboratory (NRL). On July 24, 1954, the NRL succeeded in bouncing a message off the moon. The future of satellite communications,

7-4. *Voyager 1*'s grand tour of the solar system started with a ride into space aboard a Titan-Centaur combination.

however, lay with human-fashioned rather than natural objects. In 1954, science fiction writer Arthur C. Clarke proposed a global communications network using artificial satellites. With development and improvement of rocket technology in the late 1950s, this became feasible.[92]

NASA built its own communications satellite named Echo, a giant 100-foot Mylar-coated balloon. Like the moon, it served to reflect and relay radio signals. Echo was launched from the Cape on May 13, 1960, but never reached the desired altitude because the Thor-Delta launch vehicle's second stage misfired. Echo 2 was launched on January 25, 1964, from Vandenberg, ending experiments with passive systems.[93] American telecommunications firm AT&T developed the first active relay satellite, Telstar, as part of an ambitious plan to cover the earth with communications satellites. Though it did not achieve that goal, AT&T quickly put two Telstars into orbit, paying KSC $6 million to provide launch services. This was the start of a pattern that would mark much of NASA's work in communications satellites: private-firm payloads launched by KSC on a reimbursable basis. *Telstar 1* rode atop a Delta, leaving the Cape on July 10, 1962. That same day it began broadcasting live television across the Atlantic, to great popular acclaim. The 171-pound *Telstar 1* was followed by *Telstar 2* on May 7, 1963.

The structure of the communications satellite industry changed significantly in 1962, with passage of the Communications Satellite Act. Instead of individual firms, a corporation called Comsat, privately owned but sponsored by the U.S. government, was given monopoly control of this technology. Comsat also represented the United States in Intelsat, a consortium of satellite organizations among the nations of the noncommunist world. A synchronous orbit satellite, *Syncom 1*, was launched in 1963, followed by *Syncom 2* later that year, and *Syncom 3* in 1964 to provide coverage for the Tokyo Olympics.[94] During the 1970s, KSC launched forty domestic communications satellites and fifteen more for foreign nations.[95] NASA continued to develop its own satellites, but NASA communications projects were not to compete with private ventures. Instead NASA satellites gathered useful knowledge by, for example, measuring the earth's radiation belt to prepare the way for future satellites whose delicate electronics might be disrupted by the radiation level. In 1973, budget cuts forced NASA to phase out its communications satellite program. In the period following, KSC's role in satellite launches was vastly reduced.[96]

In the meteorological field, NASA centers played a more substantial role in sponsoring and carrying out missions. Starting in 1960, the TIROS (Television Infrared Observational Satellites) missions provided weather data from earth orbit. Eight TIROS were launched between 1969 and 1978.[97] In 1970 the establishment of the National Oceanic and Atmospheric Administration (NOAA) provided a bureaucratic context for civilian funding of weather and environmental satellites. As NASA shifted focus to earth-oriented missions, NOAA teamed with NASA. The space agency provided launch and development services, and NOAA acted as administrator of a series of weather and earth- observation satellites.

The desire to address social problems such as overpopulation and pollution seemed amenable to satellites that could map, observe, and study the earth and its environment. The Earth Resources Technology Satellite or ERTS/Landsat program grew out of a multiagency effort to collect such data from space. KSC directed the launch of these earth-observing satellites from Space Launch Complex (SLC) 2 at the Western Test Range from 1964 to 1978.[98]

A thoughtful student of space science might well consider the robotic missions of these years the great unheralded triumphs of NASA. These missions, after all, not only provided an enormous amount of data for pure research on the solar system but also carried out the sort of "earth-oriented" missions that NASA was struggling to define for a skeptical Congress. Improved weather forecasting, inventories of endangered earth resources, and a vastly enhanced global communications network paid real dollar benefits. Yet they lacked the excitement that came with human space flight. Ordinary citizens outside the scientific community never embraced these missions the way they did the lunar program. NASA's place in the hearts and minds of the American people was still closely tied to sending astronauts into space. The public remained interested in space but was anticipating the next human mission.

Renewing the Space Coast

During the 1970s, KSC became firmly entrenched as the place where the public best experienced this sense of wonder and heroism in space missions. There was something about watching a rocket, pencil thin against the wide sky, as it left earth behind. Seeing it move steadily upward, knowing that it would not stop until it penetrated an alien realm, gave civilians a vicarious connection to the experience of astronauts. Facing the hard times of the 1970s, Kurt Debus saw Space Coast tourism as a means of renewal for both NASA and the KSC region. "The interest [in space] is there," he noted, "but only for the mission period."[99] To keep the fascination percolating, KSC needed more sophisticated visitor facilities.

The first KSC visitor center had opened in August 1967, in accordance with the Space Act of 1958 that required NASA to inform the public about its work. Although an improvement on the earlier self-driven tours, it had only 20,000 feet of space and parking for a maximum of 8,000 cars. The anticipated 1971 opening of Disney World in nearby Orlando was expected to increase KSC attendance, with some projections as high as 4 million people by 1975. KSC officials negotiated with Disney, which was offering package deals for tourists who came to its new Central Florida theme park. Unsure if it had sufficient attractions to keep tourists enthralled the entire week—the optimal time for a vacationer, according to Disney—the company proposed including KSC as part of its week-long ticket. A one-day charter bus would leave the theme park near Orlando and stop by for a drive-through of the Merritt Island complex before heading off for Cypress Gardens, an old-time Florida tourist spot, for the remainder of the day. KSC officials balked, however, feeling that a quick drive-through was not adequate. They planned an expanded visitor center, with a range of educational experiences appropriate for something as serious and scientific as space exploration.[100]

As predicted, Disney's opening in 1971 vastly increased attendance at the Cape, by some 30 percent over the previous year. Despite the boom, KSC officials remained conflicted about their center's relationship to the theme park. Tourists received free rental cars with Disney hotel package deals, giving them access to the Space Coast some fifty miles away. But those who arrived after their Disney experience expected the same level of entertainment and polish as at the theme park. That was not what they got. KSC displays, although technically relevant, often lacked a story line. In large part they consisted of engineering trade show exhibits donated to NASA.[101] Senator Ed Gurney led the legislative call for upgrading the visitor center.[102] Displays underwent renovation with a $2.3 million infusion of funds from Congress in 1971. KSC constructed new exhibits on the benefits of space exploration, applications, technology, and satellites, reflecting earth-focused themes as well as the already featured human exploration of the stars.

An improved visitor center gave KSC a firmer role in the economic and cultural life of a region coming to be defined as a tourist hot spot. Meanwhile, other changes in the local landscape reemphasized the launch complex's unique mixture of outlandish industrial hardware with a pristine natural environment. Indeed, the natural area around the center became more important in its relationship with the community, and an increasingly important asset to the Center generally.

Land had always been a major concern for the launch center, serving as a buffer protecting the public against accidents. In contrast to other NASA installations, KSC required substantial amounts of land to do its job, and to house the extensive facilities that went into the launch process. But how to use the land around the Center had always been an issue. Residents of Brevard County appealed for some of the "disused" land for a jetport. But in fact KSC moved in the opposite direction in this period, not turning land over to public or private developers but returning it to its natural state.

The Department of the Interior had managed the Merritt Island Wildlife Refuge since 1963. Expansion of the protected area began the following year, with an addition of 13,400 acres. In 1972 the refuge expanded again to include some 100,000 acres.[103] Establishment of a sanctuary solved NASA's immediate problem with the surrounding population and revived local support that had been eroded in the initial land acquisition. In later years, preservation of the sensitive habitat surrounding the launch areas became a political asset to the spaceport.

In 1968, hunting had returned to the wildlife area on a reservation only basis. Getting a spot at the duck blind that winter was, it turned out, harder than getting tickets to the Orange Bowl to watch Joe Namath lead the Jets to victory over the Colts in Super Bowl III. Overnight camping at Dummitt's Cove and a variety of saltwater and freshwater fishing also became available through permits. All sports activities were strictly managed in accordance with KSC needs.[104] But the reopening of lands proved a public relations coup, highlighted on November 15–17, 1968, when more than 4,000 Boy Scouts staged a camporee at the Dummitt campsite.[105] The new arrangements gave back to the northern part of Brevard County an attractive source of income to balance its slow economic growth relative to the southern half. More important, it satisfied a growing conservation movement in Florida and the nation.

Aside from ducks, some 224 other species of birds occupied the refuge area. These birds became the beloved subjects of New York ornithologist Allan D. Cruickshank and his wife, Helen. Like many migrants from northern states, the Cruickshanks came to Florida for the winter seasons, and they eventually settled permanently in Rockledge, a few miles south of the Kennedy Space Center. As leaders in the National Audubon Society since 1936, they had been among the local voices in support of creation of the wildlife refuge.[106] The Cruickshanks focused on preserving the land around the space center for birds. Perhaps no single species was more closely tied to support of refuge expansion than the southern bald eagle. Merritt Island in fact hosted a rare breeding area for the national symbol, endangered since the use of DDT had driven numbers to dangerous lows in the late 1950s.[107]

So successful was KSC in integrating with its natural environment, indeed enhancing that environment, that sometimes trouble arose over proper land use. In 1971 an interagency rivalry pitted the Bureau of Sport Fisheries and Wildlife against the National Park Service over control of the Merritt Island acreage. Birdwatchers like the Cruickshanks favored the Bureau's management because of its track record of preserving bird habitat.[108] In the U.S. Senate, Republican Gurney sponsored a bill creating the National Seashore under control of the National Park Service. Gurney looked to the seashore to help an economically beleaguered Central Florida. In a letter to NASA headquarters in Washington, KSC public affairs chief Gordon L. Harris wrote, "I honestly don't know at this point what impact a seashore activity would have upon shuttle launch operations, or vice versa."[109] Shuttle and seashore would eventually learn to coexist, though not without further con-

7-5. Bald eagles nest in the Merritt Island Refuge surrounding the Kennedy Space Center.

flict between local residents and KSC managers. More important, though, this sort of debate about land use indicated that the area around KSC had come to be more than just a buffer to protect the public from stray rockets. Rather than becoming the hub of an industrial and aerospace landscape, KSC merged its space-age technology into the natural landscape.

Transition to Shuttle

The February 1973 employee survey had been an eye-opener at KSC, and confirmed Kurt Debus's conviction that "the best motivation for creativity is a responsibility to do useful work." By November of that year there was reason for optimism. "A creative climate now exists at KSC," Debus wrote to Richard C. McCurdy, associate administrator for organization and management, "as a result of our assignment to design shuttle facilities and equipment and to participate in the design of flight hardware. This decision has stimulated KSC employees in a positive manner, with an attendant boost in morale." Debus was of course referring to the long anticipated space shuttle, and the difficult struggle that had occurred over the years regarding the form that this new space vehicle would take. Although controversial, the decision to go ahead with the shuttle and to make KSC its launch center marked a turning point for NASA and KSC in the 1970s.[110]

As with the idea of a station in space, the concept of a space shuttle had a history stretching back to the early days of space flight. From the winged rockets of the 1930s to von Braun's concept of a "cargo rocket" with a winged upper stage popularized in the *Collier's* series, a reusable craft that could transport crew and payload regularly between earth and the heavens was very much part of the vision of America's space program. It was also closely tied to the notion of astronauts living and working in space, and to future exploration of the moon and perhaps Mars as well. In a speech given in London in 1968, NASA's George Mueller outlined this link directly: "the next major thrust in space will be the development of an economical launch vehicle for shuttling between earth and the installations." Space stations would serve as "fuel and supply bases, and as transfer points en route to high or distant orbits, to lunar landings, or toward the planets." Essential to this vision, Mueller argued, would be "the capability to resupply expendables as well as to change and/or augment crews and laboratory equipment." Only an "efficient earth-to-orbit transportation system—an economical space shuttle" would do this job.[111] The shuttle itself was thus one part of a modular system that included an eventual space station serviced by the shuttle and providing economies through reusability and simplification of hardware.[112]

Mueller's words, which were echoed by subsequent NASA officials, emphasized reusability as the key to keeping mission costs down. "The shuttle ideally would be able to operate in a mode similar to that of large commercial air transports," he stated, "and be compatible with the environment of major airports." The goal was airline-type operations between earth and space. The issue of cost and reusability was an important one, given the fiscal climate. Launch vehicles used only once came with an exorbitantly high price tag: $185 million for a Saturn V, for example. Reusability came to be seen as key to driving down the cost of space flight from thousands of dollars per pound lifted to hundreds or even tens of dollars per pound.[113] This search for "orders of magnitude" reductions in cost drove NASA vehicle design work in the 1970s, and would in turn drive the work at KSC when the shuttle finally arrived there.

At first glance, one might see the shuttle's justification as a cost-saving technology in line with long-standing NASA concerns about cost and efficiency. NASA engineers had, like engineers everywhere, always taken cost as a constraint in designing equipment. How could it be otherwise, for in real life everything comes with a price tag and no one has a limitless budget, not even NASA during the flush years of the Apollo program. At KSC, Kurt Debus had developed the launch concepts for Saturn in part on cost considerations, notably the scale economies that would be realized when there were dozens of Saturns leaving the Cape each year. That never happened, of course, but it served as the basis for constructing the massive Merritt Island facilities.[114]

But in the 1970s, cost considerations took on greater significance. For one thing, it was clear that the shuttle would have to be built in a tighter budget frame, with far less toleration of cost overruns. Cost overruns had led to Congressional investigations even in the more generous Apollo era. It was certain that Congress would come down hard if the shuttle's design and construction costs could not be contained. The decision to go ahead with the shuttle was thus politically charged. The vehicle's design and concept changed to meet budgetary constraints. Indeed, only after a number of politically motivated design changes did the Space Transportation System, as it was formally called, finally get President Richard Nixon's approval on January 5, 1972.

In his official statement authorizing the shuttle, Nixon wrote that the new vehicle was "designed to help transform the space frontier of the 1970s into familiar territory, easily accessible for human endeavor in the 1980s and '90s." This economically defined goal was still harnessed to a bold vision of frontier, though one that also took into account the new emphasis on earth-oriented achievements. The shuttle would "go a long way toward delivering the rich benefits of practical space utilization and the valuable spin-offs from space efforts into the daily lives of Americans and all people," the president declared. By venturing into space in this fashion, Americans were no longer fighting a Cold War battle for the hearts and minds of allies, but rather stretching "our ability to cope with physical challenges of earth and broaden[ing] our opportunities for international cooperation in low-cost, multipurpose space missions." Could this be as inspiring as the venture to the moon? Those supporting the shuttle thought so. "Views of the earth from space have shown us how small and fragile our home planet truly is," the president continued. "We are learning the imperatives of universal brotherhood and global ecology—learning to think and act as guardians of one tiny blue and green island in the trackless oceans of the universe."[115]

With $5.5 billion promised over a six-year period, and $250 million secured in FY 1973 for start-up costs, the shuttle was now on track. Just three weeks after Nixon's decision, NASA administrator James Fletcher spoke optimistically that the 1973 budget appropriation would "enable the U.S. space program to move forward on all fronts." His confidence was not misplaced, for NASA's budget for the shuttle doubled each year from 1973 to 1976. By 1977, as funds for production of the orbiter and main engines were allocated, NASA budget appropriations rose to $3.8 billion, a figure not seen since 1969.[116]

With cost reduction the overriding goal and justification of the shuttle,

NASA centers had to develop new skills and knowledge. A report by the Space Task Group stressed how the shuttle would gain efficiency from "commonality," or the sharing of a few major systems for a variety of missions; "reusability," or employing the same systems over and over again; and "economy," in this context meaning reusable elements, simplified hardware, streamlined development, and sufficient planning from the start to reduce the need for later modifications. These were laudable goals, but they were substantially different from the earlier emphasis on research and development at NASA. Earlier, the focus had been on the creation of technology that did not yet exist for a mission that was a radical step beyond the known—a trip to the moon. By contrast, the shuttle era would be predicated on incremental development and innovation focused on cost savings. There would be plenty of new technology, to be sure, for the shuttle was a radical new design. As with any new departure in design, this meant that there was a lot to learn in both the building and the operating of the vehicle. But that learning would be done with an eye toward long-term operational efficiency.[117] And operational efficiency had important implications for KSC, NASA's launch operations center.

With the last Apollo launch in December 1972, and with Skylab terminating quickly, KSC began to define its role in the new shuttle era. The Center restructured its Design Engineering Directorate to prepare for a new type of vehicle and set up a Shuttle Projects Office.[118] The projects office was to carry out program management functions, coordinating the hardware and operational elements needed to handle a new vehicle and the new types of payloads it would be carrying. G. Merritt Preston was named shuttle project manager and Andrew Pickett deputy project manager. Grady Williams, in charge of developing the shuttle's launch processing software, moved to deputy director of Design Engineering, while Ray Clark, who designed the layout of shuttle facilities, became director.[119]

By the fall of 1973, Debus felt more secure about the Center's role in shuttle activity, but he wanted to increase the scope of KSC's responsibility. He acknowledged that KSC should "continue to be [the] systems integration and launch operations" axis, since its expertise lay "mainly in the integration, checkout and launch of space vehicles." However, once the flight hardware and ground support were worked out, Debus realized the entire Space Transportation System would need an operator. He wanted KSC to have the job. It was best placed, he believed, to treat the shuttle as an "airline" with KSC the "airport." The launch center thus would have to take an active role in shuttle development, as it had in past programs, and not merely be the "ship and shoot" point. It would need to perform "configuration management, sustaining engineering, logistics management, maintenance and

7-6. Kurt Debus,
near the time of his
retirement.

modification of flight and ground hardware, and mission planning and detailed scheduling of ground operations." KSC would also be the ideal spot for preflight training for "Shuttle experimenters and other passengers." And, as an airline operator, "KSC would schedule payloads to particular flights." Centralization of this function, Debus argued, could provide cut-rate prices to those uses that did not need priority in the schedule but could instead "operate on a space-available or deferred launch date basis." In short, Debus's objective was "to develop facilities and GSE [ground support equipment] for economical support to the Shuttle, and then to operate the airline and the airport in a cost-effective manner" in order to "support the Agency's objective of a low cost, reliable Space Transportation System."[120] To those at KSC, it seemed perfectly clear that their operational expertise was vital to a vehicle that promised operational economies.

Debus's words proved to be insightful. But he would not be there to see how things played out. He was heading toward retirement, secure at least that a major new program had been approved. Much changed in the short time between approval of the shuttle and Debus's departure. The basic organizational structure and management put into place at KSC between 1965 and 1968 shifted to reflect the new vehicle and the new mandate to lower cost through economies of scale. Longtime KSC deputy director Albert Siepert left. Rocco Petrone, whose strong-willed management had helped to get the launch facilities built and the testing and launch of the Apollo-Saturn vehicles on schedule, decamped for NASA headquarters. Some of the familiar names from the race to the moon were still in place, but Karl Sendler and Hans Gruene, both immigrants with Debus from Germany, would soon follow Debus into retirement. As the shuttle made its way through the design and construction phases and toward KSC, many of those who had led the mission to the moon would be gone, replaced by the younger generation they had trained. Debus's retirement in 1974, combined with reorganization for the shuttle, marked a turning point in the Center's leadership.

*   *   *

Kurt Debus had given the Kennedy Space Center its initial form and structure. He had shaped its role within the space program. Although, like many others at NASA, he had felt frustrated by the difficulty of securing funding for programs that might have included further exploration of the moon, of Mars, and possibly of space beyond earth's solar system, he embraced the shuttle as perhaps many did—as a necessary compromise in the post-Apollo period of tight budgets. Convinced that the public had been excited back in July 1969 because "man had left the earth" rather than because man had landed on the moon, Debus could leave KSC believing that the shuttle held out great promise in terms of recapturing the enthusiasm of Americans for the space program. He would live to see the shuttle fly, dying on Columbus Day 1983.[121]

8

✳
✳
✳

Learning to Fly the Shuttle

*"The honeymoon was over, we had
to find cheaper ways of doing things."*

Walt Kapryan

"Abandoned in place" is the military term for a facility left for scrap. By 1980
that was the fate of many of the early launchpads at the Cape, the words
stenciled on the aging blockhouses and gantries that had been used to send
Mercury and Gemini astronauts on their way. John Glenn's launchpad lay in
ruins, palmetto bugs and lizards stalking the concrete; the metal tower that
had held his rocket upright was dismantled and sold. Thirty-four launchpads
had been built on the Cape, but only nine remained in service.[1]

Not everything disappeared. Eight of the abandoned sites were named
historic landmarks, one becoming the Air Force Space and Missile Museum.
Most important, the vast Launch Complex 39 from which men left earth
for the moon was being refitted and readied for a new mission. It would be
adapted for the space shuttle, the new human space flight vehicle anxiously
awaited at Kennedy Space Center and throughout NASA. But in the refitting
much had to be changed. Outdated equipment that had participated in the
moon launch was sold, given away, or left for salvage. Objects ranging from
compact hair dryers to pallets of obsolete electronics were put up for public
auction. What role the dryers had played in the Apollo mission was unclear.[2]
Meanwhile, things were bustling at KSC as the refitting work commenced
in earnest. The Launch Control Center, VAB, and pads were made ready for
the new-generation rocket. But the 400-foot-tall, 9-million-pound launch
tower for Saturn V was gone, its resting place an empty field behind KSC
headquarters. As flowers sprouted through its steel latticework, the pace of
activity picked up dramatically in preparation for a scheduled first shuttle
launch in 1979.

The Shuttle and the Cape

Although KSC was named the launch site for the shuttle in 1972, there was much uncertainty leading up to this decision. Starting from scratch with a new vehicle design seemed an ideal opportunity to rethink launch concepts and locations. There were a wide range of factors to consider in a site: climate, altitude, latitude, environment, and existing facilities and resources. There was also politics. The chairman of the Senate Space Committee, Clinton Anderson, argued in favor of White Sands in his home state of New Mexico, a move that would have returned the space program to its place of origin. Shuttle site selection was delayed a year as Anderson pushed for White Sands. Meanwhile a task force headed by Senator Alan Cranston of California lobbied in favor of Edwards Air Force Base. Politicians in Utah and Oklahoma also offered air bases to serve as the new craft's home. Florida congressmen, backed by longtime NASA supporters in the House such as Texan Olin Teague, argued strongly in favor of using existing facilities as a cost-saving measure.[3] Before it was over, some 40 states and 150 sites would be vying for what was believed to be "the last big space money of the century."[4] Housing the launch site was expected to inject into the local economy some $1.5 billion a year for a decade and add 45,000 jobs to the winning state.

Politics seemed to favor New Mexico, with Anderson chairing a key Senate committee, followed by California, with its giant aerospace interests and huge congressional delegation. New Mexico, as well as rival Oklahoma, had another advantage—altitude. Launching from a higher altitude meant the shuttle had to travel through less of the dense near-earth atmosphere. Sitting 5,500 feet above sea level, White Sands would permit the shuttle to carry an additional three tons of cargo.[5] With all these factors in play, it soon became a gloves-off match.[6] A lot was at stake for KSC, which faced probable closure if it lost out.

Despite an altitude advantage, the inland sites had several drawbacks. The logic of shuttle economics was to have a single vehicle carry out a variety of missions to a variety of orbits, from polar to retrograde. Launching from the interior gave far fewer launch azimuths to choose from than launching from the coast. An additional consideration, also economic, soon came into play and favored coastal locations. Although the original shuttle design had called for full reusability, budget considerations mandated a modified, partially recoverable system with attached solid rocket boosters. Only flights over water would be safe for booster landing and recovery. Before that design change, KSC's location near water and its unpredictable weather had been a disadvantage. Should something go wrong and the shuttle have to ditch in the ocean, recovery would be more difficult. Now, flying over the ocean was an advantage. These factors knocked out White Sands, though Merritt Island was still competing with California as well as a possible new site on the Gulf of Mexico. The Gulf lost out when cost studies favored an existing site over a virgin one.[7] With the local population in Brevard County used to launches, there was less chance of a costly delay or disruption from public protests.[8] NASA had already received letters from citizens fearful of shuttle takeoff and landing sites right in their backyards.[9]

With only Florida and California left, there was just one more issue to consider—one launch site or two? No existing site, the Cape included, was perfect for all missions. Launching polar orbit flights from KSC, for example, meant flying over populated regions in the United States, as well as over Cuba. Certain launches for polar orbit would take the shuttle on the same trajectory as a missile attack against the Soviet Union.[10] Although a dual arrangement meant higher operating costs, there seemed no choice. Once the bicoastal option gained favor, though, saving money by reusing facilities at the Cape took on even greater significance.[11] Although NASA expected to phase out "expendable" vehicles such as Delta and Titan in favor of the shuttle, the phase-out would take time. In the meanwhile, NASA could save money by using the existing KSC facilities to launch both the shuttle and expendable vehicles.

NASA's George Low announced the decision on April 14, 1972. KSC and Vandenberg Air Force Base in California would be the launch sites for the shuttle. KSC would serve as the site for research and development launches, expected to start in 1978, and for flights launched to the east. Vandenberg would be used for polar orbit flights. Most of the needed equipment at KSC would come, initially at least, by modifying facilities built for Apollo and earlier programs. NASA was committing $150 million toward refurbishing, with design starting immediately and construction perhaps as early as the end of 1973. Work at Vandenberg, estimated to cost some $500 million, would start later and be paid for by the Department of Defense.[12]

Organizing for the Shuttle

In the years leading up to the shuttle decision, things had wound down considerably at KSC. From a high of nearly thirty launches per year in the mid-1960s, the Cape was seeing only about half that number of vehicles lift off by 1973, and the numbers would continue to fall through 1979. During the uncertain days before Low's announcement, cutbacks occurred not only in personnel but also in things that might prepare the Center for new missions. Travel was slashed, and there was little money available for training or education.[13] Now all this would be restored, and more. The Center would have to gear up quickly for the task of launching the shuttle. There was much to learn. And there were organizational changes to make. Indeed, a new culture for the new vehicle was being created at KSC, and these changes were as important as the modifications to hardware and facilities.

The organizational structure developed under Kurt Debus had emphasized hands-on knowledge acquisition. A tight focus on the clear goal of the moon launch tended to keep the Center's bureaucracy limited. So too perhaps did the youth and excitement of the men and women who came to NASA in the 1960s. They were working with a new technology and had few elders to defer to. But by the shuttle era, youth gave way to maturity and the hard lessons of politics and budget. The average age of NASA personnel in 1966 had been 38; by 1982 it would rise to 44. Thirty-seven percent of NASA employees were between 25 and 34 years old in the 1960s; by the 1980s, only 13 percent would be.[14] At KSC there was almost too much maturity. Nine percent of the workers were or would soon be at an age when they could retire at will. George English, director of KSC's executive management office, acknowledged that some workers might be "staying around for the launch" of the first shuttle, but felt confident that there would not be a "mass exodus."[15]

The Center was not only maturing; it was diversifying as well from what had once been almost exclusively the domain of white men from the American South. As hiring picked up from the doldrums of the 1970s, KSC was better able to meet mandates for diversity. Its female workforce reflected NASA-wide trends, and it was at or above the agency average in percentage of women workers through the 1970s and 1980s.[16] But KSC was still something of a southern institution. Along with the Marshall Center in Huntsville, it had the lowest percentage of minority employees in NASA.[17]

In terms of both mission and personnel, the shuttle era was bringing a more complex set of management tasks. Communications and information exchange had to be handled in more formal ways—to some, slower and more difficult ways. But there were things to be gained as well, not only in mastering the new vehicle and its many missions and payloads but in opportunities to develop new ways of working as well. The future required this sort of adaptability.

A most visible indicator of change was the new Center director, Lee Scherer. Scherer encapsulated many of the skills needed for the transition from a research and development focus to the operation of a reusable vehicle in an economically constrained environment. A 1942 graduate of the Naval Academy, he had obtained a second degree in aeronautical engineering from the Naval Postgraduate School in 1949 and a professional degree in the same field from the California Institute of Technology the following year. From 1956 to 1959 he worked on navy research and development projects, but he also gained experience dealing with budgets. Beginning in 1962 he had been responsible for management and cost control of new navy aircraft, and then was called to be program manager for the unmanned lunar orbiter whose pictures were used to select landing sites for the Apollo program. In 1964 he retired from the navy but continued to serve NASA as director of lunar programs in the Office of Space Sciences.

Scherer came to work in a reorganized executive office at KSC. Around him were a new chief counsel, a new public affairs officer, and a new equal opportunity officer. Responding to criticisms that space was too remote, too caught up with Cold War politics to meet real needs at home, KSC had also opened a new Sciences, Technology and Applications Office to deal with the large number of scientific missions studying both the solar system and planet Earth that were expected to fly on the shuttle. Other organizational changes were driven by cost considerations and a desire to meet presidential and congressional mandates to operate more efficiently. For example, a number of base support offices were closed or consolidated. Plant Engineering, Facility Maintenance, Utilities, Fire Services, and Roads and Grounds were merged into Support Operations, a second-tier directorate under Technical Support.[18] Indeed, there were so many reorganizations aimed at cost cutting that only Design Engineering and Shuttle Projects, which Debus had restructured just before his retirement, remained unchanged.[19]

Beneath these formal reorderings and beyond the consolidations and cost-saving measures were changes that reflected both the new concept embodied in the shuttle and innovations in the aerospace industry. Electrical components had improved significantly since the Apollo days, a result of the microelectronic revolution that was making computers and integrated circuits smaller and more powerful. Launch and checkout could now be done using sophisticated software programs running simulations on vehicles before they were launched. Though automated procedures were not entirely new—some had been incorporated into launch preparations as early as the Gemini program—their scale and extent vastly increased. Moreover, the opening of valves, recording pressures and temperatures, and monitoring of environmental conditions inside the spacecraft and engines were now being controlled by tiny electronic devices capable of displaying information digitally, rather than by analog devices that depended on some physical movement or reaction.[20]

Taking advantage of a fresh start, KSC moved existing personnel to new areas. Retraining and experience would be the way the organization would meet the challenges of new technology and new missions. In 1978 the Shuttle Processing Office was formed, to oversee the entire job of getting the vehicle ready to fly. There was a need for such an overarching organization to prepare a vehicle that was both booster and spacecraft. During the Apollo era, these had been treated as distinct systems. Such a distinction no longer mattered, at least in theory. The entire vehicle would leave earth, fly in space, and return, making it a booster and spacecraft all in one. The plan was that the old Spacecraft and Launch Vehicle Operations offices would be gone by 1980.

Erasing the booster-spacecraft distinction was perhaps the most radical transformation to take place at the Center. These two fundamental technologies embodied distinct traditions and were designed by different NASA installations in the years leading up to the Apollo mission. Most of the testing and preparation work on these systems had traditionally been done in separate KSC directorates. An entire set of procedures had arisen during Apollo to integrate the two as vehicles moved to the countdown phase. Designed from the start as a single integrated vehicle, the shuttle would be worked differently. Exactly how remained to be seen.

What quickly became clear was that most of the KSC people heading shuttle operations would come from the spacecraft side of the house.[21] The head of Shuttle Engineering, Ted Sasseen, had been a key Apollo spacecraft engineer. The first head of Shuttle Operations was Walt Kapryan, former Apollo launch director. Kapryan's successor was George Page, who had been in charge of Apollo testing. Page emerged as the strong leader of the shuttle program and served as the vehicle's first launch director. Running the Shuttle Program Office was Bob Sieck, who was to impart to the design of the shuttle some of the lessons he had learned working the Apollo spacecraft.[22] Bob Gray, who for years had run the unmanned vehicle program on the other side of the Cape, was made deputy director of launch operations.[23] Paul Donnelly, deputy director of launch operations in the Apollo years, headed Shuttle Processing. Given this lineup, most of the lessons carried over into the shuttle would reflect the air force–derived systems approach rather than the functional division of labor favored in the German tradition.

Meanwhile, most of the former launch vehicle people were put into the new payload processing organization. Ike Rigell, who had worked on the Saturn launch vehicle, took charge here. When the goal had been to get men on the moon, there were no "payloads" in the broader sense of the word. People and their equipment traveling in an Apollo spacecraft were the "cargo" of the Saturn booster, if one wanted to think of it that way. But the shuttle was designed to carry scientific experiments, communications satellites, military spy-in-the-sky cameras, perhaps even parts of an orbiting space station at some point. Like a commercial transport, the shuttle had a payload, and it was fully expected that in many cases the military, university scientists, or private firms would be paying NASA to carry their wares into space.

It was still not clear which payloads would be processed at the Center.[24] In January 1979 John Neilon moved from his assignment in unmanned operations to the Cargo Projects Office, where he would manage shuttle payloads. This move reflected his long experience with payload-carrying expendable vehicles, the closest analogy to what the shuttle would do. A veteran of the defunct Saturn launch vehicle organization, Andrew Pickett, headed KSC's Advance Planning and Technology Office. There he prepared studies for new ways to manage the Center in making its transition to an operational shuttle launch facility.[25]

Why this division of personnel took place remains unclear. In accordance with thinking of the shuttle as a single, integrated vehicle, a systems approach seemed to make the most sense. But tempers flared as two strong groups of engineers steeped in different traditions debated how the work should be done and who would be in charge of what.[26] The Saturn veterans who had been moved into payload operations felt that perhaps they were victims of the stronger connections in NASA forged by the Apollo spacecraft engineers. They understood, or at least believed, that the shuttle side of the organization was where the action would be. Others saw the personnel reshuffle as a creative mixing of skills. If during the lunar program the functional equivalent of a payload was the Apollo spacecraft, now the former booster engineers would learn to work payloads and the former Apollo engineers would work on the "booster." This crosscutting would prevent people from getting stuck with their old ways of thinking for a new vehicle. On the other hand, for all its newness, the shuttle would have much in common with past vehicles. It used liquid-fueled main engines plus attached solid rockets, meaning that shuttle engineers would have to work with different systems from different contractors, as had the Saturn engineers. The new vehicle would be assembled in the VAB and rolled out to the pad as Saturn had been. Most of the learning for the shuttle, how to actually fly it, would have to be acquired in practice, as had been the case with the Saturn vehicle and predecessors. There was a danger that those with only spacecraft experience might end up "reinventing the wheel" when it came to testing and launch.

A New Era

The economic logic of the shuttle was familiar to anyone who had been studying industrial technology over the previous century. In manufacturing, electric power, telecommunications, and many industries, efficiency had been achieved through economies of scale. By using expensive but essentially fixed-cost pieces of equipment to serve many customers, one could drive down prices. This was true whether the equipment was a factory turning out automobiles or an electric power grid supplying energy to a city. Once built, the system of technology would have relatively low operating costs. The longer it stayed in service and the larger the base of customers over which costs could be spread, the lower the price that could be charged. The shuttle too was a high-cost piece of equipment. It was the most sophisticated and complex flying machine yet invented. Its main engines, marvels of design and engineering, delivered the most efficient thrust of any rocket engine ever built. All this expensive hardware would pay for itself by flying many missions, perhaps one hundred for each vehicle's lifetime. Seen this way, the most dramatically new thing about the shuttle was not its marvelous hardware but its operational concept. The shuttle was to bring space travel into the same category as earthbound transportation. The economics of the shuttle were to be no different than the economics of air travel, or indeed of railroads or any form of transportation marked by heavy upfront investments, be they engines and rail lines, airplanes and terminals, or shuttles and launchpads. The entire approach was the opposite of what had been attempted in space flight up until then. Rocket science in the 1960s had meant science at the cutting edge, away from the routine.[27] But as budgets rather than technology came to drive NASA, less thought was given to science or innovation, and much more to efficient operations.

KSC's role as launch and operations center was crucial to the future of space flight defined in this way. In the debates leading up to the shuttle, again and again the phrase "like an airliner" was used, a new analogy for space flight in an era stressing the routine and cost-efficient. Tight integration of booster and spacecraft and partial reusability were seen as steps toward a vehicle that was closer to an airplane than a ballistic missile. "The Shuttle or something like the Shuttle," concluded Walt Kapryan, "will be the transportation carrier means indefinitely."[28] Befitting a space airliner, it would be prepared, serviced, readied, and launched in time measured in hours (three-digit hours, to be sure) rather than days, weeks, or months. Indeed, shuttle economics required it. Only if the vehicle could be processed quickly could it be launched enough times to reap the benefits of scale economies.

Some signs of this new way of thinking came in changes to launch and checkout procedures for the new vehicle. At the height of Apollo, KSC had employed four senior test conductors to schedule and integrate the analysis of the launch vehicle and spacecraft. Additional test conductors worked independently on readying the Apollo spacecraft. They were all integrated by test supervisors under Paul Donnelly. With the budget cutbacks, KSC reduced the number of test conductors from four to two—Norm Carlson and Gene Sestile. Sestile had managed scheduling for *Apollo 16*. When that was completed, he moved over to the newly created Shuttle Program Office, where he and other KSC engineers were to apply their expertise to the ground operations of the shuttle.[29] Unlike Apollo, where vehicle performance was key, launch operations with the shuttle had to place more emphasis on ground maintenance and turnaround times.

Ideally, operations and maintenance considerations would be included in the design of the shuttle. Earlier vehicles, derived from ballistic missiles, allowed for little thinking along these lines. They were intended to be fired once, and most of the engineering went into being sure they would fire and complete their missions. Even the Saturn and Apollo vehicles, built from scratch, gave operations little consideration in their design. The shuttle was meant to be different, and initially KSC's role in its design was expected to be significant.[30]

KSC personnel hoped to influence two areas of design: the vehicle itself and its supporting equipment on the ground. They had some success in the second area. Engineers studied every Apollo ground system, redesigning them for efficient, lower-cost operations as much as possible, given budget constraints. To a large extent, this meant reducing the "man-hours to maintain and operate the vehicle."[31] During Apollo, design responsibility for ground support equipment (GSE) was assigned to the NASA center responsible for the launch component it would service. As a result, Houston designed GSE for the command, service, and lunar modules, Marshall designed GSE for the launch vehicle, and the Kennedy Space Center designed GSE for its own ground systems. KSC had been laden with three independent systems, each which had to be separately maintained. Analysis suggested that the 6,400 racks of GSE needed to launch Saturn rockets could be reduced to about 1,600 if all ground support systems were unified under one design.[32]

Even so, KSC engineers never gained complete control over GSE integration. They sought to increase telemetry on the shuttle to permit a higher level of in-flight testing. They sought to improve access to crucial components needing testing or replacement during turnaround work. They challenged weight constraints affecting the lifting and moving of the shuttle on the ground. But by the time KSC engineers were allowed to comment on design issues, NASA was reluctant to tamper with the technology except for systems that clearly did not work.

When it came to vehicle design issues, KSC engineers were largely shunted aside. Despite the talk of airline-like operations, criteria of weight and payload capacity and above all cost drove shuttle design. "KSC proposed many changes, or opposed certain changes purely from an operational standpoint," recalled KSC director Richard Smith. Smith had taken over the leadership of KSC in 1979, after serving early in his career at Marshall and then at NASA Headquarters, where he directed the Skylab Task Force. Still, even with his wide-ranging NASA experience, Smith was unable to get a hearing for operational issues with the designers. KSC comments on design, Smith found, "to a large extent fell on deaf ears."[33] Limits of weight and budget closed off many options. KSC engineers suggested designing the shuttle so that it could be moved and stacked using simple techniques. These proposals, reflecting the operator's point of view, "would have cost more money, added more weight, or taken more time," Bob Sieck recalled. "We made some limited headway, but not near as much as we wanted."[34] Even so, the shuttle as built exceeded design weight by one-third. It could lift 60,000 pounds into low earth orbit. The Saturn V rockets that had sent men to the moon could lift 250,000 pounds into the same orbit.

Not all the issues with the shuttle reflected a conflict between design and operations, of course. It was also quite a task changing the culture of launch and vehicle operations at KSC. A frontier mentality had ruled during the early years of space flight, when engineers could truthfully say they were doing things never done before with technologies that had not even been conceived when they started. Bringing into this heady culture the idea of "routine operations" was not easy. As we shall see, much of the effort of learning to fly the shuttle at KSC went into rethinking the way things should be done.[35]

Some critics of NASA in fact proposed a radical restructuring to overcome the burden of the past. Three studies commissioned in the late 1970s recommended that the Kennedy Space Center be fully privatized. Studies from both the National Association of Public Administrators and the Aerospace Corporation considered splitting NASA into an R&D organization and an operational arm. Operations would be turned over either to the Department of Defense, to a quasi-public entity analogous to the passenger rail operator Amtrak, or to private business, regulated like the interstate bus company Greyhound. In 1981 former astronaut Thomas Stafford forwarded similar recommendations to Congress. He urged the House Space Committee to place shuttle operations in the hands of the air force and private industry, limiting NASA's role to research and development.[36]

These proposals spoke to the belief that with a well-designed shuttle vehicle emphasizing reusability, operations could be reduced to a routine matter. There was no need for government civil servants to carry out routine work, which could be handled more efficiently by a profit-oriented private firm. Only R&D, which the private sector had less incentive to perform, should use public money and civil servant time. Yet this belief in operational simplicity was quickly undercut by the hard reality of developing a radical new vehicle. Even Stafford admitted that the shuttle would only be partially "operational" during the 1980s. NASA would have to enhance the shuttle's performance by developing logistics support, increasing reliability, and minimizing turnaround time, which sounded more like research. Privatization had a catchy, favorable ring to it by the late 1970s, the beginning of the era of government deregulation. But even supporters of privatization recognized that, for a while, there was much that NASA personnel would have to figure out or learn through experience before the new spaceship could be operated as easily as an airliner.

In the short run at least, KSC's expertise in launch operations would be useful in the new era of the shuttle. During Apollo, the Center had shown it could integrate complex systems of hardware and finish work on a tight schedule. KSC personnel had learned to manage multiple time-sensitive tasks and prepare a series of vehicles for flight. They had seen how slippages in any one part of the process would tail back into the schedule and endanger not only the immediate mission but future ones as well. They had also seen how assumptions about operations as a relatively simple and routine process had been contradicted by the reality of space flight.[37]

During Apollo, for example, design engineers had thought they could deliver a stable rocket configuration to the Cape, where it would undergo relatively simple testing and verification before firing. But contrary to expectations, the fixing of configurations did not take place at the point of fabrication or at one of the design-oriented NASA centers. Only after the hardware reached the Cape was it stabilized, involving the operations end of NASA in the much more complex work of finishing the vehicle as well as testing, verifying, and launching it. As we shall see, despite the assumptions of shuttle designers and the intentions and expectations of program managers, the shuttle had KSC playing the role of finisher, much as the Center had done in the early years of space flight.

Although shuttle advocates spoke of routine operations, in the operational world "routine" did not mean simple or static technology. In fact, to make the shuttle operate like an airliner required a whole series of innovations. Some of these innovations would come in the form of improvements to shuttle systems. During the 1950s and 1960s, new booster designs and the evolution of spacecraft and other flight hardware had been significant sources of innovation. Expecting to build five orbiters, NASA would have opportunities to improve shuttle design after the first one had flown. Indeed, there would be significant changes from the first to the last orbiter, as well as periodic upgrades of all the vehicles over time. But shuttle design focused on performance—minimizing the weight and maximizing lift capacity. Specifications of hardware and engines were set. Improvements in operations would not come from spending dollars on research and development at the design and fabrication points. They would instead involve changes in ground operations and work routines at KSC.

If anything, the design process for the shuttle was placing more and more of a burden on operational innovation. When Richard Nixon approved the vehicle in 1972, he also cut the budget for the ship's design in half. This move forced designers to shift their plans from a fully reusable vehicle—a true space plane—to a partially recoverable one. A fully reusable shuttle, though expensive to design and build, had promised to be easy to operate. A partially recoverable shuttle, easier to build, would be more difficult to operate. Gaining the benefits of economies of scale now required improved operational procedures to assure fast vehicle turnaround.[38] Scheduling had a direct relationship to economics and by extension to the entire shuttle concept. Operational costs per flight appeared to be minimized with upwards of forty shuttle flights per year. Any delays in launch would reduce the annual number of shuttle flights.

Tight schedules and fast turnarounds were nothing new at KSC. But coordination and scheduling problems for the shuttle were as great as, in fact greater than, those of even giant industries such as oil and electric power; they were more akin to a military operation like D-Day. Cutting costs and speeding turnaround had to come from more efficient use of existing ground facilities, from new ways of organizing and processing work, from better logistics, from precise information. Based on the experiences of private industry, significant improvements could be expected to come through practice, or "learning by doing" as KSC started processing vehicles.

The question everyone was pondering now was, how fast could the shuttle be processed? NASA had sold the program to Congress based on a cost-minimizing forty flights per year. That flight rate required a turnaround time of 160 hours.[39] Two eight-hour shifts per day would each work forty-hour weeks to finish processing in two weeks. NASA convened a Shuttle Turnaround Analysis Group (STAG) under the authority of the shuttle program manager at the Johnson Space Center in Houston to put the 160-hour turnaround into effect. Members of this team from KSC immediately wondered why, if turnaround was so important, design engineers did not take operations into greater consideration as they worked on the vehicle. "We started looking at details of some of the designs that were coming out," recalled STAG member Gene Sestile, "and guys were saying, wait a minute, you know, there's no way. This particular system's going to take me a month the way it is right now."[40] Attachment points on the vehicle needed to be simplified, access to components made easier, replacement of parts stream-lined. But when KSC schedulers went back to the Shuttle Program Office with suggestions, they were told, "We can't afford to change that stuff." KSC workers would just have to fly the vehicle they got.[41]

Sestile and other KSC schedulers quickly concluded that the turnaround could not be accomplished in less than five weeks. Detailed charts showing 360 hours as the fastest processing time drove the point home. Even this higher figure assumed a "zero-based schedule." There would be no lost time looking for tools or changing shifts or in any other activity not directly con-nected with shuttle work.[42] It was a fanciful assumption, to say the least. As it turned out, finding and fixing problems, not routine procedures, would consume the most processing time.

Through the shuttle design phase, the two-week turnaround goal stood.[43] The shuttle program continued to advertise an orbiter that could be moved rapidly out of the processing facility and stacked. KSC analysis continued to show that each step would take longer than the schedule permitted. Adding more people would not solve the problem, either, for many jobs would take just as long whatever the number of workers. Some tasks simply could not overcome the laws of physics. As Bob Sieck pointed out, "You could have the most sophisticated equipment in the world, but it still takes so much time to get the shuttle from here to here."[44]

If the STAG analysis remained "hopeful" at best, this exercise in opera-tional planning did have a salutary effect on thinking about launch opera-tions. KSC engineers analyzed each component of shuttle processing in detail. This effort became the basis for writing processing procedures after the shuttle came to the Cape. "Had we not done [this]," Sieck recalls, "we would have been running to catch up in writing our procedures once the [shuttle] got here."[45] Meanwhile, it was taking longer than expected to get the first vehicle, *Columbia*, ready. NASA had promised Congress it would have the shuttle off the ground and quickly up to speed. But soon there were complaints about NASA's unrealistic optimism. The original schedules were thrown out and KSC's Sestile and Tip Talone presented a new one to Congress. "Everybody else in the program [was] madder than hell," Sestile recalled, because it looked like NASA had lied in its original optimistic sce-nario.[46]

Some members of the shuttle program turned the blame around and pointed to KSC. It was not poor design that would keep the shuttle from achieving its expected flight rate, it was KSC's outmoded operational con-cepts. The launch center's traditions clouded its ability to operate efficiently, critics charged.[47] The STAG chairman asserted: "Kennedy does not have an operational philosophy like the airlines do. . . . We have to educate our

R&D people to come into the operational phase."[48] Another member of the turnaround group pushed aside KSC complaints about design, noting that no matter how well designed the vehicle, "the manner in which we operate and manage our people has to be changed."[49] Critics of KSC now asked that the Center disavow its traditional belief that launch operations were part of a research and learning process. When rockets were new, perhaps such operationally based learning was needed. But not so with an advanced vehicle like the shuttle.

What the shuttle did offer was a fresh opportunity to take advantage of some recent improvements in information technology. For example, throughout Apollo, every change, every accident, every test at KSC generated a long paper trail. If a technician found something deficient during a test, he was to fill out a form that would pass up a chain of supervisors for approval. Should the supervising engineers decide a part needed to be changed, another form had to be filled out and travel through the approval process. When a technician retrieved the replacement part, he started filling out yet another series of forms detailing its movement from the warehouse to the vehicle. This tortuous process had a purpose. It helped engineers learn about the rocket. Should something go awry at launch, analysts could find the ultimate source of the problem by following the paper trail. STAG chairman Robert Buckley, who headed KSC's Operations Planning Office, wondered if this system really was needed for the shuttle. He noted that a worker at the car rental company Avis could, by looking at a computer, determine the status of any one of the cars. Why not a similar approach for the shuttle and its components? Computerizing KSC's paperwork could move the shuttle closer to an operational stage.[50]

Examples such as these supported those who believed that streamlined handling would allow KSC to meet the goal of rapid turnaround. Old ways of working reflecting an earlier era and earlier technology left many areas for improvement. But plenty of gray areas remained as well. How much of the old procedures of testing and verification that KSC personnel had performed on the Apollo program could safely be put aside for the shuttle? How much time would easy improvements, such as replacing paper with electronic record keeping, really save? How much of the turnaround problem lay with traditional thinking and organization at KSC? Debate on these issues continued to circulate between the vehicle designers at Johnson and Marshall, the aerospace firms building the shuttle, and the operational experts at KSC. None of them could be fully resolved before the shuttle arrived at the Cape. In the meantime there were other matters to consider, notably how to prepare the physical facilities to receive and process a brand-new vehicle.

Building a Launch and Landing Site

By late 1977 the Cape region had bounced back, recovering from years of reductions and economic depression that marked the transition from Apollo. More than 20,000 workers were now on NASA's and the air force's payroll, a big improvement following the loss of some 18,000 aerospace jobs and near double-digit unemployment after the postlunar shutdowns.[51] Interest in the space program, which had never really waned, continued to grow as the shuttle neared its arrival date. In 1980 the fifteen-millionth visitor walked through the gates of the KSC visitor complex. A frontier landscape of some 25,000 residents in the 1950s had matured into a region of moderate-sized towns, industry, and a quarter of a million permanent inhabitants. Reflecting the new interest in protecting the environment, residents of the area had grown more concerned with hazardous wastes, noise, and degradation of nature associated with space flight. KSC had buffered itself by creating the surrounding wildlife preserve, but residents also valued those natural resources, including the nearby Canaveral National Seashore. They wanted to be assured of continued access to them even as the shuttle began flying.[52] It would be a trickier matter than before, balancing rockets and alligators.

Reworking the equipment of launch proved to be one of the more clear-cut tasks in preparation for the shuttle. At least, that was the way it seemed to those working on this task, in comparison with the difficulties of meeting the ambitious flight schedules or dealing with a public less willing to give the space program what it wanted. Assigned to work on launchpad conversion, Tip Talone at first objected, fearing that he would be "out in left field" and no one would ever see him again. As it turned out, the five years he spent on that project were among the most rewarding of his career.[53] While his buddies were sweating over getting the shuttle to fly, he ran relatively straightforward meetings, literally helping to reshape the launch facilities for the new vehicle.

By this time, KSC had sketched out the process of preparing a shuttle for flight. The flow of processing would begin when the orbiter arrived back on earth after its mission. If it landed in California, it would be safed there, then mated to the Shuttle Carrier Aircraft (a modified 747) and flown to KSC. At the Cape, technicians would separate the orbiter from the carrier plane using a special eleven-story "demating" device. From there it would be towed to the Orbiter Processing Facility (OPF). This new building initially had two high bays with a low bay between them, and could process two shuttles at a time.[54] In 1987 a third processing bay was constructed in another building across the street.

One of the signs of change in rocket tradition at the Cape was the presence of a landing facility. Since the start of the space program, everyone had understood a rocket to be a one-time, throwaway device. Not so a reusable orbiter. Although in the first test flights the shuttle would land on a dry lake bed in California, once it was clear that a pilot could bring in the giant bird—essentially a glider as it came to earth—it would land at KSC. This would cut turnaround times by eliminating the long haul back to the Cape. In December 1973, KSC had requested bids for construction of a 15,000-foot runway, to be located northwest of the Vehicle Assembly Building.

Although the runway, OPF, and several other key pieces of shuttle-related equipment were brand new, KSC was proud of its reuse and adaption of older facilities. The reconstruction work cost only one-quarter of what it had taken to prepare the spaceport for the Apollo project.[55] Members of KSC's design engineering team reconfigured the old VAB work platforms to conform to the shape of the shuttle. They remodeled High Bays 1 and 3 to enable the stacking of the solid rocket boosters, external tanks, and orbiter that comprised the shuttle. They widened the VAB's north door by some forty feet to accommodate the larger vehicle. They turned one of the building's low bays into a workshop for inspecting the orbiter main engines.

Similar redesign took place out at the pads. Engineers used the upper portions of the old mobile launch towers as the basis for shuttle launch towers. They installed a new rotating service structure (RRS), with a payload changeout room (PCR), to handle payloads.[56] The mobile launchers from the Apollo era, now without their launch towers, were reconfigured to conform to the shuttle and became the mobile launch platforms (MLPs). Workers converted the single hole in the middle of the MLPs to three smaller holes to accommodate liftoff emissions from the shuttle's main engines and two solid rocket boosters.[57]

Other areas of the space complex were adapted to the needs of the solid rocket boosters (SRBs). The Rotation Processing and Surge Facility, a small cluster of buildings, was set up at Launch Complex 39 to receive booster segments from Utah and mate the aft segments with the SRB skirt assemblies. During flight, the booster segments were designed to fall off the vehicle and land in the ocean once they had spent their fuel. A new nautical recovery team at the Cape was prepared to go out in specially designed and rigged ships to pick them up. After recovery, they would be towed to Hangar AF at the Cape, where they were disassembled and shipped back to Utah for reloading.

Some facilities were given over to entirely new uses. The high bay and checkout areas of the Operations and Checkout Building (O&C) where Apollo spacecraft had been tested were reconfigured to accommodate the checkout of the European Space Agency's Spacelab. Spacelab components would be a frequent passenger on the shuttle in the 1980s.[58] The Spacecraft Assembly and Encapsulation Facility (SAEF-1) was remodeled and renamed the Vertical Processing Facility (VPF), where vertical payloads, and boosters that would push satellites into high earth orbit or planetary trajectories, could be checked out and processed. Apollo's parachute facilities in the industrial area were enlarged to handle the parachutes bringing the solid rocket boosters to their recovery sites in the Atlantic.[59]

Finally, the launch computer brain was reprogrammed. Reflecting the tremendous advances in computers and software since the Apollo era, the shuttle would have new, highly automated checkout and launch procedures run through a sophisticated, custom-designed Launch Processing System (LPS) software package. Starting with chalk and a blackboard, a team led by Apollo veteran Ted Sasseen got to work on this massive software project. As team member John Conway remembers, he, Tom Walton, Terry Greenfield, and a few others drew on their own expertise and their experience with the rudimentary Apollo automated systems.[60] In Apollo, the checkout and launch systems were provided by the NASA centers designing the vehicles. The automated LPS would be the first total-vehicle checkout system, integrating what had been three separate systems—launch vehicle, spacecraft, ground equipment—into a single package.[61]

The LPS promised to radically revise the work of countdown. During Apollo some 450 launch engineers and technicians looked at banks of meters and gauges and armed themselves with strip chart readouts providing a continuous stream of data on how systems were performing. To monitor the opening of a valve, they read one indicator that showed that the voltage to open it had been carried, and checked another meter to verify that the opening had occurred. Critical measures were projected on a wall for managers to see.[62] Technicians watching strip charts could discover trends in test data and check on a balky component before it reached a critical state. At key points during the countdown, systems engineers would provide "go for launch" decisions based upon their readings of the strip charts. The few automated procedures were primarily brief programs that fed information into strip charts. Evaluating the various strip charts had been an intricate process taking some twenty-eight hours.[63]

With the Launch Processing System, most of the shuttle tests would be accomplished by a computer. Even ground support equipment would be accessible via computer rather than hardwired into launch controls. The new automatic system dispensed with 1960s-era centralized mainframe architecture and became, for a time, one of the world's largest distributed computing systems.[64] Dozens of processors handling a variety of interfaces fed data to fifteen consoles, each manned by three people, one-tenth the launch control personnel that had been needed on Apollo.[65] Checking out the shuttle during the final launch countdown would take only two and a half hours, compared to Apollo's twenty-eight.[66] At the same time, the LPS provided far more data for those in the control room. Data systems would eventually incorporate information from all past shuttle flights, so that an engineer could compare what was happening with past experience to spot a problem. Advances in microprocessors now permitted far more real-time learning to go on in the launch process.[67]

As part of the refitting, engineers installed new video display screens in the old Apollo-era consoles, which were flipped upside down with new legs on the bottom. As a final gesture, the control room engineering team also turned the consoles around. In the new era, technicians monitoring the launch would be looking out the window instead of at the back wall as they had all through the Apollo years. It was a small move greatly appreciated by those who worked the shuttle launches.

For those in the LCC, automation of launch control meant a new way of working. Engineers now had to learn computer programming, and become adept at debugging complex software packages. Technicians' duties changed as well. Instead of looking at strip charts, dials, and switches, they would follow the inner workings of the shuttle on CRT screens, which projected schematics of the systems in operation. This seemingly small change in visual observation proved "a significant challenge" to those who had worked on Apollo.[68] Most of the thousands of decisions in a countdown would be automatically made by computers now, rather than by a coordinated team of technicians and engineers. Only if something went wrong would they know how to stop the countdown. The parameters of decision—whether to continue, whether to stop—were programmed ahead of time into the software. Knowledge won from years of previous experience was now built into the software that would run the shuttle countdown.

If some workers experienced this automation as a loss of responsibilities, the new computerized procedures also opened a door for new types of workers. Women were entering the technical fields in significant numbers by the late 1970s. One popular major for women engineers was computer programming. Indeed, a generation earlier, software and mathematics had been one of the few generally accepted places for scientifically and technically inclined women to work. At a time when electrical and mechanical engineering involved working with hardware, software was seen as engineering's more feminine side. By 1980, however, software was emerging as perhaps the most important facet of information technology. Women's concentration in this area redounded to their advantage. KSC managers hired a number of women computer science majors from area universities for the LPS project. "These young ladies understood how the software needed to work," remembered Charles Murphy. The hardware engineers would learn about the software from the new hires. It didn't hurt that they were young women just out of college, either. "These guys didn't mind sitting with them all day long."[69] Eventually many of the women hired to work with the new LPS moved up to become systems engineers.

Even as the Center was being refurbished, one could detect the changes in procedures and policies the shuttle would bring. The new opportunities with computers, the increasing feminization of the workforce, the new visual experience of countdown control were some of the more obvious examples. Deeper evidence could be found in how the Center was handling the entire work process. During construction of the Center in the 1960s, KSC had put into place its own site activation team under the direction of Donald Scheller. At that time the young center needed people with experience in the construction of large missile launch facilities.[70] Reconfiguring KSC for the shuttle required a somewhat different sort of team, one with expertise in modifying ground facilities for a new vehicle. Many watching the space industry assumed that this job would go to the private aerospace corporation Rockwell. Rockwell was taking the lead in designing and building the space shuttle. Presumably it knew best how to operate it. Contracting site activation to Rockwell reflected pressures on NASA to cut costs and to focus its own efforts on research and development.[71] In contrast to the preceding era, when government employees had developed key new technologies and facilities that filtered down to the aerospace industry, now knowledge was starting to flow the other way, from private industry back to the government agency.[72]

The new emphasis on contracting through private industry became one of the most important trends in the shuttle era. In the late 1970s when deregulation was winning favor, private industry was assumed to be more efficient than government. For the space industry to benefit from privatization, though, it would have to revamp its approach to contracting. KSC had used tens of thousands of contract workers during the height of facilities construction. With the shuttle, and the renewed interest in privatizing as much work as possible, contractor involvement peaked once again, reaching its highest level in ten years by 1981.[73]

The shuttle would be bigger and more complex, and therefore so would the contracting process. Apollo spacecraft personnel at KSC had largely worked with either Grumman or North American (Rockwell) personnel.

With the shuttle, civil servants would have to integrate work with Rockwell, Martin, USBI, and others—the different element contractors.[74] The complexities of an "operational" vehicle flying many missions per year required a more elaborate support infrastructure, supplied by a variety of firms. Eventually KSC would consolidate contracts among a few prime contractors and substantially change the way it did business with the private sector.

As refitting work for the shuttle moved toward completion, another change in the way things would be done emerged. The Center would have to put in place stronger environmental policies. This first became apparent in the construction of the shuttle's landing runway. Least terns, a protected species, flocked to the ends of the runway. Every time T-38 training jets took off, the terns' nests would be blown away. KSC engineers first proposed a water system to drench the nests, driving off the birds, but in the end they opted for a simpler solution—darkening the ends of the runway and providing light-colored nesting grounds at a safe distance.[75]

Working out a compromise with Albert, a fifty-year-old alligator who resided in a lake next to the shuttle runway, proved easier. The thirteen-foot-plus reptile decided to investigate a shuttle rescue test in 1980. KSC officials quickly found a new home for him at Busch Gardens.[76] A few alligators, including Kaycee, who lived in the pond in front of KSC headquarters, and Elvis, another thirteen-footer residing near the VAB, were familiar enough to get names. The rest of the 4,000 to 6,000 beasts roaming the Center's lands remained anonymous. Albert aside, most of them left shuttle operations to the humans. But some occasionally found the shuttle runway—officially the Shuttle Landing Facility (SLF)—an ideal GTF (Gator Tanning Facility). The cold-blooded reptiles were drawn to the warm cement, so before each landing a special KSC crew would be detailed to clear the runway of sunning gators.[77]

Early shuttle flights eventually would reveal a number of other environmental concerns. Sea turtles congregated in high numbers on the beaches near the launchpads. KSC instituted a turtle-watch program, modifying launch schedules to avoid periods when turtles occupied the breeding grounds.[78] Other environmental problems affected *homo sapiens*. Following some of the early launches, half a dozen launchpad crew members were briefly sent to the hospital with complaints of sore throats and dry eyes. Aluminum oxide residue from the engines' exhaust cloud had dried the workers' nasal and throat membranes. Pad crews were soon issued protective masks. Local acid rain resulting from shuttle exhaust fumes also necessitated new pad wash-down procedures. While the shuttle had been planned in an era when speed and cost were the primary factors shaping the technology, it was going to be flown in an era where environmental impact needed to be taken into consideration as well. Notions of a seamless, high-speed turnaround would be forced to confront these considerations.

✳ ✳ ✳

In 1977 work on the shuttle had progressed far enough for testing to start. A launch team headed by Walt Kapryan moved to Edwards Air Force Base. There they began working with an experimental shuttle prototype. *Enterprise*, named after the ship from the television series *Star Trek*, was built to test the flying and landing characteristics of the orbiter.[79] During these approach and landing tests (ALT), KSC personnel would also begin practicing the routine of vehicle processing they would eventually use at Merritt Island. Some seventy KSC employees, including systems and operations engineers and quality inspectors, moved with their families to Antelope Valley, California, for the next two years. Apollo veteran Paul Donnelly led the processing work, along with Don Phillips, Bob Sieck, Ted Ogelsby, Roy Tharpe, and a host of others who would become important figures in shuttle operations.

The ALT program followed the sequential development pattern established early in the space program under the methodical approach favored by Kurt Debus and Wernher von Braun. *Enterprise* was not built to ascend to space. Instead, it was carried on the back of the Shuttle Carrier Aircraft (SCA). During the "captive" flights aboard the SCA, astronauts checked out the orbiter's operational systems and KSC personnel verified the process by which the orbiter would be returned to the Cape after landing at Edwards Air Force Base. Finally *Enterprise* was released ("dropped") from the SCA for five practice landings—three on a dry lake bed and the last two on Edwards's concrete runway.

After each test Donnelly's orbiter processing team went through the maintenance, servicing, and checkout cycle. In the high desert they learned about the peculiarities of the orbiter and the sensitivities of the supplemental boosters. They practiced many of the fine details of checkout and processing. "We got a leg up" working with *Enterprise*, Bob Sieck asserted.[80] Indeed, Sieck returned to KSC as a shuttle project engineer, commanding a team whose core consisted of those he had worked with in California.[81] *Enterprise* itself provided one more valuable service. After completing its drop tests, it was flown to the Cape to serve in tests calibrating the VAB and the launchpads.[82] Like the 500-F tests in Apollo site activation, *Enterprise* verified compatibility between ground equipment and vehicle.

The Shuttle Comes to Kennedy Space Center

"Looking at that bird back there, you might think that all we need is to wipe the windshield, put it on the launchpad, and take off," astronaut John Young told reporters in a moment of understandable optimism. The space shuttle *Columbia* arrived at Kennedy Space Center in March 1979.[83] But those who had to work on the vehicle saw it from a different perspective than Young. Rather than looking buffed and ready for launch, *Columbia* looked more like "something that the cat had drug in."[84] Launch director Walt Kapryan, distraught at the decision to send an unfinished orbiter out of the Rockwell factory in Palmdale, California, exclaimed in frustration: "What was I supposed to do, stand in front of it when they towed it out?"[85]

Columbia's arrival was the first clear indication that, all public statements aside, the shuttle had not revolutionized space flight operations. As had been true during the Apollo era, it proved impossible to neatly separate the functions of design, fabrication, and operations. Indeed, even before *Columbia* arrived, KSC personnel had taken a hand in its completion. A team of engineers from the Center went out to the Rockwell factory during the last six weeks of work. Knowing that they were likely to get a less than perfect first orbiter, they scoured the manufacturer's books to see what remained to be done. They also compared the vehicle's characteristics against the specifications written by the shuttle design team. They even began testing systems, to understand how they worked and get a start on the procedures they would have to implement in launch operations.

Not all of this was unexpected. Shuttle planning had anticipated that certain work would end up being done at the launch site. No spacecraft ever arrived at KSC in a completed state, and inevitably some parts would fail quality inspections. But *Columbia* was exceptional even by this standard. KSC workers ended up managing the completion of at least seven unfinished systems.[86] They installed the aft engines, something they had never before done on a horizontal craft. They fitted the auxiliary power units, hooked up the fuel cells, and modified or replaced much of the avionics.[87] Adding to the burden was the orbiter's reusable nature. It contained much new equipment and systems never before handled by KSC personnel. Only after finishing this work could they start testing the craft, first its individual systems, then all systems together.[88]

Particularly vexing was the work remaining on the orbiter's crucial protective tiles. This new thermal protection system (TPS) was vastly different from the ablative shields used to safeguard the Apollo and earlier capsules from the searing heat of reentry. Working with the TPS required mastery of entirely new skills. "We were not fully prepared for this work by any means,"

8-1. A bedraggled-looking *Columbia* arrives at KSC unprepared for flight.

reflected Ann Montgomery, who helped manage tile installation on *Columbia*.[89] There was almost a sense of panic as a crew from Rockwell descended on the Cape to assist with tile installation.

TPS had been looming as a schedule buster even before *Columbia* left California. Unanticipated tile problems soon cascaded into a river of woe. The tiles had to be waterproof. But Rockwell engineers soon discovered that no available waterproofing technique would survive the high heat of reentry. Each time the shuttle came back to earth, the tiles would have to be waterproofed again. This work, which had to take place in a well-ventilated area, required removing the orbiter nose cone and leading-edge wing panels. It added a permanent new time wrinkle to the tight turnaround.

At least the waterproofing problem was discovered before *Columbia* left the factory. Far worse was the sudden realization that work thought completed would have to be redone at KSC. At the manufacturing plant, Rockwell had installed tiles first on the easy flat portions of *Columbia*'s underbelly, leaving only a temporary coating on those regions of the vehicle's skin not yet shielded. But during the flight from California, wind pressure stripped off many of the installed tiles.[90] Others were damaged, and still more were clearly not bonded firmly enough to withstand the pressures of a launch. By the time *Columbia* was towed into the Orbiter Processing Facility

8-2. Assembling the protective tile system of the shuttle tested KSC's workforce like few other jobs.

at the Cape, only about 1,500 of its 31,000 heat protection tiles were ready for flight, and virtually none of some 6,000 gap fillers and thermal seals between tiles had been installed.[91]

By June 1979, TPS had replaced installation of the main engines as the critical path determining the date of the first flight. Schedulers quickly produced an optimistic scenario of 600 tiles installed per week to stay on schedule. Almost overnight the OPF, designed for a crew of about 200, housed 3,000 men and women working three shifts seven days a week. Crews from KSC joined the workers flown in from Rockwell in a race to complete the shuttle. They scrambled for spaces in an unpaved parking lot and relieved themselves in Porta Potties brought in to allay the long lines at restrooms. Temporary trailers provided a minimum of office space. Adequate dining facilities were never finished.[92] Tile calibration, the delicate process of ensuring that tiles fit where they were meant to go, was carried out at first in High Bay 2 of the unfinished OPF. But it soon had to move to a renovated old building with dirt floors, to make room for other work that came on line when the OPF was activated.[93] Cultural differences quickly divided the KSC and California crews. KSC's head of security took a police dog out to the parking lot every day. Frequently the dog would uncover a stash of mari-juana in one of the cars, sending a Rockwell worker packing.[94]

All this was still not enough to meet the official NASA launch schedule. After *Columbia* arrived at KSC, Gene Sestile, whose critique of turnaround times had been the bane of the shuttle design team, returned to operations to help with completion of *Columbia*. He was now locked in a discursive battle with the program managers at the Johnson Space Center. As NASA continued to schedule launch dates that KSC would miss, Johnson direc-tor Chris Kraft had his design engineers make presentations on how KSC was going to improve. When Sestile challenged their claims, they would say, "Your experience base is bad. All you know is how not to do it." It was an-other swipe at the KSC launch culture, based presumably on the old Apollo model. Still, KSC's "experience base" from handling Apollo flows proved more realistic for assessing the shuttle than did the charts of the design en-gineers. Every Apollo spacecraft celebrated a one-year birthday at the Cape before it was launched. *Columbia* would get a second birthday there before it made it to the sky.[95]

The problem of the tiles brought out perhaps most clearly the difference between design and operations. Even from a design perspective, dealing

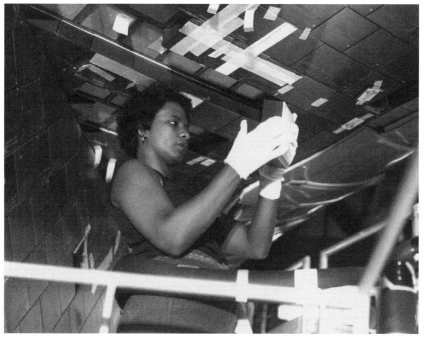

8-3. A technician carefully handles a tile, ready to install it in its precise spot on the vehicle.

8-4. Underneath the space shuttle *Columbia*, workers make progress, tile by tile.

with the 30,922 uniquely shaped tiles that made up *Columbia*'s TPS was difficult. Actually installing what was really an interacting system was enormously challenging. No two tiles were alike, and each had to be individually machined to fit its spot on the orbiter body. Differences of more than a few thousandths of an inch in the heights of adjacent tiles could result in air turbulence along the orbiter surface, which would dangerously increase the heating of tiles during reentry. Tiles also had to be installed in sequence, and work stopped if the appropriate tile was not yet ready.[96] Then there was the problem of keeping the tiles attached. Workers first treated the aluminum surface of the orbiter with a primer to facilitate bonding. Then they applied a second primer and a silicon adhesive. Meanwhile, another worker bonded a felt pad to the tile. This was designed to isolate the brittle tile from the orbiter's aluminum body, which would expand and contract with temperature changes during flight. Only at this point was the tile ready for the orbiter's skin.[97] In light of the reality of what attaching tiles required, NASA headquarters postponed the launch date once again. It was now clear that the shuttle's maiden voyage, originally slated for 1978 or 1979, would wait until the start of a new decade.[98]

The rescheduling finally gave KSC workers the time they needed to complete the crucial, painstaking tile work. But it cost a valued member of the Center his job. Walt Kapryan, head of Shuttle Launch Operations, came in for increasing criticism because of the missed launch dates. Kapryan had succeeded Rocco Petrone as launch director for *Apollo 12* and successfully guided the remainder of the Apollo-Saturn launches. Petrone was a legendary authoritarian, but Kapryan had a less confrontational management style. He found himself in a difficult position, having been asked to accept an unfinished vehicle and then told to solve the tile problem while the shuttle program as a whole was being managed at Houston. As the launch dates slipped, Kapryan was pressured to retire.

In May 1979 Kapryan stepped down, succeeded by George Page. Page, coworkers recall, was a "little Rocco." An extremely adept, well-rounded manager, he also had that ineffable quality of leadership necessary for tackling a nearly impossible task. He could "lead you through the fires of hell and you would follow him," those who worked under him would say, in part because he seemed to be working harder than anyone.[99] Page also had a

8-5. George Page took charge of shuttle operations with one goal: get *Columbia* flying.

close relationship with Rockwell, the prime orbiter contractor, but he would not take any nonsense from them or anyone else.

In the Apollo tradition, Page put together functional teams to handle the most difficult tasks. He placed Ernie Reyes in charge of the TPS problem, making him the "tile czar."[100] Reyes had been working in shuttle payloads and at first objected to the transfer. Weren't the "experts" who built the shuttle working on this problem already? But the experts from Rockwell had not succeeded, and Page insisted that Reyes had what was needed to overcome the holdup. Besides, there was no sense in his wasting time at payloads now. "If I don't have a shuttle that flies," Page pointed out, "I don't need a payload."[101]

Officially Houston was still in charge of completion of the shuttle, but effectively KSC "field engineers" had taken over much of the work under Page's direction. The hands-on guys at KSC tended to view the shuttle design engineers as prima donnas. Rockwell people, Jim Harrington recalls, saw the shuttle as their ship. They had built it, and they assumed that they knew how it operated. No NASA help was required, least of all from the bolt turners down in Florida.[102] But the procedures crafted by the design engineers for tile installation were failing. Page ordered Reyes to do "whatever you have to do" to get the tiles installed. He could change quality parameters, develop new engineering designs, cut deals with Johnson and Marshall. Whatever he and his workers thought needed to be done, Page authorized him to do. He was to report directly to Page.

Still, even with all the changes, work on the tiles moved with agonizing slowness. By June 1979, KSC workers were averaging no more than 200 tiles a week. It only got worse. By the end of the year, they were often removing more tiles than they were putting on. Over the next twenty months, workers would install some 76,000 tiles on a spacecraft using only 31,000. Just about every tile was removed at least once. Quality control remained a problem. Early estimates predicted a failure rate of 5 percent on the pull test that checked tile adhesion. The actual failure rate was nearly three times as high.[103] NASA engineers began discussing the possibility of a repair kit permitting astronauts to replace up to sixty tiles in space before concluding that if they really thought a repair kit was needed, then they shouldn't be sending the shuttle up.[104]

By January 1980, NASA executives admitted that so much attention had been placed on the thermal protection qualities of the tiles that they had failed to consider how well the tiles would stick to the orbiter once it was in flight.[105] Engineers had presumed that the tiles could be considered a unitary surface. But wind tunnel tests done after *Columbia* arrived at KSC revealed that each individual tile was a dynamic unit. As single units rather

8-6. "Tile czar" Ernie Reyes (*right*) receives an award for his work on *Columbia*.

than a continuous surface, tiles were not "dense" enough to remain attached under the stresses of launch. The tiles' silicon fibers lined up so that only the tips were glued to the orbiter. It took a long time to understand this, and then to come up with a way to make a solid surface for bonding.[106]

KSC workers suggested that the tiles be made more dense. But denser tiles would increase the weight of the already overweight vehicle. Reyes built a model of the shuttle and spent hours working out tile dynamics. Which tiles needed to be densified? How could they be installed so that the tiny gaps between them did not face directly into the superheated plasma surrounding the shuttle as it returned to earth?[107] Finally Rockwell engineers developed a process to paint the tile surfaces with a silica colloid called Ludox to increase density. KSC workers would measure the surface area of each tile and calculate the amount of Ludox needed to penetrate to about an eighth of an inch. The Ludox would be carefully brushed on by hand, in several layers, until the tile surface reached the correct density. The tiles would then be cured in an oven with waterproofing materials and reweighed to calculate the additional orbiter weight. The process was slow and cumbersome and, even when done correctly, had to be repeated if the densified tile still failed a pull test.[108]

The tile problem drew on all the resources and experience KSC could muster. For a time, workers practiced bonding and removing tiles on an old

DC-3 hung in the OPF. As they practiced, other workers tried to assess the impact of objects hitting the tiles at the high speeds of takeoff. At one point, KSC's Bob Sieck attached a tile to a race car and drove it into a line of chickens to see what would happen if birds should strike the orbiter in flight.

Columbia had spent six hundred and ten days in the OPF. Its tile work was still not done by the time it was scheduled to move to the VAB for mating with the external tank and solid rocket boosters. In two weeks KSC engineers designed access systems so that workers could continue tile application in the VAB. Meanwhile, workers from engine builder Rocketdyne and from KSC prepared the innovative space shuttle main engines (SSMEs).[109] In all, *Columbia* spent thirty-five days in the VAB. Crews worked round the clock, taking off only a half day for Christmas.[110] Just before the start of the new year, on December 29, 1980, *Columbia* finally moved from the VAB to the launchpad. Even then, workers continued to install, test, and replace tiles.[111]

First Launch

Columbia was now moving toward a definite launch date. As it did, as processing and fabricating work ended, some of the improvements in technology could come into play. Most of the shuttle countdown could use the newly installed automatic system, which would eliminate many of the old hands-on checks. During Apollo, engineers had to worry about the quality of manual procedures as they issued "call outs" requiring technicians to flip switches. Now, with the launch control rooms full of computers, all they had to do was give commands to run software.

Even in the automated launch process, though, KSC engineers had to adapt their original procedures to what they learned from experience. The shuttle blastoff began with ignition of the orbiter's liquid-fueled main engines. After they fired, the shuttle would flex or "twang" on the launchpad. Six seconds later, it would spring back to an upright position. Only then could the solid rocket boosters be ignited. KSC launch engineers developed twang tests to determine when they should light the solids. Once ignited, these giant Roman candles could not be turned off. They would burn until all fuel was consumed. If the main engines did not start, then the solid rocket boosters could not be lit. If the solid rocket boosters failed to light, then the main engines had to be shut down rapidly. Timing was everything.

Although automation promised greater efficiency and reliability, no one knew exactly how the software programs would perform in real-world conditions, when lives were at stake. KSC programmers had spent countless hours debugging the LPS, but even so many engineers distrusted it. Its first major test would come during the flight readiness firing on February 21, 1981. This firing would include all the components of the final countdown with the exception of lighting the solid rocket boosters. Even after the flight readiness test, head test director Norm Carlson still had many questions about the launch processing system. Would it automatically shut down the shuttle's main engines if the solid rocket boosters did not light? What would happen if only one SRB ignited? Many at KSC had nightmares of the main engines shutting down and the thrust from a single solid rocket cartwheeling the shuttle off the launchpad. The launch processing system might handle most contingencies, but would it handle them all, or even the most likely?[112]

Carlson wanted human backup to the LPS for the first launch. He had Tip Talone, who had spent many years as a test conductor on the Saturn, assigned as his assistant. What, Talone asked Carlson, was he to do? "You see that switch over there with the switch guard on it?" Carlson replied. "When we get down inside nine minutes, I want you to lift up that switch guard and I want you to be ready to throw that switch if I tell you to." The switch was a cutoff that Carlson had rigged. In case the launch processing system failed, he would shout "cutoff" and Talone was to flip the switch.[113]

Now all the key people were satisfied that a launch of *Columbia* could be tried. But a new delay loomed. "We run a risk of jeopardizing some of the flight hardware," an angry KSC director Dick Smith declared. What was the problem now? Eight hundred machinists and other workers employed by Boeing had just walked off their jobs. They were looking for delayed raises and cost-of-living adjustments.[114] The strike threatened to push the shuttle past its April launch date. Boeing replaced the striking workers with supervisory personnel to protect the launch schedule. Picketing workers would have to watch the first flight of *Columbia* from outside the KSC gates.

April 10, 1981, launch day, arrived only to find *Columbia* sitting on the pad as the backup flight software failed to synchronize with the four computers running the primary avionics system. KSC programmers spent the next two days poring over code line by line until they were sure they had debugged it all. Finally on April 12, just before 7 a.m., *Columbia*'s engines roared to life. The shuttle bowed as expected before coming to a straight-up position as the solid rocket boosters joined the main engines in lifting Robert Crippen and John Young into space. It was a new feeling for the astronauts, riding the shuttle. In contrast to the ponderous Saturn, the highly efficient SSMEs got the vehicle moving in a hurry. "The vehicle . . . doesn't lumber around when you light the engines," remarked Crippen. The ride was "kind of bouncy. . . . I'd liken it to me driving my old pickup down a washboard country road."[115] While the liftoff went without incident, ninety seconds before ignition a single-engine Cessna invaded the airspace surrounding the launchpad. KSC

8-7. On the first shuttle flight, *Columbia* finally leaves KSC. Note the tank painted white to help insulate the cryogenic fuel. Subsequent study showed the painting unnecessary, and it was dropped after the second flight, leaving the tank the familiar orange color.

security helicopters twice chased the airplane away from the pad before an FAA interceptor forced the craft to land at a local airport. The pilot claimed he was trying to get photographs of the launch.[116]

The strikers eventually accepted Boeing's offer a month later, after *Columbia* had landed.[117] Although a launch delay was averted, the use of replacement workers bred long-term distrust between labor and management. Workers saw the replacement as a bad-faith violation of earlier policy, which had disavowed use of scabs and lockouts. KSC engineers resented some of the shortcuts they were forced to take to keep on schedule while understaffed. To save some four days, for example, KSC personnel decided not to detank hypergolic fuels as they normally would have done after a tanking test. Hypergolics, in this case nitrogen tetroxide and monomethyl hydrazine, ignite when they come into contact, providing an extremely reliable power source for crucial engines, such as those used to maneuver the orbiter in flight. But they require extremely careful handling. They do not evaporate, so leaks would leave pools of chemicals around the shuttle, ready to ignite if the two chemicals happened to meet.[118] The decision not to detank was an added risk, especially to the workers who remained around the pad continuing last-minute work on tiles and external tank insulation.[119]

Though not related to the strike, the death of two workers during launch operations was a sober reminder of how dangerous work at KSC could be, especially in the early learning phase of a new vehicle. During the process of loading propellants, the aft section of the shuttle, which housed the main engines, was purged with nitrogen to eliminate buildup of explosive gases. Nitrogen is not toxic, and an all-clear signal had been given. But several workers, entering while nitrogen was still flowing, passed out in the low-oxygen atmosphere. Two died of asphyxiation.[120] Unlike the *Apollo 1* fire, which delayed Apollo flights for nearly a year, the deaths on the launchpad did not set back the shuttle's launch. But they raised the first questions about how safety would be balanced against the tremendous pressures of launching a vehicle expected to fly many times per year.

Before *Columbia*'s flight, no American had been in space for nearly five years. Forty-one thousand visitors watched the ship rise into the skies from viewing sites at the Kennedy Space Center. Two thousand seven hundred members of the press from as far away as Japan reported on the event. *Columbia* may not have been an Apollo moon launch, but the return to flight marked a revival of press interest in space issues.[121]

The liftoff of *Columbia* was a major milestone for KSC as well. It had taken more than two years, but KSC's personnel had completed the work on the shuttle. Now they would have to learn to process it rapidly and get it ready to return to space. As Center director Dick Smith put it, he had never "wanted to get rid of anything any worse in my life," and then "that dern thing came back and [we] got to do it all over again."[122] There was plenty to learn about the vehicle, which remained far from the space airliner everyone hoped it would become. Shuttle landings remained research and development events. At Edwards Air Force Base, KSC's Jim Harrington supervised nearly two hundred technicians to prepare for the first shuttle landing. They stood ready to receive the ship, remove any remaining toxic fuels, and mate it to the SCA for its journey back to the Cape, all procedures practiced on *Enterprise*. Airspace around the base was shut down to make way for the incoming shuttle, and the ground crew rehearsed emergency recovery procedures on the dry lake bed, integrating their work with security, fire support, and other services provided by Edwards.

Meanwhile, other NASA personnel worried about the orbiter's trip through the atmosphere. Would the troublesome tiles stay on? At KSC, the postlaunch crew had found pieces of tile on the ground after launch, adding to everyone's anxiety for the duration of the mission. Had the thermal protection system suffered a fatal breach? Fortunately, it had not. After *Columbia* landed in California, the recovery crew quickly scoured the area around the orbiter, discovering that only 16 tiles had come off during the flight. Another 143 sustained enough damage to mandate replacement. During processing back at KSC, a total of 1,500 tiles would be replaced. Postflight analysis revealed that most of the tile loss came when the vehicle was hit by an overpressure wave created by the solid rocket boosters. Joseph Mechelay, manager of mission evaluation, declared that, all in all, the problems resulting from *Columbia*'s first flight were so minor that the shuttle would be ready long before the second launch date of September 30.[123]

Mechelay's optimism spoke to the state of the orbiter. Back at KSC, others were not so sure. Pad inspectors found a "scene of devastation" after the launch. Some places looked "as if an atomic bomb had exploded nearby." Miles of electrical cables were ripped away, ducts and conduits damaged. *Columbia* had scorched the grass for a mile around and covered everything in a fine chemical dust that had to be hosed off.[124] The mission itself also showed how far NASA's infrastructure had deteriorated since Apollo. Satellite tracking stations had been lost for political and budgetary reasons. Astronauts Crippen and Young could communicate with the ground for only about 40 percent of their orbit around the earth. New tracking and satellite systems, still in development, would not be ready for many months, preventing full commercial use of the shuttle until 1983 or early 1984.[125]

Most of the damage done at the launch site was caused by the same shock wave that had loosened the tiles. Analysts determined that the wave rebounded back around the shuttle at two pounds per square inch, four times the predicted level. Though it had lasted only twenty milliseconds—too brief for the astronauts to feel—it had jarred the shuttle-tank-rocket assembly and had deflected the wing flaps six inches. It had also buckled steel on the launch tower, blown away railings, and damaged some of the umbilical connections. One railing had been driven through an elevator, putting it out of commission. The pad, not the shuttle, required redesign.[126]

In the past, KSC workers had had plenty of time to refurbish the pad after a launch. Not anymore. They would have to turn things around quickly to keep to the ambitious launch schedule. After considering major reconstruction of the pad, KSC engineers developed an improved water deflec-

8-8. Once test flights were done, the work of installing payloads to take advantage of the shuttle's massive payload capacity began.

tion mechanism to absorb the shock wave. Numerous 38-inch pipes would spray 31,250 gallons of water across the bottom of the solid rocket boosters in twenty-five seconds, deflecting the shock wave and carrying flame and exhaust along the concrete deflectors at the bottom of the pad. Permanent railings were replaced with detachable ones that could be removed before each launch.[127]

Thus far the debate about turnaround time had been a paper and ink battle.[128] Now it was possible to put "meat on the bones" of plans and schedules. "*Columbia* trained us," remarked Bob Sieck.[129] Besides proving the tile bonding process and teaching the launch team about the dangers of over-pressure, *Columbia* gave the computer programmers a real-world opportunity to debug their software. Despite many hours spent on the code, it was only after the LPS was used for the first launch that they were able to find and fix problems, rewrite procedures, and ask for changes to ground equipment.

KSC engineers had always seemed the naysayers on the turnaround issue, basing their skepticism on actual experiences from Apollo and earlier missions. Experience with *Columbia* started to provide evidence for their position. No one had expected a 160-hour turnaround after the shuttle's first flight. But earlier STAG analysts had postulated that most of the learning could be done on the first four missions. Experience now suggested that the learning process would be harder and take longer than predicted. In spite of the apparently minor repairs needed to *Columbia*, the orbiter spent three months in the OPF, moving to the VAB on August 10, 1981, for its second launch, scheduled for October 9. Then the unexpected intervened. On September 22, while fueling the shuttle's forward reaction control system, technicians spilled nitrogen tetroxide. As they dried the fuel, they felt tiles coming loose.

Some 350 tiles now had to be removed and taken to the tile processing room, where they were cleaned, waterproofed, and cured in ovens. They were again bonded to felt isolation pads and then returned to the launchpad for reattachment to the shuttle. By September 30, however, a team of sixty men and women had reattached only three of the missing tiles. Now the struggles in preparing STS-1 for launch paid off. Because technicians had already learned how to affix tile at the pad, they were able to replicate the process. A new access platform permitted reattachment of about ten tiles a day.[130] The fuel spill had delayed the shuttle's launch for a little less than a month. Then, just when it seemed that experience and hard work had done the trick, came another unplanned delay. On November 4, failure of some of the shuttle's reusable auxiliary power units pushed back launch five more days.

Joseph Engle and Richard Truly finally blasted off for the second shuttle ride on November 9.[131] The water shock suppression system that KSC had installed did its job. Analysts found the shock wave on the second liftoff to be less than 25 percent that of the first.[132] Fewer observers attended this second launch, and those with favored positions as official guests were moved back beyond the four-mile limit instead of watching the launch from in front of the Launch Control Center. NASA feared that, given the wrong wind conditions, shuttle exhaust might drift onto the observers.[133]

Two successful missions might have seemed cause for celebration. But in fact all was not well within the NASA family. The interim between the first and second shuttle flights brought renewed debate over turnaround times, with criticism pointed directly at KSC operations. Headquarters reproved the Center for its R&D approach, which required continued development and modification of the shuttle and ground support equipment. KSC personnel responded that the first two flights had only confirmed that they were still learning about the vehicle and the operations and equipment needed to process it. A week before the launch of STS-2, launch director George Page declared that the two-week turnaround time was "probably optimistic." KSC would continue to improve its turnaround time, but he concluded, "I don't think we'll ever get to two weeks."[134] Even without the delays caused by the fuel spill and malfunctions on the pad, processing for the second *Columbia* flight had taken about twenty-four weeks—thousands of hours rather than the 160 that NASA had mandated. Looking into the future, KSC planners thought that they would do no better than a ten-week turnaround by the ninth flight. These were not words NASA officials wanted to hear.

A Shuttle Turnaround Group chaired by Wes Branning worked to drive the number of hours down. Branning and his team admonished KSC to change its philosophy. They quickly found areas of operation where KSC could do better, such as the much criticized paper record system. Testing could be reduced—cut in half at least. Some shuttle components could also be redesigned for streamlined checkout and/or replacement. With the new technologies available, Branning asserted, KSC workers ought to be able to simultaneously load two types of fuel, something never attempted during the Apollo era. These seemed radical steps, but all of the proposals put forth had already been developed in industry. KSC once more was told that it could learn from industry, from the same firms that had learned from NASA's state-of-the-art procedures a generation before.[135]

Despite the lengthy processing required of *Columbia*, the imperatives of airline-like operations continued to frame discussion of the shuttle. Robert Buckley, head of KSC's Operations Planning Office, agreed with Branning that a shift from R&D to an airline operation was needed. The shuttle tiles provided a clear example. Each tile was individually designed for a spot on the Orbiter and had an individual part number. If a new tile was needed, a worker in the Orbiter Processing Facility would have to fill out a form itemizing the request. That form was read and signed by several superiors at KSC. Once an order had been approved, a requisition form was filled out and again worked its way through the signoff process. Then someone would have to get the tile, send it to the OPF, and fill out additional forms recording the tile's movement. Johnson designers had to check this paperwork too, so

8-9. Tired KSC workers call it a day.

that they could track the shuttle's status. A paper-intensive engineering process, derived from the safety-first approach instituted after the *Apollo 1* fire, contrasted sharply with practice in private industry.[136] Several suggestions came out of Buckley's planning office. KSC should reduce its paperwork by half, computerize day-to-day operations, increase automation by 25 percent, and generally reduce the role of government personnel in supervising and monitoring contractor work. Other recommendations included consolidating multiple contracts into fewer, larger ones for ease of management.[137]

Though problems with *Columbia* processing did not deflect NASA from its airliner analogy, neither did the successful launch of the shuttle silence critics of the space program. Shortly after the first liftoff, Senator William Proxmire fired off an opinion that the shuttle was being grossly oversold. "The United States is putting a truck up in the sky," he declared, "and we're being told that it's a second coming."[138] KSC personnel might well wonder what they were supposed to do, as they heard Proxmire denigrate the routine nature of shuttle flight, while being told by their own superiors that they were not making the shuttle routine enough. In fact, to someone working shuttle operations, both positions missed the mark. Proxmire clearly underestimated just how sophisticated, even revolutionary, a reusable vehicle was. But those pressuring KSC to process in a fast, streamlined manner also were missing the amount of learning to be done in handling such a sophisticated vehicle.

NASA was coming under enormous pressure even as it struggled to understand and deal with the new vehicle it had created. President Ronald Reagan's budget director David Stockman wanted NASA to slash $382 million from its 1982 budget.[139] These were serious cuts, and though they did not endanger the shuttle, several other NASA programs were decimated.[140] NASA, like other agencies, was looking for ways to preserve its budget and continue its mission in lean times. KSC officials argued, perhaps with some political naiveté, that money could be saved by moving Mission Control from Houston to Florida. The Johnson Space Center spent $500,000 to quash this proposal.[141] Fiscal tensions abated somewhat as "Boll Weevil" Democrats led by Congressman Bill Nelson, who represented Brevard County, began to reverse their overall support for Stockman's budget cuts. NASA would end up with a slight improvement in its finances after the second round of the 1982 budget battle.[142]

Learning continued with the launch of STS-3 on March 22, 1982. Wet conditions at Edwards Air Force Base forced the shuttle's landing site to shift to White Sands, New Mexico, where KSC recovery teams tried out a mobile mate-demate device for loading onto the Shuttle Carrier Aircraft. High winds at White Sands landing site extended the mission an extra day. Still, despite the irregular conditions, the shuttle moved back to KSC within seven days, the fastest time yet.[143]

Now more parts of an operational shuttle program were appearing. KSC awarded a contract to Computer Sciences Corporation for a Shuttle Inventory Management System.[144] Analogous to industry-developed methods for just-in-time manufacturing, the SIMS II program used a computerized data processing system to support inventory management at KSC, Vandenberg, and other locations.[145] STS-4 was meant to be the final official R&D flight of the shuttle *Columbia*. Launched June 27, 1982, with Thomas Mattingly and Henry Hartsfield aboard, it had achieved a turnaround time of seventy days, still far short of the 160-hour goal, or indeed the four-to-five-week turnaround that KSC schedulers believed theoretically possible. Gradually a new regime based on contracting would come to dominate launch operations, though government employees would never completely withdraw from shuttle processing. Nor would these structural changes bring launch to the Holy Grail of 160-hour turnarounds. That number, so tempting, proved an illusion.

9

*
*
*

A New Order of Things

*It must be considered that there is nothing more difficult to
carry out, nor more doubtful of success, nor more dangerous
to handle, than to initiate a new order of things.*

Niccolò Machiavelli

It was time, President Ronald Reagan said, to make the shuttle "operational."
His national security directive of 1984, issued after four test flights, deemed
the vehicle ready to carry a varied cargo into space and to carry out scientific
missions. It would fly civilians as well, all proving that space access could be
economical and routine. Declaring the shuttle operational by presidential
directive was one thing; making it fly like an airliner was another. The shuttle
still depended critically on work done on the ground at KSC, where the processing of the vehicle and its payloads occurred. The Center had significant
learning to do in meeting a schedule, serving a diverse group of users, processing payloads, and flying and maintaining a ship with millions of parts.[1]

Military and Civilian Conflicts

When Ronald Reagan entered office in 1980, many space enthusiasts expected him to revive a sagging American space program. Harrison Schmidt,
a Republican senator from New Mexico and a former astronaut, declared
that he was "really heartened by some of the scientific people on Reagan's
transition teams."[2] The new president was sure to pilot NASA out of the
doldrums it had been stuck in during the Nixon, Ford, and Carter administrations. Though Reagan was elected on a platform seeking to reduce waste
in government, Schmidt thought that his commitment to the military would
help NASA. Schmidt was right, Reagan's policies would bring more military
resources into the space program, but the impact would not be as clear-cut
as the senator had hoped.

Starting in the late 1970s and continuing during the Reagan administration, defense spending for space escalated. By 1980, Department of Defense spending on space exceeded that of NASA for the first time since 1960. The gap between military and civilian space expenditures continued to grow through the mid-1980s.[3] Reagan's policies led to closer connections between KSC and the air force launch facilities at Cape Canaveral.[4] Military support had rescued the shuttle from cancellation at a crucial moment in the 1970s, but military needs, combined with fiscal restraints, conflicted with efforts to get the shuttle program on a sound economic footing.

In 1980 Air Force Secretary Hans Mark declared that America needed at least four orbiters and that six or seven would be even better.[5] Others, including Lieutenant General Thomas P. Stafford, agreed, even suggesting that the air force should take over operation of the shuttle.[6] The shuttle program, declared Colonel Marvin Jones, commander of the Eastern Space and Missile Center at Patrick Air Force Base, "is where the air force is moving."[7] There would be even greater air force involvement after the expected 1984 opening of the Vandenberg launch site. NASA responded to the renewed military interest in space by placing Major General James Abrahamson, USAF, in charge of the shuttle program, and making Hans Mark its deputy administrator.[8]

The military presence, however, soon raised conflicts with the shuttle's goal of providing affordable space access. For the Department of Defense, the shuttle's job was to place spy satellites and other military hardware securely in orbit. DOD was leery of becoming totally dependent on a single launch vehicle outside its control. Military concerns had already shaped shuttle design, notably the inclusion of extensive cross-range cruising capacity. Should an orbiter be forced into an emergency landing while carrying secret spy hardware, military authorities wanted it to be able to glide safely to a spot within U.S. territory. Military needs placed other demands on the space vehicle as well. Spy satellites were launched into polar orbits. For polar flights, the shuttle was capable of lifting only about 30,000 pounds of payload, below the weight of some military satellites. To compensate, NASA modified launch and flight procedures, running the shuttle's main engines at 109 percent of their rated capacity. Morton Thiokol also began to build new lighter-weight solid rocket boosters, while NASA engineers worked on a version of its high-velocity liquid-oxygen-fueled Centaur vehicle that would fly aboard the shuttle and push heavy payloads into higher orbits. On the drawing board as well were plans for a fifth shuttle, lighter in weight, which would be paid for by the military.[9]

In matters of pricing and schedule, military and civilian uses of space did not neatly align. In return for supporting the shuttle, the military expected its payloads to come first in line, and even bump civilian missions from the schedule if necessary. The right to bump displeased commercial users. They could not afford to wait to get their satellites up and running. By the 1980s, they also had some choices, as an international market for launch services emerged.

To gain customers, NASA sought to price shuttle flights low enough to attract new users while competing with other launch authorities. With each shuttle mission figured to cost about $120 million, commercial clients would pay $75–90 million for a flight. Some would be charged even less. This was a sound commercial strategy with a vehicle that had large fixed costs. By undercharging initially, NASA could build up a loyal base of users and spread those fixed costs over many flights. In this way, the price of space access would fall, and the shuttle would still pay for itself. It also made sense to sell cargo space on the vehicle at a bargain price when the primary mission did not fill up the entire payload, or to charge different customers different rates reflecting their ability to pay. Critics of the shuttle and supporters of the expendable launch vehicle industry, however, argued that this pricing scheme amounted to a subsidy to shuttle users. The military took a similar view, concerned that the shuttle was pricing out of existence the Delta, Titan, and other expendables long used for military payloads.[10] Responding to recommendations not to put all its eggs into the shuttle basket, the air force reactivated the Titan program, so that it had a second heavy-lift space vehicle. This move undercut NASA hopes of flying everything on the shuttle.

In the near term, NASA could not raise prices as its critics asked. The American launch industry was facing international competition, particularly from France. The French firm Arianespace possessed an expendable booster that could be launched from Kourou in French Guiana, a position closer to the equator than Cape Canaveral. Launching closer to the equator required less energy and a smaller propulsion system to reach orbit, and hence lower operating costs. The Ariane launcher had been developed by the European Space Agency, a consortium of European nations that took advantage of the pioneering work done in America during the Apollo era to learn how to build, fly, and manage large space projects. After a few stumbles, Ariane had grown into a very credible competitive alternative to the shuttle. The launch facility at Kourou, a modern, efficient complex, also took advantage of the learning that had gone on at KSC.[11] In addition, new competition was emerging from Asia. Japanese and Chinese boosters and launch operations were poised to compete for what many believed was going to be a growing commercial satellite business in the 1980s. Foreign governments often supported or subsidized their infant commercial launch industries, to give them a chance to reach a competitive level with the United States. To be sure, the shuttle had its strong points. It could put more than 60,000 pounds in low earth orbit, considerably more than its competitors could launch. Still, only if shuttle pricing reflected the competitive market could it vie for the satellite and scientific business, and only a full manifest and many launches per year would provide the desired cost reductions through scale.[12]

These pressures forced KSC into a delicate balancing act. It had to keep the shuttle on schedule, scale up the number of flights, develop new skills in logistics to service its expanded orbiter fleet, and handle diverse payloads for a wide range of customers. At the same time, it was being pressured by the White House and Congress to keep costs down and respond to military concerns. Problems of payload processing and logistics could only be expected to grow as the flight rate rose. Most of NASA's budget was devoted to operating the shuttle, leaving little for investment in new booster technologies, major shuttle refurbishments, or new launch facilities.

One response to these pressures was to place more of the operational elements of space flight in the hands of private contractors. Beginning in the Carter administration and continuing with the election of Ronald Reagan, a new belief in deregulation and shifting tasks out of government hands and into the private sector had taken hold.[13] Conservative Republicans characterized government agencies and their civil servants as "the problem" rather than the solution to social ills and economic difficulties. As the congressional committees overseeing NASA incorporated Reagan's philosophy of privatization, they encouraged KSC to turn over more operational work to contractors.

During Apollo, NASA personnel had been proud of their role as government civil servants who worked right alongside engineers from universities and private industry in making missions go.[14] Legends of those times told of maintenance workers sweeping floors who explained what they did as "helping America get to the moon." Many at KSC believed that they had acquired valuable hands-on experience from earlier programs, experience that would be useful in managing the shuttle. But those who had once distinguished themselves from other government employees because they were "pushing beyond the frontier of science and technology . . . openly, and for the benefit of all" were now relabeled as just one more band of Washington bureaucrats.[15]

Shuttle Operations in the 1980s

KSC director Richard Smith looked over a manifest that listed some 361 shuttle flights from Cape Canaveral in the 1980s. Though only 7 missions were scheduled for 1982, that number would double to 14 the next year and increase to 18 by 1984. Launches after that would gradually rise until KSC was sending some 40 shuttles per year on their way by 1988.[16] Vandenberg Air Force Base was to launch another 4 shuttle flights beginning in 1984, with the number increasing to 15 per year by 1988. This ambitious schedule went far beyond anything that had ever been done in the history of launch operations, either at the Cape or anywhere else in the world. Meeting it required at a minimum the following: standardized processing procedures from landing to launch; equipment and parts on hand and readily available; significant local manufacturing capabilities for replacement parts; modifications and upgrades of orbiters and other equipment at the launch site rather than at the factory; expanded facilities for processing vehicles and their payloads. To avoid the week-long delay in transporting craft from California to the Cape, landings at KSC would have to become routine.

One threat to the flight schedule was kinks in the supply chain. Fuels, including hydrogen, oxygen, and hydrazine, would have to be delivered to the shuttle in increasing volumes or produced on-site. Each launch required about 500,000 gallons of liquid hydrogen to fill the shuttle's external tank. Another 75,000 to 100,000 gallons of hydrogen boiled off in the course of countdown and had to be replenished. Additional hydrogen went into the shuttle's fuel cells. Still more would be required someday to fuel the Centaur upper stage expected to boost heavy satellites into high earth or interplanetary orbits. The annual need for liquid hydrogen was forecast to grow from two to fifteen million gallons by 1990.

KSC drew its hydrogen supply from a natural gas facility in Louisiana. The liquefied gas was shipped to the Cape in 13,000-gallon tanker trucks. By the spring of 1983, specially designed 34,000-gallon rail tanks met these needs, while KSC teams under the direction of a special products development office evaluated options for local production. NASA studies reported in 1984 that the shuttle could save $750,000 to $1,000,000 per launch by constructing a coal gasification plant to produce the needed hydrogen, while generating the Center's electricity to boot. If the shuttle stayed on its launch schedule, then entirely new facilities would be going up at the Cape, transforming well-worn practices.[17]

There seemed to be a way around the supply problems, but it turned out that the critical roadblock to meeting the schedule was not processing but manufacturing. NASA officials found that they could not make the lightweight external shuttle tanks fast enough. In May 1981 they cut some seven missions from the 1982–85 manifest. Then just a month later they reduced shuttle missions by thirty more. Some of these payloads were taken by additional launches of Delta and Atlas expendable vehicles. The cuts happened so fast that customers had to scramble to decide whether they wanted to remain on the shuttle's abbreviated manifest or change over to an ELV.[18] Reductions in the shuttle's schedule reduced pressure at KSC but also undercut the strategy of shuttle use based on economies of scale.

Even with the abbreviated flight schedule, processing and turnaround problems remained. President Reagan had declared developmental flying ended with the fourth flight. But the next group of missions were hardly routine. The shuttle's design never became standardized as originally hoped. In fact, the most time-consuming part of processing was not the routine but the unplanned or unexpected problems that cropped up in each work flow. Each of these problems required time to study and resolve, and each generated its own paper trail, efforts to improve information processing notwithstanding. Soon the saying around KSC was "Until the paper is stacked as high as the VAB, you are not ready for flight."[19]

In these early years no one could be sure of fully understanding how the shuttle as a complex system behaved under real-world conditions. Everyone knew that human space vehicles had historically been more reliable than robotic ones. Despite improvements in launching unmanned vehicles, the success rate for the Deltas, Titans, and Atlases still hovered around 90–96 percent. That was good, a vast improvement over the figures from two decades earlier, but nowhere near the level of assurance needed with humans aboard. The man-rated rockets for Mercury and Gemini had performed much better than the military craft from which they were derived. The Apollo-Saturn vehicle had never lost an astronaut in flight. This was the level of assurance required for the shuttle as well. But why were the rockets that carried people more reliable than the ones that did not? Was it due to better components and hardware? More rigorous certification and testing? More careful handling? All three? Until someone could say for certain what lay behind the superior performance of human-carrying technology, it was risky to change processing and launch procedures. KSC engineers faced a potentially harrowing set of choices. You "never knew when you were going to dismantle the one thing that makes a difference."[20] This bred a reluctance to change anything. KSC would continue its policy of testing to "drive out the failure," as it had for Apollo. The sense around the Cape was, maybe someday there would be enough assurance for more streamlined operations, but not yet.

Adding to the uncertainty was the evolving nature of the orbiter itself. While much of Columbia's equipment appeared in subsequent vehicles, each new vehicle had to be tested differently from those that came before it. The first flight of Challenger, STS-6, checked out the redesigned, lighter solid rocket boosters and external tank.[21] Later vehicles were also lighter than earlier ones. Challenger weighed some 2,889 pounds less than Columbia. Discovery and Atlantis came 6,870 pounds less.[22] Lighter vehicles were structurally more sensitive and required different handling in the stacking process.

Although the newer orbiters incorporated important upgrades and arrived at the Cape in much better shape than *Columbia*, they still required a disheartening amount of finishing work. At the flight readiness firing (FRF) for *Challenger* in December 1983, technicians discovered a hydrogen leak in the number one main engine. Subsequent tests revealed that all the newer, more powerful shuttle engines had cracks in their fuel lines. Shuttle workers removed all three engines while *Challenger* sat on the pad. After extensive testing, they put two engines back in the orbiter and replaced the third. But at a second FRF on January 25, they discovered yet another leak.[23] Eventually the leaks were traced to small cracks in the number one main engine's manifold. Shuttle technicians replaced the engine.[24] Unfortunately, the replacement engine soon revealed an oxygen leak in a line to the oxygen heat exchanger. It too would have to be replaced.[25]

Even more significant, the thermal protection tiles remained unstandardized. *Challenger* required fewer tiles than *Columbia*, but each tile was still unique. *Discovery* and *Atlantis* also received individualized tile layouts. By the time KSC had a full complement of orbiters, it was tracking more than 100,000 individual tiles. These had to be kept in stock or constructed on demand. Upgrades to the thermal protection system helped somewhat here. In areas less affected by the heat of reentry, engineers were able to substitute thermal protection "blankets" for tiles. These upgrades reflected lessons learned in flying the shuttle, but they also reinforced the developmental rather than operational nature of the vehicle.

Indeed, it soon became clear that changes designed to improve vehicle operations could have untoward effects on scheduling. After the four test flights of *Columbia*, engineers felt confident enough to remove a 600-pound antigeyser line from the external tank, permitting a corresponding increase in payload. What was gained in flight performance, however, was lost in countdown time. The removal of the line increased the chances of unscheduled holds during the last nine minutes of the count.[26]

Despite the problems, turnaround times improved in the early 1980s. It had taken more than two years to ready *Columbia* for its first flight, and 213 days elapsed before NASA launched *Columbia* a second time. But turnaround between the second and third flights was cut nearly in half, to 132 days. By the time *Challenger* arrived, stacking had been standardized down to an average of about a week.

KSC executives continued to meet on the turnaround issue. They understood that their people had worked extraordinarily hard to get *Columbia* flying, but there was no way to keep up this level of motivation for all future flights. The money would not be there for such an effort, either. The shuttle program had tight limits on how many overtime hours could be charged. Accordingly, the Shuttle Turnaround Group at KSC focused on working smarter and more efficiently. Time and cost savings would have to come through innovative scheduling of personnel to assure that the right skills were on the floor when needed. Future shuttle flights would have to serve a dual purpose, both as paying operations and as learning experiments for KSC engineers. This was the only way the vehicle processors would have a chance to standardize their procedures.[27]

Some of the tasks they faced were more managerial than technical. Although the level of motivation from the first flight would naturally abate, it was still crucial to inculcate a can-do attitude among shuttle workers. This would come in part from bolstering morale and retaining key skilled people. Better scheduling to eliminate exhausting work cycles could help as well. Workers had been placed on seven-day, four-shift cycles to get *Challenger* ready for its maiden voyage in March 1983. Their workweek, during the critical period, could begin or end on any given day. Supervisors were exchanged as necessary between KSC and the various contractors. Such long hours of work burned out even the most dedicated and frayed the nerves of managers. To better control schedules, KSC set up a special control center.[28] Improved food service and transportation on night and weekend shifts helped to mollify disgruntled workers. Meanwhile, at higher levels of the organization, KSC executives worked to ensure that their engineers had "authority equal to responsibility." Frequently, KSC engineers complained, they would be given new requirements from the design centers or DOD that affected the schedule or required more resources. To minimize unplanned changes, approval of waivers would pass through KSC. A running battle for control between operations and design engineers would continue to mark the shuttle's early life.[29]

Improved work procedures allowed for more rapid processing, but now logistics held up the turnaround schedule. When the leaks on *Challenger*'s engines had appeared, there were no replacement engines in stock. Instead, one of *Columbia*'s old engines was shipped from engine builder Rocketdyne's facility in Canoga Park, California. A new engine was to be sent as well.[30] Once the new and repaired engines were reinstalled, *Challenger* was ready to fly—until technicians discovered that the TDRS satellite in its payload bay, installed during a windstorm on February 28, was contaminated. The satellite was part of a system that would permit the shuttle to communicate with the ground from anywhere in orbit. It was returned to the O&C Building, where workers cleaned and decontaminated it.[31] It was a frustrating launch, but also a good example of how problems stemming from any source—parts, work procedures, logistics—could cause delays that in turn affected other parts of the shuttle and its payload.

For example, everyone assumed that newer orbiters would have fewer problems, but logistics troubles quickly undercut this assumption. The third vehicle, *Discovery*, required completion work at KSC because it had been cannibalized while under construction to provide spares for its sister ships. *Discovery* paid the price for this service. When it arrived at the Cape, the newest orbiter went into storage in the OPF. Reporters noted how bedraggled the brand-new vehicle looked.[32] While KSC technicians could replace the items removed, they had to wait until *Challenger* returned to the Cape to complete the work, delaying *Discovery*'s move to the VAB for stacking until May 12, 1984.[33]

Cannibalization was soon a way of life with the shuttle. When an electronic circuit in *Challenger*'s toilet malfunctioned after its second flight, KSC workers replaced it with the toilet from *Discovery*.[34] *Columbia* borrowed *Discovery*'s fuel cells for STS-9.[35] Budget constraints prevented the launch center from stocking a full complement of orbiter parts. Indeed, not until 1990, with the opening of the Logistics Building, was the Center able to reduce its reliance upon a makeshift supply depot patched together from remodeled railroad cars, prefabricated buildings, and trailers.[36]

Despite its stint as a parts supplier, *Discovery* went through the smoothest flight readiness test to date. Launch manager Bob Sieck asserted that this showed the "maturity of the hardware." But hope soon faded. Within days *Discovery*'s launch was postponed to "fully analyze" the results of the FRT that had seemed to go so well. Closer inspection soon revealed that a heat shield on one of the main engines had partially debonded. While technicians checked out the mechanical and electrical connections of the payload, others replaced the engine. The replacement came from *Challenger*, then in the OPF.[37] *Discovery* failed to fly again on its rescheduled launch date when one of its onboard computers failed. This was replaced by one pulled from *Challenger*. The next day the launch was scrubbed when at T-4 seconds the number three main engine failed to ignite.[38] A pad abort with engines firing was no small matter, and it showed how far from mature the hardware on the shuttle really was.

On the positive side, the pad abort also revealed how expert KSC personnel had become in dealing with safety issues. Official news reports indicated that the crew was prepared to slide down the escape wire in the emergency escape baskets. This was a tricky maneuver to be avoided if at all possible. The walkway to the escape baskets was an open grating, heated like a grill by the hydrogen-fed flames beneath. *Discovery* was quickly doused and the pad was safed without requiring a crew escape. Following the exit of the crew, launch technicians removed liquid hydrogen and liquid oxygen from the external tank. Residual propellants boiled off overnight before technicians moved the rotating service structure back around *Discovery*.[39] Later the open grating was replaced by a solid metal walkway to lower risks to crew.[40]

KSC officials expected that they could solve the problems that had delayed *Discovery* and have the shuttle on its way by July 16, the minimum permitted turnaround time after a pad abort. It was already apparent that the delay would also postpone *Discovery*'s second launch.[41] On July 10 testing began on the main engines for leaks, in preparation for *Discovery*'s new mission, combining the payloads originally scheduled for its first and second flights. The combined mission would permit NASA to catch up with customer demand. Beginning in October 1984, KSC expected to launch one shuttle a month.[42] The fastest turnaround time thus far had been two months. Now they expected to reduce it to about thirty-five days.[43]

It was an optimistic schedule. The three satellites to fly on the modified *Discovery* mission had to be tested and mated with their payload assist modules (used to boost them into higher orbits) in the vertical processing building. They would then be rolled to the pad in the Shuttle Cargo Transport Canister, a motorized vehicle configured like the payload bay of the shuttle. Early on August 2, *Discovery* returned to the VAB for restacking. It moved to the pad on August 9. The crawler, however, set down the mobile launcher three inches out of kilter and on August 10 it returned to correct the error. The next day the payloads were installed. The countdown demonstration test (CDDT) followed on August 15 after technicians had checked out the connections for the payloads.[44] *Discovery*'s launch, set for August 29, was again delayed when during the countdown the orbiter's electronic system, which controlled the ejection of the external tank and solid rocket boosters, malfunctioned. The next day *Discovery* finally took its maiden voyage, but not before a six-minute delay while NASA helicopters chased away three curious aircraft that had invaded KSC airspace.[45]

If *Discovery* had failed to prove the shuttle a mature technology, perhaps the next orbiter would. "*Atlantis* was beautiful, I am telling you . . . absolutely spotless and pristine," remembered Conrad Nagel, who served as flow director for its first flight.[46] Compared to the earlier orbiters, it seemed almost ready to be stacked on arrival. It had a relatively trouble-free first flight (STS-51J) on October 3, 1985, after just four and a half months at the Center.[47] This orbiter, the last of the original four planned for the fleet, had been delivered to KSC functionally complete. Even so, *Atlantis* experienced delays. Between its arrival at KSC and its first launch it spent nearly a month in storage in the VAB as other orbiters filled the building's work spaces. By *Atlantis*'s second mission (STS-61B) that November, it too had to borrow parts and equipment from the other ships.[48]

Even if *Atlantis* represented the latest, most mature version of the orbiter, that did not mean that shuttle technology was stable or static. *Columbia* returned to the Cape on July 14, 1985, after a $42 million upgrade in California. KSC technicians treated the overhauled craft like a new ship. They were forced to in part because *Columbia* returned as it had arrived six years earlier, unready for flight. On the return trip from the West Coast it flew briefly through a rainstorm, damaging several hundred tiles. Workers replaced them in the OPF, continuing the rest of the refurbishment after *Columbia* moved to the VAB.[49]

Columbia's return to flight reflected the minor disruptions that continually upset the schedule. Poor weather combined with irksome problems in the aft compartment delayed launch on December 17. KSC scrubbed the launch a second time when a faulty hydraulic power unit began spinning at 10,000 rpm faster than normal.[50] While the crew waited for a third launch attempt, it had the unpleasant experience of quarantine (astronauts are commonly removed from contact with germs while awaiting flight) over the Christmas holiday. The launch was scrubbed again on January 6 when a balky fuel valve malfunctioned, dumping some 18,000 pounds of LOX on the ground. The next day saw poor weather at both transatlantic abort landing sites. This time the delay forced the crew for the next flight, of *Challenger*, back to Houston; there was no room at KSC's astronaut quarters until *Columbia*'s crew left. The launch delayed yet again when workers failed to repair another balky fuel valve in time. No one found a small temperature sensor that had broken off and lodged in a main engine LOX line valve until January 11. Not until the eighth launch attempt, on January 12, did the remodeled *Columbia* rocket into space. NASA considered shortening *Columbia*'s mission by one day to turn it around in time for its next scheduled launch. Instead poor weather at the Cape extended the mission to a January 18 landing at Edwards.[51]

Shuttle upgrades thus changed, but did not eliminate, processing headaches. Improvements eventually extended the life of key parts, such as the shuttle's brakes, reducing work and relieving pressure on the logistics system. But other complications extended processing times. In the corrosive salt air of the Cape, the shuttle's engines deteriorated faster than had been expected. Over time, work on the shuttle became more automated and integrated with the Launch Processing System. More could be done with less. But not all automation was successful. One obvious area for improvement was the time-consuming hand inspection of thermal tiles. Efforts to develop machines to automate inspection were eventually abandoned when it was found that it would take a larger crew to maintain the inspection machine than to manually inspect the tiles.[52]

Other issues simply went beyond the power of the operations experts at KSC. NASA had difficulty keeping up with its need for auxiliary power units. Each shuttle carried three hydrazine-fueled APUs. These drove the pumps that powered the shuttle's crucial hydraulic systems during liftoff and landing. Hydraulic actuators controlled the thrust vector on the main engines, powered various engine valves, moved aerosurfaces, and retracted the external tank umbilical after separation. During deorbit, they again controlled engine valves and thrusting vectors as well as the elevons, rudder, speed brake, and body flaps needed for cruising down to earth. On landing they deployed the landing gear and operated the brakes. The APUs had long been a weak point, and their problems continued to mount. As NASA ran through its supply, KSC had to shift parts, swapping APUs from one orbiter to the next.[53]

Cannibalization was becoming a long-term issue, one that prevented a faster turnaround. Each time parts were swapped, the schedule gained time. Using parts in this way also increased wear and tear, making the spares shortage even worse. But it continued because of budget cuts and pressures to lower flight costs. Focus on the ambitious schedule pushed aside long-term expenditures, such as an ample inventory of replacement parts.[54]

Although by 1985 the fast turnarounds expected for an operational shuttle had yet to appear, there was just enough sign of improvement that maybe a space airliner was still possible. It might take more time than originally thought, but eventually, optimists believed, NASA would get there. The start of shuttle landings at the Cape, for example, saved from four days to a week or more in vehicle processing. Cape landings had taken time to perfect. During the developmental period, when the behavior of the orbiter in return flight was less certain, the shuttle had touched down on the vast lake bed at Edwards, where it had a wide margin for error. A miscalculation of the approach at KSC would have the crew swimming with the alligators.

The first KSC landing occurred on the tenth shuttle mission, with *Challenger* in January 1984. When *Challenger* landed, technicians found feathers embedded in the orbiter's tiles. Commander Vance Brand reported flying through a small flock of birds coming in. More significant from KSC's perspective were the four small aircraft that violated the Center's airspace during the landing. While three were intercepted and escorted out of the restricted area by security, one flew directly over the shuttle after it had landed. All had been "sightseeing" and "photographing" the flight, but KSC security remained concerned that such intrusions revealed how a terrorist could use a small aircraft to attack the shuttle.[55]

Improvements in operations sometimes came by developing expertise in areas far removed from rocket technology. After poor weather at the Cape diverted a planned *Challenger* touchdown to Edwards in April 1984, Mission Control in Houston demanded that KSC improve its weather forecasting system.[56] Since 1983 the center's future projects office had been studying the use of artificial intelligence "expert systems" to provide twelve-hour weather prediction at the Cape.[57] NASA also continued to develop its Automatic Landing System, which would bring in the orbiter without crew intervention.[58] Weather requirements for a shuttle launch were more stringent than they had been for Apollo. An Apollo spacecraft could be launched provided it would not fly through a thunderstorm. Shuttle launch decisions, however, had to take into account not only the local weather but also conditions at abort sites in Europe and Africa. As a shuttle neared launch time, weather data from the Cape and from the emergency landing zones streamed in for close analysis. Above the Cape an astronaut flew one of the shuttle training jets, checking for high-altitude wind shear and testing the conditions for an abort back to the KSC landing strip.[59]

Shuttle missions 13 through 16 landed at Merritt Island. This regularity was short lived, however. On the next mission, STS-51D, *Discovery* suffered extensive brake damage and a blown tire while landing in high crosswinds. The crew and the craft had never been in serious danger, but NASA concluded that future orbiters would land on the Edwards lake bed until nose wheel steering was added.[60] KSC engineers fast-tracked development of a steering system, which was installed on *Challenger* and tested during a landing at Edwards in December 1985.[61] NASA predicted that KSC landings would now become 99 percent routine. However, even with the new steering system, weather derailed a planned landing of *Columbia* at the Cape in January 1986.[62]

Contractors and the Shuttle

A move toward an operational shuttle had always involved rethinking the roles of contractors and civil servants in operations. During the 1970s, and increasingly in the 1980s with the Reagan administration, policy experts argued that civil servants should get out of routine operational work, which could be done by profit-oriented contractors from the private sector. Privatization through contracting, though, created a management headache, as dozens of different firms provided a host of services and functions. These many separate contracts all had to be overseen by KSC civil servants, and their functions coordinated. It would be far simpler, it seemed, to have one prime contractor, who could add subcontractors where needed. The prime would be the main point of contact with KSC civil servants.

Studies undertaken in the 1970s and early 1980s recommended two "single point" contracts, one to handle shuttle operations, a second for shuttle payloads. A third contract, base operations, was added for the routine services, from janitorial to security to computers, needed in a vast facility employing thousands of people. The single-point contracts could be managed by KSC civil servants at a high level, and would not require the extensive coordination among different firms. They would also remove civil servants from much of the day-to-day work they had traditionally performed.

The move to contracting was controversial. In 1979 a review board chaired by General Dynamics president (and future NASA administrator) James Beggs recommended against turning the shuttle over to private contractors before the mid-1980s. The capitalization costs, the board concluded, would be too great before then to make contracting worthwhile.[63] But these warnings were pushed aside amid optimistic predictions of a rapidly rising shuttle launch rate. In 1980 NASA announced that it would eventually consolidate KSC contracts, in preparation for the time when it would be launching thirty to forty missions a year. The conservative economic philosophy of the 1980s encouraged a rapid move toward privatization. Faced with increasingly tight budgets, NASA was attracted to contracting as a way to save precious dollars.

Understandably, officials both at KSC and in industry remained unsure how or when to make the move. At one meeting KSC's Tom Utsman noted facetiously that they had begun preparing for these changes as far back as the year 1500.[64] If not a matter of centuries, the move to contracting had been under discussion for a decade or more. In 1976 KSC paid for a study by the consulting firm Booz Allen on how to transit to the operational era.[65] In 1977 the Center followed the Booz Allen study with its own operations study, prepared by Gerald Griffin, the Center's deputy director. These plans would go through several revisions, with some controversy over which contract should be let first. The Shuttle Processing Contract, or SPC, became the critical and most controversial of the three.[66]

At a 1981 meeting between KSC officials and senior industry representatives, Marvin White from Lockheed pointed out that it would be very difficult for outsiders to bid on the SPC. The shuttle's builder, Rockwell, retained significant in-house expertise and had unique firsthand knowledge of the vehicle. Though a number of big aerospace firms had shuttle-related expertise, few had any of that experience at KSC. Processing work would be highly technical, and the costs of obtaining data would be enormous.[67]

Potential bidders wondered how much autonomy they would actually be granted even if they won the contract. Then there were smaller but no less important questions. How would NASA assess contractor performance? Was the shuttle really mature technologically, or would it continue to evolve in significant ways not recognized when the contract was granted? Would NASA be able to turn over control of what, from flight experience thus far, still seemed to be an R&D vehicle?[68]

At the 1981 meeting, KSC personnel voiced their own concerns. Pressure from NASA headquarters to achieve operational status meant that the assessment time on bids would be short. How much competitive bidding would there actually be? If Rockwell formed a team with other major aerospace firms, it would be a "formidable obstacle to overcome."[69] Equally important was the question of how KSC would handle the "influence" of other centers on daily processing activities. KSC civil servants were to be the contract managers, but the work to be done involved other parts of NASA that were not directly party to the contract itself. Even at KSC such lines of responsibility posed problems. Work had to be divided among shuttle, base operations, and payload contractors, even though some work fell into more than one area. Would there have to be lines painted on the floor indicating where the base operations contract worker stopped sweeping and the shuttle processing contractor picked up the broom? (For a time, there would be!)

Questions about the role of civil servants were especially important to KSC managers. They were to be held accountable if something went wrong, but were uncertain they would have sufficient authority to supervise and direct work. Traditionally the launch director, who had final say over whether a launch was go or not, was a top-level KSC person, a government employee. Would this crucial decision now be placed in the hands of a private industry worker whose firm had been low bidder on a contract? Finally, even if all these concerns could be addressed, there was the practical matter of timing. Most argued that the shuttle would remain developmental at least for the next ten years, declarations of official policy notwithstanding. So long as it was developmental, there would be significant costs in upgrades, new learning, and troubleshooting. These might well eat into any profit the contractor could expect to realize.[70]

By the time these contract issues were being discussed, James Beggs had taken over as NASA administrator. Even as an executive of giant defense contractor General Dynamics, Beggs had doubts about the feasibility of contracting out shuttle work. He responded to pressure from above to speed up the contracting process by laying down a key condition. Something would have to be done to assure that incumbent Rockwell did not so dominate the bidding process that other potential bidders simply dropped out.[71] To give newcomers a chance, firms were invited to observe a shuttle turnaround.[72]

Some nineteen companies qualified to bid for the Shuttle Processing Contract; eight sent representatives to observe the processing of STS-3.[73] To impress potential bidders with how efficiently the work could be done, KSC set the goal of cutting STS-3's turnaround time to half that of STS-2's fifteen weeks.[74] With great pride, workers moved STS-3 from the VAB to the launchpad on February 16, 1982, five days ahead of schedule. It did not seem to matter that the schedule still came nowhere near the 160-hour turnaround. Improved processing on STS-3 saved only thirty-five days, and mostly because only 469 tiles needed to be replaced.[75]

Center director Richard Smith appointed a Procurement Development Working Group to integrate the three contracts now under consideration. Tom Utsman chaired the group, which included Bob Long from the Base Operations Procurement Development Team, George Page and C. M. Giesler from the Shuttle Processing Procurement Development Team, and Tom Walton from the Cargo Processing Procurement Development Team. Andy Pickett acted as an overall advisor.[76] Just two weeks later, they recommended a major revision of the original plan.

Base Operations, the easiest contract to integrate into the overall management structure of the Center, would be the first to go. Shuttle and Payload (or Cargo as it was then called) involved a much smaller number of potential bidders, making the competitive process less straightforward. These other contracts would rely upon the lessons learned in the Base Operations Contract experience to fine-tune their own bidding processes. Shuttle Processing would go second. Later, there would be a Cargo Processing Contract. When the process was complete, the number of contracts KSC was supervising in major work areas would drop from twenty-six to three.

Base Operations

The contracts were designed to remove KSC's research and development mentality from the day-to-day operations of the shuttle. But they had other implications. Of the existing contractors handling base services at KSC, for example, all but one would lose their jobs once the BOC was let. Some losers might become subcontractors to the primary contractor, but unions saw the entire process as a wage busting scheme. Previously, prevailing wages had been determined by an analysis of government work in Brevard County. The single-point contracts permitted wages to reflect averages in the whole country. In a conference refereed by Senator Lawton Chiles and Congressman Bill Nelson, labor unions declared that if the bidding process undercut union labor, not one shuttle would fly.[77]

For a time, it seemed that there could well be a major labor war at KSC. As bidders competed for the base operations prize, tensions rose between existing contractors and their unions. Wackenhut, which provided security, fire, and emergency medical services at KSC, locked into stalemate with the Transportation Workers Union over the proposed consolidation of fire and medical crews.[78] A strike was averted only after the union voted to extend the current contract until fifteen days after the winner of the Base Operations Contract was named.[79] The issue became moot after NASA awarded the contract to the firm EG&G, ending Wackenhut's role at the Center.[80] By the end of 1982, the first major contract was signed.

After award of the Base Operations Contract, KSC director Richard Smith announced a substantial reorganization. The Center would be restructured using seveal new directorates. Shuttle Management and Operations, under Tom Utsman, would handle processing and launch. Tom Walton would head the new Cargo Management and Operations Directorate, responsible for both shuttle and remaining ELV payloads. Bob Long took charge of Center Support Operations. Three of the four new directorates thus paralleled the proposed consolidation of KSC contracts. Center Support Operations would manage the new Base Operations Contract. Walton's Cargo Management and Operations Directorate would manage those areas slated for consolidation under the Payload Ground Operations Contract. The next step was transforming shuttle operations by contracting out most of the processing work. Utsman's Shuttle Management and Operations Directorate would supervise the bidding on this contract. Smith named Andy Pickett as the new associate deputy center director to work alongside deputy director George Page in completing this transition.[81]

The Shuttle Processing Contract

In competition for the BOC, existing contractors had scrambled to prepare strong bids. Bendix Field Engineering, Wackenhut Services, Planning Research Corporation, and Computer Sciences Corporation had formed a joint venture to pursue the consolidated contract. They were challenged by three competitors, Boeing Services International, EG&G, and Lockheed Engineering and Management Services.[82] Similar patterns were expected to emerge in the competition for the Shuttle Processing Contract.

In mid-1982, however, new questions were suddenly raised about this more significant move down the path of privatization. The new concerns

9-1. Built to launch military missions flying aboard the shuttle, these facilities at Vandenberg Air Force Base in California would never be used.

would substantially shape the way the contracting process would unfold. In Houston, members of the Johnson Space Center now believed that the shift to operational status was happening too quickly. Originally the Shuttle Processing Contract was to be bid in late 1984, so that it could commence with flight 25. This was the point at which KSC and Johnson engineers agreed the shuttle would be a stable, mature technology.[83] KSC proposed to push up the date to May 1983, nearly eighteen months sooner. There were good reasons for moving the transition forward. If contracting could save money, then the NASA budget would benefit from an earlier start date. The earlier date also would allow contract implementation to take place before launching military shuttle missions from Vandenberg began.[84]

This was a rather striking reversal of roles. KSC engineers now opined that the shuttle was maturing more rapidly than predicted. JSC engineers responded that shuttle technology was not showing early signs of stabilizing. Formerly the Johnson people had accused the Kennedy people of moving too slowly in instituting standardized rapid-processing procedures. But JSC still had on the drawing boards hardware, software, and process developments for the shuttle. The new facilities at Vandenberg needed further refinement too. And in a major concession, Johnson reviewers argued that the current shuttle configuration did not yet meet specifications and thus could not achieve the scheduled twenty-four flights per year.[85]

Despite striking the more optimistic note, KSC managers had plenty of work to finish themselves before they could turn the shuttle over to a contractor. The second Orbiter Processing Facility had just come on line at the end of 1982. A second mobile launch platform would be up only in early 1983; the third would not be ready until 1987. Firing Room 3 at the Launch Control Center was not due to open until early 1983, and Firing Room 4 not until the latter part of 1985. High Bays 1 and 2 in the VAB, the Center's software production facility, and the solid rocket motor processing facility were all awaiting completion. There were still kinks in the logistical program to iron out as well.

This pending work reinforced the belief of JSC managers that it would be at least three, possibly four years before shuttle processing became "predominantly routine." If there was still significant developmental work to be done, then moving swiftly to the contract could wreak havoc on information and communications channels between operations and design. Informal communications channels between Johnson, Marshall, and Kennedy would be lost for some period until similar informal mechanisms could be developed with the contractor.[86] Johnson estimates showed as much as a three-month slip in launches resulting from implementation of the SPC. That slip would eat up any savings gained by the early move to single-point contracting.

One way to minimize disruptions was for most of the existing shuttle labor force to transfer to the new contractor, following the precedent of the BOC. The transfer would give the new contractor full benefit of workers' experience, hands-on knowledge, and informal channels of communications. Otherwise NASA would have to take more steps to minimize the complicated finishing work that traditionally went on at KSC. New vehicles would have to be delivered to KSC with little or no open work, something that had yet to happen with the shuttle. KSC engineers could also try to write up "cookbook" procedures for processing, and could work with Johnson and Marshall in better integrating operations and design management structures. Cannibalizing of hardware had to stop, and any future enhancements of the orbiter would have to be simple and sure enough not to require major reworking at KSC.[87]

Drawing a firm line dividing development and fabrication work from operations had long been a goal of the space program, back to the first iteration of the ship-and-shoot philosophy of years before. So far, though, vehicles had never arrived at the Cape in that sort of flight-ready condition. The Johnson review team now feared that the whole SPC scenario was a "house of cards" that would "come tumbling down around our collective heads."

Too many things had to go exactly right to avoid disaster, and even a few small problems could unravel the whole fabric. The logical alternative was a phased-in contract, beginning with launch integration. Hands-on work currently undertaken by civil servants could be progressively shifted to the integration contractor over a three-year period, with a full-fledged shuttle processing contract coming in 1986.[88]

Despite the long and intense debate between Houston and KSC, financial pressures were pushing the contracting process forward. In 1982 the GAO criticized NASA for not increasing the number of contract awards. In July of that year, NASA administrator James Beggs urged Center directors to move rapidly toward increasing competitive contracting.[89] Critics of contracting had already noted a potential conflict between the profit motive of the contractor and two key NASA goals. While award fee systems promoted cost cutting, these hardly encouraged the contactor to improve technology or emphasize safety. Improvement and assurance had real dollar costs attached to them, and a single-point contract might not motivate the contractor to pursue these goals. But the advantage of competitive contracting lay in spurring higher work efficiency and lower costs, exactly the direction in which the shuttle program was now expected to move. The hope was that KSC and the design centers could make up for any loss of innovation and provide the oversight needed to assure mission success.[90]

The crucial issue was thus decided. KSC would implement the SPC. The main question now was how to attract the maximum number of competitive proposals. Incumbent experience and expertise counted heavily in the minds of members of the Shuttle Processing Contract Source Board, formed to evaluate proposals. General Dynamics, one of the eight potential bidders, had dropped out of the SPC race in February 1982, but most of the other potential bidders stayed. There was too much at stake to withdraw early. *Florida Today* quoted aerospace executives to the effect that whoever lost out on the Shuttle Processing Contract would be "left out of the largest aerospace program" in the last quarter of the twentieth century. When the air force decided to join KSC and use the same contractor for shuttle processing at Vandenberg Air Force Base, the stakes grew even larger.[91] The winner would receive a six-billion-dollar contract.[92]

Aerospace firms scrambled to organize for their bids. In November 1982 Lockheed formed a new division, Lockheed Space Operations Company, to manage its SPC application. Acknowledging the Shuttle Processing Contract as the "largest NASA competition of the decade," George Skurla, president of Grumman Aerospace Corporation, announced the following March the formation of Grumman Technical Services, to join with Lockheed. They would soon add Pan American Airlines and Morton Thiokol as partners.

In December 1982, Rockwell's space operations president George Jeffs announced the formation of Rockwell Shuttle Launch Operations Division. The next March, Martin Marietta formed Martin Marietta Launch Services to assist Rockwell's bid. This was the start of a "great partnership" with other incumbent shuttle contractors USBI, Boeing Services International, and United Airlines, which made Rockwell the most formidable competitor for the big prize.

The competing teams held widely different views on how the shuttle should be operated. Grumman and Lockheed subscribed to the view that shuttle processing was a management issue and that they were qualified on that score.[93] The Rockwell proposal was built around its experience and that of its partners. It proposed a "matrix management" structure that did little to consolidate functions or clarify lines of authority among members of the coalition. The matrix structure gave each partner its own turf, but predicted savings through the reduced oversight role of civil servants. Although the KSC evaluation panel found little in the Lockheed application to excite them—a detailed "B-grade" proposal weighing some thirty pounds—it had one big advantage. It provided clear lines of authority on functional rather than territorial grounds.[94]

Still, evaluators were unsure which submission was best. As the shuttle's builder, Rockwell clearly had the advantage in experience and knowledge. Matrix structures had been used for decades in the aerospace industry to manage complex, technically sophisticated government projects that required the integration of many skills and areas of expertise. The evaluators turned to outside experts for help. Advice was sought from General Electric CEO Jack Welch, former NASA deputy administrator George Low, and management guru Peter Drucker. Three members of the Source Board visited Drucker in his California home and laid out the Lockheed and Rockwell proposals one evening for his inspection. The famous business consultant asked for the night to think about it. The next morning he informed them that only strong leadership among the members of Rockwell's great partnership would permit such a system to work. If one of the coalition members failed to provide strong leadership or if strong leaders retired, then the partnership would fail, as had similar joint ventures in the past. The Rockwell executive who had managed his firm's operations at KSC during the moon launch, T. J. O'Malley, had just retired.[95]

That decided matters. Lockheed, not Rockwell would process the shuttle.[96] It received the award on October 1, 1983. In the end, the matrix approach of Rockwell, while perhaps viable in a research and development context, was not what NASA was looking for in an operational mode to streamlined processing. Had Rockwell won, moreover, it would have been nearly impossible for anyone to dislodge the company from its position in the future. KSC personnel would have had very little supervisory role and each of the partner contractors would retain substantial autonomy over its domain. Lockheed's functional approach was less suited perhaps to innovation and research, but that was no longer what the shuttle needed. Functional structures are designed to do the same thing over and over again, and do them well, exactly what was expected for routine shuttle operations. Worry that important expertise would be lost in the transfer to Lockheed was quelled when nearly 90 percent of the old Rockwell labor force at Merritt Island transferred to the new contractor. When the duties of shuttle processing were passed to Lockheed after the launch of STS-41B in early 1984, Tom Utsman, shuttle management and operations chief, praised the work of the outgoing contractor. One Rockwell official lamented, "I wish he'd said those things a couple of months ago."[97]

The Shuttle Processing Contract was a watershed in the development of the operational mentality long sought by NASA. But was it enough? The shuttle remained a vehicle with multiple agendas. On the one hand, it continued to be an R&D instrument for NASA in its quest to better understand space flight and related issues. On the other, it was expected to demonstrate opportunities for space commercialization through low cost, dependable launches and flights. The SPC was essential to realizing this second goal, but there had to be more streamlining of NASA management to take full advantage of it. "STS [shuttle] management must have the freedom and authority to make hard, final decisions dictated by cost and schedule objectives," wrote Jesse Moore from NASA headquarters.[98] Recognizing that the shuttle would still be serving as a research vessel, he nonetheless advocated a strong central operations manager at KSC, who had control of budget, schedule, and manifests, and supervised such functions as configuration management, sustaining engineering, and logistics.

This move would seem to imply a significantly reduced role for design centers such as JSC, "freeing [their] resources . . . for other programs."[99] Moore tempered his potentially divisive proposal with a scheme that would make the operations manager work with the other centers and let JSC retain control over its personnel and traditional functions of mission planning and management.

Moore's bold proposal for a strong operations-focused management structure would have challenged some long-standing turf divisions within NASA. It also raised once more the question of how much research and design work versus operational work the agency was to undertake. The SPC moved a significant portion of routine operations into the hands of a private firm, but as some firms had observed during the bidding process, NASA was not ready to let go control of the shuttle.

Into the Flow

The procedure of preparing a spacecraft for launch had always been called a "flow" at KSC. But even during the height of Apollo, with one vehicle after another coming down the line in the race to the moon, multiple flows had never approached the forty per year envisioned for the shuttle. With a full complement of four or possibly five vehicles, each orbiter would have to go through some eight to ten flows per year. During processing, each orbiter had a vehicle manager and an integration manager, but no one below the launch director had authority for the overall management from landing to launch. In response, KSC's George Page came up with the position of "flow director."

It was a major innovation, having a single person responsible for all the work being done on a shuttle from the time it arrived at KSC until the day it was launched into the sky. Page's concept recognized a crucial difference between the reusable shuttle and traditional expendable vehicles. The latter were built anew each time, making KSC a testing site (and frequently a building site) for the vehicles. With the shuttle, it would be more of a maintenance and supply site. Significant maintenance went into the shuttles after they returned to the Cape. This work needed its own place in the organization and its own manager who controlled the work schedule, separate from the testing and launch teams preparing for launch. Each vehicle was also a separate "flow" needing a separate manager, especially if there were several orbiters in the queue at the same time. These supervisory functions stood above or, in some cases, alongside the worker supervision provided by the contractor.

Flow directors had been in place before the SPC. Bob Sieck, the integration engineer for *Columbia*'s first flight, became the first, starting with the maiden voyage of *Challenger* in 1983. Jim Harrington, *Columbia*'s vehicle manager, took over *Columbia* with STS-9 later that year. Tip Talone managed the first flight of *Discovery* in 1984. Eventually Harrington, who had military clearance, took over *Challenger*, which flew most of the military missions.[100] The flow director concept, Harrington recalls, "worked like a charm." It provided a single point of contact for anyone at KSC, the design centers, or contractors to call for a decision on the shuttle. Flow directors had no administrative duties because no one worked for them. But they had authority, because they had final say over shuttle processing, reporting the

9-2. Preparing the space shuttle for flight in the Orbiter Processing Facility (OPF) at KSC required advanced new equipment.

state of their vehicle's fitness for launch to the launch director. It was, according to those who had the chance to be a flow director, the "best job" at the Cape "next to launch director."[101]

With the flow director, the contract, and the reorganizations, KSC had in place all the key elements for operational processing of the shuttle. In 1984, KSC director Richard Smith argued that his center would be taking over more shuttle functions from the Johnson Space Center, as Houston geared up for the next big item on NASA's agenda, a space station. The shuttle, it seemed, was now firmly on the road to becoming a routine operation, and the design-oriented centers would be moving on to new cutting-edge work.[102]

To keep the shuttle on a regular schedule, new facilities were added for rapid processing of multiple vehicles. In December 1985 a new logistics support facility at LC-39 consolidated logistics functions in one building. The

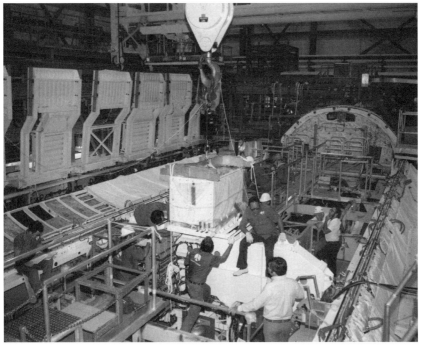

9-3. Workers process an orbiter inside the OPF.

9-4. Processing finished, the orbiter leaves the OPF for stacking in the VAB.

9-5. The orbiter arrives in the VAB, ready to be shifted to a horizontal position for stacking.

new building housed some 190,000 spare parts for the shuttles and provided office space for 550 KSC and Lockheed employees who before had been scattered in five different locations. An advanced retrieval system used robots to remove parts from their storage bins and bring them to workers.[103]

During the early years of the shuttle, components and replacement parts had been manufactured on demand at Rockwell's plants in California for shipment to the Cape. Repairs of shuttle components took from 150 to 200 days. While that time had been decreased modestly, it still remained too large. KSC added an Orbiter Maintenance and Refurbishment Facility across the street from the OPF in 1987. A Solid Rocket Booster Refurbishment Facility opened about the same time. Both were designed to expedite overhaul of shuttles on-site at the Cape. KSC subsequently upgraded the OMRF to a third Orbiter Processing Facility. Though shuttle builder Rockwell lost out on the processing contract, it expanded its presence on the Cape as it constructed new facilities to provide logistics and shuttle repair services. These were expected to reduce repair turnaround time to about thirty days.[104]

Still, none of these changes could stem the unfavorable tide of events rising outside the Center. NASA had originally scheduled forty-eight shuttle missions through 1985. Budget cuts had reduced that number, and increased turnaround times plus other constraints cut the flight rate still more.[105] Budget cuts also pushed the expected opening of the Vandenberg launch facility back from 1985 until 1986.[106] Then too, there were further unexpected

9-6. The orbiter is hoisted across the VAB transfer aisle.

9-7. The orbiter is lowered into place with its external tank and solid rocket booster stack.

9-8. Using the same crawler and same mobile launch concept devised by Kurt Debus, a now complete space shuttle or, more formally, Space Transportation System (STS) rolls out of the VAB toward the launchpad.

9-9. The shuttle on its way to the pad.

disruptions of the processing routine. In May 1985 Lockheed had to reassign three of its shuttle managers after a defective work platform fell, damaging *Discovery*'s cargo bay door. Describing the accident as a "serious breach" of NASA work procedures, NASA administrator James Beggs warned KSC management to "tighten things up."[107] Quality assurance and rapid processing remained trade-offs, and accidents could shift attention from speed to quality.

Payload Processing

KSC had always prepared payloads for launches, but payloads on the space shuttle were something else again. In earlier programs, cargo had been checked out and sealed in a spacecraft in the Operations and Checkout Building (O&C). The spacecraft was then moved to the VAB for mating with the launch vehicle. Now payloads, many of them extremely delicate scientific instruments, had to be installed in the orbiter in a clean environment. A few particles of dirt or dust could ruin a sensitive scientific experiment and foul delicate shuttle systems as well. To keep payloads clean while they were transported, KSC developed a payload canister whose interior mirrored the interior of the shuttle cargo bay.[108] Payloads that were to rest in the horizontal position were installed in the canister at the O&C building. Then a 48-wheeled transporter carried the sealed canister to the Orbiter Processing Facility, where it was transferred to the orbiter. Vertical payloads moved from the O&C building to the Vertical Processing Facility, where they were checked out in a payload canister. From there the vertical transporter took them to the launchpad, where the canister was hoisted to the level of the cargo bay doors and waited in an environmentally sealed "white room" while the bay doors opened. Finally, workers took the cargo out of the canister and transferred it to the shuttle bay.[109]

Payload processing worked with shuttle processing and the new technological elements of space launch to expand the range of missions. Some of these space ventures could be extraordinarily complex, involving the flight of a shuttle into orbit, the removal of a scientific instrument from the payload bay, and the boosting of that instrument into a higher orbit or off into space to study the solar system. KSC managers, shuttle and payload contractors, instrument builders, mission managers at NASA's Jet Propulsion Laboratory in California, the military, and university scientists worked together to move these endeavors into space. It was an excellent illustration of how the shuttle could fulfill one of its original purposes—taking on cutting-edge space missions involving close cooperation between private and public agencies.

One of the most impressive of such efforts was *Galileo*. This probe was designed to study Jupiter's atmosphere, moons, and surrounding magnetosphere. KSC had to prepare for many uncertainties in the mission. *Galileo* originally was scheduled to be launched in the early part of 1982. Delays in the development of the shuttle led to its being rescheduled for 1985, but the alignment of the planets by that date required a much more powerful booster to push *Galileo* into the proper interplanetary orbit.[110] That required some new technology.

Designed to lift payloads into low earth orbit, the shuttle was initially to be but one component in NASA's repertoire of space exploration technology. A second part was to be a "space tug" to transport cargo into orbits beyond the shuttle's range. Until the space tug was finished, other boosters would do this job. A low-powered Delta-class spinning solid upper stage (SSUS) or a payload assist module (PAM) lifted smaller satellites of 2,000–2,500 pounds into high orbits. The shuttle could carry up to four SSUSs per mission. An Atlas-Centaur-class SSUS could handle satellites up to 4,500 pounds. For still larger payloads, there was to be a powerful Interim Upper Stage (IUS).

The air force had responsibility for developing the IUS. But the air force's program was over budget and behind schedule. Faced with cost constraints,

NASA cancelled the program in January 1981.[111] Forced to find other methods, the space agency considered using its own liquid-fueled Centaur as a satellite booster.[112] A high-energy Centaur upper stage would be capable of lifting 13,000 pounds into geosynchronous orbit.[113]

Centaur seemed the ideal replacement for the ill-fated IUS. It was a powerful, reliable rocket. Despite several decades of experience with this liquid-hydrogen engine, KSC personnel faced a substantial challenge in placing such a volatile device aboard a shuttle flying people. Use of the Centaur required modifying not only the shuttle but also the mobile launcher platform and the service structures at the pad.[114] There were knotty complications for the launch control software as well. Expendable vehicles using a Centaur upper stage had been controlled through a computerized control launch set (CCLS), which had evolved from the early automated systems for these vehicles dating back to the mid-1960s. The shuttle's LPS did not yet have the track record of Centaur's CCLS. Managers from NASA Lewis Research Center responsible for Centaur and those from the Kennedy Space Center debated which launch control system should take precedence. KSC officials favored using their own LPS. They were especially concerned that employing the CCLS to load cryogenic hydrogen fuel on Centaur while using a separate system to control loading the shuttle's giant external tank would create safety hazards.[115] Centaur posed other safety issues as well. It could not be installed in the shuttle cargo bay while the orbiter was in the horizontal position. Instead, a complicated set of maneuvers required Centaur to be installed in the vertical position after the shuttle arrived at the launchpad.[116]

These intricate integration issues led some in NASA to wonder if Centaur was going to create delays and require vehicle modifications. Managers of the Galileo project, for example, suggested launching the mission aboard two shuttles and using weaker solid rocket upper stages to move *Galileo* into space. Managers of the shuttle program, on the other hand, tended to discount the near-term difficulties with using Centaur, seeing it as a long-term answer to the upper stage question.[117]

In September 1985 the first Centaur upper stage arrived at KSC in preparation for the launch of *Galileo*.[118] After workers resolved issues with the launch control program and continued modifications on the shuttle, a second Centaur arrived three months later.[119] They took advantage of a visit from the original shuttle test vehicle, *Enterprise*, to practice a KSC abort procedure of the shuttle with a Centaur on board.[120] All was now set, with *Galileo* scheduled for May of 1986 to fly to earth orbit in the shuttle payload bay, then be launched on its deep-space mission by Centaur.

There seemed to be just one more major payload question remaining:

when to implement the Payload Ground Operations Contract. This would be the most complex contract of all. Payloads came to KSC from other NASA centers, from the military, and from private firms. Each entity had its own set of requirements that had to be integrated with KSC's payload operations and with the requirements of the shuttle. More than either shuttle or base operations, payloads had to coordinate closely with the other contractors. Payload processing remained developmental, with many unknowns and more research on procedures needed.

In May 1985 when John Conway took over what was still called the Cargo Office at KSC, he faced a slew of unhappy commercial customers. All the thought and effort that had been spent on shuttle processing tended to place work emphasis on the rocket rather than what the rocket carried. Astronaut safety and a successful launch took precedence over service to users. Payload customers were irate at both KSC and Lockheed for not giving them more attention.[121] Even some KSC payload workers felt they were riding "the back of the bus," and were not that important.[122] Center director Smith quickly sent Conway to visit Chet Lee at NASA headquarters. Lee told Conway to do two things when he got back to the Cape—change the name from Cargo to Payload, and start treating the customers like they were important.[123]

Following the precedents set by the earlier contracts, KSC arranged for six companies to watch payload operations in preparation for bidding. KSC officials then narrowed the field to two, Boeing and McDonnell Douglas, who were invited to make final bids in 1986. But the day before the contract proposal was to go out, disaster struck. The space shuttle *Challenger* was lost on ascent. Now everything was on hold. When the bidding restarted, the contenders would have to propose a contract not knowing when the shuttle would fly again, but knowing that there would be tremendous pressure to clear a backlog of missions when it did.[124]

Assessing the Shuttle's First Era

In the years leading up to the *Challenger* accident, operations at KSC had yet to became standardized in the airline sense of the word. Despite improvements through late 1985, turnaround times remained much longer than the 160 hours (7–10 days) envisioned in the heyday of shuttle planning. In fact, *Challenger* consistently provided the best times, typically between 55 and 60 days, and held the record for the shortest turnaround, 26 days on STS-8. *Discovery* frequently needed 70 to 80 days from landing to launch, while the newer *Atlantis* showed promise of turnaround times between 60 and 70 days. Early flights of *Columbia* had required 90–135 days for turnaround. But the times did not improve significantly after early 1984, staying in the

9-10. Shuttle in the mist.

65–85-day range. Whenever a quicker turnaround time was needed, KSC achieved it through the use of second and third work shifts and added overtime.

Even with improvements in vehicle processing, problems either unanticipated in the original design or coming from beyond KSC's control determined how long it would take to ready a vehicle. Countdown procedures had been pretty well standardized by STS-5. But logistics remained a weak point. Should the flight rate ever reach thirty or forty per year, there would not be enough fuel, parts, and other supplies available onsite.

The growing influence of the Department of Defense forced NASA to reevaluate its relationship with the military as well. In 1979 NASA managed nearly 55 percent of the U.S. space budget. The Department of Defense handled another 42.5 percent. The remaining 2.5 percent was spread through the Departments of Energy, Commerce, Transportation, and Agriculture and the National Science Foundation. By 1981 NASA's share of the space budget had declined to 51.2 percent, while Defense's share increased to 46.9 percent.[125] The military, however, remained reluctant to commit to launching all its missions on the shuttle, a decision at odds with the supposed economies of putting everything on one craft.

The NASA-military relationship also revealed the emerging conflicts between the shuttle as an astronaut-carrying spaceship and as a payload-carrying space truck. This tension would eventually be felt by all who used the shuttle for routine space access. The Department of Defense sent up its initial payload in 1982 on STS-4, the last "developmental" mission. In a lessons-learned report put out the following November, the air force contrasted its shuttle experience with the sort of treatment it was used to from KSC's skilled launch team for expendable vehicles. While expendable vehicle launches focused on getting the satellite into its proper orbit, the shuttle, with its emphasis on human safety and return of the orbiter, demanded numerous additional tests of both vehicle and payload to protect crew and ship. The study concluded that "the spacecraft community just doesn't have the clout it is accustomed to" with the shuttle.[126] If the shuttle were to attract the military and commercial interest it required for economical flight rates, it would have to launch on a regular schedule with routine turnaround times. But in the wake of the *Challenger* disaster, that sort of routine operation seemed further away than ever.

10

*
*
*

Challenger and Beyond

On January 17, 1986, the long-awaited Centaur upper stage cleared its final major hurdle before a scheduled June launch of the *Galileo* mission to Jupiter. A few days earlier the year's first shuttle, *Columbia*, was sent on its way. KSC crews turned to the countdown test for the next mission, to fly on *Challenger*. All the parts of the shuttle system seemed to be coming together. There could still be delays, but fewer of them now were the result of unexpected hardware glitches, logistics problems, or lack of experience in handling vehicles. Only nature refused to cooperate. Dust storms in the Sahara closed a crucial abort site and forced a one-day delay for *Challenger*. The next day saw near perfect weather, but decision makers scrubbed the flight because they could not fuel the vehicle in time to meet the launch window. Then came a frustrating setback as hardware gremlins reared their heads once more. Maybe it was just a final hiccup before the flow of processing smoothed out for the year. A "door ajar" signal forced workers to reshut *Challenger*'s hatch. When they completed their task, the removable door handle would not budge. As workers wrestled with the handle, nature played havoc with human intentions yet again, and winds stirred beyond acceptable limits. The launch was rescheduled, forcing Vice President Bush to cancel his planned attendance of the blastoff. That was an unfortunate loss of good press for the program, but two days later *Challenger* was ready to go. On a chilly January 28, workers at the Kennedy Space Center walked outside at 11:38 A.M. to view the liftoff. They raised their eyes to a sight few would ever forget.[1]

Cold Fire

Temperatures at Cape Canaveral rarely dip below freezing, even in January. But a freak combination of meteorological conditions sent the mercury plummeting into the teens the night of January 27. Normally, a hard freeze presented a series of bothersome but not especially difficult chores for KSC

10-1. Ice on the pad before the launch of *Challenger*, January 1986.

crews. They drained water lines on the pads to prevent pipes from bursting. They de-iced the service structure, both for the safety of those working there and to prevent chunks of ice from falling off, shattering and possibly damaging the delicate orbiter tiles. Working outdoors hundreds of feet up on a vehicle in a stiff north wind was no fun. But rarely had such weather conditions directly affected the launch or flight of a space vehicle. That morning, with temperatures just above freezing and huge icicles on the pad and service structure around space shuttle *Challenger*, would be different.

The decisions leading up to the launch of *Challenger* have been debated, dissected, and discussed for years. The immediate cause of the accident soon became clear. At low temperatures, the normally flexible rubberized O-rings that sealed the solid rocket booster joints became hard and inflexible. In this state they did not move rapidly enough to fill the gap and secure the booster joints, which separated or "rotated" slightly on ignition. In the first few moments of firing, those giant rockets generated so much thrust that their metal skins were pushed outward. The bulging opened a gap in the rocket joints. Two O-rings stood ready to seal this gap, preventing hot gases from escaping through the joint and flaring out like a blowtorch.

The scenario of escaping gases leading to disaster was a well-known danger, but NASA engineers and engineers at the manufacturer of the solid rockets, Morton Thiokol, believed that they understood the nature of joint rotation and O-ring sealing. Despite inspections after a number of flights that showed charring on the rings, no one believed the design of the solid rockets was inherently unsafe. It was just one more real-world phenomenon not anticipated in the shuttle design phase. An "anomaly," in engineering language, but an anomaly serviceable in operations. Many aspects of the space shuttle were like that. Real-world operations revealed numerous cases where parts, components, and systems behaved unexpectedly. Solutions were worked out in practice. There was always a risk, to be sure, as there was always with many parts of the complicated vehicle. But the O-rings seemed no greater a risk—indeed, with the redundancy of two O-rings, even less of a risk—than many other critical components.[2]

It seemed that way until exactly 678 milliseconds after ignition that January day, when a single O-ring lost its race with the superheated gases. With the shuttle still building thrust but not yet moving, an inexorable chain of events began that would end with the explosion of the shuttle's external fuel tank, the disintegration of the orbiter, and the crash of the crew compartment into the sea. Fifty-eight seconds into flight, the first flare of flame appeared at the bottom of the right-hand solid rocket booster. A 5,800-degree jet of fire cut into the external tank. The flame's thrust actually broke the booster free from its mooring. As the booster careened back and forth, smashing into orbiter and external tank, the flame ignited the tank's liquid fuel. At seventy-three seconds, the flight of *Challenger* was over. In the next two and a half minutes, what remained of the orbiter plunged at two-hundred-plus miles per hour into the sea, killing all aboard.[3]

If the immediate cause was clear, the more remote causes and the accident's consequences were much less so. Had NASA sacrificed safety to meet its ambitious launch schedule? Had cutbacks in budgets forced an unholy trade-off between completing missions and reducing risks? Was private greed at work on the part of contractors? Or were contractors pressured to change their opinions about the booster's flightworthiness in cold temperatures to keep the shuttle on schedule? Were there perhaps deep, unnoticed flaws in NASA's culture and decision-making process that blinded leaders to what, in retrospect, seems so obvious?

Most of the key decisions that led to the tragedy did not directly involve the Kennedy Space Center. But KSC, like all of NASA, was deeply affected by what happened. In the wake of *Challenger*, the policy and culture that had evolved around the concept of an operational shuttle underwent radical rethinking. *Challenger* triggered a major shift in the American space program, one as significant as the decision to design and build a reusable shuttle more than a decade earlier. In this, it substantially affected KSC.

Reaction and Investigation

Immediately after the accident, speculation ran rampant. What had happened? Why? Who was to blame? President Ronald Reagan appointed William Rogers, former secretary of state, to head an independent board of inquiry. Even before the Rogers Commission released its findings, reports in the press made it clear that serious questions would be raised about NASA management, operations, and safety programs. In March, astronaut John Young charged that pressures to launch on schedule—*Challenger's* delays threatened to hold up future missions—contributed to the accident.[4] Others defended the launch decision. Famed test pilot and Rogers Commission member Chuck Yeager worried that too much "Monday morning quarterbacking" was going on. Still others believed that, tragic though it was, the *Challenger* accident was simply part of the unavoidable risk of space flight. No risk, no launch, the common wisdom at the Cape went.[5]

In the immediate aftermath, Florida congressman Bill Nelson and KSC director Richard Smith spoke to workers at the Center and framed the disaster as "an opportunity for reassessment and reeducation." Recalling the *Apollo 1* fire, they noted that KSC had emerged stronger as a result, and they expected the same this time.[6] But a rising tide of reproach in the months that followed proved them wrong. Initial optimism about a quick recovery and return to flight faded. NASA's "proud record" of past accomplishments could not overcome doubts induced by a steady drumbeat of criticism in the wake of the disaster.

It was a discouraging time for KSC workers who had been for a decade or more pushing hard to get the shuttle program up and running. Grady Williams, former director of design engineering at KSC, told *Florida Today* that the Rogers Commission ought to determine the cause of the accident before looking into management practices. "I'm sure a lot of those people are discouraged. I'm discouraged, and I haven't been out there for ten years."[7] Others noted that it was easier to see potential dangers in hindsight than beforehand, when data were confusing and contradictory. Assessment of O-ring burns on earlier flights did not reveal a consistent pattern. Some burns occurred on flights during cold weather, others when the weather was warm. Debate about potential risks among engineers was common practice and did not necessarily constitute a red flag that upper-level managers had ignored. Indeed, to NASA personnel, the intense discussions leading up to the final decision to launch *Challenger* showed the open and frank nature of communications over key matters.

Reflecting the tension, KSC director Smith spoke out publicly against what he thought was an unnecessarily harsh investigation that would leave NASA crippled for the future. Smith's unguarded remarks seemed to blame the press. On the one hand, NASA was being asked to fly the shuttle on schedule, at as low a cost as possible, and to recover as many of those costs as it could by charging customers to fly. On the other hand, NASA was rebuked every time it seemed to place schedule and economics ahead of absolute safety. In the end, the investigation would address how the shuttle should be operated, how risks should be assessed, and how NASA should make decisions with human lives at stake.[8]

As the Rogers Commission completed its work, the climate at KSC was one of sadness and gloom. Everyone present that day had heard the live broadcast of the countdown, with all the checks and reports coming back normal. They saw with their own eyes the launch and early seconds of the flight, heard those initial seconds described as normal. Then they heard the fateful words "Flight controllers here looking very carefully at the situation. Obviously a major malfunction."[9] Many of them saw the explosion of the external tank, watched as the solid rockets broke free, and followed the trails of smoke as the orbiter separated from the boosters. Most NASA people and experienced reporters knew that it was far too early in flight for normal tank separation. Many suspected that there was no way the crew would survive what was unfolding.

The loss of life weighed heavily on those who participated in the launch. Since the days of Apollo, the pad crew had established close relationships with the astronauts flying the vehicles. It was inevitable, given the need to work together on preparations, testing, and simulation exercises. Workers knew that lives were in their hands; it was embedded into the culture at KSC. One engineer suffered a heart attack upon seeing the explosion and died the next day.[10] Others were given the difficult task of speaking to the public or consoling those devastated by the event. As was common practice, KSC personnel not essential for countdown had been asked to escort VIPs and give technical briefings to the public for *Challenger*'s launch. Tom Overton's regular job was to set up the schedule of launches, so on launch days he played the role of escort. Watching *Challenger*, he was asked by Barbara Morgan, backup teacher-astronaut to Christa McAuliffe, what had happened. "They're gone, we've lost them," was all he could reply.[11] Those not working heard about the accident on the radio. Whether at home or driving, they stopped what they were doing and looked up in horror. "What did I do wrong," many asked themselves, "that might have contributed to the accident?" Overton wondered if the TDRSS satellite had come loose and fired. The efficient, lightweight space shuttle main engines, the SSMEs, had long been a concern. Engine personnel at first assumed it was their fault. Until investigators unraveled the mystery, many would not be able to shake the sense they might have been to blame in some way.[12]

For those who had been at KSC since the early years, the loss of *Challenger* was especially hard. "A lot of the fun went out of the business, with that accident," reflected John Conway, who had started at the Cape in 1966.[13] EG&G, the base operations contractor, opened a care line for KSC employees. A psychologist in the nearby city of Melbourne noted that the workers, extremely stressed by back-to-back launches, were "frightened and very numbed" after the explosion.[14] There were too many ironies, too many contingencies to let the mind rest. What if the dust storm had not appeared? What if the stuck hatch handle had been freed in time? Then *Challenger* would have got safely away before the big cold snap.

With no shuttles flying, KSC personnel had little to do. Some were occupied in the recovery of *Challenger*, but that was a mixed blessing, to say the least. On a somber March day, the USS *Preserver* pulled into Port Canaveral. On board were the flag-draped coffins holding the bodies of *Challenger*'s crew.[15] Salvaged parts of the fallen craft were brought to the logistics facility in the LC-39 area for study. Pieces continue to wash up on the Florida shore to the present.[16] Dredged up from the ocean bottom, the remains of *Challenger* were covered in barnacles. Those who worked in the hangar were working amid the smells of the sea, and the stench of decay as the barnacles died. It was "as if this spaceship [were] dying right in front of you."[17] This difficult work was a far cry from the ambitious flight schedule of a few months earlier, with teams working round the clock processing four orbiters.

Layoffs added to the depressed atmosphere at the Cape. Immediately after the disaster, USBI let some 50 employees go, followed by 120 in June. In July General Dynamics released 115 workers affiliated with the shuttle-Centaur program. The following month Lockheed, Grumman, and Morton

Thiokol added a thousand people to the unemployment lines. More would follow.[18]

Unemployed technicians wondered how long they could stretch savings until they returned to work, assuming they did return. Predictions were for a launch in 1988, but the Rogers Commission would make tough recommendations that demanded substantial ravamping, and launch schedules slipped even in the best of times. The area economy was more diversified than it had been during the Apollo era, when the cutbacks of the 1970s proved devastating to the Space Coast. But still, businesses ranging from information technology to motels felt the pinch with no rockets flying. Optimists pointed out that the Cape would survive, simply because it was one of the few places on earth for launching rockets. Unless the entire space industry disappeared, there would be a need for the sorts of specialized skills, technology, and organization accumulated there. Since Apollo, more people working at KSC or dependent on it for their livelihoods had come to see that the space business was a long-haul effort, one subject to ups and downs of policy and unexpected events, but one much more deeply entrenched politically and economically in the nation than in the days of the moon program.[19]

One aspect of Space Coast culture had taken a direct hit as a result of the accident, though. Relations with the public and press, once characterized by mutual goodwill, deteriorated. In this regard, the accident came at an especially unfortunate time for NASA. Billed as the teacher-in-space mission, STS-51L was to send high school teacher Christa McAuliffe of Concord, New Hampshire, into orbit to promote science education. The launch had drawn significantly more press interest than had other recent flights, which were losing luster as they came to be seen as routine. After the disaster, a thousand reporters descended on the region, joining those already present. All were eager for news of what had just happened. KSC officials put into motion their contingency plan for an emergency. The plan had a public relations component, but it had never been integrated with the technical parts. The need for public communications got little thought as NASA personnel rushed to secure the site, recover tapes and images, and find and protect any information that might be useful in an investigation. KSC security blocked roads, cut phone lines, and in some cases impounded reporters' cameras and film. No one was allowed into or out of the Center. Yet there was no way to keep a lid on something this big. The event, seen live on TV, quickly overloaded KSC's communications infrastructure, jamming telephone lines and forcing Southern Bell workers to manually operate the switching equipment in Orlando.[20]

As press officials clamored for information, members of NASA's and KSC's public affairs offices were unsure what to say. They had received no official word yet. It was not even clear within NASA who had responsibility for public communications in a case like this.[21] To some reporters it all began to look suspiciously like a cover-up. At the very least, it revealed a NASA, normally voluble, now for some reason suddenly reticent. Suspicion and frustration fed rumors that maybe NASA did have something to hide after all. *Challenger* would prompt significant revisions in public affairs policies and practices.

The Investigation and Its Results

When the Rogers Commission released its report in June, most of the emphasis was placed not on launch operations per se but on the booster design and the mistaken confidence of NASA and Morton Thiokol engineers that they fully understood the O-ring problem. Besides redesigning the solid rocket boosters, NASA undertook a vast number of modifications to the shuttle itself, and to ground support equipment and operational procedures. But the Rogers probe had taken up issues of organization, decision making, and safety as well. Thus all who worked for the agency felt that they bore some responsibility.

One of the most obvious areas for change was safety policy. NASA, and KSC in particular, came in for criticism on safety programs, criticism that reflected the belief that the accident's cause was as much cultural and organizational as technical. There was some evidence that, once the shuttle was deemed operational, NASA had left too few safety people in place to do an adequate job of oversight. The Headquarters Safety Office had only twenty employees, and only one assigned, a quarter of the time, to the shuttle.[22] Headquarters came under fire for not taking a stronger leadership role in safety. The Rogers Commission believed that the decentralized nature of the safety program across NASA centers contributed to the accident as well. At KSC, the commission noted, a variety of safety and quality-assurance organizations reported to those responsible for shuttle processing. The implication was that they lacked the independence to hold up work or order changes that would slow down processing.

Before *Challenger*, the normal safety procedure began with an evaluation of each component for problems, flaws, or potential failure, and assignment of a "criticality" rating to each. Criticality 1 ratings referred to those components whose failure could cause loss of life, with lower ratings following for other, less dangerous conditions. An Operations and Maintenance Instruction (OMI) provided detailed procedures for Cape technicians to abide by in flight preparations. Irregularities detected on the ground or in flight activated a reporting procedure up the chain of command. One concern revealed by *Challenger* was the difficulty of using the extensive paper trail involved in both processing the shuttle and evaluating safety and reliability issues. In operational mode, it was necessary to limit the flow of information up to the top of the hierarchy. Small issues were resolved at lower levels, so that top managers could concentrate on larger ones. Anomalies in hardware were often handled by thorough testing and maintenance, rather than fundamental redesign. This policy let NASA devote scarce resources to less easily solved problems or seemingly more pressing concerns. Despite the unexpected occurrence of joint rotation, the solid rocket booster carried a 1R criticality rating. The R indicated that it was a redundant system because of the second O-ring. Even though a booster failure could cause loss of life, the redundancy removed it from the top level of engineering concern.

Organizational features and communications patterns that pushed safety matters away from the attention of key decision makers would have to be changed. Before *Challenger*, NASA had sought to reduce shuttle turnaround times by limiting the amount of replacement and rebuilding done in launch preparation. After *Challenger*, vehicle processors would take their time, to emphasize safety and assurance. The shuttle main engines, for example, had been checked, tested, and purged at each landing, but replaced only after a few flights. Now they would be replaced after each flight, as would the crucial fuel turbo pumps.[23]

On reflection, one striking aspect of the accident was that it took place despite strong professions throughout NASA of a commitment to safety. Such a variance between rhetoric and the reality of disaster led critics to charge deceit. Had NASA merely taken a public stance in favor of safety that belied a narrowly calculated decision to accept unwarranted risks so it could meet its deadlines? The most penetrating students of the accident disputed this simplistic interpretation, noting for example that the "cost" of a single disaster, in loss of equipment, loss of public confidence, and loss of human life, far outweighed any supposed savings from cutting corners. Diane Vaughn offers a more sophisticated interpretation, which argues that risky conditions and abnormal hardware behavior became unconsciously "normalized" or accepted in the course of shuttle operation.

This problem, the unsuspected blinders that people acquire as they perform the same task over and over again, is one of the classic dilemmas of any learning organization. Getting good at one thing—flying the shuttle in this case—means ignoring other things that to outsiders might seem unusual or even potentially dangerous. Just as few of us take note of the many dangers of driving a car when we do it day in and day out, so too those operating risky technologies become inured to the very dangers that they are meant to guard against. It thus became quite natural to assume that something that had already happened (joint rotation, scorching of the O-ring) would happen again, but difficult to imagine that something that had not happened (complete O-ring failure) would occur at some point.[24] Danger signals that seem clear in retrospect were, to the engineers working on the solid rocket boosters, just one more fact of normal shuttle operations. They were deviations from the expected, to be sure, but complex technologies exhibit many deviations. The only choice is either to check, test, and finally accept livable deviations, or to wait forever for perfection. That is one reason so much learning goes on through field testing, flight, and use.

Of course, such learning, necessary though it is, can also become the slippery slope to disaster. As one NASA engineer noted, "Once you've accepted that first lack of perfection, that first anomaly, it's like you've lost your virginity."[25] People will tune out even a piercing siren of warning if it goes on long enough. When the information is weak or ambiguous, as it was with the O-rings, the chance that it will be ignored rises even higher. Stopping descent down the slippery slope is extremely difficult under these conditions, and requires a special approach to safety, one not necessarily found in normal procedures. How to prevent this taken-for-grantedness was one of the major tasks of a revamped NASA safety program.

Safety at KSC

At the Kennedy Space Center, safety programs had evolved in accordance with new missions, new hardware, and new public expectations about travel in space. In the early years of rockets, for example, the most pressing safety concern was protecting the public from errant missiles. That was one reason the Cape was the location of choice for launch operations: it was remote, relatively unpopulated, and had a vast range over the sea. The creation of a surrounding nature preserve helped to keep KSC secluded. As the Center grew during the Apollo boom, new concerns about worker safety were added as well. When humans began traveling on rockets, astronaut safety became a major area of focus. The construction of complex and expensive launch technology associated with Apollo also increased worries about the impact of accidents on crucial pieces of hardware. During the 1970s, as the KSC workforce matured, new health and safety regulations promulgated by agencies such as OSHA and EPA came on the books. More attention went to the well-being of the workforce, including those who worked in offices as well as out on the pad.

Since 1964 KSC had maintained a Safety Office, with sections devoted to flight, industrial, and explosives safety.[26] Close by Safety on the organizational chart was the related area of Quality Assurance, which held responsibility for inspecting work, materials, and hardware to see that they were up to standard. Quality Assurance and Safety would be closely aligned in KSC's history, reflecting the inherent relationship between functions aimed at preventing accidents and mishaps and functions to assure that hardware performed as it should.

This structure changed to reflect the greater scale and speed of operations as KSC geared up for the Apollo moon mission. In 1965, a much more complex safety and quality assurance program was in place. There were now four separate offices of inspection and quality control. Safety disappeared as a separate heading, except in the Reliability and Flight Safety Office. Reflecting the division of labor necessary to carry out human and robotic missions, there also were now offices for launch system reliability, vehicle inspection, testing and calibration of materials, and investigation of malfunctions, and a quality and reliability office under the Directorate of Plans, Programs and Resources. A Safety Office with separate branches for technology, industrial safety, and operations safety came under the Quality Assurance Division.

This basic structure remained in place through 1967. New departments relating to safety or quality assurance were also added for key programs and technology, such as Saturn I and Saturn V. As KSC became an operational center with the activation of the Apollo launch facilities, quality assurance, inspection, and safety functions were dispersed over several more areas, creating a decentralized structure. For example, the Technical Support, Information Systems, Support Operations, and Installation Support Directorates each had offices for quality, reliability, and/or safety.

During this period, the Center established a strong safety record, particularly considering the industrial nature of the site and the dangerous materials and machines on hand. In 1964, NASA facilities as a whole had only 2.7 disabling accidents per million person-hours worked, compared to a federal government average of approximately 8.[27] That year KSC received "honorable mention" in the President's Safety Award for all government agencies. In 1968, KSC achieved a record of 1.56 accidents per million work hours, better than the aerospace industry as a whole, which had 2.17.[28] These results were achieved despite the fact that two-thirds of KSC workers had jobs defined as high to medium hazard.[29]

Built into the launch process were also certain safety features, which evolved in the course of learning to launch during the early years. Obviously, loss of a rocket or, worse, a spacecraft carrying astronauts would be considered a major accident. In this area, safety merged with quality assurance and checkout procedures, ones that would define practice for the future. The nonroutine nature of rocket flight made it difficult to use standard statistical techniques to prove reliability, as might be done with commercial technology. Missiles therefore had to carry redundant systems. Testing supervisors concentrated heavily on areas of uncertainty. Programmers wrote special software to allow simulation and other methods of testing without introducing further faults or defects.[30] A general attitude of "make trouble your best friend" prevailed during these early, experimental years, when it was often necessary to test rockets to the point of failure to establish levels of reliability and performance.[31]

Nonetheless, safety did not always integrate smoothly into operations. KSC came in for criticism in a 1965 study, which found the Center's safety measures insufficient, particularly in light of future growth and increased hazardous operations with the scaling up of the human space program. KSC's Safety Office had only twelve civil servants, who had to oversee all operations and facilities as well as personnel. It needed at least an additional twelve to fifteen members by 1966. The report noted a "dilemma": safety would require additional workers at the very moment that President Lyndon Johnson had ordered federal agencies to "stop manpower escalation." Efforts to secure an exemption from this order for KSC failed, leading the Center to augment Safety Office staff with contractors.[32] Another report a year later made similar suggestions, including more safety personnel, fewer hours of work to reduce fatigue (a major cause of accidents), and the use of safety reviews.[33]

With the tragic *Apollo 1* fire of 1967, safety underwent a major restructuring at KSC. The central Safety Office was moved up to management level, along with Quality Assurance. Directors of these functions reported to the Center director. Greater centralization was designed to assure that responsibility for safety went right to the top of KSC. Following requirements laid down at NASA headquarters, safety programs at centers now placed more emphasis on identification of hazards, communications about jeopardous conditions, and control of known risks. Inspectors were to investigate accidents thoroughly, with prompt follow-up or remedial actions taken. Individual centers and agencies were also required to coordinate with each other. Perhaps most important, directors of safety throughout NASA were explicitly given authority to stop any work found violating safety procedures or deemed too dangerous.[34]

This basic structure, with its centralized, management-level Safety Office, remained in force for the next decade or so, with incremental modifications. In 1974 KSC added an Unmanned Launch Operations Safety Office (later Expendable Launch Vehicles), reflecting the greater number of robotic missions in the period between the end of the Apollo program and the start of the space shuttle program. By 1976 the Center's safety structure had become rather elaborate, with an office called Safety, Reliability, Quality Assurance and Protective Services. Most quality assurance functions, however, were pushed back to the directorates—for ELVs, for Space Vehicle Operations, for Design. The split between, on the one hand, safety and protective functions and, on the other, quality assurance became most pronounced in 1985, just before the *Challenger* disaster.

Critics after *Challenger* blamed the accident in part on budget cuts and financial pressures that undermined safety. But this view is too simple. History shows that even in the flush years during the Apollo program, safety existed in the context of budgets and schedule. Cuts in NASA's budget began in the late 1960s and continued through the 1970s. Yet during this time KSC also made the case that safety was a good investment, not a cost to be minimized. "I recognized that in these days of austere budgets," wrote Kurt Debus, "these approaches [to safety] may appear to require an increase in . . . cost." But, he maintained, spending money to get better flight safety data would in the end be cost effective. Investments in safety and assurance saved money by reducing the number of launch failures. Debus noted that uncertainty and doubt bred cautious behavior and expensive, "unrealistic" flight restrictions. Better data allowed more economical operations in the long run by making risks known and allowing for enabling decisions.[35]

At KSC the view that safety was a good investment generally prevailed. The "ultimate aim" of the safety program at the Center, was to "increase efficiency by reducing the number and severity of preventable accidents."[36] Reducing accidents saved money by eliminating lost time and worker compensation claims, a position that can be found in the literature on industrial safety dating back to the beginning of the twentieth century in America. Nonetheless, it was also clear that there would be points where safety had to be weighed against other considerations. "The cheapest way to launch any space vehicle is on schedule," KSC instructions told contractors. Plans for safety had to be efficient and effective. No one benefited if safety resources were used ineffectively. But the budget for safety was not limitless either. "Although expense will always be secondary to the saving of a human life, this important factor should not be neglected in preparing a safety plan."[37]

While both routine accidents and missteps in the launch process could be avoided through attention to safety and common sense, there was also recognition within KSC culture of the inherently risky nature of the business. Articles in the KSC house organ *Spaceport News* noted how people took risks even in the most mundane aspects of their lives.[38] Given the large number of failures in early rocket launches, it was natural to see risk as part of the job. Indeed, failing was often the only way to learn about an experimental technology.[39]

As the Center prepared for the new space shuttle, *Spaceport News* articles mentioned some of the special handling this new technology would require, including the immense solid rocket boosters. The new vehicle also gave safety personnel time to think more broadly about ways to minimize hazards. They gave more attention to the remote causes of accidents. "At KSC we strive to maintain safe working conditions and operations over an extremely wide spectrum of hazardous activities," noted KSC safety director John Atkins.[40] Atkins's office sought to reduce the dangers of overwork, stress, and fatigue. It put into place new programs to assist employees troubled with health problems, and provided counseling for drug and alcohol abuse, or for personal matters that might affect work performance.[41] This new approach to safety was something of a change from the Apollo era, when high-pressure work was seen as part of the invigorating environment of the space program.

The new approach did not last long, though, for when the shuttle arrived at KSC long hours and pushing oneself to the limit reappeared in the work culture. By 1980, *Spaceport News* articles spoke not of the perils of fatigue but the benefits of round-the-clock work. Intense pressure on a tight schedule could build team spirit. "Stress Can Be Good for You!" trumpeted one KSC article, which concluded that "it takes Type A personalities to launch a space shuttle."[42]

In the years leading up to *Challenger*, the safety function at KSC had evolved again in a more decentralized direction. It was treated as part of the larger engineering practice of the Center and integrated with daily operations. Such decentralization was a means of improving efficiency. Instead of having two separate organizations, one processing and another checking, the checking and processing would occur in the same organization. This move brought safety and quality inspectors right into the thick of things, giving them firsthand knowledge of what was being done and why. But it was also the structure criticized by the Rogers Commission. Safety personnel working for the shuttle office could be co-opted by their organizational peers or intimidated by their boss, who was being paid to get the shuttle ready on time.

Challenger and Change

Challenger fundamentally remapped the way NASA and the American public saw the risks and rewards of space flight. It showed that the sort of risks that might have been acceptable when test pilots were jockeying ICBMs were not acceptable on an operational vehicle flying ordinary citizens. At a deeper level, it also revealed the highly subjective and uncertain nature of a seemingly technical term like "acceptable risk." To laypeople, acceptable risk might seem a harsh and calculating approach to human life. To engineers and astronauts, it was an inescapable fact; all technologies fail sometimes. Any technologically mediated activity, from driving a car to flying in space, will always carry some risk, however careful the procedures and however robust the design. But an acceptable risk level can never be determined on technical lines alone. Hazards acceptable in one situation are not in another—the risk an adult might willingly assume is not what would be allowed for a child. Indeed, it was not even certain, based on the number of shuttle flights before *Challenger*, what the chances of an accident really were—1 in 100, 1 in 1,000?[43]

Taken to the limit, of course, the absolutely safest course was simply never to fly again. "Every time you fly," noted Gene Sestile, "you fly on waivers." He meant that during testing and launch there was always something unexpected that required someone's approval as safe to fly. One of the strongest critics of NASA on the Rogers Commission, Nobel Prize–winning physicist Richard Feynman, likened this to Russian roulette: "The argument that the same risk was flown before without failure is often accepted as an argument for the safety of accepting it again. Because of this, obvious weaknesses are accepted again and again, without a sufficiently serious attempt to remedy them."[44] One day, Feynman pointed out, the bullet was bound to be in the chamber.

Feynman and others noted that NASA's risk assessments were based on shaky assumptions about materials, components, and systems, and uncertain extrapolations from a limited number of tests. But the alternative to test data and extrapolation was knowledge gained from real-world experience, which required toleration of risks and failures.[45] An irony of working with new technology is that sometimes only failure can provide the lessons needed to understand the limits of that technology. "I think before *Challenger* we didn't know how good we were," stated KSC's John Conway. "We had these margins . . . but everything seemed to work and so you didn't know."[46] It was only through experience in test and flight that one came to know what a complex piece of technology would really do.[47] Even then, there would often be a difference of opinion among competent engineers as to what the data meant. The question always remained, how to handle the anomaly—by redesign, through more careful operations, by replacing or servicing a part more often, by not flying?

The Rogers Commission's specific recommendations were to redesign the solid boosters, review all critical items on the shuttle, install an in-flight crew escape mechanism, and create a new top-level safety office.[48] In matters of organization and communications, it wanted more astronauts in management and decision-making positions and a new plan to assure that proper maintenance was being performed. NASA headquarters responded to the Commission's recommendations with the creation of a Safety, Reliability and Quality Assurance office.[49] Headquarters also appointed General Sam Phillips to study all NASA programs and the relationship between NASA headquarters and field centers. A new Flight Safety Panel was established, which traveled to the centers to encourage "NASA and contractor employees at all levels to use their own initiative to detect, report and eliminate hazards which could adversely affect the accomplishment of manned space flight objectives." Employees were to go to their safety offices with their concerns, or if necessary bring them to the Flight Safety Panel.[50] A safety reporting system was set up and run by Batelle, an independent organization, to allow employees and contractors to report safety concerns without fear of reprisal.[51]

By 1987 KSC had centralized its safety function once more. The Safety, Reliability and Quality Assurance Directorate included separate offices of Safety and Reliability and of Quality Assurance. Under Safety and Reliability were engineering and operations divisions, payload safety, industrial safety, and systems performance analysis. Quality Assurance, which had largely been done in the line directorates, now included payload, shuttle, and support quality divisions, as well as quality engineering. The director of the entire Safety, Reliability and Quality Assurance Directorate had on staff a senior inspector as well as personnel who conducted surveys and audits and measured compliance. "Think Safety" awareness weeks, safety contests, quality days, and the like aimed to build a safety culture. As with the *Apollo 1* fire, procedures became more formal, lines of authority and coordination between different work groups tightened, and work schedules relaxed.[52] Perhaps most significant, KSC created a new Director of Space Transportation Systems Management and Operations position, which provided a single point of focus for preparing, launching, and landing the shuttle to ensure clear lines of communications.

Commission recommendations reached to the fundamentals of shuttle operations at KSC. Two weeks before *Challenger*, NASA chief astronaut John Young wrote a memo complaining that KSC's runway was unsuitable for shuttle landings.[53] His memorandum was backed by an earlier air force study that enumerated several questionable conditions. NASA officials declared the runway "safe" given good weather conditions, but the Rogers Commission disagreed. "The realities of weather cannot be ignored," the

Commission asserted, concluding that "shuttle program officials must recognize that [landing at] Edwards is a permanent, essential part of the program."[54]

Most pointly, the Rogers Commission asked NASA to reassess its optimistic flight rate for the shuttle.[55] Once, the emphasis had been on meeting the schedule and processing payloads in a timely fashion to be internationally competitive; now KSC managers began to look more closely at how the rate of flight affected safety. Before *Challenger*, overtime work was common at KSC, especially when shuttle launches occurred on weekends. Many workers put in sixty-plus hours on two consecutive weeks or even three.[56] Now there would be no more twenty-four-hour shifts for crucial personnel.[57] Some workers even left, as the new safety procedures reduced the amount of money they could earn through overtime.[58] Keenly aware that fatigue or time pressure might lead to a lapse in performance, KSC management instituted a new policy of "safety first," and replaced the schedule imperative with "doing the job right."[59] The flawed analogy to the airline industry was dead.

No more commercial payloads would fly on the shuttle. The Centaur program ended abruptly. A liquid-hydrogen rocket in the payload bay was deemed too great a risk. This cancellation was a major factor in the air force's withdrawal from the shuttle program. The Vandenberg facility for launching military missions into polar orbits was scrapped, and the military resumed using ELVs for heavy satellites.[60] Fifteen to twenty Spacelab missions, experiments that were sent up in a special canister stowed in the shuttle payload bay, were also cancelled.[61] Indeed, the entire notion that one vehicle was economical for all types of missions came into question.[62] Rather than being a frugal way to get into space, a single vehicle was now seen as complex, difficult to process, expensive to maintain, and hard to adapt for different users. As the *Challenger* accident showed, moreover, it was vulnerable to devastating costs should there be a failure—losses in human terms, to be sure, but also losses that undercut the very economic rationale for the shuttle in the first place.[63]

In two other ways that had longer-term ramifications for KSC, *Challenger* changed policy. President Reagan and congressional Republicans had been pushing for greater competition and privatization of the space business. Though not the same, strictly speaking, both agendas implied more private-sector involvement. Privatization, as we have seen, had gone forward even before *Challenger*, with the single-point contracts for shuttle processing, base operations, and payloads.[64] Competition was something new, however, and potentially more radical. It too had started before *Challenger*, with a 1983 Reagan directive pushing for commercialization of launch activities.[65]

But with a growing consensus that the shuttle could not be the sole means of access to space for military, commercial, and scientific payloads came a new belief that NASA should be "stripped of its near monopoly" over space operations.[66] International competition from France, Japan, and China had already started this ball rolling. Now within the United States there were efforts afoot to have private firms meet an expected rise in demand for satellite launches. KSC would restart its ELV program as certain payloads were moved off the shuttle manifest. In ELV operations too the Center would replace civil servants with contractors.

New Leadership

Under a new Center director, plans for return to flight at KSC were drawn up as soon as the Rogers Commission finished its report, and indeed even sooner, since many of the reasons for the disaster were already understood. Lieutenant General Forrest McCartney replaced Richard Smith in August 1986 with basically one job—get the shuttle flying again. His military background brought some rather startling changes to life at the Center. Despite its proximity to the air force base at Cape Canaveral and the flying of military payloads on the shuttle, KSC had evolved a technical, not a military, culture. From its origins in the Cold War, NASA had stressed the civilian uses of space. Civil servants now found themselves in meetings "after breakfast," which for McCartney seemed to take place sometime before dawn. KSC personnel were left wondering what to call their boss. One wag suggested either "General" or his nickname, "Sir."[67] But, in fact, fears that KSC would start the day with a bugle call proved unfounded.

The general, most of those who worked with him soon found, was really a "good guy." His military experience was in research and development. He saw it as his main task not to radically shift KSC into some sort of military operation but to rebuild people's faith in themselves. His message was, you are good at what you do; do not allow this accident to destroy your confidence.[68] There would be changes at KSC, as in all of NASA, changes in culture and organization that reflected the lessons learned from *Challenger*. But in McCartney's view, KSC was not broken and did not need fixing. The road back depended on the skills and knowledge that had otherwise served the space program well. They would be resharpened and used in the new safety-first environment to get the shuttle back in the air.

McCartney did not believe that structures mattered greatly in organizations. That might seem surprising after all the investigations of NASA's structural problems. But it rested on a solid historical fact. Processing the shuttle, as with previous launch operations, depended heavily on skills ac-

10-2. Forrest McCartney takes over as KSC director, with outgoing director Richard Smith *(right)* behind. Others pictured are James Abrahamson and James Beggs.

quired through experience—the hands-on engineering, technical, and operational knowledge that rested with the people who worked at KSC. No structure, however perfect, could by itself launch a rocket. People did that. People could make mistakes, of course, but McCartney felt that most wanted to do a good job, do what they were supposed to, most of the time. Coming on the heels of an inquiry that suggested deep structural flaws at NASA and press investigations that hinted at malfeasance, this was a breath of fresh air at the Cape. Good communications and strong positive motivations were what McCartney saw as the key to a successful return to flight. KSC workers felt much maligned by any suggestion that *Challenger* revealed incompetence or sloppy work. Getting people to feel good about themselves again meant giving them decent working conditions, and removing obstacles that hindered their performance.

As KSC had tried to meet the shuttle's ambitious schedule, its responsibilities had grown faster than its ability to accommodate new people and new operations. In September 1987 McCartney oversaw the opening of the new Orbiter Maintenance and Refurbishment Facility, which relieved pressure on the OPF. The maintenance facility would allow engineers to make modifications and upgrades to orbiters as they flew out their lifetime of one hundred missions.[69] Office space had also been put on low priority during the busy years before 1986. Workers occupied temporary facilities and made do with whatever space they could find. "KSC is not a temporary operation," McCartney announced. He cleared out the trailers and built real office and support buildings, and authorized a day care center. Taking advantage of the downtime after *Challenger*, KSC refurbished and modified its ground facilities as well.[70] There was even time at last to install a new-generation data management system to solve a problem that had been identified as much as a decade before—the tremendous paperwork involved in processing.

To McCartney and others at KSC, *Challenger* reinforced the belief that operational experience had to feed back to design. There had long been a tendency of other NASA centers to treat KSC as their "workforce." But time had shown that launch operations embodied unique skills and knowledge, ones that "belonged" to KSC and not to the other centers, even if they built the rockets and managed the missions.[71] As it turned out, post-*Challenger* efforts to promote this position were just the start of a long uphill battle that would mark operations at NASA for the next decade.

During the *Challenger* investigation there had been much speculation about why NASA had fallen so far from the successful can-do spirit of Apollo.[72] McCartney took on the task of repairing the loss of public confidence in the space program. As a military man, he had avoided the press. Now, as a civil servant, he had to cultivate good press relations. The confusion just after the accident had led to some ill will there. "I believe we have a good attitude on open communications," reported McCartney, "so I don't see any signs that disturb me."[73] Around the Cape, support for NASA and for flying the shuttle again had never waned. It seemed obvious to those who had watched the evolution of rockets: when you fall off a horse, the only answer is to get right back on again.[74] Others, following the airline analogy that had defined the shuttle, reminded skeptics that "Boeing doesn't stop flying airplanes because one 747 crashes."

Among the American public as a whole, similar attitudes prevailed. Even if *Challenger* caused some to question NASA policy, the vast majority of the public believed that the shuttle should fly again. Not surprisingly, overall support for NASA fell in the wake of *Challenger*. But on the specific question of return to flight, 70–75 percent of those asked thought the civilian space program should continue—a level of support essentially unchanged since before *Challenger*. On the specific question of flying humans in space, an overwhelming 86 percent said yes, though a similar percentage also thought that it was time to consider replacing the shuttle with a new vehicle. Even so, 79 percent were convinced that the shuttle gave good benefits and that funds should be authorized for an orbiter to replace *Challenger*. Although 44 percent feared NASA might be riding on past glories, 70 percent also rated the agency as extremely competent and at the cutting edge of technology. It remained important to Americans to get back into space, and stay ahead of Russia and Japan.[75]

Return to Flight

It took two and a half years before the shuttle was spaceborne again. During that time, the boosters were redesigned, a new crew escape mechanism was added, the KSC runway was improved, and dozens of modifications were made to the main engines, thermal protection system, wings, computers, tanks, fuel cells, and other parts and subsystems of the shuttle. Most of this work did not involve KSC directly, though the modified vehicle was tested there.[76]

Flights under the new safety procedures required a substantial amount of new learning. KSC personnel proceeded slowly, cautiously, and deliberately toward a planned summer 1988 launch of the space shuttle *Discovery*. There was absolutely no margin for error on this one, not with the whole world watching. As Center director McCartney wrote, "things are going well, but slow—*much* slower than I had anticipated." It reflected the new priority of "safety ahead of anything else."[77] Many things were proving to be bigger jobs than expected—fuel pumps, tile, the escape system for the crew. McCartney was determined to close out all the open paper before moving hardware from one station to the next, even if he had to use "tiger teams" to solve the problems.[78] *Discovery's* rollout to the pad was to take place on the symbolic date of July 4, but even that would be delayed if necessary to assure the work was done right the first time.[79]

Some of the new, extra work could be frustrating, McCartney noted. But "frustrations with the troops" was only to be expected, given the new things to be learned. Over time KSC was expected to climb a learning curve that would allow for improved processing with the new hardware and procedures as the second, third, and subsequent shuttles were prepared for flight. Morale, the director reported, was "good, as good as you would expect as we get closer to launch."[80] People let go had been hired back. Indeed, if anything, there was a shortage of key personnel, especially the new expertise needed for safety and quality assurance. KSC people now had something to do, something to look forward to. As the day of launch approached, McCartney reported, "Pride is up and that's good."[81]

Discovery rolled out of the VAB as hoped on July 4. It was "like a rebirth," remarked KSC's Tip Talone.[82] After an extremely careful set of prelaunch tests, it fired to life on September 29, 1988. Its crew of highly experienced astronauts, after nearly two years of intensive training emphasizing safety,

10-3. Tip Talone celebrates the shuttle's successful return to flight with the blastoff of *Discovery*.

rode into space wearing newly designed pressurized flight suits containing parachutes, survival equipment, and oxygen. But no one really breathed the final sigh of relief until *Discov*ery touched down on October 3 at Edwards Air Force Base. A few days later the KSC newspaper *Spaceport News* published a special edition with a full-color full-page shot of the liftoff under the banner headline "Oh, What a Feeling!" and proclaimed "the first of a new era."[83] The shuttle had returned to flight and returned safely to earth. At Cape Canaveral, the psychological pall lifted. The hiatus after *Challenger* had inflicted material and emotional damage on many Space Coast families. This flawless launch was the best medicine. "The Space Center was built for just one purpose: to launch vehicles into space." Now it had its purpose back again.[84]

The second flight, of *Atlantis*, moved more quickly. The first flow was "a bear," declared McCartney, but now it "look[s] like the learning curve is working—much easier the second time."[85] Still, improvements in processing productivity took place in a different context than in the hard-driving pre-*Challenger* era. The shortest time any shuttle spent in the OPF before *Challenger* was 26 days. Now they would be there at least 51 days, and as many as 60. Even so, preparing shuttles still required three shifts a day, seven days a week, though with more time off to prevent worker fatigue. According to

10-4. Gulls flee as *Discovery*'s engines light.

Robert Crippen, director of NASA's Space Transportation System, the work-load was no heavier than in the navy, or indeed at a commercial airline.[86] But *Challenger* allowed KSC people to "knock off the optimism" about schedule. Now it was possible to go back to the "normal" schedule pressure that was inevitably a part of flying rockets.[87]

During the space program's downtime, a substantial backlog of missions and payloads had accumulated. To clear the backlog, six shuttle missions were scheduled for 1989 and nine more during the next two years, with the numbers rising to eleven and fourteen in 1992 and 1993. But the *Challenger* accident suddenly transformed payload processing issues at KSC. Before the accident, about one-third of the shuttle manifest had gone to the Department of Defense, another third to commercial users, and the remainder to NASA missions. After *Challenger*, there would be no more commercial launches.[88] With the ending of commercial and many military flights on the shuttle, much confusion remained about how users who had contracted to fly their hardware on the shuttle would get back into space.[89]

Both the backlog and the new payload restrictions made the Payload Processing Contract an even more difficult matter than originally thought. The five years following return to flight would include the busiest and most varied manifest in KSC's history.[90] Center executives urged the head of the Source Evaluation Board, JoAnn Morgan, to move ahead as soon as she could determine the changes needed in the payload contract. Flexibility would be crucial, given all the unknowns. Yet because of *Challenger*, NASA's legal advisors wanted every "i" dotted and "t" crossed.[91] The orbiter, solid rocket boosters, and external tank had been substantially redesigned in response to the accident, forcing new requirements on the payload contractor, who now had to work with a variety of new manufactures.[92]

The issue of customer service was crucial in the decision to award the payload contract to McDonnell Douglas in 1987. Morgan was particularly impressed with their proposal. Competitor Boeing had not had much experience on the payload side of launches, while McDonnell Douglas had built the capsules for the Mercury and Gemini programs. This experience was closest to what was required in payloads, for the capsules, in contrast to the launch vehicle or rocket, carried something into space—people. McDonnell Douglas had also been involved in the construction of Spacelab and a variety of other payload projects. This experience showed in their proposal, which included special training programs for technicians to enable them to adapt to the needs of each shuttle customer.[93]

The winning contractor had little time to celebrate victory, however, for *Challenger*-bred changes had introduced a major payload-related problem. The shuttle could only loft payloads into low earth orbit, so geosynchronous satellites, which orbited at much higher altitudes, and interplanetary space probes required an additional in-orbit heave to complete their missions. When NASA canceled the shuttle's hydrogen-fueled Centaur upper stage, the only remaining option for boosting payloads was the Interim Upper Stage (later Inertial Upper Stage) developed by the military. But military satellites had priority for the IUS, and too few of them were available for the

10-5. Shuttle coming in for landing at KSC.

backlog of missions. Unless additional IUSs could be constructed quickly, many nonmilitary missions would have to wait, or even be canceled.

McDonnell Douglas volunteered its own technicians to help IUS contractor Boeing complete four additional upper stages. It was a touchy move, as Boeing had just lost the valued payload contract. Nonetheless, McDonnell Douglas technicians went to the Boeing factory to get the boosters ready, then moved back to Merritt Island to process the payloads that would use them. Very quickly the aerospace firm had grasped the need for a new way of doing business as NASA's payload contractor. The flexibility built into the contract paid off. In the first year following return to flight, seven satellites and interplanetary probes went into space. Each used an IUS to achieve high orbit.[94]

On just the sixth mission, McDonnell Douglas's payload processing team faced one of its most important challenges. The long-delayed *Galileo* spacecraft was now set to take its ride to Jupiter in 1989. The two-and-a-half-ton *Galileo* came equipped with a battery of instruments to investigate every aspect it could of Jupiter, its surrounding moons, and the planets it would fly by on its trip. Cameras, low-gain radio antennas, probes to be parachuted to the planet's surface, eleven other scientific instruments, plus fuel (some 48 pounds of plutonium), power system, computers, and control electronics were all integrated into a platform that spun on one axis to provide flight

10-6. The sophisticated *Galileo* spacecraft at KSC.

stability, while another section remained fixed to point cameras and instruments. It was the most sophisticated space probe of its time, a major achievement of NASA's Jet Propulsion Laboratory.[95]

Naturally, with this expensive piece of hardware, workers at KSC made every effort to assure that nothing went wrong. The design engineers and manufacturer of the sensitive scientific device turned over a technology that, though complete in one sense, still required assembly, checking, and integration at the launch center. With one-of-a-kind scientific payloads, final assembly and fitting work could not be predicted from past experience. Only when the equipment arrived at the launch center and met the other hardware that it would work with could the final assembly and integration stages be completed. Adding to the intensity with *Galileo* was the fact that KSC was processing multiple payloads at once to clear the backlog.

Atlantis, the shuttle that would ferry *Galileo* to its space launch point, entered the processing flow on May 16, eight days after it had touched down to earth at Edwards Air Force Base in California from its previous flight. Workers removed the orbiter's three main engines, transporting them to

10-7. Workers install the *Galileo* spacecraft in a transport container in vertical position. It will be rotated to horizontal for installation in the shuttle payload bay.

the engine shop in the VAB, where components were checked, serviced, and replaced. One important change following *Challenger* was the realization that it was actually easier and safer to remove the engines for this work, rather than to have technicians crawling around inside the narrow engine compartment filled with wires and tubing.

As work on *Atlantis* continued, KSC payload engineers serviced the *Galileo* probe. Two critical schedules, one controlling the path of the shuttle, the other controlling the preparation of *Galileo*, had to move in parallel sequence if the mission was to meet its October launch window. Since April 17, *Galileo* had been at the Spacecraft Assembly and Encapsulation Facility (SAEF). There the probe was integrated with the spacecraft that would carry it to Jupiter. This was a crucial step. When spacecraft and probe were joined and tested, all critical connections had to be verified. One failed connection could render the hardware useless. Next, everything went to the Vertical Processing Facility (VPF). At the VPF, *Galileo* received the solid-fueled Inertial Upper Stage, which would push it fully out of earth orbit and start it on its six-year journey into deep space. Once again, integrated tests had to be performed to assure that the upper stage and spacecraft worked together as they should. The most important remaining step was to place *Galileo* in the shuttle payload bay.

On August 17, *Atlantis* was rolled to the VAB, where workers were stacking the solid rocket boosters. Here they would connect the orbiter with the boosters, now redesigned to prevent another tragedy. As with the *Galileo* spacecraft, the assembled shuttle went through a series of integration tests to be sure all crucial electrical and mechanical elements worked as required. Twelve days later, *Atlantis* rolled out to Pad 39-B. On the pad, *Galileo* and the IUS were integrated into the shuttle. Orbiter and boosters, spacecraft and probe, were now all together, pointing up at space under the Florida sky. The remaining work verified the interface between the shuttle and its delicate payload, assuring that ground control would be able to communicate with the spacecraft when it was launched on its solar-system-spanning journey.

In essence, four separate systems had been processed and integrated, and then configured into one vehicle. As Shannon Bartell, then working on scientific mission payloads at KSC, noted, this process was not just technical but organizational, even cultural. Interfaces were also "people relationships" and KSC's job was to "get all these organizations to work together."[96] It added layers of complexity when different scientists and engineers from different centers with different traditions and work environments all had to agree. They had to agree to the meaning of a test, agree that their piece of the equipment was ready, agree that any problems or defects or anomalies

10-8. *Galileo* leaves earth aboard space shuttle *Atlantis*.

that appeared during the test were resolved. Different men and women, all highly trained in their fields, could easily disagree even when observing the same thing. But with the launch window approaching, the key to completion was finding some way to get beyond these differences to a point of mutual understanding. That was the crucial last stage before flight, and the main task of KSC in these sorts of missions. The specialized knowledge of the spacecraft builder was made to correspond with that of the orbiter and booster engineers and KSC ground personnel.

On October 18, 1989, *Atlantis* counted down and launched flawlessly. *Galileo* left the shuttle payload bay, the upper stage fired as designed, and the spacecraft was on its way. Six years later it rendezvoused with the solar system's largest planet and began sending back a fantastic stream of data and images. The voyage finally ended in 2003 with the spent spacecraft burning up in the thick Jovian atmosphere.

An Eye in Space

Within a few years, the procedures put into place in the wake of *Challenger* had melded into a new work routine at KSC. Clearly, *Challenger* changed things, but much of the learning about flying the shuttle and processing payloads that had been acquired before the accident continued to evolve and mature with additional experience. By 1990 the shuttle manifest was up to ten missions. The year began with the successful liftoff of *Columbia* on January 9 to launch a defense communications satellite and retrieve NASA's Long Duration Exposure Facility. Center director McCartney announced that the schedule would not pressure KSC's pace. "If there's anything we're uncomfortable with, we won't go," McCartney stated flatly. "We aren't going to push ourselves knowingly. But I'm looking forward to a very prosperous year."[97]

The new year also brought an ambitious new mission for the Center. It would exceed even *Galileo* in significance and complexity. Scheduled before *Challenger*, the Hubble Space Telescope would finally get a chance to open its penetrating eye on the stars. Conceived in the 1970s, Hubble was to soar 375 miles above the earth, away from the distorting effects of the atmosphere, and give astronomers an astonishing view of the universe. Once it was deployed from the shuttle, it would send back pictures looking farther out into space, and further back in time, than any telescope before.

This extraordinary device mandated extensive work from KSC's payload processing team. Just to transport it from Lockheed's testing facilities in California required something new. A special canister designed for the air force was used to encapsulate the sensitive instrument, which was then loaded onto an airplane.[98] John Conway noted the difficulties in handling Hubble. It came off the plane in the horizontal position and then had to be rotated at the Vertical Processing Facility, where a simulator hooked to shuttle computers could check every interface. Hubble was powered up and a mock exchange took place between the orbiter simulator and the telescope's spacecraft. In addition, Lockheed sent its people to KSC to check every aspect of the telescope with their own gear.[99] In all, the billion-dollar device would spend six months at KSC before launch, and leave a very steep warehouse bill behind. While it was on site, all burning and sandblasting at KSC ceased because of possible contamination, even in a clean room rated to allow no more than 100,000 half-micron particles per cubic meter of air.[100]

10-9. Work on the delicate Hubble Space Telescope took place in special clean rooms at KSC.

At the start of 1990, the Cape was again humming with multiple missions in various stages of completion, much as it had been before *Challenger*. *Atlantis* was scheduled to fly STS-36. It zoomed through the OPF in sixty-nine days, the most rapid turnaround since the *Challenger* disaster.[101] On January 26, *Columbia* returned to earth, touching down at Edwards.[102] Upon arriving at KSC, *Columbia* was demated from the SCA and towed the next day into the Orbiter Processing Facility. There technicians began processing *Columbia*, while other technicians were checking *Discovery*'s life support systems in preparation for the Hubble mission. Meanwhile out at the pad, technicians continued running the routine tests of *Atlantis*'s engines in preparation for its flight.

Now, however, *Atlantis* began giving the pad workers fits. Technicians replaced a turbopump after tests revealed imperfections. Parts were still in short supply, and the new safety procedures made logistics even more difficult. Norm Parmet, vice chairman of NASA's Aerospace Safety Advisory Board, groused about contractor quality assurance. "You've got a million darn inspections on these things," he asserted. "You've got to do every damn one of them."[103] It was the only way to be sure. A shortage of turbopumps resulting from the inspections led technicians to remove *Columbia*'s number two main engine so that a turbopump from *Atlantis* could be installed in *Columbia* after *Atlantis* returned.[104] At the same time, the turbopump just installed on *Atlantis* was removed for testing to ensure that it had been properly repaired. A turbopump from another of *Columbia*'s engines would replace it. Once again, parts shortages and logistics were leading to cannibalization.

At *Atlantis*'s flight readiness review, program managers discussed rescheduling subsequent launches, perhaps moving *Discovery*'s flight with the Hubble Space Telescope by a week. Over the weekend, simulated main engine starts on *Atlantis* as well as leak tests on the recently replaced turbopump continued. In the end, though, human frailty rather than spacecraft malfunction delayed the flight. *Atlantis* mission commander John Creighton came down with a sore throat on February 21, forcing two 24-hour holds. Then poor weather at the Cape delayed the launch for another three days.[105] *Atlantis* finally left on February 28, in a spectacular night launch. Workers now turned their attention to Hubble.[106]

They began the mating of the external tank and solid rocket boosters of *Discovery* on March 4. Rollout of *Discovery* to the launchpad, however, was delayed for twelve hours while workers checked the nose landing gear to determine if it had problems similar to those recently discovered in *Columbia* and *Atlantis*. All three orbiters would eventually be cleared to fly with the deviating configuration.[107] Tests on *Discovery* remained on target for an

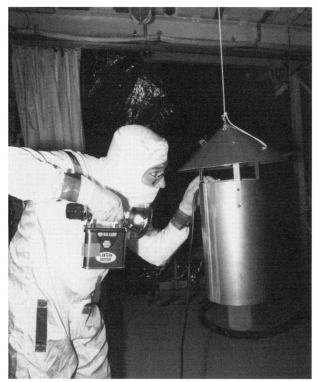

10-10. A scientist inspecting a special scientific instrument? No, a technician checking a bug trap, to keep contamination to a minimum during the Hubble Space Telescope's residence at KSC.

early launch, even though the checkout of the Hubble Space Telescope had fallen behind schedule. On April 10, *Discovery* was almost through its final countdown when, with four minutes remaining, an auxiliary power unit (APU) failed.[108] While technicians replaced the APU over the next week, Hubble's batteries were removed and recharged. KSC workers' ability to repair *Discovery* and return to launch had improved significantly in the nine years since the first shuttle launch. *Discovery*'s Hubble mission flew on April 24. It was an important demonstration of how shuttle and payload processing, flight scheduling, safety considerations, and launch operations could be meshed to prepare and fly a complex mission. It also confirmed the success of the new work routine and safety procedures put in place since the accident.

In 1991 NASA received a replacement shuttle for the fallen *Challenger*. Constructed of spare parts from *Discovery* and *Atlantis*, it was financed in part by nickels and dimes contributed by schoolchildren, who also participated in a naming competition. The name chosen was *Endeavour*, after the eighteenth-century ship commanded by English explorer James Cook. NASA thus continued its tradition of reflecting in the spacefaring ventures of the shuttle the seafaring ventures of the past.

10-11. An alligator ostentatiously pays no attention to the space shuttle.

Assessing the Impact of *Challenger*

From one perspective, the *Challenger* episode was not a sudden crises so much as the culmination of problems that had been building since the end of Apollo. In place of the clear and well-defined objective of getting to the moon, NASA had been attempting the broader, vaguer, and in many ways more difficult mission of making space flight routine and inexpensive. The operational approach had placed a premium on turnaround, schedule, and efficiency, values that seemed in conflict with space flight as a research venture into the unknown. It also implied, quite strongly, a safe vehicle, for one of the things that makes civilian airliners operational is a low risk of passenger death. Airplanes are not safe, however, because inspectors are constantly discovering and repairing defects; they are safe because the technology is well understood and safety is completely integrated with routine processing. The shuttle, however, was closer to an experimental jet fighter than to an airliner. Indeed, even as an "operational" vehicle, the shuttle had more parts than the average experimental fighter. And military test pilots fly knowing that they face a one in four chance of death in their work.[109] *Challenger* was perhaps the clearest example to date that with high-risk cutting-edge technologies, operations are sites of experimentation and learning, and not routine matters that simply follow the plans of designers.[110]

11

✳
✳
✳

Launching in a Competitive Environment

When the space shuttle started flying, many in the space program predicted that the days of old "expendable" launch vehicles were numbered. Rockets with names going back to the start of the space age—Atlas, Delta, Titan—would head for the junk pile, if not immediately, then certainly as soon as the shuttle manifest filled up. Even before the shuttle became operational, these expendable vehicles were in decline. In 1977, there had been seventeen expendable launches from Cape Canaveral; in 1978 and 1979, only five each year. With some 560 shuttle flights originally scheduled between 1980 and 1992, there would be no need for any other vehicle. Even robotic and planetary missions sent to the far reaches of the solar system would become "shuttle compliant."[1] Only those still launching expendables maintained a healthy dose of skepticism. KSC's Don Sheppard never believed that a reusable, human-rated vehicle would do everything. "We knew that wouldn't happen," he recalled. "We just laughed and said, 'We'll see.'"[2]

Launch Market

At first it appeared that shuttle supporters would get the last laugh. In October 1975, KSC downgraded Unmanned Launch Operations, making it a second-level directorate under Launch Operations.[3] Expendables would continue to fly as the Center awaited the shuttle. But the consolidation was the first step in a plan that mapped out the "completion" of the unmanned vehicle program. Completion meant termination.[4]

 Challenger changed all that, of course, but even before *Challenger* there were signs that perhaps the shuttle was not the last word in space booster technology. From 1965 to 1981, the United States launched every commercial satellite in the free world. That began to change with Ariane, the new, commercially oriented rocket developed by the European Space Agency. Before the shuttle was ready to fly, Ariane started taking on cargo. In 1979 Intelsat, the international body regulating communications satellites, agreed to use Ariane for one of its missions. NASA quickly countered by guarantee-ing the launch of two other Intelsat payloads aboard the shuttle. But it had to provide an ELV backup, so uncertain was the shuttle's first flight.[5] Then, as the date for the shuttle's maiden voyage slipped, NASA announced a two-year extension of McDonnell Douglas's contract for the Delta rocket. This mainstay of the expendable vehicle fleet, once slated for termination, was suddenly reprieved. Delays in the shuttle schedule led to a doubling of Delta production at McDonnell Douglas's California factory. Several satellite op-erators who had scheduled their hardware on the shuttle now expressed interest in the development of an upgraded Delta rocket.[6]

By January 1981 the ELV program at the Kennedy Space Center was re-covering. Fearing shuttle dependency, the military kept the heavy-lift Titan vehicle alive. NASA requested $3 million to refurbish Launch Complex 17B for Delta flights, in expectation of some ten launches there per year.[7] This revival of expendables was still seen as a stopgap measure. But as Charles Gay, KSC's director of deployable payloads, admitted, "I don't know if we'll ever do away with Delta."[8] This time, ELV supporters were right on target.

One problem with doing away with expendable vehicles was simple eco-nomics. In theory, a fully operational shuttle, with processing times reduced to the most optimistic levels, plenty of flights on the books, and no safety issues, might well underprice other forms of space transport. In theory. But expendable vehicles had not been static during the preceding twenty years. While it cost $100,000–$250,000 per pound to place objects in low earth orbit using the early Redstone, Vanguard, and Juno rockets, newer boosters cut the price to one-tenth of that. By the 1980s, demand for launch capability had also grown, brightening some of the launch vehicle horizons dimmed by the shuttle's looming presence. These prospects were brightened even more by policy initiatives taken during the Reagan administration in the early 1980s.

Until 1978, anyone in America with anything to fly in space contracted with NASA. The agency procured a launch vehicle and carried out the launch on a reimbursable basis. NASA also paid for improvements in boost-ers and maintained the launchpads. The 1984 Commercial Space Launch Act changed this long-standing policy. It aimed to eliminate NASA's "mo-nopoly" on launching. Turning regulatory powers for commercial launches over to the Department of Transportation, the act gave commercial cus-tomers greater freedom to contract directly with vehicle builders, bypass-ing NASA.[9] Private firms would be allowed to operate their own launch vehicles, and use NASA facilities for launch. NASA was told to buy launch services from private contractors, reducing the amount of hands-on work it did at KSC in preparing, testing, and launching. NASA also had to unbundle the cost of payload processing from the total cost of launch, allowing private payload handling firms to set up shop outside KSC's gates. These moves were supposed to increase efficiency, cut launching costs, and instill private-sector discipline in NASA.[10]

The private sector responded to the new opportunity. During the 1980s, space-related sales increased from 15 percent to 22 percent of total aerospace sales.[11] Some of the major contractors for rocket technology, former suppliers to both NASA and the air force, began competing in the launch vehicle market. Convair, a subsidiary of General Dynamics, came out with a new version of the Atlas and the liquid-hydrogen Centaur boosters. Transpace Carriers offered the Delta for hire, as did Martin Marietta with its Titan rocket.[12] Entirely new vehicles appeared from the private sector. In 1985, American Rocket built its own booster, seeking to undercut the costs of both existing expendables and the shuttle. Former astronaut Deke Slayton founded Space Services, arguing that its Conestoga rocket would realize cost savings through better booster design and by streamlining launch operations.[13]

For a time, NASA was able to compete by keeping the price of shuttle rides low. Promarket supporters argued this amounted to a subsidy to shuttle users, undercutting the demand for expendable vehicles. Debate over what it really cost to launch a shuttle (or an ELV) continued through the 1980s. Even without the pricing controversy, though, the launch market was restricted by still unresolved questions about legal liability for private launches.[14]

All this began to change the day *Challenger* was lost. No one vehicle, it was now argued, could be reliable enough to carry all cargo into space.[15] No user wanted to be totally shuttle-dependent again. Once dismissed as "25-year-old technology," ELVs were recast as "workhorses . . . not ready to retire into obsolescence."[16] The *Challenger* accident also allowed the Reagan administration to push its privatization agenda, demanding that NASA charge "full cost recovery" prices for the shuttle starting in 1989. As the price of shuttle rides rose, the door for ELVs opened wider.[17]

ELV Renaissance

President Reagan's national space policy of 1989 directed NASA to make ELV properties and services available to commercial users and to avoid competing with private launch operations. New launch sites were opened up for private firms, which received authorization to purchase government property and lease launchpads. As the fortunes of ELVs revived, NASA started to purchase vehicles and launch services from General Dynamics, Martin Marietta, and McDonnell Douglas.[18] In 1988, NASA had awarded its first

ELV launch services contract to General Dynamics to support Geostationary Operational Environmental Satellites (GOES). A year later, General Dynamics was carrying out missions for the navy from the Cape. McDonnell Douglas flew hardware for the British, and Martin Marietta had contracts to launch British and Japanese payloads on Titan.[19] KSC would continue to service pads and ground support equipment and act as the regulatory authority for these launches. But private contractors would do most of the testing and preparation.[20]

Reestablishing a robust ELV program required substantial work. During the early 1980s, valuable launch experience had been lost. Soon after the *Challenger* disaster, a Titan exploded after liftoff at Vandenberg Air Force Base on April 18, 1986. A few weeks later, on May 3, a Delta rocket carrying a $58 million satellite lost control after the vehicle's first-stage main engine shut down. Delta had been the most reliable of rockets, with a success rate of almost 98 percent. With the *Challenger* disaster still fresh in everyone's mind, the tumbling rocket's flight ended with a destruct order from the Cape range safety officer. It exploded over the Atlantic.[21] These accidents bred fresh doubts about the ability of the U.S. space program to carry through its planned launch schedule. With the shuttle grounded, one air force official lamented, "we have to do something because payloads are stacking up."[22] Even if those first losses were just the jitters of restarting a program, other questions remained. What would it now cost to launch payloads once expected to be driven down to rock-bottom prices by the scale economies of the shuttle?

Such concerns were pushed aside, however, as entrepreneurs responded to optimistic predictions of a growing demand for space access. Orbital Sciences Corporation developed the efficient Pegasus rocket for light satellites and scientific loads up to 1,000 pounds. Unlike ballistic missiles, Pegasus launched from beneath the "Stargazer" L-1011 airplane.[23] Pegasus's ground-based cousin Taurus joined the commercial fleet in 1994. Taurus was capable of 3,000 pounds of lift and, with two fairing sizes available, was uniquely flexible, allowing satellites to share a mission when feasible.[24]

The late 1980s were heady times for private rocket firms. "If we had evolved through as many generations of technology in launch vehicles as we have evolved through in airplanes," stated Orbital Sciences Corporation's president David Thompson, "it would be possible to launch rockets into low orbit for about three times the energy it takes to fly a [Boeing] 747 across the country."[25] Reversing the shuttle logic of a single, reusable multipurpose vehicle, Thompson and other entrepreneurs argued instead that competitive commercial operations, experimenting with many different technologies, would be the key to low-cost access.

Amendments to the Commercial Space Launch Act seemed to assure the launch entrepreneurs a favorable climate. New rules required NASA to work with the launch vehicle and satellite industries to support research into launch system technologies. Competition, supplemented by government research, would increase the performance and lower the cost of U.S. boosters to keep them internationally competitive.[26] The amendments also dealt with the liability issue, the bugaboo of all private launch firms. Before the amendment, it was extremely difficult to insure a private launch. Given that even low-cost rockets plus their cargo could cost millions of dollars, a single error put a substantial investment at risk, not to mention the danger to Cape facilities or, worse, civilian areas.[27] Potential liability seemed unlimited, and no insurer would write a policy on an unknown risk. A series of studies conducted by the Department of Transportation and NASA, however, used past experience to estimate the odds of a catastrophic loss and the damage that might result. The amended act only required private companies to purchase insurance based on these studies, which gave underwriters the certainty they needed to construct policies.[28]

This did not mean that the move to commercial, privately operated ELVs went smoothly. NASA still had priority in the use of government property for its own purposes. Moreover, ELVs and the shuttle shared some facilities. Different missions had different durations. Where complex planetary payloads might require months in payload processing facilities, commercial satellites might only require a few weeks. Commercial and national security interests could also come into conflict.[29] In July 1988 the Delta facility, Launch Complex 17, was handed over to air force custody.[30] Eventually Titan and Atlas/Delta complexes would also transition to air force management.

Commercial ventures struggled when demand for launch services unexpectedly stagnated in the 1990s.[31] Motorola's promising Iridium satellite phone network collapsed, removing a substantial piece of the launch market. It also turned out that newer-generation communications satellites lasted longer and carried more circuits, which meant that fewer were needed. At the same time, land-based fiber-optic cables cut into the satellite communications business.[32] There was suddenly a "crowded market" for launchers. Expectations were for only fifteen to eighteen commercial satellites annually during the early 1990s, with 40 percent of those going to Europe's Arianespace.

In fact the major beneficiary of the shuttle's grounding was not American launch entrepreneurs but Ariane. This vertically integrated firm had been planned from the ground up to capture the market for commercial satellite launches.[33] After *Challenger* it was inundated with orders, including some from American firms.[34] Between 1988 and 1992, Ariane launched 65 percent of the world's commercial satellites, followed by the United States (26 percent) and Japan (7 percent). NASA's longtime lead in the commercial satellite business had evaporated.[35]

By the start of the 1990s, the mainstays of the American launch fleet seemed outdated and expensive. The shuttle was back in the air, but every shuttle flight required costly arrangements for safety not necessary on ELVs.[36] At the same time, the American ELVs were hobbled by their military origins. They were designed to "throw as much payload as far as possible."[37] Ariane, by contrast, was developed specifically for commercial users. Adaptable to a wide variety of launch configurations, payloads, and prices, it was capable of carrying multiple cargos on a single trip, greatly cutting the cost to each user, while the U.S. vehicles were confined to a few configurations and could not launch multiple payloads. Despite their somewhat greater engine efficiency, U.S. vehicles could use, on average, only about 80 percent of their maximum payload capacity, compared to 90 percent for Ariane.[38] In addition, Ariane needed 15 percent less energy to reach orbit because it was launched closer to the equator than were American rockets leaving from Cape Canaveral. Even the KSC facilities, once the most advanced in the world, seemed old and cumbersome. Arianespace's Guiana site was new and purpose-built to serve the commercial market.[39] KSC's facilities dated back to the now distant moon race and had to serve both military and commercial missions. By 1994 the French booster could be launched by a crew of 100, after spending a scant ten days on the launchpad; a Delta at that time needed a crew of 300 and twenty-three pad days.[40]

As Table 1 shows, U.S. booster technology and launch operations were now contending against very efficient technologies and organizations from several nations. When the mission backlog was great, as in the late 1980s, the United States' disadvantages were not a major issue. But as booster deficit turned to booster glut, the American position declined in the face of international competition.[41] In April 1990, China launched the first satellite on its Long March rocket. It underpriced the United States by a substantial 40 percent and offered generous insurance against failure.[42] Once the loser to America in the race for space supremacy, Russia too began to reconfigure its space program for commercial users. Proven Russian technology and experienced launch crews provided a very attractive alternative to both the United States and European launch operations. The Russian Zenit booster could match America's mighty Titan rocket in sending some 31,000 pounds to low earth orbit, but for a quarter the cost and with only one day of pad time.[43] Commercial warfare had suddenly replaced the Cold War as the driving force of the space business. As Florida congressman Bill Nelson noted,

Table 1. Vehicle Operations, 1994

	Delta II	Atlas-Centaur	Titan IV	Ariane	Proton[a]	Shuttle
LEO[b] payload (lbs)	11,000	14,500	39,000	17,000	43,000	65,000
Launch cost ($ million)	50–70	70–100	350	70	—	500–700
Ground crew	300	300	1,000	100	50	hundreds
Pad time (days)	23	55	90	10	hours	30

Source: John Mintz, "Launching a Drive for Federal Help," Washington Post, January 12, 1994.
[a] Proton is the workhorse Russian rocket launched from Baikonur since 1965.
[b] LEO = low earth orbit.

"The sale of one commercial launch by a U.S. company is the equivalent of the import of 10,000 Toyotas."[44]

In the face of international competition, American ELVs had to become "cheaper and more efficient."[45] A new Atlas, using a first-stage booster derived from the older Atlas G and a Centaur for its upper stage, began flying in 1989. It was upgraded to a second-generation vehicle, Atlas II, which could be launched to highly inclined orbits.[46] A new Titan IV could boost nearly 48,000 pounds to the same orbits that the shuttle flew.[47] It was also useful for geosynchronous military satellites placed in orbit at 22,300 miles above the earth, and for NASA's own deep-space probes.[48] Though Titan remained too expensive for commercial launches, Delta's compact size, low cost, and high reliability made it popular in this market.[49] Upgrades in the 1990s significantly lowered the cost per pound of launching payloads aboard Delta.[50] By 1994, newer Deltas had dropped the price to the $3,000–$5,000-per-pound range, compared with some $10,000–$20,000 per pound for Titan.[51]

KSC's contribution to the quest for a more competitive American launch business was to automate ELV launch and ground operations, reducing labor needs.[52] This was part of a broader effort to develop Advanced Launch System (ALS) technology, which was expected to help lower the cost of space access significantly. Implied here were "significant cultural changes in the design and operations philosophy" of launching.[53] Driving down launch costs meant cooperation between vehicle designers, satellite suppliers, and payload operators at KSC. New vehicle designs would provide boosters with greater lifting power. In turn, more powerful rockets would eliminate many of the size and weight constraints that had forced payload designers to cut the weight and shape of their cargo to fit the rockets. With those limitations removed, payload engineers would be able to use conventional rather than exotic lightweight materials and simplify their satellites and scientific instruments. Greater power, better design, and new materials were expected in turn to reduce the time for testing and integrating the cargo into the rocket at KSC.[54]

NASA's contracts with rocket builders allowed KSC personnel to follow the fabrication process of the core vehicle and its adaptations, and to participate in testing and verification. Private aerospace firms supplied the basic vehicle NASA would use for a mission. But for each unique scientific or exploratory payload, special options and adaptations were needed. KSC engineers maintained sufficient insight, knowledge, and expertise to understand the hardware and software, so they could monitor construction and customization. But they did not do any of the hands-on work. Instead, through close cooperation, contractor and customer jointly figured out what was needed. As contactors saw it, they benefited from this cooperative relationship with KSC when they worked with non-NASA customers as well.[55] Thus, while KSC removed itself from much of the ELV work it had traditionally performed, the flow of information, experience, and knowledge between government and business continued, as it had for decades, though under a new organizational structure and operational philosophy.

Privatization may have been the agenda of the Reagan and Bush administrations, but it would require government work to make ELVs competitive. Teams from KSC were asked to design standard cargo interfaces, which would allow for smooth integration of vehicles, their consignments, and ground support equipment. KSC engineers carried out research on fairing designs to accommodate a range of payloads and missions. Operations engineers worked to minimize the time from a payload's delivery to KSC until it was ready to be loaded on a vehicle and launched. Other research aimed to develop standard adapters for payloads and to perform analysis of missions and operations in the search for greater efficiency.[56]

Even with all this help, though, America's aerospace firms could not stem the loss of market share to overseas competitors in the early 1990s. A downward spiral was feared, in which the United States, lacking sufficient economies of scale to price its launch services competitively, would lose more business, pushing operating costs still higher.[57] U.S. aerospace firms thus sought protection against France, China, and other nations. They argued, correctly, that those nations had benefited from generous government subsidies. The competing nations countered, also correctly, that U.S. launch facilities and rockets had benefited from significant military help since the 1950s. Both the U.S. military and NASA, moreover, continued to launch exclusively with U.S. hardware.[58]

Technology was expected to come to the rescue of U.S. firms. Policy makers pinned hopes on an ambitious project, a New Launch System (NLS). It was really a comprehensive plan for space access in the 1990s that included both the shuttle and ELVs. A November 1992 report of the Space Policy Advisory Board recommended a national space transportation architecture built around a "family" of advanced vehicles.[59] Modular in design, they would have the capacity to lift 20–50,000 pounds into low earth orbit. Another vehicle derived from the same core design and sharing components would be able to lift 135,000 pounds into orbit.[60] The shuttle would still fly, focused on safety and reliability (and, somehow, cost effectiveness too), but it would be used only for missions requiring a human presence or where national security or another compelling reason was present. Eventually, it would give way to the new family of advanced vehicles.

This bold plan was never enacted, however. With the 1992 election of Bill Clinton, military budgets were scaled back, undercutting a key source of funding for the new vehicles project. The Soviet Union, silent partner in NASA's growth over four decades, had disintegrated, and with it much of the original military impetus behind the space program. Clinton followed his predecessors in pushing a commercial agenda, particularly the movement of ELVs to contractors. He also retained Daniel Goldin, the NASA administrator named by George Bush just before he left the White House. Goldin came from TRW, where he headed the company's space and technology group. His appointment reaffirmed the shift toward a private-sector emphasis in NASA policy.[61]

A forceful manager, Goldin would end up as the longest-serving NASA administrator. Though a man of many talents, he also had an abrasive personality. He cut off those who challenged him and did not suffer fools gladly. Like many such personalities, he rarely saw a problem that he did not want to solve. But he also believed that he understood what NASA needed and what budget politics would permit. Following the decade-old direction of national policy, Goldin sought to streamline NASA operations and instill more private-sector efficiency. As part of that policy, Goldin concentrated functions and resources in those NASA centers best suited to them. With its long history of ELV testing and launching, KSC became the "lead center" for ELVs. But Goldin also picked up on criticisms of KSC operations. The 1992 Advisory Board report, for example, found that KSC still used too many operational concepts dating back to the Apollo days, resulting in a delay between the arrival of a booster and payload at the Cape and their liftoff that was unacceptably long in a tough competitive market.[62] To be sure, some of the lag stemmed from the extra testing required of rockets derived from military hardware. But with plans for improved ELVs in the works, Goldin pushed KSC to revise its launch operations and organization once more.

It was assumed that new technology would allow more efficient testing and checkout and smoother integration of payloads. As it turned out, for all the technical progress, the sort of radical shift led by revolutionary new technology that Goldin predicted never quite materialized. Instead, what carried over into the Goldin years was an abiding faith that private-sector contracting would promote efficiency.

Privatizing the Shuttle

The space shuttle, remarked KSC director Robert Crippen, "takes a lot of tender loving care," and "TLC costs money."[63] The lessons of *Challenger* were clear. Care and safety would have to come first. But the shuttle had been built on the promise of many flights per year and a fast turnaround. It had been built to provide cheap access to space. Where did those original goals now stand? During the first years after return to flight, there was still hope that a shuttle replacement, a next-generation launch vehicle, would provide the answers. Designed with rapid turnaround in mind and taking advantage of more standardized payloads, a second-generation reusable would achieve the efficiencies unobtainable by the original shuttle. But in the end, there was neither the political will nor the money to build such a vehicle.[64] Change and improvement would have to come from within, incrementally, using the same basic technology.

Accordingly, the 1990s saw a radical change in the operational logic and economics of the shuttle. If before *Challenger* the driving philosophy of shuttle operations had been to launch, launch, launch, now it would be to understand the nature of the task, do a better job at safety, and work smarter. Some 35 percent of NASA's budget, almost $5 billion a year, went to shuttle operations. A review of shuttle work in the 1980s showed that recurrent operations were by far the largest expense of flying the ship, not replacement parts or the occasional upgrade of hardware. Ground operations alone accounted for 24 percent of the bill for a flight.[65] Lowering shuttle costs meant reducing the worker-hours spent on turnaround, doing more with less. With tired workers cited as a safety hazard by the Rogers Commission, turnaround times nearly tripled in the first flights after *Challenger*. But once it was clear that the shuttle could fly safely, interest in operating it efficiently revived.[66] There would have to be new technology, new management techniques, new methods of operations, and new incentives to bring costs down.

NASA's strength had always been in the field rather than at headquarters, but this organizational structure tended to pit center against center. The Johnson Space Center managed shuttle missions, while Kennedy managed shuttle processing. In the Apollo years, NASA headquarters had tried to play a coordinating role, but Goldin's philosophy of lead centers required that the individual NASA installations figure out for themselves how to work together. The appointment of Robert Crippen to head KSC in 1994 reflected this desire to tear down institutional walls. A former shuttle astronaut, Crippen had previously worked at JSC before moving on to the Marshall Space Flight Center and spending time at NASA headquarters. Even with equipment designed and built elsewhere, Crippen noted, it was at the Cape that "the rubber hits the road."[67] He would help to remind the other parts of NASA that KSC people were the real experts in operations.

Joining Crippen in this effort was another transferee from Johnson, Jay Honeycutt. His appointment to STS Management and Operations at KSC, was, like Crippen's, designed to bridge the gap between mission and operations. Honeycutt had started his career at the Redstone Arsenal, then moved to the Johnson Space Center as a flight engineer. After a stint at NASA headquarters and a second one at Johnson as a manager in the Shuttle Program Office, he returned to headquarters in the National Space Transportation System Program Office after the *Challenger* accident. He thus brought with him the traditions of program management from his time in projects offices at JSC and headquarters, as well as the tradition of contractor management that was part of the Houston heritage. Honeycutt's background fit well with the goal of streamlining operations by relying more on the private sector.

As head of shuttle operations at KSC, Honeycutt inherited an organization that had strengthened significantly since the return to flight in 1988. Up through *Challenger*, the office had included quality assurance and surveillance branches but lacked the key component of vehicle engineering. Processing control for the vehicle was handled in other KSC directorates, which were organized along systems, functional, and disciplinary lines. Launch Support Services (which went beyond shuttle work) managed testing, logistics, site operations, facilities operations, and modifications. Launch and Landing Operations included the flow directors working on the orbiters, and other integrative work that brought the shuttle together with the payload.

The post-*Challenger* reorganization returned to the strong launch director tradition of the Apollo program. Under Honeycutt in the STS Management and Operations Directorate were now a chief engineer and a launch director. Below them was a new shuttle operations director, who coordinated the main work functions on the vehicle, including flow processing, testing, landing, and integration of payloads into the shuttle bay. Project control functions also came to STS Management and Operations. Most important, so did a budget.[68]

After return to flight, it was expected that the shuttle would fly about once a month. Budgets and personnel were keyed to this level. But in 1988 some 1.3 million person-hours were still required to prepare for a launch,

SHUTTLE OPERATIONS AT KSC

11-1. The shuttle was to provide "airline-like operations." This artist's conception vastly underestimates the work of preparing the vehicle for launch.

11-2. Similarly fanciful assumptions about low-cost operations and simplicity marked early conceptions of the ground equipment needed to service the orbiter.

11-3. The same underestimate of work requirements can be seen in assumptions about payload processing.

and that was at four flights per year. Tight schedules were met through overtime and multiple shifts. With budgets under pressure and hiring limited, the shuttle would clearly have to make do with less, without sacrificing quality or safety. The only option was reducing the time it took to process the vehicle. Improving processing efficiency was Honeycutt's first goal.

Images from the 1970s tell a fascinating story of how the designers of the shuttle envisioned processing and operations. Artists' conceptions show men in hardhats holding out plans while the spacecraft sits in front of an airplane hangar on a gleaming runway. Workers move up and down on lifts to prepare the vehicle and load its cargo. Other drawings depict the inside of the orbiter payload bay and the processing facility. A handful of workers stand on a small platform overlooking the bird while wires run from a few pieces of equipment to the vehicle to carry out tests. In another image, an overhead crane lifts the cargo in place with a few workers in attendance. If only artists' images and perhaps intended just for public relations, these pictures nonetheless illustrate the wide gulf that separated the designers' conception of the mundane work of preparing and processing from the complex reality.[69] Though the tremendous effort needed to prepare and fly the first shuttles quickly ended any flirtation with this fantasy, only in the 1990s did

11-4. Jay Honeycutt (*left*) substantially revised shuttle operations at KSC before becoming Center director.

engineers finally begin to come to grips with the fact that processing a space vehicle was every bit as complicated and required every bit as much effort and ingenuity as designing it.

Taking a "35,000-foot" view of the problem, Honeycutt sought to balance the two technical cultures that comprised the shuttle program. Engineering director Bob Lang was responsible for assuring that everything conformed to the exacting technical and engineering standards required. On these matters he had a "51% vote."[70] But his role was to support Bob Sieck, Honeycutt's right-hand man for shuttle processing. Operations would lead and engineering would support, an absolute necessity if the goal was to streamline operations. "Historically, engineering and operations tend to get a little bit grindy sometimes," Honeycutt noted, with the operations people closely attuned to schedule and budget and the engineers most concerned with following correct practice. Honeycutt was recognizing that the technical knowledge of operations stemmed not from the plans of the designer but from the experience of the operators. You had to have the right equipment, to be sure, but you also had to understand it, know how it worked, and have confidence in its performance. These could only come from operational experience.

With the form straightened out, Honeycutt could now turn to practice. The overall goal was to find and correct bottlenecks in the schedule, to allocate a limited pool of labor as efficiently as possible, and to understand where one part of the process of preparing the shuttle affected or conflicted with another. Before, KSC had tended to throw people at the schedule problem, a practice that might well lead to tired workers and unanticipated delays. There was no more labor to throw at the problem now, and a clear understanding of the overall schedule would actually improve safety by reducing any incentive to move too quickly to make up lost time.

It had been two decades since NASA engineers first sat down at the drafting table to work on the shuttle. Even if the basic vehicle configuration was going to remain the same, there had been improvements in technology that could be used to the advantage of operations. The shuttle was part of a vast technical system that stretched well beyond the orbiter's skin. Changes in even the remote branches of this system could affect key aspects of shuttle operations.

Data processing, for example, remained one of the highest-cost items on shuttle missions. Individual parts of the launch process had evolved their own computer programs. Between 1970 and 1990, data processing technology of all sorts had undergone a tremendous revolution. Rewriting cumbersome old software and providing workers with better documentation on the various data systems offered plenty of avenues for improvement.[71] Moving from old mainframe computers to networks and developing new software that could integrate existing programs while allowing decision makers access to common databases improved the flow of information.[72] Other changes came with new automated scheduling software, planning tools, and expert systems.[73]

One stinging criticism of KSC by the Rogers Commission was the lack of spare parts on-site. This had led to extensive cannibalization to fit out one vehicle at the expense of the next. Though the commission could identify no specific safety-related issue, cannibalization nonetheless was seen as inherently risky, as well as slow and inefficient.[74] It would be cheaper and faster in the long run to have a well-stocked site on the Cape for needed parts, rather than sending repair work back to Rockwell's California plant. In the early history of the shuttle, most of the emphasis and money had gone to building the vehicle and meeting the schedule. Previous NASA experience had been to build, shoot, and throw away, as with the Saturn and ELV boosters. But the orbiter consisted of hundreds of thousands of parts that periodi-

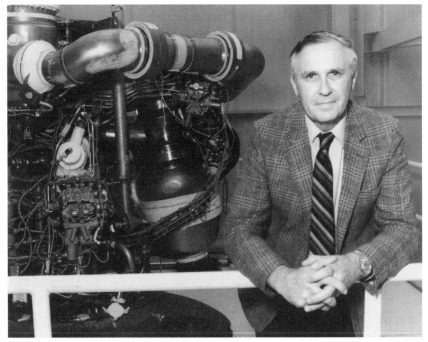

11-5. Lee Solid of Rocketdyne, the famed rocket engine builder, spent much of his career at Cape Canaveral, spanning the Mercury through shuttle eras.

cally wore out and needed replacement. Now there was time to think about stocking replacements, particularly in light of the critique by the Rogers Commission.[75] But now it might also be too late to make up for lost time.

With no new shuttles being built, Rockwell had shut down its production line. Contractors continued to service their equipment, but this work was not highly profitable. How long they would or could do it remained uncertain. KSC thus began to transfer the technical knowledge of shuttle parts to its own facility, commonly called the Depot. There technicians learned how to carry out repairs on a variety of different parts from different makers. This saved significant time in waiting for replacements or repairs from faraway factories. Perhaps even more important, it gave processing workers a ready supply of smaller parts, which actually constituted the bulk of replacement work, rather than big systems like the engines.

Before *Challenger*, there had been some twenty-five cannibalizations per flow; after, the number dropped below two.[76] Substantial time and labor was saved in doing about three-quarters of shuttle repairs on-site. The Depot thus eliminated a choke point in the flow schedule, though hopes for making KSC a center for NASA logistics were frustrated. The Depot aside, there was no single focal point for logistics within the shuttle program, and most logistics functions remained housed in the separate organizations for the orbiter, solid rocket boosters, and external tank. Potential economies through consolidation of common parts and materials in one place never materialized.[77]

Since much shuttle processing involved removing and inspecting parts, anything that reduced human handling here also had the potential to save time. Infrared inspection of electrical panels, digital images of tile gaps, acoustical, laser, microwave, and other noninvasive methods of orbiter in-

11-6. More maintenance work shifted to KSC as logistics and repair facilities allowed on-the-spot servicing of crucial parts such as the shuttle main engines.

spection were all tried.[78] By and large, though, radical improvements, such as robotic tile repair, generally proved impossible. Much still had to be done by hand. Streamlining labor-intensive processes, therefore, became the main avenue for further efficiency. Even seemingly small changes here could pay significant rewards, as when the shuttle engine shops were moved out of the VAB. The VAB had been built for an earlier generation of rocket technology. Despite its size, some tight spots allowed the big engines only a few inches of clearance. Wiping out a shuttle engine meant a $50 million bill. Engine work now went to an annex next to the Orbiter Processing Facility, which had new equipment for easier handling. The move also brought engine and orbiter refurbishment next to each other.[79] Similar changes were made in payload handling, including a new canister crate to rotate payloads from the vertical to the horizontal. This work too had been done in the VAB before, forcing payloads to compete with the booster and tank jobs for use of the big crane.

Other improvements came through identifying flow bottlenecks or uncovering poorly planned or designed work practices.[80] It had long been a hope of shuttle observers that the procedures and lessons of the airline industry could streamline operations. Under NASA administrator Goldin's "faster, better, cheaper" philosophy, private industry was to infuse the space agency with a new attitude toward efficiency. Accordingly, KSC engineers began benchmarking their work to the performance standards of industry and military programs. It was ironic in a way that the military should serve as NASA's benchmark, for even skeptics of the space program in the Apollo era had compared it favorably to the military in terms of staying on time and within budget.[81] As it turned out, in fact, most of the key techniques for improving shuttle operations did not come from outside. Rather, they came from experience, and from reflecting on that experience with what was really a unique vehicle.

It might seem that, given the number of rockets already launched from the Cape, KSC managers would have quickly developed a good sense of how to schedule processing activities. But preparing the orbiter, solid rockets, tank, and payload, bringing them all together at the correct time, testing the components both individually and as a system, was an enormous task. Pre-STS experience was certainly of value, but one could not simply extrapolate from the era of ballistic rockets to the shuttle. The shuttle's reusable nature added a level of difficulty not present in earlier programs, when preparations for each vehicle were done just once. Improvements in shuttle work mostly derived from shuttle experience. In the early years, when learning was more like research, there had been little time to study the work flow carefully. With *Challenger* and its aftermath, most of the effort went to returning to flight and assuring safety. Now it was time for an intensive study of shuttle processing work.

One of the first things Honeycutt noticed when he arrived at KSC was a tendency of different units in the shuttle program to schedule work without a clear understanding of how they were affecting the overall timetable. Directorate managers often saw no problem in accepting "parallel" assignments, meaning tasks that could be done alongside the main flow of duties needed to get an orbiter ready. The assumption was, work is work, and as long as it was not in the "serial" path to completing orbiter processing, it should be done. An admirable ethic, the tradition nonetheless cut into KSC's limited budget and personnel resources. Center directorates tended to schedule work independently of each other. The result was that if an engineer was working on shuttle hydraulics, the tile crew had to lay its tools down until the hydraulics work was completed. When the vehicle left one station, it was also common for some "open paper," or unfinished items, to travel with it. This "traveling paper" meant more leftover work to do at each subsequent stage, further degrading the processing timetable. Honeycutt instead insisted on an integrated schedule. Coordinating the various tasks as they came together in the schedule ensemble would permit a smoother, faster work flow and consume fewer resources.

One of the difficult things about any schedule is the simple fact that first things must be done first and second things second, but there is no guarantee that each step will always take the same amount of time. "Choke point," "bottleneck," "critical path," and "long pole" are all terms engineers use to describe the way schedules clog up and grind work to a halt. No one quite had a handle on how long it took for each task and how each task fit into the overall calendar. Honeycutt and his top engineers sat down and reviewed every procedure. They then assigned someone to each and gave that person a mandate to improve. The shuttle went through some 1.25 million steps between landing and launch, which were still taking about 1.25 million person-hours. With three shifts, seven days a week, and 10 percent or more overtime it was just possible to get the job done, but each orbiter flow was like "running on the beach with a backpack."[82] The goal was now a 30 percent reduction in labor time for each "bit size" chunk of work.

How would it be possible to squeeze out some 30 percent of the labor time? "It wasn't rocket science," Honeycutt later quipped.[83] He and Lang and Sieck, along with the top Lockheed manager at KSC, Dan Patterson, called in the engineers individually and asked them what they were going to do to meet the goal. The first few hemmed and hawed and then declared that it would not be possible. They were sent back and told to "try again." Pretty soon the message got around. The acceptable answer was "here's how we can," not "here's why we can't." This might seem a harsh approach to management, but actually, as Honeycutt saw it, he was relying on those who knew their jobs best to tell him what should be done. The engineers and technicians in each area understood the work better than any top manager. If anyone could figure out how to improve efficiency, they could. All Honeycutt and his team were doing was focusing them on that goal and holding their feet to the fire. Pretty soon, people began coming before Honeycutt's review board with specific suggestions and requests. They could achieve the goal if they had this or that piece of equipment, or if they could change this or that procedure first. This was exactly the right response, for it allowed the senior managers to see where the critical bottlenecks were occurring and why. From the bottom up came the needed knowledge of how to improve shuttle operations.

One of the important features of Honeycutt's tenure as head of shuttle operations was that he had control of his own budget. Previously, the budget for the shuttle was controlled at the program level, located at JSC. Now there was a budget at KSC to buy a piece of equipment if it would help process the vehicle faster. Anything that did not directly affect the orbiter itself Honeycutt could approve. This independent source of funds allowed him to cut across the basic functional structure of the Center organization and focus resources on the integrated task of processing. When, for example, engineers told him that a payload canister crane would assist processing, Honeycutt released $6 million from his office to buy it. He did not have to persuade another office to spend its money on equipment it might see as unnecessary.

In his STS Management and Operations Directorate, Honeycutt also added a small group of young engineers to work as an operations analysis detail. They were mandated to study and suggest new ways of working. This sort of industrial engineering had never been part of KSC, or indeed of NASA in general. If it existed in the space program at all, it was at the contractors' manufacturing plants. KSC did not really have an assembly line, but many of the maintenance and processing operations involved repeated movements or tasks, similar to assembly-line work. For example, one of the things that the industrial engineering group recommended was abandoning a long-standing test, the dew point measurement. In the days when shuttle tile work had been done in the un-air-conditioned VAB, engineers determined that condensation could collect on the orbiter surface while tile was being installed. Moisture weakened the tile bond, creating a potentially dangerous situation. Technicians were required to take a reading to see if the vehicle surface was damp before completing the bonding. After shuttle tile work migrated to the air-conditioned OPF, technicians found that they never had a condensation problem. Yet requirements called for performing the test just the same. Honeycutt's industrial engineers quickly saw that the test was now unnecessary. There is no better way to increase efficiency than cutting out useless work. A discussion with shuttle program engineers at JSC began. The test took only a couple of minutes, responded the program engineers; why not keep it? But from the viewpoint of work flow, those few minutes, multiplied over hundreds or thousands of tiles, could mean a significant slowdown in processing. Eventually the test was abandoned.

The incident revealed something important about the nature of work in the space program. Most procedures had not been written with overall work flow or processing in mind, but to meet a specific engineering standard or performance need. Procedures were rarely reviewed if they involved only a small allocation of time or money, even though, from the standpoint of efficiency, a small matter could have significant ramifications. Safety was frequently used as a justification for retaining such procedures. But as the dew-point debate showed, more testing did not necessarily increase safety, and it could certainly slow down work. Indeed, drawing on studies from military programs, industrial engineers at KSC noted that each operation performed on the vehicle subtracted from safety a little bit, by increasing wear and tear on components or by introducing a new risk simply in performing the test. Contrary to expectations, the same things that increased efficiency usually enhanced safety as well. This was a rather different view from that taken by the Rogers Commission investigating *Challenger*. There the recommendations had been to do more, test more, check more. This was seen as the way to increase quality and safety. But now there was a counter position, one that preserved safety by also streamlining work.

This emerging alternative point of view called into question some of the space program's founding managerial traditions. Since the beginning, a powerful assumption had been that engineers, particularly systems engineers, were the key decision makers and sources of knowledge on how to do things. They managed the technical interfaces, and thus orchestrated the specialized knowledge of functional experts through a mixture of performance, budget, and schedule criteria. That might be fine in the development phase of a project. But when work efficiency became important, so did the hands-on, often tacit knowledge of the technicians doing the work. Engineers had to get down to the shop floor and see things from the technicians' perspective, as they had during the early days of rocket launching at the Cape, when small teams working in a badgeless world did everything.

As Tim Barth, one of the young engineers Honeycutt brought into his operations analysis unit, noted, this approach was very similar to the methods long admired in Japanese factories by management consultants. Technicians and line workers did not simply carry out instructions and perform to specifications written and controlled by engineers; they provided a source of information and experience that went back to the engineers, who then modified technology, work, and product design accordingly. Though there was a temptation for the engineer to step back and do a cost-benefit analysis before recommending a change flowing up from the floor, Barth discovered that, for the most part, formal cost-benefit analysis cost more than it was worth. A lot of progress could be made simply by trusting the technicians, who knew the shuttle and the work process intimately from day-in-day-out experience. The engineer's job was to verify and assure that the suggestion did not interfere with other performance or safety requirements.

Indeed, Honeycutt began to ask engineers to think of themselves as serving a customer—the technician. This was a radical reversal of the hierarchy. Usually the systems engineer in charge thought of everyone else as working for him. But if one considered the main objective—getting the work done as quickly and efficiently as possible—then it made sense to look down the hierarchy for the true customer. All the work done above the shop floor, all the logistics, all the ground service hardware really existed to "serve" the men and women who finally put their hands on the vehicle.

Implied in this new relationship between engineer and technician was a greater degree of trust. Each hardware deviation, for example, required approval by the prime contractor or builder of the part. When something broke on the floor, work stopped, an engineer wrote up a deviation to procedure, and then everyone waited for approval from the prime contractor, who might be on the West Coast, three time zones away. Once the contractor had signed off, the deviation went to the Shuttle Program Office in Houston. It could be two or three days before all the signatures were in order. After much hard work, Honeycutt got the contractors and the Johnson Space Center to agree that they would review deviations simultaneously rather than serially. More important, he pushed hard for a policy of "assume you are going to accept it." This subtle change meant getting other centers and organizations to put their faith in the field engineers at KSC, something that design engineers had always had trouble doing. In turn, KSC engineers would be listening carefully to what their technicians told them. Such trust could make for greater efficiency. Honeycutt's long experience at Johnson and his time at headquarters may have been crucial in brokering this redrawing of assumptions. Gradually NASA was coming to invest more confidence in its operational arm, and this in turn boosted the confidence of the men and women working at the Cape.[84]

Effecting a total change in shuttle operations was beyond the power of the industrial engineering group. They could build capabilities, seed ideas, support innovation. Most important, they provided an alternative perspective on the nature of the problem that KSC and, by extension, the shuttle program really faced. Work flow and efficiency, shop-floor experience, and trust of those doing the work could now have a place alongside systems engineering, analysis, and technical specifications. Some of their influence came through published research, though more valuable were the little tweaks in procedures that took place in practice. In providing an outlet for this sort of thinking, the hope was that similar sorts of industrial engineering groups would emerge among the contractors doing the processing.[85]

SFOC

By the mid-1990s, the STS Management and Operations Directorate at KSC had introduced substantial changes, but now there were questions as to how much progress was possible. Studies showed that shuttle processing would always be limited by the design of the vehicle. The orbiter simply had not been built with processing as a primary concern. Radical changes to the vehicle were extremely expensive, and even minor retrofitting was difficult. Changes to one system or subsystem would impact others, driving up the cost.[86] The next step in efficiency, now argued some members of NASA, was a new approach to contracting. Former JSC director Chris Kraft saw in revamping contracting the best hope of getting "an operational vehicle at a reasonable price."[87] More work would have to be done by private-sector firms.

Although contractor workers had replaced civil servants in many day-to-day activities, technical control of launch operations still remained with the civil servants. The tradition from the earliest days of the space program had been a government engineer supported by a contractor technician, and backed by a contractor engineer. The 1984 SPC shifted this structure from many small, specialized contracts to one comprehensive one. Consolidation saved paperwork and time, since it was easier to manage a single large prime contract than many small ones. It also increased contractor autonomy and control over more areas of work. But SPC preserved the old pattern of both government and contractor engineers supervising the preparation of a shuttle for launch.[88]

The Space Flight Operations Contract (SFOC) proposed something more radical. Like the SPC, it would consolidate many smaller contracts, some eighty in all, into one. It would also bring together vehicle processing at KSC and mission management at Johnson. Not quite everything went into the SFOC. Marshall retained responsibility for the external tank, solid rocket boosters, and space shuttle main engines. Design engineering work stayed at the centers. But all in all, it was an extremely broad and comprehensive document, worth billions of dollars to the winning firm. In the degree of autonomy given the contractor, it went beyond anything ever tried before.

The winning contractor would take full responsibility for preparing the shuttle for flight. Managers from the contractor and NASA civil servants would set the schedule, goals, and milestones jointly, but the contractor would then be free to determine the best way to carry out the job. In contrast to the SPC, with its several thousand pages of instructions and procedures, the SFOC was a scant three hundred pages long. Most technical control passed into the hands of the contractor. Incentives rather than NASA rules and regulations would drive the labor process. NASA would evaluate performance in accordance with a set of measures, or "metrics" in the parlance of the agency. To assure safety, the contractor would follow NASA guidelines and submit to NASA inspections. But quality control—inspecting work to assure it met standards—would be placed in contractor hands. Payment would be based on how well the contractor performed, with poor-quality work and missed deadlines incurring deductions. Far less approval was required in this system, so paperwork was reduced and responsibility pushed down to those actually doing the job. In that sense, SFOC followed the course already set in operations. But it added a new wrinkle: the idea that increased efficiency flowed from the dollar incentives given to a private firm.

One necessary feature of this new regime was removal of civil servants from daily operations. No longer would KSC engineers look over the shoulders of contractors, as they had under the old dual system of responsibility. You could not have "one guy holding the wrench, one guy holding the hammer," noted Jay Honeycutt.[89] Since the contractor's work was graded, he had to have his hands on all the tools; otherwise it would be impossible to measure his performance accurately. When civil servants and contractors worked together, there was a tendency for the contractor to defer to the government engineer in technical matters, knowing that NASA held the purse strings. Under SFOC, NASA still gave out the money, but now restricted its managerial role to assessing outcomes. The technical responsibilities of civil servants shifted to research and development, working on hardware, software, and processes that could both improve shuttle operations and provide a basis for handling future vehicles.

SFOC was in many ways the culmination of all the learning about vehicle processing that had taken place over the previous two decades. No contractor would have been ready to take on this responsibility when the shuttle first started flying. There were still too many unknowns. One could not simply write a contract that said, "Deliver me a vehicle ready to go at T-0."

Specific guidance was needed. By the mid-1990s, however, accumulated knowledge and experience had greatly reduced uncertainties, such as how long parts lasted before they wore out or how to do tile maintenance. There was a lot more industry knowledge as well, with consolidations bringing together expertise that formerly had been divided among several aerospace firms. In the 1980s, contractors were like doctoral students working with a NASA professor. By the time SFOC was proposed, they were more like peers in knowledge and experience, with NASA perhaps the department chair.

Necessary to the success of the new contract were new managerial skills, which KSC personnel would have to learn. This was particularly clear in the evaluation of the award fee, the crucial payment incentives meant to spur efficiency. It was as much an art as a science. Grading performance had to be done intelligently rather than rigidly. Too stringent a measure would result in wasted time and effort. As Jay Honeycutt put it, "Look, if somebody kicked a can of paint over the OPF floor, [you] don't write that up, just get it cleaned up and go on." Everything written up had to be explained. "Some poor soul has got to go off and write up a page and a half on the impact of kicking a can of paint over."[90] But if the paint spilled on a tire and work had to stop while tires were changed, then that should be noted, because it affected time and schedule.

Initially, it was assumed that the SFOC would be let by competitive bidding. Competition was limited, however, since few aerospace firms really had the capability of being the prime contractor for shuttle processing and flight. The aerospace industry itself had been consolidating with the end of big Cold War budgets in the 1990s. In 1995 Lockheed merged with Martin-Marietta to form Lockheed Martin. Rockwell had in 1967 merged with North American Aviation, becoming for a time North American Rockwell, then Rockwell International. In 1996 Rockwell was purchased by Boeing, which acquired another aerospace giant the next year, McDonnell Douglas. By the time the SFOC was ready for bidding, only two possibilities remained, Lockheed and Boeing. Rather than compete, the two formed a joint venture called United Space Alliance, and the SFOC bidding became a formality. On October 1, 1996, the contract was signed, enthusiastically supported by NASA administrator Dan Goldin. He saw it as an important part of his agenda to bring efficiency to NASA through private-sector engagement, and to meet the goal set by President Clinton of trimming back the NASA budget by the year 2000.

While Goldin was heralding a new era in Washington, though, down at the Cape, those who had spent their careers with the shuttle were troubled. Critics asked how NASA would be able to effectively monitor work if so much of the knowledge of shuttle processing was now going over to the contractor, and to an alliance of the two largest aerospace firms at that? How would civil servants be able to undertake research without hands-on experience and knowledge of the vehicle? And how would NASA train future generations of engineers if they never laid their hands on a spacecraft?

These questions reflected a strong alternative position to the contracting philosophy, one with roots in the earliest days of rocket launches. SFOC came out of the tradition of contracting practiced in the United States Air Force. Where the German rocket tradition rested on expert penetration to the details of a technology, the air force approach argued that government officials could specify what they wanted and oversee the results. This had worked well in building military hardware such as jet fighters. It had worked in the air force's own ballistic missile program. As we have seen, many of the air force techniques were brought into NASA during the Apollo program.

Many of those who objected to SFOC had started their careers following the German tradition. They valued its methodical, incremental approach to learning. They had seen how it brought together design, operations, testing, and launch, and permitted engineers to gain a deep penetration of all aspects of rocketry. This had certainly been valuable when more was unknown than known. Like the proponents of contracting, devotees of in-house expertise could point to successful examples. Indeed, the two approaches, forming a hybrid culture, had worked well at KSC in the 1960s and 1970s, and both had helped to get Americans on the moon.[91] Contract management, on the other hand, had advantages when goals were well defined, schedules were fixed, and mission success was the primary objective, rather than learning over the long run.[92] The shift to SFOC followed this logic. If the shuttle was to finally become an operational vehicle rather than a research tool, then private sector contractors, managed by civil servants, would provide greater efficiency. Government engineers would step back and concentrate on the sort of research and development work that profit-oriented firms might not have the funds or motivation to undertake. It seemed to most of NASA's top management a perfect solution to the problems of budget, operations, and schedule they had long been wrestling with.

*   *   *

Anyone who knows Jose Garcia knows him to be blunt, forceful, and passionate. He pounds the desk when he speaks, his voice shading to the South Bronx of his youth. He relishes his reputation for speaking uncomfortable truths to superiors. As a midlevel shuttle engineer, he issued one of the most controversial critiques of SFOC. Risking his career, Garcia delivered a pointed analysis of the flaws of the plan in a letter addressed to President Bill Clinton, several high-level NASA officials, and the press months before the contract signing. The day had not yet arrived when the shuttle could be treated as a routine space transport. Maybe it never would. Half of all shuttle processing was unplanned, Garcia explained. He and his fellow engineers were "charting new waters every day," finding new problems requiring innovative solutions. Echoing the words of the Rogers Commission, Garcia concluded that the shuttle was "born a research and development vehicle and . . . will die that way."[93]

The letter aroused a brief flurry of controversy. If Garcia was right, then SFOC was the wrong way to go. The only way to assure safety in a research vessel still filled with unknowns was through the existing system of checks and balances that had grown up through the matrix of responsibility shared by civil servants and contractors.[94] NASA administrator Goldin, a strong backer of private-sector control, came out of that part of the aerospace industry that did not involve human flight. Vehicles that carried humans were not, or should not be, treated like ELVs. *Challenger* notwithstanding, the shuttle had been the most reliable spacecraft ever built, with a better than 98 percent success rate, something no ELV had yet achieved. The radical change in operations and organization that SFOC implied might well undermine the very source of the shuttle's success.

Few went as far as Garcia, but many other civil servants understood his position. They resented the loss of technical control and the abolishment of a system that had served the space program well. Others wondered how they would explain to eager young engineers arriving at the Cape that they would not be putting their hands on the shuttle, but only supervising others who did. Those pushing for the SFOC saw it as fresh, outside-the-box thinking, resisted by a stubborn older generation that would not change with the times and should be replaced with new faces from the private sector. Yet, as one of the strongest proponents of the traditional approach wondered, "are green people really better than stubborn experienced people?"[95]

Garcia did not lose his job. Even today, living in retirement in the house he built with his own hands, he stands by his words. His end run around top management angered those at NASA headquarters. But in an admirable move, the agency chose to tolerate rather than punish dissent. It did, however, answer it. No doubt, Jay Honeycutt acknowledged, one learned more by doing work oneself. But was it necessary to do the work to know how it was done and whether it was done right?[96] Roy Tharpe, who did much of the work preparing SFOC, argued that you did not need to know how a valve operated to know how it should perform. "The way you manage a valve problem is no different than the way you manage an organization. If you have project management skills, you can go in and do both of those things."[97] NASA people had to give up the old "NASA has to be involved in every aspect of processing because if they aren't it isn't being done right" attitude.[98] At any point, NASA engineers would still be able to penetrate the process. But they would relinquish "100 percent surveillance" in favor of key safety and quality inspections, samples of work performed, and data from past missions to verify that things were working as they should.[99] They would provide insight, not strive for oversight, in the more routine aspects of shuttle processing.

One thing that reassured even skeptics was a strong continuity of personnel. After SFOC, many workers stayed at Merritt Island and just changed badges, preserving much knowledge and experience. Those who had worked for Rockwell or Lockheed moved to United Space Alliance (USA). Most who worked at NASA had no desire to leave, and those whose jobs became superfluous at KSC often simply transferred to the contractor. In fact, knowledge flowed both ways, with contractor personnel keen to get government jobs when they became available. With the shift from the old government pension to a portable 401k-type retirement system, such transfers became easier. A "revolving door" between government and contractors opened up in the 1990s.

Easy movement of people between the private and public sectors was seen as a strength of the new regime. That view has been criticized on the grounds that, in the past, the revolving door between industry and government has led to cozy relations between the contractor and the agency handing out the money. Supporters of SFOC, however, pointed to the advantage. Close working relationships permitted NASA personnel to control operations at key moments.[100] But some distance was still maintained. Civil servant contract managers had to be able to step in and say to their contractor counterpart, "You're my buddy, but you didn't do that right."[101] Supporters of SFOC believed that safeguards eliminated the danger of a tight NASA-contractor relationship, while preserving the advantages of a closely integrated team effort.[102] As with the move to contracting in the ELV program, SFOC would work by making NASA a "smart buyer" of services from the contractor, and establishing close interaction between user and producer.

Assessing the New Shuttle Regime

How well, then, did the new shuttle-processing regime perform? In pure dollar terms, the budget for shuttle operations came down significantly after 1991, reduced by one-third from its $4.8 billion figure by 1996.[103] During that time, the average cost of a space shuttle mission fell from $553 million to $411 million. Many measures of performance rose, especially in the years between 1991 and 1994. Better planning cut overtime. Processing changed from three shifts, seven days a week, to a more humane two shifts, five days a week.[104] Total hours spent on an orbiter flow decreased almost 50 percent, from 1.19 million to 617,000 between 1990 and 1997.[105]

Most of these improvements, however, came before SFOC. Indeed, after the contract was signed in 1996, average mission costs again rose, reaching $688 million by 1999.[106] Despite a mandate to keep the labor hours to 581,000, United Space Alliance failed eight times to meet this goal, and the hours-worked trend showed an upward projection after 1997. Some of the deterioration in performance was due to unexpected maintenance needs on big items, such as the main engines. Some was due to problems in getting payloads ready. And some simply reflected a necessary learning curve at USA. But probably the biggest reason for performance deterioration lay outside the control of KSC or its prime contractor.

After 1997, the shuttle flight rate fell from an average of seven missions to only four per year. Most of this decline was due to delays in the International Space Station. Sending the station parts into space had become the major item on the shuttle's manifest, but those missions had to wait until the hardware was ready. Fewer missions meant that the work tended to stretch out, expanding to fit the time available. Not all of this stretching was wasteful. More time, for example, could be devoted to shuttle maintenance and refurbishment.[107] Managers found, however, that fewer than six flights per year led to inefficiency in operations.[108]

When the problems associated with the low flight rate are removed, the story looks better. By the measure of workforce size, the entire decade of the 1990s showed improvement. Between 1991 and 2000, the number of shuttle contractor workers fell from 7,800 to just under 4,000.[109] While some of the decrease reflected the lower flight rate, the number of workers was decreasing some 6 percent per year even before the flight rate fell. NASA's own shuttle workforce fell from 700 to 230 between 1994 and 2000. Labor productivity rose as each processing step took less time, at least until 1998, when the number of worker hours again started upward.[110]

The more ambitious goals of NASA administrator Goldin, however, proved elusive. Goldin had proposed reducing KSC's civil servant workforce from 2,000 to 1,400 by 1998, and perhaps as low as 1,000 eventually. When Jay Honeycutt took over as KSC director in 1995, he told the administrator that even under SFOC this could not be done. Despite all the gains in efficiency, the only way to achieve such a drastic reduction in government employment would be to redefine KSC's mission. Otherwise the cuts would make it impossible for the Center to monitor safety as it was mandated to do, and would erode "core engineering skills" and technical expertise needed to carry out research. "What I can do," Honeycutt told his boss, "is go to 200 and go out to the front gate and tack a sign that says Merritt Island Launch

Facility operated for NASA by United Space Alliance."[111] A few hundred civil servants would simply manage contracts. In the end, the KSC workforce stabilized at 1,700.

All in all, a fair assessment of the results suggests that KSC, after a slow start, did revamp its operations to achieve significant efficiencies through the mid-1990s. Its embrace of industrial engineering and operational efficiency paved the way for the move to a contractor-dominated process. But the actual savings stemming from SFOC have been less consistent or impressive. Even taking into account the declining flight rate, it does not seem that the major improvements came directly from privatization.

Contrary to what believers in the private sector may have thought, the success of the new contract rested less on competition than on cooperation. Real competition ended with the creation of USA. Performance-based contracting preserved some of the features of the marketplace by giving the firm monetary incentives to improve. Yet overall it was the formation of a new "team effort" between contractors and government employees, and the open, two-way movement of knowledge, that seems the most enduring feature of the new regime. The team concept, SFOC's strongest supporters have argued, was the real source of the efficiency gain.

For KSC, though, the SFOC had one lasting impact. The Johnson Space Center, its longtime rival, became the lead center for the shuttle after the contract was signed. Although 60 percent of SFOC monies were being spent at Merritt Island, KSC personnel no longer controlled the budget as they had when processing and flight operations were under separate contracts. It was more a loss of pride than anything else, for the work still took place at KSC—indeed, more work on refurbishing and maintaining the shuttle than ever before. But it was a blow nonetheless. At the same time, it was an opportunity. Now KSC focused on developing new methods of processing vehicles, new concepts for launch, the future. And it turned its attention to what was becoming the central technology of human space flight for the year 2000, the International Space Station.

12

*
*
*

A Station in Space

In 1977, when NASA administrator James Fletcher resigned, weary after fighting six years of declining budgets, his parting words spoke hopefully of the future of human space flight. "When people see the Space Shuttle actually building things in space . . . I'm confident that you will see increased support." America, he maintained, would eventually have a station in space, a jumping-off point for a return to the moon, a permanent lunar base, even a mission to Mars. The tremendous lifting power of the shuttle would make these things possible, Fletcher concluded, "perhaps sooner than you expect."[1]

Station Politics

A space habitat had been one of the most enduring ideas of the American space program. Even before NASA was founded, Wernher von Braun had sketched designs for a space station, a necessary feature of his plans for space exploration. Von Braun's 1953 series in *Collier's* magazine gave the American public an impressive image of a toroidal station, two giant wheels joined by an axis rotating in space to create artificial gravity. The imperatives of meeting President Kennedy's deadline for the lunar mission put von Braun's space station ideas on hold. But when NASA proposed a space shuttle in the 1970s, it used as a justification the need for a vehicle that could service a habitat in space.

Although NASA had returned briefly to the space station concept with Skylab, it was the Soviet Union that was pioneering living in space in the 1970s. Having lost glory on the moon, America's Cold War rival regained some luster with its series of Salyut space stations, beginning in April 1971. When Skylab burned up in the atmosphere in 1979, the Soviet Union's space station program was still going strong. "The Soviets can be considered ahead of the U.S. in space station operations at this time," wrote the industry paper, *Defense/Space Business Daily*. NASA had "no plans, in the foreseeable future . . . to establish a space station or settlement on the lunar surface."[2] Despite Fletcher's prediction, construction of a base in space would have to wait at least another decade.

Although political realities put the U.S. government out of the space station business, commercial interests kept the idea alive. NASA officials worried publicly about America losing out on new manufacturing opportunities taking advantage of a zero-gravity environment.[3] The General Accounting Office warned that if the United States did not double or even triple its $20 million annual budget for materials processing in space, it would lose leadership to West Germany, France, and Japan as well as the Soviet Union.[4] NASA future planner Jesco von Puttkamer pointed out: "The shuttle makes money by shuttling." Flying it on extended scientific missions in space was like parking an airliner "on the runway as an overnight trailer." A far better use of this vehicle was moving people and materials to and from earth, a mission that practically required a base in orbit.[5]

Such concerns led to at least a renewed rhetorical commitment to a space station. In a July 4, 1982, speech marking the fourth landing of *Columbia*, President Ronald Reagan called for a permanent facility above the earth. It was to promote international space activity as well as private-sector investment in space-related activities.[6] NASA's Johnson and Marshall Centers would undertake design studies for this facility, while headquarters formed a task force to define its scientific, commercial, and defense functions.[7] Two years later, NASA administrator James Beggs designated the Johnson Space Center to take the lead in space station development. The orbiting habitat had finally moved from future concept to project. But the move came at a cost. Faced with austere budgets, Beggs eliminated the proposed fifth shuttle orbiter in 1985 to focus on station construction, estimated to cost $8 billion.[8]

Almost as soon as NASA attached a dollar figure to the station, it ran into trouble. The Congressional Office of Technology Assessment attacked NASA's figures, claiming that a facility meeting all proposed needs could be built for a much more modest $2 billion. Indeed, the OTA feared that NASA's budget vastly underestimated the true cost of what was being proposed, which might run as high as $30 billion by the end of the century.[9] Within a few years, NASA's own estimates of cost rose as well. A compromise and a close vote in Congress gave NASA approval to proceed with phase one of a modified station for some $12 billion. In June 1988 Senator William Proxmire tried to kill it by slashing its budget. The cut would have left the project in caretaker status, presumably until after the 1988 election when the next president could decide its fate.[10] But the station would not die. Both presidential candidates, Vice President George Bush and Gov.

Michael Dukakis, endorsed some version of the troubled project.[11] Despite the reprieve, it remained under a cloud of doubt as Congress grappled with looming budget deficits. In light of cost concerns, President Reagan invited international cooperation in the construction of what he renamed Space Station Freedom in 1988. Fourteen foreign partners signed on to contribute components valued at $8 billion, the original estimated cost of the entire station.[12] Budget worries were not over, but now there was a firm plan for building a station as an international venture.

The Battle over Ship-and-Shoot

In some respects, NASA's approach to space station development returned to its early days, before contractors came to play such a large role in the space program. Rather than having a prime contractor, NASA would issue more than four hundred advanced technology contracts and eight to ten advanced development contracts.[13] The Johnson Space Center would provide systems engineering and integration. Gerald Griffin, Johnson's director, organized station development differently from shuttle development, seeking broader participation from other NASA installations.[14] The proposed space station was to have its own power supply, provisions for future growth, and a nearly unlimited life.[15]

Despite a promise of greater involvement by other parts of NASA, it appeared that KSC would be excluded from station design, as it had with the shuttle. KSC director Richard Smith noted that his center's role seemed to involve little "beyond launching station components aboard the space shuttle" as they were delivered from contractors and other NASA centers.[16] Budget cuts and political realities once again placed operational issues on the side, as NASA put the station through a series of redesigns. Indeed, rather than giving KSC a significant role in station planning, NASA began shifting some shuttle work from Johnson to Kennedy to allow the Houston center to concentrate more of its resources on what savvy insiders understood was now the cutting-edge work of the space program. KSC would be relegated to operating the older technology of the shuttle.[17]

With most attention focused on budget, politics, and design, KSC engineers could do little more than fight to protect processing resources for a station to be delivered years in the future. In 1982 KSC issued a request for proposals to determine the best way to process and check out space station materials.[18] In 1983 the Center sought proposals for a study of computer systems to simulate and model space station operations.[19] But overall, allocations of station money to KSC remained small. In 1985 it received only $2.85 million of the project's $150 million budget, which rose to a modest

$3.2 million the following year.[20] Most of this money went for studies. With Space Station Freedom scheduled to be operational by the early 1990s, it appeared that KSC would be forced to deal with processing issues on the run.[21]

This early phase of station development reflected a resurgence of the old ship-and-shoot mentality. Johnson design engineers foresaw only brief inspections of components at the Cape before launch. Smith and others at KSC questioned this approach. Experience had shown that hardware rarely arrived at KSC ready to fly. It seemed likely that the space station would be the same. "We will need to provide increasing support for design of facilities and ground support equipment," Smith declared, even if the budget for such work had yet to move to the top of NASA's agenda.[22]

*   *   *

To Dick Lyon, the ship-and-shoot approach seemed to miss the crucial lessons of NASA history. A thoughtful, mild-mannered engineer, he had started at the Center in 1964, rising through the engineering ranks during the Apollo era to become chief of the Shuttle Project Office for Engineering Development in 1977. By 1984 he was the Center's deputy director for engineering development. As the station moved through its design phase, Lyon moved to Payload Management and Operations. With experience in both development engineering and payloads, he was uniquely positioned to appreciate what was at stake in the issue of station processing.

So long as the development centers "did not see a need for the integrated test and checkout at KSC," Lyon realized, there was no reason to expend any funds before the station was built and ready for delivery. At planning meetings Lyon heard that KSC's role would be little more than damage inspection on arrival. Center personnel would quickly and easily load station components aboard the orbiter and move the shuttle speedily to the launchpad.[23] For this work, the only significant new equipment needed was a receiving dock for inspecting components.[24]

Experience told Dick Lyon that this was wishful thinking. A 1986 in-house study of shuttle payload processing suggested that KSC in fact played five different roles in preparing cargo for launch. The study's author, James Ragusa, concluded that, rather than becoming more routine, payload processing had become more complicated over time. KSC's processing work largely reflected customer requirements, and those requirements increased with the ambition and sophistication of the payload.[25]

Close inspection of payload history revealed that only rarely had any cargo moved to launch with the ease and simplicity implied in the ship-and-shoot model. Such payloads had strict requirements, moreover. They had

12-1. Against skeptics who did not believe testing of space station components at KSC would be needed, Dick Lyon quietly prepared for the day that this "ship and shoot" approach would prove untenable.

to be capable of remaining in the orbiter for four to six weeks without any servicing. They had to require only minimal interface testing once installed in the payload bay. They had to be tolerant of changes in schedule. Only prepackaged middeck experiments and Spacelab stowage lockers had ever met such requirements.[26] They did so in good part because the experiment builders were familiar with the design and space requirements of the shuttle middeck. This was all rather different from space station elements, which were still evolving.

History had shown that as shuttle payloads increased in complexity, KSC's role in handling and preparing them grew as well. For example, when a cargo had a tighter time frame than the middeck experiments, KSC operated in a "host" mode. The customer, not KSC, did the preparation and testing, which had to be completed within five days. As the host, KSC supported customer requirements, provided facilities, developed software, and supported payload servicing. These payloads, however, still required servicing or integrated testing after installation in the orbiter.

KSC became more involved with payloads delivered between thirty and fifty days before launch. These arrived ready to go, except for customer on-site functional buildup and checkout. They were processed in "offline" mode, as the payload owner supported experiment integration, subsystem software development, and modest integrated testing. KSC then assembled the payload to launch-ready status and finished the servicing. A few partial payloads and some commercially deployed satellites were handled this way.

Other things destined for outer space required still greater work from KSC. These included satellites, Spacelab experiments, and science and application experiments mounted on a pallet. Pallet experiments ran in the payload bay while the shuttle was in orbit, or else were deployed in space from the bay and then retrieved by Remote Manipulator System (RMS). A team of KSC and customer personnel assembled these projects, performed the integrated testing, and provided servicing at the Center. The subassemblies of these more complex payloads were built up offline. During construction, however, KSC engineers performed integrated tests at test stands, on simulators, or in the orbiter. This work helped to ensure the final product met all specifications for insertion into the shuttle. Between 15 and 20 percent of these payloads had to be rescheduled to fit launch constraints or carry out mandatory modifications.

With the most complex payloads, KSC took custody of the cargo upon its arrival at the Cape. In this case the Center became the "factory" performing operations and maintenance of hardware. Customers took a secondary role, participating and observing as KSC engineers verified each flight element. Integrated testing performed to customer specifications, first with simulators and again in the orbiter, took up to forty days to complete. To ensure flight readiness, KSC personnel might have to make between a hundred and a thousand modifications to the payload.[27]

Implied in the ship-and-shoot approach was a critique of KSC payload work, one reminiscent of the criticisms leveled at the Center's approach to shuttle processing. Field engineers were taking too much time, doing more work than necessary to get hardware ready to fly. Supporters of ship-and-shoot believed that careful design of the space station would eliminate such time-consuming tasks. History suggested otherwise. In fact, KSC had been moving steadily along the payload learning curve. Modifications to Spacelab experiments, for example, fell from 324 on the first Spacelab to 123 on the third. Modifications to the Spacelab carrier itself had been reduced 72 percent. Problem reports, reflecting anomalies discovered during payload processing, fell 81 percent between the first and third Spacelab mission. Still, for all these improvements, there remained significant operational work that could not be eliminated. After some initial improvement, for example, the number of modifications needed for Spacelab experiments stopped falling.

Even with time and improvements in work efficiency, no complex payload yet had achieved the streamlined handling being proposed for the space station. The closest analogue to space station components—satellites—were still a long way off from ship-and-shoot. In fact, even with the simplest payloads, problems and anomalies never completely disappeared. To realize the processing goals for the space station, the hardware would have to arrive

12-2. Technicians prepare for installation of payloads inside the shuttle payload bay.

needing minimal handling and permit most of the integrated preflight testing to take place in the orbiter itself. The average satellite, by way of comparison, spent 116 calendar days at KSC and required some 65 workdays
to prepare. Most of this work was performed by the customer carrying out
functional tests. Only 3 percent of the time was integrated testing in the
orbiter.[28] In all, Ragusa's report concluded, it was unlikely that space station
processing would come any closer to the ship-and-shoot standard than had
other complex payloads.[29]

Ragusa's study provided KSC members of the station development team
with powerful ammunition. Why, they could now ask, should the station
be any simpler? Driven by budget constraints, however, the design centers
largely dodged the question. The years leading up to the approval of Space
Station Freedom were fraught with peril. Congress was critical of the entire
project, and Senator Proxmire, whose committee oversaw NASA's budget,
was seeking sufficient votes to kill it altogether. NASA's efforts to protect
the orbital habitat only made matters worse. It was forced to give an embar-

rassing apology to Congress when accused of illegal lobbying through an alliance it formed with its major station contractors.[30] Although the space station program survived, it would be subject to a round of budget cuts, all of which made the designers more reluctant to allocate funds for processing. Ship-and-shoot had too much political value to be abandoned, regardless of the studies offered by KSC. The big parts of the station would arrive more or less ready to fly. Integration of experiments into payload racks would be done at the design and manufacturing originating points. KSC would do minimal processing and testing work.[31]

After Congress cut the project's 1990 allocation by $400 million, NASA began looking once more at smaller, less expensive designs. Studies now revealed a station that weighed too much, drew too much power, and required extensive maintenance by astronauts working outside in space suits.[32] A redesign reduced the station's budget from a peak of $4 billion per year to a cap of $2.6 billion.[33] Congress ended 1990 by slicing another $6 billion over the next six years.[34]

In five and a half years the space station had undergone eleven major reviews. As the National Research Council observed, the "program's entire management team [has been] consumed by phasing, re-phasing, planning, replanning, rescoping and descoping a program in ceaseless variation."[35] There had, of course, been little time to address something as remote as processing, with designs still up in the air and budgets fluctuating from year to year.

Ironically, budget uncertainty actually helped with one part of the processing question. NASA's latest design doubled the number of (now smaller) modules needed to complete the American portion of the habitat, significantly reducing the amount of construction to be done in orbit.[36] Now design engineers had to consider the problem of assembly, testing, and integration on the ground. As NASA associate administrator William Lenoir stated, "In the past, we designed a space station and then worried about how to get it into orbit. Now, we've taken all the pieces and we're assembling small spacecraft."[37] Still, even this acknowledgement did not put an end to the ship-and-shoot mentality. Integration of modules was still expected to take place at the design and manufacturing centers rather than at KSC.

There was little time for KSC engineers to debate this issue as the station's future again came into doubt. Growing federal budget deficits in 1991 prompted Congress to consider cuts in the controversial project once more.[38] Senator Dale Bumpers proposed to reduce its 1992 budget from $2 billion to a meager $100 million, effectively a death sentence. Most of the money saved would be assigned to deficit reduction.[39] After the Senate rejected this and other moves to cancel the station, the House of Representatives voted for full funding, though at the cost of taking money from other NASA programs.[40]

In 1993 NASA administrator Goldin asked for yet another station re-design. Three proposals went forward. One was to create a modest facility similar to Skylab, with a single component rocketed into space. At the other extreme was the existing station design. In between lay a modified, multi-element version.[41] A team from all NASA centers assembled at Crystal City, just outside Washington, D.C., to evaluate these proposals.

Ship-and-shoot philosophies continued to predominate in the Crystal City discussion, despite objections from KSC representatives. But ground began to give way underneath the most fervent proponents of limited ground processing. A 1991 GAO report had criticized NASA's testing standards for the station, calling them fragmented and ill defined. The four NASA centers developing station components each used their own distinct testing stan-dards, which meant a piece of hardware from one center was tested to a dif-ferent standard than an adjoining piece developed at another.[42] The notion that everything could be prepared and verified at the design and assembly points now came under hard scrutiny.

KSC representatives at the Crystal City meeting were waging a careful battle on these issues, using the lessons learned from studying the history of payload processing. "You had to be a little bit tactful," recalled Steve Fran-cois, one of the participants. "If you want[ed] to be politically acceptable, you [couldn't] exactly go tell the other guy his idea doesn't make any sense."[43] There was a natural tendency for designers to seek control over the entire project, from drawing board to fabrication to operation. They thought in terms of a completed station in orbit. Whenever they were asked to redesign the facility to reduce costs, the first thing they trimmed was ground opera-tions. Driven by budget concerns, they would ignore operations and spend the money available on station components to assure they met their perfor-mance goals once in space.[44] Maybe sometime later, this logic argued, after the project was complete, Congress would allocate more money for testing and processing. By contrast, those at KSC responsible for the station were part of the payload processing directorate. They saw it as another payload to prepare for launch. Back and forth it went. Design engineers dismissed the concerns of KSC's payload group, arguing that their contractors knew how to build the station. KSC engineers reminded the designers that both the Apollo spacecraft and the shuttles had arrived unfinished. Design engineers asked to be left alone so they could focus on building the equipment. After all, they argued, if there were no components, there would be no payload processing. KSC engineers agreed, with a subtle proviso. They acknowl-edged that ship-and-shoot was the ideal, but noted that it had never been successful in practice. They would focus their energies on getting the components into space in operating condition, and be prepared "just in case" ship-and-shoot broke down.[45]

It became an unspoken strategy of the KSC members of the redesign teams to ensure that the Center had at least the minimal facilities, equipment, and personnel they needed to check station components for shipping damage, prove that the software worked, and check component interfaces.[46] Even though the philosophy expressed by the design centers remained largely ship-and-shoot, KSC knew from experience that early elements of every space project took at least a year between their arrival at the Center and the start of their space journeys. It seemed unlikely that the space station would be different.[47] If there was a problem with a station component, what should they do? Send it back to the factory or attempt to work on it? The design centers agreed this was a problem. Perhaps KSC might need a place to work on a component rather than ship it back to the factory.

Contingency planning allowed KSC engineers to prepare for the level of station processing they felt certain would be needed.[48] Eventually they reached a tentative agreement with their counterparts at the other centers. KSC would assist the component fabricators by providing facilities for them to work on their payloads when they arrived. The Center built an "inventory of capability" that said "if you need it, we're here to help you."[49] The compromise, Francois recalled, was that KSC shifted its rhetoric away from "You just bring it and we'll do the job for you." One source of resistance to greater KSC involvement was the reluctance of contractors to turn "their" hardware over to another authority. KSC modified its approach, and began to learn that it was providing a service to customers, not taking charge of the processing entirely of its own accord.[50]

This rapprochement quelled disputes over processing philosophies. If the components could be ready to go two weeks after arrival, that would be great. But if not, KSC stood ready to help the builders do what was needed, even if it took another six months on the ground. As it turned out, the minimal-preparation compromise proved wildly optimistic. Rather than a few weeks, or even six months, the first components spent a year and a half before they were ready to fly.

A New Facility?

For several years KSC had been preparing blueprints for a new Space Station Processing Facility (SSPF). In the SSPF, components could be powered up and worked on "if needed."[52] It was a long battle to get this new facility approved. Throughout the 1980s most of the Houston design team had argued that the existing Operations and Checkout (O&C) building, which had served the Apollo spacecraft many years before, could be remodeled for the space station.[53] This approach, adaptation of existing facilities in times of lean budgets, had been used with the shuttle. But for the station, KSC argued, something different was going to be needed. During both Apollo and the shuttle, components had arrived from different contractors working for design centers. The design engineers could then test the components to their limits, and afterwards KSC engineers would ensure that the various components worked together as a system. With the space station, the need for integrated testing was likely to be much greater. Components would be arriving not only from Johnson, Goddard, and Marshall but from the international partners as well. The old O&C was not built for this sort of extensive work. It could handle only a few components at a time. It would be better in the long run to construct a new facility from the ground up. After some twenty-three presentations, KSC managers finally convinced NASA headquarters of the logic of this approach.[54]

Nonetheless, the SSPF still remained a bone of contention. "There were times we had big arguments," Shannon Bartell recalled. "I can remember people standing up in meetings saying, 'Why in the world do you need such a big building?'" KSC would never fill an SSPF that was so large it could contain 180 average-size homes.[55] With every budget cut it seemed that the new building was destined for the chopping block. Following the political trend in the Reagan years toward greater private-sector involvement, KSC sought advice from bankers, real estate investors, and aerospace companies on private financing of the facility.[56] KSC considered having a contractor build it and then lease or sell it back to the Center.[57] As it turned out, the Bush administration relaxed some of the space commercialization policies, making federal financing of an SSPF possible. It became the biggest KSC construction project since the Apollo days.[58]

During the key design meeting in Crystal City, participants had debated and analyzed various approaches to constructing a space station. Favored by KSC people was the Modular Buildup Concept, with a Combined Test Team to manage all testing.[59] Under this plan, selected KSC and contractor personnel would be assigned to each space station component as part of a factory test team. The entire group, factory testers included, would then move Merritt Island with the flight hardware to become the nucleus of the launch site processing team.[60] But the final report on the modular buildup concept ignored KSC's proposal for testing.[61] Instead flight element verification would be performed by the prime contractor. Checkout would take place in orbit.[62] No element of the space station, according to this perspective, would long remain at KSC. After perfunctory tests each would be launched quickly into space, where the final testing could be done. Once again, the old ship-and-shoot approach came to the surface.

Now the Crystal City group debated stopping construction of the SSPF. There would still be time to modify the O&C building to receive the components, saving valuable dollars for the space station program. "The good news," recalled Steve Francois, "was that it [SSPF] was half built." It was hard to make the case that shutting down a half-finished facility would save money. At Crystal City, Francois touted the SSPF's versatility as justification for moving forward. Because of the generic nature and flexibility of the work stands, any payload could be processed there. The SSPF would be useful even if the space station were eventually cancelled. This argument saved the facility once more.[63]

The Spacelab Experience

The ongoing debates over station processing reflected once again the long-standing conflict in NASA between design and operations. We have already seen how this conflict played out with the shuttle through the mid-1990s, and indeed tailed back to the Apollo years. But there was more direct and recent experience that KSC engineers looked to as they participated in discussions of space station processing. During the early shuttle years, the Center had checked out and launched Spacelab. Spacelab would influence the building of the Space Station Processing Facility as well as provide hands-on training and experience for engineers who worked on station processing.

Developed by the European Space Agency, Spacelab was a cylindrical laboratory mounted inside the shuttle's vast payload bay. While in orbit, scientists, designated on the shuttle crew list as payload specialists, performed microgravity experiments inside Spacelab. The shuttle with Spacelab aboard was in effect a temporary space station where research work could be carried out in a "shirtsleeve" environment. In this respect, it was much like the laboratory environment being designed for the space station.

From a processing point of view, Spacelab offered useful analogies to what was expected with the space station. Payload engineers at KSC checked, assembled, and integrated several large elements or modules. Experiment integration teams configured experiments to fit into the container. Then the assembled Spacelab went into the shuttle processing flow and moved via the horizontal canister transporter to the OPF where it was put aboard an orbiter. Orbiter and Spacelab next moved to the VAB for stacking, and then to the pad for launching. Upon the orbiter's return to earth, KSC teams removed or "deintegrated" the laboratory from the orbiter. Unlike other sci-

12-3. Like surgeons in an operating room, technicians ready Spacelab for flight aboard *Columbia*.

entific packages that used the shuttle to reach space, such as satellites and probes to the planets, Spacelab returned to earth for another mission.[64]

Could Spacelab serve as a model for how space station processing in the SSPF would work? It seemed to KSC people it could. In fact, with what they had learned, they believed they could do significantly better. To check out Spacelab and its experiments, KSC engineers had remodeled the O&C building, installing stands that were bolted to the floor and configured to fit the modules and pallets being tested.[65] Those who had worked in this environment quickly noted a key difference between Spacelab and what was being proposed for the station. Spacelab had standard configurations, but no two space station components were the same. Each had a different footprint and required a different service configuration. The O&C building had been built with hard stands designed for specific components. The SSPF would have to be modular and generic, so that any redesign of the space station would not significantly affect the design of the processing facility. For larger components, two or more test stands could be brought together to provide a bigger footprint. Power, plumbing, and other utilities would run through the floor and could be connected to any station configuration through flex hoses. The lessons of Spacelab argued for a configurable SSPF, which could "handle any flight hardware that came into it." Even the floor would be "clean," so that station components could be moved on hovercraft-like air-bearing pallets.[66]

Spacelab provided one more important lesson. With the shuttle, as we have seen, civil service personnel turned over hands-on work to contractors. The one exception to this general rule was the Level IV Experiment Integration Group, who did the sensitive work of placing experiments in Spacelab. It was not exactly planned this way. Originally NASA had assigned Spacelab experiment integration to the Marshall Space Flight Center. After some debate, the Level IV work went to KSC. It made little sense to test and integrate the experiments at Marshall and then move them to the Cape, argued KSC's Bill Jewell. The potential for damage in the move meant that many tests would have to be duplicated upon arrival at the launch site.[67] But having got the work, the Center found it lacked the budget to contract it out, as the prevailing privatization philosophy would otherwise have dictated. At that time, recalled Enoch Moser, civil service engineers were considered part of the infrastructure. They were there anyway, so it took no additional budget lines to move them into Level IV work. As a result of a budget quirk, civil servants gained valuable hands-on experience in experiment integration, which provided an ideal training ground for space station integration.[68]

The Level IV group employed young engineers fresh out of college. There was no better way to train new hires in the work of the Center, the argument went, than to give them hands-on experience. Assigned to different Spacelab experiments, the young engineers traveled to the source, much as flight hardware engineers traveled to the factory. There they discussed with the experiments' principal investigators the space and configuration constraints imposed by Spacelab. KSC engineers worked with the investigators, helping them design an experiment that could meet these requirements. They also reviewed the design drawings and wrote the assembly and test procedures. When the experiment arrived at KSC, they worked with contractor technicians and the principal investigators to implement those procedures.[69] Spacelab experiments were often international projects, and Level IV engineers quickly learned to operate in the international environment as well, another lesson that had relevance to the space station. For most KSC employees, the job was finished once the space shuttle launched. But Level IV personnel, because of their familiarity with both the workings of the shuttle and the experiments they had prepared for its payload, remained available to help solve any problems that might arise for the experiment in orbit.[70]

At the end of the Spacelab program in 1997, the Level IV Experiment Integration Group disbanded. Most of the program's engineers moved to

Space Station Utilization, which integrated and tested the experiments that would fly on the station.[71] Smaller numbers moved to ELV payloads, the other area where KSC still performed significant hands-on work.[72] Space Station Utilization would replace Level IV as the primary training ground for civil service engineers at the Cape.[73]

New and Old Models for Processing

The hands-on work done on Spacelab had returned KSC to its roots in the early days at Cape Canaveral. Before the Apollo program, and long before the shuttle, hands-on work by civil servants deeply involved in the building and processing of rockets had been the main method of operation. This tradition had almost completely vanished in the shuttle program in favor of contractor management. Where there was "routine" or operational work to be done, such as flying the shuttle, program management overseeing private-sector contractors was seen as the cost-saving, efficient way to go. As the Spacelab experience showed, however, new work and innovative designs could often benefit from close cooperation between civil servants and contractors, rather than just contractor management.[74]

As the space station evolved, it provided other opportunities to rethink the dominant organizational and managerial philosophies of the space program. "When we came out of Crystal City on the redesign," Steve Francois recalled, "one of the things . . . was . . . a whole new approach to management and . . . the way the program was structured."[75] The redesign team had called for a reduction of KSC civil service workers on the space station project from around 2,500 to 1,000. This proposal followed a broader NASA mandate to reduce civil service employment and turn work over to more flexible and presumably more cost-effective contractor groups. As part of that move, the multiple contracts for building what in 1993 President Clinton had renamed the International Space Station (ISS) were folded into a single prime contract let to Boeing. Boeing would manage subcontracts with the other component makers. This time, however, contracting did not simply replace civil servants with private-sector workers. It led to an important organizational innovation for NASA.[76]

The ISS organization for 1993 was modeled on the Integrated Product Teams (IPTs) Boeing had formed for its successful construction of the Boeing 777.[77] The IPT would make decisions as a group. Whereas before the program director had imposed decisions, now he or she would only coordinate decisions made by the team, a team that reflected the combined knowledge of KSC operations experts, contractor interests, and design engineers.

Decisions were made at meetings, providing communications hubs among the various team members. This cutomer-oriented or product focus aimed to eliminate mistrust, secrecy, and "silos" within a complex organization by bringing designers, operators, and customers together to make decisions that took account of the needs and drew on the specialized knowledge of each. For the space station, IPT teams would cross civil service, contractor, and center boundaries. At some NASA centers, this restructuring was largely cosmetic, but the IPT format appeared to fit the work at KSC. "That's how we finished the SSPF," Francois asserts.[78]

In the original recommendation for Boeing as the single prime contractor, NASA personnel were to reduce their technical penetration in favor of a more supervisory role.[79] In its embrace of "working together," however, IPTs became in many ways a throwback to the badgeless community of the Apollo years.[80] They differed from the earlier forms of organization in some respects. Before, NASA had retained control of the decision-making process. Now IPTs composed of KSC, design center, and contractor personnel made the decisions necessary to achieve their goals. Each team would do its work as it thought best. Each IPT worked out the mechanisms and developed the methodologies for achieving and evaluating progress. Both KSC and contractor would have insight, with the civil service personnel measuring progress and ensuring that standards were met, while the contractor workers would carry out the agreed-upon procedures.[81]

The IPT model also provided KSC with an important entrée into the design process. To the extent that IPTs functioned across center boundaries, KSC personnel were able to bring their testing insights to other organizations. Indeed, Boeing had itself used extensive testing when it developed the 777, even though the designers at the aerospace giant at first believed that superior computer-aided design technology would allow them to complete an aircraft with quality "designed in," so that it required little flight testing. Boeing management in the end abandoned the design-dominated approach, and the 777 became the most heavily tested aircraft in history.

Boeing's unexpected shift toward testing with the 777 seemed the perfect example for Dick Lyon's Space Station Project Office to challenge NASA's ship-and-shoot model. He now called for tests that would ensure that the elements connected properly and worked together—a methodology termed MEIT (Multi-Element Integrated Testing).[82] NASA, however, resisted embracing that part of Boeing's IPT experience that had recognized the critical importance of learning through testing. Although space station designers talked about the value of multiple interface tests, they never accepted KSC's proposals for MEIT at the launch site. Lyon thus could do little more than follow what was now a familiar KSC strategy for the station—quietly build up the equipment and facilities that would permit MEIT implementation should headquarters ever agree to it.[83]

As decision making shifted from the traditional, center-based, projects-office organization to the innovative IPT in early 1994, Steve Francois took over the argument for integrated testing at the launch site. At first he was no more successful than Lyon in getting MEIT approved. KSC had the facilities, but the rest of NASA would not go along. Francois backed off once more, focusing his energies on activating the still controversial SSPF. As the arrival of space station components at KSC drew nearer, though, Francois began looking at the schedule. There would be three or four components at KSC at the same time. Though it was not part of the designer's original plan, these elements could be hooked up and tested. When Francois proposed this to ISS program managers, they rejected it as unnecessary. KSC was simply trying to do, under the table, testing that had already been determined to be superfluous.[84]

Only in 1995 when George Abbey returned from NASA headquarters to become director of the Johnson Space Center did station designers finally abandon the ship-and-shoot perspective. Though JSC still had charge of the space station, Houston now had a new brief: it would run the giant Space Flight Operations Contract for the shuttle. Even with IPTs and with Boeing as the overall contractor, the station was behind schedule, over budget, and full of problems. The troubles of the station now became the focus of Abbey's concern. He imposed Saturday meetings to review progress. Francois recalls that these meetings uncovered numerous errors in both NASA and contractor programs, and revealed a schedule for delivery of elements at KSC woefully out of touch with reality.

In the spring of 1995 Abbey visited KSC and asked what the Center was doing to support the space station program. Steven Francois pointed to the construction of the work stands and power facilities. Abbey asked, what about checkout? This was a rare opportunity, and KSC personnel seized it. Francois quickly answered that the official program philosophy was ship-and-shoot, with checkout done by the customer. When asked his opinion on this by Abbey, Francois gave the standard KSC reply: if it worked, it would be good; KSC was there to help. Abbey, he recalled, went down a list of tests he thought should be included. "Well, we haven't got there yet," came back the answer, and "It's not in the program." Abbey turned to the station program managers and asked them why they had not included some check-out at KSC. Clearly the question was not so much seeking information as implying KSC should have had a foot in the door. Francois quickly offered the contingency plans KSC had been preparing, "just in case" equipment should arrive with quality deviations or other issues that designers had not foreseen. The quiet, behind-the-scenes work that Francois, Lyon, and others had been doing paid off now. Abbey authorized KSC to go forward with some of those plans.[85]

Francois proposed adding minimal testing to the space station program. KSC would use existing checkout systems at the Center so that those at the builder's factory did not have to be transported to the Cape. The testing equipment would also comport with that at the design centers.[86] He also mentioned the recently rejected idea of plugging elements together while they were awaiting launch. Of course, this would require a small amount of money and a bit more time, but no more than an extra week in the schedule. Any added expense would be offset by substantial savings if a problem were detected and fixed before launch.[87] The design engineers started listening. Abbey had also asked Francois why KSC did not have people out in the factory the way they had during Apollo and shuttle construction. By the time the meeting was over, the old ship-and-shoot justification had been shot down. Abbey asked KSC director Jay Honeycutt to form teams for visiting the factories.[88]

The Space Station Comes to KSC

Tip Talone thought nothing of it when he received a phone call from Jay Honeycutt on a Friday morning in April 1996. Talone and the Center director were old friends, so he was happy to stop by that evening at Honeycutt's home. But Talone's jaw dropped when he was asked to consider taking over the space station project at KSC. Take the weekend to think about it, Honeycutt said; don't call until Monday morning.

Happy in his job as flow director for the shuttle *Endeavour*, Talone spent two restless days composing an answer. He knew all about the troubled history of ISS. For years he had watched the funding battles. Like any smart, ambitious manager, he had given such a tenuous program a wide berth, and he wanted nothing to do with it now. After marshalling his best reasons for turning down the offer and coming up with a list of suitable substitutes, he met with his boss Monday morning. His answer would have to be no. But before he could start on the justification, Honeycutt interrupted him. "You don't understand, this isn't an invitation. I've changed the locks on your door. Your secretary's already been informed. Don't go back there, all your stuff is in an office in the SSPF."[89]

His fate sealed, Talone was savvy enough to know he could at least bargain for the best deal. Honeycutt offered him fifteen "first-round draft choices" from the KSC staff to begin his organization. Talone heard thirty. The two agreed that, whatever the actual number, the new station director got the cream of the KSC crop. And Honeycutt insisted that Talone draw his people from both the payload and shuttle directorates. "No favoritism. I need both cultures involved in this game because they both bring something different to the table."[90] Bill Parsons was sent up to Huntsville to bring back Node 1, the first space station element. Others began guiding components from their factories to KSC.[91] Honeycutt remains convinced to this day that, had KSC not followed its tradition of bringing equipment to the Center to work on, the space station would not have gotten off the ground.[92]

In this regard, Talone was the perfect man for the job. No one at KSC had more experience in bringing spacecraft from the factory to Merritt Island.[93] Moreover, his early career in the launch vehicle side of the Apollo-Saturn program left him convinced that civil servants with hands-on experience were crucial to the success of America's space program. As the shuttle transitioned to contractor management, he had found himself holding a minority view there. But Honeycutt's decision to give Talone responsibility for ISS was an acknowledgement that the hands-off management techniques were not adequate for such a new, experimental technology.

Between Talone's teams in the factory and Francois's work on the SSPF, the Center became intimately familiar with space station equipment. It was soon possible to propose tests using existing KSC facilities. Abbey imposed a monthly Space Development Operations Management meeting where managers had to stand up and indicate where they were on their schedules.[94] Francois soon had testing programs put on the agenda at these meetings, and Talone's teams at the factories began pushing the testing programs there as well.[95]

Organizationally, then, testing and integration work at KSC now had an official place in the space station program. But in day-to-day decisions, the budget still held sway. By 1996 Russia was having financial difficulties in meeting its commitments to build station components. These components had to be in orbit before the launch of NASA's Node 1. Russian delays forced delays in the shuttle launch schedule in 1997.[96] At the same time, the station was running over budget by $16 million a month, drawing fire from deficit hawks in Congress. NASA administrator Goldin complained that, if his budget were cut, "it's going to impact us and we're going to start doing dumb things."[97] His words fell on deaf ears, and NASA lost $400 million for 1997.[98] From KSC's perspective, one of those "dumb things" was a reduction in testing.[99] As so often in the past, when the budget got squeezed, KSC's work was squeezed out.

As late as March 1996, space station testing was still largely confined to the factory.[100] There was no mention of MEIT in the 1996 International Space Station Program Review, though that omission may have been strategic.[101] KSC continued to push for integrated testing.[102] In a presentation to the station program board, John Straiton characterized testing at KSC as still in its early phase. They were "just beginning to wrestle with T&V [test and verification] planning." Integrated testing, he casually remarked, was "still a possibility."[103]

In the meantime, KSC proposed a modified form of integrated testing called Cargo Integration Test Equipment. CITE proofed compatibility between payload and orbiter software. JSC engineers continued to believe that most orbiter and payload interfaces could be verified after the station parts went on the shuttle.[104] CITE they saw as only "a crutch for much of the operational community," a needless repetition of tests run at Huntsville. After the second ISS shuttle flight, software would be uploaded once the hardware was connected in orbit, so CITE would become obsolete.[105] Such confidence puzzled KSC personnel. Software and hardware arrived separately, exactly the situation that usually demanded testing on-site when they came together.[106] CITE went forward for the station's Node 1, though JSC engineers were sure it was not necessary. Meanwhile, once again behind the scenes, KSC personnel lobbied for verification tests on other critical interfaces.[107]

In April 1997 delays by Russia forced NASA to rework the schedule for station assembly and flight once more.[108] KSC took advantage of the extra time to raise again the issue of MEIT. At this point the testing plan assumed that individual devices would be examined at the factory, and integrated testing of an entire node or component would take place at both the factory and KSC. But MEIT, which included testing physical, electronic, and "plumbing" linkages between all the other parts to which a component would connect, would only be done in orbit.[109]

Then, in a brief few months, all that changed. In August 1997, Node 1 arrived at KSC. A month later, NASA once again reorganized the International Space Station program. For the first time MEIT was included in the organizational structure, placed within Talone's Space Station Hardware Integration Office. The station program now began to acknowledge the risks associated with launching components without integrated testing.[110] Unlike other space station processing work, where NASA civil servants played a limited role, MEIT was to be NASA run, with support from the element contractors.[111] The first MEIT test was scheduled for January 1999, a deadline KSC now had to scramble to meet.

Engineers at the Center had already developed a process for assembling station elements. Step by step each would be analyzed, providing a baseline for future work. To this database they would add information gathered from testing done at the factory. With all this in hand, engineers would be able to recommend further testing "based on experience." KSC teams were to identify all interfaces believed "critical to validate" and write contingency plans for unplanned tasks and late deliveries.[112]

A presentation dated April 6, 1998, reflected the pressures at KSC. Only half the MEIT team had even minimal payload processing experience. They would need six weeks of one-on-one training in the new integration test techniques to get up to speed. Command and data handler engineers would try to support both hardware and software, without help from the flight software engineers. The software requirements for the Test Control and Monitor System and the Launch Processing System remained incomplete. MEIT support, the presentation complained, was a "last minute scramble for everything." There was not enough time for thorough research and development or "engineering thought process."[113] KSC would solve some of these problems by bringing in management with experience in various aspects of the test. Shannon Bartell, Steve Francois's deputy, for example, served as a consultant on console issues. With her experience, she recalls, she had the clout to bring in "whoever they needed" if a problem arose.[114]

As KSC engineers had predicted, MEIT tests on the ground uncovered numerous problems that would have been virtually impossible to fix in orbit. Node 1 had several software incompatibilities. During the first MEIT test, when KSC tried to power it up, everything shut down. "We would have been troubleshooting for months in orbit," Francois pointed out. "Instead we found it on the ground and fixed it." As Cheryl McPhillips, one of the former Level IV engineers who had migrated to the space station, put it, "Many midnight calls were placed to engineers at Boeing in Houston, Canoga Park and Huntington Beach." But by late January, less than a month after the initiation of the first MEIT test, KSC's years of planning paid off. Most of the problems with the node were under repair.[115] Software developers were now completing their programs and getting them to KSC in time for debugging.[116] MEIT's effectiveness became so clear that it became standard operating procedure.

By 2003, ten shuttle flights had carried components to the space station. A major part of the orbital facility was aloft. Scientists were in permanent residence there, and the logistics module, Leonardo, had carried racks of experiments up to them. KSC had a state-of-the-art processing facility in the SSPF.

Drawing on its experience in Apollo and the shuttle, KSC had overcome the design centers' resistance to launch site testing and processing of hardware. For years, space station program managers had argued that extensive

12-4. Once dismissed as unneeded, the Space Station Processing Facility at KSC is filled to capacity with components to be launched into space.

ground testing was unnecessary and criticized a large new SSPF as wasted space. Node 1 went through eleven months of testing before it moved to the pad. When it finally lifted off in October 1998, the SSPF was full.[117] The size of the SSPF turned out to be a cost savings. NASA was able to draw station elements out of the factory and get the factory off its payroll by centralizing processing operations at KSC.[118] Nor did the old O&C checkout facilities go to waste. After the end of Spacelab, the O&C Building was reconfigured to check out the space station trusses.[119]

The ISS experience thus contrasts with that of the shuttle. During the 1990s, efforts to make the shuttle operational had moved the program into the hands of contractors, with NASA personnel providing insight. This withdrawal of civil servants reflected the belief that NASA scientists and engineers should be doing research, not routine operations. The shuttle was assumed to be a mature technology. Research efforts at KSC should focus on preparing to process and launch the next generation of space vehicles. The space station, by contrast, was an innovative new technology still undergoing development. Program management techniques alone would not suffice in this case. KSC personnel believed, on the basis of historical experience, that new flight hardware required significant on-the-ground processing before it could be shipped into space. In the end, the Center's argument prevailed. KSC had to gain insight into this technology to develop the tests required. Experienced hands like Tip Talone, who had long believed in the need for training government personnel through experience, were thus perfectly matched to the needs of ISS. As with most of the big programs at KSC, the work done on the space station drew on valuable insight from earlier efforts, in scientific payloads, in expendable vehicles, in Apollo and the shuttle. Bringing both shuttle and payload people into station processing, the Center once again made use of its hybrid tradition of hands-on and contract-managed work to move a project forward.

As we shall see, the assumption that NASA could draw a clear line between research work and more routine operations would continue to mark the evolution of the Center in the late 1990s. But events would also call into question the notion that anything sent into space could ever be termed routine.

13

*
*
*

Spaceport

"It's almost like going to Eden.
Living on the beach and launching rockets."

Roy Bridges

JoAnn Morgan grew up with rockets. She watched Explorer I blast into the sky as a high school student in Titusville, Florida, only a few miles from Cape Canaveral. A month later, she applied for a job at the Cape as a student engineering aide. The job started the Monday after her high school graduation. That Friday, Morgan was working on her first launch.[1] Except for the years in college, she never left.

In many respects JoAnn Morgan's career typified those who started with the early space program. Most who came in the exciting years after Sputnik never wanted to work anywhere else. "It was extremely primitive," she recalled of those days. After a launch, "debris would fall, it would catch the palmettos on fire and then the snakes would come out." Everyone learned how to fight fires, mosquitoes, and snakes.[2] Morgan was one of those who helped to lift the Center from the swamp. Gradually she rose from a junior engineer in the Apollo program, working site activation and instrumentation, to doing key development work on the shuttle's launch processing software.

Morgan also endured the routine sexism of the early space program. As one of the few women not employed in a secretarial or clerical position, she was "a pretty rare person" by her account. "I was a cute young thing with all of those engineers and soldiers," she recalled. Her worried father let her take the job only if she agreed not to fraternize with them.[3] Her first time in the firing room, someone told her bluntly, "We don't have women in the blockhouse."[4]

Still, Morgan found that competence in the end trumped prejudice. After the firing room incident, her boss told her to "just ignore him," which she did. "I ran my test and did my job and went back and gave my report." A

13-1. JoAnn Morgan was one of the pioneering women engineers at KSC.

few days later, a launch room supervisor sought her out. "You are always welcome here," he said. "I just want you to know that you're welcome here." That set the pattern for the future as far as Morgan was concerned. Do what you were asked to do, do what you were supposed to do, even if you were the only woman in the building. Even if the building had only one bathroom and the security guard had to change it temporarily from "men's" to "women's."

With a degree in mathematics, Morgan was encouraged to work with computers, software in particular. At the time, this was not considered "real" engineering work because it involved numbers and code, not big heavy pieces of equipment. Yet she found mentors and rose in the ranks. Moving into supervisory positions brought its own perils. One of the first men working under her supervision became threatening, then later attempted suicide. "Go to work for her. She'll drive you nuts," some less than sympathetic co-workers began to snicker.[5] It put her off being a supervisor, though only for a short while. Over time, Morgan moved into positions of responsibility in payloads, safety and mission assurance, and shuttle upgrades. In 1986 Center director Forrest McCartney appointed her the first woman executive at KSC.

Where women had once largely been confined to office and support functions, by the 1990s they had important positions in the main engineering areas of payload and vehicle processing. Though there had yet to be a female launch director, many women had passed through the crucial training of flow director. It was less and less likely that a female engineer would be greeted with an "excuse me, are you the girl taking notes" when she entered the room, as had been the case a decade or so before.[6]

As Morgan's story shows, in many areas KSC was a more diverse place by the 1990s. But had it changed enough? After the first black astronaut, Guion Bluford, flew on the shuttle in 1983, a wave of excitement ran through NASA's African American community. However, as in the post-Apollo phasedown, budget cuts in the 1990s came at the expense of opportunities for new minority personnel. KSC deputy director Jim Jennings found himself frustrated by the old excuse "we can't find minority engineers." Women, African Americans, and other minority groups wondered if they did not confront a glass ceiling that let them rise so high but no higher.[7] Pressures from both inside and outside the Center would gradually lead to more opportunities at KSC.

In 2000 JoAnn Morgan received a call from the Center director, Roy Bridges. Would she consider, Bridges asked, taking over a new directorate? Bridges had big plans for reorganizing KSC, and one area in particular was crucial to his strategy. Following the recent history of privatization and turning over work to contractors, he wanted KSC to be much more externally oriented. The new directorate, External Relations, not only would combine traditional education, media, legislative affairs, and public relations functions but also would promote partnerships with universities, the state of Florida, private firms, and the Department of Defense. A new unit in External Relations, the Business Development Office, would reach out to potential "customers" of the Center's services.[8]

Thinking in terms of customers, stakeholders, partners, and markets meant a major change at KSC. In accordance with the more business-oriented view of government prevalent in the 1990s, the launch center would shift from acting like a self-contained bureaucracy to positioning itself as a node in a network of relationships in the launch business. It would welcome participants from other agencies and the private sector. Bridges was not looking to turn over external functions—once considered marginal to engineering—to a traditional public affairs officer. He wanted an experienced engineer who was well known in NASA and respected within the Center to handle this work. Tapping JoAnn Morgan for the job signaled that External Relations would be more than just a support function for the "real" work of the Center. It was the start of a plan to remake KSC in light of all that had transpired over the past decade.

Spaceport Technology

Roy Bridges's new plans for KSC came to him one morning during a jog on the beach. The former shuttle pilot had never given up his training regime, maintaining astronaut trim long after he had stopped flying in space. For him the Cape, with its bright sunny days and exciting work, was the perfect job right where the exhilaration of flying in space started.[9] The seventh person to run the Center, Bridges had an impressive resume. An Air Force Academy graduate, he had successfully piloted STS-51F into orbit after the vehicle lost one of its main engines. He had also served at a number of air force facilities, including a stint as commander of Patrick Air Force Base. After retiring from the military, he was quickly asked to come back to NASA, and to apply for the directorship of KSC. He took over the position in March 1997.

When Bridges signed on, NASA, including KSC, was in the midst of downsizing under the policies of NASA administrator Dan Goldin. In 1995 Goldin had conducted a Zero Base Review, which reassessed the agency's roles and responsibilities. Goldin looked to remove NASA from operations as much as possible and hand over that work to contractors, so the agency could concentrate on research.[10] For KSC in particular, this policy had major implications. There was talk of turning the Center into a "GOCO," a government-owned, contractor-operated facility. At the extreme, this would mean perhaps a few hundred civil servants, whose only job would be to monitor the contractors doing all the launch and processing work. KSC still had some 2,000 civil servants on-site, though that number was slated to fall to about 1,400. Layoffs are never fun, and Bridges had no desire to preside over the loss of workers and closing of facilities. There was a lot of talent and experience in KSC's labor pool, but the downsizing had left many longtime workers with an unfounded belief that they added no value. Bridges had to change that outlook and rebuild morale. Even so, the Center would not be going back to where it had been a decade earlier in terms of work or mission. The new director would have to redefine the work that went on at KSC to fit the new NASA agenda.[11]

Bridges's task was to convince NASA headquarters that cutting back personnel had limits. KSC remained under a hiring freeze, and buyouts were being offered to experienced workers to get the numbers down to Goldin's figure. As Bridges pointed out, the policy of reducing numbers through early retirement meant that workers with valuable skills were walking out

13-2. As Center director in the latter half of the 1990s, Roy Bridges presided over a Kennedy Space Center with a much more diverse mission.

the door. If too many left, KSC would be no more than one person deep in some key areas, and possibly empty in others. With no new hires, it was impossible to rebalance the workforce to maintain crucial skill areas. The new vision of the Center was not going to become reality over night, but it could not happen at all if everyone was gone.

Bridges's morning run on the beach took place after a retreat he held with his top staff. His idea was simple. KSC civil servants would replace their lost operational functions with research on launch concepts and technology. It was unorthodox because, for the most part, other members of NASA treated KSC as strictly an operational arm putting into practice research and development done elsewhere in the space agency. The mandate from headquarters was clear: "Get the hell out of town and let the contractors do it."[12] As Goldin and others saw it, little that went on at KSC was important to NASA's new research emphasis. "I enthusiastically and strongly disagreed with that thinking," Bridges recalled by way of understatement.[13]

In Roy Bridges's mind the Center would become a "spaceport," not just an operations unit of the space program. Capitalizing on experience, KSC would be ready to launch any new vehicles NASA built. If NASA wanted to go to the moon, KSC would be ready to prepare and launch the vehicle to do it. If the next program were to be a second-generation reusable shuttle, no one knew better how that vehicle should be designed from an operations standpoint than KSC. There was no doubt that the other NASA centers had "great design engineers." But the real problem with the shuttle was, "it took too long to go from one flight to another. There was too much maintenance that had to be done, and that drove the costs." The next-generation vehicle would have to take full advantage of operational lessons learned by KSC if NASA was to achieve its long-sought goal of lowering the cost of space access.[14]

These ideas slowly began to receive more support within NASA. A top-level Space Transportation Architecture Study a decade earlier had found there could be "substantial, if not order-of-magnitude improvements in operational capability and cost-effectiveness" realized through incorporating operational concepts into the design of future vehicles. Among the things that should be taken into consideration were simplification and standardization of "payload-to-vehicle interfaces." Traditionally, these interface points had consumed many hours of testing and preparation. Replacing hydraulics with electromechanical moving parts, and making greater use of automated test and checkout procedures through on-board vehicle diagnostics, could also help to routinize and standardize turnaround operations.[15] Similar recommendations came out in a 1994 NASA plan. The plan suggested ways of building future vehicles for ease of operations and maintainability, suggestions that reflected an intensive "lessons learned" study.[16]

Bridges knew from firsthand experience that saving money by shifting everything to contractors was not so automatic as Goldin supposed. KSC had backed away from hands-on work in launching ELVs, for example, but still maintained a core of some two hundred engineers who had "insight and oversight" of the work done by launch service providers such as Lockheed and Boeing. From his military experience, Bridges also knew that the air force missile programs had far less in-house depth of this sort. When a number of missiles carrying spy satellites went awry, the air force actually began to study how KSC did its ELV launches, and decided it needed a similar level of penetration into the technology. It was all too easy to put a billion dollars' worth of military hardware into the drink or into a useless orbit with an errant launch. Having the capability to check what the launch contractor was doing could be an extremely valuable insurance policy.[17]

As Bridges saw it, the real strength of KSC was its people, not its location or facilities. These human resources were what kept the Center relevant to the future, whatever that future might be. "Theoretically," Bridges noted, "you could launch from an interior launch site." But even if the location moved, somebody still had to build the new launch facility, and build it in a way that incorporated lessons about how to process flight hardware and payloads efficiently. The expertise of KSC personnel would matter greatly here. The lesson of the shuttle had been that full understanding of a vehicle came not just in the design phase but in experience on the shop floor as well.

The future, Bridges hoped, would see KSC employees "working on some of the technology problems" at the point of design, "to make them more user-friendly, less maintenance-intensive, and cheaper to use."[18]

In 1997 Bridges announced his strategy in a "roadmap to the year 2025." The plan acknowledged that in the near term KSC would concentrate on improving the safety and reliability of shuttle operations, upgrading launch software and ground equipment. It would continue to push the elements of the International Space Station out the door and into orbit as well. As NASA's "lead center" for expendable vehicles, it would also provide services to a wide range of private and government users of the Cape's launch and payload facilities. At the same time, however, KSC workers would take what they learned from current operations back into research and development. Teams led by JoAnn Morgan and Loren Schriver would begin to define KSC's role in future exploration and future technologies. In External Relations, Morgan would seek new areas, "markets" where KSC's expertise could be applied. Schriver would study advanced launch and payload processing systems that could lower costs and improve efficiency. He would also establish a spaceport technology center, building partnerships outside KSC in what were likely to become key areas of research in space, such as the life sciences. Ideally, the roadmap proposed, KSC would work with developers of space transportation technology—private or international—on design, assembly, and testing.[19]

Getting to this next stage required reworking KSC's relationships with other NASA centers. It was common wisdom in NASA that Marshall and Johnson saw each other as rivals. They had talented design engineers and they competed for big projects when these became available. Kennedy as the "end of the line" tended to have a less adversarial relationship with the other centers. They needed KSC to do the launch work for their projects. But KSC still had to convince its peers at the other centers that the conventional wisdom about operations no longer applied. Even the best-designed vehicle or payload needed preparation on the ground before launch, something demonstrated once again with the International Space Station. Retrofitting and remodeling of hardware was horrendously expensive. KSC thus ended up doing substantial work in debugging equipment and finishing fabrication, as well as figuring out how best to operate it. Here Bridges's military experience gave him a valuable perspective. Military hardware must deploy. Jet fighters had to be designed to minimize logistics and maintenance problems in the field. Maintenance and operations were always considerations when the air force acquired hardware from contractors.[20]

Given that perspective, it made sense for Bridges to point the Center to the future, when it might get in on the ground floor of the design of the next generation of space vehicles. "If somebody completes a vehicle design and then they throw it over the fence to us . . . about all we can do is say, 'For that design, here's how much the ground environment's going to cost.'" That was not good enough, not if cost and budget were really major concerns. The time to start working on the ground support technology and methods of testing and launching was now, so that future vehicles could be designed around those procedures, rather than trying to build procedures around a fixed vehicle design.[21]

Moving to a new, integrated design and operations philosophy was going to require a new set of institutional relationships.[22] Budget realities made this absolutely necessary. Since funding was hard to come by, NASA tended to concentrate on getting the resources needed to design and build a project. Allocating funds up front for operations that would not begin for ten years was an extremely hard sell. Legislators who approved budgets were thinking about the next election, not the next decade. KSC would have to find partnerships outside its gates to bring the new vision to fruition.

First and foremost, though, Bridges emphasized efficient use of available resources. Personnel policy now shifted from cutting workers to moving people on to different tasks and, in some cases, even hiring new civil servants with needed skills for the future. Accordingly, Bridges sought an increase in the government payroll at the Center. In 2000 NASA authorized 150 new positions for KSC. This would increase the civil servant workforce from 1,650 to 1,800. Bridges was able to add another 71 by 2001.[23] The new hires did not simply replace those who had left. In keeping with the strategic emphasis, civil servants were to work in teams involving contractors, suppliers, and customers. Flexibility rather than bureaucratic growth was the objective. In the future, perhaps, the Center might be able to gain an even more flexible workforce through the use of temporary workers so that skills could change with missions.[24]

Labor flexibility implied a major cultural change, given that KSC personnel historically had a strong emotional attachment to the Cape. It somewhat contradicted the notion that experience and learning counted substantially for the Center's success. Much of that experience had arisen simply because so many people came, found the life and work at KSC absorbing, and never left. But given the realities of budget, that old pattern might not be sustainable. Flexibility might be the only way to assure the retention of valuable skills in the new NASA environment. And for all the value of stability and tradition, it also had a cost. People with a strong attachment to the Cape and the Center tended to become "inbred" in their thinking and too enamored of what they already knew. The signals coming from NASA headquarters were about an open and innovative culture that could learn to do things differently, more efficiently. These issues remained unresolved through 2000, but their mere presence on the table indicated how vast was the possible scope of change.

One place where questioning of the past seemed warranted was in physical facilities and hardware. Old facilities at the Center were starting to show signs of age. Rivets regularly popped off the exterior of the VAB, and a net had to be installed inside to catch pieces of the building's crumbling ceiling. In 1990 a prestigious panel chaired by Norman Augustine, CEO of the aerospace firm Martin Marietta, had produced a thorough report on future needs and directions for NASA. The influential Augustine Report recommended a substantial reinvestment in NASA's technological base. It had been "starved for well over a decade," and the agency needed to upgrade its facilities and develop a space infrastructure for the future.[25] Help started to arrive in 2002, as NASA allocated some $350 million for repairs.[26] The trend of the future, however, suggested that KSC had more facilities than it needed for the actual number of programs it operated.[27] If personnel, not hardware, was the Center's ticket to the future, it might even be time to begin closing some buildings, perhaps start from scratch with new hardware when the next generation of vehicles arrived.

One could not assume that future launch vehicles would resemble current ones, however. In the 1990s, competition from abroad in the ELV program had shown KSC it would no longer dominate the world in rocket technology. The same would likely be true of human space flight. Roy Bridges continued to emphasize the lesson that "operations knowledge enables technology development," just as "technology improves operations." The role of civil servants was to apply this experience and knowledge to future vehicles, to be "smart managers" and "smart buyers" with contractors.[28]

Though no one could say for certain what directions human space flight might take, between 1998 and 2000 there were certainly many exciting prospects under development. NASA and aerospace contractors were at work on the X-33 and X-34 space planes. These "single stage to orbit" vehicles were meant to replace the traditional multistage rocket. If successful, they implied a radical change in launch operations.[29] Bridges himself foresaw using space technology for more earthbound and commercial pursuits. A space plane that could cut a New York-to-Sydney flight to only an hour would revolutionize terrestrial travel. But such a vehicle would also require sophisticated maintenance and handling operations to keep costs down and assure the safety of commercial passengers. In outer-space travel as well, operations might actually expand significantly if new vehicles were able to dramatically reduce the cost of space access. Florida might become an "intergalactic hub" around the new generation of space planes. "You [would] have many spaceports, and so the technology customers are spread all around the domestic United States and perhaps in friendly foreign countries," speculated Bridges.[30] KSC might no longer be the sole launch site, or even a launch site at all if better locations could be found. But its knowledge and experience would be carried forward in the research it did.

Narrowing the Banana River

Military and NASA facilities had long existed side by side at the Cape. The air force and the civilian agency also had a long tradition of sharing land, range support technology, and in some cases even launchpads in the early days. But no one who worked at KSC, especially at the Merritt Island facilities built for human space flight, doubted that these were two different cultures. Neither side was eager to give up control over its domain or do business the way its neighbor did. The military was hierarchical. The commander at Patrick Air Force Base gave orders and expected them to be obeyed. NASA was decentralized. The director of KSC led by persuasion as much as command, and always expected that his top people would pose thoughtful objections if they felt a move was ill advised or technically questionable.

During the years of downsizing following Apollo, NASA had considered consolidating some operations with the air force at the Cape as a cost-saving measure.[31] Both NASA and the air force, however, backed away from this move.[32] In the end, efforts to consolidate range functions in one agency, or for NASA to operate the Eastern Test Range for the air force, were scotched and the consolidation program made little headway.[33]

Conflicts between NASA and the Department of Defense emerged in issues such as the design of the shuttle. But over time the two organizations had come to share more features. For example, NASA had used the military as its model of how to operate hardware through contractors. KSC had worked closely with the air force test range in its ELV programs. The two cultures were still distinct, but the search for efficiency began to push them closer at the Cape. During the post-*Challenger* debates on the future of space flight, one of the strongest recommendations was for greater cooperation between NASA and the military. Military and civilian space programs, it was believed, "drew from the same well." Despite differences in mission and philosophy, the two shared substantial technology, used the same industry contractors and academic institutions, and required the same human skills. A 1992 report recommended that DOD and NASA cooperate in rebuilding the "space industrial base."[34]

KSC's close proximity to a military installation made it well situated for this change. Despite conflicts over priorities, access, and procedures during the past three decades, the fact was, neither the air force nor NASA was leaving the Cape. They had reason to work out a more efficient arrangement in sharing common resources and solving common problems. Cooperation, however, could not take place in a traditional organizational hierarchy, with one person clearly in charge. It had to be across two "heads," the air force commander and the KSC director. A new Joint Base Operations and Support Contract (JBOSC) was the model for how this cooperation would work.

With his air force experience, Roy Bridges was well prepared to capitalize on opportunities for cross-agency cooperation. After months of planning with Patrick Air Force Base commander General Randy Starbuck, JBOSC was born in 1998. The Cape Canaveral Air Force Base and the Kennedy Space Center began to share operations and maintenance in a way that benefited both organizations. Why have separate fire departments, security offices, and other such activities that were common across the landscape? Bridges reckoned that the two bases could save some 30 percent by combining these and other services. As with SFOC, the JBOSC consolidated a number of separate contracts (eighteen) and was let to a consortium that included several firms that had long provided services at Cape Canaveral. A board of directors oversaw the contract and its management, with the chair and vice chair alternating between the KSC director and the commander of the 45th Space Wing.

Besides saving money immediately, the new contract furthered KSC's goal of becoming a national spaceport. No longer would users of Cape facilities go either to the air force or to NASA for what they needed. In 2000 the air force and KSC created a joint office, a "one-stop shopping place" for launch customers. Cooperation made it easier for users to get what they needed without the hassles of negotiating with two separate bureaucracies with distinct, uncoordinated procedures.[35] The joint office undertook the planning and preparation necessary to meet the needs of future commercial users as well. Formerly this sort of work had been done separately by KSC and the air force.[36]

As with research, the move to joint base operations was designed to keep the Cape competitive with other launch sites elsewhere. KSC and the air force remained separate institutions with separate missions, but now they had a framework to integrate and cooperate for the benefit of both. The contract was a great symbolic change in the relationship of two institutions that had long eyed each other warily. It was part of the cultural change Bridges sought, to get his people to think in terms of a space launch community.

Research Park of Tomorrow

Another source of resources needed to remake KSC came through partnerships with the state of Florida. The basis for cooperation here was a common interest in expanding the amount of research done at the Center and nearby. This research would include both new launch operations concepts and new methods of preparing scientific payloads for the International Space Station, once the station was fully operational. Bridges sought to create a dense network of knowledge that would draw on and enhance KSC's own skills in a new local geography of space research. He found support from a state looking to add high-paying jobs and keep competitive with other states in new technology.

In 1989 the state of Florida had started the ball rolling by creating a Spaceport Authority. Following California and Alabama, which had seen research and engineering connected to space and aerospace flourish, Florida committed public funds to build facilities, roads, and utilities. By 1998 the state had its own launchpad at the Cape. Designated Launch Complex 46, it prepared to receive new generations of commercial users flying small to medium-sized rockets.

Though the idea of a state-owned launchpad might seem a radical departure in public expenditure, Florida officials saw it as no different from a state- or county-owned airport. Federal, state, and commercial funds would come together to build an infrastructure to provide a valuable service, which would stimulate the local economy. Launch vehicle manufacturers supported the venture as a way to encourage consumption of their products. With the state acting as intermediary, competing rocket builders were assured that the funds they contributed would be available on an equal basis to all users. The new pad started out with few amenities, akin more to the early landing strips for airplanes than a modern, fully functional jetport. In accordance with the cost-consciousness of the times, its emphasized low maintenance and adoption of existing ground support equipment wherever possible. Customers were even expected to provide their own umbilical tower. This was not "a launchpad for wusses," early users noted. Later, it was hoped, funds generated by usage would allow for investment in cranes, payload clean rooms, and elevators.[37]

Working with the Spaceport Authority, KSC also began to build facilities for a research park on some 420 acres of land mainly used as orange groves. Here the Florida of the past would yield once more to a space-centered vision of the Florida of tomorrow. This Space Commerce Park would be located just outside KSC's gates, making it easily accessible to the public but close enough to the Center to take advantage of its facilities. It would support research on launch concepts and undertake projects that could benefit from the work done at KSC. For example, in cooperation with industry, researchers would perform advanced work on corrosion, cryogenics, and materials that reflected the sort of launch and processing work KSC had been doing for nearly four decades. In 2001, work also started on another new facility designed to attract outside research and investment in the area around KSC. The Space Experiment Research and Processing Laboratory was to be a "magnet facility" for the International Space Station, emphasizing research in the life sciences. Labs on the ground would complement labs in space. Scientists would have access to the space station for their research projects.[38] The hope was that firms in the pharmaceutical and related industries would choose to locate nearby.[39]

KSC 2000

By 2000, Bridges was ready to set in motion a comprehensive reorganization plan. It would support all the objectives and future initiatives he had outlined. The Center's existing organizational chart still reflected many elements of its past. Line units included Launch Operations, Shuttle Processing, Engineering, and Space Station and Shuttle Payloads. The new organizational chart would group these functions into Shuttle and International Space Station Processing, and Expendable Vehicles, capturing the major current work of the Center. A new type of future-oriented engineering would be done in a new Spaceport Engineering and Technology group. External Relations, up one level from the line directorates, would handle public affairs, but also scout new business development opportunities and external partnerships. By streamlining and reorganizing in these ways, Bridges hoped to do two things. First, he would free more personnel to work on new projects, and second, he would help shift the culture to a future orientation.[40]

Given how much of KSC's budget still came through existing programs like the shuttle, shifting to the future was going to be difficult. Crucial to KSC 2000, therefore, was creating a new approach to learning and knowledge. The plan recognized three cultures at KSC: Sustaining, Development, and Service. Each had its particular characteristics, but all three were "highly interdependent." Development work, for example, depended on knowledge and skills from operations, the "sustaining" culture. Both development and operations in turn depended on a strong, efficient institution that provided the needed resources and services. Just the same, they were distinct enough that, to be successful, they had to respect one another's uniqueness and not pit themselves one against the other.[41]

Development involved gray areas with fuzzy requirements and evolving technology and mandates. It was inherently speculative work and would end in failure probably 50 percent of the time, a necessary cost to learning new things. Only perhaps in the early years of the Center when it was still being designed and built had such a significant portion of the organization been given such a task.

By contrast, the sustaining culture emphasized consistency and completion of definite work in a definite time for existing customers. There was far less uncertainty here. Sustaining work tended to be black and white; it followed clear goals and had clear performance measures. KSC had largely been characterized by its sustaining culture, and a proud record of getting the work done, as the "end of the line" for NASA. But now it would have to make room for the greater uncertainty and speculation needed for a true development culture, without giving up its success in sustaining operations. A tall order, to be sure. KSC would continue to do the work needed to launch shuttles and complete the space station, while at the same time investigating launch concepts for vehicles not yet built.

Development work would take place in the new Spaceport Engineering and Technology Directorate. Partly a renaming of the old Design Engineering group, Spaceport Technology was mandated to prepare for the future. Among its units were offices dedicated to research on various systems—range technology, mechanical, fluid—as well as an office for vehicle processing. Spaceport Technology engineers were expected to place strong emphasis on cost-reducing, efficiency-enhancing launch operations. At the core of the new directorate was the philosophy "operations knowledge enables technology development."[42] Units doing materials testing, for example, would seek both to understand the conditions under which materials failed and to find ways to integrate new materials into future vehicles. Another part of the directorate emphasized new technology application and transfer. In keeping with the customer emphasis, there was also a projects office, the "primary point of contact" between the directorate and those needing its services.[43]

Project management had long been used at KSC to bring to bear the skills of various specialists on specific projects, but the emphasis now was moving toward serving "customers." The IPTs used for the space station were an example of this sort of customer-focused organization, but now the number of customers expanded to include a wider range of entitites: a commercial aerospace firm, the Department of Defense, and even another NASA unit. All KSC directorates were asked to see themselves as serving some final customer down the line. Rather than a top-down bureaucracy, cooperation with multiple stakeholders would be the policy. Rather than a stable institution, a network would be the organizational model. Rather than a unit in a vertically integrated NASA that did everything except build boosters, the new KSC would act as a research center, cooperate with private industry in design and operations, and use its authority to forge agreements and joint ventures with public- and private-sector partners.

How far might these changes go? With NASA's budget flat through 2001, KSC had only limited resources to move into research while fulfilling its mandate to fly the shuttle and prepare and launch the space station. Under new president George W. Bush, the Center was ordered once more to consider ways to hand over more operations to private contractors, perhaps even privatizing the shuttle fleet.[44] Before any of this could be implemented, though, fate intervened once more.

Columbia

"Has it ever struck your organizational minds that there is an answer to error or malfunction of a space craft in orbit?" began an unsigned letter to Kurt Debus in 1968. The answer, continued the writer, was "a twin standby . . . craft." A backup in case anything went wrong. So far as we know, this letter was never answered. The recommendation probably received a passing smile, if that. How could the United States afford to prepare two vehicles for every mission? The letter writer had considered that. "I know cost will be the argument; but, if it prevents loss of life," would that not be worth the cost?[45]

In one of history's ironies, this same recommendation was included among those made by the Columbia Accident Investigation Board (CAIB) probing the loss of the shuttle *Columbia* on February 1, 2003. In retrospect, of course, everything looks clear, everything obvious, everything worth the cost. In words that now look all too prophetic, however, the Augustine Committee had noted in 1990 that "statistical evidence indicates that we are likely to lose another space shuttle in the next several years."[46]

The loss of the shuttle *Columbia* again raised the question of how much care and handling a vehicle needs on the ground before it is ready to fly in outer space. "I don't care how many times it's flown, it's still a rocket," remarked Ike Rigell, veteran of the Apollo era, in the wake of the *Columbia* tragedy.[47] As he recalled, after one of the early Saturn V launches a review found that they had come within a millisecond of an engine shutdown. Loss of engine thrust during liftoff would have been a catastrophic event. All the public saw, though, was a perfect launch. Only milliseconds changed *Challenger* from an unremarkable launch to a disaster. When dealing with

13-3. The thin skin of the orbiter, protected only by delicate tiles.

technology at the extremes, milliseconds and microns can be like days and miles.

The cascading events that caused *Columbia* to break up over the southwestern United States are now clear enough. Upon launch a briefcase-sized piece of insulating foam from the shuttle's main tank broke free and struck the leading edge of the orbiter's left wing. Impact occurred 81.9 seconds into flight, with the shuttle traveling at twice the speed of sound. When the orbiter descended to earth on February 1, the hole left by the foam strike allowed superhot gases generated by the vehicle's rapid descent through the atmosphere to penetrate and destroy the wing. Dynamic stresses soon overwhelmed *Columbia*, and it broke apart over Texas, killing all seven aboard. It was the second shuttle loss in 113 missions.

As with *Challenger*, the accident investigation focused both on this immediate cause and on more remote factors, including organization, economics, and culture. Loss of foam on liftoff was a well-known, common problem, but one that NASA had come to accept as normal, much as the rotation of the solid rocket booster joint that led to *Challenger* had been normalized. Small foam strikes were seen as just a part of standard operations—a maintenance nuisance, to be sure, but nothing that endangered life or mission. NASA's "organizational culture" took the blame for this thinking. The agency had come to make assumptions and hold beliefs that, in this case, undercut its ability to see a dangerous problem.[48]

Even the CAIB, however, recognized that certain features of the shuttle just had to be lived with. It did not order NASA to eliminate all foam debris, only to mount a more aggressive campaign to minimize the risk. Other recommendations included giving the astronauts in orbit a means to inspect possible tile damage, eliminating night flights (when it would be more difficult to assess liftoff damage), and restricting the shuttle to International Space Station missions, where the crew would have a safe haven if they could not return to earth. The board also advised having a second shuttle standing by in case of emergency. These, however, were guidelines, and it remained up to NASA to decide how to proceed.

Fifteen of the board's recommendations addressed the agency's organizational and technical culture. What, the CAIB wanted to know, had turned NASA eyes away from the risks and dangers that foam presented? Among the things identified was the turmoil of Daniel Goldin's tenure as administrator, including the SFOC, the contract that privatized shuttle operations. The shuttle workforce was cut by 42 percent under Goldin, who was relentlessly committed to reducing costs.[49] NASA's overall budget was flat in the 1990s, meaning that in real dollars it went down, even while overall government spending was going up 25 percent.[50] Assumptions about the cost of operations, the board noted, may have given NASA a false sense of what it could accomplish with its lean budget. Placing all its faith in operating efficiency and private-sector competition, the agency tried to do more with fewer resources. Fewer missions and more money for maintenance, upgrades, and safety would have been the better option, the CAIB reflected.[51] Downsizing had stopped before the *Columbia* accident, and under the influence of Roy Bridges and others, the numbers had even begun to come back up at KSC.[52] But the accident quickly ended any speculations that KSC could be run as a GOCO.

One aspect of what the CAIB identified as a cultural (and also organizational) fault in NASA was failure to examine possible damage to *Columbia* by using military telescopes to view the orbiter in space. Reviewing film the day after launch, members of the Intercenter Photo Working Group were startled by the size of the foam piece, larger than any seen before, apparently striking somewhere on or near the orbiter wing. Their cameras, however, were either out of focus, in the wrong position, or of insufficient resolution to determine exactly what had happened. A Debris Assessment Team began evaluating the possible consequences of an impact. Requests for photographs were forwarded to the Department of Defense, whose high-resolution telescopes might yield a clear image of any damage. These requests did not go directly up the chain of command through NASA's mission management team, however. Whether this unorthodox move was simply a mistake or whether it reflected a belief that a direct request would be ignored remains unclear. Eventually the requests, coming from several sources, made their way to mission managers. The head of the mission management team, Linda Ham, heard from her subordinates that the photography was unnecessary. She quashed requests for photos of the damaged shuttle.

The interesting question is, why would mission managers not listen to those evaluating photography and debris at the launch site? These were, after all, NASA's designated experts on launch incidents. One possible interpretation is that this incident shows how poorly operational knowledge and expertise was integrated into NASA's structure.[53] A "party line" mentality cut off internal debate and discussion, particularly, it seems, when it came from NASA's launch operations end. Officials on the mission management team turned down the requests for not going through proper channels, but more was involved here than simple bureaucratic formality. "Communication did not flow effectively up to or down from Program managers," noted the CAIB, as managers tended to accept opinions that agreed with their own and not listen to dissenting voices.[54]

Columbia forced NASA to revisit issues of work and management that had so recently been revised with the SFOC contract. Had turning over much of the day-to-day processing of the shuttle adversely affected safety? Immediately after *Challenger*, NASA had spent considerable sums assuring that the shuttle would be operated safely after return to flight. But then the shuttle budget declined. In part, this decline reflected the enormous amount expended just after *Challenger* to institute new procedures, enact safety recommendations, and add new technology. But some of the decline was also due to the professed policy of getting operating costs down.

There was no conscious trade-off of safety for efficiency here.[55] NASA's studies had shown that moving to contractor processing would not endanger safety. Indeed, it might actually make the shuttle safer, since fewer hands would be responsible for the work (though critics noted that this also meant fewer eyes inspecting the work). The contractor, United Space Alliance, maintained that it had strong motivation to keep safety first. "If we're not able to meet the safety requirements . . . we're out of business and we know that," said a company spokesman.[56] There were dissents, however, notably from NASA's Aerospace Safety Advisory Panel. At what point might the pursuit of efficiency interfere with safety, the panel asked? No one knew. The panel especially criticized the assumption that the shuttle was a mature technology whose design could essentially be frozen and operated in this low-cost manner. As we have seen, Bridges and others at KSC had argued back to NASA headquarters about the need for government personnel to do insight and oversight work of contractors and pointed out the special type of knowledge that came from operations. *Columbia* only strengthened their argument, showing that critics who worried about the effects of contracting were not simply using safety as a shield to protect their own jobs and interests. There were genuine issues at stake here.[57]

One of the main goals of Bridges's reorganization of KSC was to assure the necessary mix of skills and experience even as the workforce changed. As part of that goal, KSC had reorganized its safety office just before *Columbia*. Safety organization at the Center had historically vacillated between centralized and decentralized forms. Each had advantages and disadvantages. An independent, centralized safety organization meant that those doing the inspecting did not report to the boss in charge of the work. But it also meant that the inspectors were somewhat removed from the day-to-day processing and preparing of the vehicle. In KSC 2000, Bridges instituted a new arrangement that preserved a central safety office, though it removed those doing quality inspection work and put them in the line directorates. The move reflected the distinctive nature of different tasks. Quality assurance personnel oversaw work and assured it was done properly. To fully understand what was going on, quality inspectors had to be part of the work flow. By contrast, the safety office made sure that workers understood the importance of avoiding accidents and kept track of dangerous situations.[58] The question was, with cutbacks and an emphasis on reducing costs, did KSC have enough people working in the independent safety office? Was that group large enough to have knowledge of the full range of operations?[59]

Nothing about the *Columbia* accident could be traced directly to these structural changes at KSC. But the CAIB addressed the larger question of how the emphasis on efficiency may have affected not just current operations but knowledge, understanding, and research.[60] Emphasizing operational efficiency necessarily meant spending less money and time performing research or making modifications. If, as critics of the SFOC and other related efficiency measures argued, the shuttle remained a "research vessel," then sacrificing research for operational efficiency might endanger overall safety, even if the work was being done as safely as possible.

The impact of *Columbia* is still being felt. What it will mean for NASA and human space flight remains uncertain at this point. But one aspect of the accident and investigation has a special bearing on the history of the Kennedy Space Center. When NASA took up the challenge of getting a man on the moon in less than a decade, it adopted procedures of program management designed to keep research within a budget and on a timetable so it could achieve its goal. Program management may have been necessary to run a large-scale engineering project like Apollo, but it also limited the amount of research that could be done on vehicles and missions, particularly at the operations end. The assumption that designers can fully understand the vehicles they build without additional knowledge from and through the operations cycle is precisely what the CAIB criticized in *Columbia*. *Columbia* thus may indicate that NASA's traditional strength in program management has exhausted its limits. Operations contains a significant amount of knowledge that penetrates to a fundamental understanding of vehicles that fly in space. The research and learning that goes on in operations may not receive its full due if all the emphasis goes to reducing costs and streamlining operations.

*   *   *

When the time came for the sad task of recovering the wreckage of *Columbia*, the recovery team was led by KSC personnel. Mike Leinbach helped to bring back twenty-seven truckloads of *Columbia* to Merritt Island. There a team led by Scott Thurston cleaned, decontaminated, and logged it into a massive database.[61] No one knew the vehicle better, had more experience with it, or understood it as well as the engineers and technicians who had tested, handled, and launched it for more than twenty years. What could better demonstrate how much knowledge of space technology resides in operations than this?

The Future of KSC?

The CAIB has argued (as many had long believed) that the shuttle, a first-generation reusable vehicle, has too many inherent limitations, too much "old" technology, ever to be operated in the stress-free, efficient manner promised when it was designed. Replacing it with something new, and seeing the shuttle as a development project, a stepping-stone, rather than an end in itself, is NASA's best hope for coming out of this moment and moving on to the future.[62] What that future will be remains uncertain, however. President Bush has outlined bold new missions to the moon, Mars, and beyond, so reminiscent of what Wernher von Braun wrote about in *Collier's* magazine decades ago. Will these missions ever come to pass? And if so, what will be the role of KSC in this future?

Launch operations now face fierce international competition. There is reason to believe that KSC will continue to hold its preeminent place in getting rockets into space. But someday there may no longer be a presumed central location for watching launches happen. The powerful, iconic image of a massive rocket slowly rising amid the smoke of its own fire may pass into oblivion just as the great iron steam trains of the nineteenth century belching fire and smoke as they left stations now exist only in paintings. Rockets will continue to fly, of course, just as trains continue to run. In the early days of commercial aviation, when cities began building airports, they built observation platforms in their terminals and carved out spots for cars to park around their perimeters. They did so to fulfill the public's apparently endless fascination with watching planes take off and land. The planes still take off and land, but few passengers on their way to their flights stop to observe. Few families park their cars and watch the comings and goings at the airport as a Sunday outing anymore. The same may one day happen to the Kennedy Space Center. People may one day stop coming to watch. If the destiny of spaceships, as many have argued, is to become more like trains, planes, and automobiles, more like other routine forms of transportation, why should they?

The land on which the Kennedy Space Center sits is fragile, a low coral and sand outcropping of delicate ecology and endangered species. But the colossal structures going back to the early space age are equally fragile. KSC's transformation of a thin strip of earth into a springboard for space was celebrated in the 1960s as the triumph of human will and technology over the natural environment. But a quick walk around the Center shows how easily the savannah can reassert itself. Notices warn walkers to beware of alligators lurking in ditches and culverts. Dozens of old launchpads now sit neglected amid the sand dunes of Cape Canaveral, rusting and crumbling. Will the VAB and the Launch Control Center suffer the same fate? They can survive the corrosive effects of salt, sand, and sea air, but only if they remain relevant to the style of launch operations of the future.

However much the work of getting into space may change, of course, there will always have to be someplace rockets leave from. That place may be a network of many launch points rather than a single center as it is now,

13-4. Shuttle at dawn or dusk.

more like a system of airports or train stations. But then again, space travel and space technology may never be fully reducible to their earth counterparts after all. While terrestrial forms of transportation have met a basic, emotional urge to move around the planet and explore, they have largely had practical, economical, and commercial purposes and payoffs. We have tried to make space into an extraterrestrial version of the same thing, and thus turn space technology into a similarly practical mode of transportation. But what if the analogy is a false one, and there will never be a payoff equivalent to what Columbus got when he landed his ships in the Caribbean? What if, in the end, the urge to explore remains the primary motive for a space program?

Astronaut Buzz Aldrin has written that "beyond all rationales, space flight is a spiritual quest in the broadest sense."[63] If he is right, then launching people out to the void will always have a spiritual element to it as well, more like a religious service than a plane flight. And if so, then there will always need to be a place where we can see it happen, even if we are not going for that particular ride. There will always be a Kennedy Space Center, even if it is not the current one, a place not just where the necessary work is performed, but where we can see and feel the process happening, and wait and watch for that final moment called "liftoff."

14

*
*
*

Conclusion

*Life, for ever dying to be born afresh, for ever young and
eager, will presently stand up on this earth as upon a
footstool, and stretch out its realm amidst the stars.*

H. G. Wells, *The Outline of History* (1920)

The Columbia Accident Investigation Board (CAIB) report asked that NASA
adopt the "best characteristics of a learning organization." It provided a list
of these characteristics, including feedback loops, a strong institutional
memory, and willingness to learn from history. It looked for the creation of
formal structures that could bring lessons learned in operations back into
engineering and management.[1] As the CAIB report acknowledged, operational understanding and learning from practice may be even more important than good design in assuring safety and reliability. This point echoes
one made a few years before by the Commission on the Future of the United
States Aerospace Industry. The commission noted that "attempts at developing breakthrough space transportation systems have proved illusory."[2] It
recommends instead that the nation base its space program more on incremental improvements. Such incremental improvements will come by
gaining a deeper, more refined appreciation of technology through use and
operations.

KSC and NASA Organization

As is true of many other complex organizations, NASA has frequently overlooked operations as a significant source of learning. The reasons for this
neglect go deep into the history of the American space program. Though
the CAIB spoke of NASA's culture, in fact the agency has many cultures.[3]
When the American space program began, no institution possessed the skills
needed for building a ship to fly in space carrying humans, or for designing

a booster to lift that spacecraft into orbit. No one knew how to construct a vehicle that could reach the lunar surface, or apparatus that would allow astronauts to survive in the airless void. The same was true of launch operations. Scaling up for the stupendous lunar mission could not be a simple linear extrapolation from previous launchpads. Early on, therefore, NASA decided to draw on existing institutions and sources of expertise for what it needed. It drew on its predecessor NACA for engineers with deep knowledge of aerospace technology. It incorporated the German scientists from the army's Redstone Arsenal. It contracted with commercial aerospace firms for engines, guidance, telemetry systems, and other hardware. It employed the Army Corps of Engineers to design and build ground facilities. As a result NASA developed a decentralized structure, with much of its expertise in its field centers. Innovation at NASA has taken place through a flow of knowledge between different organizations and across distinct cultures of work, rather than at one central location.

Like other parts of NASA, KSC nests in a complex network of institutions, organizations, agencies, and contractors. But KSC has had a dual role. It is a place of knowledge and expertise in preparing, testing, and launching rockets, and at the same time it is one of NASA's operational arms, providing "launch services" to others who design vehicles and missions.[4] The result has been something of a tension. Is KSC merely to take orders from others and do their bidding? Or does it contribute unique skills and knowledge which feed back into the design of hardware, conception of missions, and policies of the space program?

Operating may imply merely taking and fulfilling orders and following routines designated by others. Such a role would have limited KSC to what the organizational learning guru Chris Argyris calls "single loop" learning.[5] The launch center would have been responsible only for finding and correcting errors in hardware and procedures, for refining the techniques of launch, and for creating efficient routines to do its job. Important as such work is, it rarely challenges prevailing assumptions about missions or technology. It is not innovative.

More recent studies of operations, particularly operations in high-performance, high-stress environments, suggest something rather different. In nuclear power stations, aircraft carriers, and submarines, the operators of technology actually make key contributions to quality assurance and innovation. They act more like "experimenters" testing designs and gaining crucial understanding of hardware that can come only from use. They also develop shortcuts and "workarounds" not anticipated in the planning and design phase. Such operational learning and experimentation permits giant systems of technology to operate *despite* the fact that complexity inevitably breeds problems that cannot be anticipated.[6] In this the workers at KSC were more like users of commercial technology, who have been recognized recently as key actors in the innovation process. Successful firms, students of innovation now understand, interact with their customers and users in fruitful ways.[7]

From the start, the leadership of KSC proposed that it had to do more than simply "operate" space technology in the narrow sense. As Kurt Debus realized, it was necessary to "'close the loop' between development and launch operations."[8] Operations would play a key role in gaining a deeper understanding of space flight. The testing, integrating, and launching of rockets and spacecraft would provide insights not realizable in the design or even the manufacturing phase. Such knowledge would feed back to the design centers, perhaps fundamentally challenging their plans and assumptions with what was learned "on the ground," in use and practice.

The tension over KSC's function and purpose reflects the particular way NASA has conceptualized learning and innovation. The space agency has been highly innovative, but along particular channels. No one can dispute its achievement in developing, almost from scratch, the major systems and concepts necessary to take space flight from science fiction to accomplished fact. But as the Commission on the Future of the United States Aerospace Industry recognized, most innovation is not a matter of brilliant coups so much as steady incremental progress. The history of KSC suggests we need a new way to think about learning and innovation in the space program.

Organizational theorist Edgar Schein has argued that too frequently engineering and design cultures fail to acknowledge the importance of operator cultures, even though all three are really parts of a whole. Operators have local and tacit knowledge, derived directly from their hands-on experience. Designers tend to put more credence into formal rules and procedures stemming from disciplinary training. Operators, of course, depend heavily on rules and procedures as well, but they also have to live with the special pressures of finishing the job and seeing that the equipment actually operates. They understand that hardware will function differently in use than it does on the drawing board, in ways that may well violate the formal rules. Where designers and conceptual thinkers believe that success flows from excellent design and planning, operators believe that it comes from testing, proving, and trying. As Schein puts it, "No matter how carefully engineered the production process is or how carefully the routes and routines are specified, operators must have the capacity to learn and to deal with surprises."[9]

It is not always resistance from higher up the policy chain or from design engineers that blocks operator knowledge from getting through. Because operator knowledge tends to be "distributed" across the operator groups, coming as it does from their experiences in carrying out tasks rather than from studying tasks before or after they are done, it can be difficult to communicate to other parts of a complex organization. Tacit, distributed knowledge cannot be fully expressed in written, formal procedures. It is perhaps best described as a "distillation of experience combined with ingenuity."[10] Yet in times of change and uncertainty (common during innovation), operator knowledge may be more important than formal, written knowledge.[11] Failure to bring together the equally valid but different perspectives of operators with those of designers and policy makers can result in both technological malfunctions and organizational breakdown. Different groups possessing different forms of knowledge stick to their own "silos" and fail to develop the common language needed to understand a complex technology in its entirety.

Managing Technology

The uncertain place of operator knowledge within the space program reflects the dual traditions of management that have characterized NASA, and KSC in particular. As we have seen, NASA emerged from a number of predecessor organizations. But two approaches to knowledge in particular marked its early history: the German rocket tradition and the newer methods of program management inspired by the air force. Each had strengths and weaknesses, it now seems clear. The German approach stressed close vertical integration of all parts of the process of designing, fabricating, preparing, testing, and firing rockets. This allowed for careful coordination between designers, builders, testers, and operators. But it could not be used in its original form as rockets became bigger, missions more ambitious, and schedules tighter. Program management, with the reliance on private-sector contractors, provided the sort of control and discipline necessary to focus functionally arranged research and engineering departments on specific program tasks. It worked well for getting to the moon, but it was also a technique that tended to slight the sort of on-the-ground knowledge gained through operations in favor of more abstract managerial techniques.

At KSC this was somewhat less of a problem, in part because the launch center actually drew strongly on both approaches. Day-to-day work required a hybrid culture. KSC personnel used methods such as systems engineering and configuration management to handle the multiple interfaces of the Apollo spacecraft and Saturn rocket. The Cape had a program office to conform to the program management approach needed to run the lunar program. But at a finer level of detail, we can see that the informal prob-lem-solving approach remained. Teams of civil servants and contractors got together, debated, questioned, challenged, and decided.

For all the higher-level wrangling over how to do things—the air force way or the German way—in the end what was most significant was that nei-ther work tradition completely dominated at the Cape. This was true even in their respective strongholds of spacecraft and launch vehicle operations. The German-trained engineers working on the Saturn booster quickly ac-cepted the need to reorganize from functional engineering disciplines to systems engineering. They accepted contractors, quality control, and cross-checking of work. The spacecraft group ended up modifying its air force model into one approaching a system of checks and balances, with contrac-tors taking a large role but civil service engineers at KSC (and, indeed, back in Houston) having plenty of experience and knowledge of the contractor's technology.[12]

As the combined Apollo-Saturn vehicle approached launch, still more of the distinctions vanished in the process of integrating technical systems. A separate launch organization, which absorbed and understood both work cultures, took charge of the stacked rocket and moved it to the launch date. One reason that integration prevailed was the operator culture. As the "end of the line," KSC was a unique environment. Pressure to make sure that, in the end, everything worked tended to overcome any differences in peo-ple's training, culture, or background. Most of the veterans of the Apollo era recalled this quite clearly. As launch day approached, the Cape became a different place. It was like "a family" where brothers and sisters fought but then put aside their squabbles as the days counted down. The common experience and discipline of the clock moving inexorably to launch tended to make intramural matters seem rather small and insignificant. For all the differences in function and technical culture, people quickly united at mis-sion time.[13]

The merger of two traditions in this intense operator environment gave KSC a unique work culture that stood in contrast to the design centers. Vet-erans of the Apollo years came away impressed with KSC's ability to drive work on a schedule that involved coordinating the completion of multistage booster, spacecraft, ground support equipment, and other facilities. "Your work is a team effort tied together by an integrated schedule," commented John Conway.[14] That the work of each individual affected the performance of other team members was a lesson one quickly learned at KSC. Just as important was the experience of seeing something not at the early stages of concept and planning, but only at the later stages needing completion. Often hardware arrived incomplete. Knowing that there was no other place for it to go but into space gave workers their special sense of ownership of the hardware, even that produced by private firms. As Rocco Petrone put it with characteristic bluntness, when contractors came to the Cape speaking of "their" stage of the rocket, they soon learned "used to be your stage, now mine!"[15]

The on-the-ground reality of life at KSC differed significantly from how people elsewhere in NASA perceived what was going on. To those at NASA headquarters, the key to making the lunar program work—and, by extension, all human space flight—lay with the new techniques inherited from the air force. As space historian Stephen Johnson has noted, program management was an excellent device for administering research and development activities. As an operations center, however, KSC was not primarily about research and development in the *traditional* sense, but about operational learning. A thoroughgoing program management structure was too bureaucratic to deal with this sort of learning. The operating arm of NASA had to have sufficient leeway to adapt and make changes as it gained experience with the rockets it was testing and launching. Thus KSC engineers ended up going to the factories even before the rockets arrived, to work out procedures for use and testing while fabrication was taking place. They also gained more and more control over the contractors working at Merritt Island, even when those contractors reported to program managers at other centers.[16]

The Apollo program demonstrated how inadequate was the initial conception of operations in NASA's model of organization. Originally it was assumed that vehicles would simply be sent to the Cape and, after a straightforward test, set up to launch. This ship-and-shoot notion was proved wrong, with Apollo and again and again in KSC's history. In a business where people got "surprises every day," KSC had to have its own "systems engineers" with independent knowledge of hardware derived from how they used and understood it in an operations context. Operational responsibilities tended naturally to make engineers think in terms of the total system and its interactions.[17] Cooperation and coordination were built into operations, so there was no need to worry about engineers endlessly tinkering with their own piece of the puzzle at the expense of the system as a whole. Real-world pressure forced confrontations, debates, and discussions among the different work units at KSC. Perhaps that was true elsewhere, but there was no way anyone who visited the Cape could come away believing the engineers were too speculative or ivory-tower in their thinking.

In practice it was nearly impossible to draw a bright line separating research, design, and development from operations, as NASA headquarters proposed. It was also impossible to simply turn over work to contractors and manage what they did. Hands-on work remained part of what went on at KSC, despite the air force model's assumptions. At the same time, innovation and learning went on in operations, just not the same type of innovation and learning going on in the design centers. Perhaps the clearest example can be seen in a decision usually credited to the new program-management outlook—the decision to go "all up" with Apollo-Saturn launches.

When George Mueller made this decision, he was following the logic of the air force model. If one had carefully specified procedures, managed technical configurations and interfaces, and integrated the systems, then the rocket should work when all parts were brought together. Mueller was right, of course, and his decision got the United States on the moon before decade's end. But all-up testing rested on many years of previous experience that had already gone into the Saturn vehicle and its predecessors. There was plenty of penetrating knowledge of the rocket engines, stages, guidance system, and the like which had been acquired during earlier years of testing. It remains impossible to say if the all-up decision was the end of the older German-based tradition of testing, or the culmination of it.

Apollo's Legacy

Reflecting on NASA just months after the conquest of the moon, James Webb, the administrator who had made it all possible, argued that Apollo was a model for how to get things done in a modern society. Webb was on the defensive, for detractors had already begun to question the costs and benefits of the mission. *Fortune* magazine was especially critical, noting that the technical wizardry of Apollo was far less innovative than had been claimed. NASA offered little to those wrestling with civilian economic and social problems. Webb's answer was to agree with his critics on one point: the space program was much more about managing people than about science and technology. Apollo showed how a complex organization could be adaptable and flexible in pursuit of a hugely ambitious and highly uncertain goal.[18]

Webb's response echoed one given six years before by KSC deputy director Albert Siepert. Siepert too emphasized "the necessity for gradual evolution and constant improvisation to meet unforeseen administrative developments." Rather than starting with a new, centralized bureaucracy, NASA maximized technological creativity and resourcefulness through "local flexibility." Particularly important here was the "wealth of experience in the field."[19]

Both Webb and Siepert captured perfectly the on-the-ground reality at the Kennedy Space Center during the Apollo years. Perhaps nowhere else were flexibility, adaptability, and interaction with real-world conditions more evident. Following Webb's argument, then, NASA should have brought this aspect of its young history forward into the next era. The sort of operational learning that took place at KSC should have been given serious consideration. In fact, however, just the opposite happened in the shuttle era. Rather than openness, flexibility, and variation, NASA erred on the side of certainty, security, and caution.

When something big and important happens to an institution, the lessons of that event tend to leave a deep imprint.[20] Those who worked at NASA during Apollo came away thinking in terms of a big, well-defined, well-funded project. Even within KSC, the success of the Apollo program tended to harden positions. Those who had worked on the Saturn vehicle believed that its success was due to their strong hands-on tradition of work. Those who had wrestled with the Apollo spacecraft grew wedded to the air force model and came to believe that perfection would be found by the imposition of this approach to all tasks. The debates over which work culture was best for the future would continue in the 1970s and beyond, but they would take place in a much different environment.

After Apollo, NASA had to deal with an environment of political ambiguity and uncertainty. Critics of the space agency have charged that once the sense of excitement and the special ingredients of the moon race were gone, NASA acted like any other government bureau, "the post office gone to space." It protected turf, placed its survival first, and engaged in the usual Washington infighting for resources.[21] Supporters counter that once the moon was ours, we lost interest in her, and in space. No president after Lyndon Johnson put NASA high on his list of priorities, and the agency's budget shrank considerably in the 1970s. Whatever the cause, the fact was that the shuttle program operated under conditions that emphasized cost control, efficiency, and certain outcomes. These conditions undercut the very sort of learning that a center like KSC could provide.

Despite their best efforts, KSC engineers had only limited impact on shuttle design decisions. Shuttle designers argued that there was simply not enough time and money to incorporate suggestions for making the vehicle easier to process and handle on the ground. Webb had touted the ability of NASA to "spread . . . problems over the largest number of able minds and to draw upon the range of the nation's scientific and industrial competence in the locations where it existed." But political and budgetary realities of the 1970s meant that some of NASA's own minds would get very little hearing. As former NASA deputy administrator Dale Myers acknowledged much later, "had the [shuttle] design team concentrated on operations as strongly as they concentrated on development," they might well have achieved the sought-after reductions in the cost of flight.[22]

Even beyond design issues, the shuttle received limited benefit from KSC's rich operations heritage. Seen as a new technology, the shuttle was assumed operable without all the messy work that had gone into preparing Apollo-Saturn for launch. This belief had perhaps its most pernicious effect in the ill-fated attempt to reduce turnaround time for shuttle processing to a mere 160 hours. Even if unrealistic from the start, the turnaround goal spoke to a strong belief that operations was at best an unfortunate necessity, and one that should be minimized at every chance. In the interests of efficiency, the sort of penetration and learning that had gone on in the early years of launch operations was pushed aside.

The organizational embodiment of this mentality was the triumph of the air force–inspired model above the German tradition. By the time the shuttle began to fly, most of the old German rocket team was gone. Those at the Cape who had been brought up in this tradition were relegated to secondary or support roles for the new vehicle, or moved into the payloads organization. Following the air force example, NASA turned more work over to contractors. It was an odd assumption in many ways, that the efficiency sought for the shuttle would be found in the model of air force weapons procurement, usually noted for hefty budgets and cost overruns.[23]

Politics had much to do with these decisions. Budget limits forced NASA both to oversell shuttle economics and to reduce upfront expenditures. Under presidents Nixon, Carter, and Reagan, more space work was shifted to private-sector contractors, who themselves were eager to take greater control of the higher-level systems engineering functions and not just take orders from government engineers. NASA needed industry support to get the shuttle approved, and thus found itself in a more dependent relationship with contractors. It was less able to maintain the coordinating role among private actors than it had in earlier programs.[24]

Surprisingly, though, the hybrid model of work used with Apollo survived at KSC. Even though many of those responsible for flying the shuttle had grown up in the spacecraft side of the Apollo program, they inevitably brought with them aspects of both cultures, since the two had acted together during the Apollo era. If anything, over time those working on the shuttle came to appreciate the approach and some of the procedures of the German tradition. From an operations standpoint, the shuttle was not the "greenfield" technology it had once seemed. It was still a rocket. It still had to be stacked, tested, and launched against the countdown clock. It still required the often tedious and sometimes harrowing work of integrating the components into a working system. Operations learning is by nature incremental, so much of the useful past carried over into the shuttle.

KSC experiences in the 1980s kept pointing to the importance of a thorough understanding of technology gained in practice. No one yet understood why rockets flown by humans were more reliable than rockets that were not, even as the reliability of these robotic vehicles improved in 1970s and 1980s. KSC engineers thus continued to believe they had to test to "drive out failure." This caution conflicted with the desire to move the shuttle into a routine "operational" phase.[25] Design engineers, confident that they had caught all foreseeable problems, understood the need only for limited testing. KSC personnel, taking the operator perspective, did not want to back away from procedures that had worked well in the past.

For a time the *Challenger* accident settled this debate. In the wake of the tragedy, NASA was roundly criticized for, in essence, treating a research vessel as though it were an airliner. Safety now came first, and safety and quality-assurance work was centralized throughout NASA. Still, for all the impact of *Challenger*, it did not change one fundamental fact. Through the Reagan, Bush, and Clinton administrations the emphasis continued to go to reducing costs, trimming budgets, and privatizing as much work as possible. Once again, the lessons of operations were lost in a cloud of politics.

Structure versus Process

Where once efficiency was assumed to flow from rapid vehicle turnover and many flights per year, now it would come by working smarter, with fewer people. This was perhaps the most significant change in the history of shuttle operations, certainly in its history at KSC. All previous thinking had been based on designing a vehicle that would perform flawlessly, that was so well designed it could handle an ambitious schedule. The new thinking under shuttle operations chief Jay Honeycutt was that launch operations could be streamlined to minimize the cost of handling, without sacrificing quality or safety. Honeycutt looked to an industrial engineering philosophy. Not only would shuttle operations be seen in an industrial context, but the emphasis of learning would shift to the shop floor, to the workers who actually handled and processed the machine.

To a degree, the shift in outlook put more attention on operations. Systems engineering and program management dealt only with the middle and top levels of work, the white-collar engineers.[26] These management techniques provided a way to harness the engineer's expert knowledge to the overall needs of a complex system within the confines of budget and schedule. Actual hands-on work, it was assumed, could be done by almost anyone, given proper training and supervision. The new shop-floor techniques of aerospace industrial engineering, on the other hand, acknowledged there was much to be learned from those technicians. This view came closer to the German tradition, where engineers and technicians worked closely in the same organization. Under Roy Bridges, KSC took this a step further. History showed that the Center was engaged in research, though not of the kind normally seen in a laboratory or design center. The ability to capture knowledge from operations and feed it back into the design process was at the heart of Bridges's agenda, a return to what Kurt Debus had hoped would happen almost four decades earlier.

But these moves were undercut by the emphasis on shifting work from civil servants to contractors. Two logics informed this shift. Most simply, presidents were seeking ways to trim government expenditures, and cutting back the payrolls of civil servants was a way to do that. But a deeper reason lay with the unbridged gulf between what was thought of as operations and what was seen as research and development. Operations may have received more attention in the 1990s, but throughout the aerospace industry the assumption held firm that operations was one thing, research something else.

The 1996 Space Flight Operations Contract embodied this perspective. Few people at KSC had problems with the largely successful effort to streamline shuttle operations in the 1990s. But SFOC implied that the shuttle was so routine that little could be learned from operating it, and that costs could be trimmed by realigning motives and incentives. These are very strong assumptions. Most of the history of space flight argues that it is a high-risk activity, where nothing can be reduced to routine. Learning goes on constantly in operations. And perhaps most important, motivation and incentive structures have little to do with outcomes in these areas.[27] The history of shuttle processing suggests that intimate shop-floor-level knowledge made a huge difference in how efficiently the vehicle could be prepared for flight. This was less a matter of worker incentives than of gaining access to that knowledge and coordinating it through a streamlined flow of processing.

Profit-driven companies certainly have tremendous incentive to cut costs and trim excess labor: their bottom lines are directly affected by their costs.[28] A similar but less clearly articulated logic underlies the belief that profit assures safety, or at least does not contradict it. No contractor would ever want to pay the price, in both dollars and public shame, for endangering an astronaut crew. Yet SFOC came at the very moment that competition was in decline in the aerospace industry, and it gave a single giant contract to a partnership of the only two firms capable of bidding on the contract. How much competition can there be if there are no other candidates? SFOC also came after the operations work of the shuttle had been substantially streamlined through deep penetration of process and technology by teams of civil servants and contractors. Both those who favored and those who opposed privatization at KSC now agree on one point. Whoever does the work, it remains important that strong government-contractor teams cooperate and learn as much as they can in the process of operations. This was how things were done at the beginning, even if then the relative balance and position of civil servant and contractor were different. Simple monitoring without penetration to the work process limits the ability of government to control and understand what it is paying for.[29]

How well contracting can work to capture knowledge from operations remains a key question. The Center's new research focus emphasizes the value of operational knowledge. But will KSC be able to do "research" if civil servants no longer do "operations," given that it is precisely the intimate connection between research and operations that is unique to KSC? United Space Alliance, the SFOC contractor, will now presumably learn the inner details of the shuttle that once were learned by civil servants working in the processing flow. Supporters of privatization argue that the contractor–civil service team still holds, and that corporate knowledge of the vehicle can flow both ways. Where early in the shuttle's life knowledge moved from civil servant to contractor, now it can flow back from contractor to civil servant. Given the close relationship between the contractor and civil servant, they argue, learning can still go on.

In his 1968 lecture, James Webb worried over this very point. He believed that the space program had demonstrated what the *public* sector could do in orchestrating and coordinating the work of individual private companies. In the 1960s, this seemed exactly the correct role for public servants, uniting private interests, overcoming barriers put up by competition and individual self-interest to assure the smooth flow of work, knowledge, and operations for the greater good of society, in this case getting to the moon. "It is not possible," Webb warned, "to rely upon even the most complex contracting system where accountants and lawyers are the prime reliance for performance." NASA had to have in-house strength. By 2000, this position was stood on its head. Private self-interest would motivate and overcome obstacles; government was a roadblock, not an initiator, and knowledge could best be secured in private-sector companies.

Recently, SpaceShipOne and Mojave Aerospace Ventures secured the $10 million Ansari X-Prize with the first private launch of a vehicle able to carry three people into space, return, and relaunch within two weeks. A small team of talented engineers had gone where only a giant multi-billion-dollar government bureaucracy had gone before, and at far less cost, with far fewer people. Does this then vindicate the privatizers? There remains still a world, indeed several worlds, of difference between breaching the minimal boundary of space with a small, light ship and voyaging to the moon, or even into low earth orbit with a heavy-payload-lifting vehicle designed for a hundred missions. The X-Prize victor's approach to space may, however, suggest that NASA has locked itself into a very costly and narrow paradigm for space flight. Perhaps multiple vehicles and differentiated programs, rather than the all-in-one approach implied in the shuttle and similar large-scale vehicles, may actually be more efficient. Revitalization of expendable launch vehicles, competition from Ariane and other international launch programs, and now the possibility of private-sector space tourism suggest the limits of a big-engineering-project mentality. Such a mentality was hardly the monopoly of government agencies in the 1960s and 1970s. Many once-dominant private corporations from that era had to abandon the same paradigm.

Work on new vehicles implied may require a radically new design philosophy. The lesson of history, though, is that policy and conceptual innovations should be informed by the sort of operational knowledge collected at KSC. Privatization of shuttle work today relies on some twenty years of difficult learning that went on before the contractors took over. The continued vitality of civil servant–contractor teams rests on the long tradition of workers coming to and remaining at the Cape, even if they change hats from NASA to private industry and back to the government again in their careers. Much of the ability of KSC to retain penetration into the shuttle and learn from it rests on the fact that many working at the Center already possessed intimate operational knowledge, and can pass that on to a future generation. What happens when they leave and retire is uncertain.

Debate over the proper way to organize a space program has been rendered moot for the moment by the *Columbia* accident. Like *Challenger* before it, *Columbia* has reinforced the safety-first notion that human space flight is simply too different from terrestrial flight to ever be treated in routine fashion. If that is so, then continual learning during launch preparation and after return will always be a feature of a vehicle with humans aboard. It is suggestive that even while the work of shuttle processing, assumed to be well-understood, was being farmed out to contractors, KSC also argued successfully for strenuous, thorough, and integrated testing on the ground of International Space Station components. The station was new and required an operational learning process similar to what other new flight hardware had gone through. Will the skills and knowledge exist for this sort of work at KSC when the next project call comes?

What all of this suggests is that process, more than organizational structure, is the important lesson of the past forty-five years of the American space program. NASA may have become a victim of a management ideology. Systems engineering and program management using matrix forms of organization, it was believed, would solve the complex technical problems of postwar America. Military weapons, aerospace hardware, missions to the moon, even efforts to fight poverty and urban blight would benefit from these new methods of management and control.[30] It is now clear that these "formal" methodologies and structures, however rational they may have been, were not sufficient. Formal rationality needed substance, the actual learning, the ad hoc lessons, the debates and trials and retrials, the human interactions that went on day by day in the space program. After Apollo, though, this flexibility hardened into a belief that formal structures and methods alone were the "secret" to Apollo's success. The living, breathing reality of operations and the lessons learned there had been written out of the experience.[31]

Leadership and People

Where structure can never be taken as determinative, as in operations, leadership and individuals tend to matter greatly. In each of KSC's major eras, for each of its major projects, certain managers emerged who knew how to shape and use the formal structure to get the most out their workers. They did not abandon organization, but rather bent it to their purposes. They knew that communication takes place among real people who share language and experience, and they made use of the human qualities of communication to cut through formal structures when need be. They filled in the empty boxes of the organization chart with flesh-and-blood people, understanding that whatever the formal role, certain individuals would be more vital to the success of the enterprise than others. Different people had a knack for doing different things, and it was the job of the good manager to find, learn from, and promote such people.[32] This leadership strength was embodied in strong managers like Rocco Petrone during Apollo and George Page with the shuttle. It has come as well from KSC directors who, though not directly involved in the daily work, nonetheless have provided other human qualities that a complex bureaucracy needs to thrive—vision and passion for the work of getting into space.

When one turns from formal structure to individuals, from the static to the dynamic, one also turns to history. The Kennedy Space Center, like all of NASA, lives in the flow of time. Like anything that lives in history, KSC cannot simply go back and start all over again. When it was young and the American space program was young, it could learn, as one longtime member of the Center put it, like a child learns, unselfconsciously, through direct experience. Such learning becomes more difficult with maturity. The world has certain expectations of how adults behave. Where stumbling and falling the few feet to the ground rarely hurts a small child, it can break bones in an adult. So it is with mature organizations, where learning from failure becomes more costly as time goes by. Learning at KSC cannot take place as it did at the Cape in the early years, when 30 percent of launches ended in failure. But attention to the learning process remains vital.

Moving beyond the formal structure requires attention to the full range of experiences people have, down to their life in the community. If people and process matter more than (or as much as) assigned roles and bureaucratic structure, then the whole world of the Center and the Cape are the laboratory where ideas are born, exchanges take place, people figure out what they know and what they need to know. This, as observers of the Apollo program put it, was the "paradox" of "personal contact in a highly technical milieu." Top-down planning was never enough. Indeed, the more complicated the system of technology, the more human interaction and ingenuity and improvisation it required.[33]

One of the toughest problems for any complex organization is transferring this very specific and local knowledge to the higher-level policies in the organization as a whole. When change depends on bringing lessons learned in one unit to others, coordination can be a nightmare. It is far easier to simplify or to ignore one part of complex experience. NASA has not been particularly successful in overcoming the tendency, present in all complex organizations, for people to retreat into their own little cubicles, their silos and sandboxes, where they feel safe and can control their world. This tendency to compartmentalization exists, organizational theorists tell us, because when there are too many things to be learned by too many actors, when there is too much information, it is hard to sort out the noise from the signal. It becomes natural for organizations to decompose complex, interactive experience into smaller, less confusing autonomous domains.[34]

Former NASA administrator Sean O'Keefe made a strong pitch just before he left office for a single NASA identity. This "one NASA" outlook was meant to overcome rivalry, conflict, and turf battles that may have hurt the agency's efficiency and effectiveness in the past. But history shows that there are deep divisions between NASA centers. Some of the conflict that divides the agency is political (who gets what); some is historical (where you came from, who taught you). This book has been an argument in favor of understanding the KSC way of seeing the world and the unique knowledge and insight its work generates. Not because this experience is better than others, but only because it has been the easiest to ignore or push aside when heavy-going design or policy issues were on the table.

President George W. Bush's 2004 "Vision for Space Exploration" offers to NASA a fresh opportunity to rethink the role of operations in spaceflight. The learning environment of a new NASA will have to recognize that, in the real world, sharp distinctions between research and application, between design and operations, do not hold up very well. Learning takes place around and beneath the formal structures of organizations and transcends disciplinary and functional divisions of knowledge. But it also takes place through the diversity of experience that different institutions and their members have. When that happens, the unique knowledge and experience generated by space operations at the Kennedy Space Center will find its rightful place in the American space program.

Notes

Chapter 1. Moment of Truth

Epigraph source: Rocco A. Petrone, "At the Pad, Each Launching Is a 5-Month Marathon," *New York Times*, July 17, 1969.

1. Cape Canaveral—officially named Cape Kennedy from 1963 to 1973—is generically called "the Cape" throughout. The term refers to the general geographic location, midway down Florida's east coast, of Cape Canaveral Air Force Station but will also refer more generally to the location of the Kennedy Space Center. CCAFS is literally on the Cape, with the Atlantic Ocean on the east and the Banana River on the west. KSC is on Merritt Island, which has the Banana River to the east and the Indian River to the west.

2. John Noble Wilford, "A Day at the Cape: Moon Tests and Multiple Warhead Firing," *New York Times*, June 26, 1969.

3. "A New Ellington Score Marking Moon Landing," *New York Times*, July 11, 1969.

4. *Florida Today*, July 17, 1969.

5. Kennedy Space Center Archives (hereafter KSC Archives), Apollo Saturn Launches Addenda, box 2, Apollo 11 Technical Crew Debriefing, July 31, 1969, 3.1.

6. KSC Archives, Apollo Era Collection, Daily Status Report, box 6, folder 38 (February 3–28, 1969).

7. KSC Archives, Saturn/Apollo Launches, box 17, folder 160, "Apollo/Saturn V Test and Checkout Plan," May 28, 1969.

8. KSC Archives, Apollo Era Collection, Daily Status Report, box 6, folder 40, April 1–30, 1969.

9. Petrone, "At the Pad."

10. "Apollo/Saturn V Test and Checkout Plan" (see n.7).

11. Ibid.

12. Ibid.; Petrone, "At the Pad."

13. KSC Archives, Public Affairs Collection, box 5, folder 46, "Spaceport Keeps Weather Watch for Apollo 11," July 8, 1969.

14. *Florida Today*, April 30, 1969.

15. Arnold S. Levine, *Managing NASA in the Apollo Era* (Washington, D.C.: NASA, 1982), 123.

16. Ibid., 21.

17. KSC Archives, Saturn/Apollo Launches, box 17, folder 158, "Apollo 11 Flight Readiness Review Speaker's Book," June 17, 1969.

18. "Apollo/Saturn V Test and Checkout Plan." In same box, see also folder 156, "Launch Support Vehicle Operations for Support of Space Vehicle Countdown Demonstration Test and Launch Countdown," vol. 1, May 12, 1969.

19. Bernard Weinraub, "Tourists Crowd Cocoa Beach as Apollo Countdown Begins," *New York Times*, July 11, 1969.

20. KSC Archives, Apollo Era Collection, box 10, folder 241, "The Impact of Apollo 11 on Brevard County, Florida," 2–4.

21. Ibid., 1, 9.

22. Weinraub, "Tourists Crowd Cocoa Beach."

23. Ron Wiggins, "Front Row Seats Jam Packed, *Orlando Sentinel*, July 16, 1969; *Titusville Star Advocate*, July 15, 1969, 3A.

24. KSC Archives, Public Affairs Collection, box 5, folder 48, Apollo 11 Public Affairs Operations Plan. In same box, see also folder Apollo 11—VVIPs.

25. KSC Archives, Apollo Saturn Launches Addenda, Test and Checkout Procedures, box 2, "Apollo/Saturn Space Vehicle Countdown" (AS 506), July 3, 1969.

26. "Launch Support Vehicle Operations . . ." (see n.18).

27. *Titusville Star-Advocate*, July 15, 1969.

28. Duke Newcome, "Not Everyone Came to Praise the Launch," *Florida Today*, July 17, 1969.

29. On public opinion in France, see *Orlando Sentinel*, July 16, 1969, 1; in United States, see "Survey Finds Public Backs Moon Landing," *New York Times*, July 15, 1969.

30. Ralph E. Lapp, "Send Computers, Not Men, into Deep Space," *New York Times*, February 2, 1969.

31. Robert Reinhold, "Kennedy Puts Earth Needs Ahead of Space Program," *New York Times*, May 20, 1969.

32. *Titusville Star-Advocate*, July 15, 1969.

33. Bernard Weinraub, "Hundreds of Thousands Flock to Be 'There,'" *New York Times*, July 16, 1969.

34. Bob Wyrick, "Set Earth Priorities," *Florida Today*, July 17, 1969.

35. Weinraub, "Tourists Crowd Cocoa Beach."

36. John McAleenan, "Like a Mammoth Family Picnic," *Florida Today*, July 17, 1969.

37. *Titusville Star-Advocate*, July 15, 1969.

38. Skip Johnson, "Optimism Prevails on Success," *Orlando Sentinel*, July 16, 1969.

39. Eugene Sestile, interview by Orville R. Butler, July 20, 2003.

40. KSC Archives, Saturn/Apollo Launches, box 18, folder 161, "Apollo 11 Quick Look Assessment Report," July 23, 1969. In same folder, see also "Apollo/Saturn V Ground Systems Evaluation Report, Apollo 11," September 3, 1969.

41. Headline, *Orlando Sentinel*, July 16, 1969; Bernard Weinraub, "In Silence and Awe, Nearly a Million in Cape Kennedy Area Watch the Lift-Off," *New York Times*, July 17, 1969.

42. Norman Mailer, *Of a Fire on the Moon* (Boston: Little, Brown, 1970), 346, 467.

43. *Florida Today*, July 17, 1969, 9A.

44. KSC Archives, Apollo Era Collection, Daily Status Report, box 6, folder 43, July 1–31, 1969.

45. For a discussion of bureaucratization and NASA, see Howard E. McCurdy, *Inside NASA: High Technology and Organizational Change in the U.S. Space Program* (Baltimore: Johns Hopkins University Press, 1993); Levine, *Managing NASA*; Stephen B. Johnson, *The Secret of Apollo: Systems Management in American and European Space Programs* (Baltimore: Johns Hopkins University Press, 2002). For a critical view, see Malcolm McConnell, *Challenger: A Major Malfunction* (Garden City, N.Y.: Doubleday, 1987).

46. On "big science," see Peter Galison and Bruce Hevly, eds., *Big Science: The Growth of Large-Scale Research* (Stanford: Stanford University Press, 1992).

47. Individuals still matter. The X Prize competition, for example, involved a number of private individuals, groups, and small firms in a quest to build a ship that can carry three people into space. It recognizes that even with complex technologies, important breakthroughs may come from outside of existing institutions. For more information, see www.xprize.org/.

48. Johnson, *Secret of Apollo*.

49. Karl E. Weick and Kathleen M. Sutcliffe, *Managing the Unexpected: Assuring High Performance in an Age of Complexity* (San Francisco: Jossey-Bass, 2001), 12–13, 88, 99.

50. Constance Perin, "Operating as Experimenting: Synthesizing Engineering and Scientific Values in Nuclear Power Production," *Science, Technology, and Human Values* 23, no. 1 (Winter 1998), 98–128.

51. This began at a very early point with efforts to build the educational infrastructure of Central Florida to support the space program and space industry there. See *Aviation Week*, "Drive to Bring an Institution of Higher Learning . . . ," April 22, 1963.

52. Chris Argyris and Donald A. Schön, *Organizational Learning*, vol. 2, *Theory, Method and Practice* (Reading, Mass.: Addison-Wesley, 1996).

53. Barbara Levitt and James G. March, "Organizational Learning," *Annual Review of Sociology* 14 (1988): 320. How exactly organizations learn remains unclear. Some theorists posit a behavioral model, with organizations seeking to learn when performance falls below expectations. Others see it as more cognitive and reflective, a sudden break with past routines akin to a dramatic technological innovation. For more on learning, see Richard M. Cyert and James G. March, *A Behavioral Theory of the Firm*, 2nd ed. (Cambridge, Mass.: Blackwell Business, 1992); L. E. Yelle, "The Learning Curve: Historical Review and Comprehensive Survey," *Decision Science* 10 (1979): 302–28; Chris Argyris, *On Organizational Learning* (Cambridge, Mass.: Blackwell, 1992); Daniel A. Levinthal and James G. March, "The Myopia of Learning," *Strategic Management Journal* 14 (1993): 97.

54. Levitt and March, "Organizational Learning," 322.

55. C. Marlene Fiol and Marjorie A. Lyles, "Organizational Learning," *Academy of Management Review* 10, no. 4 (1985): 806.

56. An important work in this regard is William Abernathy and Kim B. Clarke, "Innovation: Mapping the Winds of Creative Destruction," *Research Policy* 14 (1985): 3–22; Anne S. Miner and Stephen J. Mezias, "Ugly Duckling No More: Pasts and Futures of

Organizational Learning Research," *Organization Science* 7 (January–February 1996), 89.

57. Levinthal and March, "The Myopia of Learning," 96.

58. Ibid., 99; Jeffrey R. Fear, "Thinking Historically about Organizational Learning," in Meinolf Dierkes et al., eds., *Handbook of Organizational Learning and Knowledge* (Oxford: Oxford University Press, 2001), 162–91.

59. Edgar H. Schein, "Three Cultures of Management: The Key to Organizational Learning," *Sloan Management Review*, Fall 1996, 9–20.

60. Perin, "Operating as Experimenting."

Chapter 2. Rockets and Alligators

1. NASA Headquarters History Office, Washington, D.C. (hereafter NASA HQ), file 4590, George A. Long, "Indian and Historic Sites Report," October 1967.

2. One burial mound from between 800 and 1500 A.D. contained two hundred skeletons.

3. Charlton W. Tebeau, *Florida from Indian Trail to Space Age: A History*, 3 vols. (Delray Beach, Fla.: Southern, 1965); Tebeau, *A History of Florida* (Coral Gables, Fla.: University of Miami Press, 1971).

4. John McAleenan, "The Past Years: Things That Have Been," *Florida Today*, April 26, 1969, 12E.

5. *From Sand to Moondust: A Narrative of Cape Canaveral from Discovery to Moon Shot* (Patrick Air Force Base, Fla.: Department of the Air Force, 1986).

6. For this paragraph and the next few following, see David Baker, *The Rocket: The History and Development of Rocket and Missile Technology* (New York: Crown, 1978), 9–15.

7. John Smith, *The General History of Virginia, New England and the Summer Isles: with the names of the adventurers, planters, and governors, from their first beginning, anno 1584, to this present 1624; with the proceedings of those several colonies, and the accidendents that befell them in all their journies and discoveries. Also, the maps and descriptions of all those countries, their commodities, people, goverment, customs, and religion, yet known. Divided into six books* (London: Longman, Hurst, Rees, and Orme, 1812), 3: 60.

8. On Goddard and Tsiolkovskiy, see Baker, *The Rocket*, 16–29.

9. For more on early American rocketry, see Ray Williamson and Roger D. Launius, "Rocketry and the Origins of Space Flight," in *To Reach the High Frontier: A History of U.S. Launch Vehicles*, ed. Roger D. Launius and Dennis R. Jenkins (Lexington: University of Kentucky, 2002), 33–69.

10. Michael J. Neufeld, *The Rocket and the Reich: Peenemünde and the Coming of the Ballistic Missile Era* (New York: Free Press, 1995).

11. Walter A. McDougall, *The Heavens and the Earth: A Political History of the Space Age* (New York: Basic Books, 1985), 42–43.

12. Herman S. Wolk, *The Struggle for Air Force Independence, 1943–47*, rev. ed. (Washington, D.C.: Air Force History and Museums Program, 1997).

13. Walter A. McDougall, "Space Flight in the Soviet Union," in *Reconsidering Sputnik: Forty Years since the Soviet Satellite*, ed. Roger D. Launius, John M. Logsdon, and Robert W. Smith (London: Routledge, 2000).

14. McDougall, *The Heavens and the Earth*, 108.

15. Roger D. Launius, *NASA: A History of the U.S. Civil Space Program* (Malabar, Fla.: Krieger, 1994), 13–14; Williamson and Launius, "Rocketry," 44–47; KSC Archives, Debus Collection addenda, box 16, interview with Kurt Debus, 1983.

16. On the work at White Sands, see KSC Archives, Historical Collection, Interviews, box 1, folder 23, Kurt Debus, August 22, 1969.

17. *NASA Historical Data Book*, vol. 2, *Programs and Projects, 1958–1968*, comp. Linda Neuman Ezell (Washington, D.C.: NASA, 1988), 330.

18. *Marshall Star*, February 1, 1967, "Debus Describes Early Days."

19. KSC Archives, Historical Collection, Interviews, box 1, folder 36, Hans Gruene, August 21, 1970; Charles D. Benson and William B. Faherty, *Gateway to the Moon: Building the Kennedy Space Center Launch Complex* (Gainesville: University Press of Florida, 2001), 250–51.

20. *NASA Historical Data Book*, 2: 29.

21. McDougall, *The Heavens and the Earth*, 107, 127–29; Thomas P. Hughes, *Rescuing Prometheus: Four Monumental Projects That Changed the Modern World* (New York: Pantheon, 1998), 69–140.

22. These early missiles using liquid-fueled engines took too long to prepare and launch in the event of attack. Beginning in 1958, the Air Force began working on a solid-fueled Minuteman missile, one that could be readied and fired in less than a minute to respond to a preemptive strike. By the mid-1960s, Minuteman deployment led to the phasing out of the Titan and Atlas designs for military use.

23. Cliff Lethbridge, "Painting by Numbers: A Statistical Analysis of Cape Canaveral Launches: The First 50 Years," spaceline.org/statistics/50-years.html.

24. *Collier's*, March 22, 1952; October 18, 1952; October 25, 1952; February 28, 1953; March 7, 1953; March 14, 1953; June 27, 1953; April 30, 1954. Indeed, he assumed that 60 percent of the cost of getting to the moon would be propellant. *Collier's*, October 18, 1952, 36.

25. *NASA Historical Data Book*, 2: 286.

26. Constance McLaughlin Green and Milton Lomask, *Vanguard: A History* (Washington, D.C.: Smithsonian Institution Press, 1971), chap. 1.

27. Ibid., chaps. 8 and 10.

28. Glen P. Wilson, "Lyndon Johnson and the Legislative Origins of NASA," *Prologue: Quarterly of the National Archives* 25 (Winter 1993): 362–72.

29. Quoted in McDougall, *The Heavens and the Earth*, 320, 387.

30. Green and Lomask, *Vanguard*, chap. 11

31. Ibid., chap. 12.

32. Wilson, "Legislative Origins of NASA"; McDougall, *The Heavens and the Earth*, 157–76.

33. *An Act to Provide for Research into Problems of Flight Within and Outside the Earth's Atmosphere, and for Other Purposes*, Public Law 85-568, 85th Cong., 2d sess. (July 29, 1958).

34. McDougall, *The Heavens and the Earth*, 180.

35. *NASA Historical Data Book*, 2: 330.

36. For more on the approach used by von Braun in Germany, see Neufeld, *The*

Rocket and The Reich, and Andrew J. Dunar and Stephen P. Waring, *Power to Explore: A History of Marshall Space Flight Center, 1960–1990* (Washington, D.C.: NASA, 1999).

37. McCurdy, *Inside NASA*, 38–39, chap. 1, n.45.

38. Roger E. Bilstein, *Stages to Saturn: A Technological History of the Apollo/Saturn Launch Vehicles* (Washington, D.C.: NASA, 1980), 45, 263; Neufeld, *The Rocket and the Reich*, 65–71, 115.

39. KSC Archives, Speeches, box 5, folder 194, Albert F. Siepert, "Administration of a Government Agency under Conditions of Rapid Change," speech before Federal Government Accountants Association, May 28, 1962.

40. J. Sterling Livingston, "Weapons System Contracting," *Harvard Business Review* 37, no. 4 (July–August 1959): 83–92.

41. Joan Lisa Bromberg, *NASA and the Space Industry* (Baltimore: Johns Hopkins University Press, 1999), 15–16, 22–26.

42. Tom Alexander, "The Unexpected Payoff from Project Apollo," *Fortune*, July 1969, 117; Harvey M. Sapolsky, *The Polaris System Development: Bureaucratic and Programmatic Success in Government* (Cambridge, Mass.: Harvard University Press, 1972) is a classic work on the role of politics in military contracting. For historical background on American thinking on the political economy of contracting, see Eric P. Rau, "The Adoption of Operations Research in the United States during World War II," in *Systems, Experts, and Computers: The Systems Approach in Management and Engineering, World War II and After*, ed. Agatha C. Hughes and Thomas P. Hughes (Cambridge, Mass.: MIT Press, 2000), 58–61.

43. McDougall, *The Heavens and the Earth*, 197.

44. Ibid., 314.

45. *NASA Historical Data Book*, 2: 52.

46. Dryden, quoted in McDougall, *The Heavens and the Earth*, 196; McCurdy, *Inside NASA*, 74.

47. Neufeld, *The Rocket and the Reich*, 158–59.

48. C. McCleskey and D. Christensen, "Dr. Kurt H. Debus: Launching a Vision," paper presented at the 35th History of Astronautics Symposium, International Academy of Astronautics, 52nd International Astronautical Congress, 1–5 October 2001, Toulouse, France, p. 10; KSC Archives, Debus Collection, box 8, folder 144, "From A-4 to Explorer I." On Debus's proposal along these lines, see same folder, Conference in Baku, USSR, October 8, 1972.

49. NASA HQ, file 4595, William Pickering to Abe Silverstein, January 23, 1959, and appendix.

50. KSC Archives, box 77-19, Debus daily journal, June 3, 1960.

51. KSC Archives, Pre-1960 Correspondence Collection, 1945–59, box 11, Functions and Authority—NASA Atlantic Missile Range Operations Office (AMROO), September 17, 1959.

52. NASA HQ, file 4595, "Functions and Authority—the NASA Launch Operations Directorate."

53. Robert Gray and Joe Nieberding, interview by Virginia Dawson, November 9, 1999; NASA, *Kennedy Space Center Story* (Kennedy Space Center, Fla.: NASA, 1972), 7–16, 211–20.

54. spaceline.org/statistics/rockets.html.

55. NASA HQ, file 4550, memo "Conference on Launching Schedules at AMR—Able, Centaur, Courier, Delta, Mercury, Midas, Tiros, Transit and Vega," July 7, 1959.

56. NASA HQ, file 4590, Hyatt memo, July 7, 1959; KSC Archives, Historical Collection, Interviews, box 3, folder 101A, Sam Snyder, July 5, 1972.

57. KSC Archives, box 77-19, Debus daily journal, May 19, 1960.

58. Loyd S. Swenson Jr., James M. Grimwood, and Charles C. Alexander, *This New Ocean: A History of Project Mercury* (Washington D.C.: NASA, 1966), 323–34.

59. McCurdy, *Inside NASA*, 63.

60. John F. Kennedy, "Special Message to the Congress on Urgent National Needs," before a joint session of Congress, May 25, 1961.

61. McDougall, *The Heavens and the Earth*, 302–3.

62. Debus interview, August 22, 1969 (see n.16).

63. NASA HQ, file 4595, Albert Siepert, memo for Associate Administrator, "Organization of NASA Activities at Cape Canaveral," June 2, 1960.

64. KSC Archives, Debus Collection, box 8, folder 157, Kurt Debus, "Proposal to Tackle the Reliability Problem Imposed by the Redstone Missile," February 1952.

65. NASA HQ, John Sloop Papers, memo of Donald Heaton, "Organization of Launch Operation at AMR and PMR," January 29, 1962.

66. Andrew Pickett, interview by Kenneth Lipartito, April 30, 2003.

67. Heaton memo (see n.65), emphasis in original.

68. KSC Archives, Debus Collection, box 8, folder 156, Kurt Debus, "A Paper on Launch and Space Flight Operations," September 27, 1961.

69. KSC Archives, Debus Collection, box 2, folder 29, Debus to Paul Styles, July 7, 1961; see also note 64.

70. NASA HQ, file 4595, Leighton Davis–Don Ostrander, April 28, 1961.

71. NASA HQ, file 4595, Harry Gorman–Albert Siepert, "LOD Administrative and Support Activities," June 6, 1961.

72. NASA HQ, file 4595, "Agreement between DOD and NASA Relating to the Launch Site for Manned Lunar Landing Program," August 24, 1961. See also NASA press release 61-189 and Debus interview, August 22, 1969.

73. Benson and Faherty, *Gateway to the Moon*, 89–90.

74. Ibid., 8–10.

75. Ibid., 91–92.

76. Ibid., 92–94.

77. Debus interview, August 22, 1969.

78. Benson and Faherty, *Gateway to the Moon*, 17–19.

79. KSC Archives, box 77-19, Debus daily journal, April 25, 1960; NASA HQ, file 4595, Don Ostrander, "Proposed Organization for Launch Activities at AMR and PMR," June 6, 1961.

80. NASA HQ, file 4595, Debus, "Proposed Organization for Launch Activities at Atlantic Missile Range and Pacific Missile Range Due to Proposed Realignment of NASA Programs," n.d.

81. Debus interview, August 22, 1969.

82. KSC Archives, Debus Collection, box 8, folder 154, Debus, "Analysis of Major Elements Regarding the Functions and Organization of Launch and Spaceflight Operations," October 10, 1961.

83. Benson and Faherty, *Gateway to the Moon*, 133–36.

84. Nicely summarized in NASA HQ, file 4595, "Major Questions on Organization of Launch Operations Assuming Major User Concept," January 26, 1962.

85. NASA HQ, file 4595, "Outline for Discussion Point up Areas Requiring Clarification in the Organization of Launch Activities at AMR," February 13, 1962.

86. Benson and Faherty, *Gateway to the Moon*, 136–37.

Chapter 3. Launch Operations Center

1. McCleskey and Christensen, "Debus: Launching a Vision," 20, chap. 2, n.48.

2. Ibid., p. 4.

3. NASA HQ, file 4590, D. Brainard Holmes, "Names for New NASA Area at Cape Canaveral," May 18, 1962.

4. "The Starry-Eyed Boss of Cape Kennedy," *Florida Accent* (*Tampa Times-Tribune*), October 8, 1972.

5. NASA HQ, file 443, Debus Biographical File, Debus, "Presentation to First World Exhibition of Transport and Communications," Munich, July 15, 1965; KSC Archives, Debus Collection, box 16, interview with Debus, 1983.

6. Roger Launius, "Public Opinion Polls and Perceptions of US Human Space flight," *Space Policy* 19 (2003): 163–75.

7. Debus, "Presentation" (see n.5). Goddard is quoted in this paper.

8. "NASA Launch Technology Detailed by LOC Director," *DATA*, October 1963, 8.

9. Benson and Faherty, *Gateway to the Moon*, 43–46, chap. 2, n.19.

10. "NASA Launch Technology Detailed," 8.

11. NASA HQ, file 4595, memo of conference, MSFC, Huntsville, April 18, 1962.

12. The JPL and Goddard, for example, wanted to set up their own independent offices, a proposal eventually rejected by Debus and NASA headquarters. KSC Archives, box 77-19, Debus daily journal, August 8, 1962.

13. Benson and Faherty, *Gateway to the Moon*, 105.

14. NASA HQ, file 4595, Agreement between DOD and NASA Relating to the Launch Site for the Manned Lunar Landing Program, August 24, 1961.

15. KSC Archives, box 77-19, Clark-Debus, December 10, 1961.

16. KSC Archives, box 77-19, Debus-Holmes, March 30, 1962; KSC Archives, box 77-19, Debus daily journal, May 6, 1962.

17. NASA HQ, file 4595, Agreement between the Department of Defense and the National Aeronautics & Space Administration Regarding Management of the Atlantic Missile Range of DOD and the Merritt Island Launch Area of NASA, January 17, 1963. See also file 4590, Holmes & Schriever–Debus, March 6, 1963.

18. KSC Archives, box 77-19, Debus-Wignall, June 6, 1962. See NASA HQ, file 4596, Webb-McNamara, July 3, 1963.

19. NASA HQ, file 4596, Basic Operating Concepts for the Launch Operations Center at Merritt Island and the Atlantic Missile Range, January 10, 1963.

20. KSC Archives, box 77-19, Debus daily journal, August 15 and October 27, 1962.

21. See note 19.

22. NASA HQ, file 4596, Basic Operating Concepts for the Launch Operations at the Atlantic Missile Range, July 19, 1962.

23. NASA HQ, file 4596, Organizational Chart, 1962.

24. As noted in NASA HQ, file 4596, Establishment of Launch Operations Center, memo "Changes and Improvements in Organization at LOC," April 15, 1963.

25. NASA HQ, file 4596, Debus-Holmes, March 1963. This relationship was "formalized" even further as "launch operations competence" was transferred from Marshall to LOC control. See file 4596, Administrators Briefing Memorandum, April 3, 1963; Rocco Petrone, interview by Eugene Emme and Tom Ray, September 17, 1970.

26. KSC Archives, Speeches, box 3, folder 127, Philip R. Maloney, "Preflight Checkout and Preparation," Spring 1964.

27. Debus, "Proposal," see chap. 2, n.64); Maloney, "Preflight Checkout and Preparation."

28. Walter Kapryan, interview by Kenneth Lipartito, April 7, 2003; KSC Archives, Historical Collection, Interviews, box 1, folder 25, "Summary of Paul Donnelly's Interview."

29. KSC Archives, Speeches, box 5, folder 210, John E. Thomas, "Evaluation Measurement for Cost-Plus-Award Fee Contracting at the Kennedy Space Center," March 31, 1965.

30. Maloney, "Preflight Checkout and Preparation."

31. Swenson, Grimwood, and Alexander, *This New Ocean*, 171, chap. 2, n.58.

32. Debus, "Proposal."

33. Swenson, Grimwood, and Alexander, *This New Ocean*, 180. On application of statistical technique in rocket launches, see Debus, "Proposal."

34. *NASA Historical Data Book*, vol. 2, 150, chap. 2, n.17.

35. KSC Archives, box 76-98, D. M. Scherer, "Fact Summary for Computer Support for Gemini Mission." In the initial missions, mission control was still located at the Cape while the building of the Manned Space Center in Houston and transfer of mission control personnel was under way.

36. KSC Archives, Historical Collection, Interviews, box 2, folder 84, G. Merritt Preston, interview by Robert Merrifield, November 12, 1969.

37. Maloney, "Preflight Checkout and Preparation."

38. Swenson, Grimwood, and Alexander, *This New Ocean*, 220.

39. Virginia P. Dawson, *Engines and Innovation: Lewis Laboratory and American Propulsion Technology* (Washington, D.C.: NASA, 1991).

40. Robert Gray and Joe Nieberding, interview by Virginia Dawson, November 9, 1999.

41. *NASA Historical Data Book*, 2: 27.

42. Terry Greenfield, interview by Henry Dethloff, Lee Snaples, and Elaine Liston, June 11, 2001.

43. KSC Archives, Historical Collection, Interviews, box 3, folder 101A, Sam Snyder, July 5, 1972.

44. KSC Archives, Historical Collection, Interviews, box 3, folder 97, memo on Conference with A. F. Siepert, January 28, 1969.

45. Siepert, "Administration," 3–4, chap. 2, n.39.

46. Gray and Nieberding, interview.

47. Ibid.

48. When trying to understand complex systems, such informality, allowing give

and take, trial and error, and face-to-face communication can be especially valuable. See Leonard R. Sayles and Margaret K. Chandler, *Managing Large Systems: Organizations for the Future* (New York: Harper and Row, 1971), 196.

49. Gray and Nieberding, interview.

50. Reflecting on the lessons of the space program after the landing on the moon, Sayles and Chandler in *Managing Large Systems* note the value of such workarounds, which they term "a distillation of experience combined with ingenuity" (264–65).

51. NASA HQ, file 4596, Robert Seamans–Director, Office of Manned Space Flight, January 10, 1963.

52. *NASA Historical Data Book*, 2: 27–28.

53. Ibid., 26; see George F. Page, interview by Launius, Dethloff, and Snaples, June 25, 2001.

54. KSC Archives, Historical Collection, Interviews, box 2, folder 74, C. C. Parker, February 13–14 and June 12, 1969.

55. As quoted in Benson and Faherty, *Gateway to the Moon*, 140.

Chapter 4. A Bridge to the Moon

1. Benson and Faherty, *Gateway to the Moon*, 67, chap. 2, n.19.

2. On Debus's justification, see *Spaceport News*, February 28, 1963; also KSC Archives, Speeches, box 1, folder 5, Aldo H. Bagnulo, "Construction of the Spaceport," October 25–27, 1964.

3. Benson and Faherty, *Gateway to the Moon*, 127.

4. KSC Archives, Debus Collection, box 8, folder 156, "A New Launch Operations Concept."

5. Benson and Faherty, *Gateway to the Moon*, 159.

6. Ibid., 126–31.

7. NASA HQ, file 4629, Launch Complex 39, Harold Finger to Clerio Pin, January 24, 1968.

8. Quoted in KSC Archives, Speeches, box 1, folder 14, Aldo H. Bagnulo, "Construction of the Spaceport," n.d.

9. KSC Archives, Historical Collection, Interviews, box 2, folder 68, Arch E. Morse, November 17, 1969.

10. KSC Archives, Historical Collection, Interviews, box 2, folder 77, William Pearson, March 6, 1969.

11. NASA HQ, file 4596, LOC Programs Briefing for George Mueller, September 12, 1963. By 1965, $830 million had been spent on LC-39 and related pad facilities. KSC Archives, 76-98, box 4, NASA Participation in Congressional Hearings.

12. KSC Archives, Land Management Collection, box 1, folder 5, "Proposed Land Acquisition," May 1961; KSC news release 189-64. The leases brought the government more than $300,000 in annual revenues. Even this did not settle matters, as growers grumbled that, lacking title, they could not be paid for improvements and investments in spraying, pruning, and cultivating the groves.

13. Gay Talese, "Nostalgia on the Beach," *New York Times*, February 16, 1962.

14. *Spaceport News*, January 3, 1963.

15. KSC Archives, Historical Collection, Interviews, box 1, folder 6, memo on interview with Col. Clarence Bidgood, November 21, 1968.

16. George E. Buker, *Sun, Sand, and Water: A History of the Jacksonville District, U.S. Army Corps of Engineers, 1821–1975* (Atlanta: GPO, 1981).

17. "Facilities Chief Has Been Soldier, Builder, Educator," *Spaceport News*, February 22, 1963.

18. Donald Buchanan, interview by Kenneth Lipartito, April 15, 2003.

19. Ibid.

20. Robert S. Kraemer, *Beyond the Moon: A Golden Age of Planetary Exploration, 1971–1978* (Washington, D.C.: Smithsonian Institution Press, 2000), 22.

21. Benson and Faherty, *Gateway to the Moon*, 141.

22. See note 15.

23. KSC Archives, Historical Collection, Interviews, box 1, folder 6, Clarence Bidgood interview by J. J. Frangie, November 15, 1968.

24. Benson and Faherty, *Gateway to the Moon*, 41.

25. *Spaceport News*, October 8, 1964.

26. KSC Archives, Uncatalogued Labor Files, box 4, folder 9, "Memorandum from Division Engineer to Chief of Engineer," September 2, 1965.

27. Senate Committee on Government Operations, Permanent Subcommittee on Investigations, *Hearings . . . Pursuant to Senate Resolution 69*, pt. 1, *Report on Work Stoppage at Missile Bases*, 87th Cong., 1st sess., April 25–June 9, 1961, 66–71.

28. Senate Committee, *Work Stoppage at Missile Bases*, 640.

29. Ibid., 427.

30. Ibid., 239

31. Ibid., 2.

32. Ibid., 500.

33. Ibid., 162.

34. KSC Archives, Debus Collection, box 2, folder 29, Styles-Debus, "Executive Order Creating Missile Sites Labor Commission," June 26, 1961; Doug Dederer, "Missile Site Labor Unit Established at Canaveral," *Cocoa Tribune*, July 12, 1961.

35. KSC Archives, Debus Collection, box 2, folder 22, Debus–George Mueller, October 26, 1966. The wage levels in the table of compensation were generally lower than prevailing craft wages in metropolitan Florida. Moreover, by standardizing wages ahead of time, it was thought that contractors would be able to prepare more realistic bids for work.

36. Senate Committee, *Work Stoppage at Missile Bases*, 131. Such weekly earnings usually required a 90-hour workweek.

37. Ibid., 44, 179–81. The pledge, issued at the international union level, was not binding on locals working the Cape, but it was believed to be very influential. NASA HQ, file 4602, KSC–Merritt Island, George Friedl Jr., "Recent History of Labor Relations Disputes at Kennedy Space Center," March 8, 1965; KSC Archives, Uncatalogued Labor Files, box 1, folder 27, "Comparison Between the First Two Years of MSLC at This Site," MSLRC Minutes 1962–63; NASA HQ, KSC Files, Labor Relations, "Chronology of Work Stoppages and Related Events KSC/NASA and AFETR, Through July, 1965," and Stuart Broad, "A Report and Chronology of KSC Labor Relations—Comments."

38. For a general study of Apollo-era engineers, see Sylvia Doughty Fries, *NASA Engineers and the Age of Apollo* (Washington, D.C.: NASA, 1992).

39. NASA HQ, file 4602, KSC–Merritt Island, Symposium on Launch Complex 39, July 8, 1984.

40. KSC Archives, Uncatalogued Labor Files, box 4, folder 8, "Report of the Fact-Finding Committee Appointed by Secretary of Labor James P. Mitchell in Connection with Dispute on Saturn Missile launching sites at Cape Canaveral, Florida."

41. KSC Archives, Debus Collection, box 2, folder 29, George C. Marshall Space Flight Center, Labor Relations Statement, August 1, 1961.

42. KSC Archives, Debus Collection, box 2, folder 29, Debus affidavit, November 18, 1960. The split here was not just along class lines. As Debus imagined it, civil servant technicians, supervised by civil servant engineers, and contractor technicians, along with contractor engineers, would handle this work. Many of the contractor technicians would be members of industrial unions, but as permanent employees working for one firm specializing in missile work, they would be better trained for the job than would trade and construction workers who moved from job to job.

43. Debus, "Labor Relations Statement," 9, in Senate Committee, *Work Stoppage at Missile Bases.*

44. KSC Archives, Historical Collection, Rocco Petrone, interview by Eugene Emme and Tom Ray, September 17, 1970.

45. Ibid.

46. A famous example of this occurred not at the Cape but at Vandenberg Air Force Base, when pipe fitters refused to relinquish their right to install manifolds for the Titan missile, even though the manifolds arrived preassembled and even though the workers were completely unfamiliar with the technology. The compromise was to have the pipe fitters "bless" the manifolds with a small marking and be paid for the time it would have taken them to pull the manifolds apart and reassemble them. Senate Committee, *Work Stoppage at Missile Bases*, 101–2.

47. KSC Archives, Debus Collection, box 2, folder 29, "Space Administration."

48. Edward W. Kiffmeyer, Labor Relations Officer, AFETR, memo for Maj. Gen. L. I. Davis, October 7, 1960, cited in NASA HQ, KSC Files, Labor Relations, George V. Hanna, Report, September 1965, 15.

49. Senate Committee, *Work Stoppage at Missile Bases*, 225.

50. The question of who was responsible for what threatened an accord struck with the air force at the Cape. According to the Joint Tenancy Agreement, NASA was in charge of labor for all NASA activities on the Atlantic Missile Range. But the air force labor relations officer there sometimes acted on his own in labor disputes, which to Debus's mind created more problems than it solved and usurped NASA management's responsibility. KSC Archives, box 77-19, Debus daily journal, April 16, 1962.

51. At the peak, 12,000–15,000 union workers were on site, according to "Chronology of Work Stoppages" (see n.37).

52. Friedl, "Recent History" (see n.37).

53. Senate Committee, *Work Stoppage at Missile Bases*, 152–53, 254.

54. KSC Archives, Uncatalogued Labor Files, box 4, folder 26, C of E Work Stoppage Reports 1964.

55. KSC Archives, Debus Collection, box 2, folder 29, Debus affidavit, June 10, 1965.

56. NASA HQ, KSC Files, Labor Relations, memo for Mr. Hilburn, January 27, 1964.

57. Ibid., memo for Mr. Hilburn, June 8, 1964.

58. Ibid., Oliver Kearns to William Pearson, June 19, 1964.

59. Ibid.

60. Friedl, "Recent History."

61. KSC Archives, Uncatalogued Labor Files, box 4, folder 9, memo from Division Engineer to Chief Engineer, September 2, 1965.

62. "Senator John L. McClellan Collection," www.obu.edu/library/mcclellancoll.htm; Friedl, "Recent History."

63. KSC Archives, Community Relations Collection, box 2, folder 17, Brevard County Planning Department, Brevard County Development Potentials Summary, 1969–1990, 10.

64. Sylvia Porter, "Apollo Booms Florida," *Washington Star*, March 12, 1962.

65. *Spaceport News*, January 3, 1963.

66. "Last Stop Before Space," *Popular Science*, March 1959.

67. Nixon Smiley, "Moon Boom Smothers Brevard," *Miami Herald*, August 20, 1963.

68. NASA HQ, file 4636, Promotional and Tourist Literature, *What to Do and See in the Cape Kennedy Area*, June 1964.

69. Gay Talese, "'Space Comics' Cheer Astronauts," *New York Times*, May 24, 1962.

70. Talese, "Nostalgia on the Beach."

71. Jerrell H. Shofner, *History of Brevard County*, vol. 2 (Brevard County Historical Commission, 1996), 207.

72. Glenn Rabac, *City of Cocoa Beach: The First Sixty Years* (Winona, Minn.: Apollo Books, 1986), 66–67.

73. Annie Mary Hartsfield, Mary Alice Griffin, and Charles M. Grigg, *NASA Impact on Brevard County: Summary Report* (Tallahassee: Institute for Social Research, Florida State University, 1966), 17.

74. KSC Archives, Community Relations Collection, box 2, folder 16, Brevard County Planning Department, "A Report on Growth in Brevard County Florida," 2.

75. Chris Butler, "East Central Florida Is Braced for Impact," *Florida Magazine* (*Orlando Sentinel*), June 2, 1962. In 1965 the JCICC was disbanded, its functions taken over by the community relations offices of NASA and the air force at the Cape.

76. NASA HQ, file 4550, Documentation, Hugh Dryden to Philip Brownstein, August 24, 1965.

77. Shofner, *History of Brevard County*, 141.

78. KSC Archives, Community Relations Collection, box 16, folder 154–155, Transcript of Public Hearing, Proposed Banana River and Pineda Expressways, Brevard County, Florida, April 6, 1965.

79. KSC Archives, Merritt Island National Wildlife Refuge, box 1, folder 6, memo from A. H. Bagnulo in response to Mr. Karl Osborne, October 14, 1963.

80. KSC Archives, Community Relations Collection, box 1, folder 8, Beach Community Hospital Feasibility Report, letter to Mrs. H. H. Eichel from Maj. Gen. D. N. Yates, USAF, May 10, 1957.

81. "Mosquito Control and Disease Prevention," *Florida Health Notes* 62 (July 1970), 175.

82. KSC Archives, Community Relations Collection, box 1, folder 9, Public Health Service and Children's Bureau, U.S. Dept. of Health Education & Welfare, Region IV, Atlanta, "Report on Florida Public Health Services to Governor LeRoy Collins," January 5, 1955.

83. KSC Archives, Community Relations Collection, box 20, folder 199, Jack Salmela and E. A. Philen, "A Cooperative Mosquito Control Plan for Cape Canaveral and the NASA Merritt Island Launch Area Involving Federal, State, and Local Agencies."

84. Ibid.

85. KSC Archives, Community Relations Collection, box 18, folder 284, "Space Age Demands on State Supported Higher Education in Florida: Florida Space Era Education Study," presented to Florida Board of Control, April 1963.

86. KSC Archives, Community Relations Collection, box 18, folder 285, *Florida's 1963–1965 Program for Higher Education: A Report to the Second Governor's Conference on Higher Education* (Tallahassee: Board of Control, January 17, 1963), 69.

87. Ibid.

88. Kenneth G. Sheinkopf, *Accent on the Individual: The First Twelve Years of Florida Technological University* (Orlando: Florida Technological University Foundation, 1976), 6.

89. Ibid., 11.

90. JoAnn Morgan, interview by Roger Launius, February 22, 2002.

91. KSC Archives, Historical Collection, Interviews, box 3, folder 105, Martin Stein, August 8, 1969; Wolf Von Eckardt, "Architects Assail Ugliness, See Model of Moonport," *Washington Post*, June 17, 1965.

92. KSC Archives, Speeches, box 1, folder 4, Aldo H. Bagnulo, "Construction of the Spaceport," April 14–15, 1964.

93. See note 8.

94. Benson and Faherty, *Gateway to the Moon*, 268–70.

95. Without the grounding, the current would have caused the steel tubes to deteriorate rapidly; see ibid., 253–56.

96. "19 Million Bid on Moon Pad," *Miami Herald*, November 6, 1963.

97. KSC Archives, Historical Collection, Interviews, box 3, folder 105, Martin Stein, August 8, 1969.

98. Von Eckardt, "Architects Assail Ugliness."

99. Kenneth Grine and Barbara Grine, interview by Patrick Moore, June 13, 2002.

100. "Spaceport USA Chronology," document in possession of Larry Mauk, project design specialist, KSC.

101. Patrick Moore, "Fueling the Fascination: Kennedy Space Center and the World's Spaceport Romance," unpublished manuscript, copy in KSC Archives.

102. KSC Archives, Visitor Information Center Collection, box 19, folder 3.

103. KSC Archives, Speeches, box 5, folder 196, Albert Siepert, February 19, 1965.

104. House Committee on Science and Astronautics, *Cape Canaveral: The Hope of the Free World*, 87th Cong., 2d sess., 1962.

105. KSC Archives, box 77-19, Debus daily journal, September 6, 1962.

106. Interview with Debus, March 31, 1964, John F. Kennedy Presidential Library, copy at NASA HQ.

107. Governor Reuben Askew and the Florida legislature restored the Cape Canaveral designation to the geographic territory in May 1973. Throughout this book we will use only the name Cape Canaveral.

108. KSC Archives, box 76-98, United States Steel news release, April 14, 1965.

109. Robert Gray and Joe Nieberding, interview by Virginia Dawson, November 9, 1999.

110. KSC Archives, box 76-98, KSC Management Board Luncheon/Meeting, September 15, 1965.

111. *Spaceport News*, May 1, 1963.

112. Ibid., May 9, 1968, 5.

113. Ann Montgomery, interview by Lipartito, March 21, 2003.

114. *Spaceport News*, January 3, January 24, and June 13, 1963.

115. Ibid., June 20, 1963.

116. Ibid.

117. Ibid.

118. KSC Archives, box 76-98, Debus memo "Equal Employment and Advancement Opportunities for Women," April 27, 1964.

119. Ibid.

120. Dunar and Waring, *Power to Explore*, 118, chap. 2, n.36.

Chapter 5. The World's Greatest Engineering Project

Epigraph source: Col. Donald R. Scheller, USAF, interview by Orville R. Butler, June 25, 2003.

1. For example, see Andrew Pickett, interview by Kenneth Lipartito, April 29, 2003; Isom A. "Ike" Rigell, interview by Lipartito, October 28, 2004.

2. KSC Archives, box 76-98, folder 5, Claire Wilkinson to Debus, February 19, 1968.

3. KSC Archives, box 76-98, folder 5, Debus to Mrs. R. L. Wilkinson, March 4, 1968.

4. KSC Archives, box 19, folder 3, Visitor Information Center Collection, "Project Justification Data, 1965."

5. KSC Archives, New Releases, box 3, folder 51, January 4, 1968; box 4, folder 87, March 5, 1971.

6. Benson and Faherty, *Gateway to the Moon*, 314–15, chap. 2, n.19.

7. Ibid., 315–16.

8. Eugene Sestile, interview by Butler, July 20, 2003; Charles Murphy, interview by Butler, April 18, 2004.

9. Sestile, interview.

10. Ibid..

11. Ibid.

12. Pickett, interview, April 29, 2003.

13. JoAnn Morgan, interview by Roger Launius, February 22, 2002.

14. Debus, "Proposal," chap. 2, n.64.

15. Richard Hartung, interview by Butler, April 20, 2004.

16. Rigell, interview, 2004.

17. Marshall Space Flight Center, *Results of the Saturn I Launch Vehicle Test Flights*, report MPR-SAT-FE-66-9, December 9, 1966; Benson and Faherty, *Gateway to the Moon*, 41–43; *NASA Historical Data Book*, vol. 2, chap. 1, 2–3, chap. 2, n.17.

18. Benson and Faherty, *Gateway to the Moon*, 244–46.

19. Rocco Petrone, interview by Eugene Emme and Tom Ray, September 17, 1970.

20. *NASA Historical Data Book*, vol. 1, *NASA Resources, 1958–1968*, comp. Jane Van Nimmen and Leonard C. Bruno (Washington, D.C.: NASA, [1976] 1988), 180, 186, 200. Nearly half the NASA money spent in the 1960s would go to California, but contractors in thirty-four states worked on the space program.

21. KSC Archives, History Collection, Interviews, box 1, folder 21, Orton Duggan, November 13, 1969.

22. John "Tip" Talone, interview by Lipartito and Butler, May 2, 2004.

23. Rigell, interview by Henry Dethloff and Lee Snaples, June 18, 2001.

24. KSC Archives, Speeches, box 1, folder 16, Walt Barney, May 21, 1965.

25. KSC Archives, Speeches, box 6, folder 247, James Webb, "NASA as an Adaptive Organization," John Diebold Lecture on Technological Change and Management, Harvard University Graduate School of Business Administration, Boston, September 30, 1968.

26. NASA HQ, file 4596, "Reorganization of John F. Kennedy Space Center," January 20, 1964. Later, General Phillips took over the role of Apollo program director.

27. *Managing the Moon Program: Lessons Learned from Project Apollo*, proceedings of a workship moderated by John M. Logsdon (Washington, D.C.: NASA, 1999), 16–18.

28. Hartung, interview.

29. Ibid.

30. On personnel, see *NASA Historical Data Book*, 1: 86–87; NASA HQ, file 4590, KSC Manpower.

31. Robert Sieck, interview by Butler, August 19, 2003.

32. Rigell, interview, 2004.

33. T. Alexander, "Unexpected Payoff" (see chap. 2 n.42), 153–54.

34. Neufeld, *The Rocket and the Reich* (see chap. 2 n.10), 224–25. On the conflict between systems engineering and the German style, see Yasushi Sato, "Local Engineering and Systems Engineering Cultural Conflict at NASA's Marshall Space Flight Center, 1960–1966," *Technology and Culture* 46, no. 3 (July 2005): 551–83.

35. In a later study of the Apollo program, *Managing Large Systems* (see chap. 3 n.48), Leonard Sayles and Margaret Chandler discovered that, contrary to expectations, significant integration work went on at the site of operations (264–65).

36. Marshall Space Flight Center, Debus Reading File, Debus to Joseph Shea, March 22, 1962.

37. KSC Archives, History Collection, Interviews, box 3, folder 113, Ladd W. Warzecha, interview by Ivan (no surname), January 14, 1970.

38. Eventually GE was constrained largely to the manufacture and testing of checkout equipment at Kennedy. See Benson and Faherty, *Gateway to the Moon*, 176–77.

39. Petrone, interview.

40. Scheller, interview, 2003.

41. Ibid.; Kearns to Pearson (see chap. 4 n.58).

42. KSC Archives, Uncatalogued Labor Files, box 1, folder 46, "NASA Work Stoppages/Strikes; 1956 Through 1982."

43. Bob Wyrick, "Stag Films at KSC," *Florida Today*, December 18, 1968; Wyrick, "8 Stag Movie Fans Fired," *Florida Today*, December 20, 1968.

44. Bilstein, *Stages to Saturn* (see chap. 2 n.38), 355.

45. KSC Archives, Debus Collection, box 8, folder 151, "Future Concepts in Launch Operations at NASA's John F. Kennedy Space Center."

46. Benson and Faherty, *Gateway to the Moon*, 109–12.

47. McCurdy, *Inside NASA* (see chap. 1 n.45), 94–96.

48. Bilstein, *Stages to Saturn*, 349.

49. National Archives and Records Administration, Eastpoint, Georgia (hereafter NARA Eastpoint), RG 255, Launch Vehicle Operations, 1956–72, box 1, folder LVO Organization, 1965–66, Debus–Director DIR, January 17, 1966.

50. NASA HQ, KSC file 4550, Documentation, Debus-Phillips, May 2, 1966.

51. *NASA Historical Data Book*, 2: 54–60.

52. Rocco Petrone, quoted in *Florida Today*, April 30, 1969.

53. This position, that NASA in these years was not bureaucratic, is revealed in McCurdy's *Inside NASA*. The idea that it was the government that overcame contractor self-interest and limitations was expressed by many who worked in Apollo; see, for example, Petrone, interview. See also Webb, "NASA as an Adaptive Organization."

54. *Spaceport News*, May 5, 1966, 1, 3; June 23, 1, 3. KSC's Western Test Range (WTR) expanded its facilities to include Delta launch capacity in addition to the Thor-Agenas that had traditionally been launched into polar orbits from the Vandenberg Air Force Base site. *Spaceport News*, November 10, 1966, 4.

55. NASA HQ file 4596, "Change in Organizational Structure," January 17, 1964.

56. KSC Archives, Debus Collection, box 16, Presentation to Congressional Subcommittee on Manned Space Flight, February 24, 1967.

57. John "Tip" Talone, interview by Butler, July 24, 2003.

58. George T. "Ted" Sasseen, interview by Butler, June 20, 2003.

59. Ibid.

60. Webb, "NASA as an Adaptive Organization."

61. Rocco Petrone, "The Cape," in *Apollo Expeditions to the Moon*, ed. Edgar M. Cortright (Washington, D.C.: NASA, 1975).

62. Gen. Sam Phillips Oral History Interview, September 28, 1989, Oral History on Space, Science, and Technology, National Air and Space Museum, www.nasm.si.edu/research/dsh/TRANSCPT/PHILLIP6.HTM; Scheller, interview, 2003.

63. Petrone, interview.

64. KSC Archives, Historical Collection, Interviews, box 3, folder 95, memo of record in Scheller interview by J. J. Frangie, October 4, 1968.

65. KSC Archives, Historical Collection, Interviews, box 2, folder 82, John Potate, interviewer unnamed, June 6, 1972.

66. Johnson, *Secret of Apollo* (see chap. 1 n.45), 63.

67. KSC Archives, Debus Collection, box 1, folder 7, letter from General Vincent G. Huston, March 26, 1965.

68. Ibid.

69. See note 64.

70. Scheller, interview, 2003.

71. Howard E. McCurdy, *Faster, Better, Cheaper: Low-Cost Innovation in the U.S. Space Program* (Baltimore: Johns Hopkins University Press, 2001), 85–86.

72. Scheller, interview, 2003.

73. KSC Archives, LC-39 Site Activation Collection, box 11, folder 202, "Apollo/ Saturn V Site Activation Board Organization and Operations Plan." In same box, see also folder 201, Scheller, "Memorandum KSC/KSC Contractor PERT/Time Level 'C' Network Integration Procedure," December 6, 1965.

74. Potate, interview (see n.65).

75. Scheller, interview, 2003.

76. Potate, interview. The most thorough study of PERT and related managerial techniques in use during this time shows that there were in fact a number of possible models, and that PERT was less significant in getting things done than its promoters believed. A similar point is made in Sapolsky, *The Polaris System Development* (see chap. 2 n.42).

77. Scheller, interview, 2003; Charles D. Benson and William B. Faherty, *Moon Launch! A History of the Saturn-Apollo Launch Operations* (Gainesville: University Press of Florida, 2001), 341–42.

78. Donald Buchanan, interview by Lipartito, April 15, 2003.

79. Scheller, interview, 2003.

80. Buchanan, interview.

81. See also Scheller, "Memorandum KSC/KSC Contractor" (n.73).

82. KSC Archives, LC-39 Site Activation Status Collection, box 1, folder 3, Scheller, "LC-39 Site Activation Status Report," February 2, 1966.

83. KSC Archives, LC-39 Site Activation Status Collection, box 2, folder 23, Scheller, "LC-39 Site Activation Status Report," April 13; box 2, folder 29, Scheller, "LC-39 Site Activation Status Report," May 4; box 4, folder 50, Scheller, "LC-39 Site Activation Status Report," August 3, 1966.

84. In his 1972 interview, John Potate asserted that engineers at Huntsville, upset with being forced to contract for GSE instead of building it in-house, created constant cosmetic changes to make construction impossible at General Electric.

85. KSC Archives, Historical Collection, Interviews, box 2, folder 95, Scheller, interview by J. J. Frangie, October 4, 1968.

86. Scheller, interview, 2003.

Chapter 6. Lunar Rendezvous

Epigraph source: Shakespeare, *King Henry IV, Part I*, act 1, scene 3.

1. KSC Archives, Speeches, Rocco Petrone, March 18–20, 1963.

2. Quotations from Paul Donnelly, interview by Orville R. Butler, August 23, 2003. See also John "Tip" Talone, interview by Kenneth Lipartito and Orville R. Butler, May 2, 2004.

3. Rocco Petrone, interview by Eugene Emme and Tom Ray, September 17, 1970. See also Petrone, quoted in *Florida Today*, April 30, 1969.

4. Robert Sieck, interview by Butler, August 19, 2003.

5. Aristoula Georgiadou and David H. J. Larmour, *Lucian's Science Fiction Novel, "True Histories": Interpretation and Commentary* (Boston: Brill, 1998).

6. Jules Verne, *From the Earth to the Moon*, trans. Lowell Bair (New York, 1993), 40.

7. Quoted in Benson and Faherty, *Gateway to the Moon* (see chap. 2 n.19), 144–46.

8. McCurdy, *Inside NASA* (see chap. 1 n.45); Launius, "Public Opinion Polls" (see chap. 3 n.6).

9. *Spaceport News*, January 24, 1963, 2; June 27, 1963, 2.

10. KSC Archives, Debus Collection, box 8, folder 153, "Initial Draft of Kissimmee Speech."

11. Petrone, "The Cape" (see chap. 5 n.61).

12. Sieck, interview.

13. Talone, interview, 2004.

14. In fact, the contractors employed their own systems engineers, overseen by a NASA systems engineer to handle the multiple interface points of the spacecraft technology. Charles Mars, interview by Butler, May 24, 2004.

15. G. T. "Ted" Sasseen, interview by Butler, June 20, 2003; Sieck, interview.

16. Charles Murphy, interview by Butler, April 18, 2004.

17. James F. Harrington III, interview by Butler, July 29, 2003.

18. Eugene Sestile, interview by Butler, July 20, 2003.

19. Talone, interview by Butler, July 24, 2003. See also Raul E. "Ernie" Reyes, interview by Carol L. Butler, Johnson Space Center, September 1, 1998.

20. Discussions of the evolution of each are found in Sestile, interview; Sieck, interview; George F. Page, interview by Roger Launius, Henry Dethloff, and Lee Snaples, June 25, 2001. In fact, by the early 1960s Marshall, the stronghold of the German engineering culture, had evolved its own matrix structure, with functional and discipline-based departments overlaid by a project structure. Bilstein, *Stages to Saturn* (see chap. 2 n.38), 266–67.

21. Sestile, interview. Sestile had come out of experience with the Department of Defense/Air Force management methods, so he may have seen less difference than others.

22. Mars, interview, 2004.

23. Even those in the spacecraft organization noted how the reality on the ground was somewhat different from the pure "air force model." At Johnson too, NASA engineers did not simply manage but worked with contractors, "share[d] their problems," and "encourage[d] a transfer of people" between agency and industry. It was a "team effort" made possible in part because NASA had in-house expertise and hands-on knowledge, and had government funding to do its own developmental work. *Managing the Moon Program* (see chap. 5 n.27), 19–21.

24. Isom "Ike" Rigell, interview by Lipartito, October 28, 2004. The real risk with all-up testing, as its advocate George Mueller pointed out, is having a failure you do not understand. See *Managing the Moon Program*, 26.

25. NARA Eastpoint, RG 255, Launch Vehicle Operations, 1959–72, box 1, folder LVO Organization, 1965–66, Gruene to Debus, March 3, 1966.

26. Ibid.

27. Sestile, interview. On how the work done actually belied many of the formal differences between management approaches, see Bilstein, *Stages to Saturn*, 272–78.

28. Sestile, interview.

29. Donnelly, interview. He had also spent several years working as a hands-on technician before getting his degree in engineering, giving him a strong appreciation for the "dirty hands" approach of the German engineering tradition.

30. Talone, interview, 2004.

31. NASA HQ, file 0443, "Notes of Interview with Kurt Debus," May 12, 1973; Siepert, "Administration" (see chap. 2 n.39). In many ways, this hybrid approach was closer to what the navy used for its successful Polaris missile program than the air force's weapons-contracting approach; cf. Sapolsky, *The Polaris System Development* (see chap. 2 n.42), 78–89.

32. KSC Archives, Historical Collection, Interviews, box 2, folder 82, John Potate, interviewer unnamed, June 6, 1972; Donald Buchanan, interview by Lipartito, April 15, 2003.

33. This follows the conclusion of the study of the Polaris missile. Sapolsky, *The Polaris System Development*, 156, notes how close relations and personal ties beyond the organizational chart were key.

34. Petrone, interview.

35. Sayles and Chandler, *Managing Large Systems* (see chap. 3 n.48), 204–13.

36. Ibid., 16; Weick and Sutcliffe, *Managing the Unexpected* (see chap. 1 n.49), 13.

37. Courtney G. Brooks, James M. Grimwood, and Loyd S. Swenson Jr., *Chariots for Apollo: A History of Manned Lunar Spacecraft* (Washington, D.C.: NASA, 1979), 228.

38. Benson and Faherty, *Moon Launch*, 382.

39. *Spaceport News*, March 16, 1967, 1.

40. KSC Archives, Debus Collection, box 8, folder 151, statement of Debus before the Subcommittee on Manned Space Flight, House Committee on Science and Astronautics, [1966].

41. NASA HQ, "The Phillips Report, 1965–1966," history.nasa.gov/Apollo204/phillip2.html.

42. Douglas R. Broome Jr., to Mgr., ASP0, "Communications Cables for Spacecraft 012 and Block II Spacecraft," January 23, 1967, cited in Brooks, Grimwood, and Swenson, *Chariots for Apollo*, 214–15.

43. Maj. Gen. John C. Shinkle, "KSC to NASA Hq., Attn.: Dir. Apollo Prog., Your Request for Results of CSM 012 Altitude Chamber Testing," January 19, 1967, cited in Brooks, Grimwood, and Swenson, *Chariots for Apollo*, 214–15.

44. KSC Archives, AS 204 Accident Collection, box 4, folder 43, Floyd L. Thompson, chairman, *Report of the Apollo 204 Review Board*, to Administrator NASA.

45. Frank Borman, interview by Catherine Harwood, April 13, 1999, Johnson Space Center Oral History Project.

46. Most stories attribute this quote to Grissom, but Ralph Sawyer attributes it to Chaffee. Ralph S. Sawyer, interview, October 7, 1999, Johnson Space Center Oral History Project.

47. There are several versions of exactly what was said on the tape of the astronauts'

voices in the burning cockpit. Resolving them is beyond the scope of this text. All agree, with minor variations.

48. Sue Hannifin Butler, interview by Patrick Moore, June 25, 2002.

49. *Spaceport News*, February 3, 1967, 1.

50. The Baron Report can be found at www.hq.nasa.gov/office/pao/History/ Apollo204/barron.html. See also Brooks, Grimwood, and Swenson, *Chariots for Apollo*.

51. Benson and Faherty, *Moon Launch*, 387–90.

52. Ibid., 398–400.

53. Daniel R. Champagne, "We've Got a Fire in the Cockpit! The Tragic Story of Apollo 1," *Quest* 9, no. 5 (2002), 27.

54. *Report of the Apollo 204 Review Board*, 6.2.

55. In 1967 Congress also created the Aerospace Safety Advisory Panel, which undertook continuous review of safety issues in NASA's flight programs. NASA headquarters formed a Crew Safety Review Board to evaluate all steps taken to protect Apollo astronauts. Some of these arrangements came under criticism as being complex and unnecessarily duplicative. The Crew Board's report found few problems. But its work reflected NASA's desire to reassure Congress and the public that it was taking safety seriously and had reformed its safety practices. See Benson and Faherty, *Moon Launch*, 400–401; KSC Archives, box 76-98, folder 5, Phillips to Debus, June 24, 1968.

56. G. Merritt Preston, interview, 1969.

57. Quoted in Benson and Faherty, *Moon Launch*, 396.

58. *Report of the Apollo 204 Review Board*, 5.12.

59. Ibid., 6.3.

60. Champagne, "We've Got a Fire in the Cockpit!," 21.

61. *Report of the Apollo 204 Review Board*, 6.3.

62. KSC Archives, Center Director Files, box 76-19, Weekly Notes to Dr. Debus, E. R. Matthews, June 23, June 30, July 20, August 3, 1967.

63. Brooks, Grimwood, and Swenson, *Chariots for Apollo*, 228.

64. KSC Archives, box 76-98, folder 6, memo "The NASA Safety Program," March 8, 1968.

65. Potate, interview (see n.32).

66. Ibid.

67. Ibid. Joe Shea described the Boeing TIE contract as "just another way of protecting your ass, so if something like that ever happened again, somebody could turn and say, 'But, gee, we had Boeing, and they didn't tell us there was a problem.'" KSC Archives, Historical Collection, Interviews, box 2, folder 94, Joseph F. Shea, interview by R. Sherrod, May 16, 1971.

68. Weekly Notes (see n.62), Van Staden, May 25, June 1, 1967; Weekly Notes, E. R. Matthews, June 16, 1967; Potate, interview.

69. Weekly Notes, E. R. Matthews, July 20, 1967. The transfer to KSC of control over the KSC portion of contracts previously let by Marshall and Houston increased KSC's clout in contract negotiations: the contractors working at KSC would begin to pay closer attention to KSC as a source of funding, according to Johnson, *Secret of Apollo* (see chap. 1 n.45), 135–42.

70. Weekly Notes, Rocco Petrone, March 10, 16, 24, April 14, 1967.

71. *Spaceport News*, November 23, 1967.

72. Benson and Faherty, *Moon Launch*, 437.

73. Weekly Notes, Rocco Petrone, January 11, 1967.

74. Benson and Faherty, *Moon Launch*, 439.

75. Ibid., 440–441.

76. Sestile, interview.

77. *Spaceport News*, October 21, 1968.

78. Jay Barbaree, interview by Patrick Moore, June 14, 2002; Howard Benedict, interview by Moore, June 11, 2002.

79. Weekly Notes, Rocco Petrone, May 2, 1968.

80. Weekly Notes, R. O. Middleton, June 6, 1968.

81. Weekly Notes, Rocco Petrone, January 18, 1968; R. O. Middleton–Center Director, January 31, 1968.

82. Fred W. Haise Jr., interview, March 23, 1999, Johnson Space Center Oral History Project; Charles Mars, interview by Lipartito, June 12, 2003.

83. Mars, interview, 2003.

84. See KSC Archives, box 76-98, folder 2, for this and many similar letters.

85. An exact accounting of how much was spent at KSC for the moon project is difficult, given the many different things going on at the same time and the question of where to divide the Apollo budget between KSC and other centers. But the one-billion figure was publicly quoted. See "Size of Kennedy Space Center Suited to Great Feats," Baltimore *Sun*, July 14, 1969.

86. Compared to a decade before, there was a substantial growth of automation in testing and checkout, with the use of digital computers to replace manual operations. But there was no master program to perform countdown operations as there would be later with the space shuttle. On automation during Apollo, see Benson and Faherty, *Moon Launch*, 347–364.

87. Petrone, interview.

88. KSC Archives, Debus Collection, box 8, folder 153, letter from Debus.

89. "3 Cars Near Apollo 13 Ignite in Vapor," *Washington Post*, March 26, 1970.

90. Benson and Faherty, *Moon Launch*, 485–87.

91. Ibid., 389–94.

Chapter 7. Transitions to the Future

Epigraph source: Margaret Mead, "Man on the Moon," *Redbook*, 1969.

1. KSC Archives, Debus Collection, box 2, folder 31, Debus memo to "My dear fellow worker," September 18, 1974.

2. KSC Archives, Debus Collection, box 7, folder 140, transcription of a 1970 interview with Debus, 63.

3. Debus memo to "My dear fellow worker."

4. Ibid.

5. Norman Augustine, *Advisory Committee on the Future of the U.S. Space Program*, (Washington, D.C.: GPO, 1990), 24.

6. KSC Archives, box 76-98, folder 2, memo from James E. Webb, January 8, 1965.

7. KSC Archives, box 76-98, folder 2, Debus to Olin Teague, October 7, 1965, emphasis in original.

8. KSC Archives, box 76-98, folder 5, "Summary: Uses of Manned Space Flight, 1975–1985" (report of conference between Science and Technology Committee and NASA Office of Manned Flight, La Jolla, December 6–9, 1968), March 19, 1969; KSC Archives, Speeches, presentation by Richard E. Dutton in Tampa, January 23, 1965.

9. Debus to Teague (see n.7).

10. KSC Archives, box 76-98, folder 2, Mueller memo, Recommendations for Apollo Applications Program Field Center Responsibilities, November 16, 1965.

11. Ibid.

12. Launius, "Public Opinion Polls" (see chap. 3 n.6).

13. Ibid. Quotations from Launius, *NASA* (see chap. 2 n.15), 93; White House Press Secretary, "The White House, Statement by the President," March 7, 1970, reprinted in Launius, *NASA*, 216.

14. "Protests Interrupt City's Welcome for 3 Astronauts," *New York Times*, March 9, 1971; NASA HQ, file 4550, Documentation, KSC Plan for Bomb Threats, July 16, 1971.

15. "Today's Picture Report," *Florida Today*, December 4, 1972, in KSC Archives, Uncatalogued Labor Files, *Labor Relations Aspects of the KSC Installation Support Contracts* (hereafter *Scrapbook*), compiled by Agnes Hough, Labor Relations Staff.

16. Joe Collum, "Strike Heads Toward Record: Machinists Reject Bendix Offer," *Florida Today*, August 5, 1974, in *Scrapbook*; Summary of 1974 Work Stoppages, January 8, 1975, in *Scrapbook*.

17. Dick Baumbach, "Strike Now Longest," *Florida Today*, January 20, 1978.

18. Moore, "Fueling the Fascination" (see chap. 4 n.101), 11–12.

19. KSC Archives, Public Affairs Collection, box 17, folder 180, "Prospectus for a Visitor Services Program at the John F. Kennedy Space Center"; "KSC Tours Rank 5th in Combined Figures," *Florida Today*, April 7, 1977; KSC news release 1-78, January 4, 1978.

20. Launius, "Public Opinion Polls."

21. Webb, "NASA as an Adaptive Organization" (see chap. 5 n.25).

22. "Summary: Uses of Manned Space Flight" (see n.8).

23. NASA HQ, file 4589, letter to Robert P. Mayo, Bureau of the Budget, re BoB's tentative budget for FY 1971, November 18, 1969.

24. Debus, interview, 1970 (see n.2), 3–4; KSC Archives, Debus Collection, box 8, folder 153, Debus, "Evolution of Launch Facilities Concepts," 11.

25. KSC Archives, box 76-98, folder 2, report by Launch Vehicle Working Group, April 17, 1968.

26. KSC Archives, box 76-98, folder 4, Debus memo to Top Managers, May 23, 1966; same box, Mueller letter to Debus and Webb memo to Mueller re budget for FY 1968 and FY 1969, October 20, 1967. A KSC Institutional Baseline Study found that a yearly budget of at least $250 million was needed at the Cape "to maintain a one billion dollar national resource as well as a stand by base from which launch activity could be supported." KSC Archives, box 76-98, folder 2, Debus to Mueller, March 29 and April 22, 1968; same folder, report from Future Studies Office to Launch Vehicle Working Group on KSC Studies, July 15, 1968.

27. KSC Archives, box 76-82, memo from Personnel Management Review Committee meeting re budget for FY 1971, June 18, 1970. See also box 76-98, folder 5, Mueller to Debus, August 14, 1968; Debus to Mueller, October 2, 1968.

28. NARA Eastpoint, RG 255, Launch Vehicle Operations, 1959–72, box 1, folder 5, Cost Reductions, Gruene-Distribution, December 10, 1969, emphasis in original.

29. Same folder, Gruene-Distribution, March 1, 1972; also December 10, 1969.

30. "The White House, Statement" (see n.13), 219.

31. Figures taken from KSC Archives, Speeches, Miles Ross, "Launch Schedule, Budget and Manpower," address to Brevard County Chambers of Commerce, September 25, 1973; *Spaceport News*, March 26, 1970, 3. KSC's budget was $490 million in 1969; $375 million in 1970; $280 million in 1971; $280 million in 1972; $285 million in 1973; $219 million in 1974. Personnel decreased in turn: 26,000 in 1969; 17,000 in 1970; 15,000 in 1971; 12,000 in 1973; 10,000 in 1974.

32. Ross, "Launch Schedule, Budget and Manpower"; *NASA Historical Data Book*, vol. 4, *NASA Resources, 1969–1978*, comp. Ihor Gawadiak with Helen Fedor (Washington, D.C.: NASA, 1994), table 3-8; Jack Hartsfield, "Study Considers Shift of Launch Activities from Cape Kennedy," *Huntsville Times*, January 8, 1971.

33. "The Future of NASA," *Time*, August 10, 1970. <http:www.time.com/time/magazine/article/0,9171,876752,00.html>.

34. Ross, "Launch Schedule, Budget and Manpower."

35. KSC Archives, box 76-82, Debus to Dale D. Myers at OMSF, July 27, 1970.

36. Ibid.

37. KSC Archives, Debus Collection addenda, box 16, "Fiscal Year 1972 Budget Briefing for Community Leaders."

38. See NARA Eastpoint, RG 255, box 1, folder 5, Cost Reductions, 1970, for samples.

39. NARA Eastpoint, RG 255, box 1, folder 7, 1970, Gruene–Chief, Requirements and Resources Office, October 9, 1970.

40. "Fiscal Year 1972 Budget Briefing" (see n.37).

41. NARA Eastpoint, RG 255, box 1, folder 5, Petrone—Kennedy Space Center, January 4, 1971. For more on the impact on personnel, see James Jennings, interview by Roger Launius, July 19, 2002.

42. NARA Eastpoint, RG 255, box 1, folder 5, Gruene, "Retention of Apollo Key Personnel," n.d.

43. James C. Fletcher to Robert Frosch, "Problems and Opportunities at NASA," May 9, 1977," reprinted in Launius, *NASA*, 237.

44. *NASA Historical Data Book*, vol. 4, tables 3-32, 3-33. The greatest increase in minority employment occurred in professional and administrative positions.

45. Marshall Space Flight Center in Alabama had only 1.6 percent minority employees at the same time; see *NASA Historical Data Book*, vol. 4, table 3-35.

46. *NASA Historical Data Book*, vol. 4, table 3-38.

47. NARA Eastpoint, RG 255, box 3, folder 4, Gruene–LO/Director of Launch Operations, April 7, 1972, with attachments.

48. *NASA Historical Data Book*, vol. 4, table 3-38.

49. Carol T. West and David G. Lenze, *Florida: Long Term Economic Forecast 2001*,

vol. 2, *State and Counties* (Gainesville: Bureau of Economic and Business Research, College of Business Administration, University of Florida, 2001), 5.

50. Ross, "Launch Schedule, Budget and Manpower."

51. Richard L. Forstall, ed., *Population of Counties by Decennial Census, 1900 to 1990* (U.S. Bureau of the Census), www.census.gov/population/cencounts/fl190090. txt.

52. Richard Pothier, "What's Ahead for Cape Kennedy?" *Miami Herald*, March 9, 1969; Martin Waldron, "Boom is 'Busted' at Cape Kennedy," *New York Times*, February 8, 1970; Edward Morgan, "Space Squeeze Hurts Florida Boomtowns," *Sunday Bulletin*, February 7, 1971; Terry Johnson King, "Space Age Has Brought a Whole Week of Fridays," *Sunday Star*, December 6, 1970; "At Space Centers, Jobs Disappear," *New York Times*, January 10, 1971.

53. Launius, *NASA*, 98–99.

54. *NASA Historical Data Book*, vol. 3, *Programs and Projects, 1969–1978*, comp. Linda Neuman Ezell (Washington, D.C.: NASA, 1988), table 2-47, "Chronology of Skylab Development and Operations."

55. Discussed in T. A. Heppenheimer, *The Space Shuttle Decision: NASA's Search for a Reusable Space Vehicle* (Washington, D.C.: NASA, 1999), 62–67.

56. NASA HQ, file 4550, Kurt Debus–Dale Myers, April 7, 1970. The Sciences and Applications Projects Office was on the same level as the new combined Apollo-Skylab Program Office and the Planning and Future Programs Office.

57. *Aeronautics and Astronautics*, October 4, 1971; October 5, 1971; February 2, 1972; December 18, 1972.

58. *Spaceport News*, December 30, 1971, 7.

59. KSC Archives, NASA Skylab News Reference, March 1973.

60. KSC Archives, Skylab, box 2, "Lessons Learned on the Skylab Program," April 1, 1974.

61. KSC Archives, Skylab, box 7, report to Administrator by NASA Aerospace Safety Advisory Panel, January 1973, 9.

62. *Spaceport News*, January 27, 1972, 3; Launius, *NASA*, 98–99. The second crew comprised Alan L. Bean, Dr. Owen K. Garriott, and Jack R. Lousma, the third crew Gerald P. Carr, Dr. Edward G. Gibson, and William R. Pogue.

63. KSC Archives, Skylab, box 5, McDonnell Douglas Astronautics, "Space Station: Analysis of Space Station Impact on KSC," December 1970.

64. See note 47.

65. KSC Archives, box 76-82, report of SYE Survey on the NASA Work Environment at the Kennedy Space Center, February 1973. The 125 young KSC professionals surveyed were randomly selected.

66. John "Tip" Talone, interview by Orville R. Butler, July 24, 2003.

67. *NASA Historical Data Book*, vol. 3, "Space Applications."

68. JoAnn Morgan, interview by Launius, February 22, 2002.

69. Baker, *The Rocket* (see chap. 2 n.6), 145.

70. Jacob Neufeld, *The Development of Ballistic Missiles in the United States Air Force, 1954–1960* (Washington, D.C.: Office of Air Force History, USAF, 1990), 147.

71. *NASA Historical Data Book*, vol. 3. Numbers on failure come from KSC Ar-

chives, document PMS 031, "Information Summaries," June 1999. There were 148 robotic launches from 1958 to 1968, of which 24 were unsuccessful.

72. John Neilon, telephone conversation with Sallie Middleton, October 16, 2003.

73. John Neilon, "Eastern Launch Facilities, Kennedy Space Center," in *Encyclopedia of Space Science and Technology*, ed. Hans Mark, vol. 1 (New York: Wiley, 2000).

74. NASA, *Kennedy Space Center Story* (Kennedy Space Center, Fla.: NASA, 1972), 65.

75. Neilon, interview by Kenneth Lipartito, March 20, 2003.

76. Neilon, telephone conversation.

77. Kraemer, *Beyond the Moon* (see chap. 4 n.20), xix.

78. *Spaceport News*, June 18, 1970.

79. Robert Gray and Joe Nieberding, interview by Virginia Dawson, November 9, 1999.

80. R. Cargill Hall, *Project Ranger: A Chronology* (Pasadena: California Institute of Technology, Jet Propulsion Laboratory, 1971), 244. Ranger experienced many failures early on, leading NASA to reorganize the Jet Propulsion Laboratory, which had responsibility for Ranger.

81. KSC Archives, "A Summary of Major NASA Launches, October 1, 1958–December 31, 1989, Eastern Test Range (ETR) Western Test Range," KSC Historical Report no. 1 (KHR-1), June 1992, I.43.

82. KSC Archives, Unmanned Launches Collection, box 32, *Technical Summary of Unmanned Launch Operations*, vol. 1 (Kennedy Space Center, Fla.: NASA, 1976), IV.44.

83. Launius, *NASA*, 51.

84. "Summary of Major NASA Launches," I.37.

85. Kraemer, *Beyond the Moon*, xv. Anticipating the first possible interstellar contact, *Pioneer 10* carried a gold-plated aluminum plaque with stylized images of a man and woman and a map showing how to find Earth.

86. Thomas A. Mutch, "The Viking Lander Imaging Investigation: An Anecdotal Account," in *The Martian Landscape* (Washington, D.C.: NASA, 1978), 4–5.

87. Mutch, "Viking Lander Imaging Investigation," 24.

88. www.robsv.com/cape/map.html.

89. "Viking Mission Established Beachhead on Mars," *Spaceport News*, August 25, 1995, 4.

90. KSC Archives, Unmanned Launches Collection, box 25, Voyager Program: Tests, Models, Schedules, "Langley Working Paper: Voyager Capsule Bus System Baseline and Mission Mode."

91. "Summary of Major NASA Launches," I.50.

92. David K. van Keuren, "Moon in Their Eyes: Moon Communication Relay at the Naval Research Laboratory, 1951–1962," in *Beyond the Ionosphere: Fifty Years of Satellite Communication*, ed. Andrew J. Butrica (Washington D.C.: NASA, 1997).

93. Donald C. Elder, "Something of Value: Echo and the Beginnings of Satellite Communications," in Butrica, *Beyond the Ionosphere*.

94. *NASA Historical Data Book*, 3: 240.

95. Ibid., 3: 236.

96. Daniel R. Glover, "NASA Experimental Communications Satellites, 1958–1995," in Butrica, *Beyond the Ionosphere.*

97. *NASA Historical Data Book*, 3: 266–68.

98. Ibid., 4: 14.

99. "Fiscal Year 1972 Budget Briefing" (see n.37).

100. Moore, "Fueling the Fascination," 38–39. See KSC Archives, Visitors Information Collection, box 12, Space Information and Education Center, July 29, 1970.

101. Larry Mauk, conversation with Middleton, June 11, 2003.

102. Dennis Beal, "Sen. Gurney Asks Center Expansion," *Orlando Sentinel*, March 19, 1971.

103. "Wildlife Refuge at KSC Expanded," *NASA News*, May 31, 1972.

104. Bill Sargent, "A Refuge for Things That Are Wild," *Florida Today*, November 21, 1968.

105. KSC Archives, Community Relations Collection, box 20, folder 193, John Nelson memo to Gordon Harris, November 18, 1968.

106. "Elegy to Allan D. Cruickshank on the Dedication of The Cruickshank Trail," document at Merritt Island National Wildlife Refuge Visitors Center.

107. Sargent, "A Refuge for Things That Are Wild."

108. KSC Archives, Community Relations Collection, box 21, folder 213, Allan D. Cruickshank to Nathaniel Reed, April 16, 1971.

109. Ibid., "Background Information re National Seashore."

110. KSC Archives, box 76-82, Debus to Richard C. McCurdy, November 30, 1973.

111. Quoted in Heppenheimer, *Space Shuttle Decision*, 93.

112. Heppenheimer, *Space Shuttle Decision*, 214.

113. Ibid., 73, 93, 246; "Summary: Uses of Manned Space Flight" (see n.8).

114. NASA report, in Space Task Group, *The Post-Apollo Space Program: Directions for the Future* (Washington, D.C., 1969), reprinted in Launius, *NASA*, 213–14.

115. Quoted in *Spaceport News*, January 13, 1972, 1–3.

116. Fletcher quoted in *Spaceport News*, January 27, 1972, 1. FY 1978 saw a budget of $4.0 billion, which rose to $4.3 in 1979.

117. NASA report (see n.114), in Launius, *NASA*, 214.

118. NASA HQ, file 4588, KSC Organizational Charts.

119. *Spaceport News*, April 20, 1972, 1, 4, 8; *Spaceport News*, August 24, 1972, 1, 4; NASA HQ, file 4590, briefing memo from Associate Administrator for Manned Space Flight re proposed KSC organization changes put forward by Debus, July 6, 1972.

120. KSC Archives, box 76-82, Debus to George Low, September 19, 1973.

121. Debus, interview, 1970, 45.

Chapter 8. Learning to Fly the Shuttle

1. David Baily, "'Abandon in Place': A Rusty Epitaph for America's Historic Launch Pads," *Florida Today*, June 1, 1970; "Dismantling of Apollo Launch Pad Starts," *Orlando Sentinel*, April 29, 1972, 13.

2. Michael Moore, "Giveaway Eats at KSC Stock," *Florida Today*, June 5, 1977. Veterans of the Apollo years recall that the dryers were used to heat-shrink material around cables and connectors.

3. *Space Business Daily*, January 6, 1971, 10; *Space Business Daily*, February 24, 1971, 243.

4. NASA HQ, file 4610, Report of the Space Shuttle Launch Site and Recovery Review Board, McConnell to Low, April 7, 1972; Jack Waugh, "Which Launching Site Is the Fairest of Them All?" *Christian Science Monitor*, February 1, 1971, 10–11.

5. William Hines, "3 Areas Contending for 'Spaceport U.S.A.,'" *Chicago Daily News*, January 16, 1971.

6. Waugh, "Which Launching Site?" 10–11.

7. *New York Times*, "Concept of Space Shuttle Points to Cape Kennedy for Launching," January 7, 1972. Preparing a shuttle port at KSC was expected to save half of what it would take to upgrade White Sands, for example; see Waugh, "Which Launching Site?" 10–11.

8. NASA HQ, file 4610, McConnell to Low, April 7, 1972.

9. NASA HQ, file 4610, Mossinghoff to McKevitt, October 22, 1971.

10. *Defense/Space Business Daily*, March 15, 1978, 84. The Site Review Board had to speculate where populations and economic activity might grow up that would make a flight path that was safe today unsafe tomorrow. Such issues could only be resolved by an imperfect science. See NASA HQ, file 4610, McConnell to Shapley, April 19, 1972.

11. NASA HQ, file 4610, "Launch Site Selection Considerations," November 23, 1970.

12. Shuttle Launch and Landing Complex, NASA press release 72-81, April 14, 1972.

13. NARA, Eastpoint, RG 255, Launch Vehicle Operations, 1956–72, box 1, folder 7, Gruene to Chief, Requirements and Resources Office, October 9, 1970.

14. McCurdy, *Inside NASA* (see chap. 1 n.45), 105.

15. *Florida Today*, August 11, 1980.

16. The presence of women in the NASA labor force grew from just over 17 percent in 1974 to 25 percent by 1985. Minority employment saw an impressive doubling from 6 percent to more than 13 percent in the same period. *NASA Historical Data Book*, vol. 4 (see chap. 7 n.32), tables 3-29, 3-34; vol. 6, *NASA Space Applications, Aeronautics and Space Research and Technology, Tracking and Data Acquisition/Support Operations, Commercial Programs, and Resources, 1979–1988*, comp. Judy A. Rumerman (Washington, D.C.: NASA, 1999), tables 7-5, 7-6.

17. *NASA Historical Data Book*, vol. 4, tables 3-33, 3-38; vol. 6, tables 7-23, 7-28.

18. *Spaceport News*, January 23, 1975, 1.

19. Ibid., February 20, 1976.

20. Ibid., February 26, 1970, 1, 4. Reflecting the new electronics was a new office of Electronic Engineering in the Design Engineering Directorate; see KSC Archives, Organizational Charts.

21. This becomes clear from a look in the telephone directories at the names listed under Shuttle Operations, Shuttle Engineering, and Shuttle Processing; see KSC Archives, Telephone Directories Collection.

22. Robert Sieck, interview by Orville R. Butler, August 19, 2003.

23. *Spaceport News*, December 31, 1970, 2.

24. Marshall Space Flight Center in Huntsville was assigned the job of preparing the scientific and technical experiments on racks for the shuttle's first three space lab

flights. Gordon Harris, "Marshall Feud with Kennedy Isn't Welcome," *Huntsville Times*, November 26, 1978.

25. KSC, NASA announcement: KSC Organizational Changes, January 19, 1979.

26. Charles Mars, interview by Butler, May 24, 2004.

27. In popular parlance, "rocket science" conflated the elegant and theoretical worlds of cosmology, astronomy, and astrophysics with the hands-on, engineering-driven space race and military and civilian rocket technology. But still, given the difficulty, in engineering terms at least, of getting to the moon, it was a conflation that to the average person made sense.

28. Quoted in "Dreary Fate for Aging Gantries," *Boston Globe*, August 12, 1977.

29. Eugene Sestile, interview by Butler, July 20, 2003.

30. Testimony of G. Merritt Preston, Kennedy Space Center Presentation for the Subcommittee on NASA Oversight of the Committee on Science and Astronautics, U.S. House of Representatives, October 20, 1971, 332.

31. Ibid., 334.

32. Testimony of Kurt Debus, ibid., 335.

33. Richard Smith, interview by Roger Launius, June 27, 2001.

34. Sieck, interview.

35. On the importance of a technological culture of frontier research, see McCurdy, *Inside NASA*, 72.

36. *Defense Daily*, September 24, 1981, 92.

37. James A. "Gene" Thomas, interview by Roger Launius, Henry Dethloff, and Lee Snaples, June 29, 2001.

38. Testimony of G. Merritt Preston (see n. 30), 334.

39. Sestile, interview.

40. Ibid.

41. Sieck, interview.

42. Ibid.

43. Ibid.

44. Ibid.

45. Ibid.

46. Sestile, interview.

47. Sieck, interview.

48. *Florida Today*, August 17, 1981, 1A, 10A.

49. Ibid.

50. Ibid.; *Florida Today*, August 18, 1981.

51. Dave Dooling, "The Cape Makes a Comeback," *Huntsville Times*, September 25, 1977.

52. Randy Zipper, "Controversy Storms over Status of Quiet Canaveral Seashore," *Orlando Sentinel-Star*, August 13, 1979.

53. John "Tip" Talone, interview by Butler, July 9, 2003.

54. KSC news release 210-77, December 19, 1977.

55. NASA news release 77-124, "Spaceport Reshaped for Role in Space Shuttle Era."

56. KSC news release 210-77, December 19, 1977.

57. Talone, interview, July 9, 2003.

58. KSC news release 210-77, December 19, 1977.

59. Ibid.

60. John Conway, interview by Butler and Sallie Middleton, March 25, 2004.

61. John Conway, interview by Kenneth Lipartito, 2003.

62. Richard Hartung, interview by Butler, April 20, 2004.

63. *Defense/Space Business Daily*, December 2, 1977; *Aviation Week & Space Technology* (hereafter *AW&ST*), April 20, 1981, 32.

64. *AW&ST*, April 20, 1981, 32.

65. KSC news release 210-77, December 19, 1977.

66. *Defense/Space Business Daily*, December 2, 1977; *AW&ST*, April 20, 1981, 32; James F. Harrington III, interview by Butler, July 29, 2003.

67. Hartung, interview.

68. Charles Murphy, interview by Butler, April 18, 2004.

69. Ibid.

70. Donald Scheller, interview by Butler, June 25, 2003.

71. KSC news release, 92–77, April 14, 2003.

72. Sieck, interview.

73. *Defense/Space Business Daily*, February 28, 1980, 305.

74. Sieck, interview. The Saturn, with its multiple stages, had involved more contractors.

75. *Defense/Space Business Daily*, April 10, 1979, 201; *Florida Today*, March 3, 1981. NASA spent another $10,000 to study how to reduce the risk of shuttle and trainer collisions with other birds nesting along KSC's runway.

76. *Florida Today*, July 10, 1980.

77. "Alligators and Rocketships with Jon Cowart," video, www-pao.ksc.nasa.gov/kscpao/visit/images/Shuttle_brief_rm.rm.

78. *Orlando Sentinel-Star*, November 10, 1980.

79. For most people the shuttle is the "orbiter," the reusable spacecraft, though in fact a complete space shuttle (or Space Transportation System) consists of orbiter, solid rocket boosters, and external tank.

80. Sieck, interview.

81. Ibid.

82. Gen. Forrest S. McCartney, USAF (Ret.), interview by Launius, Dethloff, and Lisa Malone, June 26, 2001.

83. *Defense/Space Business Daily*, March 27, 1979, 129.

84. Sestile, interview.

85. Quoted in Sestile, interview.

86. Harrington, interview.

87. Conrad G. Nagel, interview by Butler, June 24, 2003.

88. G. T. "Ted" Sasseen, interview by Butler, June 20, 2003.

89. Ann Montgomery, interview by Lipartito, March 21, 2003.

90. Kenneth S. Kleinknecht, interview by Carol L. Butler, September 10, 1998; Sestile, interview.

91. KSC Archives, box 84-79, notes to Center Director from Walter Kapryan, February 1, 1979.

92. Montgomery, interview.

93. Ibid.

94. Sasseen, interview.

95. Sestile, inverview.

96. *Defense/Space Business Daily*, June 29, 1979, 295.

97. Statement of John F. Yardley, associate administrator for Space Transportation Systems, NASA, February 5, 1980, "1981 NASA Authorization," in *Hearings Before the Subcommittee on Space Science and Applications of the Committee on Science and Technology*, U.S. House of Representatives, Ninety-sixth Congress, Second Session, on H.R. 6413, February 5, 6, 7, 11, 14, 15, 16, and 18, 1980 (no. III), 4: 1232–34.

98. *Defense/Space Business Daily*, June 29, 1979, 295.

99. Conway, interview, 2003.

100. Raul E. "Ernie" Reyes, interview by Carol L. Butler, September 1, 1998.

101. Ibid.

102. Harrington, interview.

103. *Defense/Space Business Daily*, September 26, 1979, 109, 115.

104. *Spaceport News*, October 12, 1979, 1–2; Kleinknecht, interview.

105. *Florida Today*, February 22, 1980.

106. Murphy, interview.

107. Reyes, interview.

108. Ibid.; Kleinknecht, interview.

109. Mating *Columbia* to the external tank and the solid rocket boosters required an extended learning curve as well. To fit the orbiter into its position, welders had to cut some of the existing platforms.

110. Nagel, interview. Today that same work requires less than five days, without 24-hour shifts.

111. Reyes, interview. Though the tile problem had been the worst, it was not the only work *Columbia* required at KSC. When the orbiter arrived at the Cape, cockpit installations were still not complete and the payload bay remained unfinished. KSC itself still had to finish revamping part of the launchpad. Much to the relief of those working on these tasks, the tile problem provided a "time umbrella" under which they could complete their work. Since the shuttle could not be launched until the tile problem was solved, other work, no matter how time-consuming, did not change the schedule. See Kleinknecht, interview.

112. Talone, interview, July 9, 2003.

113. Ibid.; *Washington Post*, February 21, 1981.

114. Mike Thomas, "KSC Rumors: Union May Strike," *Florida Today*, February 20, 1981.

115. Robert Crippen, interview by Launius, July 17, 2002.

116. *Baltimore Sun*, April 17, 1981.

117. *Defense Daily*, April 22, 1981, 310.

118. *Florida Today*, February 22, 1981; *Orlando Sentinel-Star*, February 24, 1981; *AW&ST*, March 2, 1981, 17, 19.

119. *Florida Today*, March 17, 1981.

120. NASA news release 81-42, March 20, 1981; *AW&ST*, April 6, 1981, 18–19.

121. *Philadelphia Inquirer*, April 29, 1981, 6A.

122. Smith, interview.

123. www.spaceflight.nasa.gov/shuttle/archives/sts-1/index.html; *Defense Daily*, April 14, 1981, 256, and April 17, 1981, 281; *Florida Today*, June 12, 1981.

124. Malcolm Browne, "Shuttle's Launching Pad Is a Scene of Devastation," *New York Times*, April 15, 1981.

125. *AW&ST*, April 20, 1981, 13.

126. *Orlando Sentinel-Star*, July 29, 1981, 2C; *AW&ST*, July 6, 1981, 21; *Defense Daily*, April 16, 1981, 273.

127. *Orlando Sentinel-Star*, July 29, 1981, 2C; *AW&ST*, April 20, 1981, 29.

128. Sestile, interview.

129. Sieck, interview.

130. *Huntsville Times*, September 23, 1981; *Florida Today*, September 30 and October 2, 1981.

131. *AW&ST*, November 9, 1981, 22.

132. *Defense Daily*, December 2, 1981, 160.

133. *Florida Today*, September 1, 1981.

134. *Defense Daily*, October 6, 1981, 156.

135. *Florida Today*, August 17, 1981, 1A, 10A.

136. Ibid., August 18, 1981, 1A.

137. Ibid., September 11, 1981, 1A; *Hearings Before the Subcommittee on Space Science and Applications of the Committee on Science and Technology,* U.S. House of Representatives, 97th Congress, first session, September 21–23, *1981*, 234–35.

138. *Defense Daily*, April 14, 1981, 257.

139. *Florida Today*, September 11, 1981, 1A.

140. *Defense Daily*, January 1, 1981, 127.

141. *Florida Today*, November 24, 1981; *AW&ST*, November 16, 1981, 16.

142. *Florida Today,* September 11, 1981, 1A.

143. Kennedy Space Center, Shuttle Mission Archive, www.nasa.gov/mission_pages/shuttle/shuttlemissions/archives/sts-3.html.

144. NASA news release 82-199, September 7, 1982; NASA news release 82-200, September 7, 1982; NASA news release 82-204, September 7, 1982; NASA news release 82-120, August 6, 1982.

145. *Defense Daily*, December 18, 1981, 250.

Chapter 9. A New Order of Things

Epigraph source: NARA Eastpoint, KSC Upper Level Management Files 88-22, box 1, A. J. Pickett, "KSC Operations Period Planning, Background, Presentation to JSC Management," March 31, 1982, quoting Niccolò Machiavelli, *The Prince*, chap. 6.

1. Reagan made this pronouncement on July 4, 1982, when he attended the fourth landing of space shuttle *Columbia* at Edwards Air Force Base in California.

2. *Orlando Sentinel-Star*, November 30, 1980.

3. NASA HQ, file 12296, Vice President's Space Policy Advisory Board, "The Future of the U.S. Space Industrial Base," November 1992, 6.

4. *Defense Daily*, December 15, 1980, 208.

5. Ibid., October 8, 1980, 193; KSC Archives, box 36-80, Center Director Staff Meeting Notes, October 9, 1980; *Defense Daily*, January 30, 1981, 150.

6. *Defense Daily*, September 24, 1981, 92.

7. *Florida Today*, October 10, 1981.

8. Ibid., October 14, 1982, 1A, 16A.

9. Joseph J. Trento, *Prescription for Disaster* (New York: Crown, 1987), 101, 204–5, 258–59.

10. Ibid., 196–98. See also Theresa M. Foley, "NASA Wins Policy Dispute over Space Shuttle Pricing," *AW&ST*, April 4, 1988.

11. Brian Harvey, *Europe's Space Programme: To Ariane and Beyond* (London: Springer, 2003), 168–72.

12. Bromberg, *NASA and the Space Industry* (see chap. 2 n.41), 114–48; John Conway, interview by Kenneth Lipartito, 2003.

13. *Defense Daily*, December 15, 1980, 208.

14. McCurdy, *Inside NASA* (see chap. 1 n.45).

15. NASA HQ, file 4629, Launch Pad 39, "Remarks by George Low, Fifth Anniversary of Manned Lunar Landing Pad 39A Dedication Ceremonies."

16. *Defense/Space Business Daily*, February 12, 1980, 222.

17. *Spaceport News*, June 25, 1982, 2; *Florida Today*, November 14, 1985, 3A; *Florida Today*, October 1, 1988, 3B; *Orlando Sentinel*, October 4, 1988, A17; NASA/KSC news release 107-87, October 5, 1987.

18. *Florida Today*, June 4, 1981.

19. Charles Murphy, interview by Orville R. Butler, April 18, 2004.

20. Ibid.

21. *Florida Today*, April 5, 1983, 1A, 14A.

22. "Challenger (STA-099, OVO-99)," science.ksc.nasa.gov/shuttle/resources/orbiters/challenger.html; "Discovery (OV-103)," science.ksc.nasa.gov/shuttle/resources/orbiters/discovery.html; "Atlantis (OV-104)," science.ksc.nasa.gov/shuttle/resources/orbiters/atlantis.html.

23. *Florida Today*, January 26, 1983, 1A, 14A.

24. Ibid.; January 30, 1983, 1A.

25. Ibid., February 15, 1983, 1A, 14A.

26. *AW&ST*, November 1, 1982, 19.

27. KSC Archives, box 84-48, Executive Staff, Shuttle Turnaround Planning, May 20, 1981.

28. *Florida Today*, February 23, 1983, 1A, 18A; "Shuttle Schedule Recovery Plan Approved," *AW&ST*, February 28, 1983, 20.

29. KSC Archives, box 84-48, Executive Staff, Shuttle Turnaround Planning, June 11, 1981.

30. "Substitute Engine Arrives," *Florida Today*, February 23, 1983, 18A; *Florida Today*, March 3, 1983, 12A; March 4, 1A, 16A; "STS-6 Mission on Track for March Launch Time," *Spaceport News*, February 18, 1983, 1. *Columbia*'s old engine was slightly less powerful than the new engines on *Challenger*, so NASA preferred to replace the malfunctioning engine with another equally powerful.

31. *Florida Today*, March 10, 1983, 1A, 16A; March 11, 1A; March 18, 16A; March 19, 1A, 10A; March 22, 12A; March 23, 1A, 18A.

440 * Notes to Pages 255–260

32. Ibid., November 11, 1983, 20A; March 1, 1984, 1A, 16A; May 1, 1984, 1A, 16A; "STS-9 Mission Is Delayed as Shuttle Returns to VAB," *Spaceport News*, October 28, 1983.

33. *Orlando Sentinel*, April 19, 1984, C2; *Florida Today*, May 9, 1984, 4A; May 13, 20A.

34. *Florida Today*, July 29, 1983, 1A, 16A.

35. Ibid., November 4, 1983, 16A.

36. Ibid., March 9, 1990, 2A.

37. Ibid., June 3, 1984, 1A, 20A; June 5, 1A; June 6, 1A; June 9, 1A, 16A; June 12, 4A.

38. *Orlando Sentinel*, June 26, 1984, A1, A6; June 27, A1, A6.

39. *Florida Today*, June 27, 1984, 12A.

40. *Orlando Sentinel*, June 27, 1984, A1, A6.

41. *Florida Today*, June 29, 1984, 14A; *AW&ST*, July 2, 1984, 16.

42. *Florida Today*, July 13, 1984, 1A.

43. *Defense Daily*, August 8, 1984, 205.

44. *Florida Today*, July 31, 1984, 12A; August 2, 10A; August 10, 13A; August 11, 1A; *Orlando Sentinel*, August 9, 1984, A9; August 16, B1.

45. *Miami Herald*, August 31, 1984, 1A, 2A.

46. Conrad Nagel, interview by Butler, June 24, 2003.

47. *Florida Today*, October 4, 1985, 1A, 2A.

48. Ibid., November 25, 1985, 1A.

49. Ibid., July 15, 1985, 5A; July 18, 5A; October 22, 5A; December 18, 1A.

50. Ibid., December 18, 1985, 1A; December 20, 1A, 2A.

51. Ibid., January 7, 1986, 1A; January 8, 1A, 6A; January 9, 1A, 2A; January 11, 1A; January 22, 3A.

52. John Conway, interview by Butler and Sallie Middleton, March 25, 2004.

53. *Florida Today*, August 2, 1990, 5A. After nose wheel steering was installed, they controlled that as well.

54. Ibid., June 12, 1986, 2A. Even after a centralized consolidated Orbiter Logistics Depot opened in May 1990, maintaining parts for the shuttle fleet remained a problem. *Florida Today*, March 24, 1990, 8A.

55. *Orlando Sentinel*, February 22, 1984, A9.

56. Ibid., April 27, 1983, A3.

57. NASA/KSC news release 250-83, October 25, 1983.

58. *Florida Today*, June 25, 1983, 6A; February 12, 1984, 1A, 20A.

59. Ibid., November 28, 1983, 1A, 10A.

60. Ibid., June 4, 1985, 1A, 12A; *AW&ST*, August 19, 1985, 13.

61. *Florida Today*, November 7, 1985, 1A.

62. *Orlando Sentinel*, January 17, 1986, A1, A9; *Florida Today*, January 19, 1986, 1A.

63. *Defense/Space Business Daily*, September 28, 1979, 126.

64. NARA Eastpoint, KSC Upper Level Management Files 88-22, box 1, A. J. Pickett, "KSC Operations Period Planning, Background, Presentation to JSC Management," March 31, 1982.

65. NARA Eastpoint, KSC Upper Level Management Files 88-23, box 1, Booz-Allen Applied Research, "STS Operations Management Study," August 25, 1977.

66. KSC Archives, box 86-35, Upper Level Management Files, John Yardley to Center Director, KSC, August 19, 1976 (copy in KSC STS Operations Period Planning, Overview, KSC Construction Unions, April 13, 1982); same box, A. M. Lovelace, Associate Director/Deputy Administrator NASA, to Center Director KSC and Associate Administrator/Director JSC, July 12, 1978.

67. Same box, KSC STS Operations Period Planning, Summary of Senior Industry Representatives Comments, September 24, 1981.

68. Ibid.

69. Same box, Assessment Team #1, Lohse/Backus.

70. Same box, Assessment Team #3, Walton.

71. KSC Archives, box 84-48, Ex/Director, Executive Management Office, memo "Shuttle Processing Contract (SPC) Briefing (on September 16, 1981)," September 22, 1981.

72. NASA/KSC news release 289-81, October 21, 1981.

73. KSC Archives, box 86-35, Upper Level Management Files, Fred Boles, KSC Procurement Officer, October 9, 1981; same box, R. G. Smith, Center Director, memo for record, December 18, 1981; *Spaceport News*, October 23, 1981, 1, 7.

74. *Orlando Sentinel-Star*, December 8, 1981.

75. *Florida Today*, February 3, 1982, 12A; February 4, 16A. Part of that difference was due to additional care in the handling of the orbiter. During the tow to the OPF following the landing of *Columbia*'s first flight, a forklift had brushed the orbiter, causing extensive tile damage.

76. KSC Archives, box 86-35, Upper Level Management Files, memo R. G. Smith, October 13, 1981.

77. *Florida Today*, January 6, 1982; NASA HQ, file 4550, Terrence Finn to Honorable Bill Nelson, February 20, 1980.

78. NASA news release 82-105, June 23, 1982.

79. *Florida Today*, October 1, 1982, 1B.

80. *Spaceport News*, December 10, 1982, 1, 6; *Florida Today*, November 30, 1982, 12A.

81. *Spaceport News*, December 10, 1982, 1.

82. NASA news release 82-105, June 23, 1982.

83. KSC Archives, box 88-22, Upper Level Management Files, Presentation [Johnson] SPC Review Team Findings to AA for STS, May 5, 1982.

84. Ibid.

85. Ibid.

86. Another fear was that a private contractor would have more difficulty communicating with civil servants at Johnson and Marshall than did the Kennedy civil servants who were replaced.

87. See note 83.

88. Ibid.

89. Same box, James Beggs to Officials-in-Charge of Headquarters Offices, Directors, NASA Field Installations, July 29, 1982.

90. Same box, "Alternative Straw Man, Work done by Jim Bone and Earl Young for June 2, 1982 Meeting."

91. *Florida Today*, February 1, 1982, 1A.

92. *Orlando Sentinel*, September 8, 1983, A1, A7.

93. *Florida Today*, December 10, 1982, 16C; March 31, 1983, 18C; May 5, 20C; *AW&ST*, September 13, 1982, 77.

94. Philip Culbertson, interview by Butler and Middleton, April 1, 2004; Conway, interview, March 2004; Andrew Pickett, telephone conversation with Butler, April 1, 2004; *Florida Today*, August 21, 1983, 1A,10A; *Orlando Sentinel*, September 8, 1983, A1, A7.

95. Culbertson, interview; Conway, interview, March 2004; Pickett, telephone conversation.

96. The complex space shuttle main engines remained outside the contract and continued to be processed by their builder, Rocketdyne, which had handled engine processing work at KSC since 1965.

97. *Orlando Sentinel*, September 8, 1983, A1, A7; *Defense Daily*, September 20, 1983, 77; *AW&ST*, September 26, 1983, 28–30; *Florida Today*, February 5, 1983, 2B.

98. KSC Archives, Upper Level Management Files, box 86-35, Board of Visitors, J. W. Moore–Center Director/KSC, May 1, 1984.

99. Ibid.

100. James F. Harrington III, interview by Butler, July 29, 2003; Robert Sieck, interview by Butler, August 19, 2003.

101. Harrington, interview.

102. *Spaceflight*, July/August 1984, 301.

103. "Logistics to Get New Home," *Star Gazer*, August 2, 1984, 8; NASA/KSC news release 239-85, November 27, 1985; "Shuttle Logistics Facility," *AW&ST*, January 20, 1986, 111.

104. *Orlando Sentinel*, May 3, 1989, B1, B6; *Florida Today*, February 27, 1986, 20C; May 3, 1989, 7A; March 24, 1990, 8A.

105. *Defense Daily*, April 8, 1981, 229; May 8, 45; June 3, 184.

106. *AW&ST*, July 6, 1981, 15.

107. *Florida Today*, March 9, 1985, 1A, 18A; March 10, 1A, 20A; March 13, 1A; March 21, 1A; April 3, 1A, 16A.

108. Wilbert "Robby" Robinson, conversation with Middleton, March 18, 2004.

109. *Spaceport News*, January 2, 1981, 3.

110. *Florida Today*, May 1, 1981, 16A.

111. *Defense Daily*, January 19, 1981, 74–75.

112. Ibid., January 12, 1981, 35; February 25, 287; March 16, 89.

113. *Defense/Space Business Daily*, September 16, 1976, 85; January 13, 1977; September 23, 1977; *Defense Daily*, January 12, 1981, 34; January 19, 74–75.

114. KSC news release 188-81, July 29, 1981.

115. KSC Archives, Upper Level Management Files, box 86-38: H. Lamberth, Shuttle/Centaur, Review of the Operational Baseline, August 1982; C. A. Bachstein, memo for file "Shuttle/Centaur Meeting with Representatives from Lewis Research Center on August 27, 1982," August 31, 1982; CCLS, NASA Lewis Research Center Space Directorate, memo for file, August 31, 1982; Shuttle/Centaur Meeting with Representatives from LRC on August 27, 1982.

116. NASA news release 77-210, December 19, 1977; NASA news release 78-183, November 2, 1978.

117. *Defense Daily*, January 12, 1981, 35. For more on KSC work to handle Centaur, see KSC news release 188-81, July 29, 1981; KSC news release 157-83, July 11, 1983; KSC news release 239-83, October 5, 1983; KSC news release 117-84, June 12, 1984; *Florida Today*, February 5, 1985, 16C; "Centaur Program," *AW&ST*, November 25, 1985, 22.

118. *AW&ST*, August 19, 1985, 25.

119. "Centaur Delivery," *AW&ST*, January 6, 1986, 26.

120. *Florida Today*, November 14, 1985, 3A.

121. JoAnn Morgan, telephone conversation with Orville R. Butler, May 20, 2004.

122. Conway, interview, 2003.

123. Ibid.; Conway, interview by Butler, April 2004.

124. Morgan, telephone conversation.

125. *Defense Daily*, December 19, 1980, 242.

126. 6555th ASTG, "82-1 Ground Processing Lessons Learned Summary," ca. November 1982, pp. T-2, O-1, summarized by Mark C. Cleary of the 45th Space Wing History Office in *The Cape: Military Space Operations 1971–1992*, https://www.patrick.af.mil/heritage/Cape/Capefram.htm.

Chapter 10. *Challenger* and Beyond

1. Almost every person interviewed about the Challenger disaster still showed deep emotion when discussing the events of that day.

2. There are many books on the events described here. The best, in our opinion, is Diane Vaughn, *The Challenger Launch Decision: Risky Technology, Culture, and Deviance at NASA* (Chicago: University of Chicago Press, 1996). Other works include Joseph J. Trento, *Prescription for Disaster* (New York: Crown, 1987), and Malcolm McConnell, *Challenger: A Major Malfunction* (Garden City, N.Y.: Doubleday, 1987).

3. Presidential Commission on the Space Shuttle Challenger Accident, *Report to the President* (hereafter *Rogers Commission Report*), 5 vols. (Washington, D.C., 1986), vol. 1, *Executive Summary*.

4. *Newsweek*, March 24, 1986, 18.

5. Robert V. Head, "NASA Probe Must Concede Decision-Making Risk," *Government Computer News*, April 25, 1986, 29.

6. *Spaceport News*, June 6, 1986, 1; February 14, 1986, 7.

7. *Florida Today*, March 17, 1986, 2A.

8. Michael Isikoff, "Space Official Criticizes Probe," *Washington Post*, March 16, 1986, 18.

9. KSC Archives, Report of the Presidential Commission, box 2, folder 8, "51L Launch from T-9."

10. *Florida Today*, January 30, 1986, 1A, 2A, 9A; *Orlando Sentinel*, February 1, 1986, A11; Thomas Overton, interview by Orville R. Butler, August 4, 2003; John "Tip" Talone, interview by Butler, July 24, 2003; *Florida Today*, January 30, 1986, 8A.

11. Overton, interview.

12. Ibid.

13. John Conway, interview by Kenneth Lipartito, 2003; see also Conway, interview by Butler, April 2004.

14. Katrina Pountney, quoted in *Florida Today*, February 6, 1986, 1A.

15. *Newsweek*, March 24, 1986.

16. William Schmidt, "Efforts Resume to Recover Shuttle Cabin," *New York Times*, March 12, 1986; "Up to 1,800 More Space Program Layoffs Expected," *Washington Post*, September 4, 1986; "Challenger Pieces Wash Up on Florida Shore," *Washington Times*, December 18, 1996.

17. Overton, interview.

18. *Florida Today*, June 20, 1986, 1A; July 30, 6A; August 15, 1A; September 5, 1A, 2A; September 19, 1A; William Broad, "NASA Cutting Work Force at Space Center in Florida," *New York Times*, September 5, 1986.

19. Fred Reed, "All Quiet on the Launch Pad," *Air & Space*, February–March 1987.

20. *Orlando Sentinel*, January 29, 1986, A3.

21. Moore, "Fueling the Fascination" (see chap. 4 n.101); Hugh Harris, interview by Roger Launius, Henry Dethloff, Lee Snaples, and Lisa Malone, June 25, 2001. It did not help that NASA administrator James Beggs was on leave of absence, under indictment for actions he had taken while at TRW. Beggs was eventually cleared, but the acting director during *Challenger*, William Graham, was inexperienced for a problem of *Challenger*'s magnitude.

22. *Rogers Commission Report*, chap. 7, "Silent Safety Program." The charge on reduction of personnel was made by Senator Albert Gore; see Ed Magnuson, "Fixing NASA," *Time*, June 9, 1986.

23. Conrad Nagel, interview by Butler, June 24, 2003.

24. Levitt and March, "Organizational Learning" (see chap. 1 n.53), 323.

25. Quoted in Diane Vaughn, "Targets for Firefighting Safety: Lessons from the Challenger Tragedy," *Wildfire*, March 1997.

26. The office may have opened even earlier, but the information is incomplete. Most likely there were similar offices and functions before KSC became an independent center. Information on safety organization at KSC used throughout this study is taken from KSC Archives, Telephone Directories File.

27. *Spaceport News*, October 1, 1964, 2.

28. Ibid., August 1, 1968, 8.

29. Ibid., December 19, 1968, 5.

30. KSC Archives, Debus Collection, box 2, folder 22, Debus- Phillips, May 2, 1966.

31. Quote from McCurdy, *Inside NASA* (see chap. 1 n.45), 65.

32. KSC Archives, Safety Collection, box 2, "Final Report: Impact of a Safety Support Contractor Group on KSC Safety Office Operations," June 1965.

33. KSC Archives, Safety Collection, box 1, "Report of the Ad Hoc Review Group of the Florida Facility Safety Program."

34. KSC Archives, 76-98, box 6, memo "The NASA Safety Program," March 8, 1968.

35. KSC Archives, Debus Collection, box 2, folder 24, Debus–David Jones, May 14, 1969; folder 24, Debus–John Clark, January 13, 1969; folder 26, Debus–David Jones, January 12, 1970.

36. KSC Archives, 76-98, box 6, Kennedy Space Center General Safety Plan, April 19, 1968.

37. KSC Archives, 76-98, box 6, Guide for Contractor Safety Plans at KSC, August 21, 1968, 2–3.

38. *Spaceport News*, December 20, 1962.

39. G. T. "Ted" Sasseen, interview by Butler, June 20, 2003.

40. *Spaceport News*, March 16, 1976, 6; December 10, 2. One cartoon showed a Frankensteinian creature with the caption "Got a Problem? See Us Before it Gets Monstrous! We Care!" See *Spaceport News*, May 27, 1977, 7.

41. *Spaceport News*, January 13, 1972, 6; May 18, 2.

42. Ibid., August 15, 1980, 1; January 21, 1983, 4.

43. *Rogers Commission Report*, app. F, Richard Feynman, "Personal Observations on Reliability of Shuttle," F-1.

44. Ibid.

45. Indeed, competition is often seen as one of the virtues of the marketplace, and NASA since the 1970s had been admonished to behave more like a private-sector firm. But marketlike processes, to discover what really works, rely heavily on trying and failing.

46. Conway, interview, 2003. In fact, one lesson from *Challenger* might be that NASA did not pay enough attention to its own accumulated operational experience, and relied too heavily on engineering tests of parts and systems. One critic has made the case that a more careful reading of the flight record might have brought into greater clarity the relationship between O-ring damage and temperature; see Frederick F. Lighthall, "Launching the Space Shuttle Challenger: Disciplinary Deficiencies in the Analysis of Engineering Data," *IEEE Transactions on Engineering Management* 38 (February 1991), 63–74.

47. Eugene Sestile, interview by Butler, July 20, 2003.

48. NASA, *Report to the President, Actions to Implement the Recommendation of the Presidential Commission on the Space Shuttle Challenger Accident: Executive Summary* (Washington, D.C., 1986).

49. *Spaceport News*, July 18, 1986, 7.

50. Ibid., May 22, 1987, 8.

51. Ibid., July 18, 1986, 2; July 19, 1987, 1.

52. Shannon Bartell, interview by Butler and Nanci Schwartz, June 26, 2003.

53. *Florida Today*, March 10, 1986, 2A.

54. Ibid., June 10, 1986, 2A; June 19, 1A; *Rogers Commission Report*, 1: 178, 192.

55. *Rogers Commission Report*, 1: 176–77, 190–91; also see vol. 2, app. G, "Human Factors Analysis."

56. "Human Factors Analysis."

57. Bartell, interview, 2003.

58. NASA HQ, file 4593, General, 1980–89, McCartney-Roe, April 21, 1988.

59. *Spaceport News*, September 25, 1987, 1.

60. *Orlando Sentinel*, June 21, 1986, A1.

61. *Florida Today*, September 2, 1986, 1A.

62. *Rogers Commission Report*, 1: 102–4.

63. The problems of the single-vehicle approach were raised strongly by the Na-

tional Academy of Sciences, which believed uncrewed vehicles were best for scientific missions. See Magnuson, "Fixing NASA."

64. *NASA Historical Data Book*, vol. 6 (see chap. 8 n.16), 463.

65. Ibid., vol. 5, *NASA Launch Systems, Space Transportation, Human Spaceflight, and Space Science, 1979–1988*, comp. Judy A. Rumerman (Washington, D.C.: NASA, 1999), 13.

66. Magnuson, "Fixing NASA."

67. Sasseen, interview.

68. Gen. Forrest S. McCartney, USAF (Ret.), interview by Launius, Dethloff, and Malone, June 26, 2001.

69. NASA HQ, file 4616, KSC Orbiter Maintenance and Refurbishment Facility.

70. NASA HQ, file 4629, Launch Pad 39, KSC news release 125-89, "Modifications Completed to Space Shuttle Launch Pad 39-A."

71. McCartney, interview.

72. Magnuson, "Fixing NASA."

73. McCartney-Roe (see n.58), April 21, 1988.

74. Reed, "All Quiet on the Launch Pad" (see n.19).

75. KSC Archives, Report of the Presidential Commission, box 2, folder 9, "Summary of Market Opinion Research Survey of American Attitudes Toward the Space Program."

76. National Transportation Systems—Overview, September 1988, "Operational Improvements and Modifications," history.nasa.gov/shuttleoverview1988/part3. htm.

77. McCartney-Roe (see n.58), July 27, 1988.

78. Ibid., February 8, 1988.

79. Ibid., April 21, 1988.

80. Ibid.

81. Ibid.

82. William Broad, "New Shuttle Is Readied for Launch Pad," *New York Times*, June 28, 1988.

83. *Spaceport News*, October 14, 1988.

84. Jon Nordheimer, "Holding Their Breath for Space Leap," *New York Times*, June 23, 1988.

85. McCartney-Roe (see n.58), July 27, 1988.

86. Edward H. Kolcum, "Managers Modernize Shuttle System to Increase Efficiency, Launch Rate," *AW&ST*, December 4, 1989, 46–47.

87. Sestile, interview.

88. *Spaceport News*, October 10, 1986, 1, 6.

89. Nagel, interview.

90. JoAnn Morgan, telephone conversation with Orville R. Butler, May 20, 2004.

91. Ibid.

92. Bobby Bruckner, interview by Dethloff, Snaples, Malone, and Elaine Liston, June 12, 2001; Conway, interview, 2003; Conway, interview, April 2004.

93. Morgan, telephone conversation.

94. Ibid.

95. NASA Facts, "Galileo Mission to Jupiter," Jet Propulsion Laboratory, Pasadena, Calif., n.d.

96. Bartell, interview, 2003.

97. "McCartney Touts Shuttle Economics," *Florida Today*, January 10, 1990, 10A.

98. *Hubble Space Telescope: Media Reference Guide* (Sunnyvale, Calif.: Lockheed Missiles & Space Company, n.d.), 1.

99. John Conway, interview by Butler and Sallie Middleton, March 25, 2004.

100. Most of KSC's clean rooms are rated 100,000; only one in the AE building is rated at 10,000, making it the cleanest room at KSC. KSC news release 29-01, March 22, 2001.

101. *Florida Today*, January 20, 1990, 4A.

102. Ibid., January 27, 1990, 5A.

103. Ibid., January 29, 1990, 4A; January 30, 1A, 4A; February 1, 1990, 10A.

104. Ibid., February 4, 1990, 8E.

105. Ibid., February 9, 1990, 4A; February 10, 5A; February 11, 1A; February 14, 6A; February 15, 11A; February 17, 2A; February 22, 1A–2A; February 24, 1A; February 27, 1A; *Orlando Sentinel*, February 25, 1990, A10; February 26, A1, A4; February 27, A10.

106. *Florida Today*, February 22, 1990, 4A.

107. Ibid., March 8, 1990, 5A; March 16, 1A; March 17, 4A; March 19, 1A; March 20, 4A; March 21, 4A; March 24, 8A.

108. Ibid., April 5, 1990, 5A; April 11, 1A, 2A, 6A.

109. Statistics cited in "No Cheers for NASA," *Newsweek*, March 24, 1986.

110. Perin, "Operating as Experimenting" (see chap. 1 n.50).

Chapter 11. Launching in a Competitive Environment

1. *Defense/Space Business Daily*, March 30, 1977.

2. Donald Sheppard, conversation with Sallie Middleton, March 25, 2004.

3. *Spaceport News*, October 31, 1975.

4. NARA Eastpoint, RG 255, KSC Upper Level Management Files, box 88-32, Unmanned Launch Vehicles, 1977, "Disposal Plan for Expendable Launch Facilities Complexes 17 & 36."

5. *Defense/Space Business Daily*, December 13, 1978, 205.

6. NASA news release 80-53, April 23, 1980; *AW&ST*, April 28, 1980, 18; *Defense Daily*, May 23, 1980, 123; *Florida Today*, August 20, 1980.

7. NASA HQ, file 4623, Launch Pad 17B, Robert Frosch to Honorable Thomas P. O'Neill, Jr., August 5, 1980.

8. *AW&ST*, February 2, 1981, 36.

9. Bromberg, *NASA and the Space Industry* (see chap. 2 n.41), 128.

10. Ibid., 118.

11. "U.S. Space Industrial Base" (see chap. 9 n.3), 10.

12. *Space: The Commercial Opportunities: Proceedings of the International Business Strategy Conference Held in London, 1984* (London: Online Conferences, 1984), 95.

13. Tom Dworetzky, "The Launching Gap," *Discovery*, July 1988, 15–18.

14. Martine Morse Wooster, "License to Launch," *Air & Space*, August–September 1991, 54–57.

15. Launius and Jenkins, *To Reach the High Frontier* (see chap. 2 n.9), 171.

16. Lee R. Scherer, "The Status of U. S. Expendable Launch Vehicles," EASCON 85; National Space Strategy—A Progress Report. Proceedings of the Eighteenth Annual Electronics and Aerospace Systems Conference, Washington, D.C., October 28–30, 1985.

17. The dispute is well covered in Foley, "NASA Wins Policy Dispute" (see chap. 9 n.10).

18. KSC Archives, box 94-100, folder 8610.3, Center Director Files, CY1989, Joseph Mahon–Stephanie Lee-Miller, May 16, 1989.

19. Irene Klotz, "Commercial Launches: Getting the Business," *Ad Astra*, April 1989, 16–19.

20. KSC Archives, box 94-100, folder 8610.3, Center Director Files, CY1989, "NASA Response to Department of Transportation Launch Site Scheduling Study," n.d.

21. John J. Glisch, "Why Delta Loss Is Still Eluding NASA," *Orlando Sentinel*, May 30, 1986.

22. George White, "Investigation Grounds Atlas Centaur: Payloads Backed Up; Military Lines up Other Launch Vehicles," *Florida Today*, May 25, 1986.

23. www.orbital.com/spacelaunch/pegasus.

24. www.orbital.com/spacelaunch/taurus.

25. Irene Klotz, "Pioneering a New Age: Commercial Launch Service," *Space World*, May 1988, 9.

26. NASA HQ, file 17152, "Expendable Launch Vehicles Technology, A Report to the United States Senate and to the U.S. House of Representatives," July 1990.

27. Klotz, "Pioneering a New Age," 7–8; "Congress Moves Toward Subsidizing ELVs," *Aerospace America*, August 1988, 8–10. By international law, the United States government was still responsible for damage outside U.S. territory, even in a private launch.

28. Wooster, "License to Launch," 54–57.

29. See note 20.

30. *NASA News*, July 15, 1988.

31. It proved harder to carry out launches than the private companies first assumed. American Rocket Company's booster exploded on its first mission. Richard Stevenson, "Private Space Rocket Is Destroyed in Blastoff," *New York Times*, October 6, 1989.

32. Tim Furniss, "Crowded Market: Commercial Launchers Come Down to Earth," *Space*, September–October 1991, 8–12; Edward Jujsak, "Can U.S. Commercial ELVs Survive?" *Space News*, May 17–23, 1993, 19.

33. John Krige, Arturo Russo, and Laurenza Sebesta, *A History of the European Space Agency, 1958–1987* (Noordwijk: European Space Agency, 2000), 2: 474–77.

34. Philip Chien, "Commercial Launch Services Big and Small," *Via Satellite*, December 1991, 32–39; Space Business News Staff, *Guide to ELVs & the Commercial Launch Market* (Arlington, Va.: Pasha Publications, 1986), 9; Lance Frazer, "Lead, Follow or Get out of the Way," *Space World*, May 1988, 12–15.

35. NASA HQ, file 17152, William Clapp, "The US Commercial Space Launch Program and the Department of Defense Dilemma," 2; "U.S. Space Industrial Base," 12.

36. Trento, *Prescription for Disaster* (see chap. 9 n.9), 185.

37. David Whitehouse, "What Cost Low-Cost?" *Space*, May–June 1989, 20–21.

38. Clapp, "Dilemma" (see n.35), 11.

39. Harvey, *Europe's Space Programme*, 175–90.

40. Launius and Jenkins, *To Reach the High Frontier*, 178.

41. "U.S. Space Industrial Base," 4–5, 7.

42. *Guide to ELVs* (see n.34), 10.

43. Melinda Gipson, "10,000 Toyotas," *Final Frontier*, July–August 1990, 40.

44. Ibid., 37.

45. Lon Rains, "NASA Struggles with Tough Issue of Private Launch Support," *Space News*, March 5–11, 1990, 1.

46. "U.S. Space Industrial Base," 8. The most recent versions are capable of lifting from 10,000 to 20,000 pounds of payload into low earth orbit; see Launius and Jenkins, *To Reach the High Frontier*, 92–98.

47. Launius and Jenkins, *To Reach the High Frontier*, 171.

48. Ibid., 173.

49. Michael Woolley, conversation with Middleton, October 26, 2003.

50. Launius and Jenkins, *To Reach the High Frontier*, 133–37.

51. See ibid., 218.

52. NASA HQ, file 17152, "Expendable Launch Vehicles Technology: A Report to the United States Senate and the U.S. House of Representatives," July 1990.

53. KSC Archives, box 94-100, folder "Advanced Launch System (ALS)," Advanced Launch System (ALS) Payload Accommodations.

54. Same file, Design Guide for ALS Payloads, October 1988.

55. Michael Benik, interview by Virginia Dawson and Joe Nieberding, November 9, 1999.

56. See note 54.

57. NASA HQ, file 12296, Statement of Dr. Alan M. Lovelace, General Dynamics Corporation, before the Subcommittee on Space, House Committee on Science Space and Technology, February 4, 1993.

58. Klotz, "Commercial Launches," 16–19; Stéphane Chenard, "The Long March to Launch Regulation," *Space Markets* 4 (1990): 193. The U.S. position was that the ESA, which charged a higher price for its own scientific missions aboard Ariane than it charged commercial users, was still subsidizing the rocket.

59. Some of the main ideas of this document found their way into the *Final Report to the President on the US Space Program*, January 1993.

60. "U.S. Space Industrial Base."

61. Bromberg, *NASA and the Space Industry*, 180.

62. "U.S. Space Industrial Base"; Bromberg, *NASA and the Space Industry*, 181.

63. Robert Crippen, interview by Roger Launius, July 17, 2002.

64. Michael Mecham, "NASA, Pentagon Urged to Focus on Cutting Launch Operations Costs," *AW&ST*, October 3, 1988, 39.

65. Ibid., 39.

66. "U.S. Space Industrial Base," 21.

67. Crippen, interview.

68. KSC Archives, Telephone Directories Collection, various years.

69. KSC Archives, Gray Photographic Collection, box 6, folder 22, Artist's Concepts. See Space Shuttle Photographs, box 1, for more.

70. Jay Honeycutt, interview by Kenneth Lipartito and Orville R. Butler, August 3, 2004.

71. Mecham, "NASA, Pentagon Urged to Focus," 39.

72. Ibid., 40. Although the flow of information during launch was considered "excellent," the problem arose in the processing work done months before.

73. KSC Archives, *KSC Research and Technology Annual Report*, 1994. Detail on improvements in the Launch Processing Software and information technology can be found in Richard Hartung, interview by Butler, April 20, 2004.

74. KSC Archives, Space Shuttle Program, box 28, Lessons Learned, "Space Transportation System Lessons Learned," December 1987.

75. Harold Heimmer, conversation with Lipartito, May 2, 2004; Ann Montgomery, interview by Lipartito, March 21, 2003.

76. Heimmer, conversation.

77. Ibid.

78. See discussion of these techniques in KSC Archives, *KSC Research and Technology Annual Report*, 1993.

79. Roy Tharpe, interview by Butler, July 23, 2004.

80. "Space Transportation System Lessons Learned" (see n. 74).

81. T. Alexander, "Unexpected Payoff" (see chap. 2 n.42), 115.

82. Honeycutt, interview.

83. Ibid.

84. Ibid. For more information on administrative streamlining, see Tharpe, interview.

85. Timothy Barth, conversation with Lipartito, October 1, 2004. More on these issues can be found in the KSC research and technology reports at rtreport.ksc.nasa.gov/.

86. Mecham, "NASA, Pentagon Urged to Focus," 39.

87. Mark Carreau, "10 Years After Challenger, NASA Feels Shuttle Safety Never Better," *Houston Chronicle*, January 19, 1996.

88. Charles Murphy, interview by Butler, April 18, 2004.

89. Honeycutt, interview.

90. Ibid.

91. Richard Smith, interview by Launius, June 27, 2001.

92. David Hounshell, "The Medium Is the Message, or How Context Matters," in Hughes and Hughes, *Systems, Experts and Computers* (see chap. 2 n.42), 255–310.

93. Carreau, "10 Years After Challenger."

94. Jose Garcia to Honorable Bill Clinton, August 29, 1995; Garcia, interview by Lipartito and Butler, September 30, 2004.

95. John "Tip" Talone, interview by Lipartito and Butler, May 2, 2004.

96. Honeycutt, interview.

97. Tharpe, interview.

98. Ibid.

99. With KSC people no longer directly involved in most processing activity, the number of inspections done by government personnel dropped from some 20,000 to about 8,000. Roy Bridges, interview by Henry Dethloff and Lee Snaples, June 17, 2001.

100. Michael Wetmore, interview by Butler, August 3, 2004.

101. Honeycutt, interview.

102. Despite the billions of dollars involved in SFOC, NASA work was far less profitable for contractors than was military work. Working for NASA gave Lockheed and Boeing prestige, cutting-edge knowledge they could apply to commercial projects, and a valuable recruiting tool. Engineers in Lockheed's space operations, for example, were paid less than engineers in the aerospace industry as a whole, but still had a much lower turnover rate. See Honeycutt, interview; Tharpe, interview.

103. Carreau, "10 Years After Challenger."

104. Wetmore, interview.

105. KSC Archives, Quarterly SFOC Planning Assessment Report, 4th Quarter Fiscal Year 2000, 21, 41, 42.

106. Launius and Jenkins, *To Reach the High Frontier*, 409.

107. Quarterly SFOC Planning Assessment Report, 23–30, 38.

108. Ibid., 41, 42.

109. Wetmore, interview.

110. Quarterly SFOC Planning Assessment Report, 45, 46.

111. Seth Borenstein, "Reducing Force a Bad Idea, Space Center Director Says," *Washington Post*, August 30, 1996; Honeycutt, interview.

Chapter 12. A Station in Space

1. *Florida Today*, May 9, 1977.

2. *Defense/Space Business Daily*, November 21, 1979, 94.

3. Ibid., November 6, 1979, 25.

4. Ibid., February 11, 1980, 213.

5. *Orlando Sentinel-Star*, December 29, 1980.

6. "Remarks by the President: Fourth Landing of the Space Shuttle Columbia, Dryden Flight Research Facility, Edwards Air Force Base, Calif., July 4, 1982," *NASA Activities* 13, no. 7 (1982): 13–14.

7. James Beggs, "1990: Year of the American Space Station," *NASA Activities* 13, no. 7 (1982): 18–20.

8. "5th Shuttle Not Needed, NASA Says," *Florida Today*, July 26, 1985, 1A.

9. "OTA Charges Space Station Flawed Without Space Goals," *Defense Daily*, February 6, 1984, 201.

10. Theresa M. Foley, "Space Station Program Faces Renewed Congressional Push to Cut Funding," *AW&ST*, June 6, 1988, 23–24.

11. "Dukakis, Republicans Pledge Support for Space Station," *AW&ST*, August 22, 1988, 27; "NASA Stresses Station Budget to Bush Team," *AW&ST*, November 14, 1988, 42.

12. KSC Archives, Space Station Collection, Statement by James B. Odom, Associate Administrator for Space Station, to Subcommittee on Space Science and Applications, House Committee on Science, Space and Technology, February 28, 1989, 2.

13. Craig Covault, "NASA Preparing 412 Space Station Contracts," *AW&ST*, September 17, 1984, 16–17.

14. Craig Covault, "NASA to Shift Focus with Space Station," *AW&ST*, March 12, 1984, 101.

15. Ibid.; Covault, "President Orders Start on Space Station," *AW&ST*, January 30, 1984, 18; Michael Feazel, "Engineers Facing Challenges in Design of Space Station," *AW&ST*, October 22, 1984, 97.

16. *Florida Today*, January 26, 1984, 1A, 16A.

17. *Orlando Sentinel*, May 4, 1984, A1, A10.

18. *Defense Daily*, July 6, 1982, 12.

19. Ibid., October 7, 1983, 182.

20. *Space Calendar*, October 28–November 3, 1985, 5; *Defense Daily*, February 2, 1984, 179.

21. In April 1985, McDonnell Douglas received a technical services contract for a one-year study of the space station's impact on KSC processing. That same year, Boeing received a contract to study KSC's role in the maintenance of the space station once it was in orbit. Yet another contract went to the Harris Corporation to evaluate KSC's role in fulfilling the station's mission requirements. *Florida Today*, April 10, 1985, 16C; April 12, 8A; "NASA Budget Boosted 3.9% to $7.491 billion in FY '85," *Defense Daily*, February 7, 1984, 179; *Orlando Sentinel*, April 27, 1984, B1, B7.

22. *Spaceflight* 26 (July–August 1984): 301.

23. Steven Francois, interview by Orville R. Butler, August 8, 2004.

24. John R. "Dick" Lyon, interview by Butler, July 23, 2004.

25. In a 1971 study looking back at the success of Apollo, *Managing Large Systems* (see chap. 3 n.48), 264–65, Sayles and Chandler noted that, contrary to the expectations of program management and systems engineering, in reality substantial integration work took place at operational sites, which was where the unexpected interface problems manifested themselves.

26. KSC Archives, James M. Ragusa, "Historical Data and Analysis for the First Five Years of KSC STS Payload Processing," NASA Technical Memorandum 83105, September 1986.

27. Ibid.

28. Ibid.

29. Ibid.

30. Theresa M. Foley, "NASA Apologizes for Illegal Lobbying to Preserve Budget, Space Station," *AW&ST*, August 31, 1987, 20; "Fiscal 1988 Station Funding Faces Battle in Senate," *AW&ST*, August 31, 1987, 21–22.

31. *Florida Today*, December 3, 1987, 4A.

32. James R. Asker, "Station Exceeds Weight, Power, EVA Limits, But NASA Says No Major Redesign Needed," *AW&ST*, July 30, 1990, 25–26.

33. Craig Covault and James R. Asker, "NASA Concept Deletes Station Truss, Changes Assembly to Solve Design Flaws," *AW&ST*, November 12, 1990, 26–27.

34. James R. Asker, "NASA to Propose Scaled-Back Station with Simpler Assembly in Space," *AW&ST*, February 25, 1991, 60.

35. James R. Asker, "Space Station Effort Enters Critical Stage," *AW&ST*, March 12, 1990, 16–18.

36. James R. Asker, "NASA Plays Down Quayle's Call for Station's 'Complete Redesign,'" *AW&ST*, December 17, 1990, 22.

37. Asker, "NASA to Propose Scaled-Back Station," 60.

38. "Space Station Survives Challenge on Senate Floor," *AW&ST*, July 22, 1991, 63; "House Bill Fully Funds Space Station But Requires Deep Cuts in NLS," *AW&ST*, October 7, 1991, 69; "Key House Panel Votes to Kill Funding for NASA Space Station," *AW&ST*, May 20, 1991, 25; Patricia A. Gilmartin, "Bush Administration Rallies Support for Space Station as Crucial Votes Near," *AW&ST*, May 27, 1991, 25; James R. Asker, "Station Work to Proceed During Funding Debate," *AW&ST*, June 3, 1991, 18–19; Asker, "House Votes to Keep Funding for Space Station in NASA Budget," *AW&ST*, June 10, 1991, 23.

39. "Space Station Survives Challenge."

40. "House Bill Fully Funds Space Station."

41. Francois, interview.

42. "GAO Faults 'Fragmented' Standards for Testing NASA Space Hardware," *AW&ST*, September 30, 1991, 23.

43. Francois, interview.

44. Shannon Bartell, interview by Butler and Nanci Schwartz, June 26, 2003.

45. Francois, interview.

46. Ibid.; Bartell, interview, 2003.

47. Eugene Sestile, interview by Butler, July 20, 2003; Francois, interview.

48. Francois, interview.

49. Ibid.

50. Ibid.

51. Ibid.

52. Ibid.

53. Ibid.

54. Lyon, interview.

55. *Florida Today*, March 30, 1998, 1A–2A; Bartell, interview, 2003.

56. Craig Covault, "Space Policy Outlines Program to Regain U.S. Leadership," *AW&ST*, February 22, 1988, 20–21.

57. *Florida Today*, May 6, 1989.

58. Ibid., February 7, 1990, 7A; "Space Station Processing Facility Contract Awarded," *Spaceport News*, February 22, 1991, 1–2.

59. KSC Archives, Space Station Collection, box 26, Bob Webster, Space Station Alpha Transition Team—Operations, "Space Station Alpha KSC Launch Site Capability Development and Processing Operations Concept White Paper," October 29, 1993.

60. "KSC Contributes to Space Station Redesign Options," *Spaceport News*, May 21, 1993, 1; Francois, interview; KSC Archives, Space Station Collection, box 26, folder C, Combined Test Team, n.d.

61. KSC Archives, Space Station Collection, box 26, folder A, Final System Review to Space Station Redesign Team, Space Station Option A, Modular Buildup Concept, Revision B, June 10, 1993.

62. Same folder, Space Station Redesign Review of Issues and Open Items to the Transition Team, July 8–9, 1993.

63. Francois, interview.

64. liftoff.msfc.nasa.gov/shuttle/spacelab/.

65. Francois, interview.

66. Ibid. Not all lessons learned in earlier processing were applied to the space station, however. As a cost-saving measure, KSC agreed to install tile floors. The first time workers ran pallets over the tile floor, "it sounded like popcorn going off." That December KSC scraped 65,000 square feet of tile off the floor and replaced it with a poured epoxy.

67. Enoch Moser, interview by Butler, July 30, 2004.

68. Shannon Bartell, interview by Butler, August 5, 2004.

69. Michael Haddad, interview by Butler, June 27, 2004.

70. Ibid.

71. Bartell, interview, 2004; Francois, interview; Jay Honeycutt, interview by Lipartito and Butler, August 3, 2004; John "Tip" Talone, interview by Lipartito and Butler, May 2, 2004.

72. Moser, interview.

73. Ibid.; Bartell, interview, 2004.

74. As Spacelab missions became routine in the mid-1990s, civil servants phased out of hands-on work here too. See KSC, Shuttle Mission Archive, STS-57, www.nasa. gov/mission_pages/shuttle/shuttlemissions/archives/sts-57.html; Spacehab, "Company History," www.spacehab.com/about/history.htm; Moser, interview; Haddad, interview.

75. Francois, interview.

76. Bromberg, *NASA and the Space Industry* (see chap. 2 n.41), 185.

77. Francois, interview.

78. Ibid.

79. Webster, "White Paper" (see n.59); Francois, interview.

80. Francois, interview.

81. Information on the IPT concept at Boeing is found in the video *777 First Flight: An Inside Look at the Innovative Production of the Boeing 777* (PBS, 1977).

82. Francois, interview.

83. Ibid.; Bartell, interview, 2004.

84. Francois, interview.

85. Ibid.

86. Ibid.

87. Ibid.

88. Ibid.; Honeycutt, interview.

89. Honeycutt, interview; Talone, interview, 2004; Talone, interview by Butler, July 9, 2003.

90. Talone interview, 2004.

91. Honeycutt, interview; Talone, interviews, 2004 and July 9, 2003; *Spaceport News*, June 6, 1997, 1–2; July 7, 1.

92. Honeycutt, interview.

93. Ibid.; Talone, interviews, 2004 and July 9, 2003; Honeycutt letter to KSC employees, April 10, 1996, quoted in KSC Chronologies, 1996, www-lib.ksc.nasa.gov/lib/archives/chronologies/1996CHRONO.PDF.

94. Francois, interview.

95. Ibid.

96. *Florida Today*, March 27, 1996, 1A; February 24, 1997, 1A, 2A; *Orlando Sen-*

tinel, February 13, 1997, A5; February 25, A1, A4; *Aerospace Daily*, March 25, 1997, 441–42.

97. *Florida Today*, May 22, 1996, 1A.

98. Ibid., November 6, 1997, 6A; *Orlando Sentinel*, November 6, 1997, A12; July 25, 1997, A4.

99. KSC Archives, Space Station Collection, box 14, folder D, KSC Launch Support IPT Position of Station to Shuttle Interface Testing, March 5, 1996.

100. Same folder, B. R. Stones, JSC Operations Position on Integrated Testing & Verification, Mission Operations Directorate, March 7, 1996.

101. KSC Archives, Space Station Collection, box 13, International Space Station POP 96 Program Review, May 21, 1996.

102. Same box, International Space Station KSC SSPF Highbay Footprint MEIT (ICM) What-If Assessment, March 17, 1997.

103. Same box, J. Straiton, Launch Support IPT POP 96 Presentation, May 21, 1996.

104. KSC Archives, Space Station Collection, box 1, folder E, Launch Site Processing Plan (LSPP) Incremental Design Review (IDR) #1 of International Space Station (ISS), February 24, 1995; box 13, John Swanson, Shuttle to Station IVT Philosophy, March 4, 1996; box 12, folder F, Tommy W. Holloway, CITE, Space Shuttle Program, NASA Johnson Space Center Houston, Texas, March 25, 1996; same folder, J. S. Swanson, "Station Integrated Verification," Space Shuttle Program, Space Shuttle Systems and Cargo Engineering Office, April 26, 1996, and Bob Webster, "Launch Site Perspective on CITE Applicability for ISS/Shuttle Verification, Response to Tommy Holloway CITE Presentation Dated 3-25-96—Preliminary," April 24, 1996.

105. Swanson, April 26, and Holloway, March 25 (see n.104).

106. Webster, April 24 (see n.104).

107. KSC Archives, Space Station Collection, box 14, KSC Launch Support IPT Position on Station to Shuttle Interface Testing, March 5, 1996; box 13, Updates to the KSC 2A Verification Assessment, April 10, 1996, 4.

108. NASA news release 97-65, April 9, 1997.

109. KSC Archives, Space Station Collection, box 18, folder I, Cheryl McPhillips, "Multiple Element Integrated Testing," Space Station Hardware Integration Office, May 8, 1997; same folder, Mark Reiber, "Element-to-Element EME Tests for MEIT," May 28, 1997.

110. KSC Archives, Space Station Collection, box 16, folder E, "Space Station Organization," August 27, 1997; Bartell, interview, 2003.

111. Bartell, interview, 2003.

112. KSC Archives, Space Station Collection, box 14, folder D, Conway/Francois, KSC Action Status: Develop Contingency Flow Planning in the Event of Hardware or Software Changes after KSC Arrival of Hardware/Software, April 1, 1996.

113. KSC Archives, Space Station Collection, box 25, folder A, Anonymous/KSC, "MEIT Concerns," April 6, 1998.

114. Bartell, interview, 2003.

115. Francois, interview; Bartell, interview, 2004; KSC news release 43-99, May 28, 1999.

116. Francois, interview.

117. *KSC Countdown*, June 24, 1997; Francois, interview.

118. Francois, interview.

119. KSC news release 46-99, June 14, 1999.

Chapter 13. Spaceport

1. JoAnn Morgan, interview by Roger Launius, February 22, 2002.

2. Ibid.

3. Ibid.

4. Ibid., June 2, 2002.

5. Ibid.

6. Shannon Bartell, interview by Orville R. Butler and Nanci Schwartz, June 26, 2003.

7. James Jennings, interview by Launius, July 19, 2002.

8. KSC Archives, "Business Objectives and Agreement for the External Relations Directorate," April 2004.

9. Roy Bridges, interview by Henry Dethloff and Lee Snaples, June 17, 2001.

10. NASA news release 95-30, May 17, 1995, "NASA Zero-Base Review Briefing Scheduled."

11. Bridges, interview Dethloff and Snaples, June 17, 2001.

12. Bridges, interview by Kenneth Lipartito, December 8, 2004.

13. Ibid.

14. Bridges, interview, 2001.

15. KSC Archives, Space Shuttle Program, box 1, folder 7, Clinton Varnado, Space Transportation Architecture Study Summary Report, May 23, 1988.

16. Same box, folder 2, NASA Implementation Plan for the National Space Transportation Policy, November 7, 1994; "Space Transportation System Lessons Learned" (see chap. 11 n.74).

17. Bridges, interview, 2004.

18. Ibid., 2001.

19. KSC Archives, Dr. Shannon Roberts Collection, folder 29, "Kennedy Space Center Roadmap."

20. Bridges, interview, 2004.

21. William Harwood, "New Spaceport Targets Cape, KSC Customers," *Space News*, July 24, 2000.

22. Jennings, interview.

23. Tom Breen, "KSC Reassigns 150 Workers," *Florida Today*, May 9, 2000.

24. Jennings, interview.

25. *Advisory Committee on the Future of the U.S. Space Program*, (see chap. 7 n.5), 2.

26. Traci Watson, "Age Catches up with Space Center," *USA Today*, May 28, 2002.

27. Jennings, interview.

28. Roy Bridges, "Kennedy Space Center" presentation, n.d., copy in possession of the authors.

29. See KSC Archives, *KSC Annual Reports*, 1997, 1998.

30. Roy Bridges, conversation with Lipartito, June 12, 2002.

31. NASA HQ, file 4589, KSC–Eastern Test Range Consolidation, T. O. Payne to Mayo, Bureau of the Budget, November 18, 1969.

32. NASA HQ, file 4589, KSC–Eastern Test Range Consolidation, Casper Weinberger–George Low, October 30, 1970.

33. Jay Silverberg, "NASA Considers Takeover," *Florida Today*, copy in NASA HQ, file 4592, General, 1971–79.

34. "U.S. Space Industrial Base" (see chap. 9 n.3), vi–vii.

35. Harwood, "New Spaceport Targets Cape, KSC Customers."

36. Jason Bates, "Air Force, KSC Create Office to Streamline Launch Operations," *Space News*, July 17, 2000.

37. Philip Chien, "Spaceport Florida: Building a Commercial Launch Pad," *Launchspace*, October–November 1997.

38. KSC Archives, *KSC Annual Report*, 2001.

39. Mike Cabbage, "Space Center Reaches for Stars," *Orlando Sentinel*, March 14, 1999.

40. KSC Archives, *KSC Annual Report*, 1999, 2001; KSC Telephone Directories.

41. KSC Archives, CD-ROM Collection, 2001-01, "KSC 2000 Cultures."

42. Ibid., KSC 2000, "Assuring Our Future."

43. KSC Archives, John F. Kennedy Space Center Business Objectives and Agreements for Spaceport Engineering and Technology Directorate, KDP-B-1034, Revision D, April 2004.

44. Steven Siceloff, "KSC Considers Privatizing Base," *Florida Today*, September 18, 2001.

45. KSC Archives, box 76-98, folder 7, unknown to Director of NASA, December 25, 1968.

46. See note 25.

47. Isom "Ike" Rigell, interview by Lipartito, October 28, 2004.

48. NASA, Columbia Accident Investigation Board, *Report* (hereafter *CAIB Report*), vol. 1 (August 2003), 97.

49. Ralph Vartabedian and Peter Pae, "Foam Was To Blame, Says Shuttle Study," *Los Angeles Times*, August 27, 2003.

50. Larry Wheeler, "Panelist Praises Space Workers," *Florida Today*, August 27, 2003.

51. *CAIB Report*, 1: 102–3.

52. Ibid., 1: 110.

53. Rob Stein, "Miscommunication, Bungling Halted Bid For Shuttle Photos," *Washington Post*, August 27, 2003. Ham has stated that she did not know the request came from the Debris Assessment Team.

54. *CAIB Report*, 1: 169.

55. Carreau, "10 Years after Challenger" (see chap. 11 n.87).

56. Dwight R. Worley, "Laid-off Shuttle Workers Worry about Safety and Slumping Morale," *Florida Today*, February 12, 1998.

57. *CAIB Report*, 1: 108.

58. Michael Wetmore, interview by Butler, August 3, 2003.

59. "Safety Concerns Prompt Close Scrutiny of NASA Layoffs," *Florida Today*, Feb-

ruary 1, 1998. Michael Cabbage and William Harwood in *Comm Check: The Final Flight of Shuttle Columbia* (New York: Free Press, 2004), 206, report that the overall shuttle workforce declined from 30,071 to 17,627. This concern was raised for NASA as a whole by the head of the CAIB, retired admiral Harold Gehman. See Traci Watson, "Records Show NASA Safety Office Cuts," *USA Today*, June 23, 2003.

60. According to Cabbage and Harwood, *Comm Check*, 213, Gehman saw the remote cause of the accident as fifteen years of squeezing and starving research and development.

61. Cabbage and Harwood, *Comm Check*, 229.

62. *CAIB Report*, 1: 6, 210–11.

63. Buzz Aldrin, "From the Moon to the Millennium," *Albuquerque Tribune*, 1999.

Chapter 14. Conclusion

1. *CAIB Report*, 1: 9, 127, 181–83, 189.

2. Commission on the Future of the United States Aerospace Industry, *Final Report* (Arlington, Va., 2002). On the general issue of breakthroughs versus incremental learning, see Richard Florida and Martin Kenney, *The Breakthrough Illusion: Corporate America's Failure to Move from Innovation to Mass Production* (New York: Basic Books, 1990).

3. A point noted by ex–shuttle commander Rick Searfoss; see his op-ed, *Orlando Sentinel*, August 27, 2003.

4. KSC is not the only part of NASA that gains knowledge from operations; Mission Control at JSC and other NASA centers that fly scientific missions do as well.

5. Chris Argyris, *On Organizational Learning* (see chap. 1 n.53).

6. Perin, "Operating as Experimenting" (see chap. 1 n.50), 100–102; Weick and Sutcliffe, *Managing the Unexpected* (see chap. 1 n.49), 12. On the problems of technological complexity, see Charles Perrow, *Normal Accidents: Living with High-Risk Technologies* (New York: Basic Books, 1984).

7. The literature on user-producer interaction is vast, but a good starting point is Eric von Hippel, *The Sources of Innovation* (Oxford: Oxford University Press, 1988). More recently, see Nelly Oudshoorn and Trevor Pinch, *How Users Matter: The Construction of Users and Technologies* (Cambridge, Mass.: MIT Press, 2003).

8. Debus, "Launch and Space Flight Operations" (see chap. 2 n.68).

9. Schein, "Three Cultures of Management" (see chap. 1 n.59).

10. Sayles and Chandler, *Managing Large Systems* (see chap. 3 n.48), 264.

11. Levitt and March, "Organizational Learning" (see chap. 1 n.53).

12. This point, about the role that civil servant knowledge as opposed to contractor knowledge played in the Apollo spacecraft at JSC, is made by Max Faget, Chris Kraft, and others in *Managing the Moon Program* (see chap. 5 n.27).

13. A point made quite forcefully in interviews, including Richard Hartung, interview by Orville R. Butler, April 20, 2004; J. R. "Dick" Lyon, interview by Butler, July 23, 2004; J. A. "Gene" Thomas, interview by Roger Launius, Henry Dethloff, and Lee Snaples, June 29, 2001.

14. John Conway, interview by Kenneth Lipartito, 2003.

15. Rocco Petrone, interview by Eugene Emme and Tom Ray, September 17, 1970.

16. Separation of launch from design placed a special emphasis on integrating mul-

tiple technologies at the launch site, since they were arriving from many different institutions and places. But since the parts would not come together until they arrived at KSC, it also meant that unexpected problems, misaligned systems, and results not anticipated in the design phase would emerge only when the rockets arrived and the preparations and testing commenced.

17. Robert Sieck, interview by Butler, August 19, 2003. A point noted in Schein, "Three Cultures of Management."

18. Webb, "NASA as an Adaptive Organization" (see chap. 5 n.25); T. Alexander, "Unexpected Payoff" (see chap. 2 n.42), 114.

19. Siepert, "Administration" (see chap. 2 n.39).

20. James March, Lee Sproull, and Michal Tamuz, "Learning From Samples of One or Fewer," *Organization Science* 2 (February 1991): 1–13; George Huber, "Organizational Learning: The Contributing Processes and the Literatures," *Organization Science* 2 (February 1991): 94.

21. McCurdy, *Inside NASA* (see chap. 1 n.45).

22. Quoted in Launius and Jenkins, *To Reach the High Frontier* (see chap. 2 n.9), 15.

23. Politics aside, one also had to assume that the approach taken to develop and manufacture ICBMs and fighter planes operating within terrestrial limits was applicable to civilian rockets and spaceships operating in outer space.

24. Bromberg, *NASA and the Space Industry* (see chap. 2 n.41), 8, 29, 41–44, 60–62, 50–53, 88–90. NASA was never meant to be a self-contained government bureaucracy, of course, and interaction between government and the private sector was seen as a strength of the American space program, in contrast to the German V-2 experience or the Russian space program. As James Webb predicted, NASA would teach private-sector firms how to work and profit through NASA contracts, though he foresaw NASA remaining in charge.

25. This informal use of the term "operational" to mean well-understood and routine reflects the problem addressed here— the assumption that the operational is not a source of learning or innovation.

26. Glenn Bugos, "Manufacturing Certainty: Testing and Program Management for the F-4 Phantom II," *Social Studies of Science* 23 (1993), 265–300.

27. Indeed, recent work on private-sector contracting has shown that parties to a contract must align not just incentives but knowledge and expectations as well. See Richard N. Langlois and Nicolai J. Foss, "Capabilities and Governance: The Rebirth of Production in the Theory of Economic Organization," Druid Working Paper 97-2, January 1997, ideas.repec.org/p/aal/abbswp/97-2.html.

28. As Sapolsky points out in *The Polaris System Development* (see chap. 2 n.42), the private sector may be quite wasteful, in that it must try many things before getting it right. During the 1950s and 1960s, in fact, Pentagon weapons system development was criticized as wasteful because it was too competitive, concurrently sponsoring multiple projects. Such concurrent development, though, could be highly innovative. Careful specification up front, detailed design work, and other planning may reduce the costs of development, or at least focus development on specific goals, but at the expense of losing the ability to respond to uncertainty and unexpected new opportunities that come with use.

29. Sapolsky makes this same point; see ibid., 209–10.

30. Hughes, *Rescuing Prometheus* (see chap. 2 n.21); David Jardini, "Out of the Blue Yonder: The Transfer of Systems Thinking from the Pentagon to the Great Society, 1961–65," in Hughes and Hughes, *Systems, Experts and Computers* (see chap. 2 n.42), 324.

31. Sapolsky, *The Polaris System Development*, notes how one method, PERT, served a well-defined and limited, and indeed political, purpose during the Polaris program, but then became written into all future programs. On the difference between formal and substantive rationality in management, see Jeffrey R. Fear, *Organizing Control: August Thyssen and the Construction of German Corporate Management* (Cambridge, Mass.: Harvard University Press, 2005), 772–73.

32. Another way of putting this is "deference to expertise," or pushing decisions to those who can best make them. Expertise does not mean formal knowledge but rather the ability in a given situation to understand what needs to be done and doing it. Weick and Sutcliffe, *Managing the Unexpected*, 48, 75.

33. Sayles and Chandler, *Managing Large Systems*, 6, 8, 16.

34. Levinthal and March, "The Myopia of Learning" (see chap. 1 n.53), 97.

Note on the Sources

Primary Sources

Most of the research for this book was conducted at the Kennedy Space Center. There we found a rich trove of materials, much untouched by historians. The essential starting point of our work was the Historical Archives in the KSC Headquarters Building. Located there are documents on almost every major project and era in the Center's history, as well as a wealth of supporting documentation, including transcripts of congressional hearings, technical reports, NASA-published monographs on a range of historical subjects, and an excellent collection of secondary works on space history and related topics. A good place to begin is with this office's ongoing annual *Chronology*, which details matters related to KSC, excerpting newspapers and industry trade publications year by year.

Particularly valuable for our work were collections denoted Apollo and Saturn, Unmanned Launches, Skylab, and International Space Station, as well as the Community Relations, LC-39 Site Activation, and Newspaper Clippings collections. Crucial for understanding the development of launch concepts, organization of the Center, and key issues of technology and management in the Apollo era are the papers of Kurt Debus, listed in our notes as the Debus Collection. These are Debus's personal papers, which were turned over to KSC. As well there are valuable collections of speeches by KSC employees and sets of older interviews conducted in the late 1960s and 1970s, some with key people no longer alive. The archives also contains some memoirs and reminiscences of former employees. Most useful for us was the autobiographical work of George "Ted" Sasseen.

The interviews we conducted, listed at the end of this essay, are also on deposit at the KSC Archives, if the interview was recorded. Just before we began our research, KSC and the NASA Headquarters History Office had conducted interviews with KSC personnel in preparation for this book project. These proved extremely useful and time-saving. Unless otherwise noted, all oral histories used in this book, whether or not conducted by the authors, are available at the KSC Archives.

Also at the KSC Archives are several other collections not formally part of the permanent holdings. One of the most valuable is the papers of Kurt Debus as KSC director, which complement Debus's personal papers. We were also fortunate to have access to several boxes of uncatalogued papers and materials from the KSC labor office, which gave us a unique perspective on labor disputes and work processes at the Center. These are referred to in the notes as Uncatalogued Labor Files. We were able to put together a preliminary list of contents of those boxes in the course of our research.

Just down the hall from the Historical Archives are the Center's library and Documents Department. There we accessed a number of technical reports, memoranda, and government documents. The library also has an extensive collection of space-related published materials, both historical and technical.

At both the Historical Archives and the KSC Press Site are enormous collections of photographs. Some of them appear in this book, but we could only begin to tap into this vast source of visual history, and much more awaits the visually oriented researcher.

The KSC Web site at www.ksc.nasa.gov/ gives a sense of the types of visual materials available, and also contains good basic information on the history of the Center and its activities. We found the Mission Chronologies particularly valuable for keeping track of human and robotic spaceflights. Other material is posted on the internal KSC Web site, accessible only at the Center. Since the content on the Web changes, it is difficult to give a precise description of what is available, but both the public and the internal Web pages are good places to find an overview of KSC and space history generally.

To get a sense of daily life at the Kennedy Space Center, the Center publication *Spaceport News*, which goes back almost to the very beginning of the institution, is invaluable. Though it must be recognized for what it is, a house organ, it can be mined for all sorts of insights about culture and life otherwise difficult to recreate from managerial or technical documents.

A second major source of primary materials was KSC's Records Management Office. The Center maintains a substantial collection of papers from its various departments or "directorates," going back to the earliest days. Many of these papers are located on-site, unfortunately in an un-air-conditioned storage facility sitting beneath the hot Central Florida sun. The information available on these holdings is limited, so we had to do a fair amount of detective work to track down those we thought might be of most use. The lists usually provide only a basic box title, such as Upper Level Management Files, sometimes including the range of dates covered. Most of the time, we were opening boxes that had not been opened since they were sent to storage. These boxes contain an abundance of history—indeed an overabundance, since there are thousands of them—that can provide crucial information on decision-making processes, research, and operational activities, plans and projects never pursued, and debates over policy and technical matters with other centers and NASA headquarters. We were only able to scratch the surface here, focusing on materials from the executive level. Much more awaits future researchers.

In addition to the large on-site collection, KSC maintains a great number of boxes off-site, at the National Archives facility in Eastpoint, Georgia. Most of these are not formally part of NARA, and so must be searched via KSC's Records Management Office. They are similar in content to the materials on-site at KSC. The facility at Eastpoint, however, does house some KSC material that has become part of the National Archives. Particularly valuable for this book were the papers from Hans Gruene's Launch Vehicle Operations organization, which tested the Saturn rocket at KSC.

NASA headquarters in Washington, D.C., also has an archives section in its History Office. Organized by topic, it contains copies of primary sources and newspaper accounts relating to the history of the space program. Particularly valuable for this book were the materials under the topical heading Kennedy Space Center, and related designations such as Florida Launch Operations. There we found headquarters-level documentation on the founding of the Center, key policy decisions bearing on the Center and launch operations, important public documents and government reports about space policy, and a wealth of material from newspapers and trade journals relating to launch operations and the changing market for launch services.

Both the Headquarters History Office and the Johnson Space Center (JSC) house some interviews of personnel connected to the Kennedy Space Center. We drew fruitfully on a number of these compiled by JSC's active oral history program. Of particular note at NASA headquarters are interviews conducted with a key KSC manager from the Apollo era, Rocco Petrone. Some of the Petrone oral histories are available at the KSC Archives as well.

NASA's *Astronautics and Aeronautics* (Washington, D.C.: NASA, various years) offers a detailed day-by-day recounting of significant events in space policy and technology. Though now several years behind schedule, this multivolume publication covers 1963 through 1995. It is an invaluable source for historians trying to reconstruct a detailed narrative. In the same vein, two industry periodicals provide detailed and in-depth coverage of almost all events of significance touching on the space business: *Defense/Space Business Daily* (after April 1980 *Defense Daily*) and *Aviation Week & Space Technology*. The Brevard County newspaper *Florida Today* has outstanding coverage of both the space industry generally and matters affecting KSC specifically.

Finally, it is worth mentioning the studies done by commissions investigating the *Challenger* and *Columbia* accidents. Reports by the Presidential Commission on the Space Shuttle Challenger Accident (Rogers Commission) and the Columbia Accident Investigation Board both provide in-depth analysis not just of the accidents but of larger matters of space operations, organization, and technology. These are widely available, and can be found at both KSC and the NASA History Office. They are certainly worth special attention from anyone seeking to understand NASA as an organization and the business of flying in space.

Secondary Sources

There is no other complete scholarly history of the Kennedy Space Center. The Center and launch operations generally are not well represented in the voluminous space history literature. However, an earlier publication on launch operations during the Apollo program was written in 1978 by Charles D. Benson and William Barnaby Faherty. Originally titled *Moonport: A History of Apollo Launch Facilities and Operations* (Washington, D.C.: NASA, 1978) and accessible online through the NASA History Office at www.hq.nasa.gov/office/pao/History/SP-4204/cover.html, it was reissued in print form as two volumes, *Gateway to the Moon: Building the Kennedy Space Center Launch Complex*, and *Moon Launch! A History of the Saturn-Apollo Launch Operations* (Gainesville: University Press of Florida, 2001). Extremely detailed and somewhat technical for the average reader, this work nonetheless is an excellent study of the early era of KSC's history, though it is largely confined to the lunar program.

Although not primarily focused on life and work at KSC, two other books on the Apollo era are required reading. Roger E. Bilstein's *Stages to Saturn: A Technological History of the Apollo/Saturn Launch Vehicles* (Washington, D.C.: NASA, 1980) details the complex history of Saturn booster technology in a fashion that is both authoritative and readable. It covers the integration, checkout, and launching procedures for this vehicle performed at KSC. Courtney G. Brooks, James M. Grimwood, and Loyd S. Swenson Jr., *Chariots for Apollo: A History of Manned Lunar Spacecraft* (Washington, D.C.: NASA, 1979), does likewise for the Apollo vehicle. Also worthwhile and with information on launch operations are Loyd S. Swenson Jr., James

M. Grimwood, and Charles C. Alexander, *This New Ocean: A History of Project Mercury* (Washington, D.C.: NASA, 1966), and Barton C. Hacker and James M. Grimwood, *On the Shoulders of Titans: A History of Project Gemini* (Washington, D.C.: NASA, 1977). Though none of these is primarily focused on KSC, they all provide valuable information on launch operations for these key programs.

The political history of the early space program is well covered in Walter A. McDougall's prizewinning *The Heavens and the Earth: A Political History of the Space Age* (New York: Basic Books, 1985). It should, however, be supplemented by other works. Roger D. Launius's *NASA: A History of the U.S. Civil Space Program* (Malabar, Fla.: Krieger, 1994) provides a good overview of NASA the government agency, supplemented by key policy documents. Roger E. Bilstein's *Orders of Magnitude: A History of the NACA and NASA, 1915–1990* (Washington, D.C.: NASA, 1990) has a longer-term perspective on the agency, going back to its prespace history. Taking a more sociological approach, Howard E. McCurdy's *Inside NASA: High Technology and Organizational Change in the U.S. Space Program* (Baltimore: Johns Hopkins University Press, 1993) looks at the problems of adjustment the organization has faced since the Apollo years and recent tribulations with the shuttle and space station. Joan Lisa Bromberg in *NASA and the Space Industry* (Baltimore: Johns Hopkins University Press, 1999) looks at NASA's relationship to private industry and the economic and business aspects of space. Finally, the NASA Headquarters History Office has published a number of excellent but more specific studies, which can be located through their Web site, www.hq.nasa.gov/office/pao/History/history.html, many available in full text online. Especially useful for statistical data are the six volumes of the *NASA Historical Data Book* (Washington, D.C.: NASA, 1988–1999), as well as the collections of primary documents in the six volumes of *Exploring the Unknown: Selected Documents in the History of the U.S. Civil Space Program* (Washington, D.C.: NASA, 1995–2004).

Important in the history of KSC launch operations is the history of launch vehicles. Roger D. Launius and Dennis R. Jenkins, eds., *To Reach the High Frontier: A History of U.S. Launch Vehicles* (Lexington: University Press of Kentucky, 2002), covers historical and recent developments in this technology. Michael J. Neufeld's prizewinning *The Rocket and the Reich: Peenemünde and the Coming of the Ballistic Missile Era* (New York: Free Press, 1995) deals insightfully with the German rocket program and many of the men who would form the nucleus of the American missile and space programs. Two older works recount the history of missiles as military weapons, which played a crucial role in early space booster technology: David Baker, *The Rocket: The History and Development of Rocket and Missile Tech-*

nology (New York: Crown, 1978), and Jacob Neufeld, *The Development of Ballistic Missiles in the United States Air Force, 1954–1960* (Washington, D.C.: Office of Air Force History, USAF, 1990). An in-depth look at NASA's main booster development center is provided in Andrew J. Dunar and Stephen P. Waring, *Power to Explore: A History of Marshall Space Flight Center, 1960–1990* (Washington, D.C.: NASA, 1999). Given KSC's historic links to Marshall, this book is also essential for understanding the early days of launch operations and the translation of the German rocket tradition to the United States.

Frederick I. Ordway III and Mitchell R. Sharpe, *The Rocket Team* (New York: Thomas Y. Crowell, 1979), makes a strong case for the innovative role of the German émigrés in the American space program. But a more recent and thoroughly researched book by Stephen B. Johnson, *The Secret of Apollo: Systems Management in American and European Space Programs* (Baltimore: Johns Hopkins University Press, 2002), effectively challenges this perspective.

Johnson's work is part of a growing literature on the new managerial structures and techniques that evolved out of early military missile programs and went on to touch many institutions in American society. For further elaboration on this, see Thomas P. Hughes, *Rescuing Prometheus: Four Monumental Projects That Changed the Modern World* (New York: Pantheon, 1998), and Agatha C. Hughes and Thomas P. Hughes, eds., *Systems, Experts, and Computers: The Systems Approach in Management and Engineering, World War II and After* (Cambridge, Mass.: MIT Press, 2000).

The recent work on systems and systems management has not fully apprehended the place of operations, however. It has also tended to privilege formal organizational structures at the expense of politics and social relationships. Harvey M. Sapolsky's classic *The Polaris System Development: Bureaucratic and Programmatic Success in Government* (Cambridge, Mass.: Harvard University Press, 1972) provides a useful corrective. A pioneering study of systems management, it offers a skeptical and sometimes wry look at the limitations of formal structure and the interweaving of politics at every level of technical management. Similarly, an often overlooked study of the early space program, Leonard R. Sayles and Margaret K. Chandler, *Managing Large Systems: Organizations for the Future* (New York: Harper and Row, 1971), recognized the disjuncture between what systems engineering and program management claimed and how they actually operated in the space program.

The literature on technology at the level of operations has begun to investigate how tacit knowledge, hands-on skills, historical experience, and informal relationships contribute to innovation and to making designs work in the real world. This literature contrasts with the literature emphasizing formal methods of management and engineering. Particularly valuable in this regard are Constance Perin, "Operating as Experimenting: Synthesizing Engineering and Scientific Values in Nuclear Power Production," *Science, Technology, and Human Values* 23, no. 1 (Winter 1998), 98–128, and Karl E. Weick and Kathleen M. Sutcliffe, *Managing the Unexpected: Assuring High Performance in an Age of Complexity* (San Francisco: Jossey-Bass, 2001).

Because accidents often uncover the messy reality and incomplete knowledge beneath seemingly rational bureaucratic structures, books dealing with accidents in the space program are especially useful. Michael Cabbage and William Harwood, *Comm Check: The Final Flight of Shuttle Columbia* (New York: Free Press, 2004), provides a balanced, detailed, and highly readable account of the *Columbia* accident. Joseph J. Trento, *Prescription for Disaster: From the Glory of Apollo to the Betrayal of the Shuttle* (New York: Crown, 1987), covers *Challenger*, but from a rather tendentious point of view. Much better, indeed one of the best studies of accidents and disasters available, is Diane Vaughn, *The Challenger Launch Decision: Risky Technology, Culture, and Deviance at NASA* (Chicago: University of Chicago Press, 1996).

Several other works deserve mention because of their coverage of key issues in space history. Roger Launius, "Public Opinion Polls and Perceptions of US Human Spaceflight," *Space Policy* 19 (2003), 163–75, provides an extremely interesting look at how Americans have thought about the value of space exploration, compiling the best available data from public opinion polls over time. T. A. Heppenheimer, *The Space Shuttle Decision: NASA's Search for a Reusable Space Vehicle* (Washington, D.C.: NASA, 1999) is a classic study that examines politics, technological choice, and culture in the space program over thirty years. And John Krige, Arturo Russo, and Laurenza Sebesta in their two-volume *A History of the European Space Agency, 1958–1987* (Noordwijk: European Space Agency, 2000) provide an authoritative look at what has become America's main competition for launch services.

People Interviewed

Bartell, Shannon	Conway, John
Barth, Timothy	Culbertson, Philip
Benik, Michael	Donnelly, Paul
Bridges, Roy	Ettinger, James
Brown, Joseph	Francois, Steven
Bruckner, Bobby	Garcia, Jose
Buchanan, Donald	Giesler, C. M.

Greenfield, Terry
Haddad, Michael
Harrington, James F., III
Hartung, Richard L.
Hattaway, James
Heimmer, Harold
Honeycutt, Jay
Jansen, Bruce
Kleinknecht, Kenneth S.
Lange, Robert
Lealman, Roy
Lugo, Raymond
Lyon, John (Dick)
Mars, Charles
Mauck, Larry
Montgomery, Ann
Morgan, JoAnn
Moser, Enoch
Murphy, Charles
Nagel, Conrad G.
Neilon, John
Nelson, Joseph
O'Malley, T. J.
Overton, Thomas
Petrone, Rocco

Pickett, Andrew
Preston, G. Merritt
Ragusa, James M.
Reed, Nathaniel
Reyes, Raul E. (Ernie)
Reynolds, Joel
Rigell, Isom (Ike)
Robinson, Wilbert (Robby)
Sasseen, George T. (Ted)
Scheller, Donald R.
Sestile, Eugene
Sheppard, Donald
Sieck, Robert
Solid, Leroy
Straiton, John
Talone, John (Tip)
Tharpe, Roy C.
Thomas, James A. (Gene)
Tucci, Larry
Utsman, Thomas
Walton, Thomas
Wetmore, Michael
Wiley, Warren I.
Woolley, Michael

Index

Kenneth Lipartito, professor of history at Florida International University, is author or editor of five books including *Investing for Middle America: John Elliott Tappan and the Origins of American Express Financial Advisors* and *Constructing Corporate America: History, Politics, Culture.*

Orville R. Butler is an associate historian in the Center for History of Physics at the American Institute of Physics and is coauthor, with Stephen Adams, of *Manufacturing the Future: A History of Western Electric.*

Related-interest titles from the University Press of Florida

"Before This Decade Is Out...": Personal Reflections on the Apollo Program
by Glen E. Swanson

Big Dish: Building America's Deep Space Connection to the Planets
by Douglas J. Mudgway

Florida's Space Coast: The Impact of NASA on the Sunshine State
by William B. Faherty

Gateway to the Moon: Building the Kennedy Space Center Launch Complex
by Charles D. Benson and William B. Faherty

International Space Commerce: Building from Scratch by Roger Handberg

Moon Launch! A History of the Saturn-Apollo Launch Operations
by Charles D. Benson and William B. Faherty

The Soviet Space Race with Apollo by Asif A. Siddiqi

Sputnik and the Soviet Space Challenge by Asif A. Siddiqi

Stages to Saturn: A Technological History of the Apollo/ Saturn Launch Vehicles by Roger E. Bilstein

A History of the Kennedy Space Center by Kenneth Lipartito and Orville R. Butler

For more information on these and other books, visit our web site at www.upf.com.